Enlightenment and Pathology

Sensibility in the Literature
and Medicine of Eighteenth-
Century France

Anne C. Vila

THE JOHNS HOPKINS UNIVERSITY PRESS
Baltimore and London

Publication of this book has been aided by the University
of Wisconsin.

© 1998 The Johns Hopkins University Press
All rights reserved. Published 1998
Printed in the United States of America on
acid-free paper
07 06 05 04 03 02 01 00 99 98   5 4 3 2 1

The Johns Hopkins University Press
2715 North Charles Street
Baltimore, Maryland 21218-4319
The Johns Hopkins Press Ltd., London

Library of Congress Cataloging-in-Publication Data will
be found at the end of this book.
A catalog record for this book is available from the British
Library.

ISBN 0-8018-5677-9
ISBN 0-8018-5809-7 (pbk.)

 *To my parents*

Contents

$\mathscr{I}$llustrations

*A*cknowledgments

I am indebted to many people for their support and interest in this book over its long gestation. For encouraging me to pursue my peculiar fascination with eighteenth-century literature and medicine, I am grateful to Wilda Anderson, Vincent Descombes, Richard Macksey, François Roustang, and most of all Josué Harari, who has been a tireless reader, an expert critic, and a generous friend from the inception of this project. I also want to thank Marie-Hélène Huet, Thomas Kavanagh, Thomas Laqueur, and Elena Russo for offering useful criticism of various parts or stages of the manuscript; Martine Debaisieux, Suzanne Desan, Richard Goodkin, Ullrich Langer, Elaine Marks, Arnold Miller, Yvonne Ozzello, Nicholas Rand, and Steven Winspur for their wise and friendly counsel as colleagues at the University of Wisconsin; and the students in my graduate courses at the University of Wisconsin, Emory University, and Stanford University for helping to sharpen my thinking on sensibility and all the areas into which it inevitably spilled over. Finally, this book would not have been possible without the patience, understanding, and steadfast moral support provided by my husband, Steven Jacobs, and everyone else in our families—including our baby daughter, Julia Suzanne, who arrived in time to keep me company as I read the page proofs. I dedicate this book to my mother, Mary Jeanette McVicar Vila, and to the memory of my father, Alan Parry Vila.

For their assistance in preparing the manuscript, I want to thank David Harrison, who efficiently tracked down existing English translations of many works and helped to assemble the bibliography; Leslie Hartness, whose word-processing services substantially expedited the writing of Part 1; and Carolyn Moser, who has been an astute, tactful, and painstaking manuscript editor. For their help in the final stages of preparing this book, I thank Michael Winston and my production editor at the Johns Hopkins University Press, Julie McCarthy.

I am grateful to the staffs of several libraries—above all the Welch at the Johns Hopkins University, the Middleton and Memorial at the University of Wisconsin, the Stanford University library system, and the Bibliothèque Nationale—whose assistance facilitated my research. I am particularly thankful to

Edward Mormon of the Institute for the History of Medicine at Johns Hopkins and to Phyllis Kauffman, Historical Librarian at Wisconsin's Health Sciences Library, both of whom graciously oversaw the photographing of illustrations from the rare medical books under their care. I would like to thank the National Library of Medicine, Bethesda, Maryland, for the illustrations from *Elementa Physiologiae Corporis Humani* and from Paulet's *L'Antimagnétisme* (used in Chapter 1 and the Conclusion, respectively); and I appreciatively acknowledge the permission of the Philadelphia Museum of Art to reproduce the illustrations of the physician curing fantasy (Chapter 3) and of the vapors (Chapter 7).

The research for and writing of this book was made possible in large measure by an Andrew W. Mellon Postdoctoral Fellowship in the Humanities at Stanford University and by summer research grants from the University of Wisconsin Graduate School. I am profoundly grateful to both for their support.

An earlier version of part of Chapter 3 appeared in *Studies in Eighteenth-Century Culture* 23 (1993, Johns Hopkins University Press) under the title "Enlightened Minds and Scholarly Bodies from Tissot to Sade"; part of Chapter 5 appeared in *Modern Language Notes* 105, no. 4 (1990, Johns Hopkins University Press) under the title "Sensible Diagnostics in Diderot's *La Religieuse*"; and a portion of Chapter 7 appeared in *Representations* 52 (1995, The Regents of the University of California) under the title "Sex and Sensibility: Pierre Roussel's *Système physique et moral de la femme*." I thank the editors for their permission to use them here.

A Note on Translations: Translations are mine unless otherwise noted. Where both an English translation and the French original are given as sources in the text, the English translation is cited first.

Enlightenment and Pathology

INTRODUCTION

On Sensibility, the Sensible Body, and the Frontiers of Literature and Medicine

This book was inspired by a sense of dissatisfaction with the partial, generally unidisciplinary explanations that have been ventured for the complex phenomenon known as "sensibility" in mid- to late-eighteenth-century France. As my title indicates, sensibility was a polysemous concept, a notion that not only cut across disciplinary boundaries, but represented several different things at once. From mid-century on, sensibility was endowed with an enormous deterministic power over both the moral and the physical natures of humankind and thus provided the philosophes with a key instrument in their efforts to improve contemporary society, along with the individuals within it. As the Chevalier de Jaucourt put it in the *Encyclopédie*, "Sensibility is the mother of humanity, of generosity; it fosters merit, aids the intelligence, and carries persuasion in its wake."[1] Yet even as they exalted sensibility, eighteenth-century authors also expressed a deep anxiety about it: moralists and physicians alike viewed sensibility as a potentially dangerous quality that could lead to emotional excess, moral degeneracy, and physical debilitation. At the height of its conceptual popularity, therefore, sensibility was situated somewhere between enlightenment and pathology: it was seen as instrumental in the quest for reason and virtue, but was also implicated in the epidemic of nervous maladies that seemed to be overtaking the population of France and of Europe in general.

What allowed sensibility to sustain both of those sets of meanings was the central role it played in fields as diverse as physiology, empiricist philosophy, sociomoral theory, medicine, aesthetics, and literature, all of which were included in the loose confederation of naturalistic discourses then known as the "sciences of man." Although this concept traversed all of those fields—and was, as I argue, especially important to eighteenth-century medicine and literature—there was not a single, monolithic discourse of sensibility: rather, there were several.[2] Those various discourses nonetheless came to converge and

I

overlap in a number of intriguing ways, making it possible to analyze them not only in the synchronic terms prescribed by Michel Foucault and his disciples, but also diachronically, so as to retrace the way that sensibility developed into a coherent conceptual and cultural construct.[3] Some scholars have characterized the jointly scientific and literary tradition that sprang up around sensibility as a *paradigm*, adapting the model that Thomas Kuhn put forth in *The Structure of Scientific Revolutions* (1962) to describe the history of scientific change.[4] Although I do not wish to abuse the rather vague (and, at this point, dated) term *paradigm*, I will employ it occasionally to refer to the distinct body of thought on sensibility that emerged in the 1750s and retained its hold on the imaginations of French writers throughout the period generally known as the Enlightenment.

To understand the sensibility paradigm fully, we must first determine what the concept meant within each of the diverse discursive fields that were preoccupied with it. In the moral and social vocabulary of eighteenth-century France, *sensibilité* belonged to the same family of words as *sens, sensation, sentiment, sentimental,* and *sensiblerie,* and was associated with notions like sympathy, virtue, pity, benevolence, tender feeling, and compassion.[5] Yet *sensibility* was also central to European physiological terminology beginning in the 1740s, when it edged out *irritability* as the word most commonly used to describe the innate capacity to react to stimuli, which was held to underlie all the phenomena of life in the human body. In fact, the various meanings attached to *sensibility* tended to be mutually permeable because eighteenth-century authors used the word as a bridging concept—a means of establishing causal connections between the physical and the moral realms.[6] From sensationalist philosophers of the intellect like Condillac, Bonnet, and Buffon, to aestheticians like Dubos and Diderot, to moralists like Duclos and Rousseau, to the vitalist theorists of the Montpellier medical school, French Enlightenment thinkers subscribed to the idea that sensibility was the essential link between the human body and the psychological, intellectual, and ethical faculties of humankind. Sensibility was thus fundamental to this period's effort to forge a global, unified understanding of human nature: it was seen as the root of all human perceptions and reflections, as the innate and active principle of sociability that gave rise to human society, as a kind of sixth sense whose special affective energy was essential both to virtue and to art, and finally, as the paradigmatic vital force whose actions could be detected in every bodily function, be it healthful or morbid. Sensibility was consequently far more than a fashionable cult of histrionic emotionalism or the self-image of a society that was peculiarly fond of shedding tears of melancholia, high-minded sympathy, or tender feeling.[7] It was also the object of a unique intellectual culture—that is, in the words of the historian G. J. Barker-Benfield, a "constellation of ideas, feelings, and events" that developed around sensibility throughout eighteenth-century Europe, albeit with often striking national differences.[8]

There were three major traits that distinguished the eighteenth-century French culture of sensibility from the ideas that surrounded the concept elsewhere in Europe. First, sensibility and sentimentalism were closely associated in France with the process of secularization that the philosophes were intent on advancing.[9] Second, French writers did not polarize sensibility in relation to sex and gender nearly as much as did their British counterparts, at least not until the last few decades of the century; rather, even the most hard-boiled philosophes prided themselves on their sensibility and saw nothing unmanly about cultivating this quality.[10] Finally, sensibility was standardly imbued by French writers with a pronounced physicalist or materialist undertone, without provoking any major outcry from the defenders of morality and religion.[11] One factor underlying the greater French tolerance for sensibility's physicalist connotations was the unusual appeal that medicine held for this nation's intellectual and social elite.[12] To get a general sense of that appeal, we need only consider the *Encyclopédie,* whose fifteenth volume (1765) contained two entries on the property: first, a lengthy medical article that affirmed sensibility's primacy in human physiology and pathology and described how it varied according to age, sex, temperament, the passions, and external factors like climate; and second, Louis de Jaucourt's one-paragraph article on sensibility's extraordinary capacity to inspire virtue, to reinforce the intellectual faculties, and to persuade by appealing to the heart. The juxtaposition of these two articles is revealing because it shows not only the proximity of sensibility's physical and moral meanings, but also the prestige that was accorded to the physicians who rallied to the cause of sensibility during the second half of the century.

In a suggestive essay on the Marquis de Sade's keen interest in contemporary medicine, David B. Morris observes: "Like theology in the Middle Ages, medicine in the Enlightenment approached the condition of a master discourse."[13] Morris also notes that the biomedical language and concepts of the era underwent a "transvaluation" in Sade's fiction—a process that, I contend, is actually much broader in eighteenth-century French literature, which appropriated many of the ideas and models promoted in contemporary medicine and other natural-philosophical discourses. For sensibility in particular, the operation of transvaluation worked both ways: the social and literary vogue that had developed around sentiment and sensibility in the late seventeenth and early eighteenth centuries played a significant part in orienting the inquiries of natural philosophers toward such questions as the physio-anatomical underpinnings of sentience, the primacy of sensation in the workings of both body and mind, and the dynamic nature of living matter. Thus, the physiological concepts of sensibility and related vital properties were, as one historian of science has put it, "infused with all the shades of meaning attached to ideas of life."[14] But so, too, were many of the ideas about sensibility that circulated in French literature after 1750, especially in the works of such novelists as Diderot, Rousseau, Laclos, and Sade—all of whom were intent on exploiting both sensibility's existing literary meanings and its recently acquired status as one of the primary conceptual metaphors of the day.

When I speak of sensibility as a conceptual metaphor, I am referring to the very particular way of seeing things that this concept afforded to eighteenth-century writers as they conducted their inquiries into the body, the mind, and contemporary civilization.[15] There are a number of ideas and theoretical suppositions involved in that way of seeing: a certain notion of how the internal space of the body was organized; an assumption that the physical and moral realms of human existence were closely interrelated; a conviction that all natural phenomena had a profound interconnection and dynamism; and a belief that there were causal structures underlying those phenomena—structures that the philosophically minded observer could uncover, provided that he had sufficient patience, perspicacity, and instinctual feeling for the operations of nature. The metaphor of the sensible body also encompassed other conceptual metaphors: for example, the idea promoted by the Swiss physiologist Albrecht von Haller that the fiber was the basic unit for all vital properties; the *sensorium commune*, a vaguely located entity held to serve as organic stand-in for the soul; the local power of "sentiment" or "taste" which the Montpellier physician-philosophers ascribed to each organ in the body; and so on. My study of sensibility is designed to retrieve these and other ideas about the organic foundations of human life because they played a crucial part in determining how human nature was perceived in eighteenth-century France.

In other words, I am attempting in this book to reach back to a time before Freud—to a moment in the history of thought when the body was not defined by the social and the psychic, but rather, vice versa. For, as Jean Starobinski has underscored, Freud effected a major shift in the manner in which the body was perceived when he forged the modern theory of the unconscious:

> Freud's original contribution was not to have spoken first of the unconscious but to have, so to speak, lifted the monopoly held on it by organic life and to have installed it within the psychic apparatus itself. It was thus at the price of abandoning the body ... that the unconscious became the custodian of a language and the producer of palimpsests or puzzles that were then open to being deciphered. Having ceased to have the life of the

body as its exclusive source, the unconscious then escaped from the exclusive competence of a medical approach and became dependent on hermeneutics.[16]

Although Freud did not entirely sever the links between psychology and biology, he did create a radically new and largely secondary role for the body in the modern understanding of human nature: "in 'dephysiologizing' psychology, Freud was 'desomatizing' the causal system commonly accepted by his predecessors" (Starobinski, 365). In the process, Freud opened up the body to a wealth of hermeneutic approaches that have greatly enriched psychoanalysis, philosophy, and not least, literary studies.[17]

Given the enormous power of Freud's somatic model over our own critical imaginations, it may be difficult for the modern reader to conceive of a time when a different model of the body held sway, this one tied primarily to physiology and the primacy of organic sensations. I nonetheless argue throughout this book that it is essential to "re-somatize" our understanding not just of eighteenth-century psychology and philosophy, but also of the period's moral theory, aesthetics, and literature, by recognizing that unicausal, organic explanations of the various phenomena of human life were common coin in all of those fields. Because of that emphasis, my analyses of the role played by the body in the literary works I study are quite different from those that have been proposed by critics who interpret them in the light of Freud, Lacan, or a related paradigm of the "body as text."[18]

The body has, of course, served since antiquity as "man's most available metaphor."[19] Each cultural-historical moment, however, has its own particular ways of using the body as a metaphor or explanatory principle—a point that has been forcefully made over the past few decades by a number of scholars, from Michel Foucault to various anthropologists, social historians, and feminist scholars.[20] The most productive and problematic somatic metaphor of the French Enlightenment was, in my view, that of the sensible or reactive body. With its heavy emphasis on the nerves and the maladies that they can incur, eighteenth-century sensibility can sound very modern in thrust.[21] Yet the paradigm of sensibility that emerged during this period also had its fair share of historical peculiarities, most particularly in the way that it was exploited by both sides in the ongoing debate over the positive versus the negative effects of civilization on human nature. Like civilized society itself, bodily sensibility was a double-edged sword: it was intimately associated not only with the much-touted principle of human perfectibility but also with the pathologies that seemed to be threatening the philosophes' programs for education and enlightenment.

Far from being limited to the medical and ethical realms, sensibility's ambiguities extended into aesthetics as well. Given its heavy emphasis on visualizing the invisible interior of the body, the physio-philosophy of sensibility was not without a certain aesthetic dimension in its own right. Equally intriguing, however, are the theories of fiction that were put forth to account for the effects of sensibility, sentiment, and sympathy upon aesthetic response. In the theoretical texts he wrote on the theater and the novel during the 1750s and 1760s, Diderot argued vehemently in favor of creating literary works that would engage the reader-spectator intimately and involuntarily in moving scenes from the drama of everyday life. One finds a similar effort in Rousseau, but with an important difference: Rousseau was so deeply suspicious of the seductive powers of conventional novels and theater that he deemed both to be beyond redemption. He thus took a dim view of other writers' efforts to transform these literary genres into forums for activating sensibility in the name of moral edification and sympathetic sociability because he maintained that those virtues could only flourish beyond the boundaries of the existing social world. At the same time, however, Rousseau played a fundamental role in popularizing the sentimentalist conception of fiction as an intensely affecting and potentially life-changing experience.

A central argument of this book is that sensibility was a property that demanded not just elucidation but control: hence the detailed programs of moral, physical, and social hygiene that pervade both the medical discourse of the French Enlightenment and its novels. It was, in fact, the jointly hygienic and anthropological thrust of La Religieuse, La Nouvelle Héloïse, Les Liaisons dangereuses, and Sade's various fictions that first prompted me to align them with contemporary medicine, and with each other, for this study. Although these novelists were often diametrically opposed to each other in their moral and social theories, they had at least one important thing in common: each defined himself not as a novelist tout court but rather as a philosophe, a figure dutybound to represent the true nature of humankind. I then realized that such an alignment might point the way to a new typology of the eighteenth-century novel—or at least, to a new understanding of the stakes and strategies involved in the novel of sensibility as it developed over the course of the century. Because it was so multifaceted, sensibility lent itself to a wide variety of literary treatments: it was central not only to the sentimental narratives that proliferated at the time, but also to the explicitly antisentimental narratives that were created by authors such as Diderot, Laclos, and Sade, each of whom was intrigued by the materialist possibilities that sensibility presented as a physicalized concept. In that sense, sensibility should be seen not as a fixed, oppressive set of literary and moral conventions that serious literary writers sought to subvert (as one feminist critic has recently asserted), but rather as a potentially subversive property in itself.[22]

Clearly, my critical approach to sensibility is grounded in the conviction that the medical and literary enterprises of eighteenth-century France were not only compatible but deeply interrelated.[23] There are, of course, important distinctions to be made between the modes of knowing and writing about human nature that were pursued in each of these fields. Yet, in addition to sharing an abiding fascination with the property of sensibility, medicine and literature were connected during this period as intellectual and social activities meant to contribute to a larger enlightenment project: namely, the effort to advance knowledge of the natural world and of human beings as feeling, thinking, and social animals. Medical and imaginative writers thus had a common view of their enterprise as fundamentally natural-philosophical and anthropological in thrust. As Sade puts it rather grandiloquently in his "Idée sur les romans,"

> the novel is—if 'tis possible to express oneself thuswise—*the representation of secular mores,* and is therefore as essential as is the knowledge of history for the philosopher who wishes to understand man . . . The novelist's brush . . . portrays man from within . . . Always bear in mind that the novelist is the child of Nature, that she has created him to be her painter; if he does not become his mother's lover the moment she gives birth to him, let him never write, for we shall never read him. But if he feels that burning need to portray everything, if, with fear and trembling, he probes into the bosom of Nature [*s'il entrouve avec frémissement le sein de la nature*] to seek his art therein and extract models to follow, if he possesses the fever of talent and the enthusiasm of genius, let him follow the hand that leads him; once having divined man, he will paint him.[24]

Above and beyond his provocative metaphor of writing as an incestuous penetration of nature, Sade's description of the novelist's mission plays upon many of the images that were typically associated with the figure of the Enlightenment philosophe: images of opening up, of uncovering what lies hidden in the interior of the human heart, mind, and body, and then of representing what one has seen with the feverish talent and enthusiasm of the natural genius. These images, and the tension they imply between what is visible and invisible in human nature, are rooted in the eighteenth-century preoccupation with visual observation and sensory detection.[25] Yet Sade's remarks also suggest that one of the best ways of performing those activities was within discourse, where representations of the human "inside" could, if conveyed with sufficient force and detail, be just as compelling as seeing the real thing. This affirmation of the powers of discourse to seize the truths of nature is related to the aesthetics of intensity that had been promoted by earlier literary author-theorists (Diderot in particular); but it is also related to a larger quest for knowledge through writing that was central to the natural-philosophical discourse of the Enlightenment. In describing the novelist's art, therefore, Sade invests it with an objective to which the period's medical authors also aspired: that of revealing and replicating the natural language that lay hidden within the recesses of the human being.[26]

One of the goals of this book is to recover the connections that existed between eighteenth-century literature and medicine as *textual* undertakings— that is, as efforts both to represent sensibility discursively and to educate or warn readers about it. This is not an exhaustive study of everything that was written about sensibility in medicine or in literature during the French Enlightenment; rather, it is a strategic consideration of the two fields both on their own terms and in interaction. I have not elaborated a general, comprehensive theory about that interaction because I believe that it is more useful to focus on the particular resonances that occur between the particular texts one is comparing.[27] To that end, I have studiously avoided the temptation to systematize the links that exist between the themes, vocabulary, or "symptoms" used in the medical and literary texts in my corpus, for fear of impoverishing the texts themselves and finding only facile equivalences between them rather than their deeper points of convergence and difference.[28] In embracing this localized methodology, I have endeavored to emulate Jean Starobinski's model of the cautious interpreter-critic, who takes pains to ensure that the language of the literary text he or she is analyzing makes a safe passage into his or her own critical language.[29] Critics who straddle the fields of literature and medicine must, likewise, ensure that the transpositions or transcodings they make between *those* two languages are valid, substantial, and productive. Such critics, in fact, have a triple task: they must read each text in their corpus with a rigorous attention to its integral nature; they must avoid simplifying either of the discursive fields involved in their inquiry; and they must, in the words of G. S. Rousseau, "become historians of science, or at least historians of science *manqué.*"[30]

In that spirit, I begin this book on a primarily historical note, with three chapters that illustrate the emergence of vital sensibility as a crucial object of investigation in eighteenth-century physiology, philosophy of mind, and philosophical medicine. In Chapter 1, I examine the landmark experimental studies of sensibility and irritability that Haller presented in his *Dissertation on the Sensible and Irritable Parts of Animals* (Latin, 1752; French, 1755) and then consider Charles Bonnet's efforts in the *Essai analytique sur les facultés de l'âme* (1759) to extend Hallerian physiology into the realm of sensationalist philosophy. In Chapter 2, I analyze how the notion of vital sensibility resounded through the philosophical medicine that was promoted between the 1750s and the 1770s by the vitalist-leaning physicians of the Montpellier school, whose leader was Théophile de Bordeu—later cast somewhat caricaturally as an interlocutor in Diderot's *Rêve de d'Alembert* (1769). The texts treated in this chapter include Louis de Lacaze's *Idée de l'homme physique et moral* (1755), several of the articles that Montpellier physicians wrote for the *Encyclopédie*, and works by Bordeu, including the *Recherches anatomiques sur la position des glandes et leur action* (1752), where Bordeu first described the organological model of bodily sensibility that would soon prove central not only to eighteenth-century medical doctrine but also to Diderot's theory of sensibility. In Chapter 3, I consider how mid-century medical writers used the new physio-philosophy of sensibility to "medicalize" the enlightenment project itself: I read, first, the optimistic plans for improving humanity's physical and intellectual capacities that were put forth in the *Médecine de l'esprit* (1753) by Antoine Le Camus, and in the *Essai sur la manière de perfectionner l'espèce humaine* (1756) by Charles Augustin Vandermonde; and second, the far less rosy picture of the quest for intellectual refinement that the Swiss physician Samuel-Auguste-André-David Tissot painted in *De la santé des gens de lettres* (1766).

In Part 2, I undertake the truly cross-disciplinary part of my study, by comparing how the physio-philosophy of sensibility was deployed as a structuring concept in selected groupings of novels and medical texts—both of which genres gave striking narrative form to the emerging models of the sensible body. Once again, my comparison of literature and medicine is strategic. That is, rather than juxtaposing texts from each field according to a strictly equal, fifty-fifty partition, I move back and forth *between* literature and medicine, using as my guiding principle the theoretical preoccupations that were common to both: for example, the epistemology and aesthetics involved in observing and interpreting bodily sensibility and in transmitting such observations in discursive form (Chapter 5); the ambiguous moral ramifications of sensibility and the efforts to control that ambiguity by hygienic means (Chapters 6 and 7); and the anthropological implications of sensibility, which became particularly pronounced in the last few decades of the century (Chapters 7 and 8). One might well ask why I single out the novel for this investigation; to be sure, sensibility was also central to eighteenth-century theater, especially to the hybrid dramatic genre known as the *drame bourgeois*. However, the literary genre in which sensibility's expanded meanings were most provocatively deployed was, without question, the novel. As I explain in Chapter 4 (where I discuss works by Crébillon, Prévost, Marivaux, and Graffigny), the representation of sensibility in the novel prior to 1750 was virtually inseparable from the social, moral, and linguistic codes of the aristocratic or worldly class. After 1750, however, literary sensibility took on new meanings, at least in the hands of certain authors: the novel became a fertile testing ground for exploring the medico-philosophical idea that all facets of human existence could, ultimately, be traced to this essential vital property.

Diderot, for example, created fictions like *La Religieuse* (1760) that both echoed and exploited the Montpellier physicians' conception of the body as a resonating sensible network; I examine that novel, along with Diderot's *Éloge de Richardson* and selected aspects of Bordeu's medical theory, in Chapter 5. Rousseau, in turn, used *La Nouvelle Héloïse* (1758) to carry out the hygienically based *morale sensitive* that he envisioned as a means of containing sensibility within wholesome, moderate bounds; in Chapter 6, I read Rousseau's fiction in juxtaposition to Tissot's like-minded medical treatise *Essai sur les maladies des gens du monde* (1770).

Pursuing my study of how physicians sought to contain sensibility's excessive manifestations, I devote Chapter 7 to the peculiar branches of eighteenth-century medical writing known as "vapors" theory and moral anthropology, where sensibility's complex relationship with sex evolved into a theory of sexual incommensurability first expressed in Pierre Roussel's *Système physique et moral de la femme* (1775). The specter of vapors introduced an unsettling note into the doctrine of sensibility, a property that had once seemed to be the unequivocally positive mark of an ungendered moral elite but was now increasingly associated with the debilitated, effeminate members of the leisure class; the theory of radical, gender-based dimorphism proposed by medical thinkers like Roussel, Paul-Victor de Sèze, and Pierre-Jean-Georges Cabanis effectively "solved" that problem by splitting sensibility's meanings differentially between women and men. In Chapter 8, I return to the novel to consider how Laclos and Sade deployed the new understanding of sensibility's "feminine" versus "masculine" forms and applied them not only to their fictional characters but also to the very act of novel-writing. Through novels that ironically mimicked the conventions of both literary sentimentalism and moral anthropology, Laclos and Sade redirected the doctrine of sensibility to support libertinism—a philosophy utterly antithetical to the social and moral meliorism which the sensibility paradigm had previously upheld. In the Conclusion, I examine what happened to sensibility in the aftermath of the Enlightenment, when the concept's meaning within specific fields became so particularized that its power as a unified conceptual construct was progressively compromised. Sensibility in its Enlightenment sense did not disappear during the nineteenth century; rather, it splintered into a number of discrete legacies and yielded its previously undisputed primacy to such new notions as *volonté*, *vie de relation*, and the renewed dualism of Romantic spiritualism.

PART I

The Making of the Sensible Body

1. Constructing a Vital Property

The New Physiology and
Psycho-Philosophy
of Sensibility

Haller and the "Discovery" of Vital Properties

To retrace the process by which sensibility became a major conceptual metaphor in eighteenth-century France, I will begin by considering the new physiological model of the body that developed in the 1740s and 1750s. We should note, first of all, that physiology did not yet exist as a field independent of medical theory at the time; very few of the authors who wrote on the functions of living bodies prior to the 1790s even called themselves physiologists.[1] Moreover, until the Swiss anatomist-physiologist Albrecht von Haller became prominent at mid-century, most physiological investigations were not specifically directed at discerning the singularity of organic, as opposed to nonorganic, phenomena.[2] The rise of sensibility thus coincided with an effort to remake physiology so that its methodology would be both more empirically grounded and better suited for discerning the vital powers that were truly immanent to the body. Fixing the nature of sensibility was a central feature of this enterprise, particularly as pursued by Haller and those who responded, favorably or otherwise, to his call for a new system of vital properties. It was also a major preoccupation of French and Francophone sensationalist philosophers like the Abbé de Condillac and Charles Bonnet, who embraced John Locke's "historical, plain" approach to the operations of the intellect.[3] Thanks to their common focus on sensibility, sensation, and the nervous system, the fields of physiology and psychological philosophy converged to a significant degree; and as a result, the concepts of body and mind were stripped of their metaphysical content and became redefined as physiological questions that could be addressed through experimental inquiry.[4]

This process of redefinition is clearly apparent in the writings of Albrecht von Haller, who was preoccupied with sensibility and its companion property, irritability, for most of his scientific career. Haller was a tireless investigator who attracted a large circle of assistants, students, and admirers, many of whom strove diligently to corroborate and augment his enormous collection of experiments on the nature of living matter.[5] He himself brought a clear sense of mission to his work as a physiologist: he sought to develop an empirically grounded understanding of how organic structure and function are integrated and thus to give the budding science of the organism a more rigorous foundation than it had previously possessed. This quest sparked an unprecedented amount of attention and debate among natural philosophers throughout Europe—not just because of Haller's exceptional methodological precision but also because he published his experiments on sensibility and irritability at a moment that was propitious in many ways. In physiology proper, the existing mechanistic systems for explaining the animal economy were beginning to seem inadequate because they relied so heavily on forces external to the body. In philosophy, the empiricist perspective popularized by Locke and others had shifted the study of the mind away from Cartesian dualism and toward an emphasis on how the intellectual faculties arise from their base in the sense organs. And in literature and moral philosophy, sensibility was taking on new and very positive connotations through its increasingly strong association with the notions of sociability, virtue, and benevolent feeling toward one's fellows. The time was thus ripe for a new, organically grounded explanation of how the human being acts, feels, and thinks. Indeed, no sooner had Haller divulged his theories on the body's essential reactive capacities than they were transposed into contexts as diverse as epistemology, psychology, disease theory, medical semiotics, and moral doctrine. Generally speaking, however, these transpositions were anything but faithful: Haller's concepts of sensibility and irritability, along with his experimental methodology, were so loosely adapted that they often became something quite different from what he had specified.

On the basis of his curriculum vitae, one might judge Haller to have been a quintessential Enlightenment scholar: in addition to writing such major physiological textbooks as *Prime Lineae Physiologiae* (1747) and the eight-volume *Elementa Physiologiae Corporis Humani* (1757–66), he was a poet, a public administrator, and a natural philosopher renowned for his vigorous exchanges with prominent contemporaries on the pressing scientific issues of the day.[6] Yet Haller had serious reservations about many of the social and scientific theories circulating at the time: he referred to the Paris of the philosophes as "the frivolous island," and strove, as principal medical contributor to the *Supplément* to the *Encyclopédie*, to refute what he considered to be the excesses of the original medical Encyclopedists.[7] Historians generally agree that Haller's most broadly influential work was his *Dissertation on the Sensible and Irritable Parts of Ani-*

mals, published in Latin in 1752, translated into French by the Swiss physician Samuel-André-Auguste-David Tissot in 1755, and then adapted to serve as the first volume of the *Mémoires sur la nature sensible et irritable des parties du corps animal* (1756–60).[8] Haller's chief aim in this text was to demonstrate the existence of irritability, the capacity to contract upon stimulation which he viewed as unique to muscle fibers. He also wanted to prove that bodily reactibility should be seen as having two utterly different modes of operation: the motile property he called irritability, and the feeling property known as sensibility. As Shirley Roe observes, "It is difficult to find a physiological or medical treatise of the late eighteenth or early nineteenth century that does not use (or misuse) irritability, and its distinction from sensibility, in some fashion."[9] Roe's remarks are, however, better suited to the mid-eighteenth century, when Haller's work was initially published and debated; for it was then that his experimental reports on sensibility and irritability aroused the most excitement among naturalists and medical experts.

Haller was recognized by his contemporaries as either a hero to be emulated or a formidable enemy to refute; he was one of the first physiologists to employ a reliable and replicable battery of experimental techniques as a means of isolating the structural anatomical unit best suited to support a given vital response.[10] By his own count, Haller performed vivisections on 190 animals for his *Dissertation* alone, in order to prove his thesis that sensibility is visibly restricted to the nerve fiber and irritability to muscle fiber. Yet that distinction was quickly blurred by his followers, both those sympathetic to his neomechanistic view of the animal economy and those opposed to it. Julien Offray de La Mettrie, for example, applied the concept of irritability to the soul in *L'Homme machine* (1748), thereby sending shock waves through the European intellectual community, not least because he slyly dedicated the work to the widely respected Baron von Haller. By associating Haller's name with his treatise, La Mettrie was not simply playing a joke on the pious (and humorless) Swiss scientist.[11] He was also using Hallerian physiology to support a materialist philosophy to which Haller was violently opposed, but which La Mettrie maintained was "the only philosophy that can here be considered, that of the human body."[12] Although most of the theorists who reacted to Haller's work were far more deferential, they too tended to adapt his ideas to suit the purposes of their own theories. Thus, as Haller's concepts of sensibility and irritability were disseminated among physiologists, physicians, and philosophes at large, his doctrine underwent a significant mutation: sensibility and irritability were fused into one reactive "superproperty," with emphasis placed variously on one term or the other.

For reasons that have as much to do with its wider cultural resonances as with physiology, sensibility—rather than irritability—became the term generally accepted by eighteenth-century thinkers to designate this all-encompassing vital property.[13] Haller's definition of sensibility was, by contrast, highly constrained, largely because he brought two rather contradictory theoretical concerns to bear upon the property. As a physiologist, Haller sought to elucidate the vital forces that inhered in the body itself. Yet as a natural philosopher with a conservative religious bent, he also sought to preserve some degree of independence for the soul, which he insisted should be seen as an immaterial entity that communicates with the body through the nerves. Because he was so intent on affirming the philosophical principle that the soul's unity of consciousness cannot be compromised by the body, Haller's criteria for "observing" the physiological operations of sensibility were quite different from those that he applied to irritability. In other words, even as he championed empirical physiological investigation as the only means of approaching vital phenomena, Haller viewed sensibility as a force that lay somewhat beyond the pale of that mode of investigation. Others, however, would not see the need for such a constricted approach to the property. These theorists—most particularly the semivitalist physicians of the Montpellier school—were those who would set the tone for the more general discourse on sensibility that predominated at the height of the French Enlightenment.

꿎 ꕤ

Historians of science generally credit Haller with ushering in a distinct era of physiological investigation, delimited as falling between the 1740s and 1770s, when biomedical thinking shifted from mechanistic models of the body towards various forms of vitalism.[14] Haller himself viewed his physiological doctrine not as a radical break with earlier systems, but as an updated recasting of the theories of his mentor, Herman Boerhaave, a famous professor of medicine and chemistry at Leyden who attracted a wider European following during the early eighteenth century than any other medical theorist.[15] Haller's first publication was, in fact, an annotated edition of Boerhaave's *Institutiones Medicae* (1708), which appeared from 1739 to 1743 as *Praelectiones Academicae in Proprias Institutiones Rei Medicae.*

In prefacing my study of Haller's physiology with a brief consideration of Boerhaave's, I do not aim to give a comprehensive account of Boerhaavian theory, nor to examine all of the many corrections Haller made on it. Rather, I seek to compare these thinkers on two select points of their respective physiological models: the vital forces they saw as crucial to the animal economy and the structural units they proposed to support those forces. One of the primary reasons that Haller's *Dissertation on the Sensible and Irritable Parts of Animals* was immediately received as groundbreaking was that he redefined the very elements of physiology. Although Haller himself was deeply skeptical about the speculative extrapolations that other thinkers made on his notions of irritability and sensibility, his realignment of the body's basic properties was nonetheless critical in establishing the conceptual framework on which the paradigm of vital sensibility would soon be built.

Like most medical thinkers of his day (with the important exception of Georg-Ernst Stahl), Boerhaave was an iatromechanist: he was convinced that, to understand the structure and action of the living body, one must look at it in terms of the geometrico-mechanical principles governing all bodies, animate and inanimate. Boerhaave therefore drew his explicative models for physiology from fields like mechanics and subscribed to the mechanistic philosophy that dominated thinking about nature and matter in the latter half of the seventeenth century.[16] Briefly described, iatromechanism had three central tenets: first, the basic activity of all material bodies is motion; second, all matter is ultimately corpuscular in composition; and third, final physical causes, like the "essence" and activating impetus of motile matter, lie beyond the purview of the experimental philosopher.[17] Boerhaave's *Institutiones Medicae*, written according to these theoretical strictures, limited physiological inquiry to examining the fundamental material attributes of the body: its elemental parts, the structural units they form, and the manner in which life is maintained by those structures.

Seen from Boerhaave's iatromechanistic perspective, the living body is made up of material corpuscles that adhere together with varying degrees of cohesiveness, depending on whether they are in a fluid or solid state (*Inst.*, 18). The function of the solid parts—which he compares to a variety of mechanical instruments, including cords, pulleys, funnels and bellows—is to support, conduct, filter, and hold the fluid parts, whose actions are to be interpreted according to the laws of hydrostatics, hydraulics, and general mechanics (18–19). Boerhaave's extensive "tool-chest" inventory of the functions of the solid parts is typical of iatromechanistic theory. He is, however, unusually careful in his attempt to coordinate the anatomical macrostructure he perceives in the body parts with their supposed invisible microstructures. To that end, he reformulates ancient solid/fluid doctrine in terms of the theory of blood circulation put forth in 1628 by William Harvey, to produce a model of the body as an essentially *vascular* machine—that is, a set of fixed (solid) and moving (fluid) parts that work together to form an elaborate hydraulic circuit encompassing digestion, blood circulation, and the transmission of the animal spirits.

Boerhaave's system is based upon a humoral teleology that reduces every physiological action to something analogous to digestion. The ultimate purpose of the living machine, he declares, is to produce and refine the three vital fluids necessary to ensure the "reciprocal commerce of the body and soul" that makes human existence possible (*Inst.*, 20). Each of these three essential fluids—chyle, blood, and nervous fluid—arises at a particular stage in the progressive grinding action exerted by the solid parts. Whether it be a primary organ (stomach, heart, lungs) or a true vessel, every solid part thus serves to carry and abrade the mixed chylous-blood fluid and then propel it on to a site of further refinement.[18] The ultimate product of this process is a "subtle humor" whose composition varies according to the gland in which it is separated out of the blood (185). Boerhaave places the nervous fluid at the top of his hierarchy of nutritive and animating fluids because he regards it as the penultimate vital force, or the closest thing to a "hidden cause" that one can discern in living matter (279). Although he does not endow nervous fluid with overtly spiritual qualities, he describes it as the only substance sufficiently fine and quick to direct the most complex operations of the living machine. That is, only nervous fluid can infiltrate muscular fibers instantaneously, overcome their natural resistance, and cause them to contract in response to the influx of blood into their hollow centers (279–80). Boerhaave's conception of muscle contraction thus corroborates his thesis that the entire solid edifice of the body consists of vessels within vessels: muscles, as he depicts them, become active motile instruments only through the agency of a hydraulic impetus that is induced and regulated by adjoining nerves.

The highly systematic approach that Boerhaave takes to physiological function and structure offers a useful counterpoint to Haller's on several counts. First, because of his preoccupation with the transformations of the body's fluid parts, Boerhaave assigns a rather passive role to their solid counterparts. Moreover, whenever he must explain a phenomenon whose intricacies surpass a simple hydrostatic or hydraulic model, he resorts to invoking what was generally viewed at the time as a quasi-metaphysical force: innervation. These tendencies are particularly apparent in his theory of muscular contraction—a theory that was also one of the few specific aspects of Boerhaavian physiology which Haller singled out as categorically wrong.[19]

As Haller relates at the end of his *Dissertation on the Sensible and Irritable Parts of Animals*, it was a disagreement with Boerhaave's explanation of the mechanism of contraction that prompted him to develop a new model for muscular action, and thus to "discover" irritability. This is how he explains his original objection—made, as he tells us, in 1739—thirteen years later:

> Dr. BOERHAAVE has acknowledged an active force in the heart, and a latent principle of motion in the pieces of it which are cut; but as he attrib-

P. F. Tardieu, after Charles Eisen, Demonstration of Physiology, *frontispiece to Albrecht von Haller,* Elementa Physiologiae Corporis Humani *(1757–1766). (Photograph courtesy of the National Library of Medicine, Bethesda, Md.)*

utes the cause of muscular motion to the nerves, this proves that he did not sufficiently know, that the cause of this motion was in the muscles themselves, that the nerves had no other office but to subject them to the will of the soul, and that they could indeed increase or diminish it, but were not the cause of it, because it is extended far beyond the nervous system . . . In my commentaries upon BOERHAAVE'S *Institutions,* published in 1739, I have expressed myself as follows, *Wherefore the heart is moved by some unknown cause, which neither depends upon the brain nor the arteries, but lays concealed in the very structure of the heart itself.* The nature of the thing obliged me to differ in opinion from my preceptor. (*Diss.,* 43–44)

Clearly, Haller's view of the body's true nature diverges from that of his mentor on both anatomical and physiological grounds. First, he disagrees with Boerhaave's structural model of the contracting muscle as a simple, hollow vessel; he refutes this notion by citing his own anatomical observations of the muscular fiber, which show it to be neither vascular, nor passive, nor significantly innervated. Second, he disputes the thesis that vital movement, the most basic of bodily actions, must depend on some means of control at a distance that is mysteriously located in the brain or arteries. For reasons that I will explore shortly, Haller emphatically rejects the idea that the brain—locus of the conscious, sentient soul—has anything to do with a vital motion like heart contraction.

Haller's forceful repudiation of Boerhaave's hypothesis on contraction in the heart reveals the fundamental principle of his own theoretical approach: namely, his conviction that, to discern the mechanisms underlying vital phenomena, one must look at the body not through the homologizing lens of traditional iatromechanistic theory, but rather, through the perspective provided by recent discoveries in anatomy, microscopy, and vivisection. In his own physiological investigations, Haller doggedly undertook to locate vital microstructures in the organic fabric itself. And to explain the reactive properties that he believed resided in those microstructures, he transformed not just the analogy-bound interpretive technique used by his predecessors, but also the basic building blocks of physiology. That is, Haller shifted the focus of physiological thinking from hydraulic forces to immanent forces, and from the vessel to the fiber—the structural unit whose anatomical and chemical organization was, in his view, more properly suited to house those forces. In the process, he effectively remapped the living body, replacing the hierarchical Boerhaavian topology of solid and fluid parts with a decentralized topology of sensible and irritable fibers and organs.

In his early physiological primer, *First Lines of Physiology* (1747), Haller starts by describing the human body as "composed either of fluids or solids"; in contrast to Boerhaave, however, he insists that what "forms the most simple and true basis of the body" are the solid parts, which, at the smallest perceptible level, are "either fibres or an unorganized concrete."[20] By "fiber," Haller means a line made up of "earthy particles" that are held together by an "intermediate glue" (*FL*, 1:10).[21] Fibers, he asserts, fall into two main categories: lineal fibers, which can align their components into arrangements of higher complexity, as in muscles and nerves; and the more amorphous "cellular" kind, which play only a supporting role in vital activities. The reactive capacity that a particular organ can possess depends, therefore, on which kind of fibers it contains and how they are disposed. This fibrillar disposition also determines the various "powers" that a given body part possesses or to which it can respond. Haller singles out three basic powers at work in the living body and illustrates each power's distinct characteristics by focusing upon the mechanism of muscular contraction.

Muscle fiber, like every animal and vegetable fiber, has a simple contractile power that is closely analogous to the elasticity of inanimate bodies (*FL*, 1:226). It also possesses a second force "more proper to life," which Haller calls the *vis insita*—an immanent excitability so "tenacious" in organs like the intestines or heart that they continue to contract after being removed from the body (233). What most distinguishes the *vis insita,* according to Haller, is its capacity to operate even when communication with the nervous system is interrupted—a point he underscores by citing the exceptionally irritable disposition of animals classified as brainless, like polyps (234).[22] The third force present in muscle fiber is the *vis nervosa,* which stimulates the fiber to carry out the brain's commands. This power can, he asserts, be turned off simply "by tying a ligature upon the nerve, by hurting the brain, or by drinking opium"—all various methods of interrupting the circuit of conscious feeling. He thus deems sentience, a power specific to the will and consciousness, to be merely incidental to the physical mechanism of motility: "The will excites and removes the nervous power, but has no power over the *vis insita*" (235). Haller declines to enter into "the direct manner by which the nerves excite motion in the muscles," for he considers it "so obscure, that we may almost for ever despair of its discovery" (236). Yet he insists that the *vis insita* and *vis nervosa* are absolutely distinct, both in their probable anatomical microstructures and in their respective modes of operation; and he suggests that the explanation of these powers that he is currently developing through experimentation is far superior to the mere "hypotheses" that others have ventured.

In presenting those 567 experiments five years later in the *Dissertation on the Sensible and Irritable Parts of Animals,* Haller calls them "the source of a great many changes in physiology, pathology, and surgery" (*Diss.,* 8). Haller's physiology is, in his own mind, different because of its fidelity to the empirical method: deploying a formidable battery of instruments and substances, he and his assistants have conducted repeated *in vivo* assays on a range of animal subjects —dogs, cats, young goats, rats, frogs, eels, and fish, used interchangeably—in order to find evidence of irritability or sensibility in each part of the body.[23] An irritable part, as Haller defines it, is one that shortens upon being touched by some foreign body, whereas a sensible part is one whose stimulation elicits a sign of pain in the feeling soul (8–9). He admits that this criterion is somewhat more difficult to apply to animals than to humans: "In brutes, in whom the existence of a soul is not so clear, I call those parts sensible, the Irritation of which occasions evident signs of pain and disquiet in the animal" (9).

Having established these working definitions, Haller proceeds to examine various body parts according to how they fit the definitions. This organic inventory, which makes up the greater part of the *Dissertation,* dwells somewhat tediously on the details of his procedures for proving or disproving rival hypotheses on the operations of the dura mater, tendons, peritoneum, and so on. It does, however, reveal an intriguing trio of assumptions on Haller's part as to what he has discovered in his laboratory investigations. First, he is confident

Albrecht von Haller and his disciples performing physiological experiments, frontispiece in Mémoires sur la nature sensible et irritable des parties du corps animal *(1756–1760). (Photograph courtesy of the Institute for the History of Medicine at the Johns Hopkins Medical Library, Baltimore, Md.)*

that he has succeeded in inducing and measuring both vital properties in a controlled experimental setting, thus providing factual grounds for his new topology of the body. Second, he believes that he has approximated, if not determined exactly, the combination of living matter in which those forces originally inhere. Finally, he is sure that his meticulous experiments will serve as an authoritative standard for speculating on the nature of the reactive forces that drive all living bodies.

The first of those assumptions—that irritability and sensibility can indeed be transformed into measurable, malleable laboratory phenomena—is apparent in the way that Haller charts the distribution of reactive properties among the body parts. For each property, he erects a scale of intensity that is calibrated according to the response he gets from an exemplary sensible or irritable organ. When testing for irritability, Haller measures the *vis insita* of each body part in relation to a standard set by the heart, diaphragm, and intestines, whose intensely irritable quality "furnishes us with a distinct character [*caractère différenciel*], between the vital organs and the others" (*Diss.*, 40). What is particular about the organs he singles out as highly irritable is not only that they are predominantly muscular, but also that their actions are entirely involuntary. In other words, Haller associates irritability strictly with the capacity to contract, and to do so independently of the dictates of the will. As for sensibility, his most dramatic experimental results are obtained in the brains and nerves themselves, which respond to his poking and prodding by throwing the poor victim into violent, spine-bending convulsions (21). He assigns the standard measure of sensibility to the skin because of its striking pattern of nerve endings: "The skin is sensible, and indeed more so than any other part of the body; for in whatever manner you irritate it, the animal makes a noise, struggles, and gives all the marks of pain that it is capable of " (10). At the end of his exhaustive survey, he concludes that, contrary to common belief, sensibility is not a significant force in the operations of most vital organs—both because he has not observed many nerve endings there, and because the "soul" does not seem to be painfully aroused when such parts are stimulated.[24]

One might argue that Haller is resorting here to the kind of analogical reasoning evident in Boerhaave's physiological system. Haller's model of the body, however, is based on not one but two different structural homologies; moreover, he uses his homologies not inclusively but *restrictively*. In the end, all of his experimental findings bear out his thesis that sensibility, the capacity to feel, and irritability, the capacity to move, are unrelated phenomena that should be treated separately. As he puts it, irritability is "so different from sensibility, that the most irritable parts are not at all sensible, and *vice versa*, the most sensible are not irritable . . . irritability does not depend upon the nerves, but on the original fabric of the parts which are susceptible of it" (*Diss.*, 25). It follows that the "original fabric" underlying each of these forces is unique, even if Haller cannot precisely determine what that primordial fabric is. Although his lamentably crude experimental techniques prevent him from seeing the submicroscopic disposition of irritability, Haller asserts confidently that it probably inheres in the elementary, invisible subparticles of muscular fibers. He is more tentative concerning sensibility: "The nerves alone are sensible of themselves, and their whole sensibility resides in their medullary part, which is a production of the internal substance of the brain" (24). Haller nevertheless considers his observations sufficiently precise to declare that sensibility has a very narrow realm of influence over the body's essential operations.

Haller's insistent elimination of sensibility as a causal factor in many essential bodily activities is inspired, in part, by his desire to refute certain aspects of Boerhaave's mechanistic physiological system, which made the entire animal economy hang upon the nerves and nervous fluid. Yet there is more to his dethroning of sentience than a mere squabble over anatomical or physiological "fact." For Haller bases his judgment of where sensibility is or is not located on a very particular notion of the soul as an immortal, indivisible, and reasoning entity. He thus finds it inappropriate, if not sacrilegious, for biomedical theorists to implicate the soul directly in such mundane activities as peristaltic movement.[25] By evacuating sensibility from all but a limited number of body parts, Haller erects what appears to be a rigid dividing line between the involuntary and voluntary sides of life—that is, between the ongoing, unconscious operations of the animal machine (the domain of irritability) and the physical activities that are willed by the soul, which uses the sensible fibers of the nerves as its medium of communication with the body.

That dividing line is most explicitly drawn at a moment in the *Dissertation* when, while describing the often gruesome vivisections he has conducted to test for irritability, Haller digresses into a philosophical meditation on the manner in which the human soul and body are connected. It is clear, given the length of this oddly placed metaphysical digression, that Haller seeks to underscore the larger philosophical framework through which he perceives the vital forces and their domain:

> The soul is a being which is conscious of itself, represents to itself the body to which it belongs, and by means of that body the whole universe. I am myself, and not another, because that which is called I, is changed by every thing that happens to my body and the parts belonging to it. If there is a muscle, or an intestine, whose suffering makes impressions upon another soul, and not upon mine, the soul of that muscle or intes-

tine is not mine, it does not belong to me. But a finger cut off from my hand, or a bit of flesh from my leg, has no connexion with me, I am not sensible of any of its changes, they can neither communicate to me idea nor sensation; wherefore it is not inhabited by my soul nor by any part of it; if it was, I should certainly be sensible of its changes. I am therefore not at all in that part that is cut off, it is entirely separated both from my soul, which remains as entire as ever, and from those of all other men. The amputation of it has not occasioned the least harm to my will, which remains quite entire, and my soul has lost nothing at all of its force, but it has no more command over that amputated part, which in the mean while continues still to be irritable. Irritability therefore is independent of the soul and the will. (*Diss.*, 28)

Haller is adamant that the soul must be viewed in strictly noncorporeal terms: that is, as an entity which depends on the body purely to receive and process information about the world around it, and whose integrity cannot be compromised by any accidents that might happen to the body with which it is associated. The soul, of course, feels the changes and variations that occur in the body's diverse parts; but, to use Haller's example, losing a finger or a leg does not affect the soul directly because the soul does not truly inhabit the flesh. By taking this staunchly spiritualist perspective, Haller finds a way to describe the soul's activities as unique and ultimately independent of the body, just as he describes the forces immanent in the body as independent of the soul.

Nowhere in the *Dissertation* is Haller's basic metaphysical stance so clear as in this excursus, after which he promptly returns to his ongoing laboratory report. That stance, however brief in its expression, is plainly pivotal to his overall doctrine of the animal economy, particularly to his view of sensibility as marginal to the body's most vital functions. Because, according to Haller's definition, sensibility is the primary force of the soul, it cannot truly inhere in the body. As a vital property, therefore, it is situated on the boundaries of physiological investigation: he can induce manifestations of sentience in his laboratory, but he will go no further in interpreting them than to label them as pain or discomfort. This extremely narrow experimental definition of sensibility provides, in Haller's eyes, a double safeguard: it both ensures the soul's noble qualities from corporeal compromise and protects his own physiological findings from undue metaphysical speculation.

This would, of course, turn out to be wishful thinking on Haller's part. By defining the reactive properties so narrowly, Haller managed to pursue his physiological investigations without endangering the principle of the unity of consciousness, but also without really tackling the perplexing question of how brain structure correlates to mental activity. Hallerian sensibility was thus, as Karl Figlio puts it, "rigorous in its experimental definition, but indefinite in its possible philosophical interpretations."[26] As a consequence of the philosophical blurriness of Haller's physiological system, the concepts of irritability and sensibility were left open to all sorts of adaptations and redefinitions.

For example, even before Haller presented in the *Dissertation* his experimental proof that the irritability of muscle fiber is self-generated, it had already attracted the notice of La Mettrie, the most notorious philosophical speculator of the day. Various scholars have drawn attention to the strong influence that the field of medicine exerted on *L'Homme machine*, where La Mettrie drew heavily on the latest physio-anatomical experiments to prove his argument that the only true philosophers are physicians.[27] In the most detailed of such studies, Aram Vartanian goes so far as to assert that "La Mettrie's conception and use of irritability was a brilliant step forward in the history of general physiology," one that "went beyond [Haller's work] . . . with respect to depth and correctness."[28] Yet we should not mistake the invocation of the physiology of irritability in *L'Homme machine* for anything more than a strategy. By making irritability the universal property of all parts of the human being, La Mettrie sought, not to contribute to contemporary physiology *per se*, but rather to exploit its radical philosophical implications, most particularly concerning such traditionally spiritualized activities as thought and virtue. It may seem curious that, of the two vital principles proposed by Haller, La Mettrie focused almost exclusively on irritability, or innate motile capacity, yet mentioned the "feeling" principle of sensibility only in a few sentimental passages on the natural benevolence he deemed common to humans and animals alike (*Man a Machine*, 116–21). That choice, too, was strategic: La Mettrie emphasized irritability because, of the two reactive properties that Haller had identified in the body, only irritability was entirely corporeal.

Haller replied to this blatantly materialist appropriation of his physiological theory in the final paragraphs of the *Dissertation on the Sensible and Irritable Parts of Animals*, where he railed against La Mettrie (who had died in 1751) for having made irritability "the basis of the system which he advanced against the spirituality of the soul" (*Diss.*, 45).[29] Haller presents La Mettrie's system here as the ultimate affront to his experiments—but not just because materialism is, in his view, metaphysically unacceptable, nor because La Mettrie had the audacity to call himself the "inventor" of the irritability principle.[30] Rather, Haller takes offense at this use of the concept on anatomical and physiological grounds. After noting that La Mettrie "founded his impious system . . . without ever having made the least experiment" on irritability, Haller launches his counterargument: "[Given that Irritability subsists after death, and occurs in] parts separate from the body, and [is] not subject to the command of the soul, [and given that] it resides everywhere in the muscular fibres, and is independent of the nerves, which are the satellites of the soul, it is evident, that it has nothing in common with the soul, and it is absolutely different from it; in a word, that neither Irritability depends on the soul, nor is the soul what we call Irritability in the body" (*Diss.*, 45–46; *Mémoires*, 1:90–91). Haller thus implies that a faithful reader of his experimental findings could not possibly ignore his distinctions of body and soul, irritability and sensibility, by linking the wrong property to the wrong entity. Yet La Mettrie did just that, precisely in order to dismantle the careful separation between physics and metaphysics that Haller was so intent on upholding.

Interestingly, in the final volume of the *Mémoires sur la nature sensible et irritable des parties du corps animal* (1760), Haller confesses that he, too, once felt the temptation to make more of the irritability principle than what had actually met his eye during his experiments: "I had worked a great deal on irritability, and particularly that of the heart, and I was keenly tempted to extend its empire and make it the source of the movement of the arteries, that of the glands, of secretions, and of fevers . . . I was ready to make it the sole motivating force [*ressort*] of the living machine. But Nature opposed the system that was beginning to get the better of me . . . Driven back by the province that I sought to conquer, I was obliged to withdraw, and content myself with the empire of the muscles" (*Mémoires*, 4:34–35). It is quite enough, in Haller's view, to have "conquered" the domain of the muscular fiber by proving that it is governed by irritability; conjecturing about the possible irritability of other body parts would take him beyond the boundaries of physio-anatomical observation (*Mémoires*, 4:96). Ironically, the urge to transform this property into *the* law of living matter is amply evident in the "Discours préliminaire" that precedes the French edition of the *Dissertation*. In this lengthy preface, the work's translator, Tissot, presents the discovery of irritability as a glorious breakthrough sure to revolutionize everything from the way laboratory inquiries are conducted, to the treatment of fevers and inflammation, to the foundations of ethics: "All of animal mechanics turns upon this principle, and it is easy to predict what a change this discovery will produce once its facts are fully explained: we owe Physics to England [that is, to Newton], but we will owe Physiology to Switzerland, and the Memoir on Irritability will be its immutable foundation . . . NATURE, that word so famous in Medicine, that word which everyone uses so often but understands so little, will be finally determined; it is *the sum of the forces of the vital principle*" (*Mémoires*, 1:xiv, xx). Thus, even Haller's translator makes assumptions about his physiological findings that go far beyond Haller's own claims: Tissot asserts, first, that there is only one reactive property—

irritability—that is truly essential to physiological activity; and second, that irritability is the long-sought vital principle, the key to nature itself.[31] The Francophone reader who begins Haller's treatise with Tissot's introduction is consequently led to interpret it in a way that contradicts all of the author's provisos, including his warning not to mistake irritability for "the sole motivating force of the living machine" (*Mémoires*, 4:35).

One might dismiss Tissot's remarks as a translator's excessive enthusiasm were it not for the fact that the "Discours préliminaire" typifies the way that Haller's experiments were received upon publication: with a rush of refutations, applications, and speculations from all sides. Some natural philosophers sought to maintain Haller's absolute distinction between the two vital properties he identified; others claimed that sensibility was the sole reactive principle of the animal economy; and still others, like La Mettrie, blithely described everything right down to the soul as "irritable." Those who went farthest in theorizing about the body's freshly discovered fibers and forces were the self-described *médecins philosophes* of Montpellier, who provide the focus of my discussion in Chapter 2. Yet physicians were not alone in leaping to speculative conclusions about the new physiology of vitality, for Haller brought forth his treatise in an era that was already acutely attuned to the way that humans respond to stimuli—whether those stimuli are organic, moral, erotic, aesthetic, or intellectual. Against this backdrop, and given the malleability that persisted in Haller's experimental definitions of irritability and sensibility, it is little wonder that his physiological concepts cropped up in all kinds of contexts. Hallerian physiology was in this sense bound to be opened up and transposed, in whole or in part, to a wider and more diverse realm. In the process, the soul/body dualism to which Haller held so tenaciously tended to soften philosophically as well as physiologically, as natural philosophers moved toward a monistic view of nature (and of human nature in particular).[32] Contributing to that trend was the emergence of physiological or quasi-physiological inquiries into the mind's functions, most of which revolved around a nebulous but conceptually fruitful entity known as the common sensorium—the semiphysical, semimetaphysical site where Hallerian sensibility supposedly originated.

The *Sensorium Commune*: Visualizing Sensibility in the Soul

The new topology that Haller proposed for the human body was both exhaustive in its details and full of holes—areas deliberately left unexplored by this most intrepid of eighteenth-century physiological investigators. Although he proudly drew attention to his discovery of the contractile power he called irritability, Haller left the nature of sensibility, the feeling power, far more undetermined. In *First Lines of Physiology*, for example, he meticulously described the configuration of the brain and nerves but refused to hypothesize about how the physical fabric of the nervous system is integrated with the operations of sensibility. All that he would assert is that this integration probably occurs at a site in the head where all of the nerves originate and the sensations of the mind are represented—that is, in the *sensorium commune,* where the soul is "present" to the brain (*FL,* 1:217–18).

Haller conceived of the common sensorium as abstractly located and anatomically simple: rejecting all of the earlier theories that had lodged the seat of the soul in a specific organ like the pineal gland or the corpus callosum, he would go no further than to say simply that the common sensorium consists of a "very soft pulp," fibrous in composition and structurally continuous with the nerves (*FL,* 1:218–24). He also defined it as functionally homogeneous in order to guarantee the unified integrity of the conscious mind, which can "entertain only one thought or idea at once" (*FL,* 2:47). In addition to suiting Haller's metaphysical notions about the soul and its mental activities, this vague locus of sensibility neatly accommodated his binary reactive topology: it allowed him to maintain that, despite the diversity of sensations evident in the body, there is only one basic mechanism for sentient reactibility. Haller thus visualized the common sensorium as an essential way station between the front-line sensory receptors (the nerves in the five sense organs), which collect and transmit the impressions of external objects, and the actual "place" of sensible reaction, the perceiving mind (*FL,* 2:33). Although he viewed the operations of the soul as "perfectly free and distinct from any corporeal faculty" (*FL,* 2:37), he made them depend upon sensibility, a property that somehow straddled the otherwise discrete domains of the physiological and the mental.

By depicting the common sensorium as a corporeal antechamber to the noncorporeal soul—an "organ" necessary for sensory perception and intellectual reflection alike—Haller struck a compromise between the empirical physiology he practiced and the dualistic metaphysics he espoused. Even when uttering the most confident pronouncements on the advances being made in contemporary physiology and anatomy (as, for example, in his articles for the *Supplément* to the *Encyclopédie*), Haller would remain vague about the composition of sensible fibers, both because their visibly soft and nondescript qualities gave no clue as to how they could support a powerful property like sensibility, and because he refused to conjecture about the mechanisms linking the body and the soul. Haller's model of the common sensorium was thus constructed (much like that of his predecessor Herman Boerhaave) on the basis not of clinical or experimental observation, but of larger theoretical concerns.[33]

During the eighteenth century, the elements of imprecision inherent in

Haller's concepts of the mind and brain tended to be remedied not within empirical physiology proper, but rather in the more speculative realms of natural philosophy and medical theory. There were two distinct groups of philosophes who took up the task of determining more exactly the nature of sensibility. First, there were the médecins philosophes, whose perspective on the interrelationship between body and mind was framed primarily by therapeutic preoccupations. Second, there were the philosophers of the sensationalist school, who took a Lockean approach to the mind that Jean d'Alembert characterized as "the experimental physics of the soul."[34] These philosophers generally shared Locke's reluctance to "meddle with the Physical consideration of the Mind";[35] at the same time, however, they were convinced that the mind's ideas were linked to certain as-yet undiscovered but regularized activities in the body. They therefore espoused the notion that somewhere in the neural substance there was a *physical* causal mechanism which, if unveiled, would undoubtedly support their fundamental thesis: all mental operations, both sentient and intellectual, could be traced back to an origin in sensation.

Modern scholars usually associate sensationalism in eighteenth-century France with Étienne Bonnot de Condillac, who refined Locke's mode of investigating the mind in works like the *Essai sur l'origine des connaissances humaines* (1746), the *Traité des sensations* (1754), and *La Logique* (1780). It was, however, Haller's faithful correspondent and fellow naturalist Charles Bonnet who strove most ambitiously to bridge the gap between metaphysical observation in the "analytic" mode popularized by Condillac and physiological observation in the style of Haller. Bonnet's *Essai analytique sur les facultés de l'âme* (1759) combined sensationalist epistemology with a Hallerian emphasis on detecting underlying reactive properties and their physical loci. Interestingly, Haller publicly endorsed his friend's efforts to extend his own meticulous laboratory observations into epistemology—or, in Bonnet's words, to "use a kind of *Physiology* that is beyond the range of the Scalpel and the Microscope."[36] Bonnet's kind of physiology entailed not only analyzing how sensations and ideas arise, but also "dissecting" the sensitive fibers that he believed were attached to each of those mental phenomena. He consequently produced both an intriguing solution to Haller's difficulties in determining the nature of sensibility and a model of the mind that was far more integrated with physiology than anything proposed by rival sensationalists.[37]

Bonnet, a widely respected Swiss naturalist best known for his exhaustive observations of insects, took up the study of metaphysics after his eyesight failed him.[38] He first sketched his plan for a full-fledged science of the soul in 1754, when he proposed aligning sensationalist philosophy and physiology under a new field he called psychology.[39] He did not, however, bring forth a definitive treatise on the subject until publishing the *Essai analytique sur les facultés de l'âme* in 1759. It is thus for reasons not of chronology but of approach that I have chosen Bonnet to represent eighteenth-century Francophone sensationalism, even though the decompositional mode of philosophical analysis he practiced is usually identified with better-known French philosophes such as Condillac, Buffon, and Diderot.[40] Like Haller, Bonnet used sensibility and the common sensorium as structuring concepts; yet he invested those concepts with far more precision than is apparent in Haller's hesitant, ambiguous account of them. What Bonnet aimed to do was, in fact, to elucidate the Hallerian model of sentience, by supplying the structure missing in the common sensorium and by "anatomizing" sensibility in his mind's eye.

Bonnet declares at the outset of his *Essai analytique* that to unlock the mysteries of "the mechanics of our ideas," one should look at ideas not in the soul itself, but rather, in "the Instrument that is used for their formation, their recollection, and their linking."[41] Real philosophy, he maintains, consists in following the methods of the empiricist observer of nature—an exemplar that is invoked throughout this text, embodied variously by Newton, Euler, Montesquieu, and Haller. Bonnet considers the process of analyzing the human being's sentient and cognitive capacities to be rigorously analogous, if not equivalent, to studying insects or plants (*EA*, vii). He thus reasons that a psycho-philosophical analysis of the mind can be accomplished by focusing on the aspects of the sentient/thinking instrument which one can "see"—that is, not ideas themselves, but the parts of the body on which they are inscribed:

> Man is a *mixed* being; he has ideas only through the intervention of the senses, and even his most abstract notions derive from the senses. It is on and through his body that the soul acts. One must therefore always return to the physical side of Man as the first origin of everything that the soul experiences. We know no better what an idea is in the soul, than what the soul itself is; but we know that ideas are attached to the workings of certain fibers: we can thus reason about these fibers because we see fibers; we can study a bit their movements, the results of their movements, and the connections they have among themselves. That is what I have tried to do in this work.   (xvi)

The simple physicalist analogy Bonnet posits here, according to which particular ideas are not merely associated with but also physically *attached* to particular fibers, is the key to the entire *Essai analytique*. For, by pursuing that analogy and all of the consequences that he can draw out of it, Bonnet is able to elaborate an extensive genealogy of sensibility—a genealogy that both explains the fibrillar derivation of all of man's higher faculties, and points the way to perfecting those faculties in the service of science, art, and morality (xxiii).[42]

This analogy permits Bonnet to have it both ways as he proceeds to "dissect" sensibility. On the one hand, he can adhere to the route for sense-based epistemological inquiries already established by Condillac, whose *Traité des sensations* set both the methodological standards for sensationalist analysis and the appropriate genre: the fable of the Statue-Man, a fictional creature whose mind is a tabula rasa which the philosopher brings into full functioning by progressively animating the sense organs (*EA*, 6).[43] It is, for example, in a Condillacian, mentalistic sense that Bonnet says "one must anatomize each fact, decompose it down to its smallest parts, and examine separately all of these parts" (ix).[44] On the other hand, Bonnet can also address the physical substrate of sensibility and propose working models of the common sensorium and its sensible fibers. When pursuing the question of anatomy in this second, more literal sense, Bonnet ventures far beyond Haller's cautious descriptions of the purported sensible body parts, yet without really transgressing the constraints that had been set on such investigations by contemporary empirical anatomists and physiologists.

Bonnet thus slips painlessly back and forth across the body/soul divide without offending anyone—in contrast to some of his more notorious fellow epistemologists, like La Mettrie and Helvétius (both of whom were widely denounced for describing the mind/soul in reductively physicalist terms). Writing in an atmosphere highly sensitive to the dangers of materialism, Bonnet avoids that pitfall by describing the union of body and soul as the product of "physical influence, occasional causes [the post-Cartesian doctrine that God intervenes in each instance where an act of mind is coordinated with a movement of the body], and preestablished Harmony" (*EA*, xxii–xxiii). Because he approaches the question through the perspective of his larger doctrine of preformed, universal harmony, Bonnet can assume that the ontological dilemma posed by the incommensurability of body and soul is already resolved. The *Essai analytique sur les facultés de l'âme* is, moreover, infused with Bonnet's overarching teleology, according to which the universe is composed of incorruptible, preformed "germs" that, although ontologically distinct (some germs are spiritual, some corporeal), obey the same natural laws of progressive development or palingenesis. Hence the *Essai*'s fundamental working hypothesis: the operations of the soul and of the common sensorium—ideas and fiber movements, respectively—are exactly coordinated (xxii).

Firm in his conviction that future discoveries in natural philosophy will bear out the divinely ordained analogies he perceives between the two sides of "the economy of our Being" (*EA*, xxi), Bonnet transforms the common sensorium from a problematic interface between mutually exclusive realms into a perfect microcosm of universal harmony. Although he uses the term *soul* throughout his treatise, he is in fact speaking of the mind, the portion of the soul which can be most readily analyzed through a naturalist's methods. In and of itself, this approach does not distinguish Bonnet from the other sensationalist philosophers of the day, all of whom similarly rejected the efforts of earlier philosophers to spiritualize man by placing as many of his faculties as possible in the immaterial soul (xxiv). However, whereas epistemologists like Locke, Berkeley, Hume, and Condillac tended to analyze the mind as if it were severed from both the soul above and the body below, Bonnet insists that natural relations exist among all three modes of human existence.

Bonnet is not, of course, literally doing physiology in the *Essai analytique*; although he sprinkles his inquiry into the inner workings of his Statue-Man with copious references to fibers, molecules, and vibrations, he uses those terms in a metaphoric sense:

> It is very important that I point out here to my reader that, by speaking so frequently of *fibers, fibrous molecules,* and *fascicles of fibers,* etc. . . . I do not claim to be using these expressions or images to determine the sort of instrument to which the production or reproduction of ideas was originally attached. I profess that I am deeply ignorant of the true nature of these infinitely small organs, which have been adapted to sensations and ideas of all sorts, and by which the Soul deploys all of its faculties. I therefore declare quite expressly that I am only using the words *fibers, fibrous molecules,* and *fascicles of fibers* in the way that Newton used the word *attraction:* that is, in order to describe an effect whose true cause is entirely unknown to me.   (*EA,* 40)

Bonnet's choice of the word *fiber* is hardly arbitrary: he clearly borrows it from the working vocabulary of Haller and other anatomists. In applying this terminology to the operations of the mind, Bonnet follows a circular logic according to which fibers must be the basic structural unit of sensibility because sensibility must have a structural unit (*EA,* 327). He likewise assumes that the common sensorium—however it may be structured—serves as the essential juncture point of the nervous system, the point where all of the sensible fibers converge and communicate both with the mind and with each other (14–15). Bonnet grants full authority to the physio-anatomical sources on which he bases his analysis; and in transposing the biological notions of sensibility, sensible fibers, and common sensorium to psychology, he endows them with such apparent precision that he and his reader tend to forget that they remain, fundamentally, unknowns.

What, then, is a sensible fiber according to Bonnet? It is "a compound of molecules or elementary parts, whose form or arrangement determines the type or the operation of the fiber . . . These molecules are small regular bodies, small strips superimposed on each other, which can glide over each other and thus lend themselves to the movements imparted to them" (*EA*, 30, 48). When an external sensory object acts upon such a fiber, it leaves an indelible imprint by rearranging the fiber's molecules, changing both its internal disposition and its position relative to adjacent fibers. Bonnet's first illustration of this process entails waving a rose under the Statue-Man's nose, which causes the "infinitely small corpuscles that emanate from the rose" to enter into the inside of his nose, where "they act on the nervous fibers that line it" (19). Those fibers in turn transmit their excitement to the common sensorium, where it is registered by the mind, causing a new "mode of being in the soul, a state that is distinct from every other state" (21). If the sensory impression is strong enough, the sensible fibers aroused in both the nose and the sensorium will be mechanically transfigured from their undifferentiated "virgin" state into fibers specifically disposed to carry out a rose-type reaction whenever any rose corpuscles come their way. This selective aptitude to vibrate only for certain objects, which Bonnet calls fibrillar "temperament" (66), is structurally reinforced in each fiber as it is nourished and grows; the fiber thus takes on particular reactive habits which gradually create the faculty of reminiscence in the burgeoning mind of the Statue-Man (30-32, 48-50). Once the Statue-Man's nose has been opened up to a slightly larger range of flower odors, the fibers in the common sensorium form distinct fascicles that have similar or sympathetic reactive habits; these fascicles come to serve as precisely fitted organic intermediaries between the order of things in nature and the types of sensations that can be excited in the mind (38-39).

Bonnet thus collects what he calls the "data" (*EA*, xxiii) of his analysis simply by tracking the stages of mechanical modification in the sensible fibers that arise from smell, the most primitive sense.[45] He then proceeds to construct an elaborate psycho-physiology that encompasses virtually every known aspect of sentient and intellectual function—from simple sensation to perception (which, in his mind, differs from sensation only "in the degree of vibration" [106]), and from elementary faculties like memory and imagination to more complex operations like desire, will, language, and the abstract ideas of succession, harmony, beauty, liberty, and self. He accomplishes all of this while his Statue-Man has not even progressed beyond comparing the odors of three different flowers (275).

Bonnet's micromechanics of sentient reactibility—which sets sensible fibers and mental "ideas" into a direct, one-to-one, unit-to-unit correspondence—adds a good deal of detail to the common sensorium, which develops over the course of his Statue-Man narrative into a perfectly functioning, multifaceted organic machine—a "miniature" of the whole nervous system, where the resonating complex of sensible fibers is coordinated with the equally resonant mechanisms of thought and language (*EA*, 15, 169). Like Condillac, Bonnet asserts that the ordering principle of the chain formed by mental associations is the phenomenon of sensory pleasure, first triggered in the Statue-Man when he is offered the scent of a carnation.[46] Bonnet, however, goes a step beyond Condillac by insisting that the mental process of pleasure is directly related to the physiological process which occurs in the fibers of the common sensorium. Sensory pleasure arises when harmonious vibratory combinations occur among specific groups of sensible fibers, prompting the mind to concentrate all of its sensibility in that part of the brain (150–51). Harmony is thus not just a state the mind experiences upon receiving the impression of a pleasing arrangement of sounds or colors; it entails a literally *instrumental* modification in the fibers of the nerves and brain.

There is, moreover, much more than pleasure at stake in the pursuit of sentient harmony; for harmony in the sensible fibers is the fundamental causal factor in exercising—and by exercising, improving—our mental faculties: "The perfecting of our faculties ultimately depends on the order in which the different fibers of each sense are put into play. The more fibers a harmony puts into play, and the more tightly it interconnects their movements, the more it perfects the exercise of our faculties in one or many genres" (*EA*, 167). For Bonnet, therefore, having a sound mind and body is dependent upon keeping the fibers in shape, whether those fibers be motile, sensible, moral, or intellectual. Out of the basic physics of harmonious fibrillar movements, he draws a number of theories: a theory of the passions (176–84); a theory of the will (184–89, 219); a theory of mental recollection (194–99); a theory of language and its salutary effects on thinking (115–43); and, most important in his view, a universal theory of education.

Education, as Bonnet describes it, consists in training the mind physically so that it can execute the most perfect, "harmonious" moral notions attainable. The superior intellect is thus formed through selective physical arousal of the sensible fibers, some of which become specialized intellectual fibers that outstrip all the others in activity (*EA*, 220). However, given the swiftness with which the force of sensibility is triggered in the typical human being, the educator must work quickly to get his pupil's brain under proper pedagogical management while it is young and malleable, before its fibers have taken on any "vicious impressions" (224). When the pedagogical experience goes smoothly, it produces a superior thinker—someone who can act as a sort of natural historian of his or her own ideas, by constantly tracing them back to their natural origins and examining their interconnections (230). All true geniuses, Bonnet asserts, excel at this type of intellectual self-analysis because they possess an exquisitely developed set of intellectual fibers (231–32). He proposes a physical analogy to explain the link between brain structure and mental function: thinking, like walking, requires strong, well-constructed, and well-exercised fibers. Yet truly perfected minds also possess a special kind of feeling that allows them to grasp "along with the main idea a host of related ideas that give rise to prompt, delicate, and subtle comparisons" (321). Under such circumstances, the common sensorium becomes a network of finely interlocking fibers capable of supporting the most complex and finely interrelated ideas.[47]

Despite the great self-assurance that informs Bonnet's physio-psychological analysis of the mind's invisible workings, a thorny question seems to nag him: if everything from brute sensation to the intellect and will can be explained in terms of fibrillar movements and resonances, what possible role is left for the incorporeal soul? Bonnet's response to that question is strategic. First, he reiterates that his analytic vocabulary is physicalist not by design but by virtue of the materially bound referential constraints of human language (*EA*, 63). Second, he points out that it was Divine Wisdom that "subordinated the activity of the soul to its sensibility, its sensibility to the play of fibers, and the play of fibers to the action of objects" (64). This, in Bonnet's view, does not compromise the soul's spirituality; for, according to his doctrine of preformed, universal harmony, the soul is guaranteed to find its fullest expression when it is housed in a properly trained sensible body.

After an excruciatingly slow process of sensory development, Bonnet's Statue-Man finally becomes a person. As Bonnet describes it, the Statue-Man can attain the status of a thinking being by acquiring an adequate bank of sensations and the use of signs (*EA*, 395); to get a human soul, however, he must be endowed with one from on high—in this case, from Bonnet—through a process of transmigration (369). What, Bonnet asks, would happen to this soul in its new lodgings, the now fully functioning brain of the Statue-Man? It would have all of the feelings, all of the faculties of memory, imagination, and so on that were exercised by the Statue-Man when he was just an automaton, "for all of that depends on the determinations that the fibers of the brain have contracted; and these determinations are independent of the soul" (370). By extension, if God had decided to experiment a bit and, say, put the soul of a Huron in Montesquieu's superior brain, then the Huron soul would have the same sentiments, perceptions, and abstract ideas as the real Montesquieu—right down to speaking French and writing *De l'esprit des lois* (370). The Montesquieu/Huron transmigration is, in fact, just one of the grafting experiments that Bonnet would eventually propose to demonstrate his psychology.[48] As he is careful to emphasize, these experiments are designed not to offend those who admire the special qualities of souls like Montesquieu's (or, one supposes, those of Native Americans), but rather, to underscore his central philosophical tenet: the quality of any soul's intellectual accomplishments is entirely determined by the fitness and training of the sensible fibers in its brain.

❦

Charles Bonnet's odd meditations on the interplay between sensible fibers and everlasting souls may seem like one man's idiosyncratic synthesis of contemporary physiology, epistemology, and cosmology. However, the *Essai analytique sur les facultés de l'âme* reflects an important development in both the philosophy of mind and the concept of sensibility at large. By using Haller's model of the body as a reactive entity in order to explain not only brute physiology but human psychology as well, Bonnet demonstrated that this model was at once paradigmatic and highly mutable. The major idea that Bonnet borrowed from Hallerian physiology was the notion that sensibility is attached to fibers; he expanded on this by maintaining that all mental events depend upon the way that these fibers are arranged and deployed. He also adapted Haller's idea that particular types of fibers have a particular, function-specific composition. Yet Bonnet so thoroughly homogenized the notion of "fiber" for the purposes of his analysis that he ascribed the same basic *modus operandi* to fibers all over the body, in the brain as in the legs: he asserted that all fibers respond to impressions through some kind of movement (contractile, vibratory, or convulsive) and then develop to the point of perfect reactive resonance. Bonnet also significantly transformed the Hallerian model of the common sensorium, carving it up into functional compartments or mini-sensoriums, each specially designed to accommodate a certain species of sensation or idea.

Although Bonnet clearly aligned himself with the Hallerian camp of natural philosophers, his modifications on Hallerian sensibility bore little resemblance to the cautious experimental proofs of vitality that were performed by the physiologists who carried on Haller's laboratory investigations (like Fontana and Caldani).[49] In his effort to "anatomize" the sentient faculties right down to their fibers, Bonnet blurred Haller's sacrosanct distinction between sensibility and irritability. In fact, by taking the notion of fiber mechanics into the seat of the soul, Bonnet contributed to the generalizing, monistic notion of vital re-actibility that was coming to dominate both philosophical and physiological thought during the 1750s. That monistic/vitalist approach emerged both because of and in spite of Haller's dynamic but rigidly binary redefinition of the reactive fibers and properties of the living body. The inevitable consequence of this shift towards organic monism was that—Haller's views notwithstanding—there was no longer any clear distinction between sentience and mobility, the properties that virtually all eighteenth-century thinkers held to be the essential attributes of animate beings. One could now refer to the basic property of reactibility as either irritability or sensibility: the fundamental mechanism was the same.

Bonnet's mode of deploying the mechanics of sensibility for pedagogical purposes illustrates a crucial transition from the idea of sensibility as a power to be observed to a vision of sensibility as a power to be harnessed and redirected. This transition had important implications for the role of the mind and soul in naturalist investigations: if the development and successful conduct of the intellect could be shown to be determined entirely by the action of fibers in the common sensorium, then the soul could be completely marginalized from discussions of human nature. It was now the body that, through its inherent reactive properties, seemed to offer the most effective site of intervention in the moral, intellectual, and physical constitution of human beings. Such intervention might be pedagogical in thrust, as it was for Bonnet, whose primary concern was with finding better ways to think; but it might also be therapeutic, as it was in the many works of physical and moral hygiene that were published during the second half of the century.

Given this general conceptual shift to the sensible body, it is not surprising that discussions of sensibility in fields ranging from physiology to metaphysics, ethics, and aesthetics should gravitate toward medicine. With its claims to privileged knowledge of the operations of the human body, medicine has always had a practical materialist side. In mid- to late-eighteenth-century France, however, it took on a very specific "philosophical" mission: medical theorists undertook to broaden the scope of their field by extending it into all areas of knowledge—and they did so largely by capitalizing on the notion of sensibility and its expanding significations. Enlightenment medical discourse consequently provided the ideal breeding ground for the continued development of sensibility as a structuring concept that could be put to a variety of purposes. As Théophile de Bordeu described it in his *Recherches sur l'histoire de la médecine* (1767), sensibility provided physicians with a global perspective on everything that occurs in the human being:

> Sensibility seems much easier to understand than irritability, and it can serve quite well as the basis for explaining all of the phenomena of life, whether it be in the state of health or in illness . . . This is therefore the way of considering the living body that has been adopted by those who, among modern thinkers, have carried their speculations beyond practical

medicine and the systems received in the schools at the beginning of the century. Such is the scope that philosophical medicine has assumed concerning the purely material functions of the body . . . The reign of feeling or sensibility is among the most extensive; feeling is involved in all the functions; it directs them all. It dominates over illnesses; it guides the action of remedies; it sometimes becomes so dependent upon the soul, that the soul's passions take the upper hand over all the changes of the body; it varies and modifies itself differently in almost all the [organic] parts.[50]

For Bordeu, therefore, the true physician was a physician-philosopher endowed with a special understanding of sensibility—a property that permitted the medical practitioner not just to direct the bodily functions in health and correct them in disease, but also to see all of the impressions, relations, and reactions to which the human being was subject, internally and externally, physically and morally, in society and in the world. Although their brand of "philosophical" medical thinking was destined to decline and eventually fall into disrepute after 1850, Bordeu and his followers nonetheless dominated French medicine for at least fifty years. They were, for example, praised by the early-nineteenth-century physiologist Xavier Bichat for having provided precisely the kind of sweeping perspective on the living body that was needed to complement Haller's experimental findings: "In the current state of physiology, the art of allying the experimental method of Haller and Spallanzani to the grand and philosophical views of Bordeu seems to me to be the approach that all judicious thinkers must take."[51]

In their writings, the médecins philosophes promoted both a holistic vision of the human being as a sensibility-driven organism, and a very precise set of techniques for observing, controlling, and correcting sensibility. The philosophical side of their doctrine can be divided into four approximate categories: (1) semiotics, or the art of deciphering the critical body language of sensibility and deploying those signs and symptoms in order to manage disease; (2) health and hygiene, or the art of cultivating a normative sensibility for each type of sensible body; (3) pedagogy, a field that encompassed cognitive, ethical, and aesthetic development; and (4) social theory, or the effort to treat the larger social body in light of the organic beings who composed it. Although I explore those categories at length in the next chapter and later chapters, it would be useful to give a brief sense here of what each entailed.

First, becoming a physician in the sensibility-oriented climate of mid-eighteenth-century France entailed undergoing a long apprenticeship both in the use of one's own senses and in the science of critical bodily signs. Proficiency in medical semiotics consequently became a question of mastering sensibility on two registers: in oneself as an observing subject and in the body under observation. Hence the emphasis placed in the *Encyclopédie* article "Observateur" on the superior physical and intellectual qualities of the true physician:

> In order to see well, or observe (I am taking these two words as synonymous), it is not enough to apply one's senses any which way; one must have senses that are well organized, well disposed not only by nature but by art and habit, and one must apply one's senses without passion, self-interest, prejudice, etc. Thus the [medical] *observer* must, first and foremost, have sense organs that are free of any vice of conformation that might impede their full and complete use; his eyes must be clear-sighted, his sense of touch fine, his sense of smell good, etc.; his senses must be suited to receiving the impressions of the [disease] phenomena that are presented, however difficult they may be to perceive, and to transmitting them unaltered to the seat of feeling, reflection and memory . . . Yet he must above all possess the science of signs and be well informed about their nature, about the way that one must proceed to grasp them correctly, about their value and their significance.[52]

According to this portrait, the physician's well-organized and properly trained sense organs—his eyes, his nose, his fingers—were just as important as his powers of reflection and memory in perceiving and deciphering the symptoms of an illness.

Once the diagnosis had been reached through proper semiotic evaluation, the physician's intervention generally consisted of dietary and hygienic prescriptions designed to restore health by correcting or redirecting underlying abnormalities in the patient's reactive spirits or fibers. Specialized treatises abounded at this time to instruct particular types of patients—hypochondriacal aristocrats, vaporous ladies, artisans, peasants, self-abusing adolescents, men of letters—on how to eat, drink, exercise, and generally conduct their daily lives. Some physician-philosophers like Antoine Le Camus, author of *La Médecine de l'esprit* (1753), optimistically asserted that most individuals (or at least, those of the male variety) could achieve unlimited physical and intellectual perfection by following the proper regimen—that is, by cultivating their sensibilities through a program based on both contemporary medical knowledge and sensationalist philosophical methods. Others, however, saw the cultivation of sensibility not as the path toward boundless perfectibility, but as a potential danger to moral and physical health. Tissot, for example, railed in *De la santé des gens de lettres* (1768) against the over-refined lifestyle of scholars and other leaders of "civilized" society, and insisted that their very table habits had pernicious, debilitating effects upon their oversensitive brains, nerves, and stomachs. Because each temperament and each profession had its own idiosyncratic pattern of sensibility, the médecin philosophe was called upon to devise specific treatments for every sensible body type across the social spectrum.

In the pedagogical and socio-theoretical registers, the médecin philosophe also assumed the task of addressing shifts in sensibility that occurred on the collective scale. For Pierre Fabre, this meant venturing into realms like the theater, an art whose edifying effects on sensible organization were not to be underestimated:

> If one considers the state of literature and the arts in France during this era [before Louis XIV], and the disposition of the French, whose sense organs—still "young," so to speak—had not yet been affected by any of those sublime objects that make such strong impressions on the sensible system, one will conclude that *Corneille* must be credited with the sudden revolution that took place in the spirit of the nation, when his tragedies appeared . . . *Racine*, born with a sensible system that tended to be more tender and less proud, became Corneille's rival . . . By multiplying in this manner, dramatic masterpieces soon developed the seed of those rare geniuses who appeared all at once in every [literary] genre. *Pascal, Molière, La Fontaine, Despréaux, Fénelon, Boussuet, Bourdaloue, Massillon,* and so on continued to excite through their diverse productions the most intense sensations in the sensible organs of the French people, according to the various modifications of their sensible system.[53]

Fabre's medical analysis of the psycho-physiological effects of great drama bears some striking resemblances to Diderot's physicalist, impression-based model of aesthetic response—a response that Diderot, too, linked to moral and intellectual edification and sought to cultivate as part of his new theory of dramatic and novelistic fiction (which I examine in Chapter 5). For Dr. Fabre, aesthetic masterpieces like those of Corneille and Racine had the power literally to remake both individual spectators and the collective body because of the manner in which those works engaged the natural force of sensibility.

We must not forget, however, that with their self-improvement programs for patients and their sense-based diagnostic apprenticeships for fledgling physicians, the physician-philosophers believed that they were simply perpetuating the positivist, empirical approach to sensibility that Haller had taken. This approach was, as we recall, inspired by the methodological conviction that one can establish "objective" scales for a reactive property and trace all reactions back to a definitive locus or point of origin in the body. When that methodology was embraced as a working assumption by natural philosophers—whether pioneers in psychology like Charles Bonnet, or medical theorists like Bordeu, Tissot, and Fabre—the concept of sensibility was opened up to three fundamental transformations. First, sensibility became the crucial link between ontologically discrete realms of nature; as some médecins philosophes would argue, what better candidate could one find for the long-sought vital principle? Second, sensibility's diverse significations (physiological, philosophical, aesthetic, and ethical) came increasingly to overlap, as focus shifted away from the reigning distinctions of those domains and onto the mechanism common to them all: the basic reactive disposition that makes things happen, move, and resonate in the body as in the soul. Finally, as these natural philosophers renounced trying to find the essence of this mysterious property, sensibility was rendered purely operational; one could therefore track its various manifestations within different types of people.

Tracking sensibility was a project that took several forms. It involved tracing the most curious and/or pathological manifestations of sensibility to their natural seats in the sensible body. It also entailed creating differential destinies for human beings according to their congenital or acquired pattern of sensibility. The médecins philosophes of the 1750s to 1790s were not alone in either of those endeavors: related speculations can be found in the works of philosophically minded novelists like Diderot, Rousseau, Laclos, and Sade. By depicting sensibility not just as a fashionable moral quality but as a bodily condition abounding in significations, these writers added new definition to the models proposed by their medical counterparts for addressing this property. Yet even as they adapted the latest medical "facts" on sensibility to their fictions, they also reclaimed the pervasive, polymorphous, and uncontrollable nature of the property. In a word, by placing the idiosyncratic living body—its pleasures and pains, its strengths and weaknesses, its inherent patterns of rhythmic vitality and mutability—at the center of narrative, these writers did more than merely emulate the contemporary physio-philosophical discourse on sensibility; rather, they transformed it and took the concept of sensibility into new, previously uncharted theoretical realms.

2. Sensibility and the Philosophical Medicine of the 1750s–1770s

Expanding on Sensibility: The Physicians-Philosophers of Montpellier

French medicine took a distinctly vitalist turn in the 1750s, as medical theorists turned away from iatromechanism and embraced instead a holistic vision of human life as a unique condition driven by its own organically rooted inner dynamics. Several factors, both conceptual and cultural, were involved in this shift of perspective. First, many physicians were growing uneasy with the therapeutic applications of iatromechanism, which often entailed aggressive treatments like copious bleedings, trephinations, and harsh purgatives; they consequently sought out more natural methods, like those inspired by the organic monism that was gaining popularity in many areas of natural philosophy.[1] Second, a campaign was afoot within medicine to revive such Hippocratic clinical notions as the belief that nature has great healing powers of its own, the theory that diseases follow inherent "critical" patterns, and the idea that the best preventive medicine consists in prudent use of the six "non-naturals"—that is, the things that affect the body's health from without: air, food and drink, sleep and wakefulness, motion and rest, evacuation and retention, and the passions of the soul.[2] Third, the influential Montpellier medical faculty had, beginning in the 1730s, become receptive to the vitalist doctrine of Georg-Ernst Stahl, who a generation earlier had undertaken to refute medical chemistry and Boerhaavian iatromechanism by arguing that all living phenomena are guided by a spiritual principle he called "anima."[3] Although mid-century Montpellier theorists like Théophile de Bordeu distanced themselves from the metaphysical aspects of Stahl's doctrine (and from Stahl's dismissal of anatomical studies as useless to the practice of medicine), they nonetheless agreed with his insistence on the singularity of life. Finally, important changes were occurring in the socioeconomic context of medical practice—changes that were transforming both the professional profile of medical practitioners and the way they interacted with their patients.[4]

French physicians were thus intent on finding a system that suited both their intellectual demand for a more dynamic explanation of the body as an organism and their clientele's apparent wish for medical guidance in maintaining their health and in achieving moral and physical self-improvement. Sensibility fit the bill on both counts because it was well established in the reigning sociomoral vocabulary and had also taken on a new significance in contemporary physiology and philosophy. When imported into medical discourse, sensibility provided a way of linking together the disparate elements then circulating in the field: the models of the body's reactive properties advanced by Haller and his rivals, theories of organic activity ranging from pure physical determinism to metaphysical cosmologism, sensationalist notions derived from empiricist philosophy, socio-anthropological ideas borrowed from Montesquieu and Buffon, and new clinical techniques for observing and treating bodily disorders. It is on these aspects of eighteenth-century French medicine that I will focus—to the neglect, admittedly, of other equally important developments, like the reform movement launched late in the century to improve the profession's teaching institutions, its language, its classificatory systems, and its methods of epidemiological surveillance.[5] Although those developments proved highly significant in institutional as well as sociopolitical terms as the Old Regime gave way to the Revolutionary period, they cannot be fully understood unless one first explores the theoretical models and metaphors on which Enlightenment physicians relied to conceive of the vital forces at work in life, health, and disease.

Thus, the concern of this chapter is the way sensibility was woven through the various layers of medical thought, just as it was woven through the larger culture of the French Enlightenment. Like their colleagues in philosophy, natural science, and literature, medical writers were singularly fascinated with sensibility and its possible implications; what they contributed to the ongoing discussion of this question was a half-scientific, half-poetic mode of discourse that seemed to reconcile the observed physical phenomena of sensibility with its more fluid and suggestive overtones. They accomplished this, in large part, by applying the recognized models of reactibility to a signifying unit far more complex than a mere fiber or isolated body part: they took on the entire human being, soma and psyche united. It was this grand-scale effort to study the multifaceted effects of sensibility in all of the various human types that made eighteenth-century medicine an overtly "philosophical," cultural endeavor.

Of course, the complex articulation which sensibility made possible between the medicine and culture of the French Enlightenment worked both ways. This chapter begins by examining how the theorists associated with the Montpellier medical school made sensibility a specifically medical concern while also promoting medicine as *the* most authoritative branch of natural philosophy—and medical semiotics as the ultimate means of "observing" sensibility by tapping into the inner voice of the sensible body. It then considers how the Montpellier theory of this property was received, both in its specifics and in its larger moral-philosophical repercussions, by a philosophe who saw sensibility as the cornerstone of philosophy and literature alike—Denis Diderot, whose text *Le Rêve de d'Alembert* stages a playful response to philosophical medicine, using Bordeu himself as a fictional interlocutor.

Much existing scholarship gives the impression that philosophical medicine was invented at the turn of the eighteenth to the nineteenth century, when the medical profession became involved in the Idéologues' efforts to transform all fields of knowledge into one harmonious "science of ideas," built on the system of Condillacian analysis.[6] However, philosophical medicine—and its implicit ambition to provide the definitive, universal theory of Man—existed well before medical theorists like Pinel and Cabanis formalized the convergence between the philosophy of sensations and the physiology of sensibility.[7] In fact, although Cabanis was the first to use the term *anthropology* to describe the project of philosophical medicine, he was not particularly innovative in the physiological concepts he espoused in his well-known treatise *Rapports du physique et du moral de l'homme* (1802), for he inherited many of his ideas from a well-established lineage of physicians like Lacaze, Le Cat, Le Camus, Bordeu, Barthez, Roussel, and Sèze, who had formed the vanguard of philosophically minded medical theorists a generation or two earlier. With a few exceptions, these theorists were trained in Montpellier between the 1740s and the 1770s and began to gravitate toward Paris, center of lucrative medical practices and intellectual renown, during the heady decades of the 1750s and 1760s.[8] Over the second half of the century, they produced a number of provocative treatises and *Encyclopédie* contributions—works intended both to stir up the Paris medical faculty and to attract an educated, increasingly health-conscious clientele. What was promulgated in those writings was a new doctrine of the reactive animal economy, declared to be truly revolutionary by its proponents. Although that doctrine drew upon a hodgepodge of ideas about fibers, humors, universal vital fluids, and competing reactive mainsprings (the diaphragm, the hypochondria, the solar plexus, and so on), it was nonetheless rooted in two firm convictions: first, and contrary to Haller's assertions, that sensibility should be seen as a primordial force pervading all vital matter; and second, that every part and function of the human being is generated and maintained by a set pattern of sensible action and reaction.

Philosophical medicine was thus undertaken to promote both a new theory of vitality and a medico-anthropological perspective on human life. The physiology of the Montpellier physicians was not a bastardized version of Hallerian physiology: to the contrary, its proponents tended to disagree vehemently with Haller's invasive means of isolating the body's *vis insita*, preferring to take the gentler route of thoughtful observation and reflection. In their view, the only useful physiology was an applied physiology, grounded in clinical observation and graced with an informed overview of the operations of life, the universe, and humanity's place in it. The natural-philosophical component of their investigations into vitality consisted, therefore, not in laboratory assays—although some of these theorists, notably Bordeu, did conduct experiments to back up their ideas—but rather, in the comprehensive accounts they proposed to explain the primary phenomena of life, like conception and embryonic organization, sentience and mobility, digestion, circulation, secretion, and interorganic sympathy and antagonism. These theorists perceived sensibility as the connecting principle for all vital processes and held it to be the communicative and coordinating force that allowed the body to function as an integrated whole.[9]

The philosophically minded physician of this period had two primary tasks to fulfill: first, to observe sensibility's myriad operations as comprehensively as possible; and second, to decipher the pathological problems that ensued when those operations went awry. Although sensibility was credited with creating all of the relations vital to human existence—the connections between molecules, body parts, the body and mind, the body and society, and the body and the universe—it was also considered a potentially destructive property. Enlightenment physicians perceived the risks involved in having such a powerful force in one's body to be numerous and serious, particularly given the onslaught of putatively unnatural stimuli to which the modern, civilized person was subject. Claude-Nicolas Le Cat, for example, underscored the potentially caustic qualities of the vital force (which he saw as a supersubtle animal fluid) and the very real risk of auto-combustion in overly vivacious subjects, like children, women, heavy drinkers, and highly emotional people.[10] Sensibility was, moreover, generally cited as the cause underlying the pervasive and troublesome condition of vapors in worldly women and men, who, out of their extreme susceptibility to the slightest irritant, suffered from hypochondria, hysterical paroxysms, or at the very least, poor digestion and enfeebled offspring. In short, life in the world of eighteenth-century France was seen as a daily battle against all kinds of potential stimuli and irritants, which could well throw a person's sensibility irreparably off balance. Exacerbating this perceived threat was the degeneration that had apparently occurred in the average Frenchman's constitution, as measured against the robust, relatively insensitive state of the nation's primitive ancestors. Bordeu described French city-dwellers in particularly dire terms in his *Recherches sur les maladies chroniques:*

> Those who live in cities . . . are all affected to some degree by a passion that holds in check the movements of the animal economy. One could compare them to sleepwalkers whose inclinations toward the natural functions are distracted and poorly directed: they only half-sleep, half-hear, and half-see; they are perpetually pressed, pulled, and irritated from the direction of the heart, from that of the heart, and from that of the stomach; they have no strength, no rest, and they are bored, exhausted and engorged with unhealthy foodstuff; they are in a perpetual turmoil of sensations, for they are agitated by projects they are forced to undertake, and crushed by losses and misfortunes that are magnified by their excessive sensibility.[11]

It was this darker side of sensibility that made a full-blown medical philosophy so crucially important for eighteenth-century society, for only the physician equipped with such a philosophy could track down all of the hidden "rallying points" in the sensible body—the organs, centers, or nerve plexuses that might become trouble spots under excessive stimulation.[12] What won sensibility so many more partisans than did irritability in the debate over the primacy of these properties was its pervasive, multiform presence in human life—along with the inner "road map" that it seemed to provide. Some theorists did, of course, attempt to construct a medical philosophy based entirely on the property of irritability; "irritability" is, for example, the term that La Mettrie favored throughout his medico-philosophical writings, including *L'Homme machine.* Yet irritability simply did not lend itself as well as did sensibility to the search for a single physical/moral vital mainspring: it was too locally restricted (to muscular fiber) and too specific in its operations (contraction). Moreover, irritability lacked the rhetorical suggestiveness and protean physiological qualities of sensibility—criteria that were equally important in the elaboration of the eighteenth century's version of philosophical medicine.

A good starting point for studying the conversion of sensibility into a key principle of philosophical medicine is the *Encyclopédie* article written by Jean-Jacques Ménuret de Chambaud on the "animal economy." After presenting this subject as the one that "of all the mysteries of nature . . . touches Man most closely, affects him most intimately, and is the most suited to attracting and satisfying his curiosity," Ménuret hints that a major step has just been made toward solving the mystery of man's physiological inner nature, by virtue of the deep, philosophical analysis that one enlightened physician has made of the "vivifying breath of the divine force [which] animates the [human] machine." What Ménuret means by "vivifying breath" is not an immaterial, superadded force, but rather "a singular property, the source of movement and sentiment, which is attached to the *organic* nature of the principles that compose the body, or rather which depends on a union of these molecules like that discovered by Glisson, who called it *irritability*, when it is, in fact, merely a mode of *sensibility*."[13] Sensibility, Ménuret insists, is evident as early as conception, when it swiftly differentiates the elementary particles of the organism into vessels, muscles, and organs—a process that creates "a like number of particular lives whose unity, interaction, and mutual support forms the general life of the entire body" ("OA," 361–62). In and of themselves, these local lives do not constitute a true animal economy; to understand that, one must seek out the fundamental cog of the human machine, which he calls "the primitive function that preceded all the others, and gave rise to them" (362). After much stalling, Ménuret finally reveals the identity of the man who has, in his view, discovered that primitive function: Louis de Lacaze—a Montpellier-trained physician who had been named *médecin ordinaire* to Louis XV in the early 1730s, and the author of the recently published treatise entitled *Specimen Novi Medicinae Conspectûs* (1750), a text better known as *Idée de l'homme physique et moral* (1755).[14]

Although it is devoid of any anatomical or clinical observations that might support its hypotheses, Lacaze's treatise merits a short detour, not least because of the heroic dimensions that the Encyclopedist Ménuret ascribes to its author. The *Idée de l'homme physique et moral* exemplifies the "genealogical" approach to the body that was popular at the time: using as his guiding principle the notion that all vital processes emanate from the mechanism which first sets life in motion, Lacaze retraces the entire formation of the human being, going back not just to the fetus but to the elementary particles contained in the "primordial soup" of humanity, the seminal fluid (Lacaze, 74–75). Semen, in his opinion, can be found in male bodies and female bodies alike; and like all vital fluids, it is animated by a universal mobilizing agent—an ethereal fluid that he holds to be electrical in nature.[15] Lacaze's embryology centers on the brain and spinal cord, which he sees as the most vitally charged organs parts because they correspond to the parts of the parent bodies that send the greatest number of "rays" to the seminal fluid at the moment of conception (96–97). By singling out sensible matter as the basic building block for the human organism, Lacaze directly challenges Haller's claim that the heart is the first organ to develop; he asserts instead that the primitive nerve cylinders of the fetus form first, after which the heart is developed and then the nutritive system (100–105). It is this triad of elemental internal parts—head, heart, and epigastrium—that provides the scaffold into which the other, more external organs are subsequently fitted (100–101, 109).

According to the central physiological thesis of the *Idée de l'homme*, what "constitute the active principle of everything that lives" are inviolable laws of antagonism, or action and reaction (Lacaze, 91). Extrapolating on this thesis, Lacaze claims that the entire animal economy hangs largely on the counterbalancing interactions between the internal versus external parts, and between the regions of the head and nerves versus the epigastrium (123, 129). The fulcrum of those interactions, or "center of reaction for all the other body parts," is the diaphragm; Lacaze views this as the "general principle underlying the workings of the animal economy, from its most important functions to the smallest of its movements" (103–4). Lacaze gives his physiological system a "philosophical" extension at the end of the treatise, when he declares that all of the interactions vital to human existence—mental, moral, and social—are regulated by the same laws of organic action and reaction as those that control human physiology (307–8, 396–99).[16]

There, in brief, are the supposedly ingenious insights that Ménuret finds in the *Idée de l'homme physique et moral*—a work that, in his eyes, has freed medicine from the theoretical errors of both the mechanistic and Stahlian-animist systems of physiology ("OA," 365). Echoing Lacaze, Ménuret describes the diaphragm as "a sort of balance wheel that sets in motion all of the organs" (366). He then proceeds to explain how this conceptual reorientation of the body's inner space has revolutionized the contemporary understanding of life and health: "The sound theory of diseases follows naturally from this brilliant and fruitful principle, which gives rise to a body of doctrine and a body of practice where everything corresponds, everything is linked, everything is simple, everything is one" (366). Ménuret is convinced that this new idea will vastly improve medical theory and practice, as well as the sciences of hygiene and morality.

Lacaze is also featured prominently in the *Encyclopédie* article "Sensibilité"—not the one-paragraph entry on moral sensibility by the Chevalier de Jaucourt, but the much longer medical article that precedes it, in which Ménuret's colleague Henri Fouquet recasts many Lacazian notions on the animal economy in even more globalizing terms. This article is not entirely devoid of the lyrical overtones that mark de Jaucourt's thoughts on the subject: Fouquet begins by identifying sensibility as "the most beautiful, the most singular phenomenon of nature."[17] He nonetheless devotes his essay primarily to showcasing current biomedical ideas about the pivotal role played by this property in the formation and ongoing economy of the human body. To that end, he reviews all of the major recent works on the subject, including Lacaze's *Idée de l'homme physique et moral*, Haller's *Mémoires sur la nature sensible et irritable des parties du corps animal*, Robert Whytt's refutations of Haller's system, and Théophile de Bordeu's various medical treatises—most particularly the *Recherches anatomiques sur la position des glandes et sur leur action* (1752) and *Recherches sur le pouls par rapport aux crises* (1757). Fouquet draws most of the "facts" he presents on sensibility's physiological and pathological manifestations from Bordeu: he cites as authoritative Bordeu's theory that sensibility operates semi-independently at the local organic level, where it forms regional centers or "departments" that play a significant role in determining how a particular disease episode unfolds. Lacaze, by contrast, serves primarily in "Sensibilité" as a foil to the methodological example set by Haller for the investigation of this vital force: "This small number of reflections will show that even the most well conceived experiments are inadequate for advancing in the knowledge of a matter whose delicate objects disappear or are denatured under the hand that seeks to work on them; that is a kind of curse attached to all human attempts of this sort . . . We must therefore content ourselves with the few fugitive forms that Nature, like a Proteus that no one can force, deigns occasionally to reveal" (Fouquet, "Sensibilité," 52). Given the range of sensibility's perceived qualities, Haller's aggressive, laboratory-bound style of studying the property's hidden nature is pointless and inhumane; far better, Fouquet suggests, for physicians to observe and reflect upon the signs of sensibility that they can discern in living bodies—without tinkering with their tissues, as Haller had done.[18]

Interestingly, neither Ménuret nor Fouquet mention the curious story that underlies the production of the *Idée de l'homme physique et moral*. In 1751, when Lacaze was adapting the Latin version of this work to make it available to a wider reading public, Bordeu had just arrived in Paris, eager to make a name for himself. As he relates in his correspondence, Bordeu was short on money and clients and therefore took up residence with Lacaze, his distant maternal cousin, who offered to hand over much of his own well-established practice to Bordeu in return for some "editorial" assistance.[19] Bordeu and another young Montpellier graduate, the chemist Gabriel Venel, were thus engaged in collaborating on the revised, French-language edition of Lacaze's book. This is how Bordeu describes the experience: "I soon realized that the physician was a crazy man fit to be put in an asylum—so crazy, in fact, that he imagined that he was inventing a new medicine and writing a book to this end; writing the book was his pressing need, and that is what attached him to me" (*Correspondance*, 115). Bordeu was apparently obliged to invent "extravagant" ideas, based loosely on his own, "in order to satisfy the appetite of this mind whose furor was increasing every day; that furor increased so much that the poor enthusiast no longer slept nor ate . . . [Lacaze] made me suffer a brand new kind of martyrdom on the subject of my own works, my theses, which he vehemently insists he wrote himself " (116–17). Despite the abuses that young Bordeu apparently suffered at the hands of his ostensible protector (whom he called an apoplectic lunatic in private [117]), he later took pains to flatter Lacaze. In his *Encyclopédie* article "Crise," for example, Bordeu praised the Latin edition of the *Idée de l'homme,* and even went so far as to call its author an "excellent and very well known [medical] observer."[20]

Whatever one makes of the stormy personal relationship between these two thinkers, the fact remains that Lacaze's treatise is sprinkled with ideas that had taken an earlier and more coherent form in Bordeu's *Recherches anatomiques sur la position des glandes et sur leur action,* composed in 1748–49 and published almost immediately upon Bordeu's arrival in Paris. One might say that Lacaze and Bordeu represent two different but not entirely incompatible styles of doing "philosophical" medicine: whereas Lacaze speculated broadly about the physical, moral, and social implications of a vitalist approach to human nature, Bordeu sought to give that approach a rigorous and systematic foundation by interconnecting anatomy, physiology, and clinical observation. To that end, Bordeu proposed new methods for observing vitality, updated the old doctrine of *crises* to fit his organological model of the animal economy, refined medical semiotics through a widely popular doctrine of pulses, and promoted innovative treatments (like hydrotherapy) for managing sensibility in the diseased state.[21] This does not means that Bordeu's ideas were devoid of speculation or that his followers refrained from making the very kind of extravagant extrapolations he himself found so maddening in Lacaze's thinking. It means, rather, that Bordeu strove to produce a comprehensive, authoritative, and practicable medical doctrine to accommodate the concept of vital sensibility.

It is this doctrine—rather than Lacaze's, which we can consider a wilder variation upon Bordeu's—that lies at the heart of the ambitious effort, conducted both within and beyond the *Encyclopédie,* to popularize the brand of medical theory that Montpellier thinkers practiced. Some historians have suggested that in its medical content, the *Encyclopédie* was primarily a work of vulgarization, designed to translate conventional medical wisdom into terms that could be grasped by a general readership.[22] I would contend, however, that the *Encyclopédie* played a substantial role not only in propagating the "revolutionary" new medicine of sensibility but also in constituting it as a unique and influential discursive practice. For, by exploiting the system of internal and external cross-references that Diderot, as editor-in-chief, had designed to aid readers in negotiating their way around this enormous work, the Montpellier medical Encyclopedists were able to create an intriguing relationship between the subject matter of their articles and the form in which that subject matter was presented.[23] In other words, these authors used the *Encyclopédie*'s cross-referencing system not only to highlight such key Montpellier principles as the organological configuration and language of the sensible body, but also to demonstrate, in a formal register, sensibility's resonating mode of communication and transmission.

"Observing" Sensibility: Medical Semiotics in the *Encyclopédie*

The campaign to use the *Encyclopédie* as a means of promoting sensibility and philosophical medicine was conducted by a mere handful of authors. The most prominent of the group was Bordeu: although he contributed only the article "Crise" to this work, he is one of the authors most frequently cited throughout the network of Montpellier-inspired medical articles. Henri Fouquet made two noteworthy contributions to the cause: "Sécrétion," an abstract of Bordeu's treatise on glands, and the long medical entry "Sensibilité." However, the true driving force behind this effort was unquestionably Ménuret de Chambaud, who wrote some eighty-five articles for the last ten volumes of the *Encyclopédie* (vols. 8–17, letters H to Z, all published in 1765). Although he was only moderately successful as a practitioner and left little else to posterity beyond his copious *Encyclopédie* contributions, Ménuret's contributions are far more significant than has generally been acknowledged.[24] Ménuret used his individual articles to maneuver medicine into a position of prominence over other, more established natural sciences, and deployed the cross-referencing system with a deftness that was, at times, worthy of Diderot.

In addition to underscoring the innovative physio-pathology on which the medicine of sensibility was based, the Montpellier Encyclopedists were intent on demonstrating its profound importance for the hermeneutic art of medical semiotics. This part of their campaign took place in a series of texts that include Ménuret's articles "Observateur," "Observation," "Pouls," and "Prognostic," as well as the anonymous essay "Séméiotique" and Bordeu's entry "Crise." The goal of these articles was twofold: they were designed, first, to publicize the new semiotic system put forth in Bordeu's *Recherches sur le pouls par rapport aux crises*, and second, to portray the médecin philosophe as a heroic figure uniquely qualified to read the natural signs that are emitted by the body.

The medical entry "Séméiotique" is relatively short, but its reformist bent is immediately apparent. The author (most probably Ménuret) begins by declaring that semiotics should not be seen as a minor subfield of physiology and pathology, but rather, recognized as a powerful instrument for penetrating into the inner recesses of the healthy or ailing body.[25] This approach to semiotics stems directly from the new Montpellier doctrine of sensibility, which invested both the patient's body and the practitioner's with a special, dynamic mode of operation—that is, with the kind of resonating topology that Ménuret describes in "Oeconomie animale." The patient's body is thus held to be driven by inner phenomena that have a "reciprocal correspondence," a "mutual linking," and a "natural gradation" ("Séméiotique," 937). The signs sent out by this body are likewise naturally interrelated, such that a physician need only follow the pattern of actions and reactions that these signs form in order to decipher what is causing the ailment with which he is confronted: "There is no part in the human body that cannot furnish some sign to the enlightened observer; all of the actions, all of the movements of this marvelous machine are to his eyes like so many mirrors, where the internal dispositions—be they natural or counter to nature—are reflected and depicted" (937). Only a certain kind of physician, however, qualifies as "enlightened" in this sense: "He alone can direct a penetrating gaze into the most hidden recesses of the body, distinguish therein the state and the disorders of the various parts, recognize through external signs the illnesses that are attacking the internal organs, and determine the particular character and seat of those illnesses." The body is a transparent machine for such a medical observer because he possesses a vision of its inner workings that goes beyond the usual limits imposed upon human understanding: "The mysterious veil that hides the knowledge of the future from frail mortals tears open before him; he sees with a confident eye the different changes that must occur in health or illness; he holds the chain that connects all events, and the first links that come into his hands reveal to him the nature of those that will come after because Nature varies only in her external appearances: deep down, she is always uniform, and always follows the same course" (937).

The science of medical semiotics is thus predicated on the assumption that every action, every movement, and every reaction of the body is a richly significant link in an ongoing chain of physiological or pathological events. The physician's task accordingly consists in garnering as much information as he can from the body's perceptible qualities and functions—its excretions and secretions, its color and heat, its respiratory rhythms, and above all its pulses. (The reader is referred at this point to "Pouls, Respiration, Sueur, Urine, etc." [938].) These signs are to be judged not by traditional symptomalogical divisions, decried here as arbitrary and "metaphysical," but rather on the basis of a painstaking observation of the same body over time—one that takes into account its temperamental type; its habits of sleep, digestion, excretion, and so on; and the illnesses it may have suffered in the past. Having assembled those facts and compared them with the signs at hand, the observing physician should be able to determine either how best to maintain that patient's health, or how best to guide him or her through an impending pathological crisis.

Although the article "Séméiotique" describes the master semiotician as a being who possesses extraordinary epistemological powers, it does not present a full picture of what those powers allow him to do as a practitioner. For that, one must consult the specific articles that are cited as cross-references—for example, the article "Prognostic," written by Ménuret. Ménuret begins by defining prognosis as a term denoting any advance knowledge obtained by a physician concerning a given sequence of pathological events.[26] He then launches into another glorifying scenario of the physician at work, this time as prognosticator:

> Prognosis is without question the most brilliant part of Medicine, and consequently the most favorable for the reputation of the practitioner: it is here that the experienced physician comes closest to being divine. The thick veil that covers future events falls before him; guided by the brilliant torch of a repeated and well-considered observation, he sees with a confident eye both preexisting objects and those that will emerge; the succession of phenomena, the increase or decrease in complications, the end of the illness, the manner in which it will take place, the corridors through which the decisive evacuation will occur—all of these elements form for him a vista that may be far off, but that is always sufficiently clear to distinguish the details . . . Through the gravest and most frightening complications, he sees that the triumph of nature and return to health are under way; and he consoles with greater sureness a shy and worried patient, reassures a desperate family, and promises without hesitating a positive outcome. (429)

As Ménuret's tableau of suffering and pathos continues, the physician becomes more and more heroic, deploying his unique divinatory talents to instill order into both the patient's illness and the familial entourage. His exceptional physical and intellectual qualities also come to the fore—and, most particularly, his uniquely attuned sense organs, which allow him to pick up on the signs of the various disease events occurring in the patient's body, to understand their natural interrelation, and to predict the manner in which the illness will be resolved through evacuation from the body. Once he has reconstructed the script that fits the patient's specific ailment, the skilled physician acts not to interfere in the illness, but rather to guide it to its most complete denouement: "Ceaselessly devoted to following nature, and to warding off anything that might delay nature's operations or prevent its success, he will skillfully proportion his assistance to both the demands of nature and the length of the illness; he will prepare from afar a complete and healthy crisis, a prompt and speedy convalescence, and firm and constant health thereafter" (429).

Ménuret thus paints a remarkably optimistic picture of medical treatment as a mutually beneficial team effort between nature and an enlightened attending physician, who deploys his semiotic talents in order to guide the patient's impending bodily crisis to a felicitous outcome. To succeed in this endeavor, the physician must be equipped with both a reliable bank of diligently reiterated clinical observations and a sure command of the body's most important signs. Those two related medical arts—observation and semiotic skill—have, Ménuret asserts, fallen into disuse since the days of Hippocrates, largely because so many theorists have promoted frivolous, arbitrary, or nonexistent signs. Fortunately, however, a handful of contemporary physicians more philosophical in temper have revived the principles of sound prognosis. "It is only recently," Ménuret notes, "that prognosis has received a new luster and greater certitude, through the observations that have been made on the pulse in relation to crises"—in obvious allusion to Bordeu's treatise on pulses, published eight years earlier ("Prognostic," 429). In Ménuret's view, one can excel in the art of prognosis only if one embraces two of the basic tenets articulated by Montpellier theorists like Bordeu: the idea that every disease state follows a specific "critical" pattern and the belief that, of all medical signs, pulses are the most significant.

Before ending the article "Prognostic," Ménuret ventures the intriguing suggestion that it might be possible to use the medically based methodology of semiotic prognosis outside the field of medicine itself: "But is prognosis only appropriate to the field of Medicine? Or, rather, might it not be possible, through a thoughtful examination of moral Man, to form a body of science that centered on the means of knowing and foreseeing the actions of men?" (430). Such a moral semiotics would, Ménuret suggests, vastly improve the understanding of human society because it would reveal "the hidden forces that motivate men"—forces that depend as much on their physical dispositions as on their present circumstances and dominant passions (430). Although Ménuret only toys with this possibility in "Prognostic," he nonetheless provides a glimpse of one of his major preoccupations as an Encyclopedist: to promote medicine, along with its divinely gifted practitioner, as exemplars for all of the human sciences.

This project is most explicitly carried out in the centerpiece article "Observation," which is designed to dramatize the "philosophical spirit" that, in Ménuret's view, has recently come to animate medical thinking.[27] As he presents it, that philosophical spirit is destined to remake the medical field from within and from without, by giving it a new place of prominence in the larger framework of human knowledge. Ménuret accordingly composes "Observation" to illustrate both aspects of this revolution: he continues his effort to maneuver semiotics into a privileged position in relation to the other branches of medicine, while redefining the general science of observation so as to depict medicine—the art of observing and coding the human body—as the alpha and omega of all natural-philosophical studies.

Although "Observation" is categorized as a medical article, medicine is not announced as its primary concern, at least not at the outset. Rather, Ménuret begins by denouncing experimental natural philosophy—a manner of regarding nature that he considers artificial and disfiguring, in marked contrast to plain and natural observation ("Observation," 313).[28] Ménuret compares the experimenter and the observer by way of synecdoche: each is reduced to the predominant sensory organ he uses for his investigations. The experimenter is thus represented by his hand—an organ that manipulates and disfigures—whereas the observer is depicted as an eye, the organ that has the most distant and unobtrusive relation to its object. Experimental methods, Ménuret insists, not only blind their practitioner to the virtues of simple observation, but also denature the object observed, producing phenomena that are artificial, arbitrary, and "ordinarily refuted by observation" (313–14). Given the multiple risks involved in experimenting on nature, Ménuret proclaims observation to be a far surer path to knowledge, for it alone produces the discoveries that constitute "the true wealth of the philosopher" (314). Following that principle, Ménuret describes a program for investigating nature that resembles Diderot's *De l'interprétation de la nature* (written a decade earlier)—with the difference that Ménuret gives a distinctly organic twist to the way that the facts of natural philosophy should interact: "Several facts taken separately appear dry, sterile, and fruitless; as soon as one brings them together, they acquire a certain action, and take on a life that arises from the mutual agreement, reciprocal support, and interrelation that ties all of them together" (314).[29] By the end of this article, the homology between the facts of organic matter and the organic-like interaction of facts themselves becomes something like a founding principle for medical discourse in general.

Ménuret's discussion in "Observation" moves steadily from fields of inorganic natural observation (astronomy, geology, physics) into the organic realm of the science of man, where the medical observer reigns supreme. "From whatever angle one envisions him," he declares, "Man is the being least suited to serving as an *experimental* subject; he is the most appropriate, most noble, and most interesting subject of *observation*, and it is only through observation that one can make any progress in the human sciences" (315). The "noble" and "divine" science of medicine is, he continues, the field that most excels in observing humankind, and thus warrants a particularly close examination. Ménuret therefore proceeds to list every type of medical observation imaginable (anatomical, physiological, hygienic, pathological, meteorological, and therapeutic) in such a way that all appear to be united under the globalizing rubric of semiotics, which he presents as a system into which every observed bodily fact can be fit (319). If it were properly designed, such a system of facts would not be a system at all, but rather "the true language of nature" (320).

Sensibility, as Ménuret describes it here, provides "a general point of view that serves as a rallying point for all of the facts that observation furnishes" (318). This theory of sensibility has, he adds, been endorsed by two distinguished contemporary thinkers:

> A famous physician (M. de Bordeu) and an illustrious physicist (M. de Maupertuis) have agreed that Man, envisioned from this brilliant and philosophical viewpoint, can be compared to a swarm of bees that undertake to attach themselves to a tree branch; one sees them pressing together, supporting each other, and forming a kind of whole, in which each part possesses its own particular mode of life but also contributes, through the correspondence and direction of its movements, to upholding this sort of *life* of the entire body, if one can use such a term to refer to a simple connection in action.   (318)

The specific works to which Ménuret is alluding in this passage are Bordeu's *Recherches anatomiques sur les glandes* (1752) and Maupertuis's *Système de la nature, ou Essai sur la formation des corps organisés* (1756), both of which use a version of the bee swarm metaphor that Diderot would later incorporate into the dialogue *Le Rêve de d'Alembert* (1769). What is most intriguing about Ménuret's use of this image in "Observation" is the manner in which he applies it not just to the organic body, but also to the body of facts that philosopher-physicians cull through their semiotic observations. A curious operational equivalence emerges in this article between the physical body being observed and the textual body that is formed by a well-assembled group of medical facts: those facts, Ménuret declares, should "communicate" via natural connections and affinities because they refer to a living body that is likewise driven by a set pattern of sympathetic physiological resonances that link its parts into an economic whole. Unlike the plain, inert theories of old-style iatromechanism—metaphorically represented here as a "flock of cranes that fly together in a certain order but without helping or depending on one another" (318)—the ideas that arise from the medicine of sensibility are destined to come to life. Ultimately, therefore, the force of bodily sensibility coordinates both the physio-pathological phenomena that the physician seeks to decipher and the way in which he obtains and disseminates his particular kind of knowledge. The bee swarm image thus figures twice in "Observation": once as a model for the animal economy and once as a model for organizing medical discourse in the most simple, natural form possible.

Ménuret's lively resonating model of medical discourse is based, in part, on an intriguing application of Condillacian analysis, in which all facts are pre-destined to take their proper, natural place in the observer's mind—in this case, because they emanate directly from a similarly ordered animal economy. It is also a particularly dynamic realization of what Diderot envisioned an encyclo-pedia to be: a work that would literally arouse its readers and stimulate them to see all sorts of new connections among ideas and in nature. The textual net-work that Ménuret and his medical collaborators construct in the *Encyclopédie* literally embodies such connections because it is composed of articles that not only describe but also mimic the active/reactive resonating quality of the sen-sible body in their "sympathetic" interactions. This is particularly apparent in articles on medical signs like "Langue," "Respiration," "Sueur," "Urine," and "Pouls," each of which was written by Ménuret, and each of which is copiously cross-referenced so as to direct the reader to Ménuret's feature article, "Pouls." In fact, whatever direction one takes in reading the Montpellier medical articles of the *Encyclopédie*, one almost invariably ends up at "Pouls"—a subject to which Ménuret devotes an unprecedented 35-page exposition in tome 13.[30] What, one might well ask, is so special about pulses that Ménuret slips in a cross-reference to this article at every possible occasion?

At first, "Pouls" appears to be a painstaking review of virtually every doc-trine that had ever been proposed to explain the information transmitted by pulses: Ménuret traces the notion from ancient theorists like Galen, to the Chi-nese (whose poetic names for pulses, like the "pulse that resembles a swimming fish," seem to strike his fancy), to the seventeenth-century iatromechanists, to musically minded contemporary physicians like François Nicolas Marquet, au-thor of the *Nouvelle méthode facile et curieuse, pour apprendre par les notes de musique à connoître le pouls de l'homme et ses différens changemens* (Nancy, 1747). The real aim in "Pouls" is not, however, to provide a comprehensive history of this medical notion. Rather, Ménuret seeks to draw attention to a new doctrine of pulses about which he is clearly excited: namely, the system proposed by Bordeu in his *Recherches sur le pouls par rapport aux crises* (1757). In the process of summarizing this treatise for the general reading public, Ménuret provides a revealing glimpse of the medical practices that were actually in use at the time—practices that, as he describes them here, seem to crystallize in the deli-cate art of tapping the resonances of the sensible body through its pulses.

Bordeu's treatise is, in fact, the source of Ménuret's general conviction that semiotic techniques like pulse-taking are the key to understanding every aspect of human physiology. As Ménuret puts it in the preface to a later version of "Pouls," "The pulse is an essential object, which is causally linked to the very constitution of the machine, to the most important and most extensive of the [physiological] functions . . . When the pulse's traits are skillfully grasped and developed, it reveals the entire interior of Man."[31] Bordeu himself provides the clearest explanation of what, precisely, is revealed through the pulse:

> The movements of the pulse depend undoubtedly on the *sensibility* of the nerves in the heart and arteries . . . Every organ being *sensible* in its *own* way, and being unable to perform its functions—particularly the most forceful—without making some impression on the entire nervous system, it is evident that each organ must make a particular impression on the *pulse:* this impression will be almost imperceptible when, as in the natural state, an organ is no more agitated than usual; by contrast, the impression will be quite evident if, as in the state of a critical effort, the organ is impeded in its functions and tries to make some extraordinary effort.[32]

For every organ or center of sensibility, there exists a corresponding pulse—for example, a "stomach pulse," a "pectoral pulse," and a "nasal pulse." Ménuret explains to his *Encyclopédie* readers that each organ-specific pulse can be further differentiated into a "pulse of irritation," a "developed pulse," and a "critical pulse," the last of which tells the physician how a disease will be resolved, by announcing when and where its critical evacuation is going to occur in the patient's body ("Pouls," 231). Of course, a pulse-based prognosis can be tricky, given that simple pulses are sometimes combined with others (235). Yet by consulting other available signs—and keeping in mind the resonating pattern of the animal economy—the medical observer can sketch a very accurate tableau of that body's natural internal order and thereby see very clearly what pathological disequilibrium is currently upsetting it (240).

The pulse, according to this doctrine, bears the signature of each organ, and thus allows the medical observer not just to translate physio-pathological phenomena into treatable terms, but to "hear" the body's inner language directly. Pulse-taking is consequently a far more incisive and reliable tool for gauging the presence of sensibility in a body part than any experimental technique deployed in Haller's laboratory, for it provides a means of retracing specific manifestations of the property back to the particular organ that is in reactive distress. Bordeu's system also entails a special map of pulse points, constructed in keeping with the various structural-functional axes that, in his view, organize the body's internal space.[33] In other words, this pulse doctrine is based upon a physio-anatomical topology that surpasses Haller's both in integration and in

NOUVELLE
METHODE
FACILE ET CURIEUSE,
POUR CONNOITRE LE POULS

PAR LES NOTES

DE LA MUSIQUE,

PAR FEU M. F. N. MARQUET.

SECONDE ÉDITION,

AUGMENTÉE DE PLUSIEURS OBSERVATIONS ET
Réflexions critiques, & d'une Differtation en forme
de Thèfe fur cette Méthode; d'un Mémoire fur la
manière de guérir la mélancolie par la Mufique, &
de l'Éloge hiftorique de M. MARQUET.

PAR M. PIERRE-JOSEPH BUCHOZ.

DOCTEUR AGGRÉGÉ AU COLLÉGE ROYAL DES
Médecins de Nancy, Médecin Botanifte Lorrain,
& Membre de plufieurs Académies.

À AMSTERDAM,
Et fe trouve à PARIS,
Chez P. Fr. DIDOT, Quai des Auguftins, à Saint-
Auguftin.

M. DCC. LXIX.

François Nicolas Marquet, Nouvelle méthode facile et curieuse, pour connoître le pouls par les notes de la musique (2d ed., 1769), title page. (Photograph courtesy of the Historical Collection of the Health Sciences Library, University of Wisconsin–Madison.)

practical applicability. What underlies that topology is the rather peculiar gland-based model of local physiological activity that Bordeu had proposed a few years earlier, in his *Recherches sur les glandes*. As we shall see shortly when we turn to that text, the Bordelian organology sheds a provocative new light on what is actually going on in an organ when a physician detects its specific pulsations.

To a certain extent, mastering the sensibility-based art of pulse-taking requires the same set of talents as those that Ménuret ascribes to the first-rate medical observer: an assiduously acquired clinical experience, a degree of in-

Exemple du poulx
naturel reglé, *from
F. N. Marquet*
Nouvelle méthode
facile et curieuse,
pour connoître le
pouls par les notes de
la musique *(2d ed.,
1769), plate.
(Photograph courtesy
of the Historical
Collection of the
Health Sciences
Library, University of
Wisconsin–Madison)*

struction in anatomy and physiology, a firm grasp of the science of pathological signs, and a refined faculty of sensory (in this case, tactile) perception. In
Bordeu's view, however, having that special manual finesse does not in and of
itself guarantee that a physician possesses the acute sensibility necessary to perceive the many nuances of organ-specific pulses. The skilled pulse-taker must
also have an exceptional cerebral finesse: "The most clear-seeing and confident
physicians in this field of knowledge are those whose heads are the most fully
furnished with the images of all the various species of pulse . . . It is for the
same reason, and by virtue of the clearness of these ideas, that the physician

whose tact is well trained can sometimes determine the state of a pulse through an initial sensation that is almost automatic and often precious: [this is] a fortunate sort of inspiration [*enthousiasme*] of which cool-headed, lazy minds are incapable, and which is only fully appreciated by connoisseurs."[34] In other words, interpreting the body via its pulses requires the physician to draw upon his keen sensory faculties and clinical acumen in order to enter into a state of fervent, enthusiastic communication with the natural phenomena unfolding before him. Interestingly, Bordeu's sole *Encyclopédie* article, "Crise," hinges upon a scenario of precisely that kind of ultrasensory enthusiasm—the trancelike condition which, he maintains, must be experienced by any physician who seeks to become a true médecin philosophe.

Bordeu's discussion in "Crise" is pertinent on several counts, not least because of its fascinating similarity to Diderot's treatment of the masterful observer of nature, which I discuss in Chapter 5. Suffice it to say, for now, that the great physician Bordeu depicts in that text outstrips Ménuret's in both the comprehensiveness and the sheer brilliance of his diagnostic capacities. Bordeu himself was notably modest, Pyrrhonist even, regarding the truth value of his own medical theories and observations. Nonetheless, he strove to be "philosophical" throughout his medical writings by grappling with the many pressing ethical and sociopolitical questions raised by life in eighteenth-century society, like the denaturing effects of worldly/urban life and the ongoing debate over the need to inoculate people against such transnational scourges as smallpox. Bordeu treats the latter subject in his *Recherches sur l'histoire de la médecine* (1767), where he presents a prolonged argument in favor of smallpox inoculation by examining it from the vantage point of every known type of physician, culminating with the médecins philosophes. What distinguishes this last group of medical thinkers, and makes their views on the question of inoculation especially authoritative, is that they "direct their views more at entire nations than at individuals or at the inhabitants of a single country."[35] Bordeu asserts that the principles which such physicians espouse in all medical matters are so broadminded that they transcend local prejudices and superstition altogether. Medical thinkers of this stature have the capacity to diagnose the ills that afflict entire nations and to perceive their underlying etiology, be it physical, moral, or social—just as Montesquieu had analyzed the entire range of existing sociopolitical systems in *De l'esprit des lois* by locating their root physical cause.[36] The médecins philosophes can, according to Bordeu, outdo Montesquieu in explaining the fundamental motors of human nature and society because they possess a more precise tool for understanding the dynamics of human nature: namely, the concept of sensibility, which not only confirms that there is a causal relation between constitution and environment, but also shows that human beings are finely tuned reactive organisms, endowed with the capacity to discern and respond selectively to the physical and moral stimuli that surround them.

The Montpellier physicians thus believed that they could serve as the ultimate *philosophes* in eighteenth-century France. It was, they claimed, the heroic persona of the physician-philosopher who held the "brilliant torch" that would eventually lead humanity out of darkness and disease by providing a natural explanation for all of the perplexing phenomena of human life, from epidemics, to Jansenist convulsions, to the worldly scourge known as the vapors.[37] Some scholars have decried the naturalist ideology that ran rampant during the eighteenth century (among other periods), viewing it as a naively anthropocentric obstacle to scientific and philosophical progress.[38] That naturalist ideology is nonetheless an integral and, I believe, benign component of both vitalist medicine and the sensibility paradigm at large.[39] Inasmuch as it allowed the fledgling human sciences to operate according to a common, coordinated set of methods and perspectives, eighteenth-century naturalism served a useful rather than hindering conceptual purpose. At the very least, this mode of naturalism allowed the physician-philosophers of the era to claim an expanded role for their ideas in the ongoing movement to "enlighten" humanity.

Later physicians would not necessarily view this expanded role with favor. For example, the nineteenth-century historian of medicine Charles Daremberg looked back with loathing upon *médecins philosophes* like Bordeu precisely because their vitalist/organicist ideas persisted so long into the next century. Along with singling out Bordeu as "a very muddled mind, an unsteady anatomist, an uncertain physiologist, a theorist who lacked any firm doctrine, a veritable syncretist, one of the most misinformed historians, a so-called scholar who vaunted incessantly empiricism and natural medicine," Daremberg condemned practically the sum total of Enlightenment medicine as "this medico-philosophical literature, this hybrid, long-winded, empty literature that had all too many representatives in France in the medicine of the late eighteenth century."[40] Above and beyond the litany of colorful invectives squeezed into those two passages, Daremberg puts his finger here on the two truly essential traits of medico-philosophical discourse: its self-proclaimed naturalism and its "literariness."

But then, what is philosophical medicine, if not a sort of literature? How does it operate, if not via an elaborate series of discursive *tableaux* of sensibility in action? In the course of our examination of the medical network of the *Encyclopédie*, we have seen how such *tableaux* could be deployed to cover every aspect of medical theory and practice: the construction of the body as a reactive animal economy, the coding of signs for deciphering that body, the organization of medical facts into a resonating body of knowledge, and finally, the depiction of the inspired medical observer engaged in diagnosis. It is, in the end, this last scenario that is the most compelling as well as most properly literary in design: for the moment of medical diagnosis hinges upon a dramatic, dynamic body-to-body engagement between two personas who represent opposite ends of the sensibility spectrum. One persona is the patient, whose sensibility is pathologically disturbed; the other is the heroic médecin philosophe, whose sensibility is both exquisitely developed and exquisitely mastered. Out of the communicative interplay between those two diametrically opposed types of sensibility is born a medico-philosophical fact, which captures sensibility and put it into words.

One might expect that this neat, harmonious discursive edifice left itself wide open to ridicule by contemporary literary wits, much as Leibniz's optimistic monadology was parodied by Voltaire in *Candide*. In fact, however, literary authors like Diderot (as well as Rousseau, Laclos, and Sade, to varying degrees) heartily embraced philosophical medicine in all of its naturalism and heroism because it provided them with just what they needed to "diagnose" sensibility on their own terms. Of course, all of these writers gave their own spin to the different elements of contemporary medico-philosophical theory: the language that the sensible body was supposedly speaking; the practice of categorizing sensibility into natural versus pathological types; and the very figure of the physician-philosopher. Yet even when they used such notions in jest or as handy conventions, eighteenth-century literary philosophes attested to the power of those ideas for framing the manner in which sensibility was understood as a force in human life.

In short, the hybrid medico-literary articulation that Daremberg so decried worked both ways, in that the medicine and the literature of sensibility overlapped not only in preoccupation, but in methodology as well. To clarify that last point, let us consider a brief passage from Jean Senebier's *Essai sur l'art d'observer* (1775). Senebier—who was, it should be noted, an ardent admirer of Haller and his methods—offers a painstaking exposition of all of the ideas and systems that had been proposed for formalizing observation into an abstract, generic art. Using Condillac's *Logique* as a foundation, he incorporates Haller, Bonnet, Ménuret's *Encyclopédie* article "Observation," and selected points from Diderot, Zimmerman, Spallanzani and other contemporaries into a medically oriented synthesis. The most intriguing aspect of this synthesis is Senebier's lengthy comparison of two seemingly heterogeneous types of observers: the observer of nature, represented in this text by the medical observer; and the keen-eyed *littérateur*. Having characterized the "observer's look" as a fine balance of attention, penetration, sagacity, and skepticism, and having found that balance in both fields, Senebier remarks that "all of these reflections suffice to show that the littérateur and the observer of nature play the same role in their research and that it is impossible to distinguish oneself in literature if one does not bring to it this observer's spirit, which is the sole source of discoveries and the guarantee of the successes that one might have."[41] In other words, the key to excelling in literature and medicine alike is having an "esprit d'observateur": that is, the ability to scrutinize the salient signs and traits of one's object step by step, as they naturally present themselves. Extrapolating from Senebier's generic model for observation, one might say that the eighteenth-century medicine of sensibility and novel of sensibility were homologous modes of a general type of diagnostics; for, after 1750, they tended to share not only a similar methodology, but the same object: sensibility, seen as a jointly physical and moral force.

Bordeu, Diderot, and the Implications of Organological Sensibility

The connections that sensibility created between medicine and literature during the second half of the eighteenth century were, of course, as diverse as the writers involved. Nowhere, however, were they more explicit than in the works of Denis Diderot, who was well versed in Montpellier medical theory, particularly as expressed by Théophile de Bordeu. Scholars of Diderot have generally interpreted his interest in Bordeu's ideas in a narrow, historiographic sense, limiting their consideration of Bordeu's medical doctrine to the "facts" that Diderot culled from that doctrine (as well as from many other works of natural philosophy and medicine) for inclusion in the *Rêve de d'Alembert* and the *Éléments de physiologie*.[42] Such an approach, however, overlooks the dramatic form that Bordeu's ideas take in the *Rêve*, where Bordeu is cast as a fictional interlocutor along with Jean d'Alembert and his mistress, Julie de l'Espinasse. In discussing this text, many critics have treated the ideas expounded there by the character Bordeu as purely Diderotian pronouncements on selected topics in natural philosophy—specifically, materialism, sensibility, generation, and teratology. Bordeu's appearance in this philosophical dialogue has thus been characterized as poetic license, on the assumption that the Bordeu persona of the *Rêve* is as unrelated to the historical Bordeu as are the fictive d'Alembert and Mlle. de l'Espinasse to their flesh-and-blood counterparts.[43] Diderot was, however, far from arbitrary or whimsical in casting Bordeu as his "modern-day Hippocrates." Rather, he very deliberately incorporated Bordeu's model of the animal economy into both the discussion and the design of the *Rêve de d'Alembert*, which one could view as an dramatization—at times parodic—of Bordeu's highly particular concept of vital sensibility.

Before considering how Diderot translates Bordeu's vision of the body into the *Rêve,* let us examine that vision on its own terms, by considering Bordeu's *Recherches anatomiques sur la position des glandes et sur leur action* (1752), which first established him as a major theorist on the French medical scene. It is here that Bordeu explains precisely what is going on inside the body whenever a sign of sensibility is given off, be it through a pulse variation, a humoral evacuation, or some other indication: somewhere in the body, an organ has been stimulated and roused into action.[44] The *Recherches sur les glandes* was, in fact, far more than a simple anatomical treatise on glands: it was a daringly innovative effort both to dismantle the accepted mechanistic (Boerhaavian) explanation of glandular function and to take on the highly limited definition of sensibility that Haller had begun to elaborate in the 1740s. Whereas Haller insisted that the reactive properties of irritability and sensibility should be seen as quite distinct, Bordeu just as insistently interconnected them; in the process, he produced a physiological system that would eventually take the form of a full-scale organological theory of vital phenomena.

Vital reactibility is, for Bordeu as for Haller, an innately organic capacity to respond to irritations emanating from an external source. Bordeu, however, locates this elemental physiological reaction not at the level of the fiber, but at that of the organ. He insists that, contrary to iatromechanistic theory, glands are not passive and compressible, but rather, able to engage in their own activities because they are richly innervated. In his view, the most illustrative gland of all is the male sexual organ, an obviously irritable body part whose mode of functioning cannot be attributed to mechanical compression: "One cannot help resorting to the sensibility and *vibratility* of the nerves . . . The convulsions and tremors that precede this excretion in most animals are familiar to everyone; an anatomically informed philosopher discovers therein a good number of subjects for meditation that elude the common herd" (*Glandes,* 125). Seminal excretion is thus the first example that Bordeu invokes to argue that the mechanistic model of glandular secretion is clearly inadequate. To reinforce his point, he proceeds to recount the steps involved in the convulsive mechanism by which semen is evacuated: the erection of the penis, which is necessary to prepare the organ for excretion; the spasm that overtakes the genital parts and everything around them when they become aroused; the *secousses* and *frottements* that "awaken" the organ into a general convulsion; and finally "the relaxation that occurs when the scene is finished" (125–26).

Bordeu concludes that this observation is "already sufficient to found a theory of the mechanism of excretion" (126). In fact, however, he uses the penis to illustrate only half of his theory of glandular function: the role of irritability, or the gland's power to perform some movement in response to a stimulus/irritant. To demonstrate the second half of that theory—the role of feeling or sensibility—Bordeu looks elsewhere in the body, to what he considers to be the feminine analogue to seminal excretion: lactation. In this observation, Bordeu describes not only the function of stimulation as carried out by the nursing infant, but also the intense, ticklish feelings that such stimulation provokes in the breast: "There is no wet nurse who has not felt this tension, and the kind of *tickling* that results from it. Most of them say that they can *feel the milk rising.* The breast becomes rounder, harder, and swollen, and there are women who endure tugging sensations that make themselves felt all the way to the shoulder and loins, and even to the arms. These tugging sensations are painful in some women; but usually they feel a more or less voluptuous titillation" (126).

The titillation that a wet nurse experiences when breast-feeding is not incidental, but rather, is crucial to the process of excreting her milk; nor is the erotic language that Bordeu uses to describe this mammary "seduction" merely coincidental. Bordeu quite consciously psychologizes and eroticizes his description of sensibility in this female gland: he depicts the breast as an organ that rather capriciously *decides* when to yield up its milk. In the next paragraph, for example, Bordeu contends that breasts only respond to the babies that excite them properly: "Wet nurses find that certain infants do not excite them enough, do not bring forth their milk, or do not provoke those *ticklings* or those *tremors* that we were discussing earlier; but there is almost no wet nurse who does not find some child that is just right for her and to whom she becomes all the more attached because he rewards her by exciting within her a sensation that is followed by tenderness" (126).[45]

Bordeu's description of how sensibility is involved in breast secretion plainly involves a strategy of provocation—a strategy that is all the more striking, given that he does not eroticize his discussion of the penis and its activities. Bordeu's correspondence contains an interesting little clue to the way that he wanted readers to respond to his *Recherches sur les glandes,* in a letter addressed to one of his younger brothers who was apparently charged with distributing the work. Bordeu asks his brother: "Have you had the work slipped into some convents? It is there, precisely, that it should wreak its effect: it must get people talking, muttering, and stirred up—particularly nuns and Beguines, right up to their wimples" (*Correspondance,* 1:138). That remark may not completely explain what Bordeu was up to in describing certain glands so pruriently, but it does suggest that he anticipated a strong response from a wide reading public—including nuns, the same segment of the population that Diderot would later address in semimedical terms in *La Religieuse.* This impression is reinforced by the pattern of strikingly popular images and terms evident throughout Bordeu's text. I shall examine that pattern momentarily; first, let us consider how Bordeu integrates the properties of sensibility and irritability in order to explain the overall mechanism of glandular function.

Unlike some medical theorists of the day, Bordeu does not so much conflate the properties of irritability and sensibility as assign them different roles in the general mechanism of local organic activity. Once he has established his model of the autonomous action of glands, Bordeu uses it to assert that glands are active organs that exhibit individual "tastes" or sentiments of their own, thanks to the nerves that innervate them and maintain their particular "tone" or "tact" (*Glandes*, 145–50). It is these local nerves—which Bordeu sees as an integral part of the gland they sensitize—that are irritated, thereby provoking the organ to manifest its "particular life" by secreting a particular humor (157). What is curious in all of this is not so much the anatomical error that, in the eyes of some of his contemporaries, Bordeu commits in constructing his glandular theory (Haller would soon refute Bordeu's thesis that the glands are heavily innervated).[46] Rather, it is the fact that Bordeu vitalizes glands by sexualizing their structure while also eroticizing both their function and the descriptive vocabulary that is to be used to analyze them. The innovative, attention-getting aspect of Bordeu's *Recherches sur les glandes* therefore resides not just in his antimechanistic model of glandular activity: it lies also in the very deliberate way that he interweaves into his physio-anatomical descriptions many of the reigning cultural ideas about sensibility, like its associations with feeling, with erotic arousal, and with women. The strikingly sexy and provocative dimension of Bordeu's biomedical theory has generally been glossed over by the historians of medicine who treat him.[47] Diderot, by contrast, was keenly aware of it.

This brings us to the question of Bordeu's often piquant descriptive vocabulary. In the course of applying his nonmechanistic, penile-based model for glandular function to all other secretory and excretory organs in the body (this includes glands proper, like the sublingual and lacrimal glands, as well as organs like the thyroid, pancreas, kidneys, and even the brain), Bordeu occasionally reminds his readers of the "glandular seduction" scenario he had sketched while explaining the secretion of milk from the breast. For example, in his discussion of the salivary glands, he depicts infant salivation as a symbiotic extension of lactation that brings the two bodies together in reciprocal glandular "sympathy" and arousal: "The infant seems to empty the ducts of all the glands that end in the mouth, in proportion to emptying the ducts of his mother's breast: *he sucks, he suckles himself*, so to speak" (*Glandes*, 148).[48] Bordeu frequently uses expressions like the "so to speak" that appears here in order to qualify his picturesque way of speaking about the dynamics of organic activity. He also sprinkles his treatise with footnotes explaining his use of particular conceptual metaphors: he qualifies his use of the terms *sensation* or *sentiment* (163), his notion of glandular taste (164), his reference to organological "departments" (178), his idea that glands follow cycles of awakening and repose (184), and his application of the word *erection* to everything from penises to the parotid glands (132). However, even as he apologizes to his reader for using such figurative expressions, Bordeu makes it clear that he finds them valuable: "I should point out that I am using the term *erection* because I have not found anything more expressive to convey the idea of what I mean by the disposition of an organ that is getting ready to make an excretion; the organ undergoes a singular sort of swelling, or increase in force; I will be obliged to use many other metaphorical terms, without which it would have been impossible for me to render my ideas clearly; I will therefore say that organs *wake up* and *go to sleep,* etc. These are figurative expressions that the reader must excuse" (*Glandes,* 132 n). For the modern reader familiar with Diderot, this caveat brings to mind the scene in the *Rêve de d'Alembert* where d'Alembert mistakes Dr. Bordeu's "technical" terms for obscenities likely to shock Mlle. de l'Espinasse.[49] It also illustrates an interesting evolution in Bordeu's vocabulary over the course of the *Recherches sur les glandes:* what had been nonmetaphorical in its original context (the description of penile excretion) becomes metaphoric when applied to more neutral glands, thus allowing Bordeu to establish a comprehensive organology out of a single, penis-based model.

To construct his organology, Bordeu must demonstrate that every gland is just as autonomous in its activities as the penis and has activities that resonate just as dramatically throughout the animal economy. He carries out this demonstration in two steps. First, he describes an active gland as a rallying point for two of the primary communicative networks of the body, the circulatory and nervous systems.[50] Bordeu claims that a secreting gland has an intensified neural activity that attracts a heavy influx of fluids through the blood, thus turning the gland into a "separate body" that is able to chose the specific humors it wants to secrete (*Glandes,* 161, 163). To illustrate how a gland can have such an independent capacity, he compares it to the polyp, a recently discovered creature that is able—even though it lacks a central nervous system—to execute very particular movements in response to the stimuli that most "interest" it (165–66). He adds that many organs of the body—such as the intestines, the stomach, and the uterus—are notoriously particular (164–65, 187, 190).

Bordeu goes on to assert that each active gland has a "department," or sphere of influence, which, in health, expresses itself at certain periods of the day. This periodicity is central to the animal economy: each gland functions according to an internal clockwork that is coordinated in relation to other glandular actions, depending on whether they are sympathetic or antagonistic. If only that natural schedule of glandular action and interaction could be charted, Bordeu reasons, an astute physician would need merely to determine which external cause had upset the patient's economy, in order to cure him (185). As an illustration, Bordeu proposes a hypothetical ideal subject, "one of those temperate and steady peasants who are only concerned with the task at hand," who, "after a diet of two days or so, . . . has slept from eight to ten hours," thus suspending all of the glandular actions that take place during the waking hours. Having set these conditions for his thought experiment, Bordeu observes his subject's glands through every stage of his daily activities:

> This subject gets up in the morning; he stretches, and *awakens,* so to speak, all of his limbs; after a few movements, his appetite begins to make itself felt, and as we observed (no. LXXIII), his parotid glands begin operating; they perform their function until the stomach is full enough; then they rest, or they only make as many secretions as is necessary . . . But then the stomach begins, in turn, to increase its action . . . Now it is time for the small intestines to become active . . . The approach of chyle toward the heart and lungs must excite the vessels and the forces of circulation; after a certain time the kidneys and skin will come to evacuate the excrements of digestion, etc.   (184–85)

Bordeu's "glandular day" has some very suggestive resonances with the famous "experimental history of a geometrist" that Diderot includes in the *Rêve de d'Alembert.* Like Bordeu's well-regulated peasant, the geometrist portrayed by the fictional Dr. Bordeu performs a preset pattern of automatic acts: "You dressed, sat at your desk, meditated, drew diagrams, worked out calculations, had your dinner, . . . went to bed and to sleep without ever having exercised the slightest willpower."[51] The difference, of course, is that the "organ" whose activities Diderot analyzes is d'Alembert's brain, which (as Diderot describes it) is no more independent in its functions than the digestive tract of Bordeu's peasant. Thus, whereas Bordeu is concerned with showing how his organological theory can be applied to ensure optimal physiological function, Diderot adapts that theory for the purposes of his materialist philosophy: he seeks to demonstrate that the will and volition are subject to the same kind of mechanical automatism as is the body because they too are *corporal* functions.[52]

To reinforce his hypothesis that a well-regulated glandular economy would exhibit an automatic harmony, Bordeu proposes two analogies, both of which reappear in the *Rêve de d'Alembert:* he compares the glands as a group to a well-regulated monastery (*Glandes,* 185–86), and he compares the human body as a whole to a swarm of bees. In Bordeu's opinion, monasteries provide the best example of a collective of physiologically well-regulated individuals, whose existences are ideally suited for maintaining the rhythmical functioning of their constituent glands or organs.[53] Bodies do not, however, always behave like monks: sometimes they act like bees. Bordeu employs the latter analogy to illustrate that the body's local and general activities are perfectly coordinated in health but lose that coordination when one part becomes weakened or antagonistic toward the others:

> In order to underscore the idea that each body part has a particular action, we will compare the living body to a swarm of bees that gather together in clusters . . . every part is, so to speak, not an animal but a sort of separate machine that contributes in its way to the *general life* of the body . . . when [the bees] all conspire to squeeze and hug each other, and in the required order and proportions, they form a whole that will subsist until the bees are disturbed.
>
> The application [of this comparison] is easy to make: the organs of the body are linked to each other; each one has its district and action; the relations between these actions, and the harmony that they create, constitute health. If this harmony is upset, either because one part weakens or because another part gains the upper hand over one that is antagonizing it, if the actions are reversed and do not follow the natural order, then these changes will constitute illnesses of varying degrees of severity. (187)

The conceptual metaphor of the bee swarm was quite popular in the 1750s and 1760s. Maupertuis used it in his *Système de la nature* to describe the genesis of an organism through the gathering of disparate psycho-physical monads,[54] and Ménuret invoked it in the *Encyclopédie* to promote the new Montpellier vision of the animal economy. Diderot employs the bee swarm metaphor for multiple purposes in the *Rêve de d'Alembert:* first, it illustrates the process by which matter shifts from mechanical contiguity to organic continuity (*RA,* 120–23); and second, once transformed into the related metaphor of the spider web with the spider in the center, it explains how sensibility and consciousness are coordinated in the human organism (141–43, 174–77).[55] The real Bordeu uses this analogy to make a medical point: each part within the body's organological federation possesses the capacity to act autonomously—that is, pathologically—and thus to disrupt the harmony which the healthy organism enjoys.

Bordeu's gland-based organology therefore entails not just a physiological doctrine, but a theory of pathology as well. Late in the *Recherches sur les glandes,* Bordeu observes that "what we have said about the particular action of organs can shed light on what happens during an inflammation" (194). The process of inflammation, he explains, is exactly analogous to what occurs when one of the

bees in a swarm becomes agitated and antagonistic—and to what happens in a
gland when it enters into a secretory crisis:

> It seems that when a part becomes inflamed, it becomes a particular or-
> gan that has its own action, circulation, and functions that are indepen-
> dent, in a certain sense, from what it receives from the general circulation
> . . . An inflamed part becomes, in a way, a *separate body,* at least for a
> time. It has a kind of action that goes beyond that which creates life; it
> creates a separate *circle* . . . in sum, what happens in this part resembles
> what goes on in glands and in other organs toward which the blood is di-
> rected, where there occur various kinds of *torrents* that medical practi-
> tioners have called *raptus.* (194–96)

A diseased state is therefore created by excessive vitality in a body part; this is
the sort of crisis that medical semioticians must decipher and treat. Pulses provide a direct indication of this process: when an organ is intensely aroused, its
surrounding nerves and blood vessels become so irritated that they divert the
circulation of blood toward that new "department," creating a special tension
or pull on the entire vascular system. This constitutes that organ's unique pulse
or signature, which the astute physician can use to trace the crisis to its specific
organic locus. By detecting a particular pulse pattern and sensing which secretory pathway seems about to be activated, the physician is able to pinpoint precisely the area of sensible disequilibrium and thereby guide the body back to
health and harmony.

   Bordeu's extension of his organological model into disease theory sheds an
intriguing new light on his entire system for diagnosing and transcribing the
bodily language of sensibility; for what that language reveals is, in essence, the
occurrence of glandular "orgasms." According to Diderot's free-wheeling application of Bordeu's physiology, if all organs in the body behave like glands,
which in turn behave like penises, there is no reason not to assert that whole organisms—people—behave the same way. The communication of sensibility
thereby becomes inherently sexual in nature, regardless of where the sensible
reaction is coming from, body or brain. The successive dialogues of the *Rêve
de d'Alembert* do, in fact, take the form of an elaborate literary demonstration
of sensibility and its seductive effects on the body and mind, as Wilda Anderson has quite persuasively shown.[56] To give that analysis a Bordelian twist, one
might call the interlocutors of the *Rêve de d'Alembert* talking glands: like the organs in Bordeu's organological confederation, they are, by turns, feverish and
inflamed in their outbursts, dormant in repose, and sympathetically resonant
through the course of their dialogues.[57] Taking this perspective on Diderot's
text, however, requires modifying one aspect of Anderson's interpretation:

namely, her insistence that "Diderot was not engaged in biological (or even physiological) reflection" when he elaborated his materialist notion of sensibility.[58] Yet what Diderot does in the *Rêve* is, precisely, to reflect upon the possibilities of Bordeu's organological theory of sensibility; in the process, he transforms the very activity of observing and musing upon sensibility into an act both of physical crisis and of "philosophical" creation.

＊＊＊

The main dialogue of the *Rêve de d'Alembert*, situated between the "Suite d'un entretien entre M. d'Alembert et M. Diderot" and the "Suite de l'entretien précédent," is set up as a physiology lesson whose ostensible purpose is to explain what organic sensibility is all about to uninformed or unconvinced characters like d'Alembert and Mlle. de l'Espinasse. Before Dr. Bordeu enters the scene, d'Alembert has spent a feverishly agitated night in the grips of sensibility, which is both the subject and the cause of his dream. He is, at the dialogue's outset, still asleep, and Mlle. de l'Espinasse is standing guard at his bedside. The presence of this sleeping interlocutor in the dialogue immediately undermines the possibility that there will be a clear, linear order to the conversation; for sleep, as Dr. Bordeu defines it, is "a condition during which the animal no longer exists as a coherent whole and in which any collaboration or subordination between parts is suspended. The master is given over to the good pleasure of his vassals and the uncontrolled energy of his own activity" (*Dream*, 215; *RA*, 182). At the same time, because dreams are also etiologically linked to "some erethism or temporary disorder" (*Dream*, 215; *RA*, 183), the setting of the *Rêve* is designed to require Dr. Bordeu's expert services: a "critical" condition like d'Alembert's passing illness calls for a physician who is able to decipher sensibility's inner workings within the body.

Dr. Bordeu is thus brought into the text as a medical practitioner who can treat d'Alembert's condition and as a *médecin philosophe* who possesses a rare capacity to interpret sensibility. His medical knowledge comes into play immediately: first, in the semiotic reading that he performs by taking d'Alembert's pulse and other vital signs ("Pulse all right . . . a bit weak . . . skin moist . . . breathing easy" [*Dream*, 165; *RA*, 115]); and second, in his ability to make sense of d'Alembert mumblings about "sensible molecules," bees, and so on. Having pronounced that the patient's physical condition is "only a bit of a temperature and there won't be any after-effects," Dr. Bordeu obligingly offers to decipher Mlle. de l'Espinasse's transcription of d'Alembert's unconscious mutterings from the night before, which she calls "some gibberish about vibrating strings and sensitive fibres" (*Dream*, 166; *RA*, 116). The gist of the mutterings transcribed by Mlle. de l'Espinasse is, precisely, the bee swarm metaphor that Bordeu had used in his *Recherches sur les glandes* to explain the problematic passage between the local sensibility of discrete vital parts (or individual "bees") and the general sensibility of a continuous living whole (like a swarm). Diderot's use of this organic metaphor demonstrates sensibility's destabilizing effects, but also its formative powers—both in the body and in the mind of the philosophical observer. By repeating and transmuting the bee swarm analogy over the course of their dialogue, the interlocutors end up elaborating a model of sensibility that seems to explain everything, including the nature of matter, organic generation, physiological functioning, disease, and the intellectual and moral capacities of human beings.

One could, of course, do a point-by-point comparison between d'Alembert's philosophical reverie on the bees he sees in his dream and Bordeu's use of the image in his treatise on glands. Such an exercise would appear all the more tempting given Mlle. de l'Espinasse's celebrated declaration, upon seeing how well Dr. Bordeu can anticipate every line of her dictation, that "I really am amazed; that's what he said, almost word for word. I can now proclaim to all the world that there is no difference at all between a doctor awake and a philosopher dreaming" (*Dream*, 170; *RA*, 122). I am more interested, however, in considering how Diderot employs the dream-state mode of thinking about living processes to present the act of observing sensibility as both highly physical and highly philosophical. This freewheeling method of analyzing vital phenomena is initiated in the *Rêve* by the sleeping d'Alembert's musings on the countless ways of "renewing the population" which the dynamic new model of sensibility makes conceivable (*Dream*, 173; *RA*, 126). It is then replayed throughout the text, in every character's observations—all of which aim to retrace the operations of this property through the full range of its imaginable effects. What Diderot's interlocutors look for during their conversations are the causal links between particular conditions of sensibility and the constitutions and behaviors that they create. The characters of the *Rêve* are themselves subject to the physical and mental effects of sensibility, yet that is not the only salient feature of Diderot's demonstration. Equally important to that demonstration is the interlocutors' behavior as investigators of sensibility—or, to put it in Diderot's terms, as thinkers who are engaged in a prolonged effort to do mentally what nature sometimes does in reality (*Dream*, 166; *RA*, 149).

The *Rêve de d'Alembert* is therefore a thought experiment on sensibility in a very literal, material sense: thinking about the property has direct consequences on both the organs of the experimenters and their understanding faculties. This is most evident in the celebrated scene of d'Alembert's "dream from the head down" [*rêve en descendant*], during which he is so stimulated by the new physiological combinations he is imagining that his own organ of generation is irritated, and he produces living matter by masturbating (*RA*, 127–29). Before that climactic manual act, however, d'Alembert had already been using his hands as investigatory instruments, to conduct his observations in a very tactile fashion. First, he asks Mlle. de l'Espinasse to take hold of the bee swarm he has envisioned in order to test it out:

> "Take this cluster of bees, there, you see it over there, and let us do an experiment."
> "How?"
> "Take your scissors; are they sharp?"
> "They cut beautifully."
> "Now, carefully, very carefully, bring your scissors to bear on these bees and cut them apart, but mind you don't cut through the middle of their bodies, cut exactly where their feet have grown together. Don't be afraid, you will hurt them a little, but you won't kill them. Good—your touch is as delicate as a fairy's." (*Dream*, 170; *RA*, 122)

Next, d'Alembert begins, in the words of Mlle. de L'Espinasse, "mumbling something or other about seeds, bits of flesh pounded up in water, different races of animals he saw coming into being and perishing one after the other" (*Dream*, 173; *RA*, 127). In this instance, d'Alembert's gestures speak far more eloquently than do his mumblings.[59] Inspired by his own gestural replication of an imagined physiological observation, d'Alembert ultimately shifts his hands downward and stimulates the source of his own microscopic "animaculae" (*Dream*, 174; *RA*, 128). By that point, however, the instrumentality of hands as organs for exploring sensibility has acquired a significance that goes beyond Diderot's salacious play on tubes, orifices, and the art of pulse-taking. (As Mlle. de l'Epinasse recounts, "I wanted to feel his pulse, but he had hidden his hand somewhere" [*Dream*, 174; *RA*, 129].) In larger terms, this series of handmade thought experiments represents a means of getting the body "into the act" of experiencing sensibility, which goes a step beyond the erotic resonances that are felt but not understood by a figure like Suzanne Simonin in *La Religieuse*, or like Mlle. de l'Espinasse for a brief moment here: "I was watching him very attentively, and felt deeply moved without knowing why; my heart was beating fast, but not with fear" (*Dream*, 175; *RA*, 129). That is, the involvement of the investigators' bodies in the *Rêve de d'Alembert* is not always an instantiation of the weak, visceral mode of sensibility characteristic of what Dr. Bordeu calls "mediocre people" (*Dream*, 212; *RA*, 178); for their physical experiences of sensibility over the course of the dialogue are not separated (as those experiences are for Suzanne Simonin) from their interpretation of the property.[60]

Moreover, everyone involved in the resonating network established by the *Rêve* is fair game for embodying any and all modes of sensibility: local organological sensibility, general sensibility, and both "higher" and "lower" sensibility. This might seem to undermine the hierarchical distinction between the weakly organized sensible being with whom Mlle. de l'Espinasse identifies and the type of cool-headed, self-controlled great man Dr. Bordeu believes himself to be (*RA*, 179–80). However, it is not so much that one kind of sensibility (lower, visceral) wins out over another (cerebral sensibility), as that all modes of sensibility become equally potent reactive forces in the federation of body parts. Thus, Diderot's experimental democratization of the susceptibility to sensibility works both ways: just as great men can be humbled by tinkering with their vigorous sensible networks, so, too, can weak souls rise above their overreactive state by following Dr. Bordeu's medical advice: "Let us build up the center of the [sensible] network, it is the best thing we can do" (*Dream*, 214; *RA*, 181).

To give just one example of that last point, let us consider Mlle. de l'Espinasse's function as subject and object of investigation. Dr. Bordeu exhibits a particular penchant for "experimenting" on Mlle. de l'Espinasse's person—and she is clearly pleased by that penchant.[61] Although she occasionally retreats into the role of oversensitive prude, delicately shying away from the morally compromising conclusions of the ideas being bandied about in the conversation (*RA*, 196), she more often behaves like someone who is working her way up the ladder of natural observers, under what Dr. Bordeu assumes to be his expert guidance: she soon becomes an observer who, in his words, can reflect on new "facts" and "draw conclusions therefrom which amaze me by their rightness" (*Dream*, 187; *RA*, 146).[62] In other words, Mlle. de l'Espinasse's sensible constitution is fortified by the practice of polishing her observational skills—just as Dr. Bordeu's is shaken when he finally realizes that he has been exchanging more than intellectual vibrations with Mlle. de l'Espinasse (*RA*, 206).[63]

In this ongoing observational free-for-all, each interlocutor's body is apt to become a physiological instrument for demonstrating the fundamental thesis of the *Rêve de d'Alembert:* namely, that everything in nature comes down to sensibility and organic movements (*RA*, 188).[64] Diderot's "everything," of course, covers a huge range of functions, including modes of procreation (126); embryonic differentiation (152); cognitive faculties like thinking, memory, the will, and the self (156–57); pathological conditions like vapors and erethism (170); the violent pleasure and pain felt by "mobile souls" during a pathetic spectacle (181); the natural underpinnings of vice and virtue (186–87); and finally, the crossbreeding of animal species (195). The discussion of all these matters consists in a basic practice of "undressing" a body by stripping it down to its origins in a rudimentary sensitive fiber or fascicle that (as in Lacaze's theory) precedes the formation of organs. That stripping-down practice is initiated in the "Entretien," where the Diderot voice recounts the story of d'Alembert's physiological conception and development as a sentient and thinking being (95–96). It is then reenacted over and over again—on Mlle. de l'Espinasse, whom Dr. Bordeu divests of her present attractive form in the name of scientific observation (145); on a Cyclops, who loses not only an eye but his nose, ears, head, hands, and feet (149); and on Newton, who is reduced to a blob of matter that retains no more than life and sensibility (188–89). This series of decompositions and recompositions, couched as they are in a peculiarly recipe-like style ("Suppress a strand of the [sensitive] fascicle . . . Double some of the strands of the fascicle . . . Disturb the strands . . . Press together two strands" [149–50]), lends a certain deterministic air to the experimental organisms that are invoked over the course of the dialogue.

Some commentators have argued that it is impossible to apply the notion of determinism to Diderot's understanding of living forms, given the radical mutability of the "vast ocean of matter" that d'Alembert contemplates at the climax of his dream (*Dream,* 174; *RA,* 128).[65] There is nonetheless a strategic *discursive* determinism at work in each physio-anatomical observation that is made in the *Rêve de d'Alembert.* That is, although the various organisms invoked by the dialogue's interlocutors are examined, manipulated, and discarded with sometimes breathtaking dispatch, the description of these creatures' physical formation follows an implacably fixed pattern. One might call the mode of talking about sentient beings that is adopted in the *Rêve* an example of the "hypervital" style that Leo Spitzer declared to be an essential Diderotian trademark.[66] Yet it can also be read as a pointed form of mimicry: the characters of the *Rêve* imitate the discursive patterns that had been popularized through the medico-philosophical writings of the day, including those of the real Bordeu.

In that sense, the "hypervital" rhythm of the *Rêve de d'Alembert* recalls the close alliance that the Montpellier physicians strove to establish between the language of the sensible body and their own descriptive language—both of which were held to operate according to the basic principle of dynamic, organic interaction. This parallel inevitably brings to mind Jean Starobinski's classic study "Le Philosophe, le géomètre, l'hybride," where he expands upon Spitzer's analysis of Diderotian language to produce a compelling reading of the stylistic, physical, and conceptual hybridization that is at work throughout this dialogue.[67] Focusing upon the sleeping d'Alembert's exalted soliloquy on life and sensibility, Starobinski finds a profound interpenetration of the lyrical and the technical: "We witness a movement of lyrical subversion, which reverses the language of scientific objectivity and confers upon it the harmony of a fervent speech" (21). The hybrid style of the passage echoes the even more extraordinary interpenetration of form and substance that is occurring within d'Alembert himself:

> The dreaming and delirious d'Alembert is the marvelous hybrid of the vital *phenomenon* (the object to be interpreted) and biological *knowledge* (the act of interpretive thinking): he presents the spectacle of a "rowdy" science—of a delirium endowed with clear-sightedness, or an idea that gets carried away with enthusiasm. Perhaps we can permit ourselves to view this momentary confusion of the subject and object (where the thought that emanates from life becomes thought about life) as a corollary to the auto-erotic agitation that overcomes the dreamer: by giving the geometrist over to his own semen, the hybridization unites the intimacy of material life and its spoken exteriorization, which is immediately reflected back upon itself. (Starobinski, 21)

On this page of Diderot, at least, "the science of nature and the intimate experience of pleasure are joined in a single source: a hylozoic androgyny where thinking matter and thinking about matter are one and the same thing" (22). The implications of this fusion, Starobinski maintains, go beyond Diderot alone: alluding to the biomedical sciences as they evolved after the eighteenth century, he asserts that "Diderot formulates the *chimera* of a [field of] knowledge in which the act of knowing would be inseparable from the expansion of life itself" (22). Yet by looking at the *Rêve de d'Alembert* as a theoretical anticipation of modern biology, Starobinski actually identifies the dream of Enlightenment philosophical medicine: the dream that medical writers might unveil the inner mysteries of the body through the pure application of their own sensibility and thereby open up new, "audacious" perspectives on the nature of life for their readers.

In a curious way, it is precisely by reducing medicine to a series of "marvelous facts" and "historical tales" (*RA*, 190) that Diderot fulfills this dream. Considered in that light, the amoral poetics that Dr. Bordeu espouses in the final dialogue in response to Mlle. de L'Espinasse's queries about mixing living species should be seen as a properly *medical* poetics: "'Your question involves physical science, morals and poetics.' 'Poetics!' 'Why not? The art of creating fictional beings in imitation of real ones is true poetry'" (*Dream*, 226; *RA*, 196–97). That is, the practice of using the concept of sensibility to create new beings, or at least to remake existing ones, was one of the principal missions of philosophical medicine during the second half of the eighteenth century. The physician-philosophers of this period sought to establish a comprehensive spectrum of possible human behaviors, a spectrum grounded in a thorough knowledge of observable sensible body types and of the conditions that lead to their creation. In the hands of Diderot, that notion takes a truly fantastical turn: it creates, for example, the indefatigable "goat-men" that Dr. Bordeu envisions in the "Suite de l'Entretien" (*Dream*, 232; *RA*, 205–6) and the procreative hothouse imagined earlier by the sleeping d'Alembert (*RA*, 127). What Diderot does at such moments is underscore the teratological possibilities of an idea that was quite common in contemporary medicine, namely, the notion that bodily sensibility could be manipulated to create certain desired combinations of physical, moral, and/or intellectual traits. The real-life physicians and hygienists of the day did not, of course, go nearly so far as Diderot's Dr. Bordeu, who at the end of the *Rêve* defends the idea that "nothing that exists can be against nature or outside nature" (*Dream*, 230; *RA*, 202). They did, however, take their own musings about sensibility's combinations and permutations among human beings to some extraordinarily imaginative lengths.

3. The Medicalization of  Enlightenment

Sensibility, Medical Therapy, and the Quest to Improve Humanity

The emergence of philosophical medicine in mid-eighteenth-century France was plainly tied to the effort to develop a comprehensive psycho-physiology that would elucidate the role of sensibility in human life. It was also clearly a product of the broader culture of the Enlightenment: the médecins philosophes saw themselves as engaged in an effort to apply their holistic, body-based vision of human nature to the full range of human experiences. Some scholars have argued that the very program of enlightenment was metaphorically medicalized by the philosophes who promoted it. Peter Gay, in particular, has underscored the rhetoric of therapy and cure that pervaded the writings of certain Enlightenment authors, who wrote to remedy the pathological excesses of a regime plagued by religious fanaticism, political injustice, and a superstitious populace.[1]

Yet the medicalization of the enlightenment project went far beyond a cluster of medical metaphors: during the decades of the *Encyclopédie*—precisely when the curative vocabulary underscored by Gay was most prevalent—physicians actively promoted the idea that enlightenment truly *was* a medical matter. By presenting philosophical medicine as the key to unlocking the secret mainsprings not just of the human body but of the human mind as well, these theorists reduced the quest to reform humanity to a single issue: isolating the physiological mechanisms by which sensibility operated in the organism when it was stimulated by outside impressions, be they physical (as in the "six things non-natural") or moral (as in passions, or ideas). Hence the thesis that, under the right physiological conditions, man's sensibility and everything connected to it could quite literally be cultivated—not in the sense of promoting good social manners, but more as one would cultivate a flower or a breed of domestic animal, through particular physical manipulations.

This thesis unfolds in the writings of a representative pair of médecins philosophes, who pursued it in two distinct but interrelated registers: first, in the individual register of self-improvement, seen as a process of transforming oneself into a great thinker; and second, in the collective register of breeding techniques that were prescribed to ameliorate both the present generation and future humankind. The physician-philosophers in question—Antoine Le Camus (1722–72) and Charles Augustin Vandermonde (1727–63)—were hardly alone in seeking concrete ways to bolster the popular quest for enlightenment. They were, however, unusually ambitious in the medical cast they gave to the idea that modern Europeans could be transformed into healthier, more virtuous, and more intelligent beings. As pursued in eighteenth-century France, that theory was predicated on two assumptions: first, that the mind and body were not only malleable, but interdependent in their malleability; and second, that enlightenment entailed a series of operations that could and should be managed, under the guidance of a qualified expert. The ranks of self-appointed experts on human perfectibility did, of course, include many celebrated nonmedical philosophes like Claude Adrienne Helvétius, Anne Robert Jacques de Turgot, and Jean-Antoine-Nicolas de Caritat de Condorcet.[2] The medical proponents of this concept nonetheless went farther in their scenarios for human progress, out of the conviction that *medicine* was the field that would eventually show exactly how to mold and maintain an improved human race. As médecins philosophes, Le Camus and Vandermonde were noteworthy on three counts: first, because of the wide scope of their schemes for bettering the species; second, in their pragmatic, physicalist approach to the mind-body link; and, finally, in the special emphasis they placed on sensibility as the primary instrument to be deployed in perfecting one's own constitution or that of one's offspring.

_9 ℰ_

Antoine Le Camus's *La Médecine de l'esprit* established him as one of the chief medical advocates of the vogue of intellectual self-improvement that apparently swept a certain segment of the French population during the 1750s and 1760s. This treatise also provides a convenient benchmark for measuring the progress of the sensibility paradigm we have been reconstructing here. Between its first edition in 1753 and its second, definitive edition of 1769, *La Médecine de l'esprit* underwent a subtle yet important transformation that attests to the spread of this concept throughout the Francophone medical establishment—including the conservative medical faculty of the University of Paris, where Le Camus held the position of "Docteur Régent." Although sensibility is never mentioned in the 1753 version, it is central to the 1769 edition of *La Médecine de l'esprit*. In this later edition, Le Camus undertook to determine "(1) the mechanism of the body that influences the functions of the soul; (2) the physical causes that make this mechanism either defective, or more perfect; (3) the means that can sustain it in its free state, and rectify it when it is hampered."[3] One might be tempted to say that the change between the two editions was purely semantic, given that the term *sensations* that Le Camus used in the early version of *La Médecine de l'esprit* is a cognate to the term *sensibilité* employed in the later edition. However, the very ease with which Le Camus incorporated the principles of the sensibility paradigm into his project is revealing, as is the sheer quantity of his references to a vital property that, by 1769, he had come to hold responsible for all human activities, from conception to cognition.

In writing *La Médecine de l'esprit* Le Camus had two primary textual antecedents, one medical and one philosophical. The first of these was Jerome Gaub's lectures on the mind-body problem, published in two consecutive essays as *De regimine mentis* (1747 and 1763), from which Le Camus drew liberally.[4] Gaub, a professor of medicine and chemistry at the University of Leiden, is generally credited with elucidating two notions that became central to the conceptual battery of the eighteenth-century physician-philosopher: the opinion that, from a medical point of view, the philosophical distinction of mind and body is a useless abstraction; and the conviction that "the mind cannot be managed properly unless account is taken of the body to which it is joined [and] in turn, the management of the mind is implicit in and bound up with the proper treatment of matters pertaining to the body" (34–35). Gaub's remarks on the first of those notions attracted the attention of a number of medical theorists, including (much to his chagrin) the materialist La Mettrie.[5] Le Camus, however, was far more interested in the second idea—the idea of devising a mental regimen by which one could maintain "the integrity of the mind . . . with the aid of salutary hygienic precepts" (Gaub, 74). In a section of *La Médecine de l'esprit* entitled "Histoire analytique des ouvrages avec lequels le nôtre a quelques rapports," Le Camus praises *De regimene mentis* as a first attempt at treating the whole human being, body and soul combined; yet he also criticizes Gaub's work, complaining that "one finds in it only general axioms, without their practical consequences" (*Méd.*, 335). It seems, then, that Le Camus wrote his own treatise in order to fill in the gap left by Gaub's, by providing his readers with all the practical elements necessary to form a comprehensive medical regimen for the mind.

However, the scope of *La Médecine de l'esprit* extends beyond the boundaries of medical inquiry and into the genre of sensationalist metaphysical analysis so popular at the time. From its preface on, Le Camus's treatise is addressed not to a narrow audience of medical students (like those addressed in Gaub's essays), but rather, to a broader public of readers acquainted with the philosophy of mind as conceived by Condillac, Diderot, Buffon, and Bonnet. Le Camus uses the conceit that his readers are themselves philosophes—that is, individuals interested in understanding both their own internal mental operations and medicine "as a field of human knowledge" (*Méd.*, 1). Although he speaks deferentially of John Locke as "the head of the Philosophers," he maintains that Locke and his followers neglected to find a natural gauge for investigating the operations of the mind. Le Camus's mission is, once again, to fill in that gap: "We want, in sum, to propose a fixed measure to which all the speculations that have been and will be made on the human understanding can be applied" (7). The fixed measure he selects is the vital property of sensibility, because "before knowing one must feel; before feeling one must be sensible . . . It is thus necessary to speak of sensibility before examining the sensations that are the principle of our knowledge" (8–9). Le Camus's plan for intellectual edification therefore begins at the point where the sensationalist philosophers generally leave off: the actual physical foundation of the mind's operations.

As Le Camus depicts it, that physical foundation is determined by sensibility at every stage of its development. He supports this claim by sketching a genealogy of sensible fluids and fibers that, like the embryology put forth by Louis de Lacaze, goes all the way back to the origins of human life. Le Camus defines organic sensibility as "the capacity to receive the impressions of objects" (*Méd.*, 9–10); that capacity is evident, first, in the primordial vital fluid that circulates within the embryo, and then in the fibers of the growing body. Interestingly, much of the basic physiology that underlies these assertions is derived directly from Boerhaave—for example, Le Camus's emphasis on solid-fluid interactions and his depiction of the brain as a filter for the vivifying humor that circulates through the nerves (12)—even though the Boerhaavian model of the body had been deemed outmoded by the time the first edition of *La Médecine de l'esprit* was published. Le Camus was clearly aware of the changes that the Hallerian and Montpellier physiologies of sensibility had wrought in medicine since the heyday of Boerhaavian iatromechanics: his treatise is filled with critical comments on everything from the purported role of the diaphragm in regulating the animal economy (26), to the debatable existence of a common sensorium (11–12, 43), to the mind-body sympathies involved in conditions like masturbation and the vapors (184, 225). Rather than proposing a radically new physiological system, Le Camus incorporates selected elements of the recently forged model of the sensible animal economy into a Boerhaavian framework. However paradoxical it may seem, this recycling of new wine in an old Boerhaavian bottle is not unusual—nor does it create any serious internal contradictions in Le Camus's explanation of the psycho-physiological mechanism that most concerns him: the creation of a well-functioning intellect out of a well-constituted body.

According to Le Camus, that mechanism first comes into play at conception: the incipient brain of a new human being is formed directly by its father's semen, a fluid that emanates from the father's brain and contains "a little brain that is the seed or kernel from which the fetus is born" (*Méd.*, 106). By positing this exact homology between spermatic fluid and cerebral fluid, Le Camus establishes the mind's first physical cause: children receive the structural seed of their brains from their fathers and therefore "resemble their father as much in [physical] organization as in intellect"; what their mothers contribute is merely the "soil" where the fledgling brain develops (107–8). The hereditary schema underlying Le Camus's model of mental development is thus overtly seminalist: the father's brain actually sends a little piece of itself through his semen into the brain of his progeny (103). He insists, however, that good parental breeding is necessary on both the paternal and maternal sides: the quality of a child's brain is determined, for better or worse, by the quality and circumstances of the parental bodies that took part in the act of creating that child. Bastards, he adds, often have "a more brilliant and lively mind" because they are "engendered in the heat of a fleeting love" (110).

The well-functioning mind thus starts with building blocks that are set before birth. The "particular genius" each person receives when he or she is conceived is nonetheless subject to a good deal of further modification, under the influence of climate, education, temperament, and sex (*Méd.*, 103–5). As with the act of generation, Le Camus approaches each of these forces as a physical cause that can profoundly affect the formation of the mind by acting upon the brain, the sensible fibers that make up the body's organs, and the vital fluids that moisten those solid parts. Curiously, Le Camus asserts that, out of all of those forces, only sex acts irrevocably upon the organization of the mind's physical substrate. He describes the effects of biological sex upon mental capacity in oppositional terms: the male mind is naturally "bold, courageous, constant, sublime, deep, and born to be free"; whereas woman, because of her "softer, finer, and more delicate fibers," has "a mind that is more lively and more fickle than that of men" (112). On this basis, Le Camus concludes that the female mind cannot support the strain of the prolonged and strenuous study for which the male mind is structurally destined (113–15). We shall come back to this highly significant differentiation of male versus female minds in Chapter 7. For now, suffice it to say that, apart from sex, all of the physical forces that modify the mind are depicted in *La Médecine de l'esprit* as susceptible to modification themselves. Climate can be changed to serve as "a physical means of correcting the faults of the mind, and for acquiring a new portion of genius" (118); education, be it moral or physical, "operates only through mechanical means" (148); temperament can be altered "to acquire intellect, or to remedy the vices of one's mind" (158); and a salutary dietary and hygienic regimen can be devised to safeguard the organic constitution of those who devote themselves to the sciences (169).

Le Camus's depiction of these physical forces as not just formative, but manipulable, is one of the most innovative features of *La Médecine de l'esprit*. For what distinguishes Le Camus's medicine of mind from the programs of mental hygiene prescribed by other eighteenth-century medical theorists is his conviction that the average man can quite literally make himself into a scholar by acting upon his body. Le Camus firmly believes that the fledgling intellectual can and should exploit his organic faculties as a means of developing his mental faculties to their fullest potential. This is, in fact, the crux of his project as he presents it in the climatic third book of *La Médecine de l'esprit*:

> We shall not speak here of the vices of the understanding and will that arise from the real illnesses of the body . . . Our project is bolder: we shall consider men who enjoy full health but are deprived of a part of the capacity and action that their souls could enjoy if they were not fettered by excessively heavy chains, and if the luminous rays of these souls could shine through their all too opaque bodies . . . It is up to those who have *the noble ambition of enjoying the full liberty of their understanding and of making themselves suitable for the Sciences and Fine Arts,* to dispose their organic constitutions such that their fibers are very sensible and that their blood receives only pure and subtle juices.   (*Méd.*, 217; my emphasis)

Le Camus's advice to those who aim to engage in lofty intellectual pursuits is this: if they truly want to enlighten their minds, they must first penetrate into what he calls "the most secret labyrinths of our constitution" (2) and then set about training the operative parts of their bodies—most particularly those involved in sensibility—to function at top capacity.

Hence the claim at the center of Le Camus's treatise: "We claim, *through purely mechanical means,* to make any man a superior thinker, or, to put it differently, to provide his soul with all of the solidity and brilliance that he wishes" (*Méd.*, 218; my emphasis). The figure of the superior thinker as Le Camus presents him is not a "scholar steeped in Greek," nor an intellectual zealot, nor a *bel esprit*; he is, rather, a man "who does not have difficulty in finding his ideas, who reasons easily, [and] who judges exactly." Noting that men often use the wrong means to acquire intelligence (like immersing themselves in great books), Le Camus proffers this simple formula for transforming a dim-witted man into an intelligent one: "First, modify his organs; next, teach him, and give him the same attention as you would accord to people who had the best [intellectual] dispositions" (219). To modify one's own organs as a means of achieving optimum mental functioning, one should select easily digestible foods (169); avoid overindulging in wine, which can dry out the body fibers (173); consume chocolate, coffee, and tea sparingly (176); exercise moderately (179); and be "neither too sparing nor too extravagant" in dispensing the vivifying fluid that is emitted during sexual intercourse (184).[6] These measures are, Le Camus assures his readers, virtually guaranteed to "make us better and more intelligent" (223).

In typical medico-philosophical fashion, Le Camus is simultaneously lyrical and physicalist when describing sensibility's influence over intelligence. Sensibility, he declares, is "the source of all our knowledge, just as it is the source of all our passions. If we were deprived of our sensibility, we would be no more than stones or metals. It is the mark of an intelligent mind, just as it is the mark of a good heart" (Méd., 221). He also holds this property responsible for a host of moral virtues: "It inspires tenderness for one's family, pity for the poor, piety for the Creator, friendship for one's fellows, love for the opposite sex, [and] gratitude toward one's benefactors." Le Camus's interest in these virtues is, however, more epistemological than moral: "What a multitude of different and often interrelated ideas must arise from all of these movements?" (221). Refined sensibility, in other words, is not just an ethical advantage, but is also a quality that the intelligent man must possess if he is to attain "this delicateness of sentiment that transmits to the soul the true nature of the impressions which the sensible qualities of objects make upon bodies" (223).

Although Le Camus emphasizes sensibility's edifying powers, he also acknowledges that the property can be unhealthy when cultivated beyond a reasonable degree—a problem he associates with vaporous women, hypochondriacs, and people who have been "agitated" by long and violent emotions. Excessive sensibility is not only "a vice that harms the mind, or that throws it into disorders that healthy reason rebukes" (Méd., 225); it also harms the body, by triggering an unnatural state of tension and stiffness in the body's fibers that prevents them from transmitting their impressions properly (223). Hence the "involuntary fits of anger," the "inappropriate gaiety," the "deep sadness over frivolous objects," and the "real inaptitude to apply oneself to any study" that one observes in vaporous patients (225). The well-constituted thinker, by contrast, possesses a sensibility that is properly proportioned and judiciously maintained through diet, hygienic practices, and strict allegiance to the rules of moral and physical moderation. Under those conditions, the sensible organs will be "delicate, sufficiently taut and susceptible to the greatest impression," the sensations experienced will be intense and distinct, and the soul will be "exactly informed about everything going on around it" (233).

In essence, Le Camus's plan for perfecting the intellectual faculties is quite simple: as long as one follows the regimen he prescribes, one's vital fluids will flow vigorously—and so will one's ideas. Intelligence thus becomes a matter of what we might call psycho-hydrodynamics: it requires "a well-organized brain in which all the movements are regulated," where high-quality animal spirits course through strong nerves, and where the fibers are "stretched to the perfect degree" (*Méd.*, 252, 259). The same physiological principles of good fluid balance and fibrillar harmony apply in Le Camus's explanation of why (contrary to popular belief) most passions aid the mind by animating the vital spirits it requires to be stimulated into action (314). Moderation and balance remain, however, the watchwords of Le Camus's recommendations to his readers: the highest virtues the intellectual can possess are prudence, fairness, temperance, and generosity (296). Health and ethics therefore overlap quite neatly in Le Camus's program for intellectual edification—a program that can, he insists, be adopted by any healthy man.

Although *La Médecine de l'esprit* deals strictly with the quest for individual improvement, there is another work by Le Camus that shows the wider applicability of his meliorist theories: the "Mémoire sur la conservation des hommes bien faits," a short, obscure text that he included in his *Mémoires sur divers sujets de médecine* of 1760. What this memoir reveals is a surprisingly radical plan for social reform: society must, Le Camus argues, remake itself to ensure that "well-made men" attend to their procreative duties.[7] Although he directs his criticisms at a number of institutions, his main target is the army, where all too many superior men perish—in part because, being more valiant, they die more readily in battle, and in part because of venereal disease, which they contract more readily than do ugly or malformed men ("Mémoire sur la conservation," 295–96). As a solution, Le Camus suggests that the government create separate "regiments of malformed men" to send off to war, rather then their better-constituted brothers (299). To defend his proposal (which he grants might seem ridiculous to some), Le Camus invokes the common medico-philosophical theme that physicians have a special responsibility to stop the degeneration that has beset the once robust human race (287). In that sense, the "Mémoire sur la conservation des hommes bien faits" directly complements *La Médecine de l'esprit*: it, too, puts forth a set of prescriptions designed to make the race better—in this case, by using the best available bodies to increase its character, its vigor, and its number.

~9 ℮~

Le Camus's "Mémoire sur la conservation des hommes bien faits" makes it clear that he envisioned the possibility of transposing his meliorist medical program from the individual to the collective scale. Such transpositions were, in fact, typical of the various discourses of the Enlightenment—medical, ethical, aesthetic and anthropological—that we shall consider in this and subsequent chapters. According to the organicist cosmology of sensibility that framed all of these discourses, the significance of the individual could only truly be conceived in terms of his or her relation to the greater, resonating whole of which he or she was a part. Hence the conceptual link that Enlightenment physicians typically made between the process of self-cultivation and the movement to reform humanity as a species. At least one theorist merged those two processes into a single operation of "good breeding": Charles Augustin Vandermonde, author of the *Essai sur la manière de perfectionner l'espèce humaine* (1756)—a work that, like *La Médecine de l'esprit*, was written to advise a philosophically minded audience on how to counteract the progressive debility that seemed to be threatening the human race.

Vandermonde, who was acquainted with Le Camus and held a similar position on the medical faculty of the University of Paris, agreed that human beings could improve themselves if they followed a basic set of principles: "I believe one can reasonable assert that our bodies do not have all the perfection of which they are capable, that we can prevent them from degenerating by following some simple rules and natural principles, and that our minds themselves must benefit greatly from the perfection of our bodies."[8] The "we" addressed in the *Essai sur la manière de perfectionner l'espèce humaine* seems, however, to have been not merely thinking men seeking to increase their mental powers, but right-minded people of both sexes who wished to improve their family stock by producing "children who are as perfect as one could desire" (*Essai,* x). Vandermonde consequently composed his *Essai* with two goals in mind: first, to show how sound hygienic practices could make health, beauty, and strength hereditary among all human beings (iii); and second, to instruct parents in the right way to train their children's minds (vii–viii).

Although the *Essai* begins on a rather grim note by underscoring man's unique tendency to degenerate from his natural, God-given conformation (iv), Vandermonde quickly assures his readers that they are not doomed to see their progeny turn out dull and enfeebled. Rather, he claims, they can act to reverse the degenerative process, provided that they go about it properly. The first step, he declares, is to improve the functioning of the human being as a sensible, vital organism: "We must replenish the corrupted source of our humours and our spirits. We must reshape our organs, and change, fortify, and improve all of the mainsprings of our machine. It is by taking this path that we will be able to break the chain of the most stubborn illnesses, and of the most tumultuous passions, by perpetuating in the human species beauty, strength, and health; [then] we could sow the seed of virtue and push the mind to its greatest force" (vi). A mission of these dimensions necessarily calls for collaborators; Vandermonde therefore enlists his readers in the cause of advancing human enlightenment by appealing to the very personal sense of pride felt by every parent for his or her particular offspring. He promises to lead them through each step of breeding a "perfect" child, from choosing a marriage partner, to conceiving, to carrying a child to term, to breastfeeding and raising the child (xii–xiii). Using this medico-philosophical spin on Locke's conceit of following a child's intellectual progress from birth onward, Vandermonde analyzes every detail necessary to produce children who are as vigorous in body and spirit as possible.

Vandermonde's discussion of good breeding habits is less concerned with the internal physiological mechanisms of generation (he defers to Buffon on that subject [*Essai*, 125]) than with the external conditions in which the act is performed. Parents seeking to create a well-made child must, he insists, attend carefully to all of those conditions: they must have "no vice of conformation, either in the parts essential to the two sexes, or in the organization of the rest of the body" (65); they must be free of deformities (like "hollow eyes" or "excessive portliness") that might be passed on from parent to child (67); they must, when carrying out their procreative duties, avoid both the extreme heat of the summer and the violent cold of winter (71); they should have intercourse in the early morning, when their bodies are refreshed and fortified (72); they must be monogamous and faithful (74); they must be old enough to procreate and not too far apart in age (77–81); they must be similar in size (85); and, finally, they should try to conceive in a rural setting (82).[9]

Having listed all of the criteria for proper procreative conduct, Vandermonde shifts into some rather bizarre speculations on the various sorts of human beings that might be produced if physicians were given full authority over the process of human breeding. His observations in this regard begin benignly enough: "If chance can cause the human race to degenerate, art can also perfect it . . . by intelligently combining the different productions of nature" (91). Yet Vandermonde's eugenic reflections become progressively bolder: "Given that we have succeeded in perfecting the stock of horses, dogs, cats, chickens, pigeons, and canaries, why wouldn't we make any [similar] attempt on the human race?" (94). Finally, he throws out some suggestions for human experimentation, imagining what would transpire if children were bred selectively for white skin, a fine singing voice, or graceful dancing (95–96). If physicians were to focus on refining the human race in this manner, conjectures Vandermonde, they could not only "perfect talents that society finds pleasing" but also produce species of human beings superior in certain chosen traits to any that have yet been seen on earth.

Of all the hereditary traits he deems desirable in human beings, Vandermonde is specific about only one: sensibility, which he considers paramount in any breeding program—be it on the grand scale of the fantastical musings cited above, or on that of a single pair of parents. Sensibility, as he defines it, is a susceptibility to impressions that resides in the nerves and sense organs—or, more precisely, in "a hermaphroditic substance, between matter and spirit" (*Essai*, 271). This substance serves to mediate between the mind and the surrounding universe and therefore plays a formative role in determining an individual's quota and type of intelligence. In a refreshing departure from many of his contemporaries, Vandermonde declares that there is little natural difference between male versus female sensibility: "Men and women all have about the same degree of sensibility. They are formed according to the same model. They have the same senses, the same organs, the same nerves" (286). He even goes so far as to assert that, were women trained early in how to make proper use of their senses, "they would take better advantage of it than do men. If their natural dispositions were cultivated, they would make more progress than we, and they would one day reunite all the advantages of the body and all the talents of the mind" (286). For Vandermonde, therefore, physical and mental cultivation is a goal that parents can set not just for their sons, but for their daughters as well.[10]

Vandermonde thus ascribes to sensibility a primordial function in education, which he sees as a process of training a child to use his or her sense organs judiciously:

Our senses are instruments that one must understand and know how to operate. Those who have been accustomed since childhood to use these instruments well, derive great benefits from them sooner or later. The more one has exercised the senses intelligently and reasonably, the less vulnerable one is to the illusions they sometimes create . . . The only ideas we should attach to all our sensations are those that are dictated by our knowledge, reason, or the unanimous agreement of our senses. If, from childhood on, this wise law had been laid down to us, we would be correct in our judgments, and we would *infinitely perfect our minds*. It is certain that the varying intelligence of men is due only to the way in which they have used their senses.   (*Essai*, 287–88; my emphasis)

Training the senses organs is, for Vandermonde, "the only means of deriving benefits from the mind and pushing it to its highest degree of force" (288). Seen from this sensationalist perspective, managing sensibility—in oneself or in one's child—becomes a process of literal mental breeding. It is, moreover, a process that is susceptible to the same sort of hygienic intervention that Vandermonde proposed earlier for the operation of physical breeding. Hence the physicalist tone with which Vandermonde discusses pedagogy: "Good education, the study of the sciences, and reading act only to rectify our sensations, and thereby open up our minds" (287). To encourage his readers to monitor every detail of their children's sensory development, he provides two handy appendices at the end of the *Essai*: one entitled "Some Rules That Parents Must Follow to Accomplish This," and another called "A Table to Consult in Order to Refine the Senses, to Make the Mind Sound, and to Give Man That Spiritual Elevation Which Characterizes Great Men."

≈ ∂ ℰ ≈

Like Le Camus, Vandermonde seems to have been inspired to take up the medicine of enlightenment out of a double conviction: first, that ameliorating the human condition was both a necessary and an attainable goal; and second, that only a médecin philosophe had the physiological and philosophical expertise required to achieve it. On that last point, at least, these two physician-philosophers won the agreement of most of their medical contemporaries. Although neither Le Camus nor Vandermonde ever attained the notoriety accorded to Helvétius for his celebrated philosophical treatise *De l'esprit* (1758), they were acknowledged by their professional colleagues to have contributed to the cause of bridging the gap between "le moral et le physique" by making sensibility the primary foundation of their meliorist regimens.[11] The general critical reaction to the medicine of enlightenment—as to the theory of human perfectibility from which this medicine drew its inspiration—was, nevertheless, decidedly mixed. However optimistic and ambitious Le Camus and Vandermonde appeared to be in proposing their respective plans for improving human beings from the body on up, they encountered resistance from some of the same contemporaries who praised their medical doctrines on other points.

Diderot, for example, borrowed considerably from Le Camus's examples of different species of mental disorder as he was composing his *Eléments de physiologie*.[12] He did not, however, place much stock in Le Camus's particular attempt at crafting a full-fledged positivistic medicine of mind—perhaps because, although he recognized that such a project was hypothetically feasible, Diderot did not feel that the medical theory of his day was up to the task.[13] Hence, perhaps, the passage in Diderot's physiological treatise in which he mocks and chastises Le Camus as "intrepid" for recommending the use of bleedings, purgatives, baths, and infusions in order to correct both bodily and mental ailments.[14] It would doubtless be rash to accuse Diderot of bad faith for reproving physician-philosophers like Le Camus and Vandermonde who strove too zealously to apply and extend their models of the sensible body— even though Diderot himself engaged in a similar type of speculation, albeit in the realm of pure fiction. Yet it is, at the very least, curious that Diderot gleaned so many passages from Le Camus on catalepsy, epilepsy, mental alienation, and other subjects for inclusion in the *Eléments de physiologie,* yet paid such scant attention to the plan for improving the mind that is the true core of *La Médecine de l'esprit.* That oversight is all the more puzzling given the very close reading that Diderot accorded to Helvétius's *De l'esprit,* a nonmedical study of the mechanisms of intellect which resembles Le Camus's and Vandermonde's on several key points. A brief consideration of Diderot's objections to *De l'esprit* will help clarify the reservations that certain eighteenth-century thinkers held about contemporary efforts to put the theories of enlightenment and human perfectibility into literal, physical practice.

Diderot's *Réflexions sur le livre "De l'esprit" par M. Helvétius* are brief but cogent, for he immediately locates the point that is both most central to Helvétius's book and most problematic: "The author of *De l'esprit* reduces all the intellectual functions to sensibility. To perceive or feel is the same thing according to him. To judge or feel is the same thing. He does not recognize any difference between man and beast beyond that of organization."[15] In fact, it is not so much the reduction to sensibility to which Diderot objects (he does more or less the same thing himself in *Le Rêve de d'Alembert*) as the casual and simplistic manner in which Helvétius performs it. Diderot's position seems to be that, in order to relate intellectual functions to the physiological functions connected with sensibility, one must have a sufficiently complex model of the physical substrate that supports those functions. Helvétius, in Diderot's view, does not have such a model: his notion of physical organization is both vague and inconsistent.

This is the criticism that underlies one of the fundamental paradoxes that Diderot finds in *De l'esprit,* concerning Helvétius's treatment of the question he raises in his third "Discours": "Whether genius [*l'esprit*] ought to be considered as a natural gift, or as an effect of education."[16] As Diderot points out, Helvétius contradicts himself when he asserts that physical organization is what distinguishes man from animals but later dismisses its role in determining different degrees of human intelligence: "Here, the author undertakes to show that of all the causes by which men can differ, organization is the least important: such that there is no man in whom passion, interest, education, and chance might not overcome the obstacles of nature and transform him into a great man; and such that there is no great man, either, in whom a lack of passion, interest, education, or certain chance events might not have turned into a stupid man, in spite of the most felicitous organization."[17] What is striking about Diderot's remarks in this passage is that as he goes about correcting Helvétius, he sketches his own theories both on congenital physical organization and on education. Diderot insists, first, that one's intellectual ability *is* largely contingent on whether one is naturally endowed with an advantageous bodily organization, and second, that education is not a monolithic force that affects all people the same way. Rather, he maintains, education is a physical cause whose modifying influence upon a person's mind varies according to the circumstances of his or her constitution—including not just temperament, but also age, state of health, emotional condition, and so on. To explain education's myriad effects, Diderot invokes a set of variables quite similar to those used by eighteenth-century physicians to explain the etiology of everything from disease to genius. In other words, in his refutation of Helvétius's shortsighted explanation of how an *homme d'esprit* is made or unmade, Diderot ends up sounding very much like a physician-philosopher—like Le Camus or Vandermonde, for example.

As Diderot reads him, Helvétius erred not because he proposed to systematize the intellect or because he approached the task with a materialist, progressionist bent, but rather, because he lacked the conceptual tools necessary to execute his project in a convincing manner. That is, Helvétius had neither a full grasp of the complexities of sensibility, nor a sense of the many factors that might impede certain people from becoming the great thinkers they aspire to be. Diderot's criticisms of *De l'esprit* also draw attention to a question that might qualify as an early version of the "nature versus nurture" debate. By underscoring the complexity of the question raised by Helvétius's third "Discours," Diderot goes to the very heart of the eighteenth-century polemic over the malleable nature of the mind. His answer to that question seems to confirm the medical opinion espoused by Le Camus and Vandermonde: to understand how intelligence come about, one must attribute some degree of formative power both to "nature," or originary physical constitution, and to "nurture," or the various impressions the mind receives from its physical and moral environment. It is, of course, purely conjectural to suggest that Diderot might have found the model of the mind promoted by these physicians to be more palatable than Helvétius's. Yet the *Réflexions sur le livre "De l'esprit"* nonetheless help us to reestablish the climate of assumptions and expectations in which Le Camus and Vandermonde carried out their respective programs for achieving intellectual edification through medical means. Within that climate, it seemed entirely plausible for physicians to claim that they could "decompose" the mind's mechanisms into its physical components and that they could act directly upon those components to improve a human being's intellectual capacities—on the condition that intelligence be seen as a complex quality, subject to a diversity of degrees and influences.[18]

For the médecins philosophes, recognizing that diversity also entailed acknowledging that the purported malleability of mind could work both ways—in other words, that tinkering with the body's sensible economy might take its owner on a direction that led not to intellectual and moral improvement, but rather to debility. This second, resoundingly pessimistic scenario of the quest for enlightenment was, in fact, just as prevalent as were the progressionist scenarios we have examined above. In a celebrated treatise on the health of men of letters, the Swiss physician Samuel-Auguste-André-David Tissot made the case that pursuing mental cultivation could be life-threatening—and he did so using a physiological model that did not differ significantly from that employed by Le Camus and Vandermonde. By comparing Tissot's theories on the physical constitutions of would-be *hommes d'esprit* with those promoted by his more optimistic fellow physicians, we shall see that the stakes of the medicine of enlightenment were not limited to eighteenth-century medical theory alone. Rather, the polemic in which these medical theorists were engaged touched upon a number of areas where "enlightenment" was pursued with equal zeal and equal ambivalence: ethics, aesthetics, and moral anthropology. In marked contrast to physicians like Le Camus and Vandermonde, who catered to the philosophes' image of themselves as infinitely enlightened and enlightenable beings, Tissot and members of his more pessimistic camp problematized the popular vogue of self-cultivation by raising questions about its consequences—questions that turned around the issue of fitness for enlightenment and what determines it.

Sensibility and the Pathologies of Scholarship:
Tissot's Warnings to Men of Letters

As the works of Le Camus and Vandermonde illustrate, sensibility could be deployed to support the notion that the human mind is readily perfectible, and

thus "enlightenable." However, even the most hopeful medical theorists recognized that reaching the fully enlightened condition—that is, the more advanced state of intellectual and moral capacity towards which the human species was purportedly progressing—could be a process fraught with risks for
the aspiring intellectual.[19] For according to the model of mind that held sway at
the time, superior mental faculties hinged ultimately upon the *physical* fitness
of the sensible fibers held to compose the body and mind alike. Managing those
fibers seemed to require expert, step-by-step guidance; hence the creation of
the genre of medical discourse I call the medicine of enlightenment. Although
this discursive genre often expressed itself in highly optimistic terms, it was
based upon two problematically related tenets: first, only those blessed with a
vigorous and well-balanced sensible system could be true philosophes; and second, the effort to cultivate such a constitution might entail considerable energy,
strain, and risk to one's health and happiness.

The ambiguity and tension implicit in the medicine of enlightenment pervades Tissot's *De la santé des gens de lettres,* a six-edition best-seller first published in Latin in 1766 and officially translated into French in 1768.[20] Tissot, a
morally conservative Swiss doctor who did his medical training in Montpellier,
was one of this period's most prolific and popular medical writers. Like other
physicians who grappled with the interrelation of mind and body, he espoused
the accepted explanation of intellectual activity as a process generated and regulated by a network of sensible fibers that conducted impressions directly from
the sense organs, to the common sensorium in the brain, to the thinking soul,
and then back again.[21] At the same time, however, he composed *De la santé des
gens de lettres* as a medical cautionary tale for those who pursued cerebral stimulation with excessive zeal. Tissot's description of the unhealthy effects of
scholarship was a strikingly pessimistic answer to the question that was, perhaps, most central to the medicine of enlightenment: namely, whether the body
should be understood as an instrument of enlightenment or as its limiting term.

The function of the body in the enlightenment process was a subject of considerable debate among eighteenth-century medical theorists. Some physicians
built their doctrines around the principle of linked physical-mental perfectibility, thereby reinforcing the contemporary fashion of engaging in the arts and
sciences in order to prove and improve one's sensibility. Others, however—
like Tissot, along with the self-appointed experts on the vapors whom I examine in Chapter 7—considered the vogue of intellectual and cultural refinement
to be inherently unhealthy, if not pathogenic. By lending his influential voice to
the latter camp with the publication of *De la santé des gens de lettres,* Tissot
played an important role in forging and disseminating the image of the intellectual that would predominate from the late eighteenth century to our day:

Mathaur Greuter, The Physician Curing Fantasy (French school, seventeenth century). (Photograph used by permission of the Philadelphia Museum of Art: SmithKline Beecham Corporation Fund.)

that of a delicate, oversensitive, borderline invalid, ill-suited to the rigors and shocks of worldly life.[22] Scholars were not the only target of Tissot's campaign to correct the pathologies of civilized existence: his collected medical writings were peopled by a gallery of dysfunctional sensible body types that also included domestic servants, debauched men, and worldly women—all of whom, in his opinion, required a physician's guidance in their physical, mental, and moral hygiene. As we shall see in later chapters, Tissot's bleak narratives of the pathologies triggered by cultivating one's sensibility did not fail to elicit some intriguing literary responses, first, from his Swiss compatriot and kindred spirit, Jean-Jacques Rousseau, and second, from the Marquis de Sade, a philosophe who embraced the tenets of the medicine of enlightenment, only to turn them on their head.

It is clear from the beginning of *De la santé des gens de lettres* that Tissot views men of letters as a sickly lot—sickly both by temperament and by vocation. He describes them in his preface as fundamentally distinct in constitution from the other social orders and as imperiled by "the dangers of a mode of life that will never be as healthy as one would wish" (*SGL*, xii–xiii). Inscribing himself in a long line of philosophers and physicians who have addressed this problem, Tissot writes in a tone that is simultaneously scolding and pedagogical: scholars must, he declares, adhere more obediently to their physicians' precepts and become better informed about the wise philosophy of body and mind that underlies those precepts (14–15). To aid his readers in those endeavors, Tissot provides them with a primer on the pathologies induced by their profession, as well as a program of sound preventive measures to follow. And to make both the primer and the hygiene program more compelling, he employs a rhetorical style that is explicitly oriented to the needs and tastes of his audience. First, he appeals directly to experiences he assumes are common to scholars: he asserts, for example, that "there is no man of letters who has not frequently left his study with a violent headache, and a great deal of heat in this [body] part" (17). Second, he liberally sprinkles his text with literary testimonials of suffering from or about a panoply of famous scholars—not just physicians, but also poets, painters, and philosophers from Plato and Aristotle to Pascal and Rousseau, whose names are capitalized for eye-catching emphasis (17, 20, 28, et passim).

Tissot's aim throughout *De la santé des gens de lettres* is to open scholars' eyes to the insidious nature of the pathologies that he sees as inextricably tied to their particular vocation. He identifies two main sources for the ailments that typically plague men of letters—"assiduous mental work, and the continual inactivity of the body; to trace an exact tableau [of these ailments] one only has to detail the dire effects of these two causes" (15). As Tissot explains it, the practice of intense thinking to which scholars devote their professional lives can, when not managed properly, become dangerous to their health because it overstimulates the brain—the body part that he colorfully calls "the theater of war" in the man of letters.

Intense mental stimulation, Tissot continues, produces a state of movement and tension in the brain that can exhaust its fibers, just as immoderate physical exertion wears out the fibers in the muscles: "The sense organs, when excited, transmit to the mind the subject of its thoughts by exciting the fibers of the brain; and, while the soul is busy with those thoughts, the organs of the brain are in a certain degree of movement and tension; these movements tire the nervous medulla, a very tender substance [that] finds itself just as exhausted after a long meditation as is a robust body after a violent exercise" (*SGL*, 16–17). Some intellectual labors are particularly apt to lead to swift brain exhaustion—for example, studying serious books, the sort that "by the power and connection of their ideas, elevate the soul outside of its usual sphere and force it to meditate, thus wearing out the spirit and exhausting the body" (19–20). Tissot adds sternly: "The keener and more sustained this pleasure is, the more deadly its consequences will be" (20). However much the scholarly soul may delight in such elevation, intense reading and meditation have an effect analogous to that of applying a ligature to the nerves leading from the brain to the body. The results are catastrophic for the animal spirits necessary to keep the organism functioning: "Meditation, by holding the nerves in a state of unrelieved action, dissipates too many of the animal spirits and also prevents the brain from preparing them; as a consequence, this precious fluid—the most pure and most refined of the entire human machine and the most necessary to our functions—is lacking and altered, which produces a multitude of disorders" (37).

It would be instructive, at this juncture, to compare Tissot's views of the basic physiological operations that underlie the act of thinking with those of his rivals—most particularly Le Camus. Using a similar model of the solid and fluid parts involved in cognitive functions, Le Camus declares that sensibility is essential for intellectuals to enjoy "the full liberty of their understanding" (*Méd.*, 217). Tissot, by contrast, emphasizes the grave dangers that accentuating the mind's sensibility creates for the rest of the human being's internal functions: any increase in sensibility, he insists, strains the entire organic system and eventually leads to its collapse. To make matters worse, says Tissot, scholars as a class typically possess the type of constitution that is least suited to tolerating "literary intemperance" (*SGL*, 29): their nerves are highly reactive, their bodies are sedentary, and their digestion is poor. (Tissot declares that "the man who thinks the most is the one who digests the most poorly" [25].)

Moreover, men of letters are notorious for their numerous bad habits—so numerous that Tissot devotes fully half of his treatise to listing them: scholars tend to isolate themselves in their stuffy *cabinets*; they eat inappropriately rich foods; they overindulge in nefarious substances like coffee, tea, wine, and tobacco; they ignore the various calls of nature for sleep, regular meals, timely evacuations, and so on; and they are lax in their personal hygiene (128–242). Little wonder, then, that "there are few men sufficiently well constituted to bear serious mental exertion with impunity" (53).

Tissot clearly designs *De la santé des gens de lettres* to give a comprehensive, sobering tableau of the health risks attendant to the life of letters.[23] To structure this tableau, he systematically classifies the various parts of the scholarly body according to the symptoms each exhibits when irritated, overtaxed, or neglected as a result of excessive studying. He also draws heavily on ominous case histories of intemperate scholars both great and small. These case histories constitute Tissot's "empirical" evidence, compiled from his own practice, from his copious correspondence with other physicians (*SGL*, 18, 22, et passim), and from reliable nonmedical sources. Tissot constructs on this basis a composite picture of the intellectual as a dysfunctional type, a being whose range of potential constitutional ailments is symptomatically mapped out with an almost exclusive focus on two centers of pathological activity: the head and the stomach.

This sort of topographical reduction of the body to a head-stomach axis was characteristic of eighteenth-century medical treatises that focused on the pathologies of the "elite" classes, including not just scholars but also men and women of leisure. Moreover, the social elite portrayed in Tissot's *Essai sur les maladies des gens du monde* have much in common with the intellectual elite he describes here. Yet his reduction of the scholarly body to little more than a stomach and a brain is particularly absolute, for it implies the functional elimination of a third center of activity, the genitals. These organs seem to be atrophied in the men of letters whom he has observed: through the attenuation of the animal spirits that is induced by intense and sustained brain activity, "seminal fluid, which several great men have believed to be quite similar to nervous juice, also loses much of its activity" (*SGL*, 77). This condition may explain, conjectures Tissot, "why it is so rare that great men have sons worthy of themselves." Add to that most scholars' tendency to eschew the joys of social intercourse for the solitary but unnatural pleasures of their studies (96–97), and you have a picture of the scholarly life as degenerating not only for the individual who pursues it, but for future generations as well. This is perhaps the point on which Tissot differs most radically from optimistic theorists like Le Camus and Vandermonde: not only does Tissot refute the notion that there is a positive connection between intellectual production and sexual production, but he also presents the typical scholar as the least suitable candidate for the sort of "great men" breeding program they promote.

By far the most dire conditions recounted in *De la santé des gens de lettres* are those that affect the organ of thinking itself: the brain. Tissot's narrative takes on a veritable life-or-death tone when he is describing how overzealous study affects this organ and the entire sensible network associated with it. Using a fiber-based physiological doctrine inspired by Haller, Tissot contends that excessive scholarly activity violates each of the three fundamental laws of the animal economy. The first law is that strong and sustained impressions leave an indelible imprint on the fibers which receive them, such that "when the soul has been long occupied and has imparted a very strong action to the brain, it is no longer able to repress it; this agitation continues involuntarily" (38). The mind, as a result, concocts delirious ideas that no longer correspond to anything in the external world. According to the second law, "humors travel to the part that is in action" (44). Therefore, during intense thought a state of humoral plethora is created in the brain, which, when allowed to persist, can lead to a number of brain ailments, including tumors, aneurisms, inflammations, *squirres,* dropsy, headaches, delirium, drowsiness, epileptic seizures, lethargy, apoplexy, and insomnia (45). The third and final law of nature that Tissot invokes is that constantly stimulated brain fibers, like all organic fibers, harden with age and exercise, eventually becoming "calloused" to the point of being nonfunctional (52).[24] Immoderate study also makes particular sense organs susceptible to disorder: Tissot claims to have treated scholars in the prime of life whose eyes became so sensitive from the irritation of continuous reading that these scholars could no longer stand the light of a thin candle (98). In short,

> if there was ever a case that called for preventive measures, it is this one; the diseases whose seat lies in the brain are hard to cure completely, and this organ is one of those that recovers its powers with the greatest difficulty; the more this organ is necessary to Men of Letters, the more they should take care of it; and it seems to me that those men who have sunk into imbecility by exhausting their faculties through excessive study, form a spectacle well suited to opening the eyes of all Men of Letters, and to giving them a most forceful lesson in moderation.   (127)

Unfortunately, the typical scholar is not a moderate creature, but rather, a type of addict who will eventually fall into a vicious circle in which "the mind harms the body, the body harms the mind, and . . . both of them contribute equally to destroying the system of nerves" (*SGL,* 77). Tissot seems convinced that the intelligentsia of the day are set on a course that leads not to enlightenment, but to self-destruction. At their worst, he declares, they are little more than chronic pleasure-seekers who strain their constitutions and sacrifice their health in pursuit of "the passion for learning, which is perhaps the blindest of all" (238). Many would-be philosophes consequently end up, not with the superior minds they had sought to acquire, but rather, with sickly and destabilized bodies that can no longer support the slightest mental effort. Throughout *De la santé des gens de lettres*, Tissot reinforces his warnings about the potentially debilitating effects of scholarship with dramatic personal observations such as this: "For twenty years, I have sadly missed a friend who was equally distinguished by his genius and character, a man born for great things, divided between the study of Letters and of Medicine, whose progress he would certainly have furthered; but he was absorbed day and night by reading, experiments, and meditations: first he lost sleep, then he had passing fits of madness, and finally he became completely insane, and it was extremely difficult to save his life" (40–41). To close this alarming anecdote, he adds, "I've seen others who were first driven frenetic and maniacal by literary studies, and who ended up becoming utter imbeciles."

Within the more general context of Tissot's medical doctrine, the slide into madness and imbecility that he describes here can also be precipitated by abusive passions that are seemingly unrelated to the noble love of letters: for example, the passion for "self-abuse," which Tissot examined in his popular and infamous treatise *De l'onanisme* (Latin edition, 1758; French edition, 1760). In Tissot's eyes, the man of letters who ends up a simpleton is just as guilty for abusing his body as is the masturbator—who, moreover, often meets an analogous fate, by violating the same physiological principles:

> The masturbator, entirely devoted to his filthy meditations, is subject to the same disorders as the man of letters, who fixes his attention on a single question; and this excess is almost constantly prejudicial. That part of the brain, which is then occupied, makes an effort similar to that of a muscle, which has been for a long time greatly extended; the consequences of which are such a continued motion in the part as cannot be stopt, or such a fixed attention, that the idea cannot be changed . . . Although exhausted by perpetual fatigue, [chronic masturbators] are seized with all the disorders incident to the brain, melancholy, catalepsy, epilepsy, imbecility, the loss of sensation, weakness of the nervous system, and a variety of similar disorders.[25]

For Tissot, therefore, the dangers of scholarship differ little from those that he associates with other forms of overstimulation. One of the trademarks of Tissot's medical writing is, in fact, his tendency to censure those who suffer from what he views as ills of excess—whether excess in intellectual pursuits, in worldly pleasure, or in sexuality. Tissot addresses the readers of virtually all of his medical treatises as wayward and irresponsible patients who have brought their bodily ills upon themselves by straining their sensible systems beyond a physiological point of no return (*SGL*, 21–22).

Despite his dire tone, Tissot remains true to his mission as a physician-philosopher and always provides his readers with a full battery of remedies for the afflictions that beset them. Given the systematic character of Tissot's physio-pathology, it is not surprising that the remedies he recommends for correcting overzealous study closely resemble those that he prescribes to cure masturbation and worldly decadence: treatment consists in soothing and fortifying the sufferer's irritated fibers, largely by restoring the proper level of sensibility to the palate and stomach through simple, wholesome, natural products. Whether he is a debilitated scholar, a *mondain*, or a masturbator, Tissot's patient should adopt a regimen of clean, balanced living (including plenty of rest, fresh air, and exercise); a milk-based, semivegetarian diet; and a program of healthy social commerce.

To demonstrate that such a regimen can be successful, and thus that it *is* possible to cultivate one's mind without damaging one's body, Tissot invokes the example of the late Fontenelle—one of the very few positive case histories furnished in *De la santé des gens de lettres*. Fontenelle was, in Tissot's eyes, a model man of letters because "he knew how to be a scholar without ceasing to be a man; he knew how to acquire the most profound and varied knowledge without sacrificing his duties to science, even while he fulfilled his duties as a citizen, a father, a professor, and a member of society" (*SGL*, 56). Fontenelle enjoyed a long, productive, and healthy career by tempering his intellectual exertions with the fruitful physical exercise he got by gardening; and he further maintained his health and cheerful disposition by "combining the delights of civil life with his literary studies" (57). Yet, Tissot underscores, Fontenelle also had a constitutional advantage: he was endowed with "that fortunate disposition of fibers that forms great men . . . [and] that makes for longevity" (54). Thus, thanks to a rare combination of a hearty constitution and a balanced, wholesome mode of life, Fontenelle proved that one can be a *philosophe* without sacrificing either one's happiness or one's health.

Lest we think that Fontenelle's success story brings Tissot closer to the progressionist theories preached by physicians like Le Camus and Vandermonde, however, we should bear in mind two things: first, Tissot takes up the Fontenelle story precisely to preempt any effort by his critics to use the tale to disprove his assertions about the dangers of study (53); and second, he insists that Fontenelle was able to avoid those dangers only by leading an exceptionally prudent and sociable existence, which mitigated the effects of his literary labors. By shifting immediately from the Fontenelle case study to censorious remarks about obsessive erudites who separate themselves from society without producing anything useful (57), Tissot makes it clear that the average intellectual of his day falls far short of his Fontenellian ideal. We should therefore classify the Fontenelle case study among the precepts, prescriptions, and exempla that constitute Tissot's general hygienic program for scholars—a program that is fundamentally corrective and restorative, in striking contrast to the eugenic regimens proposed by Le Camus and Vandermonde. Whereas those physicians view hygiene as a practical means of channelling sensibility into paths of ever-improving mental and physical functioning, Tissot employs it primarily for remedial purposes, in order to repair bodies whose sensibilities have gone awry.

Tissot ends *De la santé des gens de lettres* with a curious little caveat, made to "anticipate a sophistical objection that some might draw from this work" (243). Although he acknowledges that his treatise "offers a tableau of the ills that an excessive attachment to study produces," he denies that he regards study itself as dangerous or wishes to dissuade his readers from undertaking it whatsoever. After alluding to the famous diatribe that Rousseau made against the arts and sciences in his first *Discourse,* Tissot comments: "Even if it were true—which I do not believe—that study does not contribute to the happiness of society in general, one could hardly deny, it seems to me, that the knowledge of Letters only increases the happiness of the person who possesses it when he has acquired it neither at the expense of his duties nor at the expense of his health" (243–44). Tissot thus takes a moderate stance in the debate then raging over the relative merits and risks of striving to become learned: he argues that the pursuit of knowledge, while not entirely beneficial, can at least be benign to fledgling scholars, as long as they meet certain conditions. First, they should not become overly impassioned about their studies; second, they should not neglect their social responsibilities; and finally, they should monitor their health vigilantly —in accordance, we can assume, with the regimen Tissot details earlier in the treatise. Tissot clearly views the scholar as a type of patient who must submit to constant control, not only physical control (represented in this treatise by over a hundred pages of prescriptions for exercise, diet, sleeping, and using foreign substances like coffee, tea, and tobacco [124–242]), but also moral control, which Tissot exerts by exhorting his readers to cultivate the arts and sciences in a manner that is cool-headed, self-disciplined, and socially acceptable.[26]

The question of morality looms large in *De la santé des gens de lettres,* informing everything from the symptomatology Tissot gleans from his large collection of learned patients, to the etiological link he establishes between schol-

arship and the pathologies of his age. Ultimately, Tissot views all scholarly afflictions as stemming from a general weakening of the nervous system—a condition he labels hypochondria, whose initial signs emanate from the mind
rather than from the body: "The first symptoms that characterize the weakening of the nervous system are a kind of pusillanimity that the patient did not
have before; distrust, fear, sadness, despondency, [and] discouragement: the
man who had been the most intrepid comes to fear everything; the smallest undertaking frightens him, the slightest unforeseen event makes him tremble"
(*SGL*, 31). Far from glorifying hypochondria as the ennobling mark of a more
refined sensibility (as did contemporary English physicians like George
Cheyne),[27] Tissot charges it with a formidable battery of ignoble emotional
traits. Significantly, this passage is soon followed by a quotation Tissot takes
from Rousseau's *Préface de Narcisse*: "Library work makes men delicate, weakens their temperament, and the soul is hard pressed to retain its vigor when the
body has lost its own. Study wears out the machine, exhausts the spirits . . .
[and] makes men fainthearted, incapable of resisting both pain and the passions" (*SGL*, 33). Rousseau's absolutist portrait of the scholar as a weakened,
cowardly, and above all morally degenerate type is rendered all the more authoritative here, framed as it is by the many pathos-filled examples Tissot culls
from his medical practice. This is not the only Rousseauian moment to be
found in *De la santé des gens de lettres*, for Tissot writes his own diatribe against
the state of physical debility and moral dissolution which has, he believes, overtaken the Europeans of his generation.

Tissot attributes this condition to the nervous maladies that, he claims, "are
much more frequent and varied than they were sixty years ago" (*SGL*, 182).
Having declared that this proliferation of disorders in sensibility has reached
the proportions of a veritable plague in modern Europe, he launches into an extraordinarily long and dire commentary on its underlying causes. This commentary, made in a footnote that runs on for five pages, is a point-by-point denunciation of the unwholesome pursuits favored by those who call themselves
well-bred: activities like tea-drinking, living in luxury, carriage-riding, taking
on urbane airs, and overspicing their food (184–86). However, none of those
bad habits is quite so harmful as the ones that top Tissot's list: "the love of the
Sciences," the "much more prevalent culture of Letters," and the "reigning
mania" for learning (182). Tissot employs a chain-effect epidemiological approach to trace the deleterious repercussions of this craze throughout the social
body: excessive enthusiasm for the arts and sciences has spawned an overabun-
dance of printing presses and books, an abundance of authors "who may not
have the true attributes of Scholars, but who are more or less exposed to the ailments they experience," a "crowd of readers" to consume those authors'

books, and finally, the highly dangerous habit of ardent novel-reading—and, even worse, novel-writing—among women (183).[28] Thus, in stark contrast to the moderate stance he later takes concerning the consequences of study (243–44), Tissot does not hesitate here to draw a highly incriminating connection between the increase in nervous maladies and the contemporary scholarship craze—one of a number of cultural trends that, in his opinion, threaten the collective health and constitution of so-called civilized humanity.

What this diatribe reveals is a profound fear: the fear that all of Europe is in danger of succumbing to a kind of mass hypochondria—a collective weakening of the nervous system, brought on by culturally induced overstimulation of everyone's sensibility. *De la santé des gens de lettres* is therefore inspired by an anxiety that goes far deeper than Tissot's fretting over the poor hygiene of intellectuals; he evidently suspects that there are insidious forces of degeneration operating within the human species, which he must expose and rectify. Tissot grants that the processes of heredity and civilization make degeneration inevitable, to a degree: "Children show the effects of the ills of their fathers; our ancestors began by straying somewhat from the most healthy mode of life, [such that] our grandfathers were born a bit weaker, were raised in greater indolence, and had children even weaker than they; and we, the fourth generation, we no longer know strength and health except in octogenarians or through hearsay. For us to recover those qualities would require either a well-reasoned behavior that is too much to expect, or several centuries of barbarism for which one dares not wish" (*SGL*, 186). Yet, however pessimistic he may sound in this passage, Tissot also strives energetically to counteract the process of human decline, using philosophical medicine as a means of popularizing the very sort of reasonable behavior he declares here to be a hopeless cause.

To grasp the full significance of Tissot's medical project both within this treatise and beyond, we must consequently regard it as a mission whose primary purpose is social reform—that is, reform of the collective human constitution, body and soul. Tissot's anxiety over the ills of scholarship stems from a conviction that he must combat the degenerative tendency intrinsic to civilized people by providing a medically based plan for supervising the many risky activities associated with modern civilized life. Seen in that light, *De la santé des gens de lettres* is just one instance of a medical doctrine whose tone is unflaggingly alarmist and whose scope is impressively comprehensive. Of course, as a moralist intent on finding ways to "cure" the ills of civilization, Tissot bears more than a passing resemblance to Jean-Jacques Rousseau; one modern scholar has gone so far as to call Tissot "the Jean-Jacques of medicine."[29] I would argue, however, that Tissot's concerns with moral and physical degeneration are *not* imported from a source outside medicine; rather, they are rooted in his efforts as a theorist and practitioner working within a field that had recently undergone a conceptual revolution of major proportions.

Whatever side they took in the debate over the vital properties of irritability and sensibility, mid-eighteenth-century physicians agreed that vital reactibility was a revolutionary concept, a sort of "missing link" that would allow them to penetrate at last into the innermost workings of the human constitution. On the strength of that conviction, medicine was transformed into a properly philosophical discipline: it was now invested with a renewed theoretical vigor and with a fundamentally anthropological dimension. Although he held an opinion of humankind's ameliorative potential that differed greatly from that of Le Camus and Vandermonde, Tissot, too, considered himself entrusted by his profession with the task of addressing—and, with any luck, solving—the major problems currently confronting society. His plan for social health does indeed overlap in significant ways with the utopian vision of a perfectly regulated and salubrious domestic economy that is presented in Rousseau's *La Nouvelle Héloïse*. Yet Tissot's medical program also held great contemporary significance independently of its ties to Rousseau's social theory, for Tissot's occupation-specific approach to medicine prepared the way for a highly influential late-eighteenth-century genre of medical writing known as moral anthropology, whose proponents undertook to categorize different types of human beings according to their "natural" physico-moral traits. Moreover, Tissot's medical doctrine was a fundamental contribution both to the medicine of enlightenment as a particular discursive genre and to the effort to medicalize the enlightenment movement itself.

For those reasons, *De la santé des gens de lettres* should be seen as the centerpiece of Tissot's extensive and influential corpus of medico-philosophical writings; medicine and eighteenth-century philosophy converge within its pages in a manner that is both highly systematic and highly ambivalent. What makes this treatise so central to Tissot's mission to improve social health—just as central as his works on such pressing issues as smallpox inoculation, depopulation, and the diseases linked to poverty in the lower classes[30]—is the troubling question it raises: How might physicians act to reverse the ongoing denaturation of civilized humanity? Nowhere in Tissot's corpus is that question quite so prominent as in his treatises on the two diseases that he, effectively, invented:[31] masturbation, which he depicts in *De l'onanisme* as a devastating, contagious affliction; and scholarship, which he presents in *De la santé des gens de lettres* as an inherently pathogenic if not pathological pursuit. According to Tissot's medical theory, these two "constructed" disorders share both a common etiology (via the physio-pathological mechanism of irritability) and a number of heinous ethical attributes. Both conditions are, he insists, sterile and delusional activities whose disastrous consequences are self-inflicted. In other words, as closely related dysfunctional types, the scholar and the masturbator quite literally *embody* the denaturing effects wreaked by the insalubrious cultural trends denounced by Tissot in his Rousseauistic diatribe. Not surprisingly, these two body types are located at the point on Tissot's health scale that is farthest removed from his ideal—an ideal represented in his *Essai sur les maladies des gens du monde* by the steady-nerved, plain-living farmhand, an unenlightened figure who best approximates "true" human nature as Tissot defines it.[32]

What *De la santé des gens de lettres* demonstrates is that, for all of its relatively newfound sense of authority, medicine at the height of the Enlightenment was also filled with irresolvable tensions over the meaning of enlightenment and over the ominous specter of human degeneration. Given those tensions, it is not surprising that the scholarly body presented medical theorists with a particular quandary.[33] The popular quest to cultivate the intellect seemed to bring with it other modifications in human nature—modifications in the body, whose fibers seemed to become more irritable and more regionally specialized the more a person's vital energies were concentrated in the brain. Hence the polemic at the center of the medicine of enlightenment: What is the relation between physical vigor and intellectual vigor? Is it proportional, or inverse? Is either type of vigor *naturally* inscribed in bodies by virtue of sex, class, or birthplace? And where does "moral fiber" fit into the picture? These are some of the questions that I address in Part 2.

PART II

Narrating the Sensible Body

4. The Novel of Sensibility

 before 1750

The Ambiguities of Worldly Sensibility in Crébillon and Prévost

If the notion of vital sensibility that emerged in mid-eighteenth-century France was indeed a major conceptual paradigm, one would expect to see it at work in a broad range of fields. Thus far, we have considered how a particular model of the sensible body was forged in the experimental physiology of the late 1740s and then imported into other branches of natural philosophy like sensationalist epistemology and philosophical medicine. Now we will examine the various ways in which that idea resounded through the literature of the period—most particularly, the post-1750 novel of sensibility, a genre that casts a particularly intriguing light upon the conception of sensibility that medical theorists so insistently promoted from 1750 to 1800.

Sensibility had, of course, already been a prominent feature of the novel prior to 1750: it was a central preoccupation of such works as Prévost's *Manon Lescaut* (1731), Marivaux's *La Vie de Marianne* (1731–42), Crébillon's *Les Égarements du coeur et de l'esprit* (1737–38), and Graffigny's *Les Lettres d'une Péruvienne* (1747). Up to a point, each of these novels illustrates what Frank Baasner has called the "identification of *sensibilité* with the total of social virtues," which, he argues, dates back to the second half of the seventeenth century.[1] Sensibility's sociomoral connotations were not so much replaced as broadened in the 1750s, when novelists began to transcode the notion's recently acquired physio-philosophical overtones into their fictional writings. The novel of sensibility thereby underwent a subtle but significant transformation that, to varying degrees, reflected the new physicalist perspective on the human being.

One of my primary tasks in Part 2 will be to track the evolution of sensibility in the mid- to late-eighteenth-century French novel in order to measure the importance of literature in determining the course and fate of the larger sensibility paradigm. In this chapter I examine sensibility's literary meanings during the first half of the century. Subsequent chapters examine the "new" novel of sensibility with a focus on Diderot's *La Religieuse*, Rousseau's *La Nouvelle Héloïse*, Laclos's *Les Liaisons dangereuses*, and Sade's *Justine, ou les malheurs de la vertu*. Because these novelists quite deliberately incorporated key aspects of the contemporary biomedical model of sensibility into their fictions, I consider their works in juxtaposition to related medical texts. Such an interdisciplinary approach has two primary advantages. First, it casts each particular novel in an intriguing new light, by reconnecting it to the more general discourse on sensibility that was taking place around it. Second, it demonstrates that the post-1750 novel of sensibility played a central (and heretofore largely overlooked) role in the widespread effort to understand precisely what sensibility meant as the key factor in human nature. One might well say that the paradigm of vital sensibility reached its highest level of complexity in the novel, a genre that provided its practitioners with a battery of techniques for exploring not only sensibility's possibilities, but also its potentially troubling implications.

꿎 ꃋ

Prior to 1750, sensibility in the French novel was largely a worldly affair: upper-class sociability, as represented in fiction, was a mode of social intercourse that revolved around the acts of manifesting and deciphering such phenomena as *sensibilité, sentiments, sympathie, délicatesse, tendresse,* and *attendrissement* in oneself and in others.[2] Hence the intensive analysis of feelings that one finds in the novels of Prévost, Crébillon, Marivaux, and Graffigny, whose characters speak of sensibility in tones ranging from refined preciosity, to idealized sentimentality, to world-weary cynicism—sometimes all within the same text. What those tonal variations signal is not that these novelists were contradictory in their perspectives on the concept, but rather, that they were keenly aware that its signification was fast becoming problematic in the face of a rapidly changing world. That is, beyond their particular plots, their novels chronicle the crisis of meaning that was taking place during the first half of the century in the ethical and discursive codes used by "good company" to define itself. *Sensibility* and its cognate terms provide a ready-made barometer of that crisis, for although they carried numerous positive denotations, they also tended increasingly to connote a kind of high-born clannishness that literary authors were just as inclined to question as to embrace.

This ambivalence toward sensibility's elitist overtones is particularly apparent in Crébillon's *Les Égarements du coeur et de l'esprit* and Prévost's *Manon Lescaut*. The protagonists of both of these works are aristocrats who emphasize

their unique qualities of sensibility as a means of exciting either love or sympathy in other characters; at the same time, however, they engage in equivocal
behavior and sentimental double-talk that threaten to undermine their seemingly high-minded declarations. In contrast, one finds a concerted effort in
La Vie de Marianne and *Les Lettres d'une Péruvienne* to restore sensibility's
wavering status as an authentic, natural mark of distinction. Despite her obscure origins, Marivaux's heroine finds a place in good society by virtue of her
inborn refinement of sentiment, and Graffigny's exiled Incan princess possesses
a native, candid sensibility that is explicitly contrasted to the excessive, overly
mannered delicacy of her French hosts. Marivaux and Graffigny thereby anticipate the campaign to naturalize sensibility that became prevalent in both literature and medicine after 1750. Their novels nonetheless reflect a view of the
concept that remains rooted in the mindset represented by Crébillon and Prévost, according to which sensibility is a quality reserved for a social and/or
moral elite.

⇛ ⇚

Crébillon's *Les Égarements du coeur et de l'esprit,* a wry fictional memoir, offers
a particular lucid description of sensibility's communicative function in eighteenth-century high society. As Crébillon portrays it, worldly life is a chesslike
game of seduction and social one-upsmanship; within that game, sentiment and
sensibility are valued not so much in themselves as for providing the means by
which one player sends messages, both linguistic and physiognomic, to another.[3] The social initiation of M. de Meilcour, the novel's naïve and rather
bumbling seventeen-year-old protagonist, consequently entails not one but
two apprenticeships: first, instruction in the fine art of aristocratic lovemaking,
and second, training in the even finer art of interpreting the signs of sensibility
in those around him.

Sensibility's pivotal role in the aristocratic communicational code is most
clearly illustrated by the sequence of Meilcour's dealings with his first "tutor,"
Madame de Lursay. This highly refined woman of the world deploys sensibility, first, in her subtle mode of self-presentation: "She professed to have no
wish to please, but saw to it that she was always attractive [*en état de toucher*]."[4]
Mme. de Lursay's aim is not to seduce overtly, but rather to make selected men
vulnerable to her charms; predictably, the playfulness and tenderness that shine
in her eyes when she gazes on her fledgling suitor Meilcour serve very effectively to spark reciprocal sentiments in him. Mme. de Lursay also excels in the
highly refined manner in which high-society ladies converse about their feelings—a speaking style that causes a good deal of confusion for the as-yet un-

cultured Meilcour. As Meilcour relates it, "Among the many things I was ignorant of was the fact that in society sentiment was no more than a subject of conversation . . . Madame de Lursay . . . made out the conquest of her heart to be so difficult, required so many qualities in the object that should move her [*qui pourrait la rendre sensible*], and spoke of so singular a way of loving, that I trembled every time I thought of an attachment to her" (*Wayward*, 9–10; *ECE*, 75). However, Mme. de Lursay has no sooner made her lofty and intimidating pronouncement on the difficulty any man would have in winning her heart, than she proceeds to signal to Meilcour that she is quite disposed to be "sensible" to him. This strategy of mixed messages succeeds in arousing the young man's desire, but also leads him to be rather more constrained with the lady than she would like.

Mme. de Lursay's manner of announcing her sensibility and of inducing it in her potential partner consists of an intricate choreography of tender gazes, discreetly intimate gestures, and circuitous discourse. Were Meilcour not so naïve, Lursay's signs would have already prompted him to make the next move; however, as the older Meilcour who is narrating the tale wryly observes, "My stupidity only grew with every effort she made to open my eyes" (*Wayward*, 11). The young Meilcour is, as yet, so oblivious to the rules of the game that even when Lursay takes the risk of openly admitting her sentiments toward him, he is still confounded. His apprenticeship in the subtleties of aristocratic seduction therefore proceeds at an excruciately slow pace, largely because Mme. de Lursay must constantly adjust her system for communicating with him to overcome the handicaps presented by his lack of social knowledge and persistent reserve.

Mme. de Lursay consequently steps up her efforts to get her message across during Meilcour's next visit: "She had dressed that day in a style designed to capture both my eye and my heart. A most splendid and elegant déshabillé set off her charms; her hair was simply dressed; she wore very little rouge— everything was contrived to make her look more tender. In short, her whole toilette was of the kind that makes women dazzle the eye less, but captivate the senses more. It followed, since she had adopted it for an occasion which she regarded as highly important, that she had had previous experience of its effectiveness" (*Wayward*, 51). Although Meilcour is, at this point, somewhat distracted by his two recent encounters with a beautiful stranger who has inspired a new "tenderness" in him, he is nonetheless affected by Mme. de Lursay's fetching appearance: "Now, in spite of all the reasons I had for resistance, I was surprised by her beauty. Something inexpressibly touching and sweet shone in her eyes; all her charms were so animated by desire, and perhaps by the certainty of pleasing me, that I was moved by their vivacity" (51). Their eyes meet, and the studied languor of Mme. de Lursay's gaze—coupled with a few timely sighs—makes such a deep impression that Meilcour takes himself to be truly smitten. Despite his awkwardness, he manages to follow the stratagem she invents for them to meet alone later that evening (*ECE*, 119–27). However, when the carefully planned tête-à-tête at last arrives, Meilcour finds himself dumbstruck and trembling with fear. Once again, Mme. de Lursay must guide her would-be lover through the encounter, by coaxing the right words out of him and orchestrating a suggestive scene in which he is placed at her feet as she reclines on the sofa and plays idly with his hair. Even then, young Meilcour remains spectacularly oblivious to her intended message: "The light I saw in her eyes, which would have been a revelation to anyone else, her confusion, the change in her voice, her soft and frequent sighs—everything increased the propitiousness of the moment, but nothing made me understand it" (*Wayward*, 65). In the end, Lursay decides that she can hope for no more understanding from her naïve suitor and sends him home for the evening.

This series of impasses, which constitutes a good deal of the action of *Les Égarements du coeur et de l'esprit*, not only imbues the narrative with a sardonically comic tone but also demonstrates that worldly lovemaking is a subtle two-way system for signaling sensibility in the sense of amorous interest. What frustrates Mme. de Lursay's efforts to communicate with Meilcour is that the signs conventionally used by aristocrats to convey emotion are so discreet that they require not just an adept sender but also a properly attuned receiver. Clearly, young Meilcour still has a good deal to learn before he can read aristocratic women properly. First, he must be exposed to a wider range of *mondaines*, like the decidedly unsubtle Mme. de Senanges, who blatantly displays her erotic designs on Meilcour to the entire worldly public; and second, he must develop some of the discernment possessed by Versac, the masterful aristocrat who takes Meilcour under his wing.

Versac, who appears midway through Meilcour's apprenticeship in the ways of the world, promptly sets about disrupting Mme. de Lursay's project. As the narrator portrays him, Versac is the consummate *petit-maître*, a man who has succeeded in high society by manipulating women—that is, by reading them so well that they are powerless either to resist his advances or to counter his control over their public reputations (*ECE*, 129). Versac is intent on maintaining his extraordinary social mastery and also on being duly recognized for it; he thus wishes to punish Lursay simply because she had the nerve to scare off the young woman whom he most recently undertook to seduce. Furious at this "unpardonable" affront, Versac executes a series of strategic social strikes against Lursay by which he effectively retaliates in kind. First, he pays a social call to the Meilcour residence, where he introduces himself to young Meilcour and depicts Lursay as an aging coquette who has duped a whole series of young suitors into believing her to be unobtainable (*ECE*, 131–33). Despite the efforts of Meilcour's mother to refute this piece of malicious gossip, it has precisely the desired effect on Meilcour: "This was so just a description of my own situation that it dispelled the doubt I had hitherto been in about Versac's words. I blushed to acknowledge how thoroughly I had been taken in" (*Wayward*, 71). Next, Versac rushes over to Lursay's drawing room so as to arrive before Meilcour, the better to confirm that this young man is, indeed, the latest in her conquests. Versac clearly enjoys witnessing Lursay's discomfiture when Meilcour arrives, right on schedule: with a knowing smile on his face, Versac not only sizes up the situation perfectly but makes it clear that her carefully concealed love interest is no secret for him and will no longer be secret to anyone else, either (*ECE*, 137–38). During the interval between this episode and his return later that same evening, Versac gathers the resources he will need for the masterfully torturous scene he has planned for his enemy: he ensures that Mme. de Senanges, a potential rival for Meilcour's affections, also appears at Mme. de Lursay's for dinner; and he digs up the fatuous Marquis de Pranzi, one of Lursay's old flames, whose presence adds immeasurably to her embarrassment (*ECE*, 144, 147–49).

There is only one element of the evening that Versac has not foreseen: Mme. de Lursay's guests also include Mme. de Théville and her daughter Hortense, who turns out to be the *belle inconnue* who had captured Meilcour's eye and heart at the Opera a few days earlier. Once all of the players have assembled, there ensues a dinner party scene that illustrates the great social virtuosity of Versac, whose continual maneuvers against Mme. de Lursay frustrate her every effort to communicate with Meilcour. Lursay is forced instead to put up with the indecently familiar double entendres of Pranzi, while Mme. de Senanges is free to flirt shamelessly with Meilcour, and Versac with Hortense (*ECE*, 150, 154, 158). This scene is, as Peter Brooks has observed, designed to dramatize the intricate linguistic and gestural codes by which worldly society operates, as well as to demonstrate once again young Meilcour's problems in interpreting and participating in those codes.[5] Yet it is also significant for introducing two new deflections in the saga of Meilcour's sentimental education: Mme. de Senanges lauches her own seduction of Meilcour, by arranging for him to pay her a social call the next day (160); and Meilcour has his first occasion to pursue his nascent infatuation with Hortense, the woman whom he believes to be his one true love.

Of these two developments, the latter is unquestionably the most important to Meilcour's emerging understanding of what sentiment and sensibility truly mean—not just in terms of the worldly code followed by Versac and Mme. de

Lursay, but also according to the personal moral code Meilcour is struggling to develop. Versac does his best, during his candid exposition of his "science du monde" in part 3, to convince Meilcour that such a moral code is neither necessary nor useful for a fledgling *mondain*: "It is an error to suppose that one may preserve in the world the innocence one commonly possesses on entering it, or that one can be always virtuous and natural without risking both reputation and fortune" (*Wayward*, 160). Yet, even though Meilcour-the-narrator remarks in hindsight that Versac's lesson "had all too much influence on the conduct of my life" (159), it is not at all clear that Meilcour-the-protagonist accepts Versac's cynical insistence that sensibility is something that one should not seek to feel in the world, but rather learn to analyze and imitate. Meilcour does, of course, listen intently to the lesson; yet once it is over, he returns to his usual occupation: "Dreaming of Hortense, repining at her absence, and sighing for her return were the only things I could give my mind to" (175).

Meilcour's ardor for Hortense stands out among the novel's many amorous engagements by virtue of its apparent depth and sincerity. From the moment he lays eyes on her at the Opera, Meilcour is affected in a manner utterly different from what he feels during Mme. de Lursay's artful efforts to arouse him: "I cannot describe the strange and sudden emotion that seized me at the sight; struck by so much beauty I stood dumbfounded. My surprise was so great I was transported. I felt a disorder in my heart that spread through all my senses" (*Wayward*, 26). Each of Hortense's appearances is granted the status of a major event in the story: the narrative shifts into a detailed description of the intense inner passions she stirs up in Meilcour. This occurs, among other places, during the dinner party at Mme. de Lursay's, where Meilcour's amorous absorption is misinterpreted by both Versac (who assumes that he is distracted by Lursay) and Lursay (who believes him to be enamored of Mme. de Senanges). The inability of these otherwise hyperperceptive characters to read Meilcour correctly here provides him with a rare advantage, for it allows him to pursue, free from prying eyes, his own project of reading Hortense in the hope of penetrating her inner feelings—or more precisely, of determining whether he might just be the unidentified young man for whom she has declared herself "sensible" (*ECE*, 106–9).

Hortense, however, remains indecipherable not just for Meilcour but for the novel's readers as well: we never learn whether he succeeds in discerning her true sentiments or in winning her heart because the narrator does not reach that point in his life story before completing the tale. Instead, Meilcour's narrative ends on a note of irresolution, with the accomplishment of his long-delayed conquest of/by Mme. de Lursay. Rather than enjoying the moment, Meilcour is torn between Versacian detachment and remorseful thoughts of Hortense:

Enchanted as I was, my eyes opened at last. Without knowing what it was I lacked, I felt a blank in my heart. Only my imagination was alive [*émue*], and I had to excite that in order not to fall into listlessness. I was eager again, but less ardent. I still admired, but I was no longer moved. It was in vain that I tried to recapture my first transports. I could now only yield myself to Madame de Lursay with an air of constraint, and I reproached myself for the least desires that her beauty could still wring from me. Hortense—Hortense, whom I adored though I had so utterly forgotten her, resumed her sway over my heart.   (*Wayward*, 200; *ECE*, 246–47)[6]

Meilcour's first taste of the fruits of worldly seduction brings him undeniable sensual pleasure, but it also makes him painfully aware of the psychological contradictions inherent in living according to the codes of high society: "Torn away from pleasure by remorse, snatched from remorse by pleasure, I could not be sure of myself for a moment" (*Wayward*, 201–2). To sum up Meilcour's dilemma, his mind is willing to make the most of a social system that effectively evacuates any true sentiment from amorous encounters, but his heart urges him to believe in something quite different—namely, the "ridiculous" and "shameful" idea of being faithful in love (*ECE*, 247). Because Meilcour-the-narrator never resolves the contradictions between those two positions, we as readers are never able to tell where he, as spokesman for the novel's moral message, stands on the question of whether sensibility has any meaning in the aristocratic universe, beyond being very useful as a semiotic tool in the game of worldly sociability.

As a study in sensibility, therefore, *Les Égarements du coeur et de l'esprit* is irremediably unsettling: Versac, master seducer and manipulator of high society, situates himself entirely outside of sensibility, whereas Meilcour vacillates between his intense and seemingly genuine passion for Hortense and his keen interest in exploiting his status as worldly initiate in order to learn as much as he can about how to act and talk in the aristocratic milieu. The quality of sensibility is essential to succeeding at that task, yet it also seems in imminent danger of being stripped of any authentic emotional value. Although lovemaking is the key activity of high-society life as depicted by Crébillon, the connections that are made between his worldly lovers are standardly based not on mutual emotional affinity, but on concern with advancing their respective social positions as efficiently as possible. The purpose of cultivating sensibility in this world is therefore not so much to develop one's capacity for deep and refined feeling as to hone the observational and communicative skills that are critical to maintaining one's place in the social hierarchy.

Sensibility is also problematic, albeit in different ways, in Prévost's *Histoire du Chevalier des Grieux et de Manon Lescaut* (1731). On the face of it, these novels would seem to have little in common, beyond being fictional memoirs narrated by young noblemen. In contrast to Crébillon's narrator Meilcour, who looks back upon his social initiation with a mature and largely sardonic eye, Prévost's Chevalier des Grieux has an earnest perspective on his own tale of youthful adventures. As a protagonist, however, des Grieux is engaged in an enterprise quite similar to young Meilcour's: he, too, seeks to master the subtle communicational codes that are attached to sensibility in his elite social universe. Des Grieux is, like Meilcour, intent on using those codes to advance his love interests; but in the chevalier's case, the crucial bond that is established via sensibility is not his obsessive attachment to his mistress, Manon (a commoner), but rather his ongoing relationship with other aristocrats. In that sense, *Manon Lescaut* reflects not only the dynamics of erotic desire but also the equally complex, but more enduring, mechanism by which sensibility, sympathy, and benevolence operate within the privileged confines of the upper class.

Sensibility is first invoked in the "Avis de l'Auteur des *Mémoires d'un homme de qualité*," a liminary text that serves to frame and qualify des Grieux's first-person narrative. The "Avis," written in the name of the fictional Marquis de Renoncour, is devoted largely to addressing the moral questions raised by des Grieux's decidedly amoral tale of fatal attraction and worldly slumming. Renoncour neither defends des Grieux's questionable actions nor accepts his argument that he was the hapless victim of fate, but instead draws attention to the predicament in which this story might place its naturally sympathetic, presumably wellborn readers.[7] It is, he points out, easy for such readers to be sympathetic when they are merely contemplating abstract questions of moral philosophy: "Well-born souls feel that gentleness and humanity are attractive virtues, and are naturally inclined to practice them."[8] Exercising one's sympathetic instincts is, however, a far trickier business in real life, where "we are afraid of being duped by trying to be kind and liberal; of being considered weak by appearing too tender and emotional [*sensible*]" (*ML*, 19). The first notion associated with sensibility in *Manon Lescaut* is thus that the person who readily exhibits his sensitive qualities is potentially vulnerable to deception.[9]

What is offered in the "Avis de l'Auteur" is not a remedy to that vulnerability but rather a way of diminishing its effects: Renoncour argues, in essence, that it is better to risk being an oversensitive dupe through fiction than through real-life experience; hence the moral utility of novels, "at least when written by a person of honor and good sense" (*ML*, 19). Renoncour, however, leaves open the question of whether the fictional character des Grieux is a safe bet for exercising the reader's sympathetic sensibilities. For although the chevalier is amply endowed with the noble qualities Renoncour deems innate in persons of a high social station, he is also depicted here as a confoundingly ambiguous character:

> The man I have to portray is one young and blind, who refuses to be happy and willfully plunges headfirst into the uttermost misfortunes; who, with all the qualities that go to make up the most brilliant merit, by his own choice prefers an obscure and vagabond life to all the advantages of fortune and nature; who foresees his miseries without wanting to avoid them, without profiting by the remedies that are constantly offered him and that could end them at any moment; in short, an ambiguous character, a mixture of virtues and vices, a perpetual contrast of good sentiments and bad actions.   (18)

Although this description clearly solicits the reader's curiosity, it is far less clear whether it is meant to invite the reader to commiserate with des Grieux's sufferings, or rather, to pass judgment upon him for willfully inflicting his misfortunes upon himself. That is, although Renoncour argues that des Grieux's tale is an excellent mode of moral instruction, he does not specify precisely *what* lesson readers are supposed to draw concerning this young man; nor does he explain exactly how des Grieux's fictional adventure can serve as "a model on which to form oneself" in exercising one's virtue (19).

Interestingly, Renoncour has no sooner made his cautionary statement on sensibility and deception than he relates the automatic sympathetic response he felt upon seeing des Grieux for the first time. This reaction is detailed in the novel's opening narrative, which begins with the spectacle of the beautiful and seemingly modest Manon chained ignominiously to a band of prostitutes who are about to be shipped off from Havre-de-Grace to America: "Oh, sir," exclaims an old woman in the crowd that has gathered to gawk at the scene, "go in and see if it isn't a sight to break your heart!" (*ML*, 22). Renoncour is indeed struck by what he sees, but he is even more affected by the sight of the young man who has followed Manon all the way from Paris: "I have never seen a more living picture of grief. He was very simply dressed; but you can tell at a glance a man of birth and education. I went over to him. He got up; and I discovered in his eyes, his face, his gestures, such a refined and noble air that I felt naturally led to wish him well" (23).

Thus, although it is Manon who initially arouses Renoncour's curiosity, it is des Grieux who gets his compassion—a reaction that, as Renoncour put it, is only "natural." For, with his immediately recognizable noble bearing and fine physiognomy, des Grieux is physically constituted to touch the heartstrings of a fatherly aristocrat.[10] He speaks, moreover, in tones that are perfectly suited to an interlocutor of the marquis's elevated stature: after he tearfully tells Renoncour how he and Manon found themselves in such dire straits, the marquis promptly gives four gold pieces to des Grieux himself and six to Manon's captors, explaining simply that "this adventure seemed to me one of the most extraordinary and most touching ever" (*ML*, 24). This exchange—a moving tale proffered by a wellborn youth, in return for the sympathy and monetary aid of a rich and powerful nobleman—is critical both to the narrative contract that des Grieux will form as chief narrator of the novel and to the chevalier's *modus operandi* as a character in the world. The exact same type of exchange occurs not only a second time with Renoncour, when he again runs into des Grieux two years later in Calais, but also with every patrician character whom des Grieux meets during his adventures.

In other words, the Chevalier des Grieux's behavior as both narrator and protagonist in *Manon Lescaut* is predicated on the operation of sensibility, a quality that he expects of those of noble birth even when they are aware that he may be playing deliberately upon their sympathies. The theme of deception is, of course, central to the love story around which the novel is constructed: the chevalier's passion for Manon is constantly tempered by the fear that she is duping him (a fear that extends to his relationship with Manon's brother Lescaut). One might call des Grieux's manner of addressing that fear counterphobic, inasmuch as he strives to avoid being conned by conning everyone else. He deploys this strategy in an economic register by duplicitously cheating wealthy bourgeois at the gaming table or in their own homes, as in the episodes of MM. de G ... M ... senior and junior. But he also deploys it in a filial register: nowhere is des Grieux a bigger con artist than in his relationships with the various "fathers" and "brothers" of *Manon Lescaut,* a group that includes all of the aristocratic characters who turn up to provide sympathy—and perhaps more—every time that des Grieux needs it.

It is by no means coincidental that the chevalier systematically finds himself in conversation with a character of "quality" whenever he has gotten himself into trouble; for each of these encounters provides him with a timely opportunity to make sympathy work to his advantage. This strategy is most apparent in his dealings with the real or symbolic fathers of the novel, with whom he characteristically assumes the role of the well-bred, highborn son.[11] When engaged in such conversations, the chevalier does not ask the father in question to forgive his trangressions against familial honor or the laws of the land; rather, he embarks on a campaign of touching words and gestures that is expressly designed to soften his interlocutor's heart.

The first instance of this campaign occurs early in the novel, when the chevalier has been forcibly returned to the family home after meeting and eloping with Manon. Des Grieux senior greets his son in a warm but teasing spirit: after learning that the young man still naively believes that Manon truly loves him for himself (and not his illustrious name), the father laughs: "'Ha, ha, ha!' he exclaimed, laughing with all his might. 'That's excellent! You're a fine dupe, and I like to see those sentiments in you'" (*ML*, 41). Des Grieux junior is so mortified by his father's comic perspective on his love story that he stages a dramatic scene of tragic proportions: "I fell on the floor senseless and unconscious. Prompt aid restored me to my senses, and I opened my eyes only to shed a torrent of tears, and my mouth only to utter the saddest and most touching laments. My father, who has always loved me tenderly, tried with all his affection to console me . . . I threw myself at his knees; I conjured him, clasping my hands, to let me return to Paris and go put a dagger into B . . . " (42). The father is clearly touched by the intense sensibility exhibited by his son, for whom he feels such tender affection that he offers to find him a Manon lookalike who would be more faithful. Des Grieux senior does not, however, relent in his resolution to keep des Grieux junior away from a woman that he, like the novel's other paternal figures, judges to be "a dangerous person" (156). The chevalier's histrionics consequently fail to achieve their intended effect of restoring his freedom so that he can pursue his amorous obsession.

That does not stop des Grieux from trying the strategy again: he applies it repeatedly during his imprisonment in Saint-Lazare, which follows the unsuccessful attempt orchestrated by Manon's brother Lescaut to dupe the wealthy M. de G . . . M . . . out of a considerable sum of money and jewelry. Upon his arrival at Saint-Lazare, the chevalier is greeted cordially by its father superior, who expresses the hope that the young man will be inspired to eschew the disorders of which he is accused and embrace instead the pleasures of virtue and religion. Des Grieux reacts to this exhortation by bursting into tears and showing "all the signs of frightful despair," which moves the father superior to console the young man by reminding him of his family name and extolling his "gentle and amiable nature" and "excellent basic character" (*ML*, 82–83). Des Grieux decides to make the most of the superior's high opinion of him, as he explains in a long confessional comment that is worth quoting in its entirety:

> I was delighted to see that he had this opinion of me. I resolved to confirm it by behavior that could satisfy him completely, convinced that this was the surest way to shorten my imprisonment. I asked him for books. He was surprised that when he left me the choice of those authors that I wanted to read I decided on a few serious authors. I pretended to apply

myself to study with the utmost assiduity, and thus I gave him on every occasion, proofs of the change he wished for.

However, this was only external. I must confess it to my shame, I played a hypocrite's role at Saint-Lazare. Instead of studying, when I was alone, I did nothing but bemoan my destiny. I cursed my prison and the tyranny that detained me there . . . I had no hope except in the success of my hypocrisy. I carefully observed the Superior's face and remarks in order to make sure what he thought of me; and I made it my study to please him, as the arbiter of my destiny.   (83–84)

In fact, des Grieux's cunning and his conning tactics entail not merely pleasing the father superior but also making him so sympathetic that he will intervene with the authorities on des Grieux's behalf. This strategy works so effectively that even after des Grieux has brutally attacked M. de G . . . M . . . during a prison visit, the superior takes the side not of the victim but of the culprit; when G . . . M . . . demands that the chevalier be punished, the superior replies: "It is not with a person of the Chevalier's birth that we deal in that way. Moreover, he is so gentle and honorable that is is hard for me to understand his having gone to this extreme without strong reasons" (86). Ultimately, of course, the only reward that the father superior of Saint-Lazare gets for his sympathy is to be blamed for causing the death of the servant whom the chevalier shoots while breaking out of prison ("'See what you have caused, Father,' I said rather proudly to my guide" [96–97]).

Des Grieux does not merely exploit refined sensibility: he also claims to feel it to an extraordinary degree, not just in his great capacity for amorous passion but also in the full range of his emotions.[12] In other words, sensibility is both the active ingredient in the aristocratic code of sympathy that the chevalier exploits with characters like the father superior and the key defining term in his seemingly sincere self-image as an exceptional young nobleman. Des Grieux sketches this image while relating the Saint-Lazare episode, which he interrupts to reflect upon the intense shame and sorrow he felt upon finding himself imprisoned:

The ordinary run of men are susceptible [*sensible*] to only five or six passions, in the circle of which their lives pass, and to which all their agitations are limited. Take from them love and hate, pleasure and pain, hope and fear, and they feel nothing any more. But persons of a nobler character can be moved in a thousand different ways; it seems as though they have more than five senses and can experience ideas and sensations that go beyond the ordinary limits of nature. And since they have a sense of this greatness that raises them above the common herd, there is nothing

of which they are more jealous . . . I had this sad advantage at Saint-
Lazare.   (*ML*, 82)[13]

In his own eyes, then, the chevalier belongs to a moral elite: he wears his sensibility as a badge of honor, a mark of both his high social pedigree and the extraordinary moral-physical constitution that gives him his expanded capacity
to think and feel. The problem with this self-portrait is that it comes fast on the
heels of one of the many questionable incidents in which des Grieux is implicated, however passively, over the course of his adventures with Manon. It is,
moreover, part of a series of aggrandizing self-portrayals to which he resorts
whenever he wants to reinforce the notion that he is superior to the "ordinary
run of men"—a group represented in *Manon Lescaut* by the characters who do
not, in des Grieux's eyes, measure up to him in sensibility. No character in the
novel is immune from that assessment: the chevalier is quick to brand other
people, including his own father, as "barbarous" and insensitive when they
thwart his desires (166).

Interestingly, the character whose sensibility is most problematic is Manon,
who may resemble des Grieux in physical beauty but is no match for him in
beauty of spirit, which is the key to his vision of himself and of the world. Although the chevalier often invokes hyperbolical terms like "my dear queen"
and "angelic sweetness" to describe his charming mistress (*ML*, 50, 105), he
just as frequently excoriates her for lacking the refined sentiments necessary to
appreciate him and his extraordinary love. When faced with written proof of
Manon's practical and down-to-earth conviction that it is acceptable to sacrifice
the principle of fidelity in order to bring some money into their impoverished
household, des Grieux exclaims: "She dreads hunger. God of Love! What
coarseness of feeling! And what a bad response to my delicacy!" (72).[14] Manon,
therefore, could never be an acceptable soulmate to des Grieux—not just because his father and the other paternal figures disapprove of her, but also because she inevitably falls short when judged according to his high standards of
sensibility.

Clearly, Manon never strikes the right sympathetic cord with the men who
count; she can only raise their suspicions or affect them in an erotic manner.
And even though she dies a tragic death at the end, in the "desert" of
Louisiana, after being converted to the very image of a docile little woman, it
is not Manon but des Grieux who elicits the reader's sympathy in its conclusion. Des Grieux's moving account of Manon's hasty demise is virtually
eclipsed by his even more moving description of the exquisitely intense emotional pain he felt when she died and feels again each time that he recalls the
event. Just before getting to this part of his story, des Grieux exclaims: "For-

give me if I finish in a few words a story that kills me. I am telling you of a misfortune without precedent. My whole life is devoted to weeping over it. But although I bear it ever present in my memory, my soul seems to recoil in horror each time I try to tell of it" (*ML*, 187). The pathos of this entire episode—most particularly in the necrophilic graveside scene that follows Manon's death, when des Grieux lies down naked and suicidal upon the site where he has just buried Manon—resides, therefore, not so much in the events as in the halting and overwrought discursive representation of the chevalier's sensations. Once again, des Grieux underscores that only a man possessed of a sensibility as refined as his could possibly experience such emotions: "Do not ask me to describe my feelings or report her last words. I lost her; I received tokens of love from her even at the moment she was dying; that is all I have the strength to tell you of that fatal and deplorable event" (187–88). In death as in life, Manon's primary function is to serve as a catalyst for the expression of des Grieux's sensibility, which the novel's language presents as simultaneously admirable and excessive.[15]

Just as des Grieux's character is—in the words of the "Avis de l'auteur"— "a perpetual contrast of good sentiments and bad actions" (*ML*, 18), so, too, his use of the codes of sensibility is fundamentally ambiguous. On the one hand, des Grieux represents himself as the quintessential *homme sensible* or beautiful soul—a living embodiment of an innately noble moral property. On the other hand, he sees himself as a consummate deceiver, making his way in the world by deliberately manipulating the sensibilities of his wellborn interlocutors. Although the combination is disconcerting, it is not necessarily paradoxical; both sides of des Grieux's existence are necessary for him to function in the tragic register by which he defines his place in the world. To understand the logic of this twofold strategy, we must determine precisely where tragedy resides in this novel, and how it is connected to sensibility.

Various critics have taken up the question of the tragic dimension of *Manon Lescaut*. Thomas Kavanagh has suggested that des Grieux's struggle to survive in a world driven by the unpredictable and random forces of chance exemplifies a universal modern dilemma: "Des Grieux invites the reader's sympathetic identification not because Renoncour is careful to insist on his natural nobility and dignity but because his passivity stems, not from any fault of his own, but from his finding himself in a world ruled by chance . . . The story I tell, des Grieux invites his reader to agree, may be tragic, but it is mine and it is me. This interplay of active and passive solicits the reader's identification because its pardoning ambiguity corresponds to a need anchored in what must be the reader's own experience of the world."[16] I would contend, however, that what des Grieux solicits from his audience is not, properly speaking, identification;

for the various sympathetic interlocutors within the novel who react to des Grieux's tale (des Grieux's father, the father superior of Saint-Lazare, the Marquis de Renoncour, and so on) do not see themselves in him, largely because they do not view *their* experience of the new chance-driven world as tragic. Nor does it suffice to argue, as has Lionel Gossman, that des Grieux's tragic perspective reveals a general nostalgia for an outmoded aristocratic social order.[17] For one thing, that order is still working quite effectively to des Grieux's benefit; for another, the other noble characters of *Manon Lescaut* are just as conservative as he in their social philosophy but much more sensible (in the modern sense) and practical in their approach to contemporary social conditions.[18] Thus, the tragic element of des Grieux's story does not reside in a universal world view that he shares with his readers, be they modern or contemporary; it is, rather, part of the chevalier's more general effort to win his interlocutors' sympathy and indulgence.

Des Grieux's tragic vision of himself in the world is strategically useful because it allows him to appear and feel noble even when he is behaving quite ignobly. That strategy is strikingly illustrated by des Grieux's second-to-last encounter with his father, after the chevalier has once again been imprisoned (this time in Châtelet) for attempting to dupe the family of M. de G . . . M . . . . At the outset of this conversation, des Grieux senior is clearly fed up with his son's escapades and recognizes that des Grieux junior is trying to fool him by appearing contrite: "'How unhappy a father is when, after loving a son tenderly and sparing nothing to make him a decent man, he finally finds only a knave who dishonors him! . . . You aren't saying anything, you wretch,' he added; 'look at that counterfeit modesty and that hypocritical air of mildness; wouldn't anyone take him for the most honorable man of his family?'" (*ML*, 156).

The chevalier is unfazed by his father's insightful observations and quickly sets about changing the direction of the conversation: he insists that he has violated neither the family's honor nor his filial duty because the fault for his bad behavior lies not in himself, but in the fateful influences of passion and fortune. "It is love, you know it, that has caused all my errors," declares des Grieux, adding, "Fatal passion! Alas! . . . Love has made me too tender, too passionate, too faithful, and perhaps too indulgent toward the wishes of a wholly charming mistress: these are my crimes. Do you see one of them that dishonors you?" (156–57). This approach allows des Grieux to skirt the issue of what he actually did and emphasize instead the intense and irresistible sentiments that drove him—sentiments, he insists, that only a person endowed with his noble constitution can feel. By pleading for his father's compassion with tears in his eyes, the chevalier succeeds in winning him over: although des Grieux senior starts out in this scene seething with indignation, he ends up soft-hearted ("'Come, my poor Chevalier,' he said to me, 'come and embrace me; I do pity you'" [157]). In short, even though the father is not fooled by des Grieux's tragic pose, he nonetheless responds to it by granting all of the sympathy, and some of the aid, that his son requires.[19]

Des Grieux's recourse to the language and gestures of tragedy is therefore just one of the methods he employs for manipulating the sensibilities of the people who matter the most. As a consequence, he has not one but two means of escaping from the state of passivity in which his world seems to place him: he is active in "the control of reader and listener he achieves as the teller of his tale,"[20] and also in the control he exerts over his wellborn paternal interlocutors, whose sensible constitutions are hardwired to be touched by the tears, lamentations, and grandiose eloquence of such an attractive nobleman's son. Des Grieux does not conquer chance simply by taking charge of his life story through the act of narration: he also does so by taking charge of the sensibilities of certain key characters while he is undergoing the events of that story. This periodic activation or reactivation of his sympathetic ties to the noble class both reaffirms des Grieux's singularity and saves him from wandering too far away from that class.

Sympathetic sensibility is, in sum, the key to the special brand of solidarity that holds men of quality together as an exclusive group. To answer the question raised by the "Avis de l'auteur," it does not much matter whether des Grieux is a worthy recipient of the commiseration and compassion he elicits, for he is automatically granted the unconditional sympathy that noble fathers would grant their own children. Whether or not they are taken in by des Grieux's claims to tragic heroism, the patrician characters of the novel recognize him as one of their own and go to extraordinary lengths to draw him back into their community. Sensibility's ultimate purpose in *Manon Lescaut* is consequently to ensure the ongoing operation of a social security system for aristocrats, thanks to which des Grieux is guaranteed never to become a true victim of the outside world—a world that would have little patience for him if he were just an oversensitive fellow without an impressive family name.

"Naturalizing" Aristocratic Sensibility in Marivaux and Graffigny

Despite their considerable differences in style and tone, *Les Égarements du coeur et de l'esprit* and *Manon Lescaut* both illustrate the strategic, instrumental value that was accorded to sensibility by the elite class of early-eighteenth-century French society. For the characters who represent that social class in these novels, sensibility provides a highly effective means of communing—that is, of signaling or eliciting "interest," whether amorous or sympathetic. Yet even while they demonstrate the distinct advantages that aristocrats gain from using sensibility in this manner, Crébilllon and Prévost also suggest that such uses raise thorny ethical and psychological problems. Crébillon's aristocrats have so formalized the process by which sentiment and sensibility are communicated that the properties themselves are on the verge of losing any real moral anchor; and Prévost's, as represented by the Chevalier des Grieux, have no qualms about exploiting the mechanisms of sympathy even when their conduct is reprehensible. Although those problems are not entirely solved in Marivaux's *La Vie de Marianne* and Graffigny's *Lettres d'une Péruvienne*, they are cast in an intriguing new light. In each of these works, sensibility is not the exclusive privilege of those who belong to the insular world of the social elite. Rather, it is also ascribed to a young woman who, because she comes into that world from the outside, presents some interesting challenges to the typical operations of aristocratic sensibility.

❧ ☙

As in the novels we have just examined, the first-person narrator of *La Vie de Marianne* is amply endowed with the special qualities necessary to make an eighteenth-century fictional character "interesting." Marianne's qualities are incomplete, however: she possesses the graceful physiognomy, refined sentiments, and delicacy that mark the wellborn, yet she has been deprived of the corresponding name and social standing by an irresolvably mysterious accident of birth.[21] Marianne's saga thus concerns not just the difficulties and peripeteia of a social initiation, but also a quest for the elevated social identity to which she believes herself destined. In his meticulous stylistic study of this novel, Leo Spitzer singles out Marianne's noble, prideful *coeur* as her defining trait.[22] I would argue, however, that there is more than "heart" or courage at play in Marianne's zealous pursuit of her personal destiny: this character's very firm sense of self also draws much of its strength and direction from her sensibility. Sensibility, as represented in this novel, is at once the chief sign of Marianne's supposedly original nobleness, the major vehicle by which she recuperates that lost social quality, and the inner compass that guides her as she makes her way in the world.

Another brief critical caveat is in order here: by asserting that sensibility is central to *La Vie de Marianne*, I am not entirely contradicting Peter Brooks's argument that one should not read Marivaux as a sentimentalist, strictly speaking.[23] I wish, rather, to point out that Marivaux invests sensibility with some crucially important social and moral functions—functions that must, indeed, be understood in terms different from those commonly associated with senti-mentalism. For although Marivaux's novel abounds in scenes of effusive senti-ment, those scenes do not include a "discursive denial of the validity of social hierarchy," which David Denby identifies as one of the primary structural re-quirements of the sentimental genre of fiction that became popular in mid- to late-eighteenth-century France.[24] Far from denying the importance of social class distinctions, Marianne's narration of the overtly "touching" scenes from her past reinforces those distinctions: it is in those scenes that her *noblesse de coeur* is affirmed and put to the test. That is not to say that Denby's asser-tions about sentimentalism are wrong: the brand of melodramatically senti-mental narrative that became common in the late 1750s did, indeed, have some striking democratizing tendencies. Marivaux, however, wrote before the emer-gence of that genre; one must, therefore, recognize that the sociomoral context within which his characters speak of sentiment and sensibility remains dis-tinctly aristocratic.

In his essay "*Marianne*: The Making of an Author," John Heckman asserts that in *La Vie de Marianne*, "the appearance of sentiment represents an attempt both to create a new aristocracy and to bridge the social dichotomies exposed in various situations. It can also be an instrument of self-knowledge. In each case, however, sentiment fails to achieve its goal."[25] Although I agree with Heckman that there is something very fragile about the redefinition of nobility that Marianne's aristocratic friends promote in order to make a place for her in their world, I contend that his pessimistic view of sentiment in this novel is no more appropriate than Brooks's effort to deemphasize its significance. Mari-anne's sensibility is both heavily valorized and extremely useful to her throughout her adventures: it is fundamental both to the lucid self-awareness that allows her to negotiate the many new and disconcerting situations in which she finds herself, as well as to the mechanisms of sympathy and affinity that eventually gain her a place in the social upper class.

Marianne's sensibility first begins to function as an active faculty when she arrives in Paris at the age of fifteen: "My surprise at the sight of this noisy and populous town, at the multitude of the streets, and the magnificence of the buildings, exceeds all description. It was to me the empire of the moon: I was no longer myself, [I no longer remembered anything; I moved along], I stared at everything, I was astonished, and that was all" (*Virtuous Orphan*, 17; *VM*, 56).[26] Although her initial reaction to the noisy bustle of this new city is bewil-dered astonishment, that emotion soon gives way to an awareness of sensory pleasure: "I began to enjoy my enormous amazement: [I sensed myself mov-ing], I was charmed to find myself there, . . . the air I breathed thrilled my spir-its. There was a kind of sweet sympathy between my imagination and the objects that presented themselves to my sight" (*Virtuous Orphan*, 17; *VM*, 56). Marianne's description could come straight out of any number of contemporary treatises on the philosophy of mind; in describing her sense of a "sweet sympathy" between her imagination and the objects around her, she provides a textbook example of what eighteenth-century sensationalist thinkers perceived as the thinking subject's basic progression from pure sensations to conscious ideas.[27] Once she has experienced the sensory impressions that the stimulating milieu of Paris triggers in her, Marianne is able to imagine the countless pleasures this city undoubtedly contains. By the end of the passage, she still does not know exactly what it is that draws her to Paris, but she has developed a compelling instinctual sense that her destiny lies there. This episode, whose action consists solely in the pleasurable visceral sensations and primitive ideas that are aroused in Marianne by her first sight of Paris, is therefore an event of sensibility that initiates the process by which she gradually achieves full understanding, both of herself and of the world.

This event is quickly followed, however, by an equally intense initiatory experience, this time in the distress that sensibility can cause—a lesson Marianne learns when the woman who had raised her dies a few months after their arrival in Paris. Marianne realizes that she is utterly alone in the world, and is swiftly and violently overcome with grief: "The terror and anguish of my mind soon deprived me of my senses; [I had never in my life felt anything so terrible]; . . . I then realized how affectionately I loved her, and how much she had loved me; all of that was painted on my heart in such lively colors that the image devastated me" (*Virtuous Orphan*, 21; *VM*, 59). As she recounts this moment, Marianne-the-narrator makes an incisive reflection: "Oh, how much grief can enter into the human heart! How vast our capacity for sensibility! [*Jusqu'à quel degré peut-on être sensible!*] [I confess that my experience of the pain of which we are capable is one of the things that has most terrified me in my life, when I have thought about it; it is even responsible for my present inclination for living in seclusion . . . For my part, I think that only sentiment can give us information about ourselves that is at all trustworthy]" (*Virtuous Orphan*, 21; *VM*, 59–60). Far from being a renunciation of intellectual knowledge (as some critics, notably Georges Poulet, have maintained),[28] this passage affirms Marianne's acute capacity for deep feeling—and its formative role in the emergence of her moral, social, and intellectual character.

What transforms this capacity from something purely sentient into a social faculty is, predictably enough, social interaction. Marianne's talent for inspiring sympathetic emotions in others had been evident from the moment she was orphaned as a baby: "People came to see me from all the neighboring towns: [they wanted to see what sort of physiognomy I had] . . . Everybody took a kind of romantic fancy to me: they thought me pretty and my air engaging; and you can't imagine how much these natural accomplishments were to my advantage, or how noble and delicate it rendered the tenderness which they felt for me. They could not have caressed a little unfortunate princess with greater dignity; [the compassion I inspired was almost respect]" (*Virtuous Orphan*, 10; *VM*, 53). Although the villagers' reverent curiosity about Marianne gradually fades into the less compelling sentiment of simple charity, she continues to trigger a tender-hearted compassion in the people she meets. One of her earliest acquaintances in Paris is the kindly linen merchant Mme. Dutour, who accepts Marianne as shopgirl at the behest of her first noble benefactor, M. de Climal. Mme. Dutour sheds many a sympathetic tear for the young orphan, yet Marianne silently takes offense at Mme. Dutour's blunt manner of offering pity and consolation. This is what prompts Marianne to sense for the first time that she is out of place among those of coarse sensibilities: "I thought myself out of my true sphere and born for quite other company. Their blunt, vulgar freedom appeared very disagreeable to me; and their language was a kind of jargon, whose harshness offended the delicacy of my ears. I was already telling myself that in the polite world there must be something better than this; [I yearned for, I was sad to be deprived of this something better that I did not know. Tell me where that came from? Where had I gotten my delicacy? Was it in my blood? that may well be . . .]" (*Virtuous Orphan*, 31; *VM*, 68–69). This early realization that her sensibility is not just keen but *delicate* operates rather like an epiphany: it is what moves Marianne to embark on her lifelong quest to find *her* type of people, those whose sentiments and moral comportment truly match her own.

Marianne makes a few false starts as she pursues her quest, most notably with the duplicitous M. de Climal, a seemingly pious man who claims to be interested in the pretty but destitute young orphan simply because he is "sensitive to her misfortune" (*VM*, 65), but who turns out to have lecherous designs on her body. Although she succeeds in arousing a more welcomed interest in the young nobleman Valville during the erotically sentimental episode of her injured foot (*VM*, 93–107), Marianne does not finds a true sister soul until she meets Mme. de Miran, who by a stroke of luck shows up soon after Marianne has lost Climal's charitable support in part 3 of the novel.

In this episode, Marianne, tearful and distraught over the uncertainty of her future, seeks refuge in the chapel of a neighborhood convent, where an as-yet unidentified noblewoman just happens to be visiting; upon entering the chapel, the lady is immediately struck by the sight of Marianne absorbed in her lamentations: "She had scarcely entered when my plaintive moans reached her ears. She heard all I said, and saw me in a posture expressive of the deepest despair, while my thoughts were so swallowed up with my calamities that I even forgot where I was . . . My affliction, which appeared to her the most extreme, sensibly touched her; my youth, my shape, and perhaps, too, my dress, moved her to pity me" (*Virtuous Orphan*, 111; *VM*, 155–56). When Marianne at last senses that she is being watched, she lifts her head and meets the lady's gaze—a gaze in which Marianne is able to detect not only tender pity for her affliction, but also pleasure at her striking physiognomy. This wordless but soulful communion soon proves pivotal to the course of her life because the sympathetic compassion that she inspires in Mme. de Miran ultimately moves the lady to assume the role of Marianne's adoptive mother (*VM*, 168).[29]

Marianne's chance encounter with Mme. de Miran is central not only to her quest to find "this something better that I did not know," but also to the leitmotiv of sensibility in *La Vie de Marianne*. For what joins Marianne and Mme. de Miran is their shared *noblesse de coeur*, a quality that allows them to communicate in a manner that goes unperceived by lesser souls, like the prioress of the convent where Marianne is established as a boarder at Mme. de Miran's expense. More than words, what Marianne and her new benefactress exchange here are "tender attentions" and "secret sentimental courtesies" (*VM*, 162–63). Despite her lack of social education, young Marianne knows intuitively that Mme. de Miran is honoring her with a delicate consideration. She is therefore moved to reciprocate in kind: "I seized with transport, though very respectfully, the hand of this charming lady. I kissed it long, and bathed it with the most tender and delicious tears I ever shed in my life" (*Virtuous Orphan*, 117; *VM*, 163). Marianne's refined display of feeling is just what is needed to touch the heart of this exemplary lady, whose nobleness resides not so much in her illustrious social standing as in her extraordinarily kind, simple, and above all sensitive heart.[30]

It is Mme. de Miran's natural, uncorrupted sensibility and goodness that allow her to recognize Marianne's own exceptional qualities—a judgment that is confirmed early in part 4 during her second visit to the convent, on which she is accompanied by her friend, the equally noble-hearted Mme. Dorsin. Mme. Dorsin has no sooner set eyes on the young orphan than she remarks: "In truth, I never saw a more amiable form or an air more noble" (*Virtuous Orphan*, 131; *VM*, 174). After a few more decorous preliminaries that serve to establish a pact of mutual admiration among all three characters, the two aristocratic ladies launch into a conversation that reveals how intricately the various strands of Marianne's adventures are intertwined and also demonstrates the importance of sensibility in bringing about Marianne's rise in society.

As she listens silently to the ladies' dialogue, Marianne learns that Mme. de Miran is the mother of Valville, who has apparently been pining away in lovelorn melancholy ever since he met a mysterious young beauty with an injured foot while returning from mass. Marianne immediately realizes that she is listening to one of her own recent adventures and is greatly discomfited to hear Mme. Dorsin apply epithets like "little adventuress" and "grisette" to the mystery girl of the tale—a girl whom Mme. de Miran is determined to track down so that she might salvage the proper aristocratic marriage she has arranged for her son (*VM*, 176–78). Despairing over this latest twist in her fortunes, Marianne can no longer contain herself; in a voice broken with sobs, she confesses that she is the girl who has unwittingly stolen Valville's heart and urges her benefactress to abandon her: "It is not natural that you should preserve the character of a mother to an orphan whom you know not, whilst she afflicts you, and since a sight of her has taught your son to disobey you!" (*Virtuous Orphan*, 137; *VM*, 179).

This revelation places Mme. de Miran in a vexing predicament because it pits her sympathetic sentiments as Marianne's adoptive mother against her maternal responsibilities to Valville. Once again, however, Marianne's refined sensibility comes to the rescue: when asked whether she has heard from Valville since entering the convent, Marianne answers in a manner that is so guileless and self-effacing that she not only preserves her bond to Mme. de Miran, but also wins over Mme. Dorsin quite completely. It is here that the episode reaches its sentimental climax, with all three characters so moved that they are virtually faint with emotion: "'Yes, she is my child more than ever,' replied my benefactress, with a tenderness that would not permit her saying any more; and she immediately gave me her hand, which I took hold of as well as the grate would permit me, and kissed it for a long time [as I kneeled, so touched myself] that I was almost suffocated with tears. This was followed by a short silence which was so affecting that I can't yet think of it without feeling myself moved from the bottom of my soul" (*Virtuous Orphan*, 138; *VM*, 181). Only Mme. Dorsin can summon enough composure to express the deep feeling of the moment: "I have never in my life been so moved as I am now. I don't know which of the two I love most, the mother or the daughter."

Throughout part 4, Mme. de Miran continues to be impressed, both intellectually and viscerally, by the dignified deportment and unfailing moral generosity that Marianne exhibits even when she must tell Valville that their love is impossible: "I am ignorant to whom I owe my birth; I lost my parents without knowing them; and I have neither fortune nor relation. We are not made for each other" (*Virtuous Orphan*, 147; *VM*, 191). Marianne's blunt and concise account of her situation makes her all the more admirable and worthy—not only to Valville but to Mme. de Miran as well. Mme. de Miran therefore resolves to challenge the hierarchical dictates of aristocratic convention, which would condemn a union between Valville and Marianne as "monstrous," by giving her blessing to their marriage.[31] Marianne responds to this news in a characteristically intense, emotive manner: "Oh my dear mother . . . I am overcome; I cannot contain my gratitude and tenderness" (*Virtuous Orphan*, 156; *VM*, 200). Then she throws herself on her knees, the better to grasp Mme. de Miran's hand through the bars of the convent parlor.

Young Marianne thus begins part 4 of *La Vie de Marianne* facing the possible loss of Mme. de Miran's benevolent friendship, but ends up as Valville's intended bride and—even more importantly, according to the decorously tender language Marianne uses when addressing this lady—as Mme. de Miran's future daughter-in-law. The pattern that is now established for the events of Marianne's life unfolds as follows: she is placed in a difficult social situation, responds to it with great nobleness of spirit, gains the compassion and esteem of her aristocratic friends, and basks for a time in their appreciation of her qualities, until another potentially humiliating or catastrophic situation crops up. In all of these situations, sensibility intervenes both to save Marianne from a loss of face or position and to reaffirm and strengthen her ties to sympathetic members of the social upper class. In other words, Marivaux's novel shifts into a sentimentalist narrative style each time that Marianne is subjected to an aristocratic litmus test—that is, whenever the pressures of upper-class social convention become so intense that she and her champions must once again prove that she possesses the traits necessary to qualify as a person of "quality" worthy of marrying Valville.

These social ordeals invariably turn into teary-eyed collective testimonials to the extraordinary noble qualities that come so naturally to Marianne. The effect of such episodes is not to cast Marianne as a pathetic victim, nor to underplay the significance of her unfortunately obscured origins—narrative procedures that would become commonplace in the sentimentalist literature that became popular later in the eighteenth century. Rather, Marianne's testing scenes are designed to demonstrate that she is an exceptional being who makes such a deep impression on aristocratic hearts and minds that most, if not all, are moved to grant her the status of equal within their privileged social order.

The most decisive of such scenes occurs after Marianne is kidnapped by Mme. de Miran's relatives in part 6 and faces a long and difficult public interrogation conducted by the venerable government minister who has been enlisted as family spokesman. Although she must initially face her adversaries alone, Marianne is given an hospitable reception by the minister, who remarks with a smile: "She is very pretty, and Valville is quite excusable" (*Virtuous Orphan*, 238; *VM*, 289).[32] Most of the other assembled family members are not, however, nearly so well-disposed to Marianne because they believe that the family name will be sullied if her marriage to Valville proceeds. The leader of the hostile relatives wastes no time in making her antipathy toward Marianne obvious: she cuts short the minister's praise for the young orphan's charms and leads her cohorts in derisive laughter when Marianne responds to his questions in her standard dignified tone. This sour-tempered "harpy" endeavors throughout the episode to cut Marianne down to nonaristocratic size.[33] Fortunately, however, Mme. de Miran and Valville burst into the room at the turn of parts 6 and 7 and swiftly set about defending Marianne against those who see her as a mere social climber.

Their arrival sets the stage for the novel's climactic showdown between the aristocratic characters who are sensitive to Marianne's noble qualities and those who are not. This confrontation is also Mme. de Miran's shining moment as Marianne's protectress. Mme. de Miran explains her intense attachment to Marianne in terms not just of affection but of astonished admiration: "She has a heart, a soul, a manner of thinking which would astonish you. You know my dear child possesses nothing, and yet you can't imagine how noble, how generous, how disinterested I have found her. I esteem her even more than I love her. I have seen such instances of the greatness of her soul as have moved even the bottom of my heart" (*Virtuous Orphan*, 240; *VM*, 293). She then gives her version of Marianne's oft-recounted life story: "There is such probable evidence, as arises almost to a certainty, that her father and mother who were murdered with their attendants, when she was but two or three years old, were foreigners of the greatest distinction" (*Virtuous Orphan*, 243; *VM*, 297). Mme. de Miran ends with a resounding public testimonial to Marianne's inherent aristocratic nature: "I am sorry you force me to say before her that her person, which even to you appears agreeable, is indeed her least distinguishing feature, and I assure you that by her wit, the amiable qualities of her mind, and by the nobleness of her proceeding, she has proved herself to be as much a lady as any other person of what rank soever . . . [she owes all of this not to experience in the world, nor to the education she has received, which has been extremely simple; *it must be in her blood,* and that in my opinion is the essential thing]" (*Virtuous Orphan*, 244; *VM*, 297–98; my emphasis).

However heartfelt, Mme. de Miran's profession of faith in Marianne's nobility does not sway the audience. Although the minister grants that "from what you have told us, it is very probable that she is of noble extraction," he insists that Marianne accept an arranged marriage to a coarse young bourgeois named M. Villot, or take the veil and become a nun, or be banished from Paris (*Virtuous Orphan*, 246; *VM*, 299–300). When Marianne is called upon to announce her decision, she rises to the occasion with breathtaking magnanimity. After expressing her deep love and gratitude to Mme. de Miran for having "the generosity to love me so well, notwithstanding the efforts of those who would make you blush for it," she rejects all of the proposed options but renounces any claim to Valville's heart, out of fear that she would bring him a lifetime of public ridicule and opprobrium. And she ends her speech with "a torrent of tears" (*Virtuous Orphan*, 252–53; *VM*, 303–4).

Unlike Mme. de Miran's speech, Marianne's pathos-laced harangue is highly effective because it both resolves the Valville family dispute and prepares the episode's crowning sentimental tableau. At the center of this tableau is the minister who has overseen the meeting: after hearing Marianne's renunciation of Valville, he declares her more than worthy of Mme. de Miran's tender esteem and tells her that she is free to go. With that, he tries to withdraw but is held back by Marianne: "Seized with a sudden transport, I threw myself at his feet with a rapidity more eloquent and more expressive than all I could have said. Nor could I utter a word to thank him for the gracious sentiments he had expressed in my favor. He raised me immediately with an air that showed that this action agreeably surprised and moved him; [I noticed that it had also pleased the entire company]" (*Virtuous Orphan*, 254; *VM*, 305). It is this spontaneous outburst of sensibility that truly carries the day for Marianne and her supporters. The minister is so affected by this dramatically noble gesture that he effectively drops any official objection to the proposed marriage of Marianne and Valville. Thereafter, virtually everyone present is swept up in a collective wave of tender feelings—except for the sour-tempered relative, who comments acerbically, "I am not extremely sensitive to such romantic [*romanesques*] virtues," and then stomps out in a huff (*Virtuous Orphan*, 254; *VM*, 305). This affront is quickly covered over by the rest of the audience, who converge upon Marianne and her protectress to offer their apologies for the ordeal and their praise for Marianne's many endearing qualities.

The episode thus ends on a triumphant but somewhat ambiguous note: on the one hand, refined sensibility wins out over a formidable display of social prejudice, thanks largely to Marianne's ability to appeal to aristocratic sympathies in both her words and her actions. On the other hand, the victory falls short, because the hostile relative steadfastly refuses to be affected by Marianne in a sympathetic way. Although that woman's antipathy toward Marianne is undercut throughout the narration of the scene, her parting words are nonetheless significant. For, by declaring herself to be "insensitive" to Marianne's noble virtues and drawing attention to their *romanesque* quality, this noblewoman implies that Marianne's much-touted *noblesse de coeur* is a fictional construction created by a girl who might well be nothing but a "little adventuress." As the hostile relative puts it, soft-hearted ladies like Mme. de Miran are free to love Marianne, but they should not forget that they have "relations and allies whose honor ought not to be sullied" (*Virtuous Orphan*, 245; *VM*, 298). This argument points up a potential problem in the tender feelings that Marianne triggers in most of the aristocrats she encounters: their sympathy for her is clearly a mutually gratifying sentiment, yet it might be neither well-founded nor in the best interests of their social class.

To a degree, this conundrum recalls the question that is raised about des Grieux in the "Avis de l'auteur" in *Manon Lescaut*: should an "interesting" but ambiguous character be accorded the sympathy and compassion that sensitive persons of quality seem so eager to bestow upon him or her? In both novels, albeit it for different reasons, the answer is yes. Although Marianne, in contrast to des Grieux, is not guaranteed automatic sympathy from the aristocrats she encounters, she nonetheless generally succeeds in winning it (in part, by repeatedly demonstrating her worthiness). This is, in fact, the major thematic thread of the latter half of *La Vie de Marianne*, where, even though Marianne's fate often seems precarious, she is always assured of sympathy and admiration from some well-placed aristocrat. Even at the end of the novel, when Marianne loses Valville's heart to a rival, her *noblesse de coeur* continues to exert its powerfully touching influence over the noble characters she encounters, both old and new.

Because Marianne's story of her life does not continue after part 8 (it is replaced by the also unfinished tale of the woe-begotten nun Tervire), we as readers never know with any certainty where she ends up in the aristocratic social world. The event that dominates this part of the novel is Marianne's discovery that Valville has fallen in love with her new friend Mlle. Varthon. As Marianne-the-narrator wryly observes, her seemingly perfect lover thus turns out to be not an ideal "hero of a novel," but rather a man as fickle-hearted as any typical Frenchman of the day (*VM*, 335–36). Interestingly, she attributes Valville's infidelity to the very property that had originally drawn him to her: his ardent sensibility, which apparently made him too susceptible to new impressions to remain faithful to one woman.[34] The fading of Valville's amorous feelings for Marianne does not, however, signal a general decline in her ability to find a place in the hearts of sensitive aristocrats.[35] On the contrary, all of Marianne's experiences in part 8, where she comes to terms with the realization that she is no longer destined to be Valville's wife, confirm her unique capacity to maintain a privileged social position solely by inspiring sympathy, tenderness, and esteem in the right people. Although it is true that certain aspects of part 8 accentuate the picaresque, fate-driven quality of Marianne's life—she is even moved to consider renouncing the overly eventful world in order to become a nun (*VM*, 377)—the safety net of sympathetic sensibility surrounding her is still firmly in place. Even after Marianne has broken with the unfaithful Valville, Mme. de Miran exclaims, "Come, my dear daughter, endeavor to console thyself . . . thou hast still a mother. Dost thou esteem her as nothing?" and Mme. Dorsin joins in by declaring herself "a thousand times more her friend . . . indeed it is not her that I pity, it is Mr. de Valville. His loss is infinitely greater than hers" (*Virtuous Orphan*, 306; *VM*, 365). Marianne thus emerges from this crisis with her sentimental bonds to these noblewomen more solidly established than ever—whereas Valville loses the esteem of his mother, her friends, and even his new love interest (*VM*, 337, 371).

Soon thereafter, a new wrinkle is introduced into the plot when an unnamed aristocrat suddenly pays Mme. de Miran a social call. This friend, described as "an old friend of the family, an officer, a person of quality, and a little advanced in years," explains that his interest in Marianne has been piqued by both the "encomiums" he has heard about her and the rumors of her recent split from Valville (*Virtuous Orphan*, 311; *VM*, 371). After learning that Valville has indeed abandoned "this estimable girl, this Marianne so dear to him, and so worthy of being so," the officer receives permission from Mme. de Miran to visit Marianne at her convent. The meeting could not be more felicitous: Marianne is favorably impressed by the officer as soon as she sees his distinguished, kindly physiognomy, and he wastes no time in announcing his intentions: "I am known to be a man of honor, and a sincere, sociable, honest, plain-dealer. Ever since I heard of your character you have been the object of my esteem, my respect, my admiration. This I assure you, Mademoiselle, is strictly true. I am informed of your affairs. Mr. de Valville, unhappily for himself, is guilty of inconstancy. I am my own master, I enjoy an estate of twenty-five thousand livres a year, and I offer them to you, Mademoiselle. They shall be at your service whenever you please, after you have consulted with Mme. de Miran upon it" (*Virtuous Orphan*, 313; *VM*, 373). When Marianne discreetly asks whether he knows the whole story of her life, the officer declares that this is precisely what has moved him to make his extraordinary proposition of marriage. And when she cautions that he, like Valville, might eventually be disheartened by the thought of allying himself with a former charity case, he declares that he has come not as a lover (lovers being inconstant, by nature) but as one who admires the matchless qualities of Marianne's soul and is thus unconcerned by her lack of proper family connections (*VM*, 374).

Part 8 ends without indicating whether Marianne decides for or against the officer's proposal. However, even though the novel leaves us in suspense about Marianne's future, this non-ending also suggests that she would never lack for noble benefactors ready to replace the old ones. For what the gentlemanly military officer represents is not just a last-minute plot device, but also a ideal *type* of aristocrat: the kind who can rise above concern with the conventional marks of social legitimacy and immediately recognize Marianne's qualities. This episode makes it clear that Marianne has become something of a myth within the aristocratic social order that serves as backdrop to her tale. Her mythic quality does not render her suspect as an object of sympathy, at least not to the true aristocrats of the novel. To the contrary, it only makes her all the more admirable, in that she is able to move persons of quality who have not even met her. When characters like Mme. de Miran and the gentlemanly officer act on Marianne's behalf purely on the strength of her stirring story, they become active co-authors to the myth that comes to surround her.[36]

To the very last, therefore, Marianne remains an interesting but problematic being for the aristocrats who encounter her: although she can never prove it positively, she tends to convince the wellborn that she truly is noble because she is so effective at using her sensibility and engaging their own. Indeed, Marianne is so successful at appealing to the higher sentiments of aristocrats that the refusal to be sympathetic towards her is marked by the novel as an ill-founded impulse that is not noble but ignoble. The sentimental scenes that abound in *La Vie de Marianne* consequently serve to divide the upper-class characters into two camps, according to the sensitivity and courage that they exhibit, or fail to exhibit, in their response to the novel's young heroine. Because these scenes are dominated by the sensitive, high-minded, and perhaps gullible camp of aristocrats, Marianne's adventures become the stuff of legend within the world that is represented by the novel; the opposing camp of aristocrats, by contrast, comes across as a small group of old-school blue bloods who are simply mean-spirited, if not denatured. The "natural" sensibility that triumphs in Marivaux's novel is thus highly class-specific: it is the type of sensibility that all good aristocrats should carry within themselves, so that they can recognize exceptional souls like Marianne who just happen to have lost some of the usual marks of social distinction.

The brand of sentimentalism that one finds in *La Vie de Marianne* is thus directed not at eliminating class distinctions but rather at legitimizing them, by positing "natural" sensibility as a foolproof means of distinguishing persons of quality from commoners. It is this principle that allows Marianne to rise from obscure circumstances into the upper echelons of French society without posing an irremediable threat to the existing social order (or, at least, not in the minds of her benefactors). By the same token, "natural" sensibility serves in the novel to differentiate those who are truly noble in heart and mind from those who are aristocratic only in title. With its repeated appeals to acting upon one's most refined sentiments, the novel issues a call for reform *within* the worldly social universe it depicts. As an outsider who is accepted into aristo-

cratic society on the strength of her *noblesse de sentiment,* Marianne is a rectify-
ing, remedial agent: she effectively brings new blood, new life, into an aging
sociomoral code.

❧ ❧

Zilia, the heroine of the *Lettres d'une Péruvienne,* is even more of an outsider:
she is imported from sixteenth-century Peru into the France of the 1740s as an
Incan counterpoint to contemporary French customs and mores. She is also endowed with great natural sensibility—a quality that, interestingly, has troubled
some of the novel's recent feminist champions. Although they do not deny that
sensibility is given a privileged status in Graffigny's novel, these critics express
reservations about its connotations, largely because they view the novel of sensibility as a genre based solely on the artificial and/or superficial exaltation of
sentimentality.[37] Hence their tendency to depict Zilia not as a sentimental heroine, but rather as a cultural critic engaged in a process of philosophical "coming to consciousness."[38] Sensibility's importance in the *Lettres d'une Péruvienne*
should not, however, be so swiftly discounted because it is this concept that allows Graffigny to give a distinctly philosophical and sociocritical cast to what
might otherwise be read as a one-sided amorous correspondence.[39] Nor should
we underestimate the significance of the novel's properly sentimental aspect:
Zilia's discourse is infused with a lyrical emotional intensity that, rather than
being mawkish, has a sensual fervor which intermingles quite effectively with
the epistemological chronicle of her coming-to-consciousness. Indeed, Graffigny's manner of constructing Zilia as a sensible being reflects the full breadth
of conceptual purposes to which sensibility could be put during the first half of
the eighteenth century: Zilia is simultaneously a sentimental heroine, a philosophical subject, and a noble savage figure whose pure, uncorrupted sensibility
is systematically contrasted to the mannered delicacy of the French characters ·
she encounters.

To determine precisely how sensibility operates in this novel, one must first
consider how it is affected by Zilia's exotic status or "Peruvianness." There is,
in fact, some disagreement among the work's commentators as to whether Zilia
is exotic, and in what manner. One school of thought is represented by Julia V.
Douthwaite, who describes Zilia as a female, New World version of the "exotic
spy"—a character whom Graffigny created to correct the political and discursive injustices that earlier Europeans had committed against Peruvian culture.[40]
By contrast, Jack Undank insists that, underneath the differences the novel presents between the Peruvians and the French, "Zilia is, after all, recognizably . . .
French, an unmistakable blend of ideas promoted by Fontenelle, Fénelon,

Marivaux and others."[41] Interestingly, although these critics advance very different interpretations of Zilia's titular Peruvianness, they both find something nostalgically "primitive" about her: Douthwaite links the novel to the contemporary philosophical practice of evoking a mythical state of nature, whereas Undank sees Zilia's Peruvianness as a moral-aesthetic metaphor for a universal, feminine ideal of true feeling and transparent expression.[42] My view of Graffigny's purpose in choosing a Peruvian noblewoman as her protagonist lies somewhere in between. First, I would argue that one should not over-politicize Graffigny's recourse to primitivism, nor polemicize her relationship to Montesquieu and other male philosophes who also meditated on the meanings of such terms as *savage* versus *civilized*.[43] Second, although I agree with Undank that Graffigny uses Zilia to espouse many of the universal ethical principles central to Enlightenment thought, I contend that the sensibility Zilia embodies is not so much feminine as *different* from the denatured sensibility of the aristocratic French characters of the novel.

In the "Introduction historique" to the *Lettres d'une Péruvienne*, Graffigny provides a detailed tableau of the lost Incan civilization from which her heroine supposedly originated. Although she calls the Incas superstitious and naïve (qualities she holds responsible for their all-too-easy capitulation to Peru's Spanish invaders two centuries earlier), she praises their native intellect and simple, rational, and humane moral-social code. Graffigny's tendency to glorify Peruvian morality is most apparent in her lengthy description of their pedagogical practices:

> Young people were brought up with all the care required by the happy simplicity of their moral beliefs . . . Modesty and mutual consideration were the cornerstones of their child rearing. Those who were assigned this task were careful to correct their charges' first failings and to halt the progress of any budding passions, or to divert them to the benefit of society. There are certain virtues that imply many others. To give some idea of the Peruvians', suffice it to say that before the landing of the Spaniards, it was taken for granted that no Peruvian had ever lied.
>
> The Amautas, that nation's version of our philosophes, taught the young of the discoveries made in the sciences. Their nation was still in its infancy in that respect but in the prime of its happiness.[44]

This glowing account of the Incas' teaching methods foreshadows both of the pedagogical projects in which Zilia becomes engaged in the novel. Because her knowledge of the sciences is indeed childlike at the outset, she inevitably has much to learn when she is introduced to the more complex French civilization by Déterville, the French aristocrat who rescues her from the Spaniards. At the same time, thanks to her wholesome, natural, and well-developed moral qualities, Zilia also becomes a moral tutor to her French acquaintances. In other words, even though she spends the better part of the novel undergoing a painstaking process of intellectual enlightenment, Zilia consistently holds the status of a very un-French ethical exemplar. One might say, then, that Graffigny's purpose in harking back to sixteenth-century Peru is to locate the moral qualities she finds lacking in her so-called enlightened century: modesty, empathetic sensibility, honesty, and moderation. By bringing these virtues into contemporary French aristocratic society in the person of her exotic heroine, Graffigny both underscores their rarity and proposes an antidote to the artificial mores that have, in her mind, replaced these qualities in France.

In keeping with the allegorical tendencies of primitivist exoticism, the distance between Zilia's Peruvian moral traits and those attributed to the French is described in terms that are not so much ethnic or geographical as moral and temporal. That is, Zilia represents what the French once were naturally, and what she believes they could be again, if only they had better examples to guide them. In one of her later letters to her fiancé Aza, the Incan Sun King now exiled in Spain, Zilia characterizes the French as follows: "Naturally sensitive and moved by virtue, they are, without exception that I have seen, tender listeners to the account I am frequently compelled to give of the forthrightness of our hearts, the candor of our sentiments, and the simplicity of our manners. Were they to live among us, they would become virtuous, for example and custom are the tyrants ruling their behavior" (*LP*, letter 32, p. 138). Of course, to be able to dig beneath the surface of the French people and perceive their propensity for virtue, Zilia must first acquire sufficient linguistic and observational skills. Graffigny therefore subjects her heroine to a step-by-step apprenticeship in French language, customs, technology, and arts and sciences. As in all of her experiences, Zilia's native sensibility serves not only as her psychological, moral, and intellectual guide, but also as the force that arouses the sympathies of Déterville and his sister Céline, who make it their mission to protect her, educate her, and help her find a suitable place in French society.

Early in the novel, Zilia's acute capacity for feeling is dramatized in two distinct but interrelated psychological registers: amorous and existential. Her mood swings between great joy and suicidal despair as she tries to determine whether she will be reunited with her dear Aza, to whom she addresses the bulk of her correspondence (first via messages woven out of cords, or *quipus,* and then via letters). Zilia is nearly delirious with sensuous pleasure the first time that Aza manages to contact her after they have been separated: "The treasures of Love are open to me; I draw from them an exquisite pleasure that intoxicates my soul. As I unravel the secrets of your heart, mine bathes in a perfumed sea" (*LP*, letter 2, pp. 22–23). Soon thereafter, however, she shifts to the opposite extreme, when she realizes that she is in a "floating house" that is carrying her away from Peru: "I am losing that which I love, and the universe is destroyed for me. It is nothing more than a vast desert that I fill with the cries of my love. Hear them, dear object of my tenderness, be moved by them, allow me to die" (letter 6, p. 42). In this state, Zilia's intense sensibility is engaged at a level even more profound than that of her love for Aza: it is essential to her very sense of being. That sense of being is sorely tested throughout the novel, most particularly during Zilia's early experiences, when she struggles poignantly to make sense of the strange new objects she is encountering: "Everything that is offered to my eyes strikes, surprises, and astonishes me, leaving me with only a vague impression and a dumbfounded sense of confusion from which I do not even seek to deliver myself" (letter 10, p. 50). Zilia thus undertakes her intellectual and social journey in a state of pure, uncomprehending sentience, bewildered by the obstacles she faces both in understanding the new world around her and in communicating—be it with Aza or with the Europeans into whose midst she has been thrust.

Communication is a major theme of *Les Lettres d'une Péruvienne*, beginning with the *quipus* conceit which Graffigny uses to give a literal texture to Zilia's correspondence.[45] This conceit sets up one of the novel's central episodes: the dramatic moment when Zilia's cords run out and she is forced to master spoken and written French. When she is finally able to resume her correspondence with Aza after a lapse of six months, Zilia is exultant: "I am still barely able to form these figures that I rush to make the interpreters of my tenderness. I feel myself being brought back to life by this tender occupation. Restored to myself, I feel as if I am beginning to live again. Oh Aza, how dear you are to me, what joy I feel in telling you so, in depicting this fact, in giving this sentiment all the kinds of existence it can have!" (letter 18, p. 80).

Clearly, Zilia regards the act of writing to Aza as vital to her existence. Yet she also uses letter-writing for purposes that go beyond that of amorous effusion: writing allows her to keep a comprehensive written memoir of her life outside of Peru, to order her evolving ideas about European society, to reaffirm her native principles, and to unburden herself emotionally to a sympathetic Peruvian ear. Zilia takes comfort in the therapeutic role of her letters even during the painful periods when she is unsure of where Aza is, or whether he is still alive (letter 23, p. 103). One might even say that Zilia writes in order to correspond not just with Aza but also with her own Peruvianness. For Aza represents more than the particular Incan whom Zilia loves and hopes to marry; Aza is also the name that Zilia gives to the set of simple, absolute principles that she uses to maintain her sense of self and to judge the often reprehensible social and moral practices of the Europeans she encounters.

What Aza embodies in Zilia's mind is a universal ideal of virtue, empathetic humanity, and honesty—an ideal that she equates with the entire Peruvian culture and struggles to find in the strangers who now surround her. Sensibility is essential to this process because it provides Zilia with a seemingly infallible gauge for assessing the moral character of others. In letter 1, she portrays the Spaniards who have ravaged her country as members of a race so barbarous, cruel, and insensitive that they must be constitutionally deformed: "Far from being moved by my entreaties, my abductors are not even touched by my tears; deaf to my language, they understand no better the cries of my despair. What people is so ferocious as to be unmoved by signs of pain? What arid desert witnessed the birth of humans insensitive to the voice of nature groaning?" (letter 1, p. 18). Soon thereafter, when she passes from the hands of the "Spanish savages" into those of the French, Zilia observes a considerable improvement: the French seem kinder and more humane than her first captors, even though their behavior often perplexes her (letter 4, pp. 35–36). This use of sensibility as an absolute ethical standard pervades Zilia's judgments on Parisian aristocratic society—judgments that, however critical, reinforce her sense that the French are admirably affable, benevolent, and intelligent (letter 11, p. 56).

As in *La Vie de Marianne*, the French characters of the *Lettres d'une Péruvienne* are divided into two camps, according to whether or not they are sensitive to the plight of the heroine. Zilia immediately recognizes that Déterville is sensitive, kind, and naturally noble, even though she misinterprets his reverential treatment of her. She also instinctively perceives that Mme. Déterville is a vainglorious, denatured mother who receives her son coldly when he returns to Paris with Zilia in tow (letter 13, p. 64). Déterville's sister Céline, by contrast, embraces her brother with "natural tenderness" and treats Zilia kindly: "Although I understood nothing of what she was telling me, her eyes, filled as they were with goodness, spoke to me in the universal language of kind hearts and inspired trust and friendliness in me" (65). Zilia is so impressed by the warmth and decency with which the younger Détervilles treat her that she exclaims a few letters later that they are more Peruvian than French in character (letter 15, p. 71).

In this early stage of naïveté and linguistic incapacity, Zilia mistakes Déterville for one of Aza's subordinates who, by showering her with gifts, is simply paying tribute to her as the Sun King's intended bride (letter 15, p. 72). She remains deluded about both her situation in France and Déterville's true sentiments until she masters the French language. Doing so brings Zilia a new lucidity that she welcomes for opening up a new universe but also regrets because she realizes that she is no longer in the realm of the Peruvian Sun. She also learns that Déterville's devotion to her stems not just from his natural benevolence but also from amorous passion—a sentiment that she considers inconceivable, in the Peruvian terms she uses to judge everything. After a long debate that culminates with Zilia insisting that she could never love anyone but Aza in that way, Déterville cries out in despair: "You will come to know this heart you scorn, you will see of what efforts a love such as mine is capable, and I will force you at least to pity me" (letter 23, p. 102).

The distressing emotions inspired by this episode provoke a fever in Zilia and a general state of crisis for each member of the sympathetic trio: Céline is furious with Zilia for rejecting her brother, and Déterville is despondent. Although Zilia soon recovers both her health and Céline's friendship, she finds it considerably more difficult to mend her damaged sentimental bond with Déterville. He soon insists on having a second tête-à-tête with Zilia, which she reluctantly accords. This scene serves two important purposes: first, it informs Zilia that Aza is alive and well and living in exile at the court of Spain; and second, it prompts the second in a series of debates between Zilia and Déterville over his unrequited ardor for her. In an effort to redirect what she calls his "fruitless sensibility," Zilia admonishes Déterville to tame his excessive passions and return to what she considers to be his true moral character: "I have found only your virtues worthy of the simplicity of ours. A son of the Sun could take pride in having your sentiments. Your reason is practically that of nature . . . I find pleasing everything about you down to the nobility of your features, for friendship has eyes as well as love" (letter 31, p. 133). She adds, however, that the innocent pleasure she once took in his company has now become a painful burden because she can no longer express her own platonic tenderness toward him. In Zilia's eyes, Déterville is suffering from a disorder of sensibility: although his native moral constitution is unusually close to her Peruvian/natural ideal, he is risking both his health and their friendship by wallowing in the violent, lovelorn sentiments that now torment him.

Déterville is destined to become something tantamount to a "sister soul" to Zilia by the end of the *Lettres d'une Péruvienne*, but before that can happen, she must make a painful readjustment to her Peruvian-based system of moral judgment. That system continues to function throughout the letters in which she presents her often pointed moral and sociological observations of the French. She criticizes, among other things, the exaggerated, unnatural sentiments that are represented on the Parisian stage (letter 16); the French penchant for dramatic extremes (letter 30); and the frivolous artificiality of their social conversations (letter 32). However, Zilia's harshest criticism is directed at the unnatural way in which the French treat their women—a problem caused, in her view, by child-rearing practices that pervert native sensibility and create girls who are vain, shallow, and lacking the "tender, carefully considered goodness that causes one to do as one should with nobility and discernment, and that leads to tolerance [*humanité*] and forbearance" (letter 34, p. 145).[46] As Zilia sees them, French women are born "with all the attributes necessary to equal men in merit and virtue" but typically end up in marriages that are loveless, oppressive, and abusive (148).

To this disheartening marital scenario, Zilia contrasts the profoundly loving and sincere Peruvian-style marriage she imagines she will have with Aza, once they are are reunited: "Dearest Aza, it is you and the great extent of your love, the frankness of our hearts, and the sincerity of our feelings that have revealed to me the secrets of nature and of love . . . Oh my dear Aza! May the glittering vices of a nation so seductive in other ways not cause us to lose in any way our taste for the natural simplicity of our manners! May you never forget your obligation to be my example, my guide, and my support along the path of virtue, and may I never forget mine to maintain your esteem and your love by imitating my model" (letter 34, pp. 149–51). A true conjugal union, as Zilia envisions it, would thus be founded upon respect, sympathetic understanding, and mutual emulation between two sensitive, virtuous beings striving tirelessly to be worthy of each other. She is convinced that she will escape the fate of the married women she has observed in France by virtue of the Peruvian values she believes she and Aza share. Sadly, shortly after making this exuberant prediction of her future, Zilia is brutally disabused about Aza's true character.

When Aza finally arrives in France, he is no longer the affectionate, faithful, and upright Inca whose image she has cherished so dearly. Rather, as Zilia describes it to Déterville (to whom she addresses the last five of the novel's letters), Aza has been transformed by his assimilation into the world of the hard-hearted Spaniards. He has abandoned virtually all of the old Peruvian ways, save the Incas' rigorous candor: he bluntly announces, first, that he has come to France only to free himself from his engagement to Zilia, having converted to Catholicism (which forbids him from marrying her because she is his close blood relative); and second, that he is about to wed a young Spanish woman. Zilia is heartbroken, not only because Aza is no longer faithful but also because he is so indifferent to the pain he inflicts on her: "You saw me at your feet, barbarous Aza, you saw them bathed in my tears, and your flight . . . Terrible moment, why does your memory not tear my life from me?" (letter 39, p. 167).

Zilia is left in a state of such complete disillusion that, like so many literary heroines before and after her, she falls gravely ill, into a near-suicidal delirium. Although she is nursed back to health by Céline, she remains melancholic, unable to bear the sight of the objects in Céline's house which remind her of her terrible final scene with her perfidious ex-fiancé (letter 40, p. 169). She therefore decides to retreat to her new country house, where, thanks to the prescience of her noble French friends, she can live independently, in a château that is decorated to pay tribute to both her royal Incan birth and her status as a now-enlightened exile in France. She takes up residence in her gilded haven, alone and unmarried, disregarding the "showy decency" of the members of French society who might disapprove of a young single woman living in such a manner (170).[47]

Zilia does not, however, resolve to live out her existence in utter solitude. To the contrary, anxious to preserve the affection of "hearts sensitive to my troubles" (letter 37, p. 163), she makes a careful proposition to the ever-faithful Déterville. Although she refuses to marry him, she invites him to join her in a special kind of sympathetic partnership—a muted version of the ideal spiritual union that she had thought she would enjoy with Aza. What Zilia seeks is a friendship founded upon respect, sincerity, and the soulful understanding that can only occur between truly delicate, sensible beings; for, having renounced passionate love, the only emotion that she will allow herself to feel at this stage is friendly affection—a less intense, but safer and more enduring sentiment. To deepen that bond, Zilia suggests that they endeavor to cultivate both their intellectual sensibilities—an area in which Déterville as a Frenchman naturally excels—and their moral sensibilities, where she proposes to serve as guide. In essence, Zilia sends Déterville an invitation to draw on their respective strengths and compensate for each other's shortcomings: "You will give me some acquaintance with your sciences and your arts; you will savor the pleasure of superiority. I will regain the upper hand by developing virtues in your heart with which you are not acquainted. You will adorn my mind with that which can make it amusing, and you will take pleasure from your work; I will endeavor to make agreeable to you the childlike charms of simple friendship and will find happiness in succeeding at this" (letter 41, p. 173). Céline, too, will contribute to this union: "By sharing her tenderness with us, Céline will infuse our conversations with the merriment they might otherwise lack. What more will be left for us to desire?" (173).

The relationship on which Zilia seems to embark at the end of the novel is thus a meeting of the "French" and "Peruvian" minds—yet not in the culturally specific way that some commentators have emphasized. For although Zilia does (as Janet G. Altman puts it) represent herself "as equal partner in a reciprocal exchange of ideas," she no longer refers explicitly to her Peruvianness to describe the unique qualities she has to offer.[48] Rather, she speaks as a voice of true human nature, a person endowed with a rare understanding of the pure and innocent pleasures of sentient existence. European civilization is not at odds with those pleasures: to the contrary, Zilia seeks to make the most of Déterville's culture in order "to gain a superficial yet interesting acquaintance with the universe, my surroundings, my own existence" (*LP*, 41, p. 173). She thus acknowledges that, despite its social and moral shortcomings, intellectually enlightened France can deepen her understanding of the secrets of nature, beginning with the secret she has discovered: "The pleasure of being—a forgotten pleasure not even known to so many blind humans—that thought so sweet, that happiness so pure, 'I am, I live, I exist,' could bring happiness all by itself if one remembered it, if one enjoyed it, if one treasured it as befits its worth" (173). Ultimately, therefore, the special knowledge Zilia offers to share with Déterville has little to do with her status as a representative of the Peruvian people (whose supposedly universal moral superiority has been compromised by Aza's decidely ignoble behavior). Rather, it derives from the understanding she has acquired of sensibility—a property that she still exalts, but with a lucid, personal sense of its dangers.

In the novel's final paragraph, Zilia exhorts Déterville to join her in that understanding: "Come, Déterville, come learn from me to economize the resources of our souls and the benefits of nature. Renounce tumultuous feelings, those imperceptible destroyers of our being. Come learn to know pleasures innocent and lasting, come enjoy them with me. You will find in my heart, in my friendship, in my feelings, all that can compensate you for the ravages of love" (174). Although Zilia is still striving here to serve as a model of true virtue and sensibility, she no longer measures those qualities in explicitly Peruvian terms—that is, by constant evoking the example of Aza. Rather, having invested her sensibility too fully in a Sun King who turned out to be all too human, she seeks a more attainable mode of happy, wholesome, productive existence. The final image she paints of such an existence remains grounded in the universal principle of sentimental fellow-feeling; amorous sensibility has been abstracted out of the picture because it can easily destroy all that is good in the sensible soul. If we recall the four letters that precede this one, where Zilia expresses her acute, near-maddening pain at losing Aza, we might say that she is addressing this warning about the dangers of misdirected sensibility as much to herself as to Déterville.

In the end, Zilia moves beyond the role of primitivist critic she had initially played in Graffigny's novel and becomes a therapeutic figure—not a true insider to French society, but someone who has both a special wisdom about the workings of sensibility and sufficient empathy to guide one sensitive but flawed nobleman back to a more natural, balanced, and virtuous mode of existence.

Through the contract of reciprocal moral-intellectual enlightenment established by her last letter, Zilia not only determines her own destiny but also assumes the task of assisting Déterville in becoming a better, more noble *homme sensible* than he is at present. By offering to develop the virtues in Déterville's heart of which he himself is not aware, Zilia presents herself as the natural moral example that she earlier declared was missing in contemporary France. In return for her efforts, Zilia will get something equally valuable for the sensitive soul: an expanded knowledge of the universe and a sympathetic ear to replace the Peruvian interlocutor whom she has lost.

&9 &

On balance, Graffigny's outsider heroine is more successful than is Marivaux's in her efforts to find a stable place in the world of the eighteenth-century French aristocracy. That outcome might seem surprising, given that Zilia at first finds this world starkly alien, whereas Marianne of *La Vie de Marianne* repeatedly affirms that she feels quite at home with the subtle social delicacies of upper-class culture. Zilia does, however, have an important advantage over Marianne: whereas Marianne must constantly prove her nobility, Zilia starts out from a position of unquestionable social distinction in her native culture. Her status as an Incan princess not only adds to her exotic aura among the Parisian *beau monde* who gather in Mme. Déterville's salon, but also gives added inspiration to Déterville's earnest efforts to use his powerful social connections to assist Zilia socially and financially (*LP*, letters 21, 27, 35). Yet the differences between Zilia and Marianne are less significant than their similarity as heroines of "natural" sensibility: the adventures of both characters are scripted to affirm a notion of *noblesse de coeur* that presents itself as universal. That is not to say that this notion is, in fact, universal: to the contrary, it remains quite class-specific in both *Les Lettres d'une Péruvienne* and *La Vie de Marianne* because the sympathetic sensibility that their heroines inspire serves as a measure of the supposedly natural nobility of the French aristocrats who are moved to become their benefactors.[49] In that sense, one might characterize both of these novels as semididactic vehicles of moral instruction that were aimed at a highborn readership in order both to confirm the values of true nobility and to provide touching tableaux of refined sensibility in action. Although these works seem to advance the idea that naturally sensitive persons can and should be granted a place among the French social elite, both Zilia and Marianne are endowed with a mythic quality that actually reinforces the aristocratic myth of the privileges of birth.

Having compared the way in which Zilia and Marianne are made to embody the principle of "natural" sensibility for the world of high-society France, one might be tempted to conclude that Marivaux and Graffigny were, in essence, feminizing sensibility. That is an assumption commonly made by some Marivaux critics, who interpret Marianne's "divine natural instinct" as a sign of Marivaux's so-called feminine side—a side that they identify with his glorification of intuition, delicate passions, and spontaneity of heart.[50] However, given the overriding emphasis that Marivaux and his contemporaries placed on sensibility as a *noble* quality, the opposition between what was "feminine" versus "masculine" was quite blurred at the time and would remain so until the 1770s. Clearly, the traits that these novelists attributed to the exceptionally sensible soul—the capacity for deep feeling; the enhanced power of moral, intellectual, and social discernment; and the effort to find kindred spirits with whom one can truly communicate—are *not* presented in their works as exclusively feminine. These traits are possessed not only by Marianne, Zilia, and Mme. de Lursay, but also by des Grieux, Valville, Déterville and even the young Meilcour. In the French novel of sensibility prior to 1750, sensibility is depicted, not as gender-specific but rather, as a class-specific, singularizing moral quality, even in works that seem to take issue with the sympathetic privileges of the aristocratic social elite.

Although sensibility would continue to hold connotations of singularity and distinction after 1750, the aristocratic definition of the property that had previously imbued the novel was transformed, thanks to two major theoretical developments. One of those developments was aesthetic: a new set of emotional, dramatic, and largely private values became prevalent in literature thanks to the rise of sentimentalism, a vogue in which sensibility took on significations that were more democratic and morally unequivocal than it had held earlier. The other development occurred in the broader field of the "human sciences": philosophers and physicians alike became intensely engaged in an effort to forge a new set of body-based meanings for everything from basic sentience to complex thinking. No longer would it be necessary to introduce a foreigner like Zilia into French society to represent natural sensibility, for once it became medicalized, sensibility became natural to everyone. At the same time, however, the old classificatory impulse remained just as strong in the new theory of sensibility as it had prior to 1750: the basis of the hierarchical distinctions that were made among human beings simply shifted from the morally delicate sensitive soul to the vitally reactive sensible body.

There were, of course, a number of steps involved in the transformation of sensibility from a moral concept used to ground an aristocratic system of social distinction, into a physically based property that could supported a broad set of medical, ethical, and anthropological distinctions. Some of those steps are apparent in the works of Denis Diderot, who played a central role both in disseminating the paradigm of vital sensibility beyond the field of medicine and in codifying the new aesthetics of melodramatic sentimentalism for French theater and for the novel. There is, as we shall see, a deep and strategic connection between those two projects, for sensibility's medical and literary significations are far too intertwined in Diderot's writings to be merely coincidental.

5. Organic Sensibility in Diderot's Theory and Practice of Fiction

The Great Observer of Sensibility: Diderot's *Éloge de Richardson* and Bordeu's "Crise"

Diderot has long been recognized as one of the most encyclopedic of eighteenth-century French thinkers, a man whose readings and writings included natural philosophy, political science, ethics, art criticism, theater, and literary theory. He is also known for having taken a particularly keen interest in contemporary physiology, anatomy, psychology, and medicine; this interest culminated in his *Eléments de physiologie* but was already evident in the 1750s, when he was writing and editing articles for the *Encyclopédie*. Both Jacques Roger and Jean Mayer, the two contemporary scholars who have most closely scrutinized Diderot's philosophy of life and matter, conclude that his exposure to the medical ideas promoted in the *Encyclopédie* was seminal in the evolution of that philosophy.[1] It is therefore safe to assume that Diderot was not only aware of the new, semivitalist doctrine of sensibility that was developing during the 1750s and 1760s, but was also contemplating the broader implications of this doctrine long before he transposed it into *Le Rêve de d'Alembert* (1769).

This is important to keep in mind when considering another aspect of Diderot's intellectual endeavors from the same period: namely, the theory and practice of fiction he elaborated between 1757 and 1762, when he was clearly preoccupied with the central role that sensibility seemed to play in the aesthetic process.[2] It was during this time that Diderot became actively engaged in the two literary genres that most impassioned him: theater and the novel. Although the earnestly edifying plays that he composed in 1757 and 1758 under the titles *Le Fils naturel* and *Le Père de famille* were largely disappointing, his accompanying reflections on the aesthetic and ethical dimensions of fiction-making signaled both a major development in his thought and an important shift in the accepted understanding of how nature and human nature should be represented in art. Those reflections are contained in an important series of texts: the *Entretiens sur "Le Fils naturel"* and *De la poésie dramatique* (1757–58), where Diderot set forth the principles underlying the new genre of drama with which he wanted to reform and update French theater; the *Éloge de Richardson* (1762), in which he described the epiphanic experience of reading Samuel Richardson's intimately absorbing novels; and *La Religieuse* (1760; 1780–82), in which he explored the connections between the sympathy to which the novel of sensibility explicitly appealed and its implicit capacity to seduce its readers. Although sensibility is central to all of these works, its operations are by far the most complex—and the most explicitly physicalized—in *La Religieuse,* to which the second part of this chapter is devoted.

First, however, let us consider more closely the organic conception of the human being that underpinned the aesthetics of sensibility Diderot was developing at the time he first drafted *La Religieuse.* Diderot's probable acquaintance with contemporary medical philosophy does not, of course, suffice to explain the alternatingly erotic and clinical body language that pervades this novel—even though the work contains passages so oddly medical that one commentator has conjectured that Diderot "forgot" he was writing a novel during those moments and lapsed into the discourse of a *médecin manqué.*[3] This body language has prompted an interesting range of interpretations: some critics have viewed it as an expression of Diderot's distinctive "corporeal" writing style, while others have called it an instance of his materialism, and still others have interpreted it as signifying an obsession with something he purportedly deemed pathological—for example, hysteria, female sexuality, or femininity *tout court.*[4] Although they differ widely in emphasis, virtually all of these approaches are based on the assumption that the novel's body language is, in one way or another, metaphoric—as if Diderot's emphasis on the body parts and physio-pathological functions of cloistered human beings were really a way of alluding to something else. I contend, by contrast, that the body language of *La Religieuse* is not metaphoric but literal: the fundamental subject of this novel is the primacy of bodily sensibility in all aspects of human experience, and most particularly in the peculiarly interconnected realms of aesthetics and social hygiene.

Diderot's recourse to medical discourse for answers to the operations and enigmas of sensibility entailed a certain amount of ambivalence: as he put it toward the end of the *Eléments de physiologie,* "There are no books I read more willingly than books of medicine, and no men with whom I find it more interesting to converse than doctors—but only when I am feeling well" (*EP,* 299). In my view, it is the last part of that observation (typically omitted from most quotations) that is the most significant. For Diderot's emphasis on his own physical disposition as reader or interlocutor echoes the conviction he expressed in the *Éloge* that the act of reading could have potentially unsettling psychosomatic repercussions, particularly when it involved intensely compelling subjects, as Diderot apparently found both medicine and the Richardsonian novel to be.

What is even more curious is that Diderot devised a way to inscribe both of those reading experiences in *La Religieuse*, by introducing a distinctly medical style of discourse into an otherwise conventional sentimental narrative. This novel is clearly many things at once: a melodramatic fiction, a *conte philosophique*, and a seductive literary hoax aimed at a supposedly gullible narratee, the Marquis de Croismare.[5] One of the more perplexing traits of its long-suffering narrator-heroine Suzanne Simonin—her extraordinary capacity to provide lucid, hyperdetailed observations of bodies in states of great sensible stimulation, even while she remains incapable of interpreting the meaning of what she has observed—is a clue to how those seemingly disparate objectives are connected. Suzanne's peculiarly doubled constitution is, I shall argue, inspired by Diderot's desire to exploit simultaneously all of the multiple resonances that sensibility had recently come to acquire. The narrative language of *La Religieuse* was designed to play not only on sensibility's existing literary significations as an ambiguous force of moral sympathy and sociability, but also on the very precise clinical meanings it was given by the physiologists and medical theorists he so avidly read and consulted. By underscoring sensibility's physio-pathological operations, Diderot did not empty the property of its established ethical connotations but rather complicated them, by making the body the ultimate locus of every character's actions and reactions, whether physical or moral-intellectual. Hence the repeated occurrence, over the course of Suzanne's tale, of a distinctly clinical diagnostic scenario for "reading" organic sensibility—a scenario that seems to have been imported lock, stock, and barrel from the writings of the medical Encylopedists, most particularly Théophile de Bordeu.

Although Diderot paid his most explicit tribute to Bordeu and his provocative organological theory of sensibility in the *Rêve de d'Alembert*, it was in *La Religieuse* that he gave his most strategic response both to the physician-philosopher as a figure and to the theoretical claims and discursive practices this figure assumed. The clinical representation of sensibility in this novel is not limited to the secondary characters who are overtly diagnosed, such as Mme. ***; it is also directed at what happens to Suzanne and thus positions the novel's implied reader in a very particular manner in relation to her story. During those scenes in which Suzanne's narrative shifts overtly into a clinical register, both she and her reader become engaged in a mode of observation and interpretation that is strikingly analogous to the techniques which Bordeu recommended in his *Encyclopédie* article "Crise" for detecting and deciphering the messages that organs emit when their sensibility is critically aroused. This diagnostic activity also structures the narrative of *La Religieuse* in a larger sense: at a very fundamental level, the practice of representing the peculiar brands of sensibility encountered within cloistered walls *is* the plot of the novel. The novel's reader is thus drawn into this narrative not just because it stimulates his sensibility morally and/or erotically, but also because it obliges him to participate actively in the intellectual interpretation of sensibility's clinical signs.

Above and beyond its intriguing operation as a narrative strategy in *La Religieuse*, Diderot's literary transposition of the medicine of sensibility reflected a significant transformation of the eighteenth-century novel. Once the medical model for interpreting sensibility became so ubiquitous as to be subject to pastiche, the literary representation of the property became a far more natural-philosophical activity than it had been earlier. That transformation is also apparent in the works of such authors as Rousseau, Laclos, and Sade, who, despite their often enormous ideological differences, shared the belief promoted by the *médecins philosophes* that sensibility was the true inner language of the human being and sought to reshape their art into a vehicle for energetically conveying that truth. It was Diderot, however, who made the most concerted effort to bridge the gap between natural philosophy and literature by developing a way of representing this property that would take all of its meanings fully into account.

_9 G_

The new type of fiction promoted in the *Éloge de Richardson* is initially defined in negative terms—that is, as a rejection of the conventionally *romanesque*, and a desire to replace it with something more serious and affecting.[6] The *Éloge* begins with the then-standard attack on the novelistic genre, the better to highlight the moral and aesthetic qualities of Richardson's novels, "which elevate the mind, touch our nobler feelings, and breathe throughout a love of goodness."[7] Richardson's novels, Diderot declares, imprint a vivid image of virtue and vice upon the reader's imagination: "We see the man who is acting, we put ourselves in his place, or by his side, and we become fascinated [*on se passionne*] for or against him. If he is virtuous we sympathize with him, and if he is unjust or vicious we turn from him with indignation" ("ER," 267). He describes this mode of representation as so engagingly believable that it inspires a childlike naïveté in its readers: "Oh, Richardson! In spite of ourselves you compel us to take our part on your stage, to join in the conversations, to approve, to blame, to admire, to be angry or indignant. How often I have found myself, like a child, taken to the theater for the first time, calling out: 'Don't believe him; he is deceiving you . . . If you go there you will be lost'" (268).

This personal anecdote concerning Diderot's literal enthusiasm for Richardson—the state in which he forgets that Richardson's characters are not real beings that one can warn of impending doom—bears a striking resemblance to the many passages in his *Salons* where he recounts having become so absorbed in a given painting that he imagined he had physically entered it.[8] By accentuating the tendency of the Richardsonian reader to lose sight of the artful fictionality of what he is reading, Diderot not only affirms the seductively absorbing powers of these novels but also draws attention to their underlying mechanisms.[9] Some commentators have, in fact, seen the strategy of unveiling the mechanisms of fiction as the most significant idea put forth in the *Éloge*.[10] I would say, however, that this text contains another, equally important aesthetic notion: namely, that strongly affecting fictions require a novelist or artist capable of conveying a deeply penetrating vision of moral and physical nature, and a reader-beholder disposed to enter into that vision to the fullest degree possible.

In other words, what Diderot is defining here is fiction as a communion with nature which connects two well-constituted sensibilities—or, to use the vocabulary of many of Diderot's modern critics, fiction as a dialogical process involving two figures capable of sensing nature's truths in a profound and active manner.[11] One might assume, given the emphasis Diderot places elsewhere on the unique capacity of the creative genius to tap into nature, that he would portray the author here as the major player in that process. The *Éloge* does indeed contain multiple tributes to Richardson's extraordinary talent for observing and representing human nature in all of its complexity. Yet Diderot seems less interested here in exploring that talent than in articulating the special manner in which he believes Richardsonian fiction should be read and in distinguishing the kind of reader he deems fit to do so.

In the third paragraph of the text, Diderot declares that his own reaction of intense indignation toward Richardson's libertine characters must be a universal readerly experience: "Who has not shuddered at the character of Lovelace and Tomlinson? Who has not been filled with horror to see such a wretch feigning all the virtues with such an air of candour and dignity, with such a semblance of pathos and truth? What reader has not confessed in his inmost heart that he would be forced to fly society and to seek the solitude of the woods if there were many such dissemblers as these?" ("ER," 267). Even as he underscores the timeless, irresistible appeal of Richardson's novels, however, Diderot points out that reading Richardson requires a significant adjustment in one's idea of what a novelist should depict. For rather than terrifying his readers with the gory, fantastical, and/or exotic images typical of some contemporary novels, Richardson engages them by depicting what Peter Brooks has called "the drama of the ordinary."[12] As Diderot puts it,

> [Richardson's] stage is the real world in which we now live, the actions are true to nature, the characters live and breathe; they are the people we meet in society, and the incidents that befall them are such as might happen in any civilized country. The passions he describes are those I have felt myself; they are stirred by the same objects, and produce the results I should have expected. His characters suffer the same kinds of hindrances and griefs that constantly threaten myself; he shows me the course of events as they might be happening around me. Unless he had this skill the illusion would be but momentary, and there would be left on my mind only a feeble and passing impression.   ("ER," 268–69)

Thus, in order to read Richardson the right way, one must savor his details and identify personally with his dramatic depiction of the moral crises that fill the course of everyday life. Richardson's purpose in evoking the ordinary and familiar objects of domestic life is, maintains Diderot, not just to sustain the reader's illusion but also to plant "seeds of virtue" in the reader's unsuspecting heart—seeds that are calculated to burst into life as soon as the story reaches a crisis in which the virtuous characters are threatened with some injustice (269). All of that is impossible, however, if the reader lacks a visceral feeling for the intense and often violent energy of the passions—an energy that, Diderot contends, drives all social interactions and lies buried inside the moral "cavern" of every human being (270).

Hence this important caveat on the reception of Richardson's fiction: "The works of Richardson will please everyone, more or less, at all times and in all places, but the number of readers who can truly appreciate him will always be small; one must have too severe a taste" ("ER," 279). Although Diderot invites his compatriots to develop the asceticism necessary to read these works properly, he implies throughout the *Éloge* that contemporary French people are too frivolous and dissipated to grasp the power and complexity of Richardson's fiction. True appreciation of Richardson is thus restricted to "the quiet, solitary reader, who has known the noise and pleasures of the world, and who prefers a shady retreat where he can pass his hours profitably in sympathetic silence [*s'attendrir utilement dans le silence*]" (274).

Diderot thus suggests that although every human being stands to benefit greatly from a Richardsonian representation of the force of the passions and the vulnerability of virtue, not every reader is suited to receive that lesson. Those readers who *are* sensitive to such novels are superior not only in taste, but also in a whole series of moral and intellectual qualities: "The nobler the mind [*plus on a l'âme belle*], the more refined and the purer the taste; the more one knows nature, and the greater one loves the truth, the more one will appreciate the works of Richardson" ("ER," 273). To read Richardson well, therefore, one must possess the same characteristics that Diderot attributes elsewhere to the discriminating judge of art: a tender and honest soul, a good deal of experience in life, an elevated mind, a slightly melancholic temperament, and "delicate organs."[13]

To demonstrate how those traits come into play, Diderot presents a series of tableaux of what has happened to him or to his friends while engrossed in one of Richardson's novels. His first testimonial seems designed to refute Rousseau's notion that whatever one undergoes while engaged in a fiction leaves no lasting effect on one's "real" life.[14] Diderot, by contrast, insists that reading a novel like Richardson's *is* a real-life experience because the vision of human nature it provides is so gripping and intensely concentrated that it becomes an active moral force on its own terms.[15] He describes that operation in one of his many effusive apostrophes to this author: "My mind [while reading Richardson] was kept in perpetual agitation. How good I felt myself to be, how just, how self-satisfied after reading your books! I felt as a man does spending a day doing good works. In a few hours I had been carried through a variety of situations, greater than many ever experience in their whole life. I had listened to the true tones of passion; I had seen the springs of self-interest and self-love acting in a hundred different ways; I had become the spectator of a multitude of incidents, and I felt the richer in experience" ("ER," 268). According to Diderot, therefore, the good reader of serious fiction is anything but the passive spectator that Rousseau decries in his *Lettre à d'Alembert sur les spectacles*. Rather, by entering into the fiction, the reader/spectator of Richardson's novels is able to *hear* the true language of the emotions and *see* the usually hidden mechanisms of self-interest and pride. This reader thereby becomes physically, sensibly engaged in the multitude of situations that are evoked in these works and ends up with the sensation of having acquired real experience. That sensation is not, Diderot insists, just an illusion: great poets like Richardson rouse their readers out of their ordinary sensory oblivion to the moral and physical phenomena of the universe and literally open up their eyes and ears to the subtle physiognomy of the passions. He thus admonishes those who misjudge Richardson as a mere painter of commonplace details:

> Take care, you are condemning all the great poets when you condemn Richardson for this. You have seen the sun set and the stars rise a hundred times; and you have often heard the joyous burst of song from the

birds in the woods. But which of you has realized that it is the contrast of the noises of the daylight hours which make the silent hours of the night so impressive? And it is just the same in regard to moral phenomena; you have often seen the ebullitions of passion among men, but you could not understand all the hidden meanings in their tones or in their facial expressions. Each passion has its own mode of expression, and these different expressions may follow each other on the same countenance without its ceasing to be the same; and the art of the great poet and the great painter is to make you conscious of some quickly passing mood which had escaped your observation.   ("ER," 275)[16]

It is, Diderot emphasizes, this extraordinary power to activate its readers' senses in a very real and physical manner that makes Richardsonian fiction so valuable as an instrument of moral edification: Richardson does not simply demonstrate that virtue is more precious than life; he makes his readers *feel* that truth. Diderot declares that whenever he reads one of Richardson's novels, "without my realizing it, my sense of commiseration is exercised and strengthened," leaving him with a sensation of "delicious" melancholy that is so deeply imprinted on his face that he sometimes alarms the people who see him, long after he has put down the book (274).[17] Thus, despite all of the crying and lamenting that reading Richardson seems to provoke in the *Éloge*, a certain pleasure is ascribed to the experience of identifying sympathetically with the downtrodden. This austere, melancholic mode of communicating with the rest of suffering humanity often gives rise to a more direct kind of sociability: "I have remarked that in whatever society Richardson was read, either in public or private, the conversation became more lively and interesting. I have heard the most important points of morals and of taste seriously discussed after such readings" (277). Indeed, such discussions sometimes get so heated that they tear families asunder, by dividing their members into those who sympathize deeply with Richardson's victim characters and those who do not. Richardson's novels thus have an astonishingly powerful influence over their readers's personal lives: true enthusiasts almost inevitably come to see their acquaintances through the same polarized moral lens as that which colors Richardson's universe, deciding which real-life people are to be admired or disdained according to which of his characters those people most resemble (279).

The *Éloge* presents two perspectives on this practice of using Richardson's fiction like a secular bible, to steer oneself more surely along the morally perilous path of human life. On the one hand, Diderot claims that he, too, has fallen into the habit of judging his friends by the degree of enthusiasm they show for Richardson ("ER," 279, 283). On the other hand, he cautions against the kind of aesthetically grounded intolerance he has observed among some fellow fans, like the anonymous lady of his acquaintance who has vowed to break off her friendship with another woman because the latter had the temerity to laugh at Clarissa's afflictions (285). In the end, however, it is the zealously sensitive reader of Richardson who is celebrated in the *Éloge*, because only that type of reader displays the full, often terrible effects of the novelistic art as Diderot believes it should be practiced.

With this in mind, let us examine the text's climactic anecdote, the supposedly authentic minidrama that illustrates how the ultimate "good" reader of Richardson reacted the first time he read the scenes of Clarissa's burial and last testament (which were unknown to most French readers of *Clarissa* until the early 1760s).[18] Diderot begins by establishing the dramatis personae of the episode: the central character, who is "one of the most sensitive men I know, and an ardent admirer of Richardson" ("ER," 286), and Diderot as witness and narrator. He then gives a graphic account of how his friend behaved as he was reading: "He carried off the volume into a corner and began to read. I was watching him: first I see his tears begin to flow, he is obliged to stop, he sobs; suddenly he starts up and begins to walk about without thinking where he is going; then he bursts forth into lamentations, and utters bitter reproaches against the whole Harlowe family" (286).

This is almost a textbook example of what Diderot calls in his dramatic writings a *scène muette*, complete with agitated movements expressed through pantomime, tears and sobs, inarticulate cries, and a final eruption of bitter reproaches against the evils of the world (in this case, against the hypocritical characters in *Clarissa*).[19] What this tableau does is literally dramatize the aesthetic experience under discussion in the *Éloge*, by showing a man in whom reading has prompted a crisis just as acute as any of the domestic turmoils that Diderot depicted in his plays. Moreover, a curious *mise en abime,* or doubling strategy, is at work here: the tableau is presented as a dramatic/moving representation of the effects of a dramatic/moving representation, involving a highly sensitive reader who literally makes a scene out of himself by reading in front of a spectator-friend. One would be hard pressed to find a more succinct demonstration of sensibility's contagious effects in all of Diderot's corpus.

The final point worth mentioning about this anecdote is the intriguing position that Diderot-as-narrator assumes in it. Because he is present in the tableau only to witness the very physical symptoms of sensibility his friend exhibits while reading Richardson—without, we should note, getting physically involved himself, through words or a sympathetic embrace (something he says earlier he is *tempted* to do whenever he meets a fellow Richardson enthusiast ["ER," 283])—the persona of Diderot-as-narrator functions as a pure observer; he provides no overt interpretation and no indication of how he was affected by the scene. One could, of course, argue that this persona "catches" his friend's zealous emotion over this fiction: Diderot-as-narrator testifies repeatedly to feeling violent jolts, or shivering in horror, or having his imagination haunted by the images of Richardson's creations. There is nonetheless a peculiar disjuncture between the active enthusiasm to which Diderot professes during those purportedly autobiographical moments and his disengagement in the scene of his friend's extreme reaction to reading new passages from *Clarissa*. By positioning himself on the very margins of the tableau, Diderot-as-narrator serves as a neutral medium who transmits a pure, unmediated image of primal sensibility: his lack of participation in the action he is witnessing allows the bodily symptoms of his friend's total, devastating aesthetic absorption to speak forcefully for themselves.

One might say, then, that there are not just two but three figures depicted in the *Éloge de Richardson*, each of whom has its own distinct role to play. There is Richardson, the "true painter of nature" who brings to his craft an "astonishing knowledge of the laws and customs and manners of the human heart and of life" ("ER," 281). And there is Richardson's "good" reader, who is so acutely attuned to the language of this new brand of fiction that he or she quite literally resonates upon hearing it. Finally, there is the figure of Diderot-as-narrator, who functions alternately as the quintessential sensitive reader of Richardson and the semidetached chronicler of other people's reading experiences. Although Diderot casts himself in the second mode only at isolated moments of this text, those moments nonetheless invite comparison with the most dramatic scenes of *La Religieuse*, where the narrator character Suzanne Simonin is also oddly detached from the action. In that novel as in the *Éloge*, this third figure is the most difficult to fix, particularly in terms of the separation between the point of view of the author/actor and that of the reader/beholder, which critics have widely recognized as a central tenet of Diderot's theory of fiction.

Thus, in the *Éloge de Richardson*, Diderot ascribes certain functions to "good" readers of serious fiction. By their visible melancholy, their abundant tears, their emotional transports, and their fervent outbursts over the actions of fictional characters, the sensitive readers depicted in the *Éloge* show the powerful effects that aesthetic experience can exert upon the mind and body. They also show the effects it can exert upon society because they use what they read to create new, more morally sound types of social interaction. Richardson's novels consequently serve almost the same social function for their readers as do the touching tales recounted by one character to another in novels like *Manon Lescaut* and *La Vie de Marianne*: they test the sensibility of the individual reader or listener and determine where he or she stands in the hierarchy of sensible beings. The only obvious difference is that Diderot never mentions aristocratic birth as a precondition for possessing the innate moral-physical delicacy he deems necessary to appreciate Richardson's stories. Moreover, the experience that the sensitive Diderotian reader undergoes is, at base, fundamentally private or existential: it affirms that reader's connection not so much to a particular society as to the essential energies of nature.

Diderot's description of how reading affects both individual bodies and social bodies is, of course, far less ambiguous in the *Éloge de Richardson* than it is in his erotically and politically charged novel *La Religieuse*. That is not to say that he writes as a moralizing sentimentalist in the *Éloge*: despite its pronounced emphasis on the polarized combat between virtue and vice, this text is ultimately less concerned with defending morality than with evoking the visceral contact with nature that a certain kind of artistic representation can induce in its readers.[20] To make that contact possible, fiction must have not only a sensitive recipient but also a great visionary as its author—someone who can penetrate beneath the surface to discern the secrets that lurk within certain people or social conditions and then convey those secrets in such a way that readers feel them with maximal intensity.

❧ ❧

This account of the way a great novelist communicates with nature and with his audience is remarkably similar to the portrait Diderot sketches elsewhere of the great observer/interpreter of nature. To establish that analogy more firmly and set the stage for an analysis of the peculiarly corporeal way in which sensibility is represented in *La Religieuse*, let us recall how, precisely, a master physician-philosopher enters into contact with the natural object that most concerns him: a suffering human body. According to the scenario established by the Montpellier theorists we examined in Chapter 2, effective medical diagnosis entails a dynamic interplay between two bodily sensibilities: that of the patient and that of his or her interpreter. If the observing physician is to succeed in this process, he must not only be viscerally attuned to the patterns that sensibility follows in the pathological state but also possess an intellectual understanding of the property which far transcends the ordinary. As Théophile de Bordeu explains in his *Encyclopédie* article "Crise" (1754), balancing those two faculties is no easy trick.

Bordeu's ostensible task in "Crise" is to present an historical overview of the doctrine of crises, whose advocates maintain that diseases are scripted according to natural, numerically fixed patterns of climax and resolution. This doctrine (one of the most important aspects of Hippocratic and Galenic medicine) has, in Bordeu's view, a systematic quality that led its early proponents to venture simplistic mathematical predictions on the outcome of a given illness—for example, on the seemingly magical seventh, fourteenth, or twenty-first day. Yet even when casting ridicule upon the manner in which the notion of physiopathological crises has sometimes been applied, Bordeu recognizes and respects its enduring popularity. He therefore takes an open-minded stance toward the question of whether diseases do in fact proceed critically, and even goes so far as to suggest that the human body may indeed be susceptible to the periodic influence of an outside force—the moon, perhaps.[21] What Bordeu suggests is that the physiological and pathological functions of human beings may well follow a "critical" pattern because sensibility makes people just as receptive as other natural objects to the forces that regulate the universe. His own doctrine is, we will recall, founded on the belief that the sensible body possesses a wealth of internal rhythms that the good physician must learn to detect through such sensory-based semiotic clues as changes in the pulse, respiration, and bodily excretions.

In and of itself, however, the theory of crises is not what interests Bordeu: this article is less concerned with reconstructing what the great physicians have said about that theory than with isolating the qualities that makes them great—that is, the special powers of insight that allow them to discern the rhythms of a disease instinctively. With his antimechanistic leanings, Bordeu insists that the physician must not intervene aggressively in a disease but, rather, must listen carefully to the resonances that sensibility creates in the body, resonances that are all the more apparent when one of its organs is pathologically overstimulated. Divining those resonances requires a truly talented diagnostician with a keen observing eye, a rare sensory tact, a firm grounding in the principles of medical semiotics, and years of firsthand clinical experience, one who can sense the connections among the bodily events that point to an incipient crisis somewhere in the body: "The true physician is a man of genius who gazes firmly and resolutely upon an illness. Nature and extensive experience have together made him capable of allowing himself to be carried away by a kind of enthusiasm that is unknown to theorists: he judges the stages of an illness, so to speak, without realizing it. He may have learned everything that theory teaches, but he does not apply it; he forgets it, and decides what to do on the basis of habit and almost in spite of himself" ("Crise," 249). In practice, then, medical knowledge is not a formal theory, but a visceral understanding of another body that is born of "taste, talent, and experience"—qualities that Bordeu compares, interestingly, to those found in the great artist (250).

Visceral understanding is, however, only the first stage in the quest for full medical knowledge: "It is not just a matter of being led along *passively*, so to speak, like a practitioner, and receiving a ray of that bright light that accompanies the truth and compels one to consent. One must return from this *passive* state, and paint exactly what one has perceived in this sort of *ecstasy*, and express it in terms that are thoughtful and arranged so as to enlighten the reader just as nature would" ("Crise," 251). There, in a nutshell, is the Bordelian definition of the master physician: he is an observer who serves as an ecstatic vessel for the truths of nature at the moment of diagnosis, but he is also able to take control of this interbodily communion in order to articulate it and transcribe it for posterity. He is, in other words, a philosopher figure who operates in a manner very close to that of the great novelist Diderot describes in the *Éloge de Richardson*.

Bordeu concludes "Crise" on an elitist note: "It is necessary, to resolve or clarify the question of crises, to be *free*, and initiated in that sort of *philosophical* or *transcendent* medicine to which it is perhaps not good that all *popular* physicians—that is, *clinicians*—devote themselves" ("Crise," 252).[22] Only the truly philosophical physician has the authority to pass judgment on the questions that most concern the health and well-being of society as a whole. What endows him with this perspective is his intimate acquaintance with the force of sensibility, an acquaintance that can be attained only by passing through two stages of diagnostic engagement with this force: first, a moment of heightened but passive sensorial awareness (as in pulse-taking) and then a transcendant state of active knowledge. The ultimate médecin philosophe is a hybrid being—part supersensitive energumen and part rational philosopher, who can pull himself out of his oracular communion with the patient's particular sensible resonances and put this diagnostic experience in writing, thus producing a medical discourse that faithfully replicates what Bordeu's colleague Ménuret calls "the true language of nature."[23]

In a very substantial sense, *La Religieuse* can be seen as an answer to Bordeu's call to use the latest medical knowledge as a means of improving the human condition—not simply because Diderot grounds this novel's attack on convents so explicitly in physiology, but also because he imports so many of the theories and techniques of the médecins philosophes into this fiction.[24] Like Bordeu, Diderot depicts suffering humanity through a perspective that is inspired as much by the theory of vital sensibility as by Enlightenment social hygiene. The observations of convent life presented in *La Religieuse* are consequently predicated on the assumption that the best means of determining the soundness or insalubrity of a social institution like the convent is to analyze, through painstaking observation and decoding, how it acts upon the sensibilities of the individual bodies who dwell within it. For Diderot, however, whenever the property of sensibility is involved, reaching a detached, "objective" judgment on what one has observed is never an easy task.

Diderot explores that problem most thoroughly in his *Paradoxe sur le comédien*, where he proposes a ranking system to explain what sets apart the self-possessed sages of the world from weakly organized, run-of-the-mill "sensitive souls." Although the distinction pertains here primarily to the great versus the mediocre actor, Diderot also uses it to create a typology of great observers, whom he dubs "assiduous spectators of what is going on around them in the physical world and in the moral world."[25] Great men, Diderot declares, spend their time dispassionately observing, studying, and depicting their more sensitive, weakly constituted companions; they are able to represent what they have observed because they are "gifted with fine imagination, with great judgment, with exquisite tact, with a sure touch of taste," and above all with "no sensibility" (*PC*, 18, 14). Those qualities, whether innate or acquired through rigorous self-discipline, are the mark not only of the great actor, but also of the great prince, the great politician, the great military man, the great lawyer, and finally, the great physician. The very same list appears during one of Dr. Bordeu's lectures on sensibility in the *Rêve de d'Alembert*, a text that delves more deeply into the organic foundations of the notion that "sensibility never occurs without some weakness in constitution."[26] It is, however, the *Paradoxe* that furnishes the most thorough explanation of the *intellectual* process by which great men achieve their extraordinary sangfroid. As Diderot describes it, only through a process of cool detachment from one's human nature—that is, of willful alienation from one's own sensible body, as in the actor who gives off all of the signs of sensibility on the stage, without feeling any—can one qualify as a true sage, a great observer of nature in any field.[27]

Seen in general terms, therefore, the detachment from personal sensibility that Diderot posits in the *Paradoxe* is not so much a properly aesthetic operation as an epistemological operation strikingly similar to the step-by-step clinical apprenticeship presented in Bordeu's "Crise," where the observer is required to pass from a passive diagnostic enthusiasm to an active, masterful understanding of the sensible crisis at hand. Although all of the figures in the Diderotian typology of great men must undergo this operation to attain the coolheaded insensibility that is their mark of genius, it is especially crucial for the physician as Diderot depicts him. For of all observers of nature, the medical observer is faced with a special dilemma: he must expose himself to the potentially destabilizing effects of pathological sensibility on a daily basis, yet still maintain his detached ability to articulate the meaning of those effects in a dispassionate, clinical manner. This is, we will recall, the problem that Dr. Bordeu is made to confront in the *Rêve de d'Alembert*, where, try as he might during a prolonged consultation on sensibility to take cover behind a battery of medical anecdotes and technical terms, he fails to maintain his diagnostic detachment. Diderot also addresses that issue in *La Religieuse*, but from a different angle: although the problem of clinical insensibility is embodied by the novel's heroine, it is the work's sensitive but worldly-wise implied reader who must confront it.

Sensible Diagnostics in *La Religieuse*

As narrator of *La Religieuse*, Suzanne Simonin leads Diderot's investigation into the cruel and unnatural constraints that convent life imposes upon the bodies of those who must inhabit them. Yet as the novel's long-suffering protagonist, she is also fully subject to those constraints, and her body responds to them as any body would. Suzanne is thus a hybrid, produced by the playfully experimental fusion of two genres, the sentimental novel and medical discourse. Diderot's novel is, in this sense, a double-genre pastiche—a work that mimics both the sentimental melodrama Diderot apparently loved and the medical treatises he so relished. In fact, the elements Diderot borrows from those two genres are strategically intertwined: by embellishing on the ever-growing stock of observations on sensibility furnished by the physicians of his day, Diderot turns those observations into discursive stimuli apt to move his reader emotionally while also delivering an urgent indictment of an unhealthy social institution. The representation of sensibility is consequently also central to *La Religieuse*'s mission as a *conte philosophique*, or, as Grimm called it, "the most cruel satire that has ever been done of cloisters."[28] Yet even as it delivers its attack on convents and affirms the belief that society must recognize and respect the human being's fundamental organic nature, *La Religieuse* also complicates that message. As Herbert Josephs observes, *La Religieuse* is a highly ambiguous work, because it blurs the distinctions between libertine eroticism, Gothic pathos, and the humanitarian ethics of the Enlightenment.[29] I propose to determine what, precisely, the novel's distinctly medicalized discourse on sensibility adds to that mix.

I am, of course, not the first person to remark that there is something oddly physiological about Diderot's language in certain texts, most particularly *La Religieuse*. Leo Spitzer discusses the question in his famous study of Diderotian stylistics, where he undertakes to demonstrate that Diderot's mobile, "hypervital" writing patterns reveal "an irruption of the *physiological* rhythm of speech in writing."[30] Spitzer interprets this stylistic trait as an "innervation of language by emotion" that is most manifest when Diderot is depicting a sexual experience (Spitzer, 146). The paradigmatic, "healthy" example of this hypervital writing pattern is, Spitzer contends, the high-flown exclamatory language of the *Encyclopédie* article "Jouissance," where Spitzer finds a "psycho-physical harmony" that expresses Diderot's drive for creative expansion or self-potentiation (Spitzer, 146, 150). For contrast, Spitzer takes an "unhealthy" example of that same drive from *La Religieuse*: he picks the episode in which Mme. ***, the lesbian superior of the Sainte-Eutrope convent, responds to the woeful tale recounted by Suzanne Simonin in a manner that is not just sympathetic but erotic.

Writing in a tone full of moral outrage, Spitzer analyzes Mme. ***'s "ghastly parody" of the Christian *exercitium spirituale*, a meditative ritual designed to instill compassion through visualization, which she uses on Suzanne's body to serve the very different purposes of self-arousal (Spitzer, 146, 149). Although he claims to be concerned only with the stylistic disjuncture evident here between the superior's pious words and her impious gestures, he is plainly alarmed by the physical liberties she takes as she follows the rhythm of her sympathetic declarations: "'The brutes! Imagine binding these arms with ropes! . . . ' and she took my arms and kissed them. 'Imagine drowning these eyes in tears!' . . . and she kissed them. 'Imagine forcing complaints and groans from these lips!' and she kissed them."[31] As Spitzer reads the scene, the superior's referential "perversion" of the relation between her words and sentiments is symptomatic of a twisted, selfish, hypocritical personality (Spitzer, 149). However, he pays little attention to the ostensible victim of the episode: Suzanne Simonin, whose monotonous narration of the scene represents nothing for him but a pitifully hypnotic state. Suzanne, as Spitzer views her, is thus not stylistically interesting herself; he focuses almost entirely on Mme. ***, the party responsible for the "evil automatism" that takes over the language of this episode.

There is nonetheless an equally striking automatism to much of Suzanne's narrative language that cannot be explained by Spitzer's interpretation. This automatism is most manifest during the seduction scenes that occur, on a regular and ever more intimate basis, between Mme. *** and Suzanne after the episode Spitzer singles out. In those celebrated passages, Suzanne's words belong not to a bewildered ingenue but, rather, to a detached observer who exhibits an uncanny clinical acumen at precisely those moments when she is supposed to be least aware of what is going on. In fact, such scenes tend to undermine both the moralism of Spitzer's reading of Diderot and the kind of physiological style that he interprets as typically Diderotian. For, to put it in Spitzer's terms, there is no emotion impelling the *style coupé* that appears in those episodes, no exultant *jouissance* on the speaker's part; rather, Suzanne's highly detailed, anatomically fixated description of the symptoms of erotic sensibility she observes in Mme. *** is strangely de-eroticized, deliberately out of sync with what is going on in its object.

My intent here is neither to "correct" Spitzer's overall reading of Diderot (which, despite its quaint moral overtones, is often highly astute and, one might even say, sensitive) nor to address the stylistic fallacy that imbues it *per se*.[32] I wish, rather, to point out that considerations of style can only take one so far in understanding the narrative strategies involved in *La Religieuse*, particularly as they concern the tricky property of sensibility. To see how Diderot sets up the effects that surround this property in this novel, one must consider not only its language but also the figure of Suzanne, the character assigned to enunciate it. Suzanne's characterization as a "reserved" persona holds the key to her strikingly reserved performance in depicting the tortured sensitive souls she has encountered in convent life.

Before she begins to function as an observer of other people's sensibilities, Suzanne Simonin spends a good deal of time depicting herself. The pathetic tale of Suzanne's multiple sufferings is explicitly constructed around her classically sentimentalist image as victim-heroine, abandoned by her family and shunned by society because she is a "natural," or illegitimate, daughter. From the very first page of the novel, Suzanne describes her many "interesting" qualities: she is pretty, smart, and talented—far more so than her two sisters—as well as naïve, frank, and effusively grateful for the attention of the honorable and sensitive Marquis de Croismare, to whom she is writing her story (*Rel.*, 81–83).[33] Suzanne thus has all the traits that are guaranteed, by the rules of the sentimental genre, to elicit great empathy in the reader (just as they move Mme. *** in the scene that so scandalized Leo Spitzer). This part of *La Religieuse* is coded quite faithfully to fit the conventions of the sentimental novel à la Richardson: Suzanne tells the marquis at regular intervals, "My face is an interesting one," "I have a touching voice" (*Nun*, 91), and so forth—thereby reminding him that he has every reason to be tenderly moved by her exceptional physical persona and all the more unsettled by her ghastly misfortunes. Suzanne's status as victim comes to the forefront in the scenes in which, despite being in a state that would touch "souls of bronze" (*Rel.*, 140), she fails to elicit sympathetic responses from the characters who determine her fate—for example, her mother, M. Simonin, and Soeur Sainte-Christine (the second mother superior of Longchamp), who has Suzanne tortured by her band of nasty sycophants. However, the image of Suzanne as victim is truly sealed by the moments in her tale when she loses consciousness in public, leaving her suffering body to speak pathetically for itself.

Suzanne's description of how she fell into a state of physical alienation while taking her religious vows is, in fact, one of the first times that her narrative discourse assumes the external focalization that will later be put to clinical purposes:

> They took off my religious habit and redressed me in the clothes of the world; this is a custom with which you are acquainted. I understood nothing of what was being said around me. I had become practically an automaton. I was aware of nothing, save that from time to time I had a kind of small convulsive fit. They told me what was to be done; and they were often obliged to repeat themselves as I understood nothing the first time. It was not that I was thinking about anything else, but that I was completely rapt . . . They did with me what they would all that morning, which has been erased from my life, for that period of time has never passed into my consciousness. I do not know what I did or what I said. No doubt I was questioned and no doubt I answered. I pronounced my vows, but cannot remember doing so, and I became a nun as unconsciously [*innocemment*] as I had become a Christian.   (*Nun,* 44; *Rel.,* 123–24)

The great expressive power that this tableau assigns to Suzanne's body brings to mind a particular aspect of the theory of absorption popular in eighteenth-century French art: namely, the tendency to single out images of obliviousness or unconsciousness as particularly persuasive.[34] At the same time, there is a curious double vision at work in this passage. On the one hand, Suzanne uses what Jay Caplan identifies as hypotyposis (a discursive rendering of a visually striking object) in order to "present her interlocutor [M. de Croismare] with one of the trials she has undergone in the hope that he will be moved to free her from the convent."[35] On the other hand, this is a *scène muette* in which Suzanne-as-narrator is peculiarly objective and detached from what she, as a protagonist, was experiencing at the time.[36] This rather odd mode of self-description has a distinct purpose in relation to the story's plot: it disposes the sympathetic reader to accept the argument Suzanne employs in a later conversation with Soeur Sainte-Christine that her religious vows are meaningless because she was not really "present" at the ceremony where she took the veil (*Rel.,* 152). It also suggests that alienation is not so much a psychological condition in Suzanne as a condition of her very specific double function as both a conventional victim-heroine and a very unconventional narrator.

Interestingly, the act of reading Suzanne's physiognomy extends beyond her own effort to throw an extra note of pathos into her story: she is also intensely scrutinized by the inhabitants of every new convent she enters, who quite literally "assay" her, sizing her up in body and mind. The observations that other characters make on Suzanne's moral and physical traits inscribe a second level of semiotics—or *sondage*, to use Suzanne's term—in the novel, which only truly comes into play when Suzanne arrives at the convent of Sainte-Eutrope, where Mme. *** presides in her inimitably "bizarre" fashion. This is how Suzanne describes the examination to which she is initially subjected by the resident nuns of that convent: "The first moments passed in reciprocal compliments, questions on the House I had left, trials of my character, my inclinations, my tastes, and my mind. They feel you out all over . . . They sound your feelings about morals, devoutness, the world, religion, the monastic life, and everything; and these repeated experiments result in an epithet which sums you up and is attached as a surname to the one you bear. Thus I was called Saint Suzanne the Reserved" (*Nun*, 125).

This scene represents more than just one in the long series of personal interrogations that Suzanne undergoes in the course of her travels, for the grammatical shift from "I" to "you" as direct object of the nuns' inquiries indicates that "experiments" of this sort are not isolated acts inflicted upon Suzanne to demonstrate her singularity, but rather standard rites of passage, necessary to place any new arrival properly within the economy of the religious household. Probing other characters is thus established as an institutional practice, which formalizes the observations conducted within the convent into a fine art of soliciting certain reactions and deciphering particular signs. That semiotic art becomes downright clinical a few pages later, when Suzanne is examined once again—this time by Mme. *** herself, who assesses Suzanne's character and finds it calm ("Cold even" [*Nun*, 145]), asks her what arouses her and discovers nothing, and even takes Suzanne's pulse: "How calm your pulse is! How regular! Nothing stirs it!" (150).

Together, these tests of Suzanne's character produce a second portrait of her that seems incommensurate with the one she overtly gives to the Marquis de Croismare. The self-described Suzanne has abundant physical charms, an instinctive sense of compassion toward others, and a visceral emotive tendency that sometimes causes her to pass out at key moments. Yet the Suzanne diagnosed by other nuns—even her ardent admirer, Mme. ***—is everything that her epithet of "reserved" implies: implacably calm, collected, and unreactive. Some might interpret this clash as yet another point of incongruity in Diderot's composition of his heroine and attribute Suzanne's reserve to the peculiar innocence and ignorance she professes (or feigns?) in all compromising situations.[37] There is nonetheless more at issue in Suzanne's reserve than simple ignorance, for reserve has a special meaning in the Diderotian typecasting of sensible constitutions. It is reserve—or conscious resistance to provocative stimuli, whether they are discursive (the nuns' battery of questions) or physical (Mme. ∗∗∗'s attempts to arouse Suzanne)—that allows Suzanne to record, in painstakingly objective detail, her observations of the odd actions and reactions going on around her. At the same time, the instinctively compassionate side of Suzanne's character is equally important to the tale of sensibility that she is narrating, for if Suzanne's consciousness is safely detached or "alienated" from those events, her body most certainly is not.

To see the two-sided constitution of Suzanne in action, let us consider more closely how she, and her narration of herself, operate in the famous series of episodes involving her and Mme. ∗∗∗. Suzanne prepares us for her increasingly intimate encounters with this hypersensible creature by giving a detailed report on the superior's physiognomy and general physical appearance:

> I cannot resist the temptation of describing her before going any further. She is a quite round little woman, but quick and lively in her movements, her head is never still on her shoulders; there is always something wrong with her dress. Her face is agreeable rather than the reverse. Her eyes, of which one, the right one, is higher and larger than the other, are full of fire, and yet wandering. When she walks she throws her arms backwards and forwards: if she wants to say something she opens her mouth before she has planned out her ideas and so she stammers a little. When seated, she fidgets on her chair as though something were making her uncomfortable . . . Her distorted face reflects everything that is disjointed in her mind and uneven in her temperament. In consequence order and disorder reigned alternately in the House.   (*Nun,* 120–21)[38]

As diagnostic indices, the elements of this portrait form a cluster of symptoms that point to a certain type of potentially pathological sensibility. Mme. ∗∗∗'s agitated, disorderly body—an awkward amalgam of mismatched body parts and clothes, jerky appendages, disjointed speech and thoughts—represents a mode of sensible organization that is unhealthy both for its own internal economy and for the economy of the collective body she oversees. For, as Suzanne points out a few lines later, "Women like this are very difficult to live with. One never knows what they will like or dislike, what you must do or not do. Nothing is regulated" (122). By virtue of the highly deterministic aetiological link that it establishes between a certain type of sensible woman and a certain kind of institutional disorder, Suzanne's portrait of Mme. ∗∗∗ diagnoses sensibility in its extreme form as a force that produces not harmonious (or "sympathetic") connection, but rather, contagious, chaotic disconnection and instability. And as Suzanne's closing observation emphasizes, there is no sure means of immunizing oneself or the larger social body against the secondary effects of such a rampantly oversensitive constitution.

Suzanne, however, seems to change that for a time: both she and the rest of the nuns remark a greater regularity in the character of Mme. *** after her sensibility is "fixed" by fixing on Suzanne. ("The community had never been so happy as it was since my arrival. The Superior appeared to have lost her temperamental lack of balance. People said I had a settling effect on her" [*Nun*, 148].) The "therapeutic" influence exerted by Suzanne's presence at Sainte-Eutrope stems not just from the fact that Mme. *** becomes enamored of Suzanne, but also, and more fundamentally, from the special resonating dynamic that is established between their two counterbalancing sensibilities over the course of their many *tête-à-tête*. With her two unconnected modes of sensibility—conscious reserve on the one hand and unconscious compassion on the other—Suzanne is uniquely constituted to strike a rare balance between intimacy and distance in dealing with Mme. ***. This does not fully immunize her against the contagious effects of the superior's "incredible sensibility," but it does afford Suzanne a means of transcribing each of their intimate encounters in an utterly factual and unfeeling light, even as her own physical sensibility comes to resonate with Mme. ***'s more and more strongly. By following the interplay of dueling sensibilities that occurs within Suzanne during these scenes, one begins to detect a special logic to her bedside observations. That logic, I contend, concerns more than Diderot's desire to blur the distinction between sympathy and seduction: it relates directly to his theoretical views on observers of nature and the special problems they confront.

Of course, the section of *La Religieuse* in which these encounters occur is also one of Diderot's most artful explorations of the equivocal effects involved in such conventionally "touching" experiences as having music lessons, seeing a pathetic tableau, or listening to a tale of misfortunes. Suzanne's narrative in these pages broadly exploits the ambiguous link between the mechanisms of spiritual sympathy and erotic arousal. Mme. ***'s sensibility toward Suzanne is initially sparked while listening to her play a few pieces by Couperin, Rameau, and Scarlatti, which inspire her to express her emotion in a tactile way: "Meanwhile she had lifted a corner of my neckerchief, her hand was placed on my bare shoulder, and the end of her fingers rested on my breast. She sighed and seemed oppressed; her breathing became irregular, the hand, which she kept on my shoulder, first pressed it hard and then not at all, as though she were without force or life, and her head fell on mine. Really the silly woman had an incredible sensibility and the most lively appreciation of music. I have never known anyone on whom it produced such singular effects" (*Nun*, 135).

Although she graphically recounts the effects that music triggers in her listener, Suzanne makes no connection between them and her own considerable charms (underscored so coquettishly elsewhere in the novel), and she takes no

pleasure herself in the musical interlude. During their next encounter, however, with no music-playing to explain the effects that are again triggered in
Mme. ***, even Suzanne cannot help suspecting that something besides her
own proficiency on the clavichord is responsible for the Mother Superior's
sighs and trembling. Unable to fathom what may be the cause—"I try to guess
and cannot" (*Nun*, 138)—Suzanne resorts once again to her monotonous case-
history narrative style to record the scene, and thus effectively takes herself out
of it as a conscious participant. At the same time, she is participating physically
in their mutual caresses and, despite her intellectual confoundment, detects effects in her body that resonate exactly with what seems to be happening to her
companion.

Now, such passages can be read ironically or psychoanalytically to demonstrate Diderot's salacious libertinism, or Suzanne's psychic repression, or the
tragedy of unavowed lesbianism. However, what interest me about these scenes
is the "schizophrenic" way that Suzanne operates in them: she is split between
her insensibility as a conscious observing subject and her clearly reactive sensibility as an observed object. This split is not, I hasten to add, a mind/body
schism; it is, rather, Diderot's way of deploying the two seemingly incommensurate types of sensibility that he needs to make *La Religieuse* work on its
reader at both a visceral and a cerebral level.

To see precisely how that strategy operates, let us consider the purpose of
the clinical language Suzanne uses to describe what is happening both in Mme.
***'s body, and in her own, during their second intimate encounter. At one
level, Suzanne's peculiarly clipped discursive style allows her to assume the position of an innocent bystander, sufficiently removed from the proceedings that
she cannot be implicated in the sexual causality of the superior's sensible effects. On another level, it allows her to collect with admirable thoroughness all
of the signs of an impending crisis of sensibility: "Then came a moment, I
know not if it was pleasure or pain, when she turned pale as death: her eyes
closed, all her body stiffened violently, her lips first were tightened and then
wet as if with a light froth; then her mouth opened slightly and she seemed to
me to die, as she uttered a deep sigh" (*Nun*, 138). Concluding that these signs
point to an illness of some sort, Suzanne responds, appropriately enough, by
trying to summon some medical help: "I got up quickly: I thought she was ill.
I wished to go out and call for help." Mme. ***, naturally, stops her—giving
Suzanne the occasion to complete her observations and extend them to herself:
"I then perceived, from the trembling that seized her, from her troubled
speech, the wildness of her eyes and hands, from the warmth with which she
hugged me, the violence with which her arms embraced me, that her illness
would not be long in coming again. I do not know what was happening inside

me, but I was seized with a terror, a trembling, and a desire to swoon which verified my suspicion that her illness was contagious" (143).[39]

From this point on, Suzanne will persist, with the same clinical precision, in diagnosing both the mother superior's symptoms and her own as a contagious malady, which she tries to figure out during her moments of reflection, but fails to decipher as more than a simple assembly of related bodily phenomena (*Rel.*, 230). Catching the illness of sensibility does not, however, prevent Suzanne from continuing to record her observations in an orderly, progressive fashion. Even at the height of her own crises, Suzanne manages to keep her wits about her, thanks to her unique capacity for alienation, or separation of her mental activities from her body—the hallmark, we may recall, of all assiduous observers in the Diderotian typology. The key to this delicate narrative balancing act is the language that Suzanne uses: she speaks, not in the "language of the senses" in which Mme. *** is so fluent (*Nun*, 146), but in the discourse of semiotic pathology. Given the painstaking attention with which she collects signs of critical sensibility both in herself and in Mme. ***, Suzanne might have made an excellent "witness of particular facts," the entry-level position on the hierarchy of medical observers proposed at the end of Bordeu's article "Crise" (252).

But what, one might ask, is the purpose of importing the clinical language associated with sensibility into a novelistic genre more standardly concerned with evoking precisely the sensual language that Suzanne cannot read or speak? One could conclude that Diderot invented this peculiar narrative operation, by which psychological interpretation is replaced with a purely empirical physical diagnosis, as a stratagem to allow Suzanne to elide the taboo subject of sexuality. Yet Diderot's recourse to a clinical mode of discourse is more than just a device for ensuring his heroine's innocence while simultaneously titillating his reader. Even as Suzanne's "compassionate" nature moves the story along by getting her involved in the sensibilities of other convent residents, her reserved, insensible voice allows the signs they emit to be articulated in graphically objective detail. It is thus precisely by reducing all of its characters, including Suzanne, from psychological beings to physiological beings that *La Religieuse* succeeds in one of its primary philosophical tasks: providing a broader perspective on sensibility than is typical in the conventional novel.

What, then, is that perspective, and who is supposed to have it? Clearly, it is not Suzanne herself, for although her decodings of sensibility are always thorough and precise, there is a peculiar gap between the signs she gathers and the interpretations she reaches using them. Although Mme. *** does her level best to teach Suzanne to speak the language that would have expanded her interpretive understanding, Suzanne quite obstinately refuses to learn it: "I know nothing about the language of the senses . . . I know nothing and would rather remain ignorant than acquire knowledge that would perhaps make me more to be pitied than I am already" (*Nun*, 146). It is not simply because she would bemoan her cloistered existence all the more, or lose her much-vaunted innocence, that Suzanne must reject that fuller understanding of sensibility. Rather, it is because she would lose her effectiveness as a narrator.

Other critics have established that Suzanne's lack of knowledge is a cunning rhetorical device, one that obliges the reader to provide a more worldly interpretation of the novel's sexually compromising scenes.[40] What remains to be explained is the epistemological value that the novel gains by having Suzanne stick to the clinical facts on sensibility. Suzanne pathologizes sexuality not only to de-eroticize it, but also to provide an impartial empirical account of the extraordinary sensible phenomena she has observed inside convent walls. That impartiality serves two purposes, one rhetorical, the other more philosophical (or sociopolitical, in modern terms). First, because of the deliberate disjuncture that is created in the *tête-à-tête* episodes between Suzanne's masterfully impersonal technical language and her interpretative naïveté, the reader must provide the speculative connections among her facts and reach his own erotic conclusions as to what is going on. This act of interpretation guarantees that he (as the reader inscribed in the novel should probably be designated) will be sensibly affected by those episodes. Diderot therefore deprives Suzanne, as narrator, of her own knowing enjoyment—that is, the ability to interpret—so as to make it impossible for the reader to maintain the insensibility that Suzanne consciously assumes. In the process, the reader becomes suspended between intellectual insight into the causality that links together Suzanne's impersonal and incomplete observations, and a sensual response to the sensibility of the fictional bodies he is beholding. Thus, according to Diderot's paradoxical narrative enactment of sensibility, it is the reader who must ultimately resolve the dilemma implicit to understanding sensibility—a property that must be directly *experienced* to be fully fathomed, yet also observed from a distance to be articulated. It is a seductive, and confounding, strategy indeed.

At the same time, Diderot provides a way out of the epistemological impasse posed by *La Religieuse* through the very "clinical" language by which he had created it. For one can also approach the rhetorical operation sketched above in terms of the extended metaphor of contagion that permeates the novel: as a carrier of sensibility, Suzanne manifests some of its symptoms (i.e., physical arousal) but is free of others, namely the pleasure triggered by recognizing that one has had a moving experience. We can also apply that model to the reader: although it is through the agency of Suzanne that the reader contracts sensibility in all of its irresistible moral and physical resonances, it is nonetheless also through Suzanne that he is able in some way to ascend to a larger philosophical perspective on the events recounted in *La Religieuse*. What those events add up to is, by design, an inside picture of the profoundly unhealthy disequilibrium of convent life as an institution. That disequilibrium is, moreover, grounded in the literally pathological side of sensibility that is inscribed as the text's main "lesson"—the lesson through which Diderot's novel of sensibility rejoins philosophical medicine as an enlightening brand of discourse.

Let us therefore leave the reader for a moment in his uncomfortable fix and turn to the larger message about sensibility that *La Religieuse* is designed to impart. Suzanne's writings are composed as a formal plea to be rescued from her unfortunate circumstances; they thus serve a purpose similar to that of the memoirs written by M. Manouri, the lawyer who represents Suzanne in her legal request to be released from her vows. Manouri's first memoir is built around the central premise that "no one knows the story of these retreats" (*Nun*, 100)—implying that were this story to be known, claustral life and the vows associated with it would be proven criminal in the terms of both social and natural law. Lying at the heart of Manouri's impassioned criticism of convents is the question of constitution: first, the constitution of the state, to which convents may not be as essential as some believe (*Rel.*, 182); and second, the constitution of the individuals who, by force or imprudence, take up monastic vows. As Manouri argues,

> Can these vows, which go against the whole grain of our nature, ever be properly observed except by a few ill-constituted creatures in whom the seeds of passion are withered and whom we should properly class among the monsters, if our knowledge permitted us to know as easily or as well the internal as the external structure of man? Can the animal functions be suspended by the gloomy ceremonies observed at the donning of the habit or at the moment of profession when a man or woman is consecrated to monasticism and misery? . . . Where is it that Nature, revolted by a constraint for which she is not intended, breaks down the obstacles that oppose her, goes mad, and throws the whole animal system into a disorder for which there is no remedy? (*Nun*, 99–100)

Manouri's questions lead inexorably to the conclusion that the entire human system—organic as well as psychological—is placed into jeopardy when people are committed to the disordering misery of monastic life. Only monstrously organized, passionless creatures can possibly obey such impossible vows, and those who are not so organized at the outset become monsters after a certain time. In short, he declares, "the cloistered life is fit only for the fanatic and the hypocrite" (*Nun*, 101) because it obliges its followers either to deafen themselves to the bodily language that demands to be heeded or to devise hypocritically veiled ways of speaking it. Hence Mme. ✳✳✳, whom Suzanne calls a prime example of "the strangeness of the female mind" and of "the effect of retiring from the world" (136). And hence the urgency of liberating a delicate creature like Suzanne (as well as her potential offspring, according to the populationist bent of the argument) from a setting that fosters, not the spiritual values of poverty, chastity, and obedience, but rather, "discomfort, nausea, and the vapors . . . servitude and despotism . . . hates that never die . . . passions nurtured in silence" (100).

Unfortunately, compelling as it may be, Manouri's first memoir makes "only a slight sensation" (*Rel.*, 182), and his second results only in an unsuccessful trial that officially seals Suzanne's fate of remaining within one convent or another. Suzanne comments after the fact that Manouri's legal memoirs failed to make her case convincingly because they contained "too much wit and not enough pathos" (181). These memoirs succeed, however, in establishing that the "philosophical" way to confront the institution of monastic life is to view it through the lens of *natural* history—an approach that calls for close examination of the internal structure both of the institution and of the bodies trapped within it. A truly enlightening case against institutional religious life would thus be based not so much upon the particulars of one inhabitant's circumstances (he makes no mention of Suzanne's family or current cloister) as upon multiple firsthand observations of the constitutional disorders that inevitably arise when people are forced to live in unnatural conditions of prolonged silence, celibacy, and solitude (184). Such an investigation would therefore entail not psychological profiles, but a series of case histories that would reveal the full spectrum of physio-pathological *types* that convent life produces. Focused as it is on the dangerously constraining effects of religious vows upon the natural inclinations of the human body, Manouri's proposed history of convents requires a very special kind of clinical historian, one who could both decipher the signs of a body's internal functions and diagnose the resonances of those functions within a societal context. Yet, given the very secrecy and closure of the institution he would like to bring to light, that historian would also have to be an insider—in this case, a nun. With her peculiarly detached observational acumen, yet direct experience with the most extreme cases of denatured sensibility observed in three different convents, Suzanne is uniquely suited for the task.

In that sense, Suzanne's narrative presents exactly what her lawyer had called for in the public condemnation of convents by which he hoped to win her case and free her from her vows. All that Manouri's memoirs needed, in theory, was the right kind of historian, able both to present the observations he had proposed and to give them a more stirringly pathetic tone. By setting down her own life story, Suzanne is in essence rearguing her own case from the privileged vantage point of a "natural," disingenuous young woman who functions as a clinical observer garbed in a nun's habit. As a natural history, her memoirs consist of an accumulation of medical semiotic studies, using as specimens the variously disordered sensible creatures she encounters during her successive internments. And as a pathetic personal history, Suzanne's story is both a deposition and an appeal for help to sympathetic outside parties, represented here by the shadowy Présidente de *** (a friend of Suzanne's friend Soeur Sainte-Ursule, who had hired Manouri on Suzanne's behalf [*Rel.*, 149, 204–5]) as well as by the Marquis de Croismare.

Because of Suzanne's limited understanding of sensibility, she cannot fully articulate the novel's plea to emancipate innocent victims like her from the denaturing institution of religious claustration. It is for that reason that other, more worldy-wise characters are brought in to explain the severity of the situation—characters like Manouri, and like Dom Morel, the new confessor who is introduced at the novel's end. Dom Morel presides over the final stage of the drama surrounding Mme. ***, whose excessive sensibility turns into an irreparably fatal disorder when church authorities forbid her to see Suzanne (*Rel.*, 252–61). In addition to hearing Mme. ***'s last, damning confession of her sins (273–74), Dom Morel provides Suzanne with a new sympathetic ear and the reader with additional insights into the fundamental unhealthfulness of monastic existence. Like Suzanne, Dom Morel is a monastic insider who is profoundly unhappy with his condition. His tale of personal misfortune naturally strikes a chord with Suzanne, and his explanation of the pathological nature of Mme. ***'s present constitution serves to complete the novel's warnings on the dangers of cloistered life.[41] Moved by the sympathy she feels toward Dom Morel—as well as by the fear of falling victim to the madness that, he asserts, afflicts all nuns who are not suited for claustration (271–72)—Suzanne resolves in the last, fragmented pages of her memoirs to escape from Sainte-Eutrope with a "young Benedictine" who is probably none other than Dom Morel. Unfortunately, she is no sooner outside the walls of the convent than she discovers that her sympathetic liberator is in truth a scoundrel who wants to seduce her (281–82).

However heinous, Dom Morel's behavior in that briefly sketched plot turn is less important than the fact that he is introduced to express, more eloquently and insightfully than could Suzanne, the pathogenic powers of an unnatural mode of existence; it is he who makes the novel's final appeal for abolishing all convents. Dom Morel may turn out to have the usual dark designs on Suzanne's body (inevitable, it seems, given her many charms); but that only makes his denunciation of monastic life all the more convincing for the reader of *La Religieuse*. Dom Morel is, like Manouri, a character too minor and too interested in Suzanne to be a true philosophe within the novel. He does, however, serve both as a case in point and as mouthpiece for the more global aetiology that is necessary to turn Suzanne's isolated clinical decodings into a grave diagnosis of the monastic institution.

Diderot's *La Religieuse* consequently demonstrates that a novel of sensibility can be just as effective in serving philosophical or sociopolitical ends as it is in eliciting the "touching" moral responses associated with sentimental narrative. Given the clinical tone that is adopted not just by the narrator but also by characters like M. Manouri and Dom Morel, it might be more appropriate to call the ends of this novel medico-philosophical; for both the social and the literary projects implicit to *La Religieuse* are pursued through a discourse on sensibility that is rooted as much in contemporary physiology and pathology as in sentimentalist aesthetics. Indeed, one might say that *La Religieuse* surpasses the ambitions of philosophically minded physicians like Bordeu: this novel deploys knowledge of the body as a means not only of understanding the physical consequences that ensue when human beings are subjected to certain social conditions, but also of legislating social reform.

As for the reader of *La Religieuse*, although he is destined to fall prey to the various seductive traps that are set by the narrative (the blurring of sympathetic and erotic response and of the boundary between reality and fiction), he is nonetheless afforded a rare glimpse into the singular effects that convent life exerts on the fundamental property of human nature: sensibility. He is also positioned, by virtue of the incompleteness of Suzanne's observations, to reach his own active judgments as to the causes and repercussions of those effects. To reach the right judgments, the reader must possess the proper moral-physical disposition; it is thus no coincidence that the novel's fictional reader, the Marquis de Croismare, bears a close resemblance to the *Éloge de Richardson*'s "quiet, solitary reader . . . who likes to pass his hours profitably in sympathetic silence" ("ER," 274). That is not to say that the marquis is presented as immune to the more equivocal effects of reading a story such as Suzanne's, for there are, as Diderot emphasizes in the *Éloge*, moral "caverns" within every human heart—including perhaps the marquis's, as Suzanne acknowledges in her postscript: "Can it be that we think men less sensitive to the picture of our sufferings than to the image of our charms? Do we say to ourselves that it is easier to seduce them than to stir their hearts?" (*Nun*, 193). Given what Diderot insisted was the double-edged, contagious nature of sensibility, none of the figures involved in this novel—neither author, narrator, character, or reader—is able to maintain the dispassionate, transcendant perspective on the property to which the great actor-observer of the *Paradoxe sur le comédien* as well as the contemporary *médecin philosophe* aspired.[42]

On balance, then, one must say that the "knower of sensibility" is in Diderot's works a constructed or ideal position, impossible and necessary at the same time. For while no one can fully and truly hold that position, it is still possible to make well-grounded observations on sensibility's myriad operations for the benefit of suffering humanity. In this sense, the diagnostic mode of narrative employed in *La Religieuse* should be characterized as natural-philosophical in orientation: it corresponds directly to the program for natural philosophy that Diderot sketches in *De l'interprétation de la nature*, according to which the only means of glimpsing nature's underlying laws is to amass observations into an ever-expanding bank of facts and then to "sniff out" the vital connections among them.[43] It also corresponds to the period's larger debate over how sensibility can or should be managed in order to advance the cause of enlightenment.

The complex operations of sensibility in *La Religieuse*—and in Diderot's general theory of the purposes and effects of serious fiction—create some intriguing resonances between the two other concepts that are announced in the title of my book: enlightenment and pathology. The project of enlightenment is unquestionably central to all of Diderot's writings, even the most pessimistic or licentious.[44] The desire to enlighten obviously informs Diderot's description of how great fiction works upon its reader: he invests the experience of reading Richardson with an extraordinary capacity both to improve the moral character of the individual reader and to make that reader's social interactions more wholesome. Yet one can see the same desire at work in the far more morally ambiguous *La Religieuse*, a novel in which the graphic representation of sensibility's pathological capacities unveils, with maximal intensity, one of the hidden moral dramas that Diderot believed was taking place out of sight of most philosophes. Diderot does not depict either sensibility or sexuality, in themselves, as pathological: he reserves that label for certain social practices and prejudices that no enlightened society should, in his mind, tolerate.

꒰ ꒱

Although his concerns were not, properly speaking, medical, Diderot did find inspiration in two of the notions championed by Enlightenment *médecins philosophes*. The first was their dynamic new topology of the body—its reactive centers, its economic actions and reactions, and its inherent capacity for arousal and redirection. This physiological model of sensibility plainly fascinated Diderot and fit nicely into his more general efforts to forge a comprehensive system of vibrant materialism. The second was the idea that vital sensibility had ramifications for every aspect of human experience—including intellectual functioning, moral feelings, and social interactions—all of which could be controlled and improved through proper individual and social hygiene. Diderot did not, of course, always take that enterprise seriously: witness the salacious turn that the discussion of social hygiene takes at the end of the *Rêve de d'Alembert,* and the reservations Diderot expressed about Helvétius's mechanistic reduction of all intellectual functions to sensibility in *De l'esprit.* Diderot's meditations on art and fiction nevertheless illustrate that he perceived sensibility both as a crucial aesthetic and moral tool, and as a means of carrying out the central activity of all philosophes: communicating with nature, within oneself and in one's fellows.

Before leaving Diderot, we should note that literary historians have more commonly credited Rousseau for moving the eighteenth-century French novel away from the "detached, intellectual, evaluative" values that Peter Brooks ascribes to the novel of worldliness, and toward the intense emotional values associated with sentimentalism.[45] Diderot's role in this process should not, however, be underemphasized; for it was he, and not Rousseau, who issued a call to other writers to take up the cause of reforming the principles of fiction in both the novel and the theater. That is not to refute the undeniably huge importance of Rousseau's *La Nouvelle Héloïse* for novelists of the next generation—Laclos, Sade, Bernardin de Saint-Pierre, Rétif de la Bretonne, and others.[46] Rousseau, however, was clearly too disgusted with contemporary civilized society by the time he wrote that novel to place any faith in the philosophes' effort to foster moral-intellectual edification by improving literature and other cultural institutions. I therefore consider him to be less a founder than a participant in the physicalization of sensibility in the novel after 1750 and the effort to use the novel as a natural-philosophical vehicle for furthering enlightenment. As we shall see, Rousseau took part in this development in his own, idiosyncratic manner: he embraced a theory of moral sensibility that was rooted in a peculiar brand of moral-physical hygiene, and he designed *La Nouvelle Héloïse* in order to put that theory into fictional practice.

6. The Moral Hygiene of Sensibility

 Rousseau and Tissot

Prescriptions for Wholesomeness: The *morale sensitive*

Because it fell on both sides of the famous eighteenth-century dyad known as "the physical and the moral," sensibility played a central role in Enlightenment ethics; it even gave rise to its own genre of moralist discourse, known as *la morale sensitive*—a system of morals based largely if not exclusively on regulating sensibility's effects on moral behavior. The writers who contributed to this genre sought both to determine sensibility's moral ramifications and to use it as a natural means of making human beings more virtuous. As in the theories of intellectual edification we examined in Chapter 3, the campaign for moral edification was fundamentally physicalist: the chief instrument its proponents employed for improving man's moral nature was the sensible body, deemed to be the locus of all the impressions to which the human being was subject. However, the *morale sensitive* theorists sought to restrict rather than expand and cultivate those impressions; for, in pointed opposition to those who assumed that the advancement of civilized society would automatically bring about moral improvement, these theorists saw the civilizing process as a grave threat to virtue. That is, they saw civilized society as an intrinsically unwholesome force that acted not to improve human nature but to corrupt it, by overstimulating and denaturing the sensible constitution. For such moral philosophers, therefore, the sensible body was the potential cause or site of an alarming ethical ill; yet it was also the primary means of remedying that ill.

Not surprisingly, the *morale sensitive* school of thought is closely associated with Jean-Jacques Rousseau, who invented its name, if not its basic principles. Although Rousseau never carried out his plan to write a book on how to regulate morality by controlling sensibility, its underlying tenets pervaded his writings.[1] Rousseau's interest in a sensibility-based moral hygiene was evident as early as his first and second *Discourses,* where he advanced the historical-anthropological theory that, buried under social man's factitious and corrupted moral constitution, there exists a virtuous nature that can and should be retrieved.[2] This was the first expression of the Rousseauian myth of the primitive *homme sensible,* an antiprogressionist construct that was also central to the sympathetic self-portrait he presented in his autobiographical works. However, the *morale sensitive* project was hardly exclusive to Rousseau; it was equally evident in the theories of Enlightenment medical hygienists, who sought to manage sensibility to ensure health and to restore what they saw as the proper moral order of human life.

Because Rousseau's model of a *morale sensitive* is crucial for understanding the deep resonances between his views and those of contemporary médecins philosophes, it is an appropriate place to begin our study of the hygiene-based ethics of sensibility. That model is found in a rather short passage in the ninth book of the *Confessions,* where Rousseau recounts what occurred in his life from early April 1756 to December 1757, when, having definitively renounced city life, he took up residence at the Ermitage and (when not distracted by his personal dramas) devoted himself to writing.[3] Among the works Rousseau planned to compose during this time was one tentatively entitled *Morale sensitive, ou Le Matérialisme du sage,* which he envisioned as the ultimate fusion of physics and metaphysics. Acting as the wise materialist of his title, Rousseau imagined undertaking a painstaking study of how his "different manners of being" are triggered through the impressions made upon his sensitive system by such external forces as "the seasons, sounds, colors, darkness, light, the elements, food, noise, silence, motion, rest" (*Conf.,* 343). Having made those observations, he would be able to trace his changing moral dispositions back to their physical origins and, from there, develop "an external regimen which—varied according to circumstances—could put or maintain the soul in the condition most favorable to virtue" (343). In theory, Rousseau would then possess a full knowledge both of the human being's sensitive faculties and of the myriad objects that inspire the sentiments "by which we let ourselves be dominated." Such knowledge would, he underscores, be of inestimable value to the quest for virtue: "From how many errors would reason be saved, how many vices would be kept from being born, if we knew how to force the animal economy to favor the moral order it so often troubles!" (343). In other words, Rousseau's *morale sensitive* would provide the key for making people virtuous not by training their minds, but rather, by carefully controlling the impressions made upon their bodies—or more precisely, upon their sensitive systems.

The *morale sensitive* as Rousseau conceived it was thus a hybrid brand of moral-physical analysis, grounded in materialism yet given a pronounced moralist twist. Vestiges of this project are evident in virtually all of the works Rousseau wrote during or after his Ermitage sojourn, and most particularly in two: *La Nouvelle Héloïse* (1756–57) and the *Dialogues, ou Rousseau Juge de Jean-Jacques* (1772–76), where he gave his most extensive definition of sensibility in both general and personal terms. That definition appears in the *Deuxième Dialogue*, where the interlocutor designated as "Rousseau" tries to explain the singular temperament of "Jean-Jacques" to an interlocutor dubbed "Le Français."[4] Although the *Deuxième Dialogue* appears at first glance to offer little more than testimony to Rousseau's intense paranoia and egocentrism, it contains another critical component of his sensibility theory and therefore warrants a close and careful look.

The discussion of sensibility in this dialogue begins as an effort to rebut the apparently widespread opinion that Jean-Jacques's sensibility is excessive, vicious, and therefore "monstrous."[5] That malicious criticism has, asserts the Rousseau interlocutor, been levied by people who misunderstand Jean-Jacques as well as the multifaceted nature of sensibility itself.[6] Sensibility, Rousseau explains, has many different, and at times contradictory, manners of operating—physical versus moral and positive versus negative:

> Sensibility is the principle of all action . . . All men are sensitive, and perhaps to the same degree, but not in the same manner. There is a purely passive physical and organic sensibility which seems to have as its end only the preservation of our bodies and of our species through the direction of pleasure and pain. There is another sensibility that I call active and moral which is nothing other than the faculty of attaching our affections to beings who are foreign to us. This type, about which the study of nerve pairs teaches nothing, seems to offer a fairly clear analogy for souls to the magnetic faculty of bodies. Its strength is in proportion to the relationships we feel between ourselves and other beings, and depending on the nature of these relationships it sometimes acts positively by attraction, sometimes negatively by repulsion, like the poles of a magnet. (*Judge*, 112)

What is most significant about this passage is its concluding metaphor: the sensitive soul, like the body, operates mechanically, in keeping with the laws of physical attraction. That magnetic metaphor allows Rousseau to keep physical and moral sensibility distinct but analogous, and also to posit the existence of two subspecies of moral sensibility—positive and negative—which are then aligned with his more general distinction between *amour de soi-même* and *amour propre*. *Amour de soi-même*, as defined here, is an instinctive urge to "extend one's being and one's enjoyments"; *amour propre*, by contrast, is a "de-

generated" mode of self-love that prompts human beings to reflect and compare themselves constantly with their fellows (112). Translated into mechanical terms, *amour propre* produces a type of moral sensibility that only acts neg-
atively. This "repulsive" kind of sensibility, declares Rousseau, arises not from
nature but "from social relations, from the progress of ideas, and from the cultivation of the mind," all of which alienate people from those around them. He
finds *amour propre* to be particularly rampant among "witty people and especially men of letters" (113).

Having combined these distinctions into a multitiered model of sensibility,
the Rousseau interlocutor proceeds to apply it to the case of Jean-Jacques:

> Jean-Jacques seems to me to be endowed with physical sensibility to a
> rather high degree. He depends a great deal on his senses, and he would
> depend on them even more if his moral sensibility did not often divert
> him. Indeed, it is frequently through the latter that the former exerts such
> a lively effect on him. Beautiful sounds, a beautiful sky, a beautiful land-
> scape, a beautiful lake, flowers, scents, beautiful eyes, a gentle look: all
> these react so strongly on his senses only when they have in some way
> gotten through to his heart . . . It is the mixture in most of his sensations
> that tempers them; and because his purely material sensations are de-
> prived of the seductive attraction the others exert, all sensations act more
> moderately on him.   (*Judge*, 114)

Jean-Jacques's physical sensibility, however intense and voluptuous it may
seem, should therefore not be confused with the "depraved" and showy sensu-
ality characteristic of worldly people, for it is tempered through a special system of internal wiring which ensures that his tastes remain "healthy, even delicate, but not refined" (114).[7] The same "naturalness" is evident in the moral
register: "As for his moral sensibility, I never knew any man so subjugated by
it, but here it is necessary to understand what I mean, for I have found in him
only that which acts positively, which comes from nature" (115–16). Jean-
Jacques's sensibility is thus unique not because it is excessive but because it is
unsocialized: it is radically different from "the repelling sensibility which becomes exalted in society" (116). Jean-Jacques should, by consequence, be recognized not as a monster, but rather as the sole living example of a truly sensitive and warm-hearted man—a being whose sensibility operates only in the
positive magnetic register. What is truly monstrous, insists the Rousseau interlocutor, is worldly life, a mode of existence that turns sensibility into a negative
and literally unattractive source of moral energy.

In addition to clarifying Rousseau's complex attitude toward sensibility and
its various registers, this discussion gives us a sense of how he might have put

his *morale sensitive* to autobiographical use. The Rousseau interlocutor of the *Dialogues* concludes that if one really wants to understand Jean-Jacques's seemingly extraordinary behavior—including his admitted lack of virtue, as conventionally understood—one must do a thoroughgoing examination of "his temperament, his moral temper, his entire constitution" (*Judge,* 156). This sort of constitutionally based analysis of moral character is the first step in the *morale sensitive* sketched in the *Confessions.* In the *Dialogues,* however, the analysis stops there: the Rousseau interlocutor does not use his material knowledge of Jean-Jacques's unique sensibility to propose a moral regimen by which it might be better controlled. That, the *Dialogues* suggest, would be futile for Jean-Jacques, who could not and would not adapt to a world that is so radically unsuited to an *homme sensible* like him.

This impasse is predictable: the *Dialogues* are designed to explain and ex-culpate Jean-Jacques, and not to rehabilitate him. It does not, moreover, ex-clude the possibility that Rousseau may have used a different literary vehicle to carry out his vision of a fully executed *morale sensitive.* That is precisely the mission attached to *La Nouvelle Héloïse,* a fiction written as an imaginary real-ization of Rousseau's quest for a world fit for true sensibility. In that world, the natural-born sensitive man would not be forced to comply with the perverse demands of contemporary society; instead, he would find everything in his en-vironment—all physical and moral stimuli—perfectly adapted to his special mode of physical and moral functioning. Under such circumstances, positive sensibility could reign supreme, and one would only have to *feel,* in the most profound and authentic sense, to attain the state of virtue.

꧁ ꧂

Numerous critics have, of course, ventured interpretations of how the quest for virtue is woven into the plot of *La Nouvelle Héloïse:* they tend primarily to cite Wolmar's "cure" of the two erstwhile lovers, Julie and Saint-Preux, a cure fre-quently compared to modern psychoanalytic techniques of psychic condition-ing.[8] I would argue, however, that this novel's plan for effecting moral reform is best understood by recourse not to twentieth-century psychoanalytic theory, but to eighteenth-century medical theory. For, like Rousseau, Enlightenment physicians believed that morality could be achieved through material means—that is, by proper understanding and treatment of the body. They also per-ceived an implicit connection between the medical profession and the philoso-phy and practice of morality. In the eyes of some, the connection was chiefly methodological: medical semioticians like Ménuret de Chambaud and Sénebier asserted that their observational techniques held revolutionary implications for medical and moral theory alike.[9] For others, the link seemed to be etiological—that is, rooted in the necessary correspondence between physical constitution and moral disposition. Diderot echoed this view in *Les Eléments de physiologie* when he maintained that "when national mores are pure, bodies are healthy and illnesses are simple."[10] However they established the connection, most medical theorists endorsed the notion that, as Tissot declared in *De la santé des gens de lettres,* there is "a close union, a perfect interlinking, a reciprocal dependence between the science of morals and the science of health."[11] Health was thus to be viewed as a matter involving not merely an individual's body, but his or her entire sensible economy—an economy that many physicians saw as sorely tested by the insalubrious conditions of contemporary society.

Any study of the health prescriptions put forth by Enlightenment physicians would thus be incomplete if it did not take into consideration the more general code of ethics to which they subscribed. Tissot's medical doctrine is particularly instructive for understanding this aspect of philosophical medicine because it was built upon a system of socially determined body types ranging from the peasants to high society, with scholars, artisans, and masturbators situated at various points in between. His concern with morality was most obvious in his use of hygiene as a social cure-all—that is, a means of guiding the various members of the social collective back to a more "natural" state of human health and happiness. This manner of interconnecting hygiene and social theory reflected three larger developments in eighteenth-century thinking. The first was the overt effort on the part of medical theorists to revive the ancient doctrine of the non-naturals in order to appeal to a newly health-conscious popular clientele and its concerns with strength, happiness, and longevity.[12] The second was the tendency on the part of physicians and moralists alike to view sensibility as a natural, secular force that could be tapped to improve the moral fitness of the human race.[13] The third was the period's growing anxiety over the ambiguous effects of the civilizing process, a process that most philosophes (including physician-philosophers) saw as nearing completion in their "enlightened" century, but not necessarily for the better.[14]

Those conceptual trends coalesce dramatically in Tissot's *Essai sur les maladies des gens du monde* (1770), a work that I shall treat as a medical complement to *La Nouvelle Héloïse.* In making that comparison, I am not overlooking Rousseau's deep skepticism regarding contemporary medicine, a sentiment that he obligingly illustrates in the third dialogue of *Rousseau Juge de Jean-Jacques* by compiling the many antimedical passages of the *Emile.*[15] We should note, however, that Rousseau exempted Tissot from his more general condemnation of medicine and medical practitioners. In June 1762, moved to express his admiration for Tissot's recently published *Avis au peuple* (1761), Rousseau initiated a very cordial correspondence with his Swiss compatriot that lasted until Rousseau's death. One of Rousseau's last letters to Tissot (February 1, 1769) is particularly revealing in this regard, because it demonstrates that Rousseau not only considered Tissot a kindred spirit, but hoped that the doctor's prescriptions for healthful living might offer him some relief from his "cruel illness" of chronic intestinal and urinary ailments.[16]

There was thus a personal underpinning to the intellectual sympathy that Rousseau and Tissot expressed for each other.[17] For our purposes, however, the most important aspect of the Rousseau-Tissot relation is the connection that exists between their ideas, and most particularly between their respective models for a *morale sensitive*. In comparing those models, we should take care not to reduce either author to a mere disciple of the other—for example, by calling Tissot a "medical Rousseau," or by treating Rousseau as an amateur medical theorist, as at least one well-intentioned reader of *La Nouvelle Héloïse* has done.[18] To avoid those pitfalls, I approach Tissot's *Essai sur les maladies des gens du monde* as an intertext for Rousseau's novel and underscore the striking resonances that become evident when one juxtaposes these texts. Tissot's treatise contains multiple passages that echo key moments in Rousseau's work; it also demonstrates that Rousseau's notion of sensibility was closely linked to an important trend in contemporary medical philosophy.

❧ ☙

One of the most intriguing aspects of the model of "healthy" sensibility promoted by Tissot and Rousseau alike is its extreme degree of ascetic constraint. That asceticism might seem all the more remarkable in the *Essai sur les maladies des gens du monde* when one considers its intended audience: the putatively unconstrained and pleasure-loving urban elite. Yet Tissot's exacting medical plan for the rich and worldly class differed only in degree from those recommended by other physicians of his day, who agreed that *gens du monde* were, by constitution and by habit, excessively delicate, and hence, unnaturally sensitive to the outside impressions produced by the complex world in which they lived.[19] The frailty of the upper class was worrisome to Tissot and his colleagues not simply because it endangered the individual, but because it also threatened the greater social body, whole segments of which seemed to be chronically incapacitated.[20] These médecins philosophes thus used hygiene as an instrument of active social edification: they sought to instruct weak members of society in how to fortify themselves, so that they might be less vulnerable to the sensory overload associated with civilized life.

This is the theoretical climate within which Tissot composed his *Essai sur les maladies des gens du monde,* a treatise that interweaves notions of health, morality, lifestyle, and sensibility into a single conceptual continuum. Tissot's purpose in writing this essay is not simply to advise worldly people on matters of health: he also seeks to issue a warning about the fundamental insalubrity of their mode of life. Tissot employs two interrelated programs to correct this state of affairs. The first is a rhetorical program of persuasion, designed to awaken his readers to the health risks they incur through their dissipated, extravagant, and unnatural living habits. The second is a therapeutic program for improving the oversensitive constitution of the typical *mondain.* Although he grounds his therapy in contemporary hygienic doctrine, Tissot does not use that doctrine neutrally: to the contrary, he deploys it in order to advance a social theory that is clearly hostile to most of the values then associated with "polite" living. Indeed, the *Essai* represents the strongest and most pronounced expression of the antiworldly ideology that pervades Tissot's entire theoretical edifice—an edifice constructed, like Rousseau's, on a series of polarities that grow out of the geographic and moral distinction of Switzerland versus Paris, and which serve to invest such antithetical terms as "natural" versus "unnatural" and *campagnard* versus *citadin* with intense polemical meaning.

Tissot's discourse is thus contrapuntal in form, a stylistic trait that links him not just to Rousseau but to a number of nonmedical theorists of the period. For example, his method of dividing the population into specific groups bears a strong resemblance to the Physiocratic classification of the social orders into *classes stériles* and *classes productives.*[21] Like the Physiocrats, Tissot argues in favor of correcting the current social conditions that have led to a concentration of wealth, bodies, and moral/cultural authority in the cities, while the countryside has been depopulated and devalorized.[22] Tissot, however, gives a peculiarly medical twist to the Physiocratic "back to the country" campaign: placing hygiene before economics, he argues that the necessary first step in social reform is to improve the health of society's most exclusive, and most denatured, branch.

As Tissot explains in his preface, he undertook the *Essai sur les maladies des gens du monde* in order to fill in a lacuna in the existing medical literature, which lacked any treatise on the social order "whose health is the most impaired."[23] He goes to great pains to position himself as an outsider to high society: a work of this sort, he declares, should really have been written by physicians living at the center of the worldly *tourbillon,* whose situation would have produced a store of pathological observations "that mine, fortunately, prevents me from having in such great quantity" (*MGM,* xii).[24] Having scolded high-society doctors for neglecting their duty to address their patients' "errors in regimen," Tissot levies an even harsher reproach on the patients themselves:

> The persons whose health is the object of this work almost always have help readily available to them . . . But because they are accustomed to having others do a great deal for them, often without doing anything themselves, they would like to subject Medicine to the same docility, and thus persuade themselves that medicine should heal them without their getting involved. They think that they have done quite a lot by agreeing to take a few remedies, but they do not want to disturb the way of life that is killing them; they would like to be healed while working towards the ruin of their health, and after having done everything to make themselves sick, they do not want to do anything to recover.   (xix)

With its unrelenting denunciation of the willful and imperious attitude that worldly people generally take toward their health, this paragraph establishes Tissot's own decidedly undocile attitude toward the intended readers of his *Essai*. Rather than humoring the highborn in the manner to which they are accustomed, Tissot turns the tables on them: he declares that the careless medical arrangement to which they are accustomed is "impossible" and warns that they had better improve their behavior if they want to improve their well-being (xx). The first step in that direction is to reverse the balance of power between worldly patients and their physicians: in the new arrangement that Tissot proposes, the medical expert is an all-powerful healer and tutor, whereas the *mondain* is demoted to the rank of a docile and contrite pupil.

Clearly, Tissot views *gens du monde* as a singularly troublesome group of patients whose high-living proclivities lead systematically to delicateness, which is just a step away from pathological disorder: "Delicate people are often fit, but are never sure of being fit for long, because their health is too dependent on foreign circumstances. This way of existing is most unfortunate: it is a type of perpetual slavery, in which one is always obliged to fix one's attention on oneself, to seek to avoid anything harmful without necessarily knowing what that is" (*MGM*, 2). The robust person, by contrast, is virtually impervious to such outside impressions because he or she is endowed with a constitution that meets the three basic conditions Tissot considers essential to good health: first, "a strong fiber, which provides all the vessels and viscera with adequate action, and thus supports the regularity of the bodily functions" (4); second, "an even transpiration," which maintains a necessary equilibrium between what the body takes in through food and drink, and what it expels (5); and finally, "firm nerves—that is, nerves that being no more sensitive to impressions than they should be, only transmit them such as they are to the organ of sentiment, and do not upset the entire body for a very minor cause" (5–6). Tissot's robust person is, in short, literally firm of both fiber and nerve: he or she possesses precisely the right degree of both irritability and sensibility. The delicate person, on the other hand, lacks both firmness and reactive equilibrium and is consequently doomed to degenerate easily into a valetudinarian state.

Tissot perceives both sickliness and healthfulness as socially contingent phenomena: "The number of delicate and valetudinarian persons is not equally distributed among the different orders of society. There is one that contains a far greater proportion of them" (*MGM*, 3). The unfortunate social order that Tissot singles out here is, obviously, that of the high-society people to whom this treatise is addressed. On the other end of the spectrum is a class strikingly free of sickly members: namely, that to which farmhands belong. Tissot admits, however, that the present-day peasantry is a flawed embodiment of ideal robust health: the laboring class is "unfortunately very inferior to what it once was, in the time when it did nothing but till the soil" (7). This decline stems not from the peasant lifestyle itself, but rather from the pernicious effects of social climbing and urbanization: cities have lured hearty peasants away from their fields and into an unwholesome urban environment, where, engaged in worldly professions like domestic service, "they have weakened their health . . . and brought into their villages some of the customs of the city" (8).

Thus, according to Tissot's historical scenario, the health of the peasants he would like to use as his physiological ideal has deteriorated in direct relation to their exposure to city life. Along with furnishing a medical justification for the argument that the health of a nation is contingent upon the health of its agricultural bases, this scenario marks the urbane activities generally associated with "polite" living as quintessentially pathological and denaturing—in pointed contrast to the simple and natural life led in the countryside. Using that fundamental opposition as his basis, Tissot proceeds to construct a new social hierarchy in which physical robustness, rather than prestige, determines one's rightful rank. He consequently gives pride of place to the heretofore humble peasant as healthiest human being and ranks all of the remaining social groups in descending order:

> The further one moves away from their state [that of the peasant], health seems to diminish by degrees . . . The various artisans who work to serve the needs of city-dwellers not only suffer ills related to their vocation, but alter their health even more by straying from the simplicity of country habits and manners, which, being dictated by nature itself, are those that suit our constitution the best.
>
> The distance from this simple way of life increases even more in the next social order, that of the bourgeois, and their health diminishes proportionately; . . . finally, it is as great as possible among the worldly—a

class that, relative to health, necessarily includes all the people who, even if they do not have the same rank, lead the same mode of life.   (*MGM*, 9–10)

This scale reveals the essence of the medical ethics at play in the *Essai*: the urban/worldly mode of life lies at the point on Tissot's scale that is farthest removed from man's "natural" state, and is therefore antithetical to sound physical and moral health. Worldliness, he insists, saps the strength of those born to it and of those who aspire to it, for it has unleashed an epidemic of false pleasures, perverted moral values, and bad physical habits that has spread throughout society. To correct this problem, Tissot aims to reverse the direction of influence between the social orders by illustrating to his sophisticated urban readers that they have a great deal to learn from the more healthful habits of their country cousins.[25]

With this purpose in mind, Tissot employs an extended point/counterpoint comparison of two diametrically opposed personae: first, the *homme du monde*, a delicate figure who embodies all that is most frivolous in the lifestyle of the social elite; and second, the farmhand, depicted here as the closest living embodiment of robust health, economic productivity, and sound hygiene. He devotes the first six chapters of his *Essai* to a study of how the various non-naturals—food, drink, air, exercise, secretions, and the passions—are used and experienced by the typical worldly person versus the typical farmhand. On every count, the worldly person is deemed either reckless in his habits or imperiled by his urban surroundings, whereas the peasant is held to be both hygienically responsible and environmentally blessed.

The chapter "Of Food and Drink" begins with a glowing picture of the farmhand's plain, natural, and economical diet: he consumes coarse bread, a good deal of milk and bland vegetables, but very little meat; he uses very few spices and drinks virtually nothing but water; and he and his wife "suffice to plant, harvest, and prepare all his meals" (*MGM*, 12–13). The wealthy urbanite, meanwhile, indulges in a diet that is driven by excess and extravagance: "The most succulent meats he can procure for himself, the most tasty game birds, the most delicate fish cooked in the most fragrant wines—made even more heady by the seasonings used, poultry, crayfish in their bisque, gravies extracted in different ways from the meat juices, eggs, truffles, the most flavorsome vegetables, the most piquant spices lavished onto everything, jams of all sorts brought from every corner of the globe, infinitely varied sweets, pastries, fried foods, cream desserts, the most pungent cheeses—these are the only foods that such people eat" (13–14).[26] What seems to irk Tissot most about these eating habits is their unnaturalness: worldly people eat not out of hunger but rather fashion, and they do not chew or digest properly (16–17). Above all, says Tissot, they are the very opposite of self-sufficient in their methods of procuring the unhealthy delicacies that form their repasts: "When one calculates the number of hands that are used when a rich man eats even a second-rate meal, one sees that they add up to several hundreds; one would have to count them by the thousands for big feasts. How many lives have even been sacrificed to go to the limits of the earth in order to find these tasty fish that we swallow with delight, and that carry into our veins the seeds of languor, sadness, illness, and a premature death!" (15).

In sum, worldly people violate two basic principles of domestic economy that are dear to Tissot, and that we shall encounter again when examining the hygienic program followed in *La Nouvelle Héloïse*. The first is that one should ingest only what the body needs for the animal economy to function efficiently, lest the digestive process become instead a process of "corruption" (*MGM*, 17). The second is that one should consume only frugal and home-grown products. The worldly diet as Tissot portrays it clearly fails in both regards: it overtaxes the physical system, causing first the stomach and then the entire body to become so excessively sensitive that "all the functions are upset and disorder reigns throughout the animal economy" (16); it is, moreover, exotic and costly in both money and lives, in that (by Tissot's melodramatic count) several hundred anonymous hands are required to produce the simplest worldly repast. Hence Tissot's conclusion that "the first of these diets [that of the farmhand] favors all the conditions required for good health, whereas the second destroys them all" (18).

This polarity between worldliness and unworldliness is even more pronounced in the domain of moral regimen, which Tissot takes up in the chapter "Des Passions." He views the passions as the most influential of the non-natural agents that affect the human constitution—and also the most significant source of difference between the worldly and the unworldly man: "If one compares the state of the *homme du monde* to that of peasants in regard to the passions, the difference will be more extreme than in any other register" (*MGM*, 26). Tissot's *homme du monde* is plagued by three principal passions: ambition, the desire for distinction and honor, and the desire for fortune—three intense and destructive emotions that are, he asserts, endemic to the treacherous social milieu in which the worldly person functions (28–29). Moreover, under the onslaught of the relentless barrage of impressions, interests and anxieties characteristic of high society, the intellectual faculties of the worldly man operate in a chronic state of tension and agitation that saps the vigor of the entire organism (27). The peasant, by contrast, is immune to such excesses of feeling and thinking, for he aspires to little beyond a good crop: blissfully ignorant of anything beyond his menial tasks, he can perform them virtually without reflection, "like a true automaton." The peasant is thus frugal not only in how much he consumes but also in how much he thinks—an "economy of ideas" that Tissot sees as "one of the best ways to preserve one's health, which is almost always inversely proportional to the exercise of the mental faculties" (27).

The unworldly moral regimen is not, however, a resoundingly positive example in Tissot's eyes; for what makes this regimen so healthful is the dampening effect it exerts upon the sensibility of the peasant who follows it. Tissot depicts the typical peasant as so naturally impassive or *insensible* that "the loss of the people dearest to him hardly touches him at all; the loss of his worldly goods does not affect him much more" (*MGM*, 35). The very opposite is true of worldly people, whose susceptibility to affect makes them both sublime and pathetic: "Because of their great sensibility, worldly people are also the victims of their most honorable affections; everything that afflicts or threatens those close to them, all of the misfortunes of humanity and of virtue, are for them real pains that often torment them more than their own pains, and that directly harm their health" (36). It would seem, then, that Tissot considers *gens du monde* to be genuinely superior to their country brethren on at least one count: their exquisitely cultivated sensibility expands their capacity for empathetic personal suffering to the collective realm. This heightened moral capacity is, of course, bought at a price, for it victimizes worldly people by making them impressionable in a manner that overpowers their sensible systems—systems, Tissot reminds us, that have already been weakened by their ill-advised habits of eating, drinking, sleeping, breathing, dressing, exercising, and so on.

In short, although Tissot's tableau of peasant life appears rosy when he is describing such subjects as diet and exercise, it turns distinctly grey when he takes up the question of the higher human faculties that are most directly related to sensibility in the ethical sense. The farmhand's impassive moral regimen may fit the *Essai*'s hygienic standards, yet it comes across as less than fully human when juxtaposed with the moral character of *gens du monde*. As Tissot later underscores, genteel existence does have some important advantages over the life of the farmhand: only highborn people can experience "two classes of very intense pleasure, which have their source in the cultivation of the mind and the exercise of feeling" (*MGM*, 85). All too often, however, the heightened moral sensibility of worldly folk leads to nervous illness, "one of the cruelest plagues afflicting worldly persons" (109).

Having by now sufficiently traumatized his readers through alarmist tableaux of their bad habits and humiliating comparisons between them and hearty peasants, Tissot undertakes in the long chapter entitled "Des Préservatifs" to offer them some helpful advice. What he recommends here is not that worldly people revert to the ways of "savages," nor even to the peasant existence he has vaunted throughout the *Essai* (*MGM*, 84). Rather, he proposes a sort of *morale sensitive* that is tailored to suit both the strengths and weaknesses of this group's typically heightened sensibility. As Tissot describes them here, *gens du monde* would seem to have everything going for them: "The great qualities, the great virtues, the pleasures of society, and the charms of the mind and figure should, in the natural order of things, be found in the most well-educated men" (86). Although the poor health that is chronic among members of the social elite casts a pall over those qualities and charms, Tissot insists that this need not be the case: worldly people are not doomed to bad health by virtue of their station in life. All that they need do to break the causal link between their lifestyle and pathology is adopt a hygienic plan that recognizes the peculiarities of worldly sensibilities. Although he grants that his program is ascetic, Tissot assures his readers that it will not reduce their pleasures; rather, it will increase them. According to his philosophy, when one carefully regulates the impressions one allows the body to experience, one discovers a higher, purer mode of sensibility: "The more that one seeks out exquisite pleasures, the more one strays away from them; the organs become difficult the more that one indulges them; it is only by adhering strictly to simplicity that one can be sure to enjoy constant pleasure" (93). It thus behooves those who are most sensitive to the highest civilized pleasures to embrace the simplest and most carefully regulated regimen and to stick to it vigilantly.

Tissot's plan for wholesome living thus recognizes both the advantages and drawbacks of a highly developed sensibility, and seeks to control them through a painstaking, medically based plan for impression management. Several of the principles and practices involved in this plan bear a striking resemblance to those that are followed by the Clarens household in *La Nouvelle Héloïse*. However, the concluding remarks to the *Essai sur les maladies des gens du monde* indicate that Tissot did not fully endorse Rousseau's sweepingly censorious view of high society and its inhabitants. Tissot finishes his treatise by softening the reproachful tone he has used to address his worldly audience: rather than lecturing his readers here, he appeals to their admirable force of will, their superior intellectual capacities, and the important role they play in society in order to persuade them to take better care of their health (171–72). This shift from chastisement to placation is not merely rhetorical. Rather, it suggests that, in Tissot's view, a truly enlightened civilized life need not be synonymous with worldliness, the contemporary epidemic whose ill effects he has just chronicled. Ultimately, therefore, Tissot's perspective on high society is redemptive:

he seeks to rehabilitate his worldly patients so that, with their high sensibility held properly in check, they may be morally and physically fit to occupy the privileged place they enjoy in the social hierarchy.

In sum, Tissot depicts sensibility as simultaneously natural and unnatural, as a vital property that, although congenitally determined, is also profoundly and pathologically affected by the worldly social milieu. To temper and "naturalize" the intense sensibility characteristic of *gens du monde*, he proposes a comprehensive plan for plain and wholesome living: his worldly reader-patients are instructed to follow the simple, bland diet he prescribes, to adhere to his detailed guidelines for sleep, proper exercise, and so on, and to control their passions. Tissot tells his audience that they *can* enjoy the higher pleasures of civilized life without falling victim to pathological overstimulation, as long as they take care to protect their sensible systems by practicing good hygiene of body and mind. Tissot's *morale sensitive* for worldly people is therefore an attempt to accommodate the ideal of natural living with the reality of worldliness: he lauds the simple peasant lifestyle but also respects the civilized person's constitutional need for a more refined moral-intellectual existence.

❧ ❧

It is perhaps on this point that Rousseau's notion of sensibility most differs from Tissot's: rather than seeking to reconcile sensibility with the worldly influences that affect it, Rousseau constructs a *morale sensitive* in which worldliness is systematically excluded. Like Tissot, Rousseau subscribes to a plan for controlling sensibility that recognizes the needs of the refined soul, yet his *belles âmes*—whether they be the characters of *La Nouvelle Héloïse*, or the "Jean-Jacques" of his *Dialogues*—are plainly not of this world. Rousseau adheres to a Tissot-like conception of moral and physical health but employs it to ground the representation of an alternative universe, one in which a positive, uncorrupted, and spiritually directed form of sensibility could at last flourish. Seen in this light, *La Nouvelle Héloïse* assumes the status of a literary experiment in Rousseauian sensibility theory. Although the aim of that experiment is explicitly ethical, its form is implicitly medical, by virtue of its deep structural analogies with contemporary hygienic discourse like that of Tissot.

To perceive those analogies and follow the stages by which this experiment proceeds, we must, of course, single out the experiment's locus. Because Rousseau's "wise materialism" is so fundamental to the *morale sensitive* he practices in *La Nouvelle Héloïse*, that locus is necessarily material. In other words, we should not be misled by the novel's repeated invocations of the sensitive soul—as, for example, in the axiom popularized by this novel, "what a fatal gift from

Heaven is a sensitive soul!"[27] For the characters of *La Nouvelle Héloïse* are far from ethereal souls suffering celestial torments. To the contrary, Saint-Preux, Julie, and company are quite literally what they eat, drink, and otherwise experience through their bodies—bodies whose most significant quality is their highly developed sensibility. One must, therefore, recognize the pivotal and very precise function that is accorded to bodily sensibility in Rousseau's novel if one wants to understand how its characters interact as lovers, moral beings, and members of a carefully constructed social economy.

The role of the body in *La Nouvelle Héloïse* has already attracted some attention in recent criticism, most notably in books by Anne Deneys-Tunney and Peter Brooks.[28] Although distinct in their particulars, these analyses share an assumption, derived from the psychoanalytic theories to which both of these critics subscribe, that the body in this novel is first and foremost the site of amorous desire. That critical scenario casts Saint-Preux as desiring subject, and Julie as the body desired. Brooks, for example, asserts that "Julie's body becomes the obsessive object of a massive writing project originating from its presentation by way of its impress or imprint, so that it becomes a kind of allegory of the relation of representation to desire and its objects" (47). Deneys-Tunney, citing Lacan as her prime theoretical inspiration, likewise approaches Julie's body as an entity that is inscribed in a complex chiasmatic relationship with writing and desire (197). By taking such an overridingly psycho-sexual approach, both critics produce readings of *La Nouvelle Héloïse* that are elegant and compelling on their own terms; yet they also modernize Julie's body to such a degree that it does, indeed, appear to function as a dematerialized tissue of words and frustrated erotic drives. I would argue, however, that the body is anything but absent or dematerialized in this novel: to the contrary, the body's very physical, sensible presence weighs heavily upon the structure of Rousseau's narrative. There are, moreover, multiple bodies at play here, which act and interact as much in a hygienic register as in an erotic register. Finally, the body in *La Nouvelle Héloïse* is indeed "made semiotic," as Brooks asserts (38); yet that operation has less to do with semiotics in the modern, linguistic sense than with the very particular brand of semiotics to which sensibility gave rise in eighteenth-century medicine and literature.

That semiotics, which I discussed earlier, was a decoding system designed to diagnose the signs the sensible body emitted when touched, pained, or aroused. The two underlying assumptions of this semiotics were, first, that all bodies and body parts were interconnected via an ongoing exchange of sensible actions and reactions; and second, that language was the last and always inadequate vehicle for communicating messages about sensibility. The bodies in *La Nouvelle Héloïse* are consequently involved in a semiotic network that is far more pervasive and intricate than one might think if one considered only the work's epistolary form. Writing—specifically, letter-writing—is, of course, the novel's most prominent means of communication; yet it is by no means the only one. For the message of all the transmissions that occur in this novel is too fundamental for mere words. That message, as Rousseau represents it in this novel, *is* sensibility—a magnetically resonating force that both binds the novel's characters together into a single sphere of reciprocal influence and provides them with the various modes (verbal as well as nonverbal) by which they communicate. It is thus not enough to examine (in the manner of Paul de Man)[29] the problematics of language in *La Nouvelle Héloïse*: one must also examine the problematics of the very distinctive *body* language by which sensibility is expressed in this novel.

"Natural" Sensibility and Domestic Hygiene in *La Nouvelle Héloïse*

At first blush, *La Nouvelle Héloïse* would seem to be a classic eighteenth-century tale of a sensitive man at odds with the world around him. Indeed, the long-suffering Saint-Preux bears a certain resemblance to earlier literary figures of misplaced sensibility. He uses much the same fatalistic, languorous vocabulary to describe his amorous predicament as does des Grieux of Prévost's *Manon Lescaut*: "I wish only to be cured or to die"; "I languish and waste away. The fire runs in my veins"; and so on (*New Eloise* 27, 46; *NH*, 1.1.33, 1.10.54). Moreover, as with Marianne of *La Vie de Marianne*, Saint-Preux's highborn friends like Milord Edouard see him as a deep-feeling *belle âme* who just happens to be in modest social circumstances. There is, however, a critical difference between Saint-Preux and his literary predecessors: whereas des Grieux and (most probably) Marianne are noble, Saint-Preux is a commoner, "an inconsiderable bourgeois without fortune," in the words of Julie's cousin Claire (*New Eloise*, 39; *NH*, 1.7.45). As Marie-Hélène Huet has argued, Saint-Preux's lack or refusal of any social identity makes him a "hero" only in the formal sense, in that it is he who provokes the crisis of moral values around which the novel is constructed.[30] The manner in which Saint-Preux qualifies as an *homme sensible* is therefore rather more complex than in the case of Prévost's and Marivaux's protagonists.

That is, whereas des Grieux's sensibility is a quality intrinsic to his status as the son of the aristocracy, and Marianne can attribute her sensibility and innate *noblesse de coeur* to lost noble origins, Saint-Preux has nothing but "nature" on which to stake his claim to the property. On the one hand, by claiming the designation of *sensible* for commoners like himself, Saint-Preux confirms the emerging view that sensibility is a sign not of extraordinary birth class, but rather of extraordinary natural constitution. On the other hand, neither Saint-Preux nor anyone else in *La Nouvelle Héloïse* is a social egalitarian: the Wolmar household at Clarens is nothing if not hierarchical, and the place to which Saint-Preux is relegated there is that not of an equal to the masters of the house, but rather of a childlike dependent. Thus, although Saint-Preux seems to embody the natural, unsocialized sensibility Rousseau associates in his *Dialogues* with the misunderstood "Jean-Jacques," that sensibility is *not* given free reign in Rousseau's novelistic universe. To the contrary, the natural sensibility of both Saint-Preux and Julie, his wellborn sister soul, is only allowed to operate on the condition that it be strictly controlled. Like his literary predecessors, Rousseau invokes a particular institution to exert that control and to define the meaning of true sensibility. The institution he designates is, however, not social class but the domestic milieu—a milieu that must, like sensibility itself, be constantly regulated.[31]

The sensitive beings of *La Nouvelle Héloïse* are therefore subject to an ongoing process of domestication that fulfills two primary purposes: first, it accords a place to all worthy souls, including the social misfit Saint-Preux, within a privileged, familial circle; and second, it ensures that the sensibility of the novel's characters functions in a properly wholesome and edifying register. The domestication process is only fully instituted in the novel's second half, the part of the book that is, significantly, presented in the "Seconde Préface de *Julie*" as the morally edifying "remedy" to the scandalous and tumultuous first half (*NH*, 17). This explicit division of the novel into two discrete halves is used by the preface's interlocutors, "R" and "N," to draw a clear moral distinction between the unmarried Julie d'Etange who falls into dishonor in parts 1–3, and the married, redeemed Julie de Wolmar who dominates parts 4–6 ("the chaste and sensible wife, the worthy matron, obliterate the remembrance of the guilty lover" [*Eloisa*, 1:10; *NH*, 17]). At the same time, this structural division allows Rousseau to represent and contrast two radically distinct modes of sensibility—one involuntary and untamed, the other voluntary and carefully contained. In other words, the acute and contagious sensibility that runs rampant in the first half of *La Nouvelle Héloïse* is the necessary and instructive ill that the second half serves to remedy, by providing a comprehensive program designed to reform the novel's wayward characters and to keep their vulnerable sensibilities in vigilant, virtuous check.

The metaphoric relationship of malady to remedy that the "Seconde Préface" establishes between the two halves of the novel warrants further scrutiny. According to this medical metaphor, the novel is designed as a gilded pill—the pill being the edifying second half, and the gilding the titillating but dangerous first half. This division suggests a fundamental ambivalence on Rousseau's part about the property of sensibility itself, for it implies that the uncontrolled sensibility of parts 1–3 is more dangerous but also more aesthetically engaging than the managed sensibility of parts 4–6. Moreover, it sets the stage for a major point of discussion regarding the novel's moral utility: as the interlocutor "R" contends, *La Nouvelle Héloïse* is a uniquely edifying work because it exerts a literally tonic effect upon its readers—or at least, on some of them.

"R" begins by arguing that sophisticated readers like "N" are mistaken in criticizing the novel according to Parisian-based standards of literary value because those criteria are inappropriate for a work that was not written by, for, or about the worldly (*NH*, 14–16). Rather, this correspondence, whether real or fictitious, should only be judged according to the response it triggers among a particular audience: the audience of "real country-folks," who, although usually overlooked and misserved by the literary establishment, are precisely the readers on whom this work will make a true impression (*Eloisa*, 1:17; *NH*, 20). To illustrate this assertion, "R" sketches an ideal scenario for the novel's reading:

> I like to imagine a married couple reading this novel together, imbibing fresh courage to support their common labours, and perhaps new designs to render them useful. How can they possibly contemplate the representation of a happy family without attempting to imitate the pleasing model? How can they be affected with the charms of conjugal union, even where love is wanting, without increasing and confirming their own attachment? In quitting their book, they will neither be discontented with their situation, nor disgusted at their labour: on the contrary, every object around them will assume a more delightful aspect; their duties will seem ennobled; their taste for the pleasures of nature will revive; her genuine sensations will be rekindled in their hearts, and, perceiving happiness within their reach, they will learn to taste it as they ought. They will perform the same functions, but with another soul; and what they did before as peasants only, they will now transact as real patriarchs. (*Eloisa*, 1:18; *NH*, 23)

The intended audience of *Julie* is thus embodied by a happily married provincial couple reading the correspondence together. And, as this scenario depicts it, the value of the novel—most particularly its seemingly off-putting second half—resides in its power to engage those readers in an experience that is both aesthetic and moral, in that it exposes them to the representation of the objects, duties and simple pleasures associated not with glitzy Parisian life (the standard subject matter of most novels [*NH*, 19–20]) but rather with their own condition. As a result of that engagement—which, we should note, operates via the same means of *attendrissement* and identification we saw at work in Diderot's

theory of the novel—these country-folks will emerge with their homey sentiments stimulated and reinforced because they will draw edifying lessons for
their own domestic lives from the "pleasing model" the novel proffers.

The novelistic genre, as Rousseau practices it, is thus invested with a new
mission: to "reduce all things to a state of nature, make mankind in love with a
life of peace and simplicity . . . and instead of exciting people to crowd into
large cities, persuade them to spread themselves all over the kingdom, that
every part may be equally enlivened" (*Eloisa*, 1:15–16; *NH*, 21). This statement
of purpose both recalls the Physiocratic pro-rural campaign and anticipates the
language of Rousseau's medical counterpart Tissot, who likewise seeks to
change the direction of cultural influence between the worldly and unworldly
milieux. The interlocutor "R," however, does not include the worldly in the
circle of readers for whom *La Nouvelle Héloïse* is destined: worldly readers are,
he argues, ill-disposed by both temperament and condition to understand the
inelegant but authentic language of true sentiment and passion (*NH*, 14–15).
They are therefore incapable of appreciating the novel's simple but sensitive
young protagonists, who "finding nothing that corresponds with their own
feelings, . . . detach themselves from the rest of the universe [to] create in their
separate society a little world different from ours, which presents an entirely
new spectacle" (*Eloisa*, 1:10; *NH*, 16–17). In other words, only readers who are
already detached from the world, both in spirit and in milieu, can truly sympathize with the distinctive manner in which this novel's characters think, feel,
and speak.

This brings us to a last noteworthy aspect of the "Seconde Préface": this
preface contains the same metaphor of magnetic attraction Rousseau uses to
define sensibility in his *Deuxième Dialogue*. Here, it is invoked by "N" to explain the stylistic monotony of the novel's letters, which he attributes to Julie's
"enchanting" influence on everyone around her: "This Julie, as she is represented, must be an absolute enchantress; all who approach her must immediately resemble her; all her friends should speak one language" (*Eloisa*, 1:25;
NH, 28). Julie is therefore characterized from the very outset as a pole of irresistible attraction—the mode of operation Rousseau associates in the *Deuxième
Dialogue* with natural, positive sensibility—and as a transforming influence on
others. Indeed, by the second half of the novel, Julie comes to function literally
as the organic center of the domestic economy that is instituted at Clarens: she
is the source of its vital energy and the figure that holds all of its parts together.
In order to occupy that position, however, Julie must be proven worthy, by
passing through a prolonged series of moral-physical crises.

It is this trial process that structures the plot of the first three parts of the
novel and makes Julie the dramatic center of all the peripeteia that occur there,

leading up to her "conversion" into Julie de Wolmar. Although the unmarried Julie already exerts a remarkable effect upon everyone who enters her sphere, neither her sensibility nor the magnetic influence it produces are fully healthy at this stage. For, as long as she is Mlle. d'Etange, her sensibility bears too close a resemblance to that of her lover Saint-Preux, which is in a perpetual state of crisis and excess throughout the novel. Julie's natural sensible constitution must be tested, stabilized and "cured" before the domestic *morale sensitive* that dominates parts 4–6 can be set into play.

As initially represented in *La Nouvelle Héloïse*, the notion of sensibility is inseparable from the theme of amorous passion, the force that binds the two young lovers together in an ostensibly spiritual kind of fatal attraction. As Julie puts it in an early letter to Saint-Preux, "In spite of fortune, parents, and ourselves, our fates are forever united . . . Our souls, if I may use the expression, touch in all points, and we feel an entire coherence . . . Henceforth our pains and pleasures must be mutual; and like the magnets, of which I have heard you speak, that have the same motion, though in different places, we would feel the same sensations at the two extremities of the world" (*Eloisa*, 1:83; *NH*, 1.11.55). Yet even as they exult in their "adhesion" as natural soul mates, both Julie and Saint-Preux employ a distinctly pathological vocabulary to describe their dangerously intense, immoderate amorous sentiments; Julie speaks, for example, of "the poison which destroys my sense and my reason" (*New Eloise*, 32; *NH*, 1.4.39). This characterization of love as pathology is more than just a timeworn literary trope, for it serves to introduce into the novel a key component of Rousseau's "vital impression" theory of sensibility. All passions, according to that theory, are stimulants that act in a *mechanical* way upon the sensible system; love is the most powerful passion because it makes the deepest sensible impression. Saint-Preux provides a dramatic illustration of this mechanism in the letter he writes after having received the kiss that Julie and Claire stage for him in the grove: "What have you done, my Julie? You wanted to reward me and you have destroyed me. I am drunk, or rather, I am insane. My senses are disordered; all my faculties are disturbed by that fatal kiss . . . I have scarcely known what has happened to me since that fatal moment. The deep impression that it made will never be effaced" (*New Eloise*, 52–53; *NH*, 1.14.63–65). What makes the two lovers so susceptible is, as Julie explains, the rare temper of their sensible souls: "I see, my friend, by the temper of our souls and by the agreement of our dispositions, that love will be the great business of our lives. Whenever love has once made the deep impressions that we have felt, it must extinguish or absorb every other passion" (*New Eloise*, 90; *NH*, 1.35.109). Their extraordinary capacity to feel is thus exalted as the force that brings Julie and Saint-Preux together; yet it is also bemoaned, for it can only lead them into pathological crises as long as it uncontrolled.

This dilemma is clearly evident in the case of Saint-Preux, who, deprived by birth of the means necessary to attain social distinction, instead seeks distinction in the superior qualities of his exquisitely sensitive soul. He thus devotes most of his letters in parts 1–3 to detailing "the situation of my soul" as he travels about, enduring his exile from Julie and receiving noteworthy impressions from the various settings he encounters (*New Eloise*, 63; *NH*, 1.23.76). One of the first and most significant letters in this vein is written during Saint-Preux's journey through the mountains of the Valais, which he describes almost entirely in terms of the successive sensations and sentiments he experiences along the way. He starts out his journey melancholic, "in a certain languid state that is not without charm for a sensitive heart" (*New Eloise*, 64; *NH*, 1.23.77); yet he soon feels both his mood and his bodily state change markedly for the better as he climbs higher into this daunting, sublime wilderness. As he searches for the cause of this change, Saint-Preux observes that the mountain air and setting exert a remarkably therapeutic effect on both his passions and his organic constitution:

> In the high mountains where the air is pure and thin, one breathes more easily, one's body is lighter and the mind is more serene. Pleasures are less ardent there, the passions more moderate. Meditations take on . . . an indefinable, tranquil voluptuousness which has nothing of the pungent and sensual. It seems that in being lifted above human society, one leaves below all base and terrestrial sentiments, and that as one approaches the ethereal regions, one's soul acquires something of their eternal purity . . . It is in this way that a pleasing climate causes the passions, which elsewhere constitute man's torment, to contribute to his happiness.   (*New Eloise*, 65; *NH*, 1.23.78)

He even ventures to suggest that his discovery should become a general therapeutic principle: "I doubt whether any violent agitation or any vaporous sickness could withstand a prolonged stay in the mountains, and I am surprised that baths of salutary and beneficial mountain air are not one of the major remedies used in medicine and morality" (*New Eloise*, 65–66; *NH*, 1.23.78–79). It seems, therefore, that this quintessential *homme sensible* has not only found his element—a milieu that truly suits him—but also discovered the secret of putting his sensitive acuity to philosophical, moral use. However, no sooner does Saint-Preux establish the principles that would seem to offer him a fail-safe method of staying happy, calm, and virtuous, than he reveals the character trait than makes it impossible for him to adhere to his own doctrine: Saint-Preux can never "forget himself" (*Eloisa*, 1:36; *NH*, 1.23.79) because, even in the spiritual ecstasy he feels amidst the Valais mountains, he cannot forget Julie, the being who has left a permanent and indelible imprint upon his oversensitive soul.

Thus, rather than losing himself and his ardent passions in the healthful Valaisian milieu, Saint-Preux inscribes the image of Julie upon each and every object there:

> I led you everywhere with me. I did not take a step without you. I did not admire a view without hurrying to show it to you. All the trees that I encountered lent you their shade; all the grassy banks served you as a bench ... Everything in this peaceful place reminded me of you. The striking natural beauty, the invariable purity of the air, the simple manners of the people, their constant and sure wisdom, the amiable modesty of the women and their innocent graces—in short, all that gave me pleasure to my eye and my heart reminded them only of her whom they constantly seek.   (*New Eloise*, 66; *NH*, 1.23.83)

Clearly, the calm and edifying effect that the natural objects of the Valais exert on his moral disposition is compromised by his irresistible urge to intermingle the image of those objects with that of Julie. As a consequence, rather than curing Saint-Preux of his passionate affliction, this seemingly wholesome setting becomes marked as the space of his Edenic fantasy of union with Julie. As soon as he recalls the impossibility of that union, Saint-Preux's "delicious" sense of being one with nature turns sour, as is evident a few letters later when he writes from Meillerie.[32]

In Meillerie, Saint-Preux finds a small esplanade from which, through a telescope, he can gaze across the lake at Julie's happy town. These are the ideal circumstances for pursuing the next stage in his exercise of inscribing his passion for Julie both onto nature, and onto paper: "I have taken such a liking to this wild place that I even bring ink and paper here, and I am now writing this letter on a slab of rock that the ice has detached from a nearby crag" (*New Eloise*, 73; *NH*, 1.26.90–91). From this bleak vantage point, he gazes obsessively upon the place from which he is exiled; he travels in his mind's eye right into Julie's bedroom, such that the recollected images of the minute details of her daily routine (including the image of Julie reading one of her lover's letters) become inextricably intertwined with his current surroundings. This obsessive exercise, coupled with his despair at being so close yet so far from his beloved, prompts Saint-Preux to lapse into a melancholia that is now suicidal: "Since I have come back near you, my mind dwells only on distressing thoughts. Perhaps the place where I am contributes to this melancholy. It is sad and dreadful. But it is thus more suited to the state of my soul, and so I stay more patiently here than I would in a more pleasant place" (*New Eloise*, 72; *NH*, 1.26.90). It is here that Saint-Preux exclaims, "Oh, Julie, what a fatal gift from Heaven is a sensitive soul!"—by which he means that the sensitive soul is not nature's moral partner, but rather nature's helpless and hapless victim: "The lowly plaything of the air and the seasons, his fate is determined by sunlight or mists, cloudy or clear weather, and he will be content or sad as the winds blow" (*New Eloise*, 71; *NH*, 1.26.89).

I have examined letters 23 and 26 of part 1 at some length because their significance is twofold. First, they set the stage for the crisis that ends part 4 of *La Nouvelle Héloïse*, when Wolmar's carefully calculated cure of the erstwhile lovers is put to dramatic test. Second, they provide a most revealing demonstration of Saint-Preux's modus operandi as an *homme sensible*: he experiences his sensibility intensely and involuntarily, giving himself over both to his passions and to the impressions made by nature. One might say that Saint-Preux uses his acute capacities of feeling as a means of eroticizing the *morale sensitive* doctrine: rather than using the milieu as a means of keeping his soul in the state most propitious for virtue, he inscribes his passions upon the objects in that milieu so as to feed his soul's amorous ardor. Thus, even though Saint-Preux is the first character in *La Nouvelle Héloïse* to articulate the novel's very particular brand of applied materialism, he does so in a manner that is diametrically opposed to the moral hygiene Julie and her entourage will later practice at Clarens.

That is, whereas Julie's sensibility evolves significantly over the first half of the novel, Saint-Preux's remains in a state of arrested development: although both of the lovers undergo repeated ordeals as they endure the pains of separation and the dangerous fervor of reunion, Julie emerges from each one stronger and more resolved, while Saint-Preux wallows in moral extremes. What makes Julie's mode of sensibility so different from that of Saint-Preux is not that she has a constitution fundamentally different from his; for the two lovers are cut from the same "extraordinary" mold (*New Eloise*, 163; *NH*, 2.2.193). Rather, Julie's sensibility is necessarily more constricted and self-controlled because she is, as Saint-Preux underscores, situated in a very precise and privileged social milieu:

> What a difference there is between your situation and mine! . . . I am not speaking of rank and fortune; honor and love suffice for want of all that. But you are surrounded by people whom you cherish and who adore you. The attentions of a tender mother and of a father for whom you are the only hope, the friendship of a cousin who seems to live only for your

sake, a whole family for whom you constitute the ornament, an entire town proud of having seen you born there—all these people occupy and share your sensibility . . . But I, Julie, alas! Wandering, without a family and almost without a country, I have no one on this earth but you. Love alone is all I possess.   (*New Eloise*, 61; *NH*, 1.21.73)

Thus, whereas Saint-Preux's sensibility operates in a state of permanent detachment and itinerancy, Julie's is framed from the outset by her domestic role and responsibilities, which impose constraints upon her actions and provide a context for her very special magnetic influence. Julie must consequently deal with her sentiments and sensations in a manner that is, according to the novel's vocabulary, more "heroic," "resistant," and "firm" than that of Saint-Preux. If she were to yield as readily as does her lover to the impulses of her passions and sentient impressions, she would lose not only her honor and social standing, but also the sole theater in which her exquisite soul can exercise what Claire calls its "sphere of activity"—an irresistible power of sensibility that compels all of Julie's family, friends, and acquaintances to emulate her (*NH*, 2.5.204). It is this positive sensibility, along with the social position that gives it meaning, that Julie and her devoted cousin Claire struggle valiantly to preserve over the course of parts 1–3.

Whenever the word "heroic" occurs in the first half of *La Nouvelle Héloïse*, it always describes Julie; and there is, indeed, an epic quality to her attempts to overcome the dangers of her amorous attachment to Saint-Preux. Although she tries to muster a "heroic resistance" when first separated from Saint-Preux, the effort literally makes her ill (*New Eloise*, 75; *NH*, 1.27.93). Fearing for Julie's life, Claire summons Saint-Preux back from exile. Soon thereafter, Julie loses her innocence, yielding to the "dangerous spectacle" of her lover convulsing in passion at her feet (*NH*, 1.29.96). This first crisis—the "crise de l'amour," or crisis of sexual possession (*NH*, 1.9.51, 1.28.95)—is constructed according to a direct moral-physical causality that also pervades the many crises that follow.

Although these crises are explicitly designed to test Julie's acutely sensitive soul, it is invariably Julie's body that suffers the most dramatic consequences. When, having gotten pregnant by Saint-Preux, Julie resists her father's plans to marry her to his friend Wolmar, she finds herself in a "critical moment," paralyzed by "a sort of stupidity which renders me almost insensible and permits me to use neither my passions nor my reason" (*New Eloise*, 145; *NH*, 1.63.177). In the postscript that ends letter 63 of part 1, she announces to Claire the signs of an impending miscarriage—the "tragic consequence" of the violent scene she has just had with her outraged father (*NH*, 1.63.174–75, 178). Later, after

Julie's mother has discovered the letters that reveal her daughter's illicit liaison, the mother promptly falls mortally ill of chagrin, which plunges Julie into a new bout of moral/physical affliction. Claire diagnoses Julie's condition as a sheer exhaustion of the heart and senses, brought on by an excess of sentiment:

> The extreme dejection of my poor cousin cannot be imagined. You must see her to realize it. Her heart seems suffocated by grief, and the violence of the sentiments which oppress her gives her a stunned manner [*un air de stupidité*], more frightful than piercing cries. She remains day and night on her knees at her mother's bedside, with a mournful look and her eyes fixed on the ground, keeping a profound silence. She serves her with more attention and vivacity than ever, then immediately relapses into a state of dejection which would cause one to mistake her for another person. (*New Eloise*, 227–28; *NH*, 3.1.307–8)

What makes these crises so terribly dangerous, in Claire's opinion, is the risk that they may alter Julie's constitution altogether by robbing her of her positive, resonating energies. That fear is underscored in this letter's conclusion: "How dulled is her brightness! . . . Alas, what has become of that fond and sensitive character, that pure taste for virtuous things, that tender interest in the pains and pleasures of others? . . . Those sublime sentiments have grown weak, that divine flame has cooled, and that angel is now no more than an ordinary woman. Ah, what a soul you have seduced away from virtue!" (*New Eloise*, 230; *NH*, 3.1.310). For Julie to be reduced to the level of an ordinary woman, stripped of her sublime sentiments and "divine flame," is not only pathological: it would also be a catastrophic loss for everyone who lives within her warm, edifying sphere. And, as Claire makes clear in her parting words, there is one person responsible for this impending catastrophe: Saint-Preux.

Claire, however, places great faith in the power of her mortifying rhetoric on Saint-Preux and in the heroic quality of Julie's sensitive faculties. A few letters later, after recounting to Saint-Preux a tear-jerking scene of Julie attending to her dying mother—"What regret, what tears, what affecting caresses, what unwearied sensibility! . . . I never saw any person enter my aunt's chamber during the last days, without being moved even to tears at this most affecting spectacle" (*Eloisa*, 2:84–85; *NH*, 3.7.322)—she expresses guarded optimism about Julie's prognosis: "Her heroic faculties are not however annihilated, but suspended: a momentary crisis may restore them to their full vigor, or totally destroy their existence. One step farther in this gloomy path, and she is lost; but if her incomparable soul should recover herself, she will be greater, more heroic, more virtuous than ever, and there will be no danger of a relapse" (*Eloisa*, 2:87; *NH*, 3.7.324). Sure enough, Claire's prediction that there is a decisive crisis coming is proven right: the rest of part 3 chronicles Julie's last ordeal as a single girl.

The first stage in this ordeal repeats the etiological pattern established by Julie's preceding tribulations: as soon as Julie accepts her father's wishes that she renounce Saint-Preux and marry Wolmar (*NH*, pt. 3, letters 9–10), she falls ill with smallpox (*NH*, pt. 3, letter 12). During her illness, Saint-Preux returns and contracts it, too, through an "inoculation of love" (*Eloisa*, 2:99; *NH*, 3.14.333). This medical crisis, which Julie interprets as a reaffirmation of nature's dictate that her heart (if not her hand) will always belong to Saint-Preux (*NH*, 3.15.334–35), is no sooner resolved than Julie undergoes her definitive moral crisis: her marriage to Wolmar. What happens to her during and after her wedding ceremony is nothing less than a total conversion that, despite its unmistakable religious overtones, is as much physical as spiritual. Although this conversion operates upon Julie's soul, it does so by means of the three-step mechanism of stimulus, impression, and inscription that is always associated in this novel with a profound experience of sensibility.

Julie details the stages of her conversion in a letter to Saint-Preux that takes the form of a long recapitulation of "every inward sentiment" she has felt over the course of her life (*Eloisa*, 2:140; *NH*, 3.18.364). Musing over the crises through which she has passed, Julie confirms that sensibility was the root cause of all her past afflictions: "You know, my dear friend, that my constitution, which is strong enough to endure fatigue and inclemency of weather, is not able to resist the violence of passion, and that too exquisite a sensibility is the source of all the evils which have afflicted my mind and body" (*Eloisa*, 2:122; *NH*, 3.18.351). As soon as she enters the church for her wedding ceremony, however, all of that changes: "I felt a sort of emotion that I had never experienced . . . An inconceivable terror seized my mind in that solemn and august place, which was full of the Being worshipped there." She describes the elements that compose the scene—"the gloomy light of the temple, the profound silence of the spectators, their decent and contemplative deportment, the train of all my relations, the imposing look of my venerable father," and most particularly, the moving sight of Claire and her husband—as a series of impressive "objects" that reinforce the words of the minister concerning the sanctity of the marriage vows. Julie is profoundly affected by the milieu and the moment: "I felt a thorough revolution within me. An invisible power seemed suddenly to rectify the disorder of my affections, and to settle them according to the laws of duty and nature" (*Eloisa*, 2:126–27; *NH*, 3.18.353–54). Her agitation consequently gives way to a sense of peace and tranquillity throughout her being, which persists even after she has put her sensibility to the test by deliberately conjuring up the image of Saint-Preux.

Marriage gives Julie the ultimate reinforcement for her previously faltering moral character: she now has both a dignified wifely status and a divine "internal principle" that gives her "the strength to resist my own heart, which I could not find within myself " (*Eloisa*, 2:131; *NH*, 3.18.357). As she portrays herself now, she is literally reborn: the "violent shock" that brought about her conversion has restored the firm, healthy, and radiant constitution she originally received from nature (*New Eloise*, 255–56; NH 3.18.364). It follows that Saint-Preux must undergo a radical change as well: "Everything is changed between us, and your heart must accommodate itself to the change. The wife of M. Wolmar is not your Julie; your change of sentiment with regard to her is unavoidable; all that you can do now is honor this change, according to the election you make of vice or virtue" (*Eloisa*, 2:139; *NH*, 3.18.363). If Saint-Preux is to recover the virtue and vigor of his own *belle âme*, he must alter both the nature and direction of his feelings for Julie—something that (as she underscores in her last letter to him) can be achieved only through a comprehensive cure (*NH*, 3.20.375).

It is at this point that Julie introduces Wolmar, the man uniquely suited to lead the effort to restore Saint-Preux's sensibility to a state of firmness, health, and virtue. Wolmar's coolheaded constitution provides the perfect complement to Julie: "If he had a heart as tender as mine, it would be impossible for so much sensitivity on both sides not to come sometimes into collision and for quarrels not to result" (*New Eloise*, 262; *NH*, 3.20.373). In fact, Wolmar's philosophical distance from sensibility makes him the constitutional analogue of the médecin philosophe figure we analyzed earlier. That similarity becomes even more apparent in Wolmar's self-portrait in part 4:

> I am one of those men whom people think they are truly insulting when they call them insensible, that is, when they say they have no passion which diverts them from following the true direction of mankind. Little susceptible of pleasure and of grief, I even experience only very faintly that sentiment of self-interest and of humanitarianism which makes the affections of others our own . . . My only active principle is a natural love of order . . . If I have any ruling passion, it is that of observation. I like to read the hearts of men. Since my own gives me few illusions, since I observe coolly and without self-interest, and since long experience has given me some insight, I am hardly ever mistaken in my judgments . . . Society is agreeable to me for the sake of contemplation, not as a member of it. If I could alter the nature of my being and become a living eye, I willingly would make this exchange. (*New Eloise*, 317; *NH*, 4.12. 490–91)

Wolmar is physically incapable of experiencing sensibility and the sympathetic connections it creates among human beings; yet he sees this insensibility as a virtue rather than a flaw. For being insensitive allows him to exercise his keen observational skills and natural taste for order, the better both to contemplate human nature and to control it.

Thus, by the end of part 3 of *La Nouvelle Héloïse*, the stage has been set for putting the novel's *morale sensitive* into play: Julie's sensibility has been transformed into a vigorous, stable, and unquestionably virtuous force; the wise, dispassionate Wolmar has been introduced; and Saint-Preux has been sent off to seek out new "objects" and impressions that will replace those he associates with his passion for the old Julie (*NH*, 3.23.394). To bring us to this point, Rousseau uses what we might call a teleology of crisis: the acute sensibility that runs rampant through the first half of the work plunges the two young lovers into one crisis after another, until Julie's matrimonial conversion puts an abrupt end to the cycle. It is those crises, and the questionable moral climate they create, that represent the *mal* to which the interlocutors of the "Seconde Préface de Julie" refer. Having passed through their many ordeals, the novel's protagonists are now disposed both to administer and to receive the "remedy" provided by the wholesome domestic milieu of the Clarens estate, a setting that is designed both to foster sensibility and to keep it in its place.

꧁ ꧂

One of the most striking aspects of life at Clarens is that, even though Wolmar is the all-seeing master of the house, it is Julie who is exercises an absolute, natural empire over everyone else: she holds, among other things, exclusive maternal powers, Claire having ceded them so that her daughter might be transformed into another Julie (*NH*, 4.9.439). Julie's central role in the Clarens community has, of course, attracted considerable critical attention—notably from Jean Starobinski, who describes Julie as the omnipresent soul of the idyllic little closed society that surrounds her.[33] I, however, see Julie's function at Clarens as more than moral or philosophical: it is truly organic. That is, Julie is not just the soul but also the central body part of Clarens, because—as Claire puts it—she literally vivifies all of the other members of the household: "My Julie, you were born to rule. Your empire is the most absolute that I know. It extends even over the will of others, and I am sensible of it more than any one . . . This is because your heart gives life to all the hearts that surround it, and gives them a kind of new existence, for which they are bound to adore yours, since they derive it entirely from you" (*Eloisa*, 2:200–201; *NH*, 4.2.409). Julie is, in effect, the "queen bee" of Clarens: to recall the bee swarm metaphor used in both the medical articles of the *Encyclopédie* and in Diderot's *Rêve de d'Alembert,* her extraordinarily resonant sensibility not only draws those around her but also structures their every action and reaction. As Saint-Preux observes, Julie regards all of her "worker bees"—"laborers, domestics, everyone who has ever served her, if only for a single day"—as her children, and actively intervenes in their daily affairs; and they, in turn, happily swarm around her (*Eloisa,* 2:246; *NH,* 4.10.444). However, in order to wield this sympathetic empire, Julie must stay strong, virtuous, and healthy; if she were to falter, morally or physically, the network of positive sensibility that holds her community together might well fall into disarray.

It is for this reason that the second half of *La Nouvelle Héloïse,* most particularly parts 4 and 5, is imbued with a distinctly hygienic tone: the domestic economy of Clarens is, in essence, a hygiene program no less comprehensive than that detailed in Tissot's *Essai sur les maladies des gens du monde.* Thanks to that program, Julie functions up until her death as both the primary subject and the primary agent of the organic network of sensibility that binds her household together. The true key to the operation of sympathy in this novel, and to the socioeconomic practices that are so rigorously followed at Clarens, is the care and maintenance of Julie's sensibility. For, without that, nothing else— not the creation of robust rural workers, nor Clarens' wholesome rustic regimen, nor the "wordless communication" enjoyed by the sensitive souls who inhabit it, nor the prolonged cure of Saint-Preux—would be either necessary or possible.

The Clarens program is based on a set of principles that is virtually identical to Tissot's: utility, simplicity, and frugality; the consumption of wholesome, home-grown products; the condemnation of urban habits and mores; and above all, moderation in the enjoyment of all pleasures. And, as in Tissot, the ascetic rules imposed at Clarens are justified by appealing to the higher principle of physical and moral health: each and every activity pursued in this household "nourishes the inclination for seclusion, work and temperance, and preserves, in whoever applies himself to them, a healthy mind and a heart free from the disturbance of the passions" (*New Eloise,* 304; *NH,* 4.11.470). Moreover, in the eyes of the superior souls who reside in this rustic haven, work itself is a pleasure: "Everything that contributes to our well-being becomes our amusement" (*Eloisa,* 3:49; *NH,* 5.2.549). In other words, health, happiness, and virtue are simultaneously induced at Clarens, through a system that micromanages every aspect of the domestic milieu that might leave an impression on the sensibilities of its inhabitants.

No one embraces this system with greater method or conviction than Julie, who exercises strict discipline over herself and the stimuli that might arouse her senses beyond what is strictly salubrious. She does so, Saint-Preux explains, as a means of tempering her acutely delicate and sensitive constitution:

> Julie's mind and body are equally sensible. The same delicacy prevails in her sentiments and in her organs. She was formed to know and taste every pleasure, and for a long time she only cherished virtue so dearly because she regarded it as the most refined of all delights [*voluptés*]. Now that she is able to enjoy that supreme pleasure peacefully, she refuses herself none that are consistent with it; but her method of enjoying them resembles the austerity of those who deny themselves such pleasures, such that the art of enjoyment [*l'art de jouir*] is for her an art of privation . . . This is how her simple soul preserves its first vigour; her taste is not spoiled by use; she never needs to excite it by excess; and I have often seen her take exquisite delight in a childish diversion, which would be insipid to any other person on earth.   (*Eloisa*, 3:39; *NH*, 5.2.541–42)

Julie's ascetic *art de jouir* is based on two assumptions: first, that to stay healthy and robust, the soul should enjoy only carefully metered doses of sensible pleasures; and second, that to stay virtuous, one must constantly subordinate one's desires and passions to the rule of reason. It is amusing to note, in passing, that Julie's program for controlling her sensibility bears a remarkable resemblance to that which Tissot proposed as a cure for masturbation—right down to its emphasis on milk and dairy products.[34]

Julie thus rules her powerful sensibility with an iron will, the better to "remain mistress of herself" (*Eloisa*, 3:39; *NH*, 5.2.542). Nowhere is this force of will more apparent than in her diet: "Though she is sensuous and *gourmande* in her meals, yet she does not love meat, ragouts or salt, and has never tasted wine by itself. Some excellent vegetables, eggs, cream and fruit, compose her ordinary diet, and was it not for fish, of which she is likewise very fond, she would be a perfect Pythagorean" (*Eloisa*, 2:258; *NH*, 4.10.453). This diet demonstrates Julie's great self-control as well as her exemplary "femininity," as the novel defines it. For Julie's dietary choices are presented as proof that certain foodstuffs are not only naturally preferred by women, but also reinforce their "natural" moral attributes: "Milk and sugar are naturally suited to the taste of the fair-sex, and may be deemed the symbols of innocence and sweetness, which are their most becoming ornaments" (*Eloisa*, 2:257; *NH*, 4.10.452). In Julie's case, this "you are what you eat" logic has a circular quality: while she is inclined by nature to consume only those foods that foster her delicate, womanly qualities, she also imposes them upon herself in order to keep her sensible constitution in top form.[35]

Julie's dietary rules, and those that she follows in planning meals for her entourage, also serve the larger purpose of keeping the Clarens household as self-sufficient as possible: one never finds any foreign products on Julie's table, only "a particular choice vegetable of the country; fine greens of our own gardens; fish from the lake, dressed in a special manner; cheese from our mountains; a German pasty, or game caught by some of the domestics" (*Eloisa*, 3:41; *NH*, 5.2.543). More important than the frugality evident in these selections is their repeatedly underscored homegrown quality: all of the food consumed by the residents of Clarens is domestically produced or obtained to guarantee that they are never exposed to any denaturing outside stimuli. As Wolmar points out, this rule extends to every object in the house:

> Our table is furnished with nothing but viands of our own growth; our dress and furniture are almost all composed of the manufactures of the country: nothing is despised with us because it is common, nor held in esteem because it is scarce. As every thing that comes from abroad is liable to be disguised or adulterated, we confine ourselves, as much through nicety as moderation, to the choice of the best home-commodities, the quality of which is never suspect. Our meals are plain, but choice; and nothing is wanting to make ours a sumptuous table, but the transporting it a hundred leagues off; in which case every thing would be delicate, every thing would be rare, and even our trouts of the lake would be thought infinitely better, were they to be eaten at Paris. (*Eloisa*, 3:49–50; *NH*, 5.2.549–50)

Domestically produced goods are therefore preferred at Clarens not only because they are more authentic and economical, but also because they better suit the residents' simple, wholesome temperaments than would products chosen according to the snobbish, worldly Parisian standards of rarity and exoticism. By purposely eschewing those standards, the Wolmars are better integrated into the general economy of their rural surroundings and also healthier in body and spirit.

It is Julie who oversees the process of domesticating all of the food and drink consumed at Clarens: she is both mistress of the house and its chief dairy-woman (*NH*, 4.10.452) and wine-maker. Although wine is presented in *La Nouvelle Héloïse* as a potentially risky substance—Saint-Preux has a couple of drunken misadventures in parts 1 and 2 (*NH*, pt. 1, letters 50–52; pt. 2, letter 26)—it is also held to be a "non-natural" necessary to the constitution of real men, most particularly Swiss men (*NH*, 1.23.81, 4.10.452). One of Julie's principal duties is thus to convert the grapes cultivated at Clarens into wine, for the enjoyment of the men of the estate. For the fieldhands taking part in the harvest, she transforms the grapes of a single vineyard into at least seven different preparations, each unique and "healthy and natural" (*NH*, 5.6.606). For her husband and her father, Julie deploys the same powers of magical transformation but at a more refined level: "They both love to sit a little after meals, in the manner of the Swiss; on which occasions, particularly after supper, she seldom fails to treat them with a bottle of wine more old and delicate than common" (*Eloisa*, 3:53; *NH*, 5.2.552). As Saint-Preux relates, the "pompous" foreign names of these wines at first dismayed him, because he thought that Julie had flagrantly violated the Clarens homegrown rule. But she explains: "The Lisbon, the Sherry, the Malaga, the Champagne, the Syracuse, which you have drunk here with so much pleasure, are all, in fact, no other than wines of this country, and you can see from here the vineyard that produced them. If they are inferior in quality to the celebrated wines whose names they bear, they are also without their inconveniences; and as one is certain of the materials of which they are composed, they may be drunk without risk" (*Eloisa*, 3:53; *NH*, 5.2.552–553).[36] With her wondrous domesticating touch, Julie succeeds in turning the very substance of intoxication into something natural and wholesome for her men. Her wines are, moreover, imbued with an added moral quality; as Wolmar attests, they "have a taste which pleases us better than any others, and that arises from the pleasure she takes in preparing them" (*Eloisa*, 3:53; *NH*, 5.2.553).

All of this work on the objects consumed at Clarens would nonetheless be futile if the estate's inhabitants were not properly disposed to benefit from it. Hence the great care that is taken in choosing domestic servants, who must be "honest" people able to assume a role in the extended Clarens family. It is of paramount importance, as Saint-Preux explains, that Clarens be protected against the unsavory, ruinous riffraff who are typically hired for domestic service in cities like Paris and London (*NH*, 4.10.445). To that end, "they have omitted no precaution to prevent the vices of the town from creeping into a family, where the master and mistress are strangers to them, and will not suffer them under their roof" (*Eloisa*, 2:252; *NH*, 4.10.449). Accordingly, the Wolmars' strategy for selecting and training their servants is devised in pointed opposition to worldly practices: "They do not take them from town, but from the country. This is the first place they live in, and it will assuredly be the last if they are good for anything. They take them out of some numerous family overstocked with children, whose parents come to offer them of their own accord. They choose them young, well-made, healthy, and of a pleasant countenance" (*Eloisa*, 2:247; *NH*, 4.10.445). Having narrowed the field to young, robust persons of good peasant stock, M. and Mme. de Wolmar take an equal part in interviewing candidates and in guiding them through the initial apprenticeship. Their greatest concern during this stage is to ensure that their apprentice servants not become corrupted: "They are not suffered to be enervated by idleness, the parent of vice. They do not allow them to become gentlemen, and to grow proud in their service. They continue to work as they did with their own family; in fact, they do but change their father and mother, and get more wealthy parents. They do not, therefore, hold their old rustic employments in contempt. If they were ever to leave this place, there is not one of them who would not rather turn peasant, than take any other employment" (*Eloisa*, 2:248; *NH*, 4.10.445).

The Wolmars therefore strive to maintain a household ambience that is explicitly paternalistic, rustic, and closed to the outside world. They are motivated, in part, by the same concern that Dr. Tissot voices about the degenerative influence of domestic service on the peasants who enter it; but their more general aim is to safeguard Clarens against contamination by vice. The Wolmars go to extraordinary lengths to control the behavior and character of their servants: they watch them vigilantly to ensure that all are zealous and industrious, and back up their own efforts by hiring overseers and encouraging useful informants (*NH*, 4.10.443, 465); they carefully restrict contact between the sexes, to keep the women chaste and the men virile and honest (*NH*, 4.10.449–54); and they provide organized recreational activities like games on Sundays and dances in the winter, which Julie always attends "in order to preserve decorum and modesty by her presence" (*Eloisa*, 2:261; *NH*, 4.10.456). In sum, the Wolmars function as benevolent, all-seeing, totalitarian parents who plan every aspect of their servants' lives so as to keep them morally upright and true to their original rustic nature. In fact, the Wolmars do nature one better: their servants not only retain their natural peasant roots, but also emerge from domestic service as outstanding citizens who are remarkably healthy and fit for a range of honorable endeavors (*NH*, 4.10.455).

Thus, just as Julie manages to create wines free of wine's usual insalubrious effects, so she and her husband manage to create a mode of domestic service that is immunized against the risks typically associated with it. Through a training system constructed entirely on the principle of moral hygiene, the Wolmars forge a domestic milieu in which order and sensibility not only coexist but reinforce each other. The servants of Clarens are quite literally the creation of their masters: "One might say that part of the master's intelligence, and of the mistress's sensibility, was conveyed to each of their servants; they seem so judicious, benevolent, honest, and so much above their station" (*Eloisa*, 2:280; *NH*, 4.10.470). These servants demonstrate how profoundly edifying a domestic *morale sensitive* can be on a collective scale, when it is administered by the proper social architects.

What Julie and Wolmar practice at Clarens does, indeed, have a distinct architectural component, in the sense that they carefully design certain spaces to serve particular sociomoral purposes: for example, Julie's "little Gynaeceum," where all the women of the household assemble after Sunday evening services (*NH*, 4.10.451–52); the "salon of Apollo," where only members of the Wolmars' intimate society are invited to dine (*NH*, 5.2.543–44); and the Elysée, Julie's artificially created "natural" garden (*NH*, pt. 4, letter 11). By stimulating the sensibilities of their inhabitants, these spaces "attach" them more closely to the pleasures of true nature, to the moral philosophy of Clarens, and to the rest of the community (*NH*, 4.10.452). These are, therefore, deliberately edifying milieux, which operate by triggering impressions that channel sensibility into the directions desired by the Wolmars.

It is within such settings that Julie's radiant motherly influence is most fully evident: the Gynaeceum, for example, is actually her children's bedroom, and the weekly gathering held there always begins with some game of skill meant to amuse and instruct the little ones (*NH*, 4.10.451). The game is followed by a light refreshment consisting of dairy products and sweets, "as suits the taste of women and children." Although, as a general rule, both wine and men are systematically excluded from these all-female festivities, Saint-Preux is granted the rare favor of accompanying Julie there one Sunday. The scene that follows is significant in light both of Saint-Preux's excessively enthusiastic reaction to the refreshments and of Julie's corrective counter-reaction:

> I made a most delicious repast with them. Where could you find such cream cakes as we have here? Imagine what they must be, made in a dairy where Julie presides, and eaten in her company. Fanchon presented me with some cream, some seed-cake, and other little comfits. All was gone in an instant. Julie smiled at my appetite. "I find (said she, giving me another plate of cream), that your stomach does you credit every where, and that you make as good a figure among a club of females, as you do among the Valaisans [identified earlier (*NH*, 1.23.81) as hearty drinkers]." "But I do not (answered I) make the repast with more impunity; the one may be attended with intoxication as well as the other; and reason may be as much distracted in a nursery as in a wine-cellar." She cast her eyes down without making any reply, blushed, and began to cuddle her children. This was enough to sting me with remorse. This, my Lord, was the first indiscretion, and I hope it will be the last. (*Eloisa*, 2:256–57; *NH*, 4.10.452)

Despite the edifying effects of the setting, Saint-Preux literally takes what he is consuming the wrong way: as he gorges himself with dairy treats, he symbolically turns them into wine—the quintessentially male, intoxicating substance that has caused some of his excesses in the past. Julie, disconcerted by a gaffe that stirs up disturbing old erotic memories (specifically, of the chalet where she had once tried to arrange a tryst with her erstwhile lover [*NH*, pt. 1, letter 36]), responds by hugging her children. Her overtly maternal gesture reminds Saint-Preux that he must rid himself of the vision of the old Julie which has resurfaced in his imagination and strive to redirect his sensibilities to suit the domestic ambience that has been so meticulously created at Clarens.

A similar scene occurs when Saint-Preux is given a tour of the Elysée by M. and Mme. de Wolmar. During their prolonged explanation of the "refound" naturalness of this garden, the Wolmars repeatedly underscore Julie's virtuous intentions in designing it: this garden is a monument to familial happiness, from the happy bird families who thrive in Julie's aviary (*NH*, 4.11.476–77) to the Wolmar children who play there (*NH*, 4.11.485–86). When, at the end of the tour, Saint-Preux indiscreetly asks why Julie favors this new garden over the charming groves on the other side of the house, Wolmar reproachfully reminds him of the troubling history of that place (where Saint-Preux and Julie first kissed), and adds, "Learn to respect the spot where you are; it has been planted by the hands of virtue" (*Eloisa*, 2:300; *NH*, 4.11.485). Wolmar's admonition is promptly followed by the entrance of Julie's little family. Once again, the touching spectacle of Julie surrounded by her children is employed to reinforce a lesson for Saint-Preux: what he should see when he contemplates the objects in the Elysée is an image of Julie not as his former mistress, but rather as "the most respectable mother" on earth (*NH*, 4.11.470).

That object lesson is put to the test at the end of the Elysée episode, when Saint-Preux returns there alone the next morning. Although he approaches the garden imagining that he will see the old Julie in every flower, he recalls Wolmar's admonition the minute he steps inside:

> The recollection of that single word instantly changed my whole frame of mind. I thought that I beheld the image of virtue, where I expected to find that of pleasure. That image intruded upon my imagination with the charms of Mrs. Wolmar, and for the first time since my return, I saw Julie in her absence—not such as she appeared to me formerly, and as I still love to represent her, but such as she appears to my eyes every day. My Lord, I imagined that I beheld that amiable, that chaste, that virtuous woman, in the midst of the retinue which surrounded her yesterday. I saw those three lovely children, those honorable and precious pledges of conjugal union and tender friendship, play about her, and give and receive a thousand affecting embraces. At her side I beheld the grave Wolmar, that husband so beloved, so happy, and so worthy of felicity. I imag-

ined that I could perceive his judicious and penetrating eye pierce to the
very bottom of my soul, and make me blush again.   (*Eloisa*, 2:302; *NH*,
4.11.486–87)

The Elysée thereby wields its intended effect, and Saint-Preux duly absorbs its
carefully staged message. The moment is "critical" for Saint-Preux—but this
time, in a positive, healing sense: "There was nothing, even to the very name
of Elysium, but what contributed to rectify my rambling imagination, and to
inspire my soul with a calm far preferable to the agitation of the most seductive
passions" (*Eloisa*, 2:303; *NH*, 4.11.487). Saint-Preux has at last made some
progress in his struggle to recover from his tumultuous past, and he has done
so largely through the positive reinforcement furnished by Julie's garden. The
scene thus marks the true beginning of his moral recuperation—that is, his
evolution from a figure whose overwrought sensibility disrupts the existing social and moral order to a fully incorporated member of the wholesome Clarens
household.

    The lesson that Wolmar administers in the Elysée preludes the official role
he will henceforth assume in the orchestration of Saint-Preux's cure. Wolmar
explains this project in the conversation with Julie and Saint-Preux that he
stages in the very grove where, as Julie puts it, "all the misfortunes of my life
commenced" (*Eloisa*, 2:306; *NH*, 4.12.489). Once seated in the grove between
the two erstwhile lovers, Wolmar takes them each by the hand, addresses them
as "my children," and makes two important revelations. First, he tells them that
he has known all along about their old liaison, which in Wolmar's judgment
arose from a "deceptive enthusiasm [that] only operates on beautiful souls"
(*Eloisa*, 2:314; *NH*, 4.12.495). Second, he announces that he is determined to
use their old affections to forge a new domestic arrangement: "We three may
be connected by a lasting attachment, capable of promoting our common good,
and procuring me some comfort to alleviate the troubles of approaching old
age" (*Eloisa*, 2:307; *NH*, 4.12.490). It was with that goal in mind that Wolmar
first undertook to cure Julie and now undertakes to cure Saint-Preux, by "regulating" their attachment rather than destroying it. Saint-Preux, in Wolmar's
sagacious eyes, has great potential: "Though you are not yet what you ought to
be, I find you more improved than you imagine, and I am better satisfied with
you than you are with yourself" (*Eloisa*, 2:315; *NH*, 4.12.496). Having said
that, Wolmar executes the next stage of the cure: he orchestrates a new kiss between the old lovers in the grove with the express intent of "profaning" it—
that is, of stripping this "fatal spot" of its old, passionate resonances, and replacing them with new, calm, innocuous associations. The technique is quite
effective, at least for Julie: "The kiss was nothing like that which rendered the

grove terrible to me. I silently congratulated myself, and I found that my heart was more changed than I had hitherto dared to imagine" (*Eloisa,* 2:315; *NH,* 4.12.496).

In overseeing the cure of Julie and Saint-Preux, Wolmar is therefore one part stage director and one part experimental scientist, testing out a theory of sensibility management that is a logical extension of the *morale sensitive* Clarens is designed to foster. Wolmar's therapeutic instruments consist primarily of the carefully crafted objects and spaces of Clarens, which he exploits in order to makes a precise impression on the sensibilities of his two young subjects. He sizes them up in a letter to Claire near the end of part 4: although "my two young people are more in love than ever," they are, he declares, "perfectly cured," in that their love is fast being converted into an "honest" attachment (*Eloisa,* 2:331; *NH,* 4.14.508). As for Saint-Preux, even though he is still deeply enamored of Julie, "he loves her in the time past"; thus, reasons Wolmar, "deprive him of his memory, and he will no longer be in love" (*Eloisa,* 2:332; *NH,* 4.14.509). In short, Wolmar's entire therapeutic strategy consists in adroitly replacing Saint-Preux's old ideas about Julie with new ideas (*NH,* 4.14.510).

One of those new ideas involves Claire: she, suggests Wolmar, should return to Clarens to marry Saint-Preux and allow him to take the final step in his recovery. (This is an idea that both M. and Mme. de Wolmar promote repeatedly in the second half of the novel [*NH,* pt. 5, letter 13; pt. 6, letter 6].) In the meantime, Wolmar uses other objects to carry out his "image replacement" therapy: "I endeavor to make the objects of his dread familiar to him, by presenting them to him in such a manner, that he may no longer think them dangerous. He is impetuous, but tractable, and easily managed. I avail myself of this advantage to give a turn to his imagination. Instead of letting him imagine his mistress, I compel him always to look at the wife of his friend, and the mother of my children; I efface one picture by another, and hide the past with the present" (*Eloisa,* 2:334–35; *NH,* 4.14.510–11). Saint-Preux's sensibility at this stage is as ardent as ever; but it is also weak and easy to control, particularly through techniques of "object impression" that act directly on his imagination without his knowing it. Wolmar is so confident that his curative plan is fail-safe that he deliberately leaves Julie and Saint-Preux alone together for eight days, "to teach them to sort out their true sentiments, and to know in what relation they really stand to each other" (*Eloisa,* 2:335; *NH,* 4.14.511). It is during Wolmar's absence that the two old lovers undergo the definitive crisis of the second half of the novel: the second episode at Meillerie, which puts both Saint-Preux's cure and the entire domestic *morale sensitive* program to the test.

This episode, which starts out as an innocent boat outing on Lake Geneva, takes a dramatic turn when Julie, Saint-Preux, and their boatmen are forced by a sudden windstorm to go ashore at Meillerie. Recounting the scene to Milord Edouard, Saint-Preux confesses that he had a secret motive in planning this outing: he wanted to "visit this cherished spot, in a more pleasant season and with her whose image formerly dwelled there with me" (*New Eloise*, 335; *NH*, 4.17.517). He thus persuades Julie to accompany him on a hike up to the esplanade from which he had once spent long days pining after his beloved—a place, he exclaims, "so full of you" (*New Eloise*, 336; *NH*, 4.17.519). And with that, Saint-Preux seems to regress into the mode of living through involuntary impressions that he had followed in parts 1-3 of *La Nouvelle Héloïse*: upon seeing the rock where he had engraved Julie's initials in a thousand different places, "I felt how much the sight of things can powerfully rekindle the violent sentiments with which we were once shaken near those very things." He points out every spot where he once sat to write to Julie, or read her letters, or gaze upon her residence in the distance; and he works himself up into such a desperate frenzy that Julie finally intervenes, saying with emotion: "Let us go, my friend. The air of this place is not good for me" (*New Eloise*, 336; *NH*, 4.17.519-20). He leaves with her, speechless but moaning; and they return to the port, where they set out to return to Clarens.

It is in the boat, on the journey home, that Saint-Preux has his definitive crisis of memory: "I began by remembering a similar outing made once before with her during the rapture of our early love. All the delightful sentiments which then filled my soul were recalled to my mind, in order to afflict me; all the events of our youth, our studies, our conversations, our letters, our trysts, our pleasures . . . those hundreds of little things which brought back the image of my past happiness—all returned, taking a place in my memory and increasing my present sorrow" (*New Eloise*, 337; *NH*, 4.17.520). The force of this onslaught of old, painful objects, coupled with the bitter reflections he makes upon them, throws Saint-Preux into a fit of desperate rage in which he is tempted to hurl himself overboard with Julie in his arms. Fortunately, his "agitations" soon change course, and his suicidal despair gives way to tearful, tender feeling. When he sees that Julie has also been moved to tears, Saint-Preux murmurs "I see that our hearts have never ceased to understand each other!" and Julie replies: " 'It is true,' she said in a changed voice, 'but let this be the last time that they will speak in this manner.' " Saint-Preux ends by declaring that this was "the day in which, without exception, I have felt the most intense emotions of my life," adding, "I hope that they will constitute the crisis which will restore me completely to myself" (*New Eloise*, 338; *NH*, 4.17.521).

It does indeed seem, as Saint-Preux says in his next letter to Edouard, that "the scene at Meillerie has been the crisis of my folly and my misfortunes." For from this point on, he regards Wolmar not as a rival, but as a dear friend, healer, and paternal benefactor, thanks to whom "this excessively feeble heart is cured, as completely as it can be" (*New Eloise*, 344; *NH*, 5.2.527). This suggests not only that Wolmar fully anticipated the perilous Meillerie episode as part of his therapeutic project, but also that Saint-Preux has willingly embraced his aggressive, risky healing techniques: "Enjoy, my dear Wolmar, the fruit of your labor. Accept the homage of a purified heart, which you have taken so many pains to make worthy of being offered to you. Never did a man undertake what you have undertaken; never did a man attempt what you have executed. Never did a grateful and sensitive soul feel what you have inspired in me. Mine had lost its force, its vigor, its being; you have restored them all. I was dead to virtue as well as to happiness; I owe you this moral life to which I feel myself reborn" (*New Eloise*, 360; *NH*, 5.8.611). Having undergone his cure, Saint-Preux now regards himself as a full-fledged member of the Clarens community because his soul is at last in harmony with the serenity that reigns there: "I am beginning to see myself here without uneasiness, to live here as if in my own home; and if I do not have the complete authority of a master in it, I feel even more pleasure in considering myself as a child of the house." He is now completely under the sway of the Wolmars: passing his days "amid practical reason and sensitive virtue," Saint-Preux observes that this couple's irresistible influence over him is so powerful that "my heart is put gradually into harmony with theirs" (*New Eloise*, 345; *NH*, 5.2.527). Saint-Preux has, in short, been fully integrated into the network of sensibility that binds the residents of Clarens together into an organic unity.

One might say that Saint-Preux has been tamed, domesticated, and thereby rendered harmless—just like Julie's wine. But he has also been rendered socially useful for the first time in his life: not only is he entrusted with the duty of educating the Wolmar's children (*NH*, pt. 5, letters 2 and 8), but he can now take part in the wordless communication that the true initiates of Clarens enjoy in their most intimate moments. A major instance of this communication occurs in part 5 after some out-of-town visitors have just left Clarens, leaving the inner circle alone to pass an afternoon enjoying the quiet pleasures of true friendship. The scene begins as a tableau of domestic contentment: the children are playing happily together, Mme. de Wolmar is doing her embroidery next to them, and the two men are reading aloud from the gazette. Then Julie is struck by a story concerning the illness of the French king, to whom the people of France seem so singularly attached. When Wolmar replies, "You have no need to envy a sovereign, you who have so long had us all for your subjects," she drops her embroidery and looks at her husband with "a look so touching and tender, that I quivered myself at it." Without a word, the three adults exchange a round of deep, telling gazes, and Saint-Preux remarks, "I could sense, by the manner in which her husband pressed my hand, that the same emotion had affected us all three, and that the delightful influence of her expansive heart was diffusing itself around her, and triumphing over insensibility itself" (*Eloisa*, 3:61; *NH*, 5.3.559). It is as if the positive resonating powers of Julie's sensibility have been turned on full force: her feelings are contagiously transmitted to her soul mates, and everyone, including the children, is so moved that they fall into an immobile ecstasy that lasts for two hours. Looking back on the scene, Saint-Preux exclaims: "How many things were said without anyone opening his lips! How warm the sentiments that were communicated, without the cold interposition of speech! . . . Julie's eyes were fixed on her three children; and her heart, ravished with the most enchanting ecstasy, animated her charming features with all the affecting sweetness of maternal tenderness" (*Eloisa*, 3:62; *NH*, 5.3.560).

The saga of Julie's sensibility reaches its climax here: she is in her ultimate earthly element, exerting her tender, vivifying influence over everyone around her (*NH*, 6.11.730). As she writes to Saint-Preux just before the accident that will make her a martyr to maternal devotion, Julie is now situated at the very center of her sympathetic universe:

> I am here surrounded by every thing that interests me . . . all that is dear to my heart, and perhaps all that is desirable in this world . . . The whole universe to me is in this little spot. I enjoy at once my attachment to my friends, that which they have to me, and that which they have to each other; their mutual good-will either comes from, or relates to me; everything I see extends my being, and nothing divides it. I exist in all those who are around me . . . I have nothing more to desire; to feel and to be happy [*sentir et jouir*] are with me the same thing; I live at once in all that I love; I am replete with happiness, and satisfied with life: come, death, when thou wilt! I have no new feelings to experience now. (*Eloisa*, 3:230; *NH*, 6.8.689)

Julie has, in her own mind, performed her task on earth: she has created a deep and enduring "mutual good-will" among the other residents of Clarens and has herself felt all of the sentiments that a single soul can feel. All that is left for her is to die: that is, to go off into the great beyond in order to find an eternal mode of sensitive communication, this time with God.[37]

So it is that the very next letter of the novel announces the accident that will soon prove fatal to Julie: she throws herself into the lake to save her youngest son, succeeds in that mission, but falls mortally ill in the process (*NH*, 6.9.702–3). Julie nonetheless strives before dying to ensure that she—or at least, the network of sensibility she has created at Clarens—will live on even after her death. She therefore writes to Saint-Preux from her deathbed to urge him to carry out her final wishes: "You are losing of Julie only that which you have for a long time lost. The best of her remains for you. Come, rejoin her family. Let her heart dwell among you. Let all those she loved gather together to give her a new existence. Your duties, your pleasures, your friendship—all will be her work. The bond of your union formed by her will give her new life; she will expire only when the last one of all is dead" (*New Eloise*, 406; *NH*, 6.12.741). This is, perhaps, Saint-Preux's true function at the end of the novel: to maintain the bond of sympathetic affection among Julie's survivors, by seeing to it not only that her loved ones stay physically together but also that "another Julie"—Claire, her faithful cousin and sister soul—steps in to provide the group with another center of sensibility that can organize and vivify it. Julie's last wish is for Saint-Preux to come back to Clarens and marry Claire: "Each of you is going to lose half of his life; join together in order to preserve the other. The only way left for you both to survive me is by serving my family and my children. Would that I could invent still stronger bonds in order to unite everything that is dear to me!" (*New Eloise*, 406; *NH*, 6.12.742).

According to the final letter of *La Nouvelle Héloïse*, however, the union of Saint-Preux and Claire does not seem likely: Claire, too, urges Saint-Preux to return with Milord Édouard in order to rejoin all that remains of Julie, but she refuses to entertain the notion of marrying him or any other man. The conclusion of the novel is therefore marked by a note of anxious uncertainty over the viability of the community, now that Julie is no longer physically present. On the one hand, Claire attests to the continuing power of Julie's magnetic sensibility: "I like to believe that from the place where she is dwelling, from the place of eternal peace, her soul, still loving and sensitive, takes pleasure in returning among us, in finding her friends again full of memories of her, in seeing them imitate her virtues . . . No, she has not forsaken this place, which she made so delightful for us. It is still full of her. I see her in every object; I perceive her at every step. At every instant of the day I hear the accents of her voice" (*New Eloise*, 409; *NH*, 6.13.745). Julie's sensible image therefore seems indelibly inscribed upon all of the people and objects that make up the Clarens household. Yet, on the other hand, Claire's final words are fragmented and suicidally melancholic—recalling Saint-Preux's own episode of desperate, dejected obsession at Meillerie in part 1, when he sees the image of Julie in the objects around him but knows that he cannot possess her (*NH*, 1.26.89–93). Thus, in the absence of the extraordinary sensible being that had provided Clarens with its vivifying energy, both the estate's domestic economy and its unique moral ambience seem threatened with extinction; for the material objects and sites that had once made Clarens a rigorously edifying embodiment of a *morale sensitive* now seem to wreak the opposite effect on Julie's survivors (*NH*, 6.13.745).

Julie's death is, in short, the ultimate crisis for Saint-Preux and Claire, the two supersensitive souls she leaves behind. Given their inferiority to Julie in matters of moral heroism and the grieving Claire's tendency to yield to an uncontrolled, excessive mode of sensibility reminiscent of the novel's "unhealthy" first half (*NH*, 6.11.738–39), one might conclude that Rousseau's literary experiment in instituting a *morale sensitive* is also killed off in the end of *La Nouvelle Héloïse*. Or rather, one might say that his experiment really is just a fiction—an impossible dream of a world perfectly designed, down to the last moral and physical detail, to foster true sensibility. In order to function, the world imagined by Rousseau must have at its center a sensible being who, although quite organic, is nonetheless otherworldly: Julie, who is mythic even as a cadaver (*NH*, 6.11.736–37). Once she is gone, that world reverts to its cold, mundane condition; and the sensitive souls who remain behind seem doomed to become, once again, the helpless victims of their own vulnerable natures.

7. Moral Anthropology

Sensibility and the
New Biology of
Enlightenment

Sex, Sensibility, and the Vapors

No discussion of the meanings of sensibility in eighteenth-century France would be complete if it did not address the subject of sex—or more precisely, the subject of women and the "exquisite" sensibility that physicians and other philosophes generally associated with them. During the first three-quarters of the century, women's sensibility was almost always ascribed a special intensity, yet the significance attributed to that intensity often varied so widely as to be contradictory. To cite some of the literary examples we have examined, "feminine" sensibility could be represented as a refined moral sense (as with Marianne of *La Vie de Marianne*), or as a pathological hypersusceptibility to stimulation (as with Mme. *** of *La Religieuse*), or as an extraordinary influence over others (as with Julie of *La Nouvelle Héloïse*). Clearly, the relationship between sex and sensibility during this period was pervaded by the same ambiguities as those that characterized women's status in Enlightenment culture up to the 1770s. In the last few decades of the century, however, the complexity and contradictions that had previously marked that relationship subsided, in keeping with the shift that took place in the accepted understanding of woman's so-called nature and of her place in society. This shift, which has been keenly scrutinized in recent feminist studies of the history of gender, occurred in a broad range of discursive fields, including moral and political philosophy, physiology, anatomy, botany, and zoology. Yet nowhere was it more pronounced than in the field of biomedical theory, where an obsession with defining woman's essential nature in narrowly domestic terms spawned a highly teleological subgenre of medical discourse known as moral anthropology.

The discourse of moral anthropology was generally conducted in three interconnected genres: the sex-specific natural history, the sex-specific hygienic tract, and the medico-philosophical treatise on "the physical and the moral." The medical authors who wrote in this vein include Pierre Roussel, Paul-Victor de Sèze, Pierre-Jean-Georges Cabanis, and (pursuing the genre into the nineteenth century) Jacques-Louis Moreau de la Sarthe, G. Jouard, Jean-Baptiste Mège, Julien-Joseph Virey, and C. Lachaise.[1] Today, moral anthropology is usually approached as one of several scientific theories that were used to promote the restrictive image of women's physical and mental capacities which held sway in Europe at the end of the eighteenth century and throughout much of the next. In his provocative study *Making Sex: Body and Gender from the Greeks to Freud*, the historian Thomas Laqueur describes the intellectual climate of this period as follows:

> By around 1800, writers of all sorts were determined to base what they insisted were fundamental differences between the male and female sexes, and thus between man and woman, on discoverable biological distinctions ... Thus the old [Galenic] model, in which men and women were arrayed according to their degree of metaphysical perfection, their vital heat, along an axis whose telos was male, gave way by the late eighteenth century to a new model of radical dimorphism, of biological divergence. An anatomy and physiology of incommensurability replaced a metaphysics of hierarchy in the representation of woman in relation to man.[2]

Responding to Laqueur's thesis, Londa Schiebinger agrees that a major shift occurred during the eighteenth century toward a paradigm of sexual incommensurability, or complementarity, as she prefers to call it; however, she maintains that this shift was under way as early as 1730.[3] Read in tandem, these historical analyses provide a compelling picture of how the quest for sexual divergence led anatomists and physiologists to perceive clear-cut sexual oppositions in everything from the genital organs, to bones and skulls, to brains.[4] Within the field of moral anthropology, however, the story is somewhat more complicated; although biological distinctions between the sexes also preoccupied these medical theorists, the primary locus of sexual difference was, in their eyes, not any particular organ or bone, but rather the entire sensible system.

Bodily sensibility was, in fact, the principal site on which the shift toward sexual incommensurability was played out within moral anthropology—a doctrine whose advent is critically important not only for the representation of sex and gender, but also for the theory of sensibility whose evolution I have charted in this book. From its very inception with the publication of Pierre Roussel's best-selling *Système physique et moral de la femme* in 1775, moral anthropology was invested with the dual task of defining the nature of women versus men while also refining the current medical model of sensibility along new, neatly divided anthropological lines. That mission was not confined to medicine alone: it is also strikingly apparent in the libertine novel of the late eighteenth century, particularly the novels of Laclos and Sade, whose fictional universes are, like moral anthropology, peopled by beings with sensibilities so physically and morally distinct as to be incommensurate.

Roussel's *Système physique et moral de la femme* has been given a prominent place in recent discussions of the history of sex, gender, and the body largely because many twentieth-century scholars have taken their cue from his nineteenth-century hagiographers and declared him to be the founder of an entirely new school of medical theory—one that is now considered notoriously misogynist and reactionary.[5] Several modern commentators have asserted that Roussel wrote his *Système* in the service of a particular political agenda: for example, to lend medical weight to the constraints that were imposed upon women in the public sphere during the French Revolution and under the Napoleonic Civil Code.[6] It is, however, misleading (and somewhat anachronistic) to read the medical works of Roussel and his followers in the light of contemporary political events; for, although moral anthropology undoubtedly contributed to the cultural climate that prompted the French authorities to legislate strict sociopolitical boundaries between the sexes, it was devised to serve a theoretical agenda specific to philosophical medicine. This theoretical agenda was, as I will argue, concerned less with sex or gender *per se* than with sensibility. What Roussel himself viewed as groundbreaking in his work was its innovative model of sensibility, a model in which the physical and moral were fully integrated, and in which male and female sensibility were kept neatly separated on different developmental tracks. One cannot, therefore, begin to address the gender politics involved in Roussel's work or in the larger field of moral anthropology without first considering the theoretical sources and repercussions of this bifurcated, sex-specific model of vital sensibility.

The discussion of sex and sensibility that took place in moral anthropology was rooted in three different conceptual traditions. The first, and most important, was the Montpellier school of medical theory. Roussel culled much of his medical doctrine from the vitalist model of the sensible body popularized by his mentor Bordeu. The second tradition was philosophical anthropology as conceived by Buffon, on the one hand, and Rousseau on the other. Buffon's *Histoire naturelle de l'homme* (1749–78) provided moral anthropologists with the naturalist methodology they used to classify sensible bodies according to variations in age, climate, temperament, and sex; and Rousseau's tale of Sophie in the fifth book of *Emile* set the tone for their differential perspective on the "natural" moral-physical development of girls versus boys.[7] Finally, moral anthropology was an outgrowth of the large body of medical writing that was devoted to the health and illnesses of women during the second half of the century. Because a certain realignment of sex and sensibility was already afoot in these texts, I will preface my analysis of Roussel and his followers with a selective survey of this medical literature, focusing on the lively debate that began in the mid-1750s over the apparent epidemic of vapors and other nervous maladies which was afflicting the inhabitants of France's large cities, most particularly their rich female residents.

Various critics have ventured interpretations of the vapors' significance for eighteenth-century representations of women. The most influential is undoubtedly Michel Foucault, who broaches the subject in *Histoire de la folie à l'âge classique* while discussing hysteria, hypochondria, and the evolving notion of nervous illness. Women, Foucault emphasizes, were seen as particularly susceptible to these ailments by physicians of the so-called classical age: "The entire female body is riddled by obscure but strangely direct paths of sympathy; it is always in an immediate complicity with itself, to the point of forming a kind of absolutely privileged site for the sympathies; from one extremity of its organic space to the other, it encloses a perpetual possibility of hysteria. The sympathetic sensibility of her organism, radiating through her entire body, condemns woman to those diseases of the nerves that are called vapors."[8] As is typical of Foucault's treatment of eighteenth-century medical thought, his observations on the vapors are at once insightful and misleading—insightful because he identifies the major conceptual and social tensions that pervade this discourse, but misleading because his interpretation of their significance is overly generalized and, at times, chronologically or geographically skewed.[9] Although the organic sympathy that he singles out was sometimes invoked to explain why effeminate constitutions were prone to become vaporous, it was not the sole component of the model of sensibility that was at play in the vapors theory of eighteenth-century France. Nor, contrary to the suggestion of Foucault and others, was the female body *tout court* marked as pathological by virtue of its heightened susceptibility to impression: rather, the vapors specialists tended to pathologize only a certain type of femininity or effeminacy.[10] Finally, sensibility's significations within the discourse on vapors had repercussions that extended beyond the evolving theory of madness that preoccupies Foucault, in that the sickly, putatively "feminine" sensibility that vapors theorists constructed in their treatises helped to frame the normative representation of women's healthful nature put forth by Roussel and other moral anthropologists.

My study of moral anthropology proper concentrates upon the works of three illustrative members of the first generation of medico-moral anthropologists, focusing primarily on Pierre Roussel, author of the *Système physique et moral de la femme* as well as the uncompleted *Fragment du "Système physique et moral de l'homme"* and *Essai sur la sensibilité*. Roussel's doctrine was extended and refined by Paul-Victor de Sèze, who included a long chapter on sex in his *Recherches physiologiques et philosophiques sur la sensibilité ou la vie animale* (1786), and by Pierre-Jean-Georges Cabanis, who devoted the fifth memoir of his *Rapports du physique et du moral de l'homme* (1802) to sexual difference. Cabanis, writing at the very end of the period that interests us, is significant both because he synthesized the various strands of the medicine and philosophy of sensibility and because he established the Rousselian model of women as canonical for the next generation of moral anthropologists.[11] What emerged from these works was not just a new model of sex, but also a new biology of enlightenment—that is, a doctrine according to which it seemed possible to invoke sex-based distinctions in sensibility to argue who was capable of full enlightenment and who was not.

Women's health was a rich but confounding subject for eighteenth-century medical writers, one that inspired discussions and polemics that now seem quaint, if not downright bizarre.[12] One of the most curious of those debates concerned the affliction known as the vapors, which many physicians in the second half of the century viewed as a peculiarly modern, urban scourge. As Joseph Raulin puts it in his *Traité des affections vaporeuses du sexe* (1758), "For at least a century now, vapors have been endemic in large cities; most women who enjoy the comforts of life are vaporous—one might say that they pay for the pleasure of wealth with a succession of languors."[13] That is not to say that men were seen as immune from this condition, for most vapors specialists of this period dismissed the ancient notion that actual vapors arise from the uterus, favoring instead a neural explanation of the ailment that could apply to both sexes.[14] Thus, Raulin insisted that "men become vaporous just like women when their nerves lose their natural firmness"; and Pierre Pomme, writing two years later, explicitly entitled his work *Traité des affections vaporeuses des deux sexes* (1760).[15] Eighteenth-century medical theorists did not, moreover, label all women vaporous: only wealthy, urban-dwelling women, and men who had "degenerated" to a similarly delicate temperament, got the vapors. For a certain time, therefore, being vaporous had more to do with a mode of life that physicians viewed as overrefined and soft, than it did with biological sex.

When Enlightenment physicians spoke of the vapors, they referred to a disease also called hypochondria, hysteria, uterine furors, and nymphomania, depending on the type and severity of the affliction in question; all of these conditions were commonly placed under the umbrella of "nervous affections" and

Alexandre Colin, The Vapors, from Album comique (1823). (Photograph used by permission of the Philadelphia Museum of Art: SmithKline Beecham Corporation Fund for the Ars Medica Collection.)

judged to stem from a pathological oversensitivity of the nervous system. The symptoms associated with the vapors consequently covered quite a range of complaints, including melancholic lethargy, spasms and convulsions, humoral plethora, excessive nervousness, overactive imagination, nausea, headaches, and indigestion. It is not my purpose here to explain the rather convoluted nosology of vapors and related disorders, nor to confirm the thesis advanced by some commentators that eighteenth-century medical thought moved progressively away from organic models of the vapors and toward a psychogenetic interpretation of the condition.[16] For what one actually finds in these writings is not so much a progression as a persistent oscillation between organic and psycho-pathological explanations, reflecting the period's more general tendency to depict sensibility as a property that partook of *both* the material and the mental registers. The progressionist historical approach is, moreover, not necessarily the most productive mode of inquiry into this subject, largely because the vapors were so heavily invested with the period's social concerns that the question of their actual locus is somewhat secondary. At the heart of those concerns was the widely decried phenomenon of excessively luxurious living among the upper classes—an issue so fundamental to the discourse on vapors that the disease virtually disappeared from the medical horizon after the Old Regime had been dismantled.[17] My aim in analyzing the vapors debate is to determine how the vapors were constructed as a *cultural* problem, one that involved questions of sex, gender, ethics, hygiene, and above all sensibility.

We can situate the debate on vapors in eighteenth-century French medical discourse fairly precisely: it was conducted in about a dozen treatises devoted in part or in whole to the subject, beginning in 1756 with Pierre Hunauld's *Dissertation sur les vapeurs et les pertes de sang,* and ending approximately in 1789 with M. Bressy's *Recherches sur les vapeurs.* The treatises written in this genre were generally written for a mixed audience that included both medical practitioners and the vaporous themselves.[18] All of the vapor theorists were convinced that there was something decidedly new and alarming about the nervous disorders that were apparently rampant in certain French cities, Paris in particular. In the words of the Montpellier physician Edme-Pierre Chauvot de Beauchêne, "Vaporous illnesses are new; their progress has followed that of luxury, and of the immense population of Paris."[19] Bressy, also of Montpellier, likewise depicts the vapors, which he also calls "melancholia" and "hypochondria," as a modern plague and issues a call to medical action: "Melancholia is not exactly a new illness, but in no other century has it been so general or had such intensity; it can thus be regarded as a new plague. We must consequently join all our efforts to annihilate it, as we have succeeded in doing for venereal illnesses."[20] These treatises were therefore conceived in response to what was widely seen as a serious crisis in social health. What they present to address that crisis is both a panoply of often hair-raising curative therapies and a scathing critique of certain pathogenic aspects of contemporary French society.

This social critique, a prominent feature of every treatise on the vapors, is significant on several counts. First, it recalls Tissot's broad indictment of worldliness in the *Essai sur les maladies des gens du monde*, which we examined earlier.[21] But whereas Tissot used the figure of the sickly *homme du monde* to structure his treatise, the vapors theorists focused instead on the worldly woman, who most fully embodied the sedentary, luxurious lifestyle they associated with the privilege, wealth, and idleness enjoyed by a particular class of city-dwellers. In other words, these physicians represented worldliness as a gendered mode of life that created the same type of excessive effeminacy in everyone who adopted it. Their perspective on the urban elite was thus highly attuned to the feminizing effects of the worldly lifestyle, signs of which included an exaggerated moral and physical delicacy (Pomme, 14; Beauchêne, 1–2 et passim), oversensitivity to the least little stimulant (Hunauld, 40; Raulin, 114–15), and a dangerously fragile animal economy.[22] Although they derived their physiological notions from the Montpellier model of sensibility, these theorists applied that model in a particular manner, by placing special emphasis on "the sensibility attached to the essence of women, or to particular constitutions that are more susceptible to it than others" (Raulin, xix).

Typically, after espousing the consensus view that the vapors stem from the sensibility or irritability of the nervous system, each vapor theorist puts forth his particular theory on which body parts are actively involved in sensitizing the human being. While some single out humors (Hunauld, 92; Bressy, 46), others emphasize fibers, either those that compose the viscera (Raulin, xxiv–xxvi), or those that make up the nerves (Pomme, 13; Pressavin, 7). Many of these writers also attribute a major causal function to stimulating moral causes like "the effervescence of the passions" (Pressavin, 218–20) or an overactive imagination.[23] We should note, however, that the imagination is never treated by the vapors theorists as independent from its material substrate; rather, it is viewed as an organ among others in the overall economy of vital sensibility.

The vapor theorists venture a variety of hypotheses concerning the organic seat of the sensibility that is at play in this ailment, ranging from visceral organs like the uterus and the stomach (Raulin, xxvi; Pomme, 11), to the general epigastric region (Pressavin, 148), to the vagina (Bienville, 3), to any organ where a "vitiated humour" settles (Bressy, 16; Beauchêne, 47). They are, however, in solid agreement that certain people are more inclined by nature to fall victim to the vapors: "Children, persons of the fair sex, and men of a delicate temperament naturally have a more mobile and sensitive nervous system, and are consequently more subject to nervous illnesses than are adults and men of robust constitution" (Pressavin, 203). The temperamental qualities associated with the vapors are not, in themselves, deemed incompatible with health; on the contrary, they define certain natural conditions, like femininity: "The delicate organization of women provides them with the sensibility that nature has placed in them to make us happy; and yet, such is their physical disposition that, despite the delicateness of their organs, nature gives to their passions, and to their sensibility, an energy and expansive force of which men are not capable" (Beauchêne, 11). At the same time, however, enhanced sensibility makes one's constitution especially vulnerable to being altered by the denaturing effects of culture.

It is this kind of reasoning that underlies the strong disapproval the vapors theorists express for the city, a setting that epitomizes culture in all of its negative aspects. In the eyes of these physicians, the city is a place where wealthy people lead a reprehensibly soft life (Pomme, 14); where they intensify their violent passions by novel-reading, gambling, and theater (Beauchêne, 31–34); where the air is bad and the diet pernicious (Raulin, 40, 56); where residents commonly commit excesses of both study and debauchery, and overindulge in substances like tobacco, chocolate, coffee, and fermented liquor, thereby sapping the very life force of the human race and contributed to hereditary debility (Pomme, 15; Raulin, 46–48; Pressavin, 212); and where men and women alike have become so denatured that some have taken up the perverse art of "vaporizing" just to be fashionable (Hunauld, 34). Raulin blames the debility that has overtaken the affluent inhabitants of France's cities not on nature, but on the perverse mode of corporal "education" favored by high-society ladies: "The rich women who live in big cities and have been raised in idlenesss are delicate, weak, and valetudinary . . . After such an education, full of so many inappropriate abuses, the nervous system—especially in women—is weak, feeble, delicate, and sensitive, and can only perform its functions halfway; the least little thing aggravates it, irritates it, and causes irregular movements within it. This gradually results in bad digestion, obstructions in the viscera, difficulties in the secretions . . . and finally vapors, phthisis, and so on" (Raulin, 40–41). He adds that the same sort of transformation can and does occur in some men, who become vaporous or hypochondriacal "through debauchery, exhaustion, idleness, excessive mental exertion, and so on" (Raulin, 42). In its male victims, the vapors create an unsettling gender indeterminacy: speaking of the symptoms he has observed in male patients, Raulin exclaims, "I would have sworn that they were women, if I had not been certain of their sex" (Raulin, 42). The vapors are thus a disorder that both accentuates effeminacy and blurs the natural lines between the sexes.[24]

When a woman embraces a worldly lifestyle, she disrupts the fragile equilibrium that exists among her organs, between her body and her passions, and between her organism and the outside world. Like a sensitive plant whose leaves wither and fall off when one touches it, a vaporous woman become incapable of withstanding the slightest stimulus—even the religious music played during mass—without fainting (Raulin, 115). Most of the vapors theorists insist, however, that such excessive sensibility results not from female nature but from the way that women live in high society—a point they commonly illustrate by underscoring the stark difference between *mondaines* and their rural counterparts (Hunauld, 193; Raulin, 41; Pomme, 14–15; Pressavin, 209; Beauchêne, 2–3, 19–20). Jean-André Venel is particular absolute in his distinction between the two lifestyles: "A comparison between the physical state of the most civilized women with that of the women who are closest to the state of nature offers the most striking and alarming contrasts."[25] Raulin goes so far in emphasizing the superior robustness of country women as to declare that "illnesses are spawned by society—they are hardly ever seen in savage peoples" (Raulin, 41).

Like Tissot, therefore, the vapors theorists use a rural ideal of good hygiene as the basis of the remedies they propose for an affliction they view as a social disease—that is, an unnatural disease caused by too much civilized living. As the discourse on vapors evolved from the 1750s on, it became increasingly preoccupied with curing the disease by returning each sex to its "natural" condition. Hence, perhaps, the increasingly domestic tone of the remedies devised for vaporous women. Bressy, for example, prescribes for his women patients a lactation remedy that would consist of drawing the vitiated menstrual blood that he considers responsible for the vapors to the breasts, where it would naturally be converted into milk and safely evacuated (Bressy, 135–40). Breast-feeding, he insists, is the most effective and natural method of accomplishing this: "Breast-feed, call your milk back to your breasts, and your happiness will lack for nothing; loving and virtuous wives, tender and beloved mothers, you will be the symbol of perfection, and your life will be the model of felicity" (141). Health and happiness for women therefore depend ultimately on devotion to their familial duties, which Bressy represents here metonymically, via the mammary synecdoche favored in many late Enlightenment writings on women and nature.[26]

No physician, however, goes quite so far as Beauchêne in promoting women's absolute domestication as a prophylactic measure against the vapors. His *De l'influence des affections de l'âme dans les maladies nerveuses des femmes* (1781) brought a distinctly new tone to the discussion of vapors, for it was clearly written in the wake of Roussel's *Système physique et moral de la femme*.

Beauchêne explicitly borrows from Roussel when he insists that woman's entire constitution is "altogether different from that of man" (Beauchêne, 12); he
then proceeds to use Roussel's sex-specific sensibility theory to construct his
own explanation of the vapors. Female sensibility, Beauchêne maintains, is
acute, energetic, and expansive; but "this expansion of the soul which is natural
to women, is often harmful to their tranquillity" (211). Male sensibility, by contrast, operates by means of slower and better-regulated movements, affecting
the constitution in a far less intense manner (13). Hence the new distinction that
Beauchêne introduces into the existing theory of the vapors: this disease is, he
asserts, rare and mild in men, even those who lead lives of dissipation; and it is
virtually absent in "natural" women, because their robust and productive lives
immunize them against oversensitivity (1–2). However, the vapors are ubiquitous and serious among women who lead the rich, idle life typical of France's
cities: "The vaporous maladies of the fair sex . . . have become so general and
so serious in big cities, especially Paris, that they almost always have a major
effect on the length of women's lives, and on the time it takes to cure the other
illnesses that afflict them" (6). High living is, he insists, downright lethal for
women because it weakens their organs, aggravates their passions, and height-
ens their sensibility to a degree that is both physically and morally perilous.

Beauchêne thus breaks with certain of his predecessors by insisting that the
vapors are a properly *female* disorder—a condition that is determined not
merely by a feminine or effeminate lifestyle, but also by a peculiarly female
susceptibility to a certain mode of denatured sensibility. By taking this tack,
which is clearly informed by the set of sexual distinctions recently popularized
by Roussel, Beauchêne gives new specificity and direction to the established
Enlightenment thesis that the vapors are an affliction of the social elite. He approaches the vapors as a condition in which worldliness and femaleness collide,
with disastrous consequences both for women's health and for their morality.
And to demonstrate his thesis, Beauchêne undertakes a "day-in-the-life"
chronicle of worldly existence that pinpoints the precise activities most likely
to bring on the vapors in women.

Beauchêne sees cities like Paris as full of wealthy ladies who eat, drink,
sleep, move, and think in a manner that is "almost always in conflict with nature" (Beauchêne, 214). Because such women are freed of any child-rearing duties or the need to earn their substinence, they exist in a state of perpetual *ennui*, with little to do but seek diversion: "Women with nothing to do are
reduced to seeking new pleasures in the inexhaustible resources of the imagination; the more the imagination works, the more it weakens the organs it
dominates" (4).[27] Driven by this perpetual quest for amusement, worldly
women follow a routine that revolves around a trio of unwholesome milieux:

the overladen dining table (32, 35); the salon, where they stir up their passions and imaginations (36); and, worst of all, the theater. The theater is not the only aesthetic practice that Beauchêne singles out as pathogenic over the course of his social critique: he also has harsh words for the excessively sentimental novels so popular among the women of his day (37). His comments on the theater are, however, far more detailed, largely because he seeks to lend medical authority to the antitheatrical argument made by Rousseau in his *Lettre à d'Alembert sur les spectacles*.[28] Beauchêne expresses astonishment that Rousseau, "who knew women so well, particularly city women," neglected to mention the most worrisome effect of French theater: its direct causal role in the epidemic of vapors among worldly women (35). Since Rousseau himself failed to point out this problem, Dr. Beauchêne obligingly does it for him, and thus launches a rather extraordinary medical excursion into theater criticism.

Beauchêne's primary objection to theater-going is that the practice is physically and morally unhygienic, especially for its avid female fans. First, he confirms Rousseau's observation that the French-style theater is a somber and distressing place, where people sit for hours, inactive and silent, "imprisoned" in a cramped and stuffy room that barely allows one to breathe (Beauchêne, 33). Second, he maintains that worldly ladies rush off to the theater without having properly digested their rich meals and leave it only to head for the gaming table, a source of further nervous agitation (35). Beauchêne acknowledges that some kinds of theatrical production can have a benign or even edifying effect upon the spectator's constitution by reinforcing the reasoning faculties. These, however, are not the plays most in favor among sophisticated Parisian women, who flock precisely to the genre of spectacle that is most likely to overstimulate their sensibilities, the *drame bourgeois*, which Diderot had championed as a vehicle for moral edification but which Beauchêne regards as a primary cause in the spread of vapors because it is expressly designed to elicit a weepy physical reaction.

Curiously, Beauchêne's attack on the *drame bourgeois* is based upon the very same principle that informs the aesthetic theory Diderot had deployed in texts like the *Entretiens sur "Le Fils naturel"* to promote this hybrid genre: namely, the notion that the *drame bourgeois* possesses a special capacity to engage its spectators because it so thoroughly absorbs their attentions and arouses their sympathies that their entire sensible systems are physically affected. That aesthetic operation is, in Beachêne's analysis, all too effective in female spectators: "The sensibility of women, focused on a small number of objects [the pathetic figures and actions being represented on the stage], is set in play through all sorts of means. The soul is so strongly stirred that it produces in their nerves a commotion that is brief, in truth, but whose consequences are ordinarily grave;

the momentary loss of their senses, the tears they shed during the performance of our modern tragedies, are the least of the accidents that can result" (Beauchêne, 33). So profound is the commotion induced in the delicate sensibilities of women playgoers that symptoms persists for months: "Observe them several months after this performance, and you will soon be sure that it has produced in them an agitation that is very difficult to ease, and that will frequently even cause them very violent pains in the nerves. Even those women who do not immediately show the effects of what they have seen in the theater conserve in their minds a ready disposition for new troubles, which can recur spontaneously and without any known cause" (33).

Theatergoing, pleasure-seeking, and other forms of high living thus combine to wreak a devastating effect upon the sensible systems of wealthy Parisian ladies: "If some passion seizes them in the midst of these occupations, these ideas, this mode of life, their blood is altogether inflamed; their nerves are strained to the highest degree, and as soon as the passion demands some effort on their part, the vapors ensue" (Beauchêne, 38). He describes the onset of the vapors in graphic and alarming terms: what begins as a tendency toward languor, melancholy, swooning, and inexplicable crying jags escalates into frightful nervous contractions that trigger loss of consciousness and of feeling. Patients in the throes of such a crisis may then regain their senses, only to start wailing in a dreadful manner and tearing out their hair. These fits are soon followed by deep moaning and "torrents of tears," which are sometimes accompanied by screaming, teeth-grinding, and general convulsions (39).

Beauchêne ends his dramatic symptomological tableau with a telling apostrophe: "Come, amiable and pleasure-loving women, come contemplate this spectacle, if there is still time . . . Shun henceforth false pleasures, ardent passions, idleness and indolence; follow your young husbands into the countryside and on their travels, and come back to Paris fit to provide your fellow women with an example of the exercises and occupations that suit your sex; above all, love and raise your children yourselves" (39). His advice to worldly women is categorical: if they want to protect themselves against this terrible nervous affliction, they must abandon their relentless pursuit of urban cultural diversions and retreat instead into the country—accompanied, of course, by their husbands.[29] For what Paris needs, in his view, are fewer overstimulating theatrical spectacles and more living examples of maternal devotion. Like Rousseau, therefore, Beauchêne undertakes to cure women of the effects of civilization by transforming them into paragons of natural virtue and wholesomeness—beings who will no longer be passive spectators of artificial worldly spectacles, but rather, active participants in their own domestic scene.[30]

Beauchêne's plan for treating the vapors thus entails an ambitious program of social reform—reform in both the definition of women's social role and in the social institutions with which they should be associated. It is not enough, in his eyes, for women to modify their tastes and habits; men must also take an aggressive role in the preservation of their wives' health:

> I could tell men: build your houses a different way, change your style of life, ensure the morals and happiness of your wives by keeping them busy in a pleasant and useful manner, and by not leaving them any time to develop desires; destroy your theaters, or at least banish from them dramas, or modern tragedies; burn all of those little novels whose least faults are affectation of style, outlandish plots, and the exaggeration of feelings; tell your children to stick close to their mother: her affection for them will soon become the most intense of all her affections; such a pure feeling will never cause migraines, vapors, or melancholia.   (Beauchêne, 7)

Ultimately, then, the task of eradicating the vapors falls to men in their capacity as builders of society and as *paterfamilias*. It is up to men to change the denaturing mode of life that has become endemic in France's cities by dismantling the cultural institutions that make their women weak and vaporous. And it is up to men to orchestrate, with the assistance of their children, their wives' return to the maternal occupations that will safeguard their health and happiness.

_9 &_

Beauchêne's *De l'influence des affections de l'âme dans les maladies nerveuses des femmes* established a new and intriguing set of connections among the various ingredients common to the discourse on vapors: gender, sex, sensibility, culture, and pathology. By approaching the vapors as a pathological condition induced in women by the overstimulating effects of high society, Beauchêne sought to provide medical grounds for the emerging conviction that worldly culture was incompatible with women's "nature," as that nature had come to be defined by a confederation of theorists, including Rousseau and the moral anthropologist Roussel. Within the discourse on vapors, Beauchêne's work signaled a shift away from the gender-based indeterminacy of effeminacy as the mark of worldliness and toward a far more clear-cut distinction between women as victims of the vapors and men as their healers. The threat of vapors therefore came to be used as a means of justifying the increasingly narrow limits that were placed upon women's activities in the last decades of the eighteenth century; as Beauchêne's cautionary tale makes clear, serious disorder would ensue if women strayed beyond those limits.

This selective realignment of sex and worldly culture was, of course, bound up with what Michel Foucault has labeled the "ethics" of nervous sensibility that came to dominate the general theory of nervous disorders by the end of the French Enlightenment. Although Foucault is a bit too quick to equate that theory with madness, he very aptly identifies the profound moral ambivalence that was associated with "falling ill from feeling too much."[31] As soon as general sensibility was singled out as the root cause of nervous illness, the person afflicted with this type of disease was seen as simultaneously more innocent and more guilty:

> More innocent, because one was swept by the total irritation of the nervous system into an unconsciousness whose severity increased in proportion to one's disease. But more guilty, much more guilty, because everything to which one was attached in the world, the life one had led, the affections one had had, the passions and the imaginations one had cultivated too complacently—all combined in the irritation of the nerves, finding there both their natural effect and their moral punishment ... The innocence of the nervous sufferer, who no longer even feels the irritation of his nerves, is at bottom simply the fitting punishment for a deeper guilt: the guilt which makes him prefer the world to nature. (Foucault, 157)

What Foucault does not mention, however, is that the attribution of guilt for preferring worldliness over nature eventually came to fall overwhelmingly upon high-society women. Nor does he give sufficient weight to the energetic effort made by physicians like Beauchêne to "rescue" such women from worldly culture and return them to their supposedly originary maternal nature—the only state in which female sensibility could, in their minds, be properly exercised.

The "back-to-nature" therapies promoted by the vapors theorists ultimately came to overlap with the normative, nonpathological model of women's nature that was then emerging in moral anthropology. The advent of this model signaled a significant shift in the general medical representation of women, for rather than emphasizing the pathologies to which women were deemed vulnerable, the moral anthropologists strove to define female nature in its most perfect, healthy state. In a sense, these theorists skirted the entire issue of civilization's debilitating influence on the "fair sex," by defining women in such a manner that their engagement in certain worldly activities was simply inconceivable. That is not to say that pathology is absent from the discourse of moral anthropology, but simply that its proponents were preoccupied with fixing the conditions most conducive to allowing each sex to fulfill its unique, natural destiny. In other words, the moral anthropologists were intent on saving both human nature *and* society from the threat of pathology. To that end, they redistributed the various labors associated with human existence—such as child-rearing versus intellectual advancement—along sexually incommensurate lines. It might be tempting to sum up this redistribution by saying that the moral anthropologists reserved "nature" for women, and "culture" for men; in truth, however, the relationship they established among those terms was more complicated than that. The dualist or complementarian style of thinking that informed moral anthropology did not oppose nature and culture but, rather, prescribed sex-specific roles in both realms. The concept of sensibility is, as I will argue, the best means of working one's way through the moral anthropologists' web of conceptual pairings, because these theorists deployed the property on *both* sides of their rigid sexual divide.

Defining Sex, Refining Sensibility

Before considering how sexual difference was defined by the moral anthropologists of late-eighteenth-century France, we should first establish how they defined their theoretical enterprise. As their treatise titles and prefaces attest, these physicians saw themselves as carrying on the philosophical brand of medical theory that had been promoted a few decades earlier by the medical faculties of Montpellier and Paris, both of which are cited in glowing terms by Roussel in his preface to the *Système physique et moral de la femme*.[32] Roussel describes the concept of vital sensibility as a discovery that allowed physicians to dispense with the old, outmoded iatromechanistic models, to break down the barriers between medicine and philosophy, and thus to forge "a more simple, enlightening, and *spiritualized* plan for medicine" (*SF*, lv). Sensibility is accorded the same lavish rhetorical treatment in de Sèze's pedagogically oriented *Recherches physiologiques et philosophiques sur la sensibilité ou la vie animale*,[33] and in the *Rapports du physique et du moral de l'homme*, where Cabanis ambitiously aims to use the concept in order to synthesize the work of the physician, the sensationalist psychologist, and the moralist into one grand "SCIENCE OF MAN . . . [which] the Germans call ANTHROPOLOGIE."[34] Cabanis sums up sensibility's primordial nature, and its multifaceted importance for the medico-moral observer, in his first memoir: "Physical sensibility is the last term at which one arrives in the study of the phenomena of life and in the methodical search to determine their true sequence. It is also the last result, or . . . the most general principle furnished by the analysis of the intellectual faculties and of the soul's affections. The physical and the ethical natures [of humankind] thus merge at their beginning, or, to put it more accurately, the ethical is only the physical nature considered from certain particular points of view" (Cabanis, 1:50). The principal concern of moral anthropology was therefore not sex but sensibility, the vital principle that these theorists deemed responsible for determining all aspects of human life and all variations thereon. For what made humankind worthy of study in the first place was, in their eyes, the species' "eminent sensibility" (Cabanis, 1:217)—the quality that placed Man at the top of the pyramid of living beings.

The sensibility paradigm framed moral anthropology in ways that are both explicit and implicit; it is evident, first of all, in the monistic vitalism that informs this opening statement in Roussel's *Système physique et moral de la femme*: "After having considered the physical side of Woman, I have examined her moral side. In so doing, I have undoubtedly restored to medicine something that rightfully belongs there. I have always been convinced that it is only within medicine that one finds the foundations for good moral philosophy, and that if anything can lead medicine to a state of perfection, it will be the care that medical thinkers take never to lose sight of the internal force that governs animated beings" (*SF*, xl). The moral anthropologists' totalizing approach to women's nature was thus inspired, in part at least, by the philosophical aspirations that had become characteristic of medical theorists: like the médecins philosophes who preceded them, Roussel and his colleagues believed that the mysteries of both medicine and morality could be solved through sufficient attention to the inner laws of vitality on which human existence seemed to be predicated. Yet they also strove to bring greater precision to the existing theory of sensibility by determining exactly how the property took the various forms that they perceived in different types of people. "Sensibility," says Roussel in his *Essai sur la sensibilité*, is "different in different species of animals because of their constitution, and among different individuals of the same species as a result of their temperament, mores, occupations and habits" (359). Hence the anthropological dimension of moral anthropology: its practitioners undertook to study temperament, climate, age, illness, regimen, and above all sex as a means of charting the patterns in sensibility that they deemed to be most regular and most significant in the human species.

The format of these treatises might create the impression that sex was merely one of several factors that the moral anthropologists took into consideration: take, for example, the seemingly neutral way that Cabanis inserts "Of the Influences of the Sexes on the Character of the Ideas and of the Moral Affections" in the midst of his discussion of human variability.[35] Yet sex was endowed by these theorists with a uniquely powerful influence over the workings of sensibility in the human body and mind. Thomas Laqueur has interpreted this period's special focus on sex as an epistemological shift of major proportions:

> Sometime in the eighteenth century, sex as we know it was invented. The
> reproductive organs went from being paradigmatic sites for displaying
> hierarchy, resonant throughout the cosmos, to being the foundation of
> incommensurable difference ... While the one-flesh [Galenic] model did
> not die—it lives today in many guises—two fleshes, two new distinct
> and opposite sexes, would increasingly be read into the body. No longer
> would those who think about such matters regard women as a lesser ver-
> sion of man along a vertical axis of infinite gradations, but rather as an al-
> together different creature along a horizontal axis whose middle ground
> was largely empty.   (Laqueur, 148–49)

Although Laqueur's argument is compelling, it only partially explains how the
moral anthropologists read sexual incommensurability into the sensible bodies
they sought to analyze. The conceptual cosmology within which these physicians worked produced its own neo-Aristotelian teleology, according to which
every human body could be situated somewhere along a spectrum of physical
and moral being, according to his or her type and dose of vital sensibility. In
French medicine, therefore, the two-sex model developed out of the various di-
chotomous scales that theorists of sensibility had long used to differentiate
physiological types as peasant or urban, laboring or scholarly, or even Swiss or
Parisian. The moral anthropologists did significantly sharpen the line of difference between the sexes; yet they nonetheless continued to theorize according to a one-flesh model of the body because they subscribed to the idea that all
bodies are composed of the same basic sensible matter.

　The late-eighteenth-century medical doctrine of sexual incommensurability
did not, therefore, represent a radical break with the epistemology inherited
from the ancients. Rather, as Londa Schiebinger describes it, the old hierarchical thinking about the sexes not only persisted, but gained new force as it was
incorporated into emerging evolutionary theories—many of which were directly applied to human development and used to argue that men are more
fully evolved human beings than women.[36] This sort of logic is particularly
conspicuous in moral anthropology, whose proponents sought to advance the
contemporary doctrine of sensibility while also masculinizing the particular
brand of the property that was required to perform the higher human functions. They consequently recast sensibility along sexually dimorphic lines—
not, I would argue, to legitimize misogyny, but rather, to resolve some of the
inherently paradoxical qualities of sensibility that had vexed theorists since the
concept's very inception. For its early medical and philosophical champions,
sensibility was a creative, malleable force that drove everything from the rudi-
ments of thinking, to the inception and regulation of physiological function, to

humankind's most basic ethical and aesthetic responses. Yet sensibility also seemed to have a potent capacity to induce physical frailty, moral perversion, and even hereditary degeneration when overdeveloped or misdirected. By the 1770s, when Roussel first appeared on the scene, the ambiguity of vital sensibility seemed so acute that a redefinition of the property was virtually inevitable.

So it was that, without altering the basic ingredients of the Montpellier doctrine of sensible matter, Roussel and his followers modified that doctrine's implications, by emphasizing the significance of sexual variability. The sexually dimorphic model of sensibility they created was a new means of arranging sensibility's diverse effects into categories far neater than anything that had been proposed before. At the same time, their model was explicitly designed to establish the rightful place of men and women, respectively, on a naturally determined chain of moral and intellectual being. Seen from that perspective, moral anthropology might appear to be a mere reprisal of the age-old tendency to represent reason as a "manly" enterprise. However, this medical theory is highly specific to the waning years of eighteenth-century France and represents one of the final instances of that period's defining project: the effort to determine precisely how sensibility is involved in advancing, or hindering, the cause of human enlightenment.

❧ ☙

Roussel begins his *Système physique et moral de la femme* with the following explanation of sexual difference:

> Nature, which works in so many different ways to favor the reproduction of the species, dictated that the human race would owe its reproduction to the union of two individuals who are similar in the most general traits of their organization, but destined to cooperate in this task through means that are particular to each one. The difference between these means constitutes sex, whose essence is not limited to a single organ, but rather extends, through more or less evident nuances, to all the body parts. As a result, woman is not woman in one place alone, but also in all the facets through which she can be envisaged.   (*SF,* 1)

Sexual difference is thus to be seen as an essential part of nature's plan for humanity—a plan that is not only useful but "perfect," because it so neatly ensures both the survival of the species and the happiness of its particular members (de Sèze, 218). Indeed, the related teleological values of propagation and happiness are so central to the discourse of moral anthropology that they are invoked to ground virtually every assertion that Roussel and his followers make about the biological and moral necessity of the traits they ascribe to each sex. Some modern commentators have maintained that these theorists do not apply their teleological thinking as heavily to men as they do to women—a contention that might seem valid if one considers only the highly restrictive social roles to which they relegate women.[37] However, the moral anthropologists are nothing if not strictly and systematically complementarian in their approach to each sex's biologically determined "natural" role: every physical and moral trait that they discuss in one sex has an exactly reciprocal counterpart in the other.

The moral anthropologists have also been taken to task for their peculiar manner of mixing up gender and sexual traits; Michèle Le Doeuff makes such an argument in her well-known essay "Pierre Roussel's Chiasmas."[38] Le Doeuff views Roussel's theory of female nature as the creation of a sexually repressed charlatan who, because he is incapable of dealing with the properly female traits of the female body, remakes it by means of an elaborate and cleverly concealed chiasmatic model. As she describes it, this chiasmatic treatment of woman entails two paradoxical conceptual maneuvers: genitalizing the entire female body *except* in the female genitals (LD, 245), and inverting the qualities that "should" be assigned to woman's physical and moral registers, respectively, and ascribing each, instead, to the opposite register (LD, 142–43). Le Doeuff's characterization of Roussel's method as "chiasmatic" is provocative, but her analysis of the particular points of his text is misleading and historically misdirected. For when one scrutinizes the moments in Roussel's treatise that she deems most egregiously phallocentric—for example, his purported deemphasis of anatomical differences between female and male pelvic bones,[39] or his assertion that menstruation is a social condition brought on by "psycho-historical" causes[40]—it becomes apparent that Le Doeuff is misinterpreting the stakes involved in Roussel's use of the chiasma figure.

The chiasma *is* a central operation in Roussel's medical doctrine, but not because of the phallocentrist social bias against women that Le Doeuff supposes to be his prime theoretical motivation. Rather, his tendency to moralize about physio-anatomical details, while also biologizing particular moral characteristics, is a strategy fundamental to his entire corpus—indeed, to all of moral anthropology; it is, moreover, applied just as systematically to man as to woman. Le Doeuff, unfortunately, does not give sufficient attention to the other side of Roussel's theoretical coin: namely, his chiasmatic, teleological model of male nature. When she broaches Roussel's model of man as a point of comparison, it is only to make the unfounded claim that the male body is spared from his strategy of pan-sexualization and to imply that his medical doctrine is no more

Woman, from Pierre Roussel, Système physique et moral de la femme, *frontispiece (7th ed., 1820). (Photograph courtesy of the Historical Collection of the Health Sciences Library, University of Wisconsin–Madison)*

than an elaboration on Rousseau's shibboleth that there is "no parity between the sexes as regards the consequences of sex."[41] However, as with Tissot, Beauchêne, and some of the other medical authors we have encountered, the sympathy that Roussel and his disciples express for certain of Rousseau's ideas does not mean that they were slavishly devoted to them. In fact, there is a good deal of parity in the manner in which the moral anthropologists treat the sexes—a parity inspired by the desire to determine not only how the sexes differ, but also how they complement each other in body and in mind and thereby realize "their special and respective perfection" (Cabanis, 1:219).

According to the moral anthropologists, the sexes start out with the same basic constitutional ingredients, the most important of which is a substance Roussel calls the mucus or cellular tissue, a concept first promoted by Bordeu in his *Recherches sur le tissu muqueux, ou l'organe cellulaire* (1767).[42] What these theorists mean by that term is the matter wrapped around the body's fibers and organs which provides them with a link and means of communication (*SF*, 3). Mucus tissue is, by their lights, the substance that determines where and how a given body will be sensible because it determines how easily sensibility can be communicated from organ to organ and fiber to fiber. It is thus a primary agent in the workings of the animal economy, serving as a conduit for two things: first, the tonic motion triggered by the action of a fiber or organ that has been aroused by an impression; and second, the fluids that such an organ secretes— for example, menstrual fluid and milk from the properly female organs (*SF*, 10–12). In other words, everything in the physical system of human beings— the fibrillar makeup of their organs, the way those organs and their fluids communicate, and the resulting bodily temperament—ultimately depends upon the relative quantity and quality of their mucus tissue. This tissue therefore plays a central role in sexual differentiation. In women, explains de Sèze, the mucus tissue "expands more easily, is more porous, and consequently hampers less the vibrations of the fibers" (de Sèze, 220); this exposes female fibers to irritations and makes them more mobile and reactive. In men, by contrast, "this tissue thickens, its sheets stick together, and it consequently forms a layer around the nervous fiber which is less abundant but more compact, and which, by dulling that fiber's sensibility, adds to its strength" (de Sèze, 220). In other words, men's nerves require a stronger irritation to be aroused, but register that impression in a more powerful and durable manner.

At a primordial level, then, sexual difference is inscribed in the organic substance that envelopes all the body parts and connects them as a coherent, resonating whole. Yet the physio-anatomical theory underlying moral anthropology also incorporates the Montpellier notion that there are organological centers, or "departments," of heightened sensibility within the body—centers that change with each successive stage in human development.[43] Age is not, however, the only factor that alters the locations of these centers (de Sèze, 185–99); sex does, too. Hence the importance that Roussel and his followers accord to the reproductive organs as agents not only of sexual difference, but also of the communication of maleness and femaleness throughout the body (*SF*, 84–85; Cabanis, 1:222–27). Hence also their insistence that, during childhood, when the reproductive organs have not yet become active, males and females are seemingly undistinguishable: boys and girls are more or less equally delicate, soft, and sensitive (*SF*, 2–3; Cabanis, 1:219; de Sèze, 188). All similarities end, however, with puberty, which these theorists depict as the critical moment when the nature of each sex truly emerges.

The scenario of puberty is what best reveals why these medical theorists call themselves anthropologists, for it is here that their concept of sexual complementarity takes on its unique evolutionary cast. Puberty is, according to these physicians, a veritable "crisis" in the vitalist sense of the term—an event that rearranges the order of each individual's entire animal economy. Pubescent girls experience a rechanneling of their vital fluids toward a new organic center: "Toward the age of fourteen, a girl's body develops a new order of functions: an organ that had not been active before now awakens, and the oscillations of the nerves direct themselves toward it, carrying with them the blood and humors that always follow the nerves' current" (de Sèze, 222). The fledgling woman does not, however, advance very far beyond the "primitive" constitution she had as a child: "Delicate and tender, she always retains something of the temperament proper to children" (*SF*, 4). Indeed, not only do a woman's organs retain their softness, but her mucus tissue actually increases both in quantity and sponginess as her body parts are redesigned to suit the "new chain of physical and moral relations" to which women alone are subject (*SF*, 4).

The pubescent male, by contrast, undergoes far more dramatic alterations as he takes on the physical and moral traits that announce his natural destination. First, his body becomes stronger, shedding the girlish delicateness that had marked him as a child: "His limbs lose the softness and the round shape that they had shared with those of the female body: his muscles, which are the principal instruments of animal strength, eliminate or reduce through their reiterated contractions the mucus tissue that had filled their interstices and weakened them" (*SF*, 2). Second, his face and voice become more manly, as does his character: "The shyness of childhood gives way to an instinct that leads him to brave every peril; he does not fear anything, because the hot blood that is surging through his veins . . . makes him believe that he can do anything" (4). In short, declares Roussel, everything about the pubescent male—his taller stature, his proud demeanor, his confident movements, and his new tastes and ideas—"retraces in him the image of strength, and bears the imprint of the sex that must master and protect the other one" (4).

Thus, from puberty on, from their soul to their toes, men are literally firm and resistant, thanks to their vigorously developed organs and minimum of mucus tissue; women, by contrast, remain the soft, vulnerable, and oversensitive beings they were as children. Having established that basic constitutional difference, Roussel promptly invests each sex's body with a set of gender-specific behavioral qualities: "Nature, in man, seems to overcome the obstacles that hamper it, through strength and activity; in woman, nature seems to elude those obstacles by submitting to them. If strength is essential to man, it seems that a certain weakness contributes to the perfection of woman. This is even more true in the moral register than in the physical" (*SF*, 11). Nature thereby dictates that, in their physiology and moral comportment alike, men naturally resist or overcome unwelcome irritants and obstacles, whereas women cede involuntarily to the multiple stimuli to which they are subject because they have no more power to resist than do children. Clearly, the moral anthropologists relegate women to a less developed type of anatomical composition than men; yet they also take pains to point out that a weak, reactive, and yielding constitution is the most advantageous kind imaginable for women, given their peculiarly unstable physiology: "It is certain that the sex of woman subjects her to revolutions that might upset all of her organs, if they offered too strong a resistance" (17). They emphasize, moreover, that the anatomical distinctness of each sex reinforces the complementarian notion that men and women are two halves of a natural whole, "one of which possesses strength and toughness, while the other is marked by weakness and sweetness; in isolation, these qualities are worth nothing, but when they are reunited, they support and temper each other" (de Sèze, 218).

The moral anthropologists extend this complementarian logic as far as they deem conceivable. They apply it liberally to human anatomy, attributing a masculine or feminine quality not just to the reproductive organs but also to certain nonreproductive body parts; the historian Ludmilla Jordanova refers to this kind of selective sexualization when she speaks of "the feminization of the nervous system and the masculinization of the musculature" that was commonplace in eighteenth-century writings on women (particularly those of the middle and upper classes).[44] In truth, these medical theorists do not so much feminize the nervous system as carve it up into weak/effeminate versus strong/virile parts, the most masculine part being the brain. The essential object of the moral anthropologists' complementarian perspective is sensibility: "Ultimately, there is more variety than inequality in the gift that Nature has given the two sexes in the form of these precious quality . . . they differ less in their degree of feeling than in its effects" (de Sèze, 217). In other words, the two sexes are equally sensible, but sensible in different, complementary ways. Cabanis explains the sexual division of sensibility in terms of the role that each sex plays in fulfilling his or her natural destination: "A sensibility that retains profoundly the impressions of objects, and whence results durable impressions, is thus appropriate to the man's role. But a lighter sensibility that permits the impressions to succeed one another rapidly, that almost always lets the latest impression predominate, is the only one that is appropriate to the woman's role" (Cabanis, 1:237). Thus, far from being a purely feminine quality, sensibility is a critical ingredient in the ideal functioning of man and woman alike. There is, moreover, a very precise fit between the genre of sensibility characteristic of each sex and the role to which each sex is assigned in the physico-moral order that regulates human existence.

As Jordanova has rightly observed, the teleological emphasis that these medical theorists placed on the propagation of the species led them to view women strictly as wives and mothers: "Women's capacity to bear and suckle children was taken to define their physical, psychological and social lives," whereas men, because their role in propagation and child-raising was perceived as far more limited, had a potentially unlimited sphere of psycho-social activity.[45] Yet what is most interesting about the moral anthropologists' definition of women's existence is its extraordinarily physicalist slant: using the putative physio-anatomical properties of sensibility, weakness, and capriciousness, these physicians construct an image of women's normative constitution that makes the maternal state not just preferable, but biologically necessary. As de Sèze puts it,

> It was necessary for woman to be sensitive so that the cries of the child to whom she gives life would deeply move her heart, forcing her to forget her own needs and devote herself fully to his needs; it was necessary that she be weak so that the fear of outside dangers would keep her within the home and help her endure the sedentary life that maternal duties require; it was necessary that she be fickle so that her first child would not absorb all of her tenderness, and that she might transfer some of its effects to the new beings who clamor for her attention.   (de Sèze, 219)[46]

The acute but fast-changing sensibility that characterizes the female constitution is therefore the perfect vehicle for accomplishing some of the most fundamental tasks that nature assigns to the human race—but certainly not all of those tasks.

To determine how the moral anthropologists divide up the rest of the physico-moral qualities they see as natural to humankind, let us turn to the other sphere of activity for which sensibility is deemed necessary: mental function. As one might expect, given their globalizing view of sensibility, the moral anthropologists subscribe to the sensationalist theory of the mind. Hence their emphasis on the common sensorium, center of the highest reasoning and moral faculties. Roussel devotes a long chapter of his *Fragment du "Système physique et moral de l'homme"* to demonstrating that the common sensorium acts both as "the center where all of the impressions received by the individual converge" (*FH,* 300) and as the part of the brain that coordinates the activities of the organism as a whole. In an individual endowed with a superior organization, sensibility is selectively channeled to this brain center, where it stimulates the soul to express itself (228–29). Under these constitutional conditions, sensibility realizes its full potential as an animating, expansive life force: "It is from this material foundation . . . that the soul rises to the most important vital functions, and to the most sublime operations of intelligence" (236). When the soul is functioning at this level, the human being is a sublime figure that looms large on the stage of nature: "This important object, which captivates and fixes the gazes [of the other living beings], is man . . . He reigns over them all, through his intelligence" (227–29).

Intelligence is therefore the ultimate manifestation of sensibility's power in the human being—and the most dazzling expression of humanity's rightful dominance over the rest of nature. Full intellectual development is, however, represented by the moral anthropologists as an exclusively masculine achievement. First, as de Sèze describes it, the stage of life known variously as the age of reason or "virile age" can be attained only when sensibility is so fully centered in the brain that it reigns supreme over the rest of the body (de Sèze, 194). Sustained thinking is, moreover, an exercise that requires both a strong will and considerable physical fortitude: "At the moment when a man fixes all of his attention on the object of his research, his brain swells: its fibers stretch and attract a greater portion of the body's general activity, such that the humors are carried to the brain in greater abundance. However, the action of the brain does not suffice on its own: it must be reinforced by a strong tension in the phrenic center, in the intestines, and in all of the viscera of the lower abdomen" (de Sèze, 226–27). Clearly, in the eyes of these physicians, not all human beings meet those criteria: the viscera may be too weak to sustain the tension that thinking causes in the epigastric region, as often occurs in hypochondriacal persons (de Sèze, 227–28); or the common sensorium might have to compete for its dose of sensibility with another, less elevated center of vital activity, like the womb (*SF,* 59); or the "cerebral pulp" may simply be too soft, as Cabanis maintains when speaking about female brains (Cabanis, 1:227).

Men and women are thus deemed to be just as distinct in their moral and in-

Man, from Pierre Roussel, Fragment du "Système physique et moral de l'homme" *(1820), frontispiece. (Photograph courtesy of the Historical Collection of the Health Sciences Library, University of Wisconsin–Madison)*

tellectual functioning as they are in their physical makeup. Being sensitive, sedentary, and soft-brained is, however, presented as a real advantage for women: "More sensitive than robust, more animated than capable of moving, woman possesses all of the vital qualities in the most exquisite degree, but with very limited physical capacities; such that her existence consists more in sensations, than in ideas and bodily movements . . . We shall see that woman, in whom the very range of sensations ensures that no sensation will linger long, and who is thereby saved from the unrelenting reflections that torment so many thinking beings, is perhaps closer than is man to the bliss that accompanies natural human existence" (*SF*, 17). Woman's soft physique makes her soul as well as her body sanguine: "Supple fibers that are easy to arouse must require a type of sensibility that is acute but short-lived; this facilitates the various operations of nature and accustoms the soul to a feeling of confidence that inspires cheerfulness" (*SF*, 39). Women consequently tend to live longer than do men (de Sèze, 229) and suffer fewer chronic illnesses (*SF*, 124). Moreover, woman's heightened sensibility disposes her, far more effectively than would "cold reason," to approach her maternal functions with extraordinary instinct, energy and patience (*SF*, 29). We can sum up the consequences of the moral system that Roussel and his colleagues assign to woman as follows: although woman's hyper-receptive system is aroused by everything, nothing—not passion, not tears, and certainly not ideas—ever leaves a strong impression on it.

There is, of course, a curiously circular causality at work in the manner in which the moral anthropologists collapse the moral traits of feminine gender onto woman's physical substrate. That circularity is evident in Roussel's explanation of why healthy women are almost universally sanguine in bodily temperament, whereas entire ethnic groups may, under the influence of climate and alimentary intake (*SF*, 37), collectively lean toward one or another of the four standard temperamental types (sanguine, phlegmatic, melancholic, and bilious [33–35]). The lack of temperamental variation among women stems, says Roussel, "from the uniformity of their occupations, or, as I will soon explain, from the fact that the same temperament is common to almost all women" (37). We can interpret this causal logic in one of two ways: Roussel may be implying that there is only one "climate" that truly influences women: the domestic sphere, which would therefore take on the deterministic proportions of a natural force. Or he may simply be taking circularity to its extreme here and asserting that the temperament of women rarely varies because they all have the same temperament. Indeed, Roussel seems to lapse into the same type of "chicken and egg" reasoning each time he undertakes to prove that a given moral quality is both predetermined by, and predetermines, woman's physical system.[47] It is as if nature and social structure have collaborated so effectively in shaping woman's sensible constitution that Roussel seems hard-pressed to say with any certainty *which* force is primordial—or, indeed, whether the two are even separate forces. Clearly, an odd sort of double-standard, socionaturalist determinism informs these texts: for, if one follows the moral anthropologists' reasoning to its logical conclusion, they are arguing that female sensibility is the product of nature collaborating directly and harmoniously with society—whereas male sensibility, by its naturally superior force and irrepressible activity, always hovers somewhere beyond societal bounds.

We find a striking example of that double-standard determinism in Roussel's explanation of each sex's characteristic type of mind. Although some of his remarks on human intellect reveal a Rousseauistic skepticism about the moral advantages of enlightenment (*FH*, 231), Roussel nevertheless declares in his *Fragment du "Système physique et moral de l'homme"* that man's intellectual faculties are indefinitely perfectible, particularly when cultivated at a collective level: "There are some fields of knowledge that require the cooperation of several men . . . it is society that increases their scope. Once man's faculties have thus been set in motion, they display a singular disposition to be constantly sharpened and extended, and this is what has truly expanded his being" (233–34). The capacity to improve and expand is therefore a normal, natural condition for the fully human mind, as described in Roussel's *Fragment*. However, it is neither normal nor natural for the female mind as Roussel depicts it in the *Système physique et moral de la femme*.

This discussion occurs in the climactic seventh chapter of the *Système de la femme*, entitled "Des moyens naturels qui conservent, et des causes accidentelles qui peuvent changer ou faire dégénérer le tempérament de la femme" ("Of the natural means that preserve, and of the accidental causes that can change or corrupt the temperament of woman") (*SF*, 53–79). Along with exercise, diet, and the passions, the activity of thinking is presented here as a practice that, although necessary to female existence, must nonetheless be pursued in moderation, lest a woman denature her temperament by overtaxing her delicate sensible system. Once again, Roussel explains that, constitutionally, women are ideally suited to a life that is circumscribed by familial and social duties: their tissues are appropriately soft and yielding, and their minds are too. In this healthy state, "the mind of women, uncultivated but sparkling, shines all the more when it is not weighed down by undigested knowledge . . . Their ideas have nothing stilted or constrained about them; their expressions are the true image of their soul: irregular, but full of life and naturalness; their conversation, which is always lively and animated, can do without science, and has its own kind of interest that all the resources of erudition could not give it" (64–65). Women excel in the type of thinking that requires a keen "esprit de société," that is, a sagacious understanding of the proprieties and conventions which drive society (65). The female mind is therefore suited for the little details of social and domestic life—and not, Roussel underscores, for the "more sweeping views of politics" and the "great principles of ethics" that rightfully occupy the male mind (19).

In historical terms, Roussel's restrictive account of woman's intellectual existence was probably the single most influential element of his *Système physique et moral de la femme*; for it would be repeated, in one form or another, by medical theorists well into the next century.[48] Roussel's followers are, in fact, far less generous than he in the degree of intellectual capacity they accord to women: de Sèze, for example, declares that women are physiologically incapable of the "strong action of the brain" that is required to excel in the imaginative arts, in profound philosophical meditation, and in the sciences (de Sèze, 225–26). And Cabanis dismisses *femmes savantes* as deluded women who lose all of their feminine qualities and acquire nothing but the pedantry and ridiculous idiosyncracies of scholars (Cabanis, 1:241–43). Rejecting the notion that poor education is the reason behind women's inferior intellectual performance, these physicians issue dire medical warnings to those women who might be foolish enough to undertake mental activities that are inappropriate for their sex. Roussel argues that the same constitutional reasons that make vigorous physical exercise inadvisable for women "also prohibit them from pursuing the even more dangerous labors involved in intense study" (*SF,* 59). Women would, he adds, have little to gain and much to lose by pursuing scholarship because intense study draws most of the vital forces to the head and thus inevitably disrupts all of the other bodily functions (61). Ultimately, the body either languishes under the strain of scholarship or deteriorates into the nervous agitation known as vapors or hypochondriasis—a condition that would, Roussel opines, be "an even more natural and inevitable consequence of serious study in those women foolish enough to undertake it" (62).[49]

Thus, despite his footnote caveat that "we are not saying this in order to discourage women from seeking an honest degree of intellectual refinement" (*SF,* 64), Roussel is clearly convinced that women can remain healthy only by devoting themselves entirely to motherhood and light, mindless social interaction. Women, he stresses, would be particularly misguided to emulate men of letters, whom he depicts as notoriously unsociable and guilty of neglecting all social niceties out of their immoderate desire for self-instruction (63). Cabanis takes up this theme by declaring that the only women who have succeeded in rigorous scholarly endeavors are not truly women at all, but rather "ambiguous beings who are, properly speaking, of neither sex" and who will surely fail at their wifely and maternal duties, if they ever succeed in catching a husband (Cabanis, 1:242).

Having thereby branded women who deviate from nature's plan as akin to monsters—that is, as beings who are incapable of reproducing normally, according to Roussel's definition (*SF*, 8)—these physicians reaffirm their conviction that women's natural destination is to bear children, to be sociable, and to "please through their physical charms and natural grace" (62–63). The complementarian trade-off that the moral anthrolopogists propose for women thus comes down to this: although women are not able to enjoy "the lofty conceptions of a mind that can soar to the greatest heights of nature," they are abundantly endowed with the sweet, natural empathy that is the basis of all the social virtues (17). Nature, asserts Roussel, has done quite enough for women as it is: "it would be an affront to [nature] to stigmatize the gifts that women owe to her" by madly undertaking sustained intellectual labor (61). Women must, in short, respect the nonintellectual direction in which their sensibility leads them, not only in order to preserve their health, but also to uphold the natural and social order, and guarantee the "privileged" place that they occupy therein.[50]

꿎 ꕔ

Although it plainly had repercussions that went far beyond medicine, moral anthropology was, first and foremost, a medical theory. That is, the effort undertaken by Roussel and his followers to define the essential nature of each sex was part of a larger medico-philosophical attempt to fix the various characteristics of sensibility by assigning them selectively to distinct body types. This undertaking was a significant development in the history of sensibility and physiology not merely because it radically biologized the gender traits then ascribed to women and men, but also because it transformed the particular brand of sensibility with which women were supposedly endowed into an absolute limiting term for their human capacities—most particularly, their capacity for mental improvement. In addition to serving as the major impetus for a new field of medical discourse, that transformation affected all the fields in late-eighteenth-century French thought in which sensibility was commonly invoked to explain human nature. Here again, however, the gender politics involved in the conceptual shift initiated by moral anthropology must be understood in the light of theoretical tensions that go beyond gender alone.

In effect, by "double-tracking" sensibility along incommensurate sex lines, the moral anthropologists struck a compromise between two opposing views of human nature that were then circulating in the various human sciences. One view could be called the meliorist or Condorcetian perspective, according to which the key characteristic of human nature is its positive and boundless potential for progress and enlightenment. As Jean-Antoine-Nicolas de Caritat de Condorcet expressed it, "The perfectibility of man is truly indefinite . . . the progress of this perfectibility, from now onwards independent of any power that might wish to halt it, has no other limit than the duration of the globe upon which nature has cast us."[51] According to the other view, which I shall refer to as the Rousseauistic perspective, the human race seemed not to be improving but rather degenerating—and degenerating precisely because of its capacity for ever-increasing refinement. Speaking of perfectibility in his second *Discourse*, Rousseau remarked: "It would be sad for us to be forced to agree that this distinctive and almost unlimited faculty is the source of all man's misfortunes; that it is this faculty which, by dint of time, draws him out of that original condition in which he would pass tranquil and innocent days; that it is this faculty which, bringing to flower over the centuries his enlightenment and his errors, his vices and his virtues, in the long run makes him the tyrant of himself and of Nature."[52] From this perspective, perfectibility appeared to be as much of a double-edged sword as sensibility itself: although the drive for physical and intellectual self-improvement seemed essential to humanity's basic makeup, it was actually an instrument of unhappiness and injustice and, as such, was deeply implicated in the ongoing denaturation of civilized man.[53]

These two stances on humankind's perfectible nature—Condorcet's optimistic faith in its progressive capacities, versus Rousseau's condemnation of it as a bane for all of humanity—represent the two extreme poles of the Enlightenment dialectic that we have been studying throughout this book. The moral anthropologists did not resolve the tension between those poles; rather, they devised a model of sensibility that allowed them to deflect that tension by displacing it onto the question of sexual difference. Although these medical theorists adopted a modified version of the optimistic, Condorcetian position for the male mind and sensible constitution, they took a pessimistic, Rousseauistic, *fixist* stance toward the female mind and sensible constitution.[54] This bifurcation, which made the quest for enlightenment natural to man's constitution but pathological to woman's, was a direct result of the more obvious bifurcation in bodily sensibility forged by Roussel's medical doctrine. I would therefore contend that what prompted Roussel and his followers to separate the sexes in both sensibility and intellectual capacity was not (in most cases) overt ideological misogyny, but rather, a need to save the reigning medical model of sensibility from its own internal contradictions.

By dividing the attributes of sensibility into complementary but incommensurate sets (feminine versus masculine, yielding versus resistant, womb-based versus cerebral), the moral anthropologists effectively resolved a theoretical quandary within philosophical medicine concerning sensibility—a vital property that had, by the 1770s, come dangerously close to meaning too many things at once. By virtue of the new, two-tracked model, all of the "bad" qualities and "inferior" patterns of sensibility (vapors, melancholy, erotomania, and so on), which theorists a generation earlier had seen as possible in all body types, now seemed to reside almost exclusively in the female body—although male bodies that were allowed to degenerate into effeminacy might still be susceptible to them, too. The now inherently hypersensitive female body was consequently doomed, by its very makeup and development, to stray from the path to a fully enlightened mode of existence. According to the medico-anthropological scenario first proffered by Roussel, man could aspire to a virtually unlimited degree of mental elevation, provided he cultivate his constitution correctly (*FH*, 234); woman, on the other hand, was developmentally arrested at a more primitive bodily stage. This scenario was destined to be reiterated in even harsher terms by the next generation of biomedical theorists, who used not only sexual but also racial difference as an excuse for excluding from the quest for reason those beings who seemed to deviate from or fall short of certain physiological and moral norms.[55]

Thus, at the heart of the medical theory written during the last years of the enlightenment movement, one finds a project that might be dubbed the biomedical engineering of sensibility. The moral anthropologists took up the cause of enlightenment by typecasting men and women physically, the better to insert them into a fixed hierarchy of moral-intellectual being. What I would suggest, however, is that sex was not the "bottom line" in the making of the masterful, enlightened being; rather, *type* of sensibility was. This becomes clearer if we recall that philosophical medicine was not the only discourse in late-eighteenth-century France to elaborate a deterministic system of bodily typecasting as a means of grounding an intellectually elitist philosophy: the same phenomenon can be seen at work in the libertine novel, whose most notable practitioners used sensibility for distinctly hierarchical purposes but often subverted the sexual distinctions that had been made conventional by both medical and nonmedical theorists. In the following chapter, I consider the manner in which Laclos and Sade transposed the models of contemporary natural philosophy and medicine in their libertine fictions to create characters who pursued sex and enlightenment in ways that contemporary medical experts deemed biologically impossible.

8. Sensibility, Anthropology, and *Libertinage* in Laclos and Sade

The Libertine Novelist as Natural Philosopher

Despite their obvious differences in style and purpose, the late-eighteenth-century libertine novel and the medical doctrine of moral anthropology had some interesting interconnections, most particularly in the deterministic, complementarian perspective each took on the questions of sensibility, moral nature, and organic constitution. The theory of complementarity that became prevalent during the 1770s was itself the product of some creative connections; as Ludmilla Jordanova observes,

> The radical boundary drawn between the sexes through life-style and occupation was based on a physiology that was sensitive to the interweaving of physical and moral, mind and body. The language of this physiology brought together biological, psychological and social considerations largely through the use of bridging concepts such as "temperament," "habit," "constitution" and "sensibility," which were technically medical terms. This framework offered a naturalistic account of gender, race and class differences, which captured the complexity of individual lives while also offering avenues for detailed medical investigations.[1]

Of the various bridging concepts Jordanova mentions here, sensibility was the most powerful because it not only blended biological, psychological, and social interests, but also created intriguing alignments between diverse discursive fields—for example, philosophical medicine and the philosophical novel. During the last few decades of the eighteenth-century, the most important contributors to the latter genre were Pierre-Ambroise-François Choderlos de Laclos, author of the masterful epistolary fiction *Les Liaisons dangereuses* (1782), and Donatien-Alphonse-François de Sade. Laclos, a self-styled moralist and disciple of Jean-Jacques Rousseau, was less overtly libertine than Sade in his philosophy: although the protagonists of his novel are clearly libertine in their principles and behavior, the novel is cloaked in so many layers of irony that it is virtually impossible to fix either its ultimate meaning or Laclos's authorial position in relation to the work.[2] Laclos nonetheless shared with Sade a cynical view of traditional morality and social institutions, as well as a particular vision of himself as a novelist: each characterized novel-writing as an enterprise akin to doing natural philosophy and deployed the novel as a means of exploring the physical, moral, and intellectual implications of sensibility in various types of human beings.

In that sense, the discourse on sensibility contained in the writings of Laclos and Sade was deeply resonant with the ideas on the property that were circulating in the medical discourse of the day—even though these authors usually put their commentaries on sensibility in the mouths of "monstrous" characters whose ideas on society and nature were radically subversive of mainstream Enlightenment thinking. The complementarian philosophy represented in their fictions often follows the lines of the medico-moral doctrine that Roussel had recently expounded in his *Système physique et moral de la femme,* but Laclos and Sade did not necessarily use that philosophy to support the sexual oppositions central to moral anthropology. Rather, they deployed complementarianism to serve two somewhat contradictory ends: to typologize the human race by dividing it into irreconcilably opposing camps, and to create libertine characters of both sexes who insist on their own individual complexity and exception. The determinism that pervades the works of Laclos and Sade is thus dimorphic in itself, for reasons that have less to do with gender, class, psychology, or conventional social dictates (topics that figure prominently in many critical studies of these authors) than with the physico-moral distinctions implicit to libertine philosophy—a vision of human nature that both authors derived, in large part, from contemporary anthropology and medical anthropology.

Clearly, the libertine adaptation or co-optation of sensibility had some important implications for the larger project to promote enlightenment, personal self-improvement, and a judicious return to "natural" living. As interpreted by the moral anthropologists of late-eighteenth-century France, the quest for enlightenment was natural for a certain type of sensible constitution (man's) but unhealthy if not impossible for the other (woman's). Laclos and Sade provide an intriguing counterpoint to that interpretation: they demonstrate that the notion of sensibility could be applied to support a properly libertine conception of enlightenment—one that not only severed all the traditional ties between intellectual strength, bodily fitness, and moral ideals like propriety and moderation, but also went beyond gender in its relentless pursuit of sex.

❧ ☙

Both Laclos and Sade evidently felt the need to justify their particular enter-prises as novelists. Laclos took pains to explain himself in a series of letters ex-changed in April 1782 with his fellow novelist Mme. Riccoboni, who had ex-pressed her indignation over the *Liaisons dangereuses*; and Sade used the publication of his novella collection *Les Crimes de l'amour* as an occasion to pre-sent his theory of literature, in the form of a literary-historical preface entitled "Idée sur les romans." In relating these texts, I am not attempting to resolve the perplexing question of why, out of all the seventeenth-and eighteenth-century French novelists that Sade reviewed in the "Idée sur les romans," Laclos was practically the only one excluded from mention.[3] I seek, rather, to explore the analogy that both novelists established between the art of the novel and the practice of "philosophical" observation as applied to libertines and other dis-turbing creations of nature.

Because Laclos makes his reflections on novel-writing in a bantering style meant to charm and disarm the outraged Mme. Riccoboni, his remarks are not as fully developed as are those of Sade, whose "Idée sur les romans" is com-posed in the solemn, erudite manner of a literary scholar.[4] Laclos nonetheless furnishes an interesting response to the question that is most central to Sade's essay: What is the purpose of novels? Laclos's initial aim in his letters to Ric-coboni is, of course, to explain the purpose of one particular novel, the *Liaisons dangereuses*, which Riccoboni has politely denounced for giving foreigners "such a revolting idea of the morals of [Laclos's] nation and of the taste of his compatriots," adding, "We do not need to safeguard ourselves against charac-ter traits that cannot exist, and I beseech M. de Laclos never to adorn vice with the charms he gave to Mme. de Merteuil."[5] The first question raised in this epistolary polemic thus regards both the verisimilitude and the usefulness of Laclos's representation of his novel's most striking character: the Marquise de Merteuil, whose seductively pleasing exterior succeeds in masking her wicked inner nature until the novel's end.

Picking up on the last sentence in Riccoboni's letter, Laclos replies:

> M. de Laclos begins by congratulating Mme. Riccoboni for not believing in the existence of mean and depraved women. He, who has been enlight-ened by a more unhappy experience, assures her with chagrin, but with sincerity, that he could not erase any of the traits that he assembled in the person of Mme. de Merteuil without lying to his conscience, or at least without suppressing a part of what he has seen. Would it thus be wrong to have wanted, out of indignation at these horrors, to expose them, com-bat them, and perhaps prevent similar horrors? ("R-L," 758)

What is interesting in this reply is not just Laclos's tone—a combination of flattery of Riccoboni, and moralistic self-defense—but also his contention that women like Merteuil do indeed exist because he himself has seen them and, apparently, suffered at their hands. In composing the character of Merteuil, Laclos declares, he has no more besmirched the image of the women of his country than did the creator of Lovelace (Richardson, in *Clarissa*) or the author of the *Égarements du coeur et de l'esprit* ("R-L," 758).[6] Laclos's conscious effort to align himself with Richardson and Crébillon is significant, not least because it culminates in the intriguing division of novelistic labor that he posits at the end of this letter, where he suggests that male and female authors have very different tasks to fulfill in writing.

Laclos makes this argument by way of a compliment to Mme. Riccoboni, whose "charming" fictional tableaux of women's virtue and tenderness should provide readers with an antidote to his own stark depiction of human nature ("R-L," 758–59). Using Riccoboni's works (like the *Histoire d'Ernestine* [1765] and the *Lettres de Mistriss Fanny Butlerd* [1757]) as a model, Laclos ascribes a particular role to the woman novelist: "Only women possess that precious sensibility, that easy and light-hearted imagination that embellishes everything it touches and creates objects such as they should be." Men, by contrast, are "condemned to a more severe task": their purpose in writing literature is not to improve on nature but to represent it "with exactitude and accuracy" (759). Only male novelists, by implication, can see and represent the objects in nature as they truly are; moreover, they gain this capacity through a loss—that is, by their constitutional lack of the "precious sensibility" that Laclos finds so admirable in the fair sex.[7]

Laclos reiterates and expands on this definition of the male novelist's particular constitution throughout his ongoing defense of Merteuil's verisimilitude. In his next letter, he takes issue with Riccoboni's suggestion that Merteuil is a monster that exists only in Laclos's imagination; he replies that he has no more invented his notorious heroine out of thin air than did Molière when he forged the character Tartuffe on the basis of the many hypocrites he had observed among his contemporaries ("R-L," 761). Laclos thus provides a strategic response to the question of Merteuil's putative monstrosity: he does not deny that she is monstrous, but he places the responsibility for that monstrosity on nature, not on himself. As for the question of whether this "depraved" female is an affront to the honor of French womanhood, he explains: "Mme. de Merteuil is no more a Frenchwoman than a woman from any other country. Wherever a woman is born with active senses and a heart that is incapable of love, some intelligence and a vile soul, a woman who is cruel but whose cruelness lacks efficiency [*énergie*], there Mme. de Merteuil will exist, whatever the guise she assumes" (762).[8] Once again, Laclos insists that creatures like Merteuil are out there lurking in society; to recognize them, however, one must have a particularly deep and penetrating gaze: "The practiced eye easily uncovers the model, and recognizes it in its *naked* state" (762; Laclos's emphasis). It is thus Laclos's clear-eyed, coolheaded, sagacious temperament that allows him to perceive the nasty human types who remain hidden for other people. By contrast, honest and delicate women like Riccoboni remain blind to such beings because their active sensibility—interestingly, the only trait that Laclos accords both to Merteuil and to "good" women—colors their vision to such an extent that they cannot see the world as it truly is.

These remarks prompt a third letter of protestation from Mme. Riccoboni, who (writing at this point in the name of all decent women) persists in her contention that the character Merteuil is not only utterly lacking in verisimilitude, but is also so vile, depraved, and exaggerated that no reader could possibly derive any useful lessons from her ("R-L," 763).[9] In his two successive letters of reply, Laclos returns to the theme of what male versus female authors can and should depict in their novels. He declares here that men are simply not as capable of representing the strength, grace, courage, easy wit, tenderness, modesty, and other virtues of ideal womanhood; even Rousseau, despite all of his enthusiasm, fell short in his literary portrait of Julie (765). Depicting women in their ideal light requires distinctly feminine qualities: "A woman, born with a beautiful soul, a sensitive heart and a delicate mind, can undoubtedly imbue the portraits she traces with some of the charm she herself possesses" (765). This sort of literary enterprise, Laclos suggests, is effortless for a woman writer because she is, after all, only composing a likeness of herself; most men, however, would lose their composure if they undertook to paint woman in all of her enchanting charms.

The purpose of novel-writing is, therefore, fundamentally different for the two sexes: women writers, as Laclos describes them, are suited for producing charming, touching, and reassuring images of the best aspects of human nature, which he consistently associates with "good" femininity; whereas male writers have a less pleasant and more difficult mission that entails depicting the despicable mores and "guilty artifices" of creatures like Merteuil—who, however, monstrous, are nonetheless quite real ("R-L," 760). Laclos concludes his defense of *Les Liaisons dangereuses* by obstinately repeating: "The tableau [of such mores] is saddening, I admit, but it is true" (767). In Laclos's view, the "virile" kind of novel he has produced is not only true; it is also singularly useful because its depiction of the carefully masked vices of certain members of society arouses a healthy sense of indignation in the reading public—as Riccoboni's own reaction to this novel attests.

Laclos thus inscribes *Les Liaisons dangereuses* in the tradition of the edifying, corrective kind of literary representation at which Molière excelled in the dramatic genre, and Richardson in the novelistic genre. Interestingly, Laclos makes his case using a mode of argument much like that which Diderot had employed twenty years earlier to describe the philosophical qualities of the serious, Richardsonian novel. Laclos portrays himself to Mme. Riccoboni as a keen-eyed, morally upright observer of human life in all its facets; and he presents his novel as the kind of fiction that is most apt to elicit the intense ethical reaction necessary to alert contemporary readers to the often seamy side of human nature—the "cavern" of the human soul, to recall Diderot's language.[10] The primary difference between Diderot's theory of serious fiction and the one that Laclos elaborates here is that Laclos's is quite distinctly *gendered,* in part because of the sexual and professional tensions that pervade his combative exchange with Mme. Riccoboni. It is gendered, moreover, in a manner that is strikingly evocative of the sexually dimorphic model of male versus female sensibilities put forth in the texts of the moral anthropologists, according to whom women are constitutionally suited for engaging in light and pleasing modes of cultural activity, rather than the "more sweeping views of politics" and "great principles of ethics" associated with men.[11] One could say, then, that Laclos uses a logic very similar to that of the moral anthropologists in order to masculinize the theory of the novel which Diderot had advanced in the *Éloge de Richardson*: the novel, Laclos maintains, should convey a penetrating image of society and the principles that drive it, but only male novelists are suited for the task.

The unfailingly courteous, chivalrous, and bantering tone that Laclos assumes in his letters to Mme. Riccoboni makes it somewhat difficult to be sure whether his complementarian perspective on novel-writing is based on a deep aesthetic conviction, or whether it is just a rhetorical strategy that he employs to win his epistolary skirmish with Riccoboni over the value of *Les Liaisons dangereuses*. I would maintain, however, that complementarianism pervades all of Laclos's writings, including his three uncompleted essays on women, written in 1783 in response to a question proposed by the Academy of Châlons-sur-Marne on the best means of improving women's education.[12] Given the fragmented, inconsistent, and often derivative nature of these essays, I will not venture to analyze them in detail; instead, let us focus on the aspects of these texts that show the interconnection between Laclos's theory of the novel and his interest in contemporary natural philosophy.[13]

In the first place, Laclos's purpose in composing these essays is evidently to affirm and extend Rousseau's anthropological myth of the state of nature, this time with a focus on women; his discussion is thus centered on an idealizing tableau of "natural" woman designed to refute Buffon's theory that human sociability is natural in itself ("Des femmes," 392–422). As part of that tableau, Laclos sketches a natural history of human development that echoes the writings not only of Rousseau and Buffon, but also of contemporary physician-philosophers like Roussel. He describes puberty as a process which is accelerated by the various moral and physical stimuli of civilized life and which brings about a radical differentiation between the sexes by setting women—or at least, natural women—on a path that leads inevitably to maternity (398–402). Moreover, Laclos denounces the sedentary, worldly lifestyle for making women's bodies more delicate, sensitive, and disease-prone than is natural; his recommendations for correcting this problem (430–32) conform closely to the hygienic programs of physicians like Tissot, Tronchin, and the various vapors theorists of the day. Finally, Laclos proposes an educational plan that is strictly tailored to women's particular moral needs (434–43). Although his list of recommended books bears an ironic resemblance to the readings that Mme. de Merteuil describes in her famous autobiographical letter 81, it is also notable for its Rousseauistic emphasis on the dangers that a young woman faces when she reads any novel, unless she is properly supervised and guided in her interpretation (440).

Clearly, then, Laclos uses the same system of sexual dimorphism to frame his views both of literature and of human nature in the broader, anthropological sense popular in his day. In his correspondence, as in his essays on women, Laclos comes across as a moralist à la Rousseau. The moral component of Laclos's aesthetics and of his anthropology is complicated, however, by the ambiguous sexual dynamics that pervade the *Liaisons dangereuses* and by the philosophy of libertinism to which its main characters subscribe. Before taking up those questions in the novel itself, let us first examine how Sade likewise interweaves morality, anthropology, and libertinism in his "Idée sur les romans," a text that replicates and expands on many of Laclos's ideas concerning the purpose of novels.

و۹ ۀ

Like Laclos, Sade adapts selected elements of the sentimentalist aesthetics that had emerged in the 1750s—most particularly, the notion that the novel should be reshaped so as to represent the true, unvarnished nature of human life. The novelist, as Sade describes him, must be a philosophe capable of carrying out a deep and thoroughgoing scrutiny of his fellow human beings; yet he must also be a natural artistic genius who can convey what he has observed to his readers with maximal dramatic vigor, energy, and interest.[14] Those are, in fact, the three key words in Sade's aesthetic vocabulary, and they all come into play midway through his essay, when, after having done a rapid historical survey of the evolution of the novel, Sade arrives at his principal task: answering the question "Of what use are novels?"—a question he assumes is foremost in the minds of the "hypocritical and perverse men" who distrust or disdain this genre ("Reflections," 109).

The first lines of that answer take shape a few pages earlier, in Sade's short but impassioned tribute to the "vigorous" English novels of Richardson and Fielding: "'Tis Richardson, 'tis Fielding, who have taught us that the profound study of man's heart—Nature's veritable labyrinth—alone can inspire the novelist, whose work must make us see man not only as he is, or as he purports to be—that is the duty of the historian—but as he is capable of being, as he must be when subjected to the modifying influences of vice and all the commotion caused by the passions. Therefore we must know them all, we must employ every passion and vice, if we wish to labor in this field" ("Reflections," 106). Although Sade employs a comparison rather different from Laclos's to develop his model of the novelist—Laclos uses the woman writer as his counterexample, whereas Sade uses the historian—both argue that only the genuine philosopher-novelist is capable of revealing the "truth" about human nature.[15] Sade pursues his opposition between history and fiction a few pages later, once again assigning a greater truth value to the novel than to historical writing: whereas history depicts only man's external appearance, the novelist's brush "seizes him when he drops this mask, and the description, which is far more interesting, is at the same time more faithful. This, then, is the usefulness of novels" (109–10). What Sade means by "true" here is not a slavish devotion to the everyday, but rather, the capacity to render as energetically as possible a certain notion of nature.[16] Thus, when Sade characterizes that truth by evoking what man *might* be, he is clearly not referring to the pleasing, tasteful, moralizing image that women authors tend to put forth (Sade echoes Laclos on this point), but rather to a very different sort of possibility that lies hidden within the labyrinth of the human heart—namely, the natural capacity of all human beings to be radically transformed by vice and by the violence of the passions.

Every human heart, Sade contends, contains an astounding range of modes that the novelist must know and employ in his works: "'Tis therefore Nature that must be seized when one labors in the field of fiction, 'tis the heart of man, the most remarkable of her works, and in no wise virtue because virtue, however becoming, however necessary it may be, is yet but one of the many facets of this amazing heart, whereof the profound study is so necessary to the novelist, and the novel, the faithful mirror of this heart, must perforce explore its every fold" ("Reflections," 107). According to Sade, vice is not only just as intrinsic to human nature as is virtue, it is also more *interesting*. It follows that the triumph of virtue is less important to the novel than the capacity to move one's readers to the depths of their being: "If, after the most severe trials and tribulations, we finally witness virtue overwhelmed by vice, our hearts are inevitably rent asunder, and the work having moved us excessively, having, as Diderot was wont to say, *smitten* [*ensanglanté*] our hearts in reverse, must inevitably arouse that interest which alone can assure the writer of his laurels" ("Reflections," 107).

What Sade is doing here is applying, somewhat hyperbolically, Diderot's idea that effective fiction operates by engaging its readers intensely and involuntarily in the dramatic conflict between virtue and vice. Sade, however, uses that idea not to foster a new and improved sense of community through sympathetic identification with suffering virtue, but rather to underscore the superior energy and interest of vice. In other words, he takes to an extreme the ethical polarization that is implicit to sentimentalist aesthetics, arguing that the fundamental truth of human life is the systematic triumph of vice over virtue—a notion that is played out repeatedly in all of his narratives, be they "respectable" works like the stories in *Les Crimes de l'amour* or his blatantly pornographic texts like *Les Cent vingt journées de Sodome* or *L'Histoire de Juliette*. In his dedication to *Justine*, for example, Sade declares that his fiction takes a route exactly opposite to that of most works in the genre: rather than telling a story in which suffering virtue is ultimately compensated and evil punished, he wants "to present Vice triumphant and Virtue a victim of its sacrifices, to exhibit a wretched creature wandering from one misery to the next; the toy of villainy; the target of every debauch; exposed to the most barbarous, the most monstrous caprices."[17] The only arms that his virtuous heroine has to defend herself are "a sensitive soul, her natural intelligence, and a good deal of courage" ("Justine," 455). This, Sade maintains, is the best way to teach his fellow men a truly "sublime" moral lesson—one in which the conventional values of virtue and sensibility are indeed affirmed, but as qualities that doom the characters who embody them to unrelenting pain and persecution.

I shall return later to the manner in which the conventional sensibility of the Sadian victim is exploited in *Justine* both to render his fiction as "interesting" as possible and to demonstrate the existence of beings whose sensibilities are constructed in an entirely different way. There remain, in the meantime, a few more aspects of Sade's literary theory to consider. The "Idée sur les romans" contains three striking metaphors for nature: first, the image of the heart of man—his moral inside—as a maze that the novelist must devote himself to studying ("Idée," 40); second, the notion of nature as an enormous, roiling volcano whose energy, however terrible or "bizarre" in its effects, is admirable and worthy of artistic emulation (47–48); and third, the famous incestuous metaphor of nature as Mother Nature—an entity that the novelist must seek to know, love, and penetrate in a quasi-sexual way (44). The novelist's relationship with nature is somewhat different in each of these metaphors: he is by turns an observer of nature, an artistic apprentice to nature, and a creature and actor within nature.[18] Sade adds yet another image to this gallery: the novelist as itinerant anthropologist—someone who travels the world in search of the truth of human nature.

As Sade describes it, there are only two ways for the novelist to acquire his deep, philosophical knowledge of the human heart—by suffering and by traveling: "One must have seen men of all nations in order to know them well, and one must have suffered at their hands in order to learn how to judge and evaluate them; the hand of misfortune, by ennobling the character of him whom she crushes, places him at that proper perspective from which it is essential to study men; from this perspective, he views them as a traveler perceives the wild waves crashing against the reefs whereon the tempest has tossed him" ("Reflections," 110). It is not enough for the novelist-as-anthropologist to study his fellow human beings; he must also become their victim. Only then, asserts Sade, can the novelist appreciate human nature for what it is and gain the philosophical perspective necessary to excel in his art. The novelist thus occupies a position in the Sadian universe analogous to that of the woe-begotten heroine of *Justine*: he must be tossed about by life, suffer persecution at the hands of his fellows, and (according to the final image of the passage) end up as a lonely castaway, stranded by the ferocious tempest of the passions.

The notion of travel that Sade evokes here can, of course, be seen as a variation on a classic Enlightenment conceit, made famous by the philosophical *récits de voyage* of Montesquieu and Voltaire, and a conceit Sade himself employs in both *Aline et Valcour* and the various tales of *Les Crimes de l'amour*.[19] Yet Sade is doing more in the passage cited above than simply exploiting a popular literary trope: he is also sketching the fundamentally dimorphic division of the human race that underlies his entire novelistic universe, whether the fiction in question is situated in France, in Sweden (as in *Ernestine*), or on the utopian island of Tamoé (one of the sites visited by the traveling character Sainville of *Aline et Valcour*). We need not, therefore, restrict ourselves to one of Sade's explicitly "exotic" narratives to see the anthropological structure of Sadian narrative at work. For, wherever they are located, all of his characters inevitably fall into one of two camps: they are either libertines born and bred, or they are virtuous people who will necessarily fall victim to the first group.

In the "Idée sur les romans," that division separates the novelist—a virtuous victim—from humanity at large, which according to Sade is evolving toward a disquieting mixture of increased liberty, intellectual enlightenment, and energy, but also increased moral corruption:

> As minds grow increasingly corrupt, as a nation grows older, by virtue of the fact that Nature is increasingly studied and better analyzed, and prejudice increasingly eradicated, Nature must be made more widely known . . . In the state wherein we live today, let us always start from this principle: when man has weighed and considered all his restrictions, when, with a audacious look, his eyes gauge his barriers, when, like the Titans, he dares to raise his bold hand to heaven and, armed with his passions, as the Titans were armed with the lavas of Vesuvius, he no longer fears to declare war against those who in times past were a source of fear and trembling to him, when his *aberrations* now seem to him naught but *errors* rendered legitimate by his studies—should we then not speak to him with the same fervor [*énergie*] as he employs in his own behavior? In a word, is eighteenth-century man identical with the man of the eleventh century?   ("Reflections," 113–14)

At a certain level, Sade employs this socio-anthropological observation on humankind's present state in order to reinforce his insistence on aspiring to maximal aesthetic intensity in literature; yet at another level, he uses it to give a extremely dire moral cast to the entire Enlightenment project of promoting knowledge, emancipation, and humane understanding. Sade clearly agrees with the philosophes that eighteenth-century man is more advanced than his ancestors, thanks to his greater understanding of nature and his refusal to submit to the religious and political constraints that once made men tremble. In Sade's view, however, all of this progress had led to a volcanic unleashing of the passions and an "audacious" tendency on the part of modern man to justify his moral lapses as simply natural. That is, the end result of the Enlightenment pursuit of human rights and perfectibility is, according to Sade, a return to nature unlike anything the philosophes imagined: the truly enlightened, truly natural human being is, he maintains, necessarily a libertine.

Sade ends the "Idée sur les romans" by situating himself as a serious man of letters in relation to the libertine characters that his philosophical calling obliges him to depict. In defense of the vivid manner in which he depicts crime and corruption, Sade declares: "Never shall I portray crime other than clothed in the colors of hell. I wish people to see crime laid bare [*à nu*], I want them to fear it and detest it, and I know no other way to achieve this end than to paint it in all its horror" ("Reflections," 116). Much like Laclos, therefore, Sade justifies his novelistic enterprise by characterizing himself as a moralist and philosophe—that is, as a brave, high-minded man who recognizes and exposes the monstrous libertine creations of Mother Nature in their "naked" state. In their theoretical reflections on their art, both novelists take pains to denounce libertines as abhorrent, but both plainly view them as more interesting than morally upright human beings. Laclos and Sade thus take a distance from their more unsavory fictional characters, for reasons that are not just moralistic but strategic: that distance allows them to align their mode of literature with natural philosophy and anthropology, fields from which these writers draw both respectability and an authoritative set of "facts" on human nature.[20]

Many of those "facts," as we shall see when we broach their respective fictions in detail, concern the different modes and meanings of sensibility in different sorts of human beings. Generally speaking, the dividing line that Laclos and Sade draw between libertine sensibility and nonlibertine sensibility corresponds to the sex-based oppositions favored by the moral anthropologists of the period: their victims are female, and their libertines predominately male. This correlation between sex and libertine sensibility does not, however, always prove true in Sade's novels—and it is most certainly turned upside in the case of Mme. de Merteuil, who is unquestionably the superior libertine of Laclos's *Liaisons dangereuses*. For Merteuil as for Sade's master libertines, reaching the condition of maximal philosophical enlightenment entails redefining both sex and sensibility not just in moral and social terms, but in constitutional terms as well.

Sensibility, Libertinism, and Determinism in *Les Liaisons dangereuses* and *Justine*

In the eyes of the physician-philosophers of eighteenth-century France, understanding human nature entailed two things: first, taking a holistic perspective on the physical and moral aspects of human existence; and second, constructing stable, physiologically based categories to explain the full range of human constitutions, temperaments, proclivities, and capacities. What Pierre Roussel and his followers did was develop the anthropological thrust of philosophical medicine, by typologizing human beings in a far more definitive manner than had been done before. Along with sex, sensibility was the key term in the moral anthropologists' doctrine of human types: human constitution, on this theory, could be reduced to two basic modes of sensibility—one soft, womb-based, and feminine; the other firm, cerebral, and masculine. This distinction, the moral anthropologists contended, stemmed not from culture but from nature; for although an individual's "natural" moral and physical qualities might be modified by life in the world, they were nonetheless grounded in biological organization, which was generally held to be immutable.

Given that eighteenth-century libertinism was, like the medicine of the day, a discourse that purported to reflect the true nature of humankind, it is perhaps not surprising to find a similar insistence on predetermined distinctions among the human types represented in Laclos's *Les Liaisons dangereuses*. There is, of course, no "natural" man or woman in this novel that might correspond to the ideal categories posited by the moral anthropologists—or, for that matter, to the mythical natural being that Laclos himself sketched in his essays on women. Yet Laclos's fictional characters are not determined solely by the forces of social convention, either. The *Liaisons dangereuses* has standardly been interpreted as a novel about the complex mores, manners, and practices of worldly eighteenth-century society; but it is even more fundamentally a novel about sensibility, its deterministic implications, and its capacity to be not only manipulated but transformed.

In that sense, critics who concentrate on the social forces, gender tensions, and strategies of seduction that inform *Les Liaisons dangereuses* are only addressing the side effects of a larger exploration of the role played by sex, sensibility, and moral-physical organization in contemporary human life. Several different kinds of "fatality" have been ascribed to this novel: the determinism of social convention; the superhuman power that the novel's libertine masterminds assume over everyone else's destiny; the inexorable, militaristic driving force of the libertines' projects; and the fatefulness of the very act of writing letters.[21] All of Laclos's characters are, however, constructed in terms of a *constitutional* determinism which follows a rigorously systematic logic similar to that seen in contemporary moral anthropology. That is, the *type* of sensible constitution with which the novel's characters are endowed is what determines how they function in the world: they either resist the moral and physical stimuli that surround them, or they give in to them. Resistance is thus not a mere strategy that the *roués* of the novel adopt for self-defense, nor does it necessarily correspond to the conventional definitions that the novel gives to masculinity versus femininity.[22] Rather, resistance—or the lack thereof—is a constitutional quality that defines every character's fate.

One way in which this constitutional determinism manifests itself in Laclos's novel is through the technique of the literary portrait, by which the various characters are sized up according to their supposedly essential attributes. Charles Baudelaire, perhaps the first critic to note the importance of portraiture as a structuring principle of *Les Liaisons dangereuses*, exploits it himself to give a thumbnail sketch of each of the work's major players: Cécile de Volanges is the "perfect type of the detestable young girl, silly and sensual"; the Présidente de Tourvel is a "simple, grandiose, and touching type"; Danceny is an "man of honor, a poet and smooth talker"; and Valmont is a "vain person," a "Don Juan on the way to becoming a Tartuffe, and who is charitable out of self-interest."[23] Baudelaire's description of the Marquise de Merteuil is rather less precise: he characterizes her as a "female Tartuffe" and "a satanic Eve" (333–34), but he also notes Merteuil's wit, her good sense, her own talent for portraits and self-portraits, and above all her superiority over Valmont—who has, in Baudelaire's words, "some remaining sensibility that makes him inferior to Merteuil, in whom everything that is human has been burnt to a cinder" (336). As Baudelaire reads the novel, all of the characters except Merteuil embody a predictable trait of personality, moral character, or sentiment: what allows Merteuil, far more than Valmont, to escape being reduced to a stereotype is her "superior" constitution, in which all human qualities—most particularly, sensibility—have been willfully incinerated.

Although I disagree with Baudelaire's assertion that sensibility is absent in Merteuil, I find his remarks quite useful in establishing the proximity between the art of portraiture as practiced in the *Liaisons dangereuses* and type-casting. As Peter Brooks observes, the novel's most cunning characters practice portraiture to demonstrate the control they exert over all the other characters, whom they typologize according to "an ideological conception of self as a completely systematic being."[24] In my view, sensibility is the key element in the reductive conception of self that Merteuil and Valmont apply to everyone else: being sensitive in a soft, "feminine," involuntary way means being utterly predictable in the eyes of these roués and virtually defenseless when subject to their manipulations of language, setting, and situation. The novel's libertines clearly use an entirely different conception of self in composing their self-portraits: they see themselves as beings who are matchlessly clever, invulnerable to easy sentiment, impervious to outside influence, and coolheaded in all of their adventures. What makes all that possible is the radically unconventional kind of sensibility Merteuil and Valmont claim to possess: they have cultivated an intense capacity for feeling that is evident in their relentless search for new modes of erotic pleasure, yet they exercise a rigorously willful control over their sensibility so as to ensure that it remains centered not in their hearts or senses but rather in their minds alone.

Valmont seems, at the outset, to embody those masterful qualities: he enjoys both a public reputation and a self-image as the consummately cerebral, ever-calculating libertine. Mme. de Volanges furnishes Valmont's public image in her letter of warning to the Présidente de Tourvel: "He's even more deceitful and dangerous than he is pleasant and seductive. From his earliest youth he has never made the slightest move or uttered a single word without having some evil or criminal intent . . . His despicable behavior is a matter of principle. He calculates precisely how far he can pursue his abominable conduct without compromising himself; and to gratify his cruel and wicked nature without any risk, he's chosen to prey on women."[25] Valmont himself delights in boasting about his principled detachment from the seductions he undertakes: he insists throughout his liaison with Tourvel that he has pursued her purely out of curiosity, as a means of determining just how far he could go in reducing a truly pious, virtuous, faithful married woman to total amorous subjugation to him (*LLD*, letter 7, p. 20). Tourvel's stereotypically "prudish" traits add to Valmont's cynical delight in seducing her; yet it is her astonishing sensibility—expansive enough, Valmont notes sardonically to Merteuil, to be lavished even on Tourvel's husband—that really makes her the perfect experimental subject in Valmont's eyes: "For my investigation, I needed a woman with a delicate, sensitive nature, who would devote herself completely and utterly to love" (letter 133, p. 298). Valmont thus claims to occupy the position of dispassionate observer in relation to Mme. de Tourvel; and when Merteuil protests that he is taking too long to carry out this project, Valmont rationalizes his slowness by invoking the intense cerebral pleasure he takes in watching the process.[26]

Valmont clearly possesses the libertine's sense of superiority over the mere mortals of the novel. For example, he says dismissively of Danceny: "I've finally gotten to know him thoroughly well, this wonderful novelistic hero! He no longer has any secrets from me" (*LLD*, letter 57, p. 109); and he vows that the "celestial" Mme. de Tourvel will be no more than "a woman like all the rest" once he has finished with her (letter 96, p. 204). Yet however much Valmont may boast, his actions and principles are consistently undermined by what Merteuil views as grave character flaws: first, his lack of originality in the strategies he uses to execute his projects, a problem that Merteuil judges to be typical of male libertines (letters 81 and 113); and second and more importantly, his inability to resist the amorous sentiments and the sympathy that Tourvel arouses within him. It might be argued that this lack of resistance is merely one of the many ploys Valmont uses to disarm his virtuous victim, Tourvel: he does, indeed, play upon it when writing to her, declaring at one point that he fell into libertinism as a youth because of his "delicate and sensitive" character ("After all, what was I doing but failing to resist the whirlwind into which I'd been plunged?" [letter 52, p. 103]).[27] That interpretation fails to account, however, for the many occasions when Valmont really *does* goes involuntarily soft in his dealings with Tourvel. Although he expresses a certain sense of wonder at the pleasure he experiences when gripped by a feeling of genuine tenderness, passion, or commiseration, he is nonetheless plainly perturbed by such emotions because they are utterly incompatible with the cynical, clear-eyed detachment on which he prides himself—and on which his radically nonconventional libertine pact with Merteuil depends.

Valmont seems lighthearted as he recounts his first episode of unplanned feeling, which takes place in the midst of an act of "public edification" in which he deliberately saves a local peasant family from eviction in order to make a good impression on Mme. de Tourvel (*LLD*, letter 21). As the scene unfolds, Valmont finds himself in the middle of a veritable Greuzian tableau, surrounded by a grizzled old patriarch and his tearful wife and children, all kneeling before their savior. He comments, "I must confess to a moment of weakness: my eyes filled with tears and I felt an involuntary but delicious emotion stirring inside me" (letter 21, p. 43). He is considerably less sanguine, however, when describing the episode's epilogue: his tête-à-tête later that day with the duly impressed Tourvel, during which he confesses both that he had planned the whole scene of public benevolence and that he is passionately in love with her. When Tourvel bursts into tears at the latter piece of news, Valmont almost loses control at the sight of "her lovely face, made even lovelier by the potent charm of tears" (letter 23, p. 48). He congratulates himself as he writes for having overcome his "weakness"—that is, his temptation to take advantage of Tourvel in a moment when he was too hotheaded and she too pliable to put up any real resistance. Yet Valmont continues to be plagued by that sort of weakness whenever he is in Tourvel's presence: many letters later, when he detects the literally spasmodic symptoms of yielding in Tourvel and knows that his master project is about to succeed, he is so "intensely moved" that he ceases and desists (letter 99, p. 214). Merteuil sardonically points out that Valmont exhibits his own symptoms of yielding each time that he relates one of these tender scenes (letter 106, p. 234).

Valmont's predicament, one of the most intriguing of the novel, has been viewed by some critics as representing a redemption of sorts—precisely what Tourvel hopes to accomplish by undertaking to convert Valmont to the cause of piety, virtue, and selfless friendship (*LLD*, letters 22, 67, and 124). Yet such a view is problematic because it is based either on what Joan DeJean describes as a Rousseauian effort to "redeem the *Liaisons* by placing it in a moral context," or on the *libertin* analogy that Irving Wolfarth has identified as common to much Laclos criticism.[28] Those who adhere to that analogy tend to perceive a fundamental affinity or doubling between the novel's libertine protagonist— standardly assumed to be Valmont—and its author; they therefore maintain that Laclos's project in writing this novel is itself experimental and manipulative, in that he aims to "test the *libertin* project" only to undermine it in the end.[29] Although Valmont's project is indeed undermined, this does not necessarily imply that the novel subverts libertinism itself; for that would require us to assume that Valmont is the true "hero" of *Les Liaisons dangereuses*. Such an assumption is, of course, made within the novel by Danceny and Mme. de

Rosemonde, two of the characters who survive its final debacle; yet taking at face value the moralizing spin which they give to the story's final events means assenting not only to an "Aesopian" kind of morality that is excessively focused on the work's ending (Wolfarth, 273), but also to a male-centered definition of libertinism and mastery that the Marquise de Merteuil seeks insistently to correct in her correspondence with Valmont. That male-centered definition is clearly not part of the exactingly frank pact of mutual understanding that allows Valmont and Merteuil to function for three-quarters of the novel as members of an exclusive intellectual elite. Rather, it stems from the purely conventional notion of the eighteenth-century roué, which both the all-seeing Merteuil and the partially blinded Mme. de Volanges recognize as an all-too-common type in their society.[30]

Interpreting Valmont as a libertine who is redeemed by love is therefore tantamount to reducing him to a conventional category which, for most of the novel, he strives to resist, for fear of losing the "mythological" status he believes he shares with Merteuil.[31] It is also tantamount to ignoring at least one-half of the experiment that is, indeed, taking place in *Les Liaisons dangereuses*: namely, Merteuil's construction as an entirely unconventional kind of libertine, a being who upsets all of the conventional notions of sex, sensibility, and libertinism. Laclos's exploration of those notions has a built-in quality of scandal to it, but not for the reason that Jean Giraudoux suggests when he asserts that "it is by completing forgetting or neglecting the legend of feminine resistance that Laclos's book is compromising for humanity."[32] Rather, what this novel undoes is the contemporary moral-anthropological myth of *masculine* resistance and *feminine* yielding—a myth that was central to the manner in which eighteenth-century natural philosophers (including Laclos, in his extraliterary writings) viewed the sexes.

When one considers Valmont's struggle over sensibility in the light of that context, it becomes apparent that he, as much as Tourvel, suffers the classically feminine fate that Merteuil sketches in her celebrated diatribe against "those restless, idle females whom you call *sensitive* and who fall so easily and so helplessly into the grip of love" (*LLD*, letter 81, p. 162). Valmont may start out as a detached observer intent on executing a seduction so glorious that it will immortalize his reputation as master of all Parisian roués (letter 115); he becomes, however, the "sensitive," "delicate" object with which he had sought to experiment, his soft head and heart unable to resist the contagious sensibility he has caught by falling in love with Tourvel. Valmont remains perspicacious enough to be aware of what is happening to him: in the midst of a letter in which he rages at having been outsmarted by Tourvel (who has just succeeded in fleeing from Mme. de Rosemonde's estate, without his knowing it), he asks: "But what fatal force binds me to this woman? . . . My happiness and peace of mind are utterly dependent on possessing this woman, whom I love and hate with equal furor" (letter 100, p. 217). Valmont is clearly unable to overcome his obsessive attachment to Tourvel: he succeeds in proving himself irresistible to her, but so does she for him.

Valmont's letters to Merteuil concerning Tourvel are thus marked by an odd mixture of cynical lucidity, on the one hand, and thinly veiled alarm that he is losing his sangfroid—that is, his capacity to control his own sensibility at will and thus to qualify for membership in the community of roués. Despite the bluster Valmont standardly employs when relating his exploits to Merteuil, his discourse is also distinctly confessional: even as he brags about his masterful techniques, his purity of method, and his unwavering observational powers, Valmont lingers just as long over the description of his own emotions as he does over those he detects in the Présidente. This is particularly apparent in letter 125 (the dramatic opening of part 4 of the novel), where Valmont describes in painstaking detail his long-awaited physical conquest of Tourvel. The letter begins with some triumphant gloating: "Well, fair lady, take a look now at that haughty woman who was rash enough to imagine she could resist me! There she is: I have conquered her . . . it's a crushing victory, achieved by a hard-fought campaign and clinched by clever manoeuvres" (*LLD,* letter 125, pp. 276–77). Yet no sooner has Valmont proclaimed his victory, than a note of simultaneous wonder and worry creeps into his writing:

> I'm still too overcome by my good fortune to be able to appreciate it; but I am amazed by the strange charm which I felt . . . haven't I felt the charm I mentioned with other women? Yet it's not the charm of love either because after all, if I did experience with this astonishing woman a few moments of weakness with some apparent similarity to that anemic passion, I was always able to overcome them and return to my principles . . . Yet that same charm still lingers on. I confess I should find it rather agreeable to go on enjoying it if it didn't make me feel rather uneasy. Am I going to be overpowered at my age, by an involuntary and unfamiliar emotion, like some schoolboy? Certainly not! I must, above all, fight it and analyze it more closely.   (letter 125, p. 276)

The surprise that Valmont expresses here over discovering the enduring "charm" of love is, as Laurent Versini underscores, a libertine leitmotif probably inspired by novels such as those of Crébillon and Duclos.[33] Valmont's response is also typical of that literary tradition: he undertakes to combat his persistent, involuntary amorous sentiments for Tourvel, first by deriding them as weakhearted and unheroic, and then by analyzing them out of existence. Valmont thus reinterprets the intense pleasure he experienced with Tourvel as "the sweet taste of the feeling of victory"—a way of looking at the situation that, in his words, "saves me from the humiliating idea that I might somehow be dependent on the very slave whom I've just subjugated; or that my great happiness lies anywhere but in myself; or that my ability to enjoy it fully is restricted to one particular woman to the exclusion of any other" (277). Clearly, however, Valmont's analysis only confirms what he fears: his pleasure and newfound happiness derive not from his own will but rather from the "extraordinary" woman he has just conquered, and no amount of cynical rationalization can alter that.

There is consequently a schizophrenic quality to the rest of this letter: as Valmont recounts how he finally overcame Tourvel's resistance by staging a dramatic scene of suicidal despair, he simultaneously boasts about the dispassionate attitude he maintained underneath his distraught mask and yet demonstrates that he neither experienced the seduction episode nor writes about it afterwards from an exclusively libertine point of view. This is clear in the very wording of Valmont's observations: although he describes with clinical precision the signs of moral-physical crisis evident in Tourvel ("Her body was swaying, her breath coming in gasps, her muscles contracted, her trembling arms half-raised . . . gasps, convulsions, sobs" and so on), he also exalts her grandiloquently as "the Frightened Beauty," "the Timorous Lover," and "the adorable woman" (*LLD*, letter 125, pp. 280–83). Valmont even typologizes himself as "the New Lover"—a man who has, for the first time in his life, experienced a complete and reciprocal ecstasy that lingered on after the sexual act itself: "I left her arms only to fall at her feet and swear eternal love. I must not hide anything: I meant what I said" (283).

As Roy Roussel notes in his analysis of *Les Liaisons dangereuses,* letter 125 reflects a fundamental change both in Valmont's character and in his friendship with Merteuil: Valmont has fallen not only in love, but also under the spell of the traditional image of the triumphant masculine lover, whose pleasure (according to Mme. de Rosemonde's tableau of conventional male-female relationships) is entirely self-directed, unlike the vicarious happiness that women, with their putatively greater sensibility, supposedly experience.[34] Roussel describes Valmont's transformation in these terms: "His affair with Tourvel is no longer an experiment in the manipulation of signs but rather a clichéd seduction in which the woman is sacrificed in order to certify the man's power . . . The ironic distance which, within the context of his friendship with Merteuil, Valmont maintained toward his own masculinity has disappeared" (Roussel, 109–10). Merteuil immediately realizes that the Valmont of bygone days has disappeared: in her delayed reply to letter 125, she gleans out the most self-aggrandizing and hypocritical sentences in Valmont's epistle and throws them back at him.

Thus begins the mortal combat between Valmont and Merteuil that takes over the novel in part 4: that is, the fight to determine which of the two will prove to be truly superior, in the sense of exerting greater control over "*the adorable, the divine* Madame de Tourvel," "*the endearing* Cécile," "*the schoolboy, the soppy* Danceny" (*LLD*, letter 127, pp. 286–87). Valmont, as Merteuil caustically underscores, not only has an overblown opinion of himself now that he has executed both his own project (the seduction of Tourvel) and the project in which Merteuil had engaged him (the seduction of Cécile de Volanges), but also far too little esteem for Merteuil, whom he apparently wants to place in the number three position in his budding harem of sexual conquests. Merteuil indignantly insists that she will not be cast in a minor, conventional feminine role by any man: "You certainly have a plentiful supply of self-conceit; but apparently modesty is less plentiful with me because however hard I look at myself, I fail to believe that I could have fallen that low . . . *Goodbye, as in the old days,* you say? But in the old days you used to think rather more highly of me; you hadn't yet relegated me completely to supporting roles; and above all you were prepared to wait until I said yes before being sure I'd agree" (287).

Although Valmont attempts to repair his damaged relationship with Merteuil in his next letter, he never goes back to being the old, purely cerebral roué he was at the outset of the novel. Instead, he embraces the powers attendant to his new self-definition as a traditional masculine lover. Even as he claims to be continuing his love affair with Tourvel simply to pursue his libertine "work" on her (*LLD*, letter 133, p. 299), Valmont exhibits all the symptoms of total sentimental infatuation. This is certainly not lost on Merteuil, who forces him to recognize his bad faith by underscoring the hyperbolic language he persistently uses to describe Tourvel (letter 134, pp. 300–301). The only trait that Valmont retains from his old self is his vanity—a quality that prompts him to do everything possible to disprove Merteuil's contention that he is hopelessly in love, right down to sacrificing the Présidente by sending her a word-for-word copy of the cruel "epistolary model" Merteuil had composed for that very purpose (letter 142, p. 319). Once again, however, Valmont's attempt to prove his libertine mettle is half-hearted: immediately after breaking off his liaison with Tourvel, he suggests trying to win her back (on the pretext that this might be a good way of prolonging the original experiment). Merteuil responds by gleefully revealing that she has played on Valmont's vanity to force him to abandon Tourvel, who is by now so gravely wounded that she has retreated altogether from the world and taken refuge in a convent (letter 145, pp. 320–21).

Valmont's transformation from unconventional libertine to hotheaded, heartsmitten, and vainglorious male lover is significant not only because it brings disaster for everyone around him, but also because it represents a self-betrayal. For when he shifts into the traditional male role in the last part of the *Liaisons*—right down to flying into a jealous rage and sending Merteuil "the most husband-like letter possible" after discovering her in an intimate tête-à-tête with Danceny—Valmont commits what Merteuil rightly calls "a real infidelity" against his old self (*LLD*, letter 152, pp. 335-36). Valmont has not only lost the playful and often self-mocking humor that once marked his exchanges with Merteuil; he has also violated the libertine principles that had bonded the two together as superior beings. In part 4 of the novel, therefore, he is not redeemed but reduced, at least in terms of the libertine philosophical system to which he had previously subscribed.

Valmont continues to exert a good deal of control over events, even in his death scene, which simultaneously seals his final image as a gallant man and true lover of Tourvel, and sets into circulation the letters that he knows will condemn Merteuil in the public eye. As he lays dying after his duel with the Chevalier Danceny (with Mme. de Rosemonde's devoted *intendant* M. de Bertrand as witness), Valmont nobly forgives Danceny for mortally wounding him (letter 163). He then entrusts the chevalier with what turns out to be the most crucial part of the voluminous correspondence Valmont had maintained with Merteuil. One might read these very deliberate final acts as Valmont's ultimate coup against Merteuil, and thus as proof that he remains a libertine to the end, were it not for the fact that Valmont remains *inside* the system of social conventions here. It is, at the very least, ironic that he selects Danceny—a young man he had ridiculed just a few weeks earlier as a backward *sentimentaire* (letter 144, p. 323)—to have himself killed off. One could say, however, that Danceny's ultimate function in *Les Liaisons dangereuses* is to redeem Valmont's manhood, first on a symbolic level by dealing him a heroic death by the sword, and second on a social level, by promoting the official, "pro-Valmont," pro-masculine interpretation of the novel's events that dominates the work's conclusion.

Only Merteuil, therefore, comes across in the end as a monster—not because she is literally a hermaphrodite (to cite Aram Vartanian's provocative but problematic 1963 interpretation of this work),[35] but because, within Laclos's novelistic universe, there is no conventional social role into which a self-defined female libertine can fall once she has been unmasked. For that reason, as well as for her unwavering fidelity to the principles she has forged for herself, Merteuil is a being utterly distinct from her erstwhile fellow roué Valmont. Merteuil is thus not merely boasting when, in her famous autobiographical letter 81, she sets herself radically apart from all existing categories of women.

Rather, she truly is a whole new species unto herself, one that did not exist until she, with her unique capacities and inclinations, came along.

Letter 81 is not a mini-confession but a prideful and defiant self-portrait. In response to Valmont's intimation that she might be taking too great a risk in leading on the formidable lady-killer Prévan (who has accepted a public challenge to make Merteuil "sensitive" to his charms [letter 70]), Merteuil writes a long epistle to demonstrate her superiority over everyone in her social universe—the arrogant roués Prévan and Valmont included. The first four pages of letter 81 are given over to a devastating series of typologies, starting with a reductive portrait of Valmont himself (*LLD*, 160). Both to deflate Valmont's ego and to provide a frame of reference for her own libertine merits, Merteuil paints a dismissive picture of male libertines in general, who, given the decadent nature of contemporary society, face no real difficulties or obstacles in pursuing their sexual conquests. Conventional women, of course, are just as worthy of contempt in Merteuil's eyes—whether they are "those frenzied women, self-styled women of feeling," whom she derides for their utter lack of reflection and deluded faith in their sensations, or those idle women who idealize their sensibility to such an extent that they write imprudently effusive love letters to the men who are sure to betray them eventually (162). It is above all on intellectual grounds that Merteuil declares her radical difference from any of these types: she, in contrast both to traditional roués and traditional women, adheres strictly to a set of principles that are "the fruit of my deep cogitations: I created them, and can truly say that I am my own invention" (163).

Given Merteuil's scathing typological opinion of the rest of humanity, we must take care in interpreting her famous assertion that she was born to "avenge my sex and subjugate yours" (162). For Merteuil's purpose in making that remark is not to declare herself a feminist but rather, to affirm her singularity as a literally self-made libertine woman—someone who has come into existence through a unique process of natural-historical development, one that she herself directed. To explain the principles underlying that process, Merteuil retraces her evolution from the moment of her symbolic birth, when she entered the social world at adolescence (always a seminal phase in eighteenth-century naturalist discourse), up to her present state as a perfectly formed libertine philosopher. Merteuil's autobiographical tale has often been compared to a discourse on method à la Descartes or the philosophes.[36] Few Laclos scholars, however, have noticed that what Merteuil describes here is a *hygienic* regimen designed to act upon the particular sensible substrate with which she was born—that of a naïve and powerless fifteen-year-old girl. This kind of mental-physical constitution, according to Laclos's representation of young girls, is certainly as complete a tabula rasa as any that appear in the genealogies of the intellect proposed by sensationalist philosophers like Condillac, Bonnet, or Buffon. Much like the Statue-Man who serves as protagonist for those writers, the young Merteuil acquires her knowledge of the social world through careful, step-by-step observation and reflection on the sensations to which she is progressively exposed. She, however, evolves into a fully thinking being on the basis of a constitution that is classically female at the outset.[37] Clearly, then, far from alienating herself from her naturally sensitive female constitution, the young Merteuil uses that constitution to strategic effect, in order to become a philosopher like none seen before.

As Merteuil describes it, she embarked on her personal quest for enlightenment out of a visceral sense of indignation that society would deny her the possibility of thinking independently, simply because she was born female: "I was still young and not very interesting; but my thoughts were the only things that belonged to me, and I felt indignant that someone might snatch them from me or detect them against my will" (164). To protect herself from falling into the stereotype of the mindless young girl, the adolescent Merteuil became a discreetly self-taught, scientifically methodical student of human nature—beginning with her own. The first of the human sciences that she undertook to master was that of physiognomy: she learned how to control her gaze so as to appear too distracted to be noticing what was transpiring around her, and then determined how to "regulate, in a similar fashion, the various movements of my face" (173). Merteuil underscores the central role her physical constitution played in this enterprise: "I even went so far as to cause myself deliberate pain and practice looking pleased at the same time. I made a similar effort, though this was harder, to repress the outward signs of any unexpected joy" (163).[38] The young Merteuil thus achieved a progressive mastery over herself by experimenting first on her body—her facial expressions, and her gestures—and then on her speech, all of which she manipulated according to circumstances or whim, in order to maintain a facade so unassuming that no one had any idea what sorts of ideas were going through her head. Underneath that facade, however, Merteuil was steadily developing her powers of physiognomic observation and interpretation of others: "The work I had done on myself had made me interested in faces and the way that physiognomy reveals character; it gave me that penetrating gaze which . . . has rarely let me down" (164).

The next stage in Merteuil's libertine apprenticeship entailed the science of sensations, by which she means the physical pleasures associated with lovemaking. Even as an ignorant adolescent, Merteuil had an acute interest in those pleasures, which she now attributes to nature: "It seemed almost as if Nature was working silently to bring her work to perfection. My head alone was in ferment: I didn't seek physical pleasure, I sought knowledge. This desire for information suggested to me how I might approach the matter" (164). Merteuil was thus disposed from an early age to channel her sensibility or capacity for erotic pleasure to her head—without, for all that, evacuating it from her body. This is important distinction, and it is reinforced in Merteuil's account of her wedding night, which she describes as if she were, indeed, the statue in a sensationalist thought experiment: "That first night, which girls normally anticipate as something either very horrid or very nice, represented nothing more for me than a chance to gain experience: I took accurate note of everything, the pain and the pleasure, and saw my various sensations merely as a means of gathering information for later evaluation" (165). One of the facts that Merteuil discovered that night was that sex is intensely pleasurable—a discovery which prompted her to make a precociously libertine resolution regarding her husband: "I resolved, precisely because I was sensitive [to sexual pleasure], to show myself as completely unfeeling with him" (165).

Given the significance that Merteuil accords to sensibility in this important passage, it is all the more curious that so many Laclos critics have interpreted her as a fundamentally insensitive creature.[39] Far from suppressing her sensibility when feigning frigidity in front of her husband, the young Merteuil simply concealed it, so as to cultivate more freely the proclivities and ambitions of her "active head" (166). As Merteuil recounts, she pursued that self-cultivation on her husband's country estate, where, in the company of the local peasants she enlisted as her assistants, she expanded the range of her erotic experimentations. This furnished her with a useful stock of empirical observations on sexuality and human nature, which she fortified by reading up on the mores and practices of contemporary society (166). When she finally grew bored with these "rustic pleasures," Merteuil decided to apply what she had learned, and thus ventured, now as a young widow, onto her true testing ground: the great theater of high society.

At this point in letter 81, Merteuil abandons her pastiche of the scientific language of the natural philosopher and shifts instead into a more theatrical discourse, better suited for describing the various social roles she has learned to play. Upon reappearing on the Parisian social scene after observing the requisite period of mourning for her late husband, Mme. de Merteuil quickly realized that she would have to modulate the impression she made in public in order to attract the right kind of suitors, while also gaining the sympathy of "the whole tribe of puritans" (167). To that end, she cloaked herself in a mode of sensibility rather different from what she had displayed to her husband: "I presented myself as a woman who was impressionable [*une femme sensible*] but difficult to please, a woman whose extreme delicateness shielded her from love" (167). She thus acquired the reputation of an *invincible,* a veritable paragon of female resistance. To strengthen that reputation, Merteuil publicly encouraged only the men she did not like and disarmed each of her real lovers by uncovering his deepest secret, such that he would have neither the desire nor the power to betray hers (167–68).[40] That principle held true in the case of Valmont, about whom Merteuil says: "I wanted you even before I met you. Having been seduced by your reputation, I saw it as the only thing missing from my glory; I longed to combat you hand-to-hand [corps-à-corps]" (168). Once again, Merteuil underscores the particular direction of her sensibility: it is both intensely erotic and intensely cerebral, in that what initially attracted Merteuil to Valmont was not his physical person but his renown as a libertine. As she describes their subsequent relationship, Merteuil admits (in a rare compliment to Valmont) that "you are the only one of my flames that ever for a second gained a hold over me" (168). She nevertheless took the necessary measures to ensure that neither Valmont nor anyone else—including her chambermaid (aptly named Victoire)—could ever compromise her carefully cultivated public persona, even if they knew the truth of her actions.

Having thus enlightened Valmont about her rigorous principles and ingenious resources as a libertine, Merteuil returns to the defiant tone she had used at the letter's outset: "But to imagine that I've taken such care only to fail to reap the fruits of my labours; that having raised myself with such arduous efforts above the ordinary run of women, I could ever consent to cringe like them, wavering between cowardice and recklessness, and above all that I could be so scared of any man as to flee for my life, no Vicomte, never, never! I must conquer or die in the attempt" (169). Merteuil clearly wants recognition for the painstaking efforts she has taken to raise herself to a position of absolute invulnerability to the roués of the world. She concludes by declaring that she will *have* Prévan, savor the adventure, and emerge triumphant because she will make him powerless to ruin her reputation afterward. This is exactly what happens in the episode recounted a few letters later, where Merteuil relates one of the novel's finest examples of the high theater of worldly social intercourse (letter 85).

Letter 81 demonstrates that Merteuil's highly particular sensible constitution is crucial both in predisposing her to become a great libertine in her thoughts and actions, and in effecting her willful self-transformation. By "evolving" into a libertine mastermind, Merteuil not only redefines the meaning of sex as it applies to her, but also remakes sensibility into a principle not of vulnerability but of strength. First, the knowledge Merteuil acquires of her own natural sensuous proclivities is instrumental to her quest for enlightenment, power, and emancipation; and second, she masters the art of manipulating the feelings and psychological vulnerabilities of others so effectively that they are usually completely unaware of it.[41] This brings us to a question that has been much debated in Laclos criticism: can we judge Merteuil in the traditional moralist terms that she uses to place others in a stable psychological category, or should we call her "mythical," as both Merteuil herself and numerous critics suggest? The answer depends, of course, on what one means by "mythical."[42] I will define the term by saying that Merteuil exists *outside* of the theoretical frame standardly used in Laclos's day to explain both human nature and sensibility: by situating herself above not only all other women but also all existing categories of human types, Merteuil defies both the sociomoral conventions and the natural-philosophical theories of late-eighteenth-century France. She functions instead within a very different theoretical frame: philosophical libertinism, a system that exploits those same conventions and theories, but to serve opposite ends.

In this light, if one accepts the notion that Merteuil embodies something monstrous, what is teratological about her is not that she is a female libertine but rather that she is a *true* libertine—someone who is constitutionally hard-wired to embrace vice as a higher, more truthful, and more intensely satisfying mode of being. Some critics, applying a Hegelian dialectic to *Les Liaisons dangereuses,* insist that there is an essential weak spot in Merteuil's carefully elaborated armature: they argue that she needs Valmont to give substance to her glorious self-image by recognizing her as a superior, omnipotent being.[43] Although I agree that Merteuil requires allies to carry out her projects, I do not believe that she absolutely needs Valmont—that is, a man—to valorize her as an exceptional, libertine woman. For the novel entertains another possibility until the middle of part 3: the possibility that Cécile might eventually replace Valmont as confidant and accomplice to Merteuil, and thus become the second member of Merteuil's new libertine master race.

Merteuil expresses high hopes for Cécile in this regard early in the novel: "The child is adorable and I'm quite infatuated. Unless I'm mistaken, she's shaping up to become one of our very smartest women. I can see her little heart starting to open up and it's a delight to watch . . . I've often been tempted to make her my student" (*LLD,* letter 20, p. 41). Merteuil is still very optimistic about this pedagogical project in part 2: "I've promised her that I would educate her, and that's a promise I think I will keep. I've often felt the need for a confidante and I'd sooner have her than anyone else" (letter 54, pp. 105–6). The advantage that Merteuil would procure from having Cécile in her confidence is clear: such a alliance could not be contaminated by the traditional male-female sexual dynamic that ultimately spoils her friendship with Valmont. Moreover, as Merteuil envisions things at this point, a libertine Cécile would be a clone of Merteuil herself—a young woman raised according to the same methods and principles of self-mastery that Merteuil employed to become what she is. She adds, however, that her education of Cécile can only truly start after Valmont has initiated Cécile's sexual education: "But I can't do a thing with her until she's done . . . what she's got to do" (106). Merteuil thus counts on Cécile's deflowering as the moment when she can begin to replicate herself, or at least create a "junior intriguer" able to play a secondary role in Merteuil's sophisticated sexual adventures (letter 106, p. 239). In the meantime, she conducts some subtle tests to measure Cécile's capacities both for sexual pleasure and, equally important, for resistance to an erotic advance: "On a whim, I decided to find out in person what sort of defense she actually was capable of putting up: with one thing leading to another, I got that girl so worked up . . . and I'm a mere woman" (letter 54, p. 105).[44]

Unfortunately for Merteuil, Cécile turns out to be seriously lacking in what it takes to be a libertine—despite the best efforts of both roués and despite what would seem to be optimal conditions for repeating Merteuil's self-taught methods of libertine education: age, active sensibility, and an inattentive mother. When Cécile fails to respond properly to being seduced by Valmont, Merteuil writes to her: "But seriously, how can a girl who's past her fifteenth birthday be so positively childish? . . . If you don't educate yourself better, what on earth can you expect other people to do for you? What hope is there, if the act that opens other girls' eyes seems instead to blind yours?" (letter 105, p. 231). Although she gives Cécile several bits of advice in the rest of this letter—urging her, for example, to recognize the advantages of her new liaison with Valmont, to learn how to hide her feelings better, and to stop writing like a child—Merteuil is clearly disgusted with the dismal performance of her would-be protégée during her moment of sexual truth.

Merteuil expresses her bitter disappointment in her next letter to Valmont, where she says of Cécile: "I have absolutely no further interest in her . . . I see now that she doesn't have what it takes [il n'y a pas d'étoffe]" (letter 106, p. 235). She goes on to diagnose Cécile's constitutional deficiencies in pseudo-medical terms: "She suffers from a stupid sort of ingenuousness that didn't even respond to your specific treatment, though that rarely fails; to my mind, that's the most dangerous disease a woman can have. In particular, it points to a character weakness that is well-nigh incurable" (235). Cécile, in other words, can never be anything more than an easy woman because she has only one, typically female center of sensible pleasure, and it isn't her head. Merteuil concludes by reducing Cécile to the lowest species of female: the "pleasure machine," a being too dim-witted to resist or master the bodily sensibility that is naturally aroused during a seduction (235).[45]

Thus, while Cécile starts out as the focus of Merteuil's efforts to recreate her own innovative, cerebral mode of sensibility, she ends up branded with the most contemptible, involuntary, typically female form of the property. But what, we might ask, really happens to her would-be mentor, the mastermind Merteuil? She, as everyone knows, falls victim at the end of the novel to small-pox, the favorite disease of eighteenth-century literature. Although Merteuil recovers, she is, as Mme. de Volanges recounts, "terribly disfigured; in partic-ular, she has lost one eye" (letter 175, p. 370). However *postiche* this conclusion may be, the novelistic defiguration that is finally visited on Merteuil is fitting in its way. Not only is it an appropriate means of undoing a self-proclaimed mas-ter of physiognomies, but it also uses as its agent Merteuil's own body, just as she had done when she made herself into a libertine. In Merteuil's original ex-periment on herself (as recounted in letter 81), she employed the physiognomic science of figures not in its usual sense—as a means of revealing the soul—but rather to hide, under a proper and pleasing feminine exterior, the inner being that she was radically reconstituting by channeling all of her sensibility to her head. It is the *physical* part of Merteuil's constitution that fails her in the end: by failing to resist the attack of the most eminently communicable disease of the century, Merteuil's body literally undoes her because it strips her of the facade she needs in order to cover up her uncommonly powerful mind.[46]

The hideous appearance with which the Marquise de Merteuil emerges after her bout with smallpox—which claims, significantly, one of her penetratingly analytic eyes—effectively destroys her viability as a functioning male/female hybrid; she can only continue to exist by being generally recognized as patho-logical and taken out of social circulation. The ending of *Les Liaisons dan-gereuses* therefore serves to terminate an ambitious attempt to challenge the constitutional determinism that pervades every other aspect of the novel. If Merteuil's defeat were purely the result of a social logic that reaffirms itself in the novel's conclusion, it might have been accomplished without recourse to a symbolic physical undoing like death or disease. This suggests that something other than social logic is at play in the conclusion that Laclos gives to his novel: namely, a physiological logic analogous to that which informed thinking about sex and sensibility in contemporary medico-moral philosophy, according to which a strict conceptual limit had to be placed on the constitutions deemed possible for women versus for men. It is that logic which triumphs at the end of Laclos's novel—bringing with it, not coincidentally, a return to conventional social order.

Physiology and its clearly defined set of normative constitutions emerge in *Les Liaisons dangereuses* at those moments when the ongoing experiment in lib-ertine sensibility seems to be succeeding too well. In the end, that physiologi-cal logic acts to transform the novel's experimental subjects into a predictable gallery of case histories, all ravaged by some sudden and merciless blow to their sensible bodies: Valmont gets "two sword thrusts in the body" (letter 163, p. 349), Cécile has a miscarriage, the exquisitely sensitive Tourvel fades away into a delirious death, and Merteuil is undone by smallpox. Up until Merteuil's final transformation, however, she embodies a truly novel mode of experimenting with the existing meanings and possibilities of sensibility. For Merteuil's painstaking work on herself consists not just in analyzing the social world à la Condillac or Buffon, but also in cultivating a cerebrally based mode of *jouissance* that brings her brand of sensualist philosophy closer to that of Sade. Despite her fate in the novel's conclusion, Merteuil succeeds for a while in secretly bucking the complementarian determinism of mainstream natural and social philosophy—not because she represses her feminine sensibility, but because she *improves* on it. Because she never yields, never ceases to adhere to the superior, intellectual kind of sensibility that only men were supposed to have at the time, Merteuil proves herself to be by far the most compelling (and ultimately unknowable) creature represented in *Les Liaisons dangereuses*. Although she defines herself in ironic relationship to the highly codified conventions of her society, the manner in which she pursues her personal "evolution" takes her right off of that society's conceptual and moral map. In that sense, Merteuil is anomalous within Laclos's anthropological system, and belongs instead in Sade's: with her exceptional physico-mental constitution and diabolically active sensibility, Merteuil would be well suited for dwelling among Sade's master libertine-philosophers.

و۹ و۔

The function of sensibility in Sade's writings has generally been a conundrum for Sade critics: even those who have elaborated the most subtle interpretations of his peculiar system of libertinism have tended to regard sensibility as either absent in his libertine characters or as paradoxical.[47] There are, of course, moments in Sade's texts that would seem to support both hypotheses: the argument that the Sadian libertine is fundamentally insensible is espoused by the victim character Justine of *Justine, ou Les Malheurs de la vertu*, who declares that "a libertine is rarely a man of sensibility" (*Justine*, 506); and the paradox theory seems confirmed by Sade's notion of apathy—that "happy" state that allows libertine masters like Mme. de Clairwil of *Juliette, ou Les Prospérités du vice* to commit their crimes in absolute sangfroid even while deriving exquisite voluptuous stimulation from them.[48] Critical efforts to explain that paradox have, however, not adequately addressed two important questions. First, what precisely is the theoretical origin of Sade's insistence that libertines must (as Philippe Roger puts it) "reconvert" their sensibility in order to stay true to their philosophy?[49] And second, if sensibility is so suppressed in Sade, then why do his novels repeatedly stage a confrontation between conventional sensibility as embodied by Sade's virtuous victim characters and the radically unconventional sensibility of his libertines?

To resolve those questions, one must consider Sade's deployment of this property in the larger context of late Enlightenment sensibility theory—a theory that, as I have contended, was dominated by the moral-anthropological branch of philosophical medicine that emerged through the writings of Pierre Roussel and his followers. Various scholars, noting the preeminence of La Mettrie's works in Sade's library, have singled out *L'Homme machine* (1747) as central for understanding Sade's brand of libertine materialism.[50] Yet La Mettrie's iatromechanical model—outmoded by the time Sade was composing his fictions—is less pertinent to the operation of sensibility in Sadian libertinism than are models furnished by more contemporary medical thinking. As we have seen, the medical theory of sensibility evolved significantly in the latter half of the eighteenth century, as médecins philosophes endeavored to cultivate sensibility's good qualities (like its formative role in the development of the enlightened mind) while controlling its dangerous, ignoble, and/or contradictory attributes. The solution proposed by the medical theorists of the 1770s was essentially anthropological: sensibility was to be understood as a property that follows distinct tracks of development in distinct species of human beings. In other words, every body was still seen as sensible, but sensible in a manner distinct to its basic nature—a nature held to be utterly different depending on whether one was robust or delicate, male or female, a country-dweller or an urbanite, a manual laborer or a scholar, and so on.

The anthropological multiplication of types of sensibility that occurred in the late eighteenth century was, as I have argued, an attempt to salvage the notion that man is a perfectible, enlightenable being. Rather than continuing to promote this idea as universal for human beings, medical theorists like Roussel, de Sèze, and Cabanis argued instead that the quest for intellectual enlightenment was still possible, but that it should be limited to those who were constitutionally suited to withstand its rigors. On their analysis, the key physio-anatomical quality for enlightenment was a refined and resistant sensibility that could be trained to foster higher sensations and cognitive activities. When one considers Sade's treatment of sensibility in this theoretical context, it becomes clear that his libertine materialism was a cunning turn not just on Enlightenment philosophy, but also on Enlightenment medical philosophy. For Sade, too, elaborated a two-tracked model of the human race; he, however, based that model on one, and only one, anthropological opposition: libertine master versus hapless victim.

I therefore interpret Sadian libertinism, and the peculiar sensibility associated with it, as a jointly medical and philosophical condition. For the Sadian libertine, physio-anatomical constitution is both a biological and an intellectual destiny: the libertine's body is his primary instrument for acceding to knowledge, as well as for acting on libertine principles. In that sense, the body of the Sadian libertine is not so much reduced as reconstructed, along lines quite similar to—and yet quite distinct from—contemporary medical treatments of sensibility. Sade is thus an active participant in the ongoing effort to "improve" the latest theoretical models of the sensible body and to fit that body to certain principles and beliefs about human nature.

Sade, like Laclos, has two distinct ways of deploying sensibility in his fictions. For Sade's libertine philosophes, sensibility operates as a boundlessly energetic instrument for cultivating the erotic intellect; for his victim characters, by contrast, it is an inexorably fatalistic force that dooms them to the worst kinds of moral and physical suffering. Sade's novels are standardly plotted as a running debate between those two oppositionally constituted camps of beings. That structure is particularly pronounced in *Justine, ou Les malheurs de la vertu*, which accords a bit more space than usual to the arguments of the virtuous, sympathetically sensitive camp because it features a heroine who is judged by her libertine persecutors to be more intelligent than their typical voiceless victims.[51] The libertines of this novel are thus intent both on deriving intense sexual pleasure from Justine/Thérèse's classically "interesting" body[52] and on seducing her intellectually—that is, enlightening her as to the illusions of virtue and the superiority of libertinism. The latter seduction is, of course, doomed to failure, for two reasons. First, Justine/Thérèse steadfastly refuses to be disabused about the moral conventions she holds dear: she continues to be amazed, for example, when her persecutors are not moved but rather aroused or irritated by her tears and her endless panegyrics to virtue, religion, benevolence, and so on. Second, it is predetermined from the start that Justine/Thérèse will no more succeed in "converting" to libertinism than she will convince her libertine opponents that the mainstream philosophy she espouses is preferable to theirs. Her moral-philosophical position consequently holds little weight in her debates with the various adversaries she encounters because the libertines' arguments—like their bodies—are quite simply stronger and more energetic.

The inveterate deflowerer Saint-Florent of *Justine* provides this succinct explanation of the constitutional difference between the "weak individual" like the novel's heroine and stronger souls like him: "Vigorous souls, who are far more delighted by powerful shocks imparted to what surrounds them than they would be by the delicate impressions felt by the feeble creatures in their midst, inevitably prefer, as befits their constitution, what affects others painfully over what would only touch them in a gentler manner: this is the only difference between the cruel and the meek; both groups are endowed with sensibility, but each is endowed with it in a special manner" (*Justine*, 661–62). Saint-Florent grants that each class of beings has its own distinct *jouissances*, but he insists that cruel people experience pleasures that are more intense and thus "doubtless more authentic, since they characterize the penchants of all men who are still creatures of Nature" (662). Conventional pleasures like piety, charity, and compassion are, by contrast, "deceiving and vapid delights" because they derive not from nature but from civilization—an artificial state that is to be condemned for hampering the fundamental principles of nature. In their quest to stay true to nature, Sade's libertine philosophes heed nothing but the demands of their bodies; as a result, they have so "perfected" their sensible systems that they can withstand the most intense and exquisite sensations conceivable to their equally singular minds. In this universe, therefore, physical sensibility is quite literally instrumental for experiencing what Sade proclaims to be the ultimate truth of existence: sensation, *tout court*.

As the fledgling libertine Léonore explains to her mother in *Aline et Valcour*, certain souls feel differently than most because they are organized differently: "Are all our souls made in the same manner? Must all of them feel the same things? Pity only acts on souls in proportion to their softness; the more vigorous the individual, the less he is susceptible to being shaken in that way."[53] What Léonore concludes from this very Rousselian constitutional distinction is that there is a radical incommensurability between "souls of a certain mettle" and common, conventional souls (*Aline et Valcour*, 260). The former class of beings have a different neuro-physiological destiny: they can feel "sensations that are not *known* by everyone else" (260); and they are "irritated" or stimulated by precisely those things that revolt or overwhelm their more primitive counterparts. In other words, libertine souls have access through their unusually vigorous sensibilities to knowledge that is unattainable for anyone else.

However, developing a truly advanced sensibility, according to Sade, entails more than being constituted to feel things in a singularly intense manner. It also requires that one concentrate all of one's energies and reflections exclusively, solipsistically, on that heightened capacity for physical feeling. To do that, Sadian libertines must (rather like Mme. de Merteuil of Laclos's *Liaisons dangereuses*) put themselves through a long course of pedagogical training and self-discipline, whose purpose is to dull the "mediocre" kind of sensibility that leads toward virtue while cultivating the violently energetic form of the property that leads to vice, crime, and the most extreme forms of libertine atrocity. Clairwil of *L'Histoire de Juliette* provides a neuro-physiological explanation of the latter, vicious kind of sensibility: "If . . . foreign objects act in a forceful manner upon our organs, if they penetrate them violently, if they stir into brisk motion the neural fluid particles which circulate in the hollow of the nerves, then our sensibility is such as to dispose us to vice. If the foreign objects' action is stronger yet, it leads us to crime, and finally to atrocities, if the effect attains its ultimate intensity" (*Juliette*, 278). Only after they have rechanneled their sensibilities in this manner—and undergone the necessary training of their imaginations—can libertines practice a full-fledged philosophy of heightened *jouissance*.[54]

The bandit la Dubois of *Justine* explains the principle of studied physicality that underlies this philosophy in terms of proportion: "There is no rational proportionate relation between what affects us and what affects others; the first we sense physically, the other only touches us morally, and moral feelings are deceiving; none but physical sensations are authentic" (*Justine*, 491). What Sade effectively does in this and similar passages is to break the link that traditional Enlightenment theorists had established between three forms of sensibility: intellectual refinement, moral sympathy, and constitutional delicacy. Each of those terms is transformed in his libertine system: intellectual refinement comes to mean adherence to the more immediate and active natural principles of physical sensation and the circulation of matter; the sympathetic "moral fiber" conventionally invoked to uphold the institutions of social law, morality, and religion is rejected as illusory and irrelevant; and the constitutional delicacy traditionally regarded as a mark of superiority in the other two registers is here replaced by selective, organ-specific physical vigor.

On that last point, there is a curious and striking structural homology between Sade's portrait of the truly "enlightened" being and those put forth by the mainstream philosophes and médecins philosophes of the eighteenth century: the Sadian libertine, much like the scholar portrayed in works like Le Camus's *Médecine de l'esprit* or Tissot's *De la santé des gens de lettres*, has streamlined his or her sensible economy to one central reactive axis, formed by the organs essential to certain activities. In the case of Sade's libertine philosophes, that axis consists of the brain, stomach, and genital organs—the last of which are often prodigious in size and vigor.[55] These "fearsome organizations" (so markedly different from the atrophied genitalia Tissot ascribes to scholars) are essential prerequisites for becoming a libertine in Sade's system; they would be meaningless, however, were they not attached to an equally prodigious mental organization.[56] Sadian libertines thus mimic and subvert the medicine of enlightenment that was so popular in Sade's day: they cultivate an ethic of pure vigor of body and mind, follow exact regimens for literally sensational living, and transform intemperance into a principled, philosophical virtue.

The physio-philosophical training that a libertine must undergo in Sade's system can be seen as an instance of the operation of transvaluation that the critic David Morris has proposed to describe how biomedical language and concepts pass into Sade's fiction.[57] I believe, however, that the notion of transvaluation should be applied in a manner broader than it is in Morris's essay, which focuses almost exclusively on Sade's appropriation of the contemporary medical theory of pleasure and pain. It is not so much pain as sensibility, in all of its modes, that serves as "a comprehensive metaphor for truth" in Sadian natural philosophy (Morris, 314). Sade's libertines search tirelessly both for ever more intense sensations and for all the "facts" about the body's reactive properties that they can glean from contemporary medical theory. The purpose of these investigations is to gain greater understanding of their own extraordinary sensible constitutions while also confirming the soundness of their philosophical beliefs. For example, the monk Clément of *Justine* gleefully awaits further advances in anatomy to nullify the institutions of social law, morality, and religion:

> When the study of anatomy reaches perfection, they will without any trouble be able to demonstrate the relationship of the human constitution to the tastes which affect it. Ah, you pedants, hangmen, turnkeys, lawmakers, you tonsured rabble, what will you do when we have arrived there? What will become of your laws, your ethics, your religion, your gallows, your Gods and your Heavens and your Hell, when it shall be proven that this or that flow of liquids, this variety of fibers, that degree of pungency in the blood or in the animal spirits are sufficient to make a man the object of your punishments or of your rewards?   (*Justine*, 603)

The libertine surgeon Rodin, also of *Justine,* is so anxious to bring about this "enlightened" state of affairs that he devotes his life (and that of his unfortunate daughter Rosalie) to perfecting anatomy—in this case, by performing autopsies on the genitals of prepubescent virgins who have died a cruel death.[58] In this parodically eroticized turn on the penetrating gaze of the Enlightenment physician, the entire epistemology of the *médecins philosophes* is turned upside down. That is, knowing the sensible body, for a Sadian medical observer, does not mean gently coaxing out its secrets (as it had for the Montpellier vitalists), but rather subjecting it to the most violent outrages imaginable.

Finally, however, the most significant idea that Sade transvalues from eighteenth-century medical theory is anthropological: the dimorphic model of sensible constitution that had recently become paradigmatic in philosophical medicine plays a critical role in structuring Sade's narratives, just as it does in Laclos's *Liaisons dangereuses.* The battle between "good" sensibility and "evil" sensibility that informs the late-eighteenth-century libertine novel is therefore rooted not just in the moral-aesthetic principles of literary sentimentalism, but also in a divided vision of human nature that typologizes one half of the human race as constitutionally fixed and depicts the other half as limitless in its ability to pursue and attain what passes for the state of enlightenment. In Laclos and Sade, only libertines occupy the second category: these authors' libertine characters, whatever their sex, are endowed with the capacity to remake themselves into higher, purely voluntary beings; whereas their delicate, virtuous, and compassionate victim characters are constitutionally destined to suffer intense and heart-rending torments of body and soul.

In short, when they created their libertine characters, Laclos and Sade embraced the latest natural-philosophical notions of sex, sensibility, and enlightenability but used them to support a philosophy utterly antithetical to the sociomoral conventions that those notions had been designed to uphold. These writers imported both anthropological dimorphism, with its neat plan for distributing sensibility among opposing body types, and the new biology of enlightenment into their fictions; yet they also created some exceptional female characters like Merteuil or Clairwil, whose special sensibilities allow them to defy the limits of their sex and thus become philosophes in their own right. It is, in the last analysis, these female libertines who represent the most daring libertine transvaluation of all: they embody the conceptually monstrous possibility that the reigning theory of complementarity could just as easily be deployed to support libertinism as to uphold the traditional philosophy of enlightenment. One might say, therefore, that the ultimate "victim" of libertine literature is the Enlightenment theory of sensibility itself—a theory which was designed to contain, control, and edify human nature by medicalizing it, but which ended up, in this literary genre, taking a wild and ultimately pathological turn.

CONCLUSION

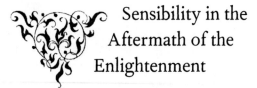 Sensibility in the
Aftermath of the
Enlightenment

Given the dimorphic manner in which sensibility was treated in both moral-anthropological medicine and libertine fiction, it seems evident that the Enlightenment concept of sensibility was headed for a sort of theoretical implosion at
the end of the eighteenth century. Implosion, in this case, does not mean that
sensibility lost its pertinence in the various fields which, up to then, had used it
as paradigmatic. Rather, it means that the idea of sensibility which had created
such dynamic interconnections among the fields of physiology, medicine, philosophy, ethics, anthropology, aesthetics, and literature began progressively to
splinter into discrete, specialized ideas about the property's particular signification in particular contexts. Paradoxically, perhaps, this mutation was already
at work in the writings of physicians like Roussel and Cabanis, for despite their
firm allegiance to the holistic, monistic, semivitalist theory of sensibility they
had inherited from the médecins philosophes and sensationalist philosophers of
the preceding generation, these theorists effectively split sensibility into radically different modes of expression. The increasingly pronounced tendency to
subdivide sensibility into incommensurate modes or types in the aftermath of
the Enlightenment movement ran directly counter to the philosophes' attempts
to devise a unified vision of humankind in which everything human could be
seen as linked together in a seamless natural continuum. Sensibility and the
strange hodgepodge of sentimentalist, vitalist, and materialist ideas related to it
remained popular, even at the violent heights of the French Revolution. Yet as
nineteenth-century thinkers refined the meaning of sensibility for their respective fields, the old consensus over the property's integrated physico-moral-
intellectual nature not only weakened, but was, in some cases, rejected out-
right.

Clearly, some unusual interdisciplinary convergences had arisen out of the
philosophes' effort to expand sensibility's explanatory power by applying it

simultaneously to matters of the heart, head, and body, thus creating such odd bedfellows as physiology and metaphysics, medical diagnostics and aesthetics, hygiene and ethics, and anthropology, sentimentalism, and libertinism. Although eighteenth-century authors were often well aware of the tensions that attended such convergences, they nonetheless perceived the general alignment of the physical and the moral to be richly productive, both for their own fields and for the greater cause of the so-called human sciences. The spatial metaphor of "between" that I use in the title of this book consequently describes not only the two poles of meaning that framed the eighteenth-century concept of sensibility—enlightenment and pathology—but also the terminological borrowings, conceptual transcodings, and philosophical transvaluations which this property inspired across the boundaries of diverse discursive fields. That metaphor, however, loses a good deal of its viability when we take up the question of what, exactly, happened to sensibility in the following century, when literature, medicine, physiology, and philosophy each underwent major changes that necessarily affected the conceptual and semantic relations that had once existed among them.

Before I embark on a brief historical overview of the various legacies of eighteenth-century sensibility, I should perhaps say a word about history itself—or at least, about the manner in which I have been practicing it in this book. It may well be that by elaborating my own, at times idiosyncratic narrative of the evolving meanings that were attached to sensibility in eighteenth-century France, I have opened myself up to objections from purists in both literary studies and the history of science. There is doubtless something a bit arbitrary about the choices I have made in composing my literary corpus; I have, admittedly, neglected some of the genres in which sensibility played a significant role, such as theater and dramatic poetics, nonfictional and non-medical moralist writing, and the treacly novels of minor sentimental authors like Baculard d'Arnaud, whose saga *Les Délassements de l'homme sensible* (1783–87) was peculiarly popular at the time.[1] Moreover, by presenting an account of eighteenth-century medicine and physiology that focuses almost exclusively on the subject of sensibility, I have not addressed some of the other important debates going on in those fields over such questions as the nature of respiration, digestion, circulation, and generation; the naming and classifying of diseases; the relationship between the medical and surgical professions; and the perceived need to reform both the teaching and the institutional organization of biomedical science.[2]

My selection of subject and texts was, however, dictated by more than just my personal tastes as a literary scholar and amateur medical historian: the works on which I have focused are those that best illustrate the extraordinary power with which the conceptual metaphor of sensibility was invested in both the medicine and the literature of this period. If the historical component of my study seems to be heavily weighted toward sensibility's emergent significations in medicine and natural philosophy, that is not because I seek to subordinate literature to those fields. Rather, it is because I wish, above all, to demonstrate that the literature of sensibility which flourished during this period was remarkably open to productive contamination by ideas from the medical and natural-philosophical discourses of the day. It is this quality, perhaps more than anything else, that distinguishes eighteenth-century literary sensibility from its nineteenth-century incarnations.

In his appraisal of the mutations that literary sensibility underwent at the turning point of the eighteenth and nineteenth centuries, Frank Baasner points to three developments that undermined the concept's authority. First, sensibility was trivialized by both the kitschy excesses of sentimentalism and the waggish delight that certain eighteenth-century wits like Collé took in poking fun at the earnestly "scientific" language often used to discuss the property. Second, sensibility acquired unsettlingly amoral connotations when it was appropriated by libertine writers like Laclos and Sade. And finally, the eighteenth-century cult of tender feeling became untenable when pursued amidst the ferocious public bloodletting that marked the darkest days of the French Revolution.[3] As the eighteenth century drew to its painful close, many writers thus turned away from the optimistic, sentimentalist, parody-prone conception of sensibility that had become pervasive in popular culture. Yet rather than rejecting sensibility altogether, the anti-Revolutionary and generally antiphilosophe authors who launched the fledgling Romantic movement took pains to redefine the concept in terms that were more restrictive, moralizing, and private. As a result, literary sensibility became endowed with religious, melancholic, and at times antisocial overtones that it had not had in the previous century outside of Rousseau's writings.

François René, vicomte de Chateaubriand, for example, declared categorically, "We cannot be too fervent in urging our century to embrace this truth: without religion, *there is no sensibility*."[4] Germaine de Staël retained the Enlightenment notion that "sensibility, imagination and reason lend each other mutual support";[5] at the same time, however, she expressed grave reservations about the use of sentimental rhetoric in a violent, mob-driven society like that of revolutionary France and sought to rehabilitate moral sensibility by taking it in a transcendent, Protestant direction. Pierre Simon Ballanche undertook to correct Rousseau's misanthropic condemnation of the arts by championing "the singular phenomenon of that kind of sensibility which literature and the arts develop within us";[6] yet Ballanche oscillated between a persistent adherence to the philosophes' belief in art's socially edifying powers and a Romantic proclivity for glorifying melancholy and grandiose contrasts as a source of poetic inspiration.[7] Étienne de Senancour, lastly, endeavored to sever sensibility's old ties with society and sociability and return the property instead to nature—that is, to a nature that only the "primitive," unsentimental man could experience: "This vast, delicate, and deep sensibility, this interior sense that can be affected in countless ways, consumes and shortens the existence it expands . . . Sensibility is not merely tender or painful emotion, it is also the faculty given to the perfectly constituted man to receive deep impressions from everything that can act upon human organs. The truly sensitive man is not the one who is moved, who cries; rather, it is the man who receives sensations where others would only find indifferent perceptions."[8] All of these writers strove in various ways to rescue sensibility from the moral and aesthetic ambivalence it had acquired in the waning years of the eighteenth century; they thus helped to shape the quest for a new moral world which became one of the defining leitmotifs of nineteenth-century literary and philosophical discourse.[9]

That quest was informed by several other notions also inherited from the French Enlightenment—most particularly that of regeneration. As the historian Mona Ozouf underscores, this idea was not entirely new to the Revolutionary period, but rather, can be traced back to the primitivist fables of "natural man," which had proliferated in France ever since the publication of Lahontan's *Dialogues curieux* (1703), and to the philosophes' debates over the nature of human perfectibility.[10] Ozouf argues that the notion of creating a new, uncorrupted, regenerated type of human being was pursued with special intensity during the 1790s, under the joint influences of the Revolutionary program for radical social reform and the resurgent Christianity promoted by some of the Revolution's harshest critics (Ozouf, 129–30). We should note, however, that the dream of forging such a superior human type is already apparent in the scenarios of masterful sensibility that proliferated in the anthropological medicine and libertine fiction of the late Enlightenment. In an important sense, therefore, the Revolutionary and Romantic vision of regeneration was an outgrowth of the Enlightenment's many hygienicist projects for using sensibility as a means of edifying the human race.

Clearly, any effort to reconstruct what happened to the eighteenth-century idea of sensibility must involve a consideration not just of literary, philosophical, and moralist writings but also of the scientific and pseudoscientific discourses that emerged in the early nineteenth century. In a way, the disintegration of the philosophes' organically rooted conception of this property is paradoxical, given that organicist ideas like "Naturphilosophie" were streaming into France from German philosophers like Goethe, Schelling, Herder, and

Steffens.[11] Yet even the most overtly vitalist biomedical thinkers of early-nineteenth-century France were careful not to align their theories too closely with *Naturphilosophie*: although they were keenly interested in developing a totalizing, unified science of man in relation to nature, society, and the cosmos, they were often virulently opposed to anything that might be considered materialist.[12] The idea of interconnecting all of the various human sciences under a single superscience thus remained compelling for nineteenth-century thinkers, but in a manner rather different from that of both the eighteenth-century philosophes and the Idéologues—a group of thinkers who, between approximately 1794 and 1807, undertook to consolidate all the branches of knowledge through a sensationalist epistemology inspired by Condillac.[13] During the period when *Idéologie* dominated the newly reorganized institutions of learning, the fields of physiology, philosophy, psychology, and moral theory continued to be closely aligned, and the proponents of philosophical medicine continued to promote it as an all-encompassing anthropological project.[14] However, the Idéologues' efforts to advance the ongoing unification of knowledge by reconfiguring France's intellectual institutions ended, for all practical purposes, with the new repartition of academic chairs in 1811.[15] Moreover, even before then, there emerged influential conceptual currents that tended to undermine the staunchly physicalist foundations of the old Enlightenment order of things.

It is instructive, in this regard, to compare the role played by eighteenth-century sensibility theory in two of the major medical controversies of the century's last two decades: the debate over the cult of mesmerism that became popular in Paris during the 1780s and the heated attack on the guillotine that was led in the 1790s by physicians like Cabanis and Jean-Jacques Süe. Süe's position on the latter issue was directly derived from the Montpellier vitalist model of the human body as a federation of locally sensible parts; he used this model to argue that execution by guillotine was not the painless process its inventor, Dr. Guillotin, had claimed it to be, but rather a horrible experience for the decapitated head, which undoubtedly retained both its consciousness and its capacity for physical suffering for several minutes after being separated from its body.[16] The integrated physico-moral concept of sensibility that had become standard during the Enlightenment thus continued to be pressed into service by the mainstream medical theorists of the Revolutionary era—but it was also exploited by healers of a very different persuasion, like Franz Anton Mesmer.

The semifluidist, semielectrical doctrine of therapeutic crises promoted by Mesmer and his followers was more than just pseudoscience or charlatanism; rather, it was a cunning recasting of mainstream Enlightenment medical ideas concerning the "sympathetic" manner in which an individual sensible body

Jean-Jacques Paulet, Satire on Animal Magnetism, *from* L'Antimagnétisme
*(1784), frontispiece. (Photograph courtesy of the National Library of Medicine,
Bethesda, Md.)*

acts and reacts in relation to external forces like the "non-naturals."[17] As François Azouvi has noted, French proponents of mesmerism such as Nicolas Bergasse systematically inverted the terms that contemporary vitalist physicians used to describe how the inside of the human organism interacts with the surrounding natural world: "Rather than making the internal principle the principal site of the vital reaction, as did the vitalists, [Bergasse] attributed to the individual a tendency to disorganization, and to the universe the inverse tendency to restore equilibriums . . . In this entirely new and unprecedented therapeutic process, it was the amplification of sensibility that explained the amplification of consciousness."[18] In other words, rather than perceiving vital sensibility as a preservative and restorative internal force that enabled the individual body to retain its integrity in the face of disruptive impressions introduced from the outside, the mesmerists viewed it as the painful sign of a pathological imbalance that had been triggered by a lack of harmony between the body's energies and those of the cosmos. Only the magnetizer, according to this theoretical scenario, could correct the problem, thanks to his ability to act as a "conductor" of animal magnetism—a fluidlike force that supposedly effected the salutary crises which were needed to bring the ailing individual back into healthy resonance with the universe.[19]

Mesmer's disciples in late-eighteenth-century France therefore used selected elements of mainstream medical vitalism in order to construct a new, mystically tinged therapeutic doctrine that mixed medicine, physics, occultism, Rousseauistic moral theory, and politics in a manner that was rightly viewed as radical by French authorities.[20] The most significant aspect of mesmerist thinking, for my purposes, is the way that it mimicked the eighteenth-century medical concept of sensibility while stripping it of its positivistic, monistic foundations: the mesmerists were far less interested in visualizing the actual internal workings of the sensible body than in confirming their belief that all human beings should be seen as part of a larger, harmonically resonating *Tout*—a cosmos that expressed itself in an organic register but also transcended the merely organic. In that sense, one can compare this peculiar brand of natural philosophy to the metaphysical doctrine that was elaborated by one of the few nineteenth-century philosophers who addressed mesmerism critically: Maine de Biran, who refuted the pseudoscientific aspects of Mesmer's doctrine, but also espoused a dualistic and ultimately transcendent vision of the human being.[21] Biran was among the earliest nineteenth-century philosophers to undertake an antimaterialist reinterpretation of sensibility, which in his mind was necessary in order to correct the reductiveness of sensationalism as practiced by Condillac, Bonnet, and the Idéologues. In the process, he effectively demoted sensibility to an essentially passive role in the operations of cognitive perception and moral consciousness and struck a serious blow to the pervasive eighteenth-century assumption that everything human could ultimately be ascribed to a corporeal foundation.[22]

The turn of the eighteenth to nineteenth centuries was thus marked by a general movement toward a new, far less monolithically physicalist vision of the human interior—a movement that created new terms like "hypersensible" (coined by Biran), new systems for categorizing the vital forces at work in the human being, and new conceptual grids for conceiving the relations that existed among the body, mind, and soul. That is not to say that the body—sensible or otherwise—was repudiated; rather, it was accorded a less prominent role in certain areas of inquiry (like psychology, ethics, and epistemology), while also being subject to new modes of investigation in the fields that dealt with it most directly, namely physiology and medicine. In the realm of physiology, Xavier Bichat deserves special mention for developing a more empirically grounded system for conceptualizing vitality, which he presented in his *Recherches physiologiques sur la vie et la mort* (1800), published shortly before his death at the age of thirty-three.

In Bichat's system, sensibility—along with irritability, now renamed contractility—was subdivided into two distinct modes: the inferior, involuntary kind of sensibility characteristic of the organic or passional life, versus the highly developed, voluntary kind associated with the animal or intellectual life.[23] Although Bichat's physiological doctrine was designed as a refinement on the organicist-vitalist theories put forth by Montpellier physicians like Bordeu, it nonetheless reintroduced a kind of dualism into physiological thinking. This was not, we should note, a mind-body dualism; for, as Elizabeth Williams observes, "Bichat did believe intellectual function to be dependent on material structures."[24] Rather, it was a way of rearranging the various human faculties to suit, first, Bichat's idea that vital energy is distributed in limited doses to the different parts of the animal economy; and second, his schematization of human temperamental types, according to which some people have highly developed intellectual faculties because their animal sensibility reigns supreme, whereas others are held in the sway of their passions because they are dominated by the "organic" life.[25]

Several elements of Bichat's physiological doctrine left their mark on nineteenth-century medical thinking. For example, his principle of limited vital energy obviously informed Julien-Joseph Virey's medico-philosophical discourse "Du contraste entre le pôle génital et le pôle cérébral dans l'homme et dans la série des animaux" (1840), where it was used to support an opposition between the sexes far more absolutist than anything that had been written by earlier moral anthropologists.[26] Thanks in part to the greater precision that Bichat brought to organicist vitalism, the old monistic, physiologically based vision of sensibility persisted in medical theory well into the 1830s.[27] However, this notion of sensibility encountered stiff opposition from rival biomedical theorists of a dualist and politically conservative bent. Some physicians, like J. L. Alibert, continued to promote medicine as the ultimate science of sensibility—a field that "would be the beacon for metaphysics[,] . . . lead in analyzing and treating the mental illnesses that were inimical to human progress, . . . ground all future work on 'sympathy' and 'sociability,' and forge a new alliance with politics to assist in the campaign for comprehensive public hygiene."[28] Yet many nineteenth-century physicians, like Fréderic Bérard, took a decidedly spiritualist approach toward sensibility: Bérard insisted that "sensibility must be ascribed to 'a particular force, distinct from all the others,' which metaphysicians called the *moi*"[29]—rather than to an organ, as had been common among eighteenth-century médecins philosophes.

There were, of course, a number of different theoretical and ideological concerns involved in the reaction that occurred in many nineteenth-century fields, including medicine, against much that was judged to be materialist in the ideas inherited from the preceding century. Despite this reaction, many physicians on both sides of the new physicalist-spiritualist divide continued to place a great deal of faith in the optimistic idea of perfecting humankind via physical and moral education. This contributed to the proliferation of new hygienicist discourses on the effects that civilized society supposedly made upon human nature; but it also triggered the invention of the more restricted, hierarchical notions of perfectibility and human types that became prevalent in nineteenth-century biomedical science and anthropology proper—ideas like degeneration, which gained great popularity in Europe in the second half of the century.[30] Concerning sensibility, one might say that two ideas took over much of the conceptual work that this idea had done in the previous century: the principle of *volonté*, which was championed by philosophers, psychologists, and poets alike; and the notion of *vie de relation*, which was central not both to Bichatian physiology and to contemporary social theory—including, not coincidentally, the kind found in Balzac's *Etudes philosophiques* and *Etudes analytiques*, all published in the 1830s. Given his expressed desire to depict, as he put it, "the general physiology of human destiny," Balzac is a fitting figure on which to end my reflections on the legacies left by the eighteenth-century medical notion of sensibility.[31]

Let us take as an example Balzac's philosophical novella *La Peau de chagrin*, which was composed as a fictional exploration of both the principle of *volonté* and the concept of *vie de relation*. Among other things, this work contains a wonderful scene of medical consultation, in which the ailing hero Raphael summons not one but three different medical experts, each of whom represents a distinct medical system. First, there is "Brisset," a thinly veiled caricature of François-Joseph-Victor Broussais, "head of the so-called organic school, and successor to such men as Cabanis and Bichat; he was the positivist, the materialist, seeing in man a finite being, subject exclusively to the laws of his organization." Second, there is "Caméristus," or J. C. A. Récamier, "leader of the 'vitalists,' the enthusiastic champion of the abstract doctrines of Van Helmont; he saw in human life a lofty, mysterious principle . . . a kind of intangible, invisible flame governed by some divine law." And, finally, there is "Maugrédie," or the strictly pragmatic experimental physiologist François Magendie, "a man of distinguished intellect but also of a skeptical and satirical turn of mind, who trusted only in the surgeon's knife."[32] Because it ends in an utter impasse, this scene dramatizes both the uncomfortable coexistence of the three main schools of medical thought that emerged in nineteenth-century France and Balzac's own abiding fascination with medicine, with the idea of vitality, and with the impossible dream of forging a unitary science of human nature.

In sum, the old integrated conception of sensibility fell victim after the end of the *ancien régime* to social upheaval, politics, new theoretical developments, and a pervasive urge to resacralize many of the aspects of human experience that had been desacralized during the Enlightenment: consciousness, personality, ethical imperatives, and, in some cases, the living process itself. Sensibility did not disappear in nineteenth-century France, but it did take a distinctly different form, most particularly in literature, philosophy, and aesthetics, where it became associated not with the rational and sociable qualities of humankind but rather with imagination, mysticism, and the idiosyncrasies of artistic temperament. Hence the emergence of a new dichotomy between sensibility and reason—a dichotomy that has since come to be applied to eighteenth-century France, with the result that this period has, at times, been anachronistically labeled "Preromantic."[33] Yet that dichotomy does not at all suffice to explain the complexity of sensibility in the eighteenth century (or in the nineteenth, for that matter). For eighteenth-century sensibility had its own distinct history, one that ran parallel to that of the Enlightenment itself—the period when *sensibilité* truly flourished, enjoying a conceptual dynamism and breadth of meaning that have, for better or worse, since been lost.

 *N*otes

Introduction

1. Louis de Jaucourt, "Sensibilité (Morale)," in *Encyclopédie, ou Dictionnaire raisonné des sciences, des arts et des métiers,* ed. Denis Diderot and Jean d'Alembert, 17 tomes (1751–65; reprint, New York: Pergamon Press, 1969), vol. 3, tome 15, p. 52; my translation.

2. G. S. Rousseau provides an overview of the various discourses that circulated during the early modern period on melancholy, hysteria, the nerves, and sensibility, in "Discourses of the Nerve," in *Literature and Science as Modes of Expression,* ed. Frederick Amrine (Dordrecht: Kluwer Academic Publishers, 1989), 29–60.

3. See Foucault, *L'Archéologie du savoir* (Paris: Gallimard, 1969), esp. 29–54, and *L'Ordre du discours* (Paris: Gallimard, 1971). The scholarly reaction to Foucault's conception of intellectual history has, of course, been enormous among philosophers, historians, and literary critics alike. Historians of the human sciences have particularly taken umbrage at the reductive manner in which the eighteenth century and its major figures are treated in Foucault's *Les Mots et les choses* (1966). See, for example, John Christie, "The Human Sciences: Origins and Histories," *History of the Human Sciences* 6, no. 1 (1993), 1–12; and Michèle Duchet's remarks on Foucault in her chapter on Buffon in *Anthropologie et histoire au siècle des Lumières* (Paris: Maspero, 1971), 229–79. Elizabeth A. Williams offers some concise insights into the strengths and weaknesses of Foucauldian discourse analysis for understanding eighteenth-century medical science in *The Physical and the Moral: Anthropology, Physiology, and Philosophical Medicine in France, 1750–1850* (Cambridge: Cambridge University Press, 1994), 3–8.

4. See R. F. Brissenden's brief discussion of how eighteenth-century concepts like sympathy and sensibility could be approached paradigmatically, in *Virtue in Distress* (London: Macmillan Press, 1974), 20–22; and G. S. Rousseau's more extensive application of Kuhn's methodology in "Nerves, Spirits, and Fibres: Towards Defining the Origins of Sensibility," in *Studies in the Eighteenth Century, III: Papers Presented at the Third David Nichol Smith Memorial Seminar, Canberra, 1973,* ed. R. F. Brissenden and J. Eade (Canberra: Australian National University Press, 1976), 137–58 (reprinted with a postscript in *The Blue Guitar* 2 [1976], 125–53). There is something inherently problematic about transposing the Kuhnian notion of paradigm to a broad-based cultural and conceptual phenomenon because Kuhn's thesis is based on a pattern of collective assent, crisis, and revolution that he viewed as specific to scientific fields like astron-

omy, physics, and chemistry; see Thomas Kuhn, *The Structure of Scientific Revolutions*, 2d ed. (Chicago: University of Chicago Press, 1970), viii. Kuhn addresses the excessive terminological and conceptual plasticity of this notion in "Second Thoughts on Paradigms," in *The Essential Tension: Selected Studies in Scientific Tradition and Change* (Chicago: University of Chicago Press, 1977), 293–319.

5. Frank Baasner underscores that "many elements of the eighteenth-century definition of 'sensibilité' were inherent in the [term's] seventeenth-century connotations," although its exalted socio-moral meanings were not fully developed until about 1750. "The Changing Meaning of 'Sensibilité': 1654 till 1704," *Studies in Eighteenth-Century Culture* 15 (1986), 78. On the timing of the sensibility movement in French literature, see also Geoffroy Atkinson, *The Sentimental Revolution: French Writers of 1690–1740* (Seattle: University of Washington Press, 1965); John S. Spink, "'Sentiment,' 'sensible,' 'sensibilité': Les Mots, les idées, d'après les 'moralistes' français et britanniques du début du dix-huitième siècle," *Zagadnienia Rodzajów Literackich* 20 (1977), 33–47; and Brissenden, *Virtue in Distress*, 11–55. As Brissenden notes, the semantic history of *sensibility* and *sentiment* in eighteenth-century England is related but not identical to the terms' meaning in France. On the meanings of *sentimental* in the British context, see Erik Erämetsä, "A Study of the Word 'Sentimental' and of other Linguistic Characteristics of Eighteenth-Century Sentimentalism in England," *Annales Academiae Scientiarum Fennicae*, ser. B, 74, no. 1 (1951).

6. I borrow the term "bridging concept" from Ludmilla Jordanova; see her essay "Natural Facts: An Historical Perspective on Science and Sexuality," in *Sexual Visions: Images of Gender in Science and Medicine between the Eighteenth and Twentieth Centuries* (Madison: University of Wisconsin Press, 1989), 19–42.

7. On the eighteenth-century predilection for crying over novels, plays, and touching real-life spectacles, see Anne Vincent-Buffault's entertaining study *Histoire des larmes, XVIIIe–XIXe siècles* (Paris: Editions Rivages, 1986), and Robert Mauzi's "Les Maladies de l'âme au XVIIIe siècle," *Revue des sciences humaines* 100 (1960), 459–93. Some literary critics have dismissed the cult of sensibility as artificial and histrionic: see, for example, Arthur M. Wilson, Jr., "Sensibility in France in the Eighteenth Century: A Study in Word History," *French Quarterly* 13 (1931), 35–46, and I. H. Smith, "The Concept 'Sensibilité' and the Enlightenment," *Journal of the Australasian Universities Language and Literature Association*, no. 27 (1967), 5–17. One might call this the Lansonian view of sensibility, after the nineteenth-century literary historian Gustave Lanson, who persistently derided eighteenth-century sentimental literature in studies like *Nivelle de la Chaussée et la comédie larmoyante* (Paris: Hachette, 1887) and *Histoire de la littérature française* (Paris: Hachette, 1912). Lanson's attacks inspired Pierre Trahard to rise to a passionate four-volume defense of that literature in *Les Maîtres de la sensibilité française au XVIIIe siècle (1715–1789)* (Paris: Boivin, 1931–33); see esp. ch. 1, "Prédominance de la sensibilité au XVIIIe siècle," 7–28.

8. See G. J. Barker-Benfield, *The Culture of Sensibility: Sex and Society in Eighteenth-Century Britain* (Chicago: University of Chicago Press, 1992), xix. See also John Mullan's elegant literary analysis of the eighteenth-century British preoccupation with

the ambiguities of sensibility, sentiment, and society in *Sentiment and Sociability: The Language of Feeling in the Eighteenth Century* (Oxford: Clarendon Press, 1988), and Chris Jones, *Radical Sensibility: Literature and Ideas in the 1790s* (London: Routledge, 1993).

9. David Denby examines the connection between sentimentalism, secularization, and the Enlightenment project in *Sentimental Narrative and the Social Order in France, 1760–1820* (Cambridge: Cambridge University Press, 1994). See also Peter Brooks's comments on the Romantic reaction to Enlightenment desacralization, in his introduction to *The Melodramatic Imagination: Balzac, Henry James, Melodrama, and the Mode of Excess* (New Haven: Yale University Press, 1976), 1–23.

10. This is the central argument of R. S. Ridgeway's *Voltaire and Sensibility* (Montreal: McGill-Queen University Press, 1973), where Ridgeway persuasively demonstrates why Voltaire must be understood as a "man of feeling." See also Roland Mortier, "Unité ou scission du siècle des Lumières?" in *Clartés et ombres du siècle des Lumières* (Geneva: Droz, 1969), 114–24.

11. In England, by contrast, writers like Mary Wollstonecraft condemned sensibility's mindless, materialist, and potentially immoral connotations; see Barker-Benfield, *The Culture of Sensibility*, 351–95. See also the chapter "The Attack on Sensibility," in Janet Todd, *Sensibility: An Introduction* (London: Methuen, 1986), 129–46.

12. See William Coleman, "Health and Hygiene in the *Encyclopédie*: A Medical Doctrine for the Bourgeoisie," *Journal of the History of Medicine* 29 (1974), 399–421; Antoinette Emch-Dériaz, *Tissot, Physician of the Enlightenment* (New York: Peter Lang, 1992); Roy Porter's introduction to *The Popularization of Medicine, 1650–1850*, ed. Roy Porter (London: Routledge, 1992), 1–16; and Colin Jones, "Montpellier Medical Students and the Medicalisation of Eighteenth-Century France," in *Problems and Methods in the History of Medicine*, ed. Roy Porter and Andrew Wear (London: Croom Helm, 1987), 57–80. Peter Gay describes the affinity between eighteenth-century medicine and the project of enlightenment in more metaphorical terms; see "The Enlightenment as Medicine and as Cure," in *The Age of Enlightenment: Studies Presented to Theodore Besterman*, ed. W. H. Barber (Edinburgh: St. Andrews University Publications, 1967), 375–86.

13. David B. Morris, "The Marquis de Sade and the Discourses of Pain: Literature and Medicine at the Revolution," in *The Languages of Psyche: Mind and Body in Enlightenment Thought*, ed. G. S. Rousseau (Berkeley and Los Angeles: University of California Press, 1990), 297.

14. Karl M. Figlio, "The Metaphor of Organization: An Historiographical Perspective on the Bio-Medical Sciences of the Early Eighteenth Century," *History of Science* 14 (1976), 26.

15. On the heuristic value of metaphors and other "discursive elaborations" in scientific and sociopolitical thought, see Judith Schlanger, *Les Métaphores de l'organisme* (Paris: Vrin, 1971), and *L'Invention intellectuelle* (Paris: Fayard, 1983), esp. 182–206.

16. Jean Starobinski, "A Short History of Bodily Sensation," in *Fragments for a History of the Human Body*, ed. Michael Feher, vol. 3 (New York: Zone, 1989), 364. See also Starobinki's second essay in this collection, "Monsieur Teste Confronting Pain," 371–405.

17. The scholarly studies that reflect Freud's somatic model are too numerous to cite exhaustively. I will, however, mention two recent works that are pertinent for eighteenth-century France: Peter Brooks, *Body Work: Objects of Desire in Modern Narrative* (Cambridge: Harvard University Press, 1993), and Marie-Hélène Huet, *Monstrous Imagination* (Cambridge: Harvard University Press, 1993).

18. The most recent example of this approach to eighteenth-century French fiction is Anne Deneys-Tunney's *Ecritures du corps: De Descartes à Laclos* (Paris: Presses Universitaires de France, 1992). I do not mean to imply that there is anything wrong with this critical approach, but I agree with Roy Porter and G. S. Rousseau that when rhetoric, language, gender, and psycho-erotics become the "informing structures" for literary analysis of the body, "the human body is abandoned, and discourses consulting the human *form* rather than the 'body as text' or the 'body as trope' become increasingly rare." Porter and Rousseau, "Introduction: Toward a Natural History of Mind and Body," in Rousseau, *The Languages of Psyche,* 12 n. 16.

19. Roger Cooter, "The Power of the Body: The Early Nineteenth Century," in *Natural Order: Historical Studies of Scientific Culture,* ed. Barry Barnes and Steven Shapin (Beverly Hills, Calif.: Sage Publications, 1979), 73.

20. See the introduction by Catherine Gallagher and Thomas Laqueur to *The Making of the Modern Body: Sexuality and Society in the Nineteenth Century* (Berkeley and Los Angeles: University of California Press, 1987), vi–xv. Foucault's most important works on the body in cultural context are *La Naissance de la clinique* (1963), *Histoire de la folie à l'âge classique* (1961), *Histoire de la sexualité,* 3 vols. (1976–84), and *Surveiller et punir* (1975). Norbert Elias is also an important figure in the twentieth-century rediscovery of the body's history; see his multivolume study *The Civilizing Process,* trans. Edmund Jephcott (New York: Urizen Books, 1978). Dorinda Outram does a highly polemical overview of Foucault, Elias, and other historians of the body in *The Body and the French Revolution: Sex, Class, and Political Culture* (New Haven: Yale University Press, 1989), 6–26. See also Barbara Duden, "A Repertory of Body History," in Feher, *Fragments for a History of the Human Body,* 470–554.

21. Approaching the concept in this light, Syndy McMillen Conger asserts that "eighteenth-century sensibility . . . ushered in the era of a new consciousness, a modern consciousness that was emotionally and intellectually sensitive to both internal and external stimuli, and self-conscious and reflective about those stimuli: newly uncertain about the nature and boundaries of the self." *Sensibility in Transformation: Creative Resistance to Sentiment from the Augustans to the Romantics,* ed. Syndy McMillen Conger (Rutherford, N.J.: Fairleigh Dickinson University Press, 1990), 16.

22. Cf. Joan Hinde Stewart, who begins her study *Gynographs: French Novels by Women of the Late Eighteenth Century* (Lincoln: University of Nebraska Press, 1993) by asserting: "None of the novels discussed in this study may be handily categorized as a 'typical' novel of sensibility, for although the novels participate extensively in the conventions of such literature, they often revise or subvert those conventions. A close reading suggests that women organized their understanding of the ambivalence of their status around the concept of *sensibilité,* which they seemingly adopted but routinely

undercut. That is to say, the superficial sentimentality that novels extolled and exalted sometimes masked other, less admissible tendencies. If women writers helped glorify *sensibilité*, they also made legible its symbiosis with oppression" (7). Such a description of sensibility underestimates the complexity and richness of the concept itself, which should not be equated with the "superficial sentimentality" from which Hinde Stewart seeks to dissociate eighteenth-century women's writing.

23. Marie Mulvey Roberts and Roy Porter make a similar point in their introduction to *Literature and Medicine during the Eighteenth Century,* ed. Marie Mulvey Roberts and Roy Porter (London: Routledge, 1993), 1–23.

24. Donatien-Alphonse-François de Sade, "Idée sur les romans," in *Les Crimes de l'amour* (1800), published in English as "Reflections on the Novel," in *The 120 Days of Sodom and Other Writings,* trans. Austryn Wainhouse and Richard Seaver (New York: Grove Press, 1966), 109–11. I have slightly modified the English translation.

25. Barbara Marie Stafford analyzes the period's preoccupation with "visibilizing the invisible" in *Body Criticism: Imaging the Unseen in Enlightenment Art and Medicine* (Cambridge: MIT Press, 1991).

26. Lawrence Rothfield makes some suggestive observations about the "mimetic impulse" that marked both the clinical medicine and the realist novel of the nineteenth century: see his introductory chapter "Medicine and Mimesis" in *Vital Signs: Medical Realism in Nineteenth-Century Fiction* (Princeton: Princeton University Press, 1992), 3–14.

27. Some scholars have urged those interested in either literature and medicine or literature and science as a field to develop a general theory before undertaking further scholarly practice. See particularly the series of essays that G. S. Rousseau has devoted to this issue, including "Medicine and Literature: The State of the Field," *Isis* 72 (1981), 406–24; "Literature and Medicine: Towards a Simultaneity of Theory and Practice," *Literature and Medicine* 5 (1986), 152–81; and "Medicine and Literature: Notes on Their Overlaps and Reciprocities," *Gesnerus* 43 (1986), 33–46. See also Frederick Amrine's "Introduction: The Evolution of Literature and Science as a Discipline," in *Literature and Science as Modes of Expression,* xiii–xxv; Stephen L. Daniel, "Literature and Medicine: In Quest of Method," *Literature and Medicine* 6 (1987), 1–12; and the remarks made by Marie Mulvey Roberts and Roy Porter in *Literature and Medicine during the Enlightenment,* 12–13. Like Roberts and Porter, I would argue that rigorous local practice of the kind of cross-disciplinary analysis involved in "doing" literature and medicine is at least as valuable as theorizing about it in the abstract. See their excellent bibliography of the many articles, books, and essay collections that have appeared in recent years on the interplay between these two fields.

28. John Mullan makes some cogent comments on this problem in *Sentiment and Sociability,* 224–28.

29. Starobinski writes: "The word *interpres* originally signified someone who acts as a mediator in a transaction, a person whose assistance is necessary in order for an object to change hands, on the condition of payment of a fair price. Thus the *interpres* assures a *passage.* At the same time, he assures that the exact value of the exchanged object is recognized, and participates in the transmission process in order to vouch that

the object is passed on to its new owner in its *integrity*." Jean Starobinski, "La Littéra-ture, le texte et l'interprète," in *Faire de l'histoire: Nouvelle approches,* ed. Jacques Le Goff and Pierre Nora (Paris: Gallimard, 1974), 2:180, cited in Josué Harari, *Scenarios of the Imaginary: Theorizing the French Enlightenment* (Ithaca, N.Y.: Cornell University Press, 1987), 24–25. Elaborating on Starobinki's point, Harari proposes a critical ap-proach he calls "transcoding," which I have tried to adopt here.

30. G. S. Rousseau, "Discourses of the Nerve," 51.

Chapter 1: Constructing a Vital Property

1. John Lesch points out that most eighteenth-century physiological researchers were known either as physicians or as naturalists; see *Science and Medicine in France: The Emergence of Experimental Physiology, 1790–1855* (Cambridge: Harvard Univer-sity Press, 1984), 15–16.

2. See Georges Canguilhem's essay "La Constitution de la physiologie comme sci-ence," in *Etudes d'histoire et de philosophie des sciences,* 5th ed. (Paris: Vrin, 1983), 226–73.

3. See John Locke's introduction to *An Essay Concerning Human Understanding* (1689), ed. Peter H. Nidditch (Oxford: Clarendon Press, 1975), 43–48.

4. See Karl M. Figlio's excellent study "Theories of Perception and the Physiology of Mind in the Late Eighteenth Century," *History of Science* 12 (1975), 177–212. See also Gary Hatfield, "Remaking the Science of Mind: Psychology as Natural Science," in *Inventing Human Science: Eighteenth-Century Domains,* ed. Christopher Fox, Roy Porter, and Robert Wokler (Berkeley and Los Angeles: University of California Press, 1995), 184–231.

5. See Lester King's biographical introduction to the reprinted 1786 English trans-lation of Haller's *First Lines of Physiology* (New York: Johnson Reprint Corp., 1966), ix–lxxii.

6. Haller had a prolonged dispute with the English physiologist Robert Whytt over the nature of sentient function; see R. K. French, *Robert Whytt, the Soul, and Med-icine* (London: Wellcome Institute for the History of Medicine, 1969), 63–76, and François Duchesneau, *La Physiologie des Lumières: Empirisme, modèles, et théories* (The Hague: Martinus Nijhoff Publishers, 1982), 171–234. He also opposed Georges-Louis Leclerc de Buffon's ideas on reproduction; see his *Réflexions sur le système de la généra-tion de M. de Buffon* (Geneva, 1751). Finally, he maintained a correspondence with his friend and fellow naturalist Charles Bonnet for nearly twenty-four years; see *The Cor-respondence between Albrecht von Haller and Charles Bonnet,* ed. Otto Sontag (Vienna: Hans Huber Publishers, 1983).

7. Haller had a pronounced personal antipathy toward the original Encyclopedists; see his letter to Bonnet of October 30, 1759, in Sontag, *The Correspondence between Haller and Bonnet,* 179.

8. My citations are taken from the anonymous 1755 English translation of Tissot's translation, reprinted in 1936 with an introduction by Owsei Temkin; see Albrecht von Haller, *A Dissertation on the Sensible and Irritable Parts of Animals* (Baltimore: Johns

Hopkins Press, 1936), hereafter cited as *Diss.* Because the English translation of the *Dissertation* is sometimes incomplete, I have incorporated missing portions of the work in brackets. Those passages, which I have translated, are taken from Haller's expanded, four-volume *Mémoires sur la nature sensible et irritable des parties du corps animal* (Lausanne, 1756–60), hereafter cited as *Mémoires.*

9. Shirley A. Roe, ed., *The Natural Philosophy of Albrecht von Haller* (New York: Arno Press, 1981), vi.

10. On the methodological significance of Haller's work in the history of physiology, see Owsei Temkin's Introduction to *Diss.*, 1–5, and Gerhard Rudolph, "La Méthode hallérienne en physiologie," *Dix-huitième siècle* 23 (1991), 75–84. John Lesch notes that "Haller's physiological writings embodied at least seven distinct research approaches," including experiments with opium that he conducted on himself. Lesch, *Science and Medicine in France,* 20.

11. La Mettrie's dedication to Haller is a striking example of eighteenth-century libertine writing, in that it transforms the study of nature into a properly voluptuous pursuit—with Haller cast as the exemplary "lover" of nature, one intimately acquainted with the stimulating pleasures of the mind. This dedication (not included in most English translations of the treatise) is accompanied by a useful set of commentaries by Paul-Laurent Assoun in *L'Homme machine* (Paris: Editions Denoël/Gonthier, 1981), 85–91.

12. Julien Offray de la Mettrie, *Man a Machine,* trans. Gertrude Bussey and M. W. Calkins (La Salle, Ill.: Open Court Publishing Co., 1943), 149.

13. G. S. Rousseau suggests that Haller's investigations into sensibility were directly influenced by the property's preexisting cultural meanings. Rousseau, "Discourses of the Nerve," in *Literature and Science as Modes of Expression,* ed. Frederick Amrine (Dordrecht: Kluwer Academic Publishers, 1989), esp. 46–48.

14. For various perspectives on this shift, see Thomas Hall, *Ideas of Life and Matter: Studies in the History of General Physiology, 600 B.C.–1900 A.D.* (Chicago: University of Chicago Press, 1969), 2:5–118; Theodore M. Brown, "From Mechanism to Vitalism in Eighteenth-Century English Physiology," *Journal of the History of Biology* 7, no. 2 (1974), 179–216; Sergio Moravia, "From *Homme Machine* to *Homme Sensible*: Changing Eighteenth-Century Models of Man's Image," *Journal of the History of Ideas* 39, no. 1 (1978), 45–60; and Claire Salomon-Bayet, *L'Institution de la science et l'expérience du vivant* (Paris: Flammarion, 1978).

15. Boerhaave combined a practical clinical manner with a modest, Newtonian-style insistence on demonstrating any theory on nature "empirically"—that is, through the highly revered laws of mechanics. See François Duchesneau's analysis of Boerhaave's physiological system in *La Physiologie des Lumières,* 104–16; see also G. A. Lindeboom, *Hermann Boerhaave: The Man and His Work* (London: Methuen, 1968), 264–82. Haller himself offered a nostalgic tribute to his master Boerhaave in the article "Physiologie" that he contributed to the *Supplément* to the *Encyclopédie* (1777; reprint, New York: Pergamon Press, 1969), vol. 5, tome 4, p. 354.

16. See Marie Boas's classic essay "The Establishment of the Mechanical Philoso-

phy," *Osiris* 10 (1952), 412–541. See also Thomas S. Hall's study of how Isaac Newton's scientific and philosophical ideas influenced mid- to late-eighteenth-century physiologists, in "On Biological Analogs of Newtonian Paradigms," *Philosophy of Science* 35, no. 1 (1968), 6–27.

17. In his preface to the *Institutions*, Boerhaave seconds Newton's rejection of the search for first causes, declaring that "it is neither useful, nor necessary, nor even possible for a physician to inquire into them. The physician must follow nothing but what pure and simple experiments have truly demonstrated in anatomy, chemistry, mechanics, and physics." *Institutions de médecine*, trans. Julien Offray de La Mettrie (Paris, 1743–50), 1:14; my translation. Hereafter cited as *Inst.*

18. See G. A. Lindeboom, "Boerhaave's Concept of the Basic Structure of the Body," *Clio Medica* 5 (1970), 203–8.

19. Although Haller was ambivalent toward iatromechanism as a theory, he transcribed virtually unaltered Boerhaave's explanations of such processes as digestion, the humoral composition of the blood, internal feeling, and the composition of nervous liquid; see Duchesneau, *La Physiologie des Lumières*, 103.

20. Albrecht von Haller, *First Lines of Physiology* (New York: Johnson Reprint Corp., 1966), 1:9, hereafter cited as *FL.*

21. Haller later reformulated this idea in his *Elementa physiologiae* as "Fibra enim physiologo id est, quod linea geometrae"—an idea that some commentators have interpreted as proof that he had a fundamentally rationalist, mechanistic bent. François Duchesneau, however, argues that Haller did not use this image to make a literal comparison between geometric bodies and animate bodies, but rather, to isolate the basic physiological component; see *La Physiologie des Lumières*, 130.

22. Trembley's discovery of the polyp in 1740, made not long before Haller wrote the *First Lines of Physiology*, aroused keen interest. See Aram Vartanian, "Trembley's Polyp, La Mettrie, and Eighteenth-Century French Materialism," *Journal of the History of Ideas* 11, no. 3 (1950), 259–86, and Virginia Dawson, *Nature's Enigma: The Problem of the Polyp in the Letters of Bonnet, Trembley, and Réaumur* (Philadelphia: American Philosophical Society, 1987).

23. Haller tells his reader exactly how he conducted each of his physiological assays: by laceration, ligature, burning, pricking with an iron probe, or the application of irritants like "blowing, heat, spirit of wine, the scalpel, *lapis infinalis*, oil of vitriol, and butter of antimony" (*Diss.*, 10). Barbara Stafford underscores the ironies implicit to the sadistic experimental techniques Haller used to find the deep seat of pleasure and pain; see *Body Criticism: Imaging the Unseen in Enlightenment Art and Medicine* (Cambridge: MIT Press, 1991), 411–13.

24. Haller concludes on these grounds that arteries and veins, visceral organs, and glands are insensitive because they are virtually devoid of visible nerve endings (*Diss.*, 37–40). He scornfully refutes Théophile de Bordeu's recently published treatise *Recherches anatomiques sur la position des glandes et sur leur action* (1751), which advanced a staunchly antimechanistic theory of glandular activity based on the idea that

glands have their own way of "sensing" when it is appropriate to react to a secretory stimulus. I examine Bordeu's theories of sensibility and glandular secretion in Chapter 2.

25. It is on these grounds that Haller later condemns the "active sentient principle" proposed by his rival Robert Whytt, whom he accuses of attempting to "reclaim for the soul forces that I find in the body." Haller, "Réponse générale aux objections," *Mémoires*, 4:96; my translation.

26. Figlio, "Theories of Perception," 187. In a separate study, Figlio stresses the "productive ambiguity" inherent in biological concepts like Hallerian irritability and sensibility, noting that thanks to "the investment of different meanings in the same terms, . . . physiological work could proceed in an area burdened with paradox." Figlio, "The Metaphor of Organization: An Historiographical Perspective on the Bio-medical Sciences of the Early Eighteenth Century," *History of Science* 14 (1976), 26.

27. From the very outset of *L'Homme machine*, La Mettrie opposes physicians to theologians, using the argument that "experience and observation should . . . be our only guides here. Both are to be found throughout the records of physicians who were philosophers, and not in the works of the philosophers who were not physicians. The former have traveled through and illuminated the labyrinth of man; they alone have laid bare to us those springs [of life] hidden under the external integument which conceals so many wonders from our eyes" (*Man a Machine*, 88).

28. Aram Vartanian, *La Mettrie's "L'Homme Machine": A Study in the Origins of an Idea* (Princeton: Princeton University Press, 1960), 82. Vartanian nonetheless provides some useful background information on the tense rapport between La Mettrie and Haller and on their shared iatromechanistic heritage (82–89). See also Kathleen Wellman, *La Mettrie: Medicine, Philosophy, and Enlightenment* (Durham, N.C.: Duke University Press, 1992).

29. Haller had already written two letters of protest over being associated with *L'Homme machine* through its dedication; see Paul-Laurent Assoun's summary of this dispute in *L'Homme machine*, 167–70. La Mettrie responded to Haller's complaints with a now-obscure satire entitled "Le Petit Homme à longue queue" (1751), where Haller appears as an aging *roué* fond of supping with prostitutes while discussing the many "marvels" of nature. This work is reprinted with an introduction by Pierre Lemée in *Corpus*, nos. 5/6 (1987), 181–93.

30. Haller's severe assessment of La Mettrie was vigorously seconded by Charles Bonnet, who wrote, "La Mettrie was an excrement of the literary world; but this excrement had an agreable odor for some noses that were not made like yours and mine." Bonnet to Haller, February 7, 1758, in *Correspondence between Haller and Bonnet*, 132; my translation.

31. Haller's correspondent Bonnet expressed reservations about Tissot's "Discours préliminaire," commenting that "he indulged too much in the pleasure of expounding; if only he had limited himself to expounding on the practical consequences [of Haller's experiments]." Bonnet to Haller, January 27, 1755, in *Correspondence between Haller and Bonnet*, 59–60. Bonnet and Haller nonetheless took to heart the special dietary pre-

scriptions Tissot made for scholars in his medical bestseller, *De la santé des gens de lettres*; Bonnet to Haller, June 21, 1768, in *Correspondence*, 759.

32. Figlio, "Theories of Perception," 200.

33. For a useful summary of Boerhaave's and Haller's respective approaches to the common sensorium, along with an overview of the many theories that have been put forth on this subject from antiquity onward, see K. D. Keele's chapter "The Search for the Sensorium Commune," in *Anatomies of Pain* (Springfield, Ill.: Charles C. Thomas, 1957), 55–101. See also Georges Canguilhem's discussion of the function of the common sensorium in eighteenth-century neurology, in *La Formation du concept de réflexe aux XVIIe et XVIIIe siècles*, 2d ed. (Paris: Vrin, 1977), 96–107.

34. This passage is part of d'Alembert's homage to Locke in the *Preliminary Discourse to the Encyclopedia of Diderot*, trans. Richard N. Schwab with the collaboration of Walter E. Rex (Indianapolis: Bobbs-Merrill, 1963), 84.

35. Locke, *An Essay concerning Human Understanding*, bk. 1, ch. 2, p. 2. Later in this work, however, Locke asserts that when the impression of an external object strikes our senses, "'tis evident, that some motion must be thence continued by our Nerves, or animal Spirits, there to *produce in our Minds the particular Ideas we have of them.*" *Essay*, bk. 2, ch. 8, p. 12.

36. Bonnet to Haller, July 25, 1961, in *Correspondence between Haller and Bonnet*, 240; my translation. Haller gave his seal of approval to the recently published *Essai analytique* in his article "Physiologie" for the *Supplément* to the *Encyclopédie*, where he elected Bonnet to the ranks of the most noteworthy physiologists of the day and praised Bonnet's treatise on the soul as "a mechanical explanation of its most hidden functions." *Encyclopédie*, vol. 5, tome 4, p. 359.

37. Condillac was as hesitant as Locke to delve into the physical underpinnings of the mind: although he asserted in the *Traité des sensations* that "I have a sensation when a movement in one of my sense organs is transmitted to the brain," he refused to hazard any further conjectures about the mechanism involved, concluding simply that "these facts authorize me to suppose that our statue, being organized like ourselves, is like us, capable of memory." *Condillac's Treatise on the Sensations*, trans. Geraldine Carr (Los Angeles: School of Philosophy, University of Southern California, 1930), 22. Bonnet did have an English counterpart in his endeavor to fuse philosophy and physiology: Dr. David Hartley devoted his *Observations on Man* (1749) to demonstrating that vibrations in the medullary substance of the nerves and brain are directly associated with ideas in the mind. However, the physical medium underlying Hartley's dual doctrines of vibrations and associationism consisted, not of "fibers," as in Bonnet, but of vessels and circulating fluids—an old hydraulic notion adapted from Newton and Boerhaave.

38. For more on how Bonnet incorporated his early naturalist observations into his later preformationist contemplations on nature, see Lorin Anderson, *Charles Bonnet and the Order of the Known* (Dordrecht: D. Reidel Publishing Co., 1982). For a less sympathetic view, see F. J. Cole's remarks about Bonnet's "perverse" natural philosophy in *Early Theories of Sexual Generation* (Oxford: Clarendon Press, 1930), 86–131,

197–210. On Bonnet's hostility toward the enlightenment program of the Parisian philosophes, see Jacques Marx, *Charles Bonnet contre les Lumières, 1738–1850*, vols. 156–57 of *Studies on Voltaire and the Eighteenth Century* (1976).

39. Bonnet's *Essai de psychologie*, written anonymously in 1751 and published in 1754, is significant for containing the first use in French of the term *psychology*. On the semantic and conceptual evolution of this term, see Georges Canguilhem, "Qu'est-ce que la psychologie?" *Cahiers pour l'analyse*, nos. 1–2 (1966), 77–93. Bonnet frequently mentioned the *Essai de psychologie* in the *Essai analytique sur les facultés de l'âme* but pretended that it had been written by someone else; on his apparent embarrassment over this work, see Anderson, *Charles Bonnet and the Order of the Known*, 16–17. See also John C. O'Neal's discussion of Bonnet in *The Authority of Experience: Sensationist Theory in the French Enlightenment* (University Park: Pennsylvania State University Press, 1996), 62–82.

40. Denis Diderot is usually credited with first proposing this type of "metaphysical anatomy" in his *Lettre sur les sourds et muets* (1751), where he suggests that someone should "decompose a man, so to speak, and consider what he gets from each of the senses he possesses." Diderot, *Oeuvres complètes*, ed. Herbert Dieckmann et al. (Paris: Hermann, 1975–), 4:140. Buffon included a version of this epistemological scenario in the third volume of his *Histoire naturelle* (1750), which preceded Condillac's *Traité des sensations* by four years; see the *Oeuvres philosophiques de Buffon* (Paris: Presses Universitaires de France, 1954), 309–12. A few philosophes actually tried to enact such thought experiments by manipulating the sensory experiences of living subjects who lacked the use of one or more sense organs. The Chevalier de Mérian, for one, proposed a chilling study in which indigent children were to be raised in a state of artificial blindness until adulthood, to determine which abstract ideas they could develop under such conditions; see his *Histoire du problème de Molyneux* of 1772, presented by Alain Grosrichard in "Une Expérience psychologique au dix-huitième siècle," *Cahiers pour l'analyse*, nos. 1–2 (1966), 101–24.

41. Charles Bonnet, *Essai analytique sur les facultés de l'âme* in *Oeuvres d'histoire naturelle et de philosophie* (Neuchâtel, 1779–83), 6:viii, hereafter cited as *EA*. All translations are my own.

42. See also Bonnet's "Essai d'application des principes psychologiques de l'auteur," in *Oeuvres d'histoire naturelle et de philosophie*, 7:97–104.

43. Although Bonnet insists that he struck independently upon the idea of using a fictive Statue-Man to track the "natural" generation of ideas, he acknowledges his debt to Condillac and follows the order used in the *Traité des sensations* (a work that he considers too cursory; *EA*, 7–8).

44. Condillac's use of such analytic terms as *décomposer* and *anatomiser* was purely figurative; he used them to refer to the mental operations that organize sensory "facts" into knowledge. Some scholars have nonetheless underscored the materialist aspects of Condillac's psycho-physiology: see, for example, Sylvain Auroux, "Condillac, inventeur d'un nouveau matérialisme," *Dix-huitième siècle* 24 (1992), 153–63, and Gianni Paganini, "Psychologie et physiologie de l'entendement chez Condillac," ibid., 165–78.

45. In keeping with Condillac, Bonnet asserts that smell is the sense with which one should start a decompositional analysis of sentience and thought (*EA*, 18). Pierre Maine de Biran would later criticize both thinkers for choosing smell as a departure point, arguing that this sense is too primitive to generate the faculty of "modal reminiscence" that must exist for a subject to develop reflection and memory; see *Mémoire sur la décomposition de la pensée* (1805) in Pierre Maine de Biran, *Oeuvres* (Paris: Vrin, 1984), 3:161.

46. See Condillac's explanation of how pleasure and pain function as developmental motors for his Statue-Man, in the *Traité des sensations* (Paris: Fayard, 1984), 18.

47. Bonnet illustrates this point in a curious footnote added to the 1772 edition of the *Essai analytique*, where, speaking of the now-deceased philosophers Leibniz, Wolf, and Haller, he asserts: "The brain of these rare men was a sort of genealogical tree where ideas of all kinds arose through prodigiously numerous natural filiations" (*EA*, 391–92).

48. In his "Analyse abrégée de l'*Essai analytique*," for example, Bonnet muses over what would happen to a human soul stuck in an oyster—or to Newton's stuck in the body of a Californian. He concludes that neither soul could develop its faculties beyond what its restrictive cerebral casing allowed. Bonnet, "Analyse abrégée de l'*Essai analytique* où l'on trouve quelques éclaircissemens sur les principes psychologiques de l'auteur," in *Oeuvres d'histoire naturelle et de philosophie*, 7:21, 24–25.

49. See François Duchesneau's assessment of these physiologists in *La Physiologie des Lumières*, 156–70. The nineteenth-century medical historian Charles Daremberg divided the biomedical theorists of the eighteenth century into two diametrically opposed groups: the "phalanx of true scholars, experimenters, observers, positivist men" who emulated Haller and Morgagni, and the médecins philosophes, who "relied more on their imaginations than their senses." *Histoire des sciences médicales* (Paris: Baillière, 1870), 2:1019; my translation. Elizabeth Williams points out that Daremberg's medical history was part of an ideological effort waged after 1850 "to undermine 'philosophical medicine' in general and vitalism in particular." *The Physical and the Moral: Anthropology, Physiology, and Philosophical Medicine in France, 1750–1850* (Cambridge: Cambridge University Press, 1994), 20–21.

50. Théophile de Bordeu, *Recherches sur l'histoire de la médecine*, in *Oeuvres complètes* (Paris, 1818), 2:668–69; my translation.

51. Xavier Bichat, cited by Duchesneau, *La Physiologie des Lumières*, 362.

52. Ménuret de Chambaud, "Observateur," in *Encyclopédie, ou Dictionnaire raisonné des sciences, des arts et des métiers* (Paris, 1751–65; reprint, New York: Pergamon Press, 1969), vol. 2, tome 11, p. 311.

53. Pierre Fabre, *Essai sur les facultés de l'âme, considérées dans leur rapport avec la sensibilité et l'irritabilité de nos organes* (Paris, 1785), 151–54. See my essay "The *Médecin Philosophe* as Drama Critic: Pierre Fabre's Natural History of French Theatre," *Studies on Voltaire and the Eighteenth Century* 314 (1993), 231–48.

Chapter 2: Sensibility and the Philosophical Medicine of the 1750s–1770s

1. For more on the development of vitalism and organic monism in and around medicine, see Thomas S. Hall, *Ideas of Life and Matter: Studies in the History of General Physiology, 600 B.C.–1900 A.D.* (Chicago: University of Chicago Press, 1969), 2:5–118; Karl Figlio, "The Historiography of Scientific Medicine," *Comparative Studies in Society and History* 19 (1977), 262–86; Figlio, "The Metaphor of Organization: An Historiographical Perspective on the Bio-medical Sciences of the Early Eighteenth Century," *History of Science* 14 (1976), 17–53; Jacques Roger, *Les Sciences de la vie dans la pensée française au XVIIIe siècle* (Paris: Albin Michel, 1963), 457–779; Georges Gusdorf, "Le Progrès de la conscience médicale," in *Dieu, la nature, l'homme au siècle des Lumières* (Paris: Payot, 1972), 424–525; Sergio Moravia, "From *Homme Machine* to *Homme Sensible*: Changing Eighteenth-Century Models of Man's Image," *Journal of the History of Ideas* 39, no. 1 (1978), 45–60; and Elizabeth Haigh, "Vitalism, the Soul, and Sensibility: The Physiology of Théophile Bordeu," *Journal of the History of Medicine* 31 (January 1976), 30–41.

2. Dr. Anne-Charles Lorry, for example, published a two-volume *Essai sur les aliments, pour servir de commentaire aux livres diétiques d'Hippocrates* (Paris, 1757) to update ancient hygienic prescriptions for the benefit of the contemporary public.

3. François Boissier de la Croix de Sauvages is generally cited as the Montpellier professor who taught Stahlianism most enthusiastically, in order to support his argument that medicine would be more effective if physicians viewed and classified diseases as excesses or deficits in vital force. See two articles by Lester S. King: "Boissier de Sauvages and Eighteenth-Century Nosology," *Bulletin of the History of Medicine* 11 (1966), 43–51, and "Stahl and Hoffmann: A Study in Eighteenth-Century Animism," *Journal of the History of Medicine* 19 (1964), 118–30. Also see François Duchesneau, *La Physiologie des Lumières: Empirisme, modèles, et théories* (The Hague: Martinus Nijhoff Publishers, 1982), 1–31 and 361–430.

4. See William Coleman, "Health and Hygiene in the *Encyclopédie:* A Medical Doctrine for the Bourgeoisie," *Journal of the History of Medicine* 29 (October 1974), 399–421; Matthew Ramsey, "The Popularization of Medicine in France, 1650–1700," in *The Popularization of Medicine, 1650–1850*, ed. Roy Porter (London: Routledge, 1992), 97–133; J. P. Goubert, ed., *La Médicalisation de la société française, 1770–1830* (Waterloo, Ont.: Historical Reflections Press, 1982); Toby Gelfand, "The Decline of the Ordinary Practitioner and the Rise of the Modern Medical Profession," in *Doctors, Patients, and Society: Power and Authority in Medical Care*, ed. M. S. Staum and D. E. Larsen (Waterloo, Ont.: Historical Reflections Press, 1981), 106–29; and Colin Jones, "Montpellier Medical Students and the Medicalisation of 18th-Century France," in *Problems and Methods in the History of Medicine*, ed. Roy Porter and Andrew Wear (London: Croom Helm, 1987), 57–80.

5. That reform movement was the subject of numerous historical studies during the 1960s and 1970s. See, for example, Michel Foucault, *Naissance de la clinique* (Paris:

Presses Universitaires de France, 1963); François Dagognet, *Le Catalogue de la vie* (Paris: Presses Universitaires de France, 1970); Jean-Pierre Peter, "Malade et maladies à la fin du XVIIIème siècle," *Annales E.S.C.* 22, no. 4 (1967), 711–51, and "Les Mots et les objets de la maladie: Remarques sur les épidémies et la médecine dans la société française du XVIIIème siècle," *Revue historique* 246 (1971), 13–38; the collective work *Médecins, climat, et épidémies à la fin du XVIIIème siècle* (Paris: Mouton et Ecole Pratique des Hautes Etudes, 1972) by the *Annales* historians Jean-Paul Desaive, Jean-Pierre Goubert, Emmanuel Le Roy Ladurie, Jean Meyer, Otto Muller, and Jean-Pierre Peter; and Caroline Hannaway, "The Société Royale de Médecine and Epidemics in the Ancien Régime," *Bulletin of the History of Medicine* 46 (1972), 257–73. A more recent study is James C. Riley's *The Eighteenth-Century Campaign to Avoid Disease* (Basingstoke, Hampshire: Macmillan, 1987).

6. See, for example, Sergio Moravia, "Philosophie et médecine à la fin du XVIIIème siècle," *Studies on Voltaire and the Eighteenth Century* 89 (1972), 1089–1151; George Rosen, "The Philosophy of Ideology and the Emergence of Modern Medicine in France," *Bulletin of the History of Medicine* 20, no. 2 (1946), 328–39; Owsei Temkin, "The Philosophical Background of Magendie's Physiology," *Bulletin of the History of Medicine* 20, no. 1 (1946), 10–35; and the chapter entitled "Medicine and Ideology: The Methodology and Epistemology of the Sensationalists" in Elizabeth Haigh's *Xavier Bichat and the Medical Theory of the Eighteenth Century* (London: Wellcome Institute for the History of Medicine, 1984), 66–86. As Elizabeth A. Williams notes in her introduction to *The Physical and the Moral: Anthropology, Physiology, and Philosophical Medicine in France, 1750–1850* (Cambridge: Cambridge University Press, 1994), 1–3, the "philosophical" or "anthropological" medicine that became prevalent during the Revolution and the postrevolutionary era has a history that began some forty to fifty years earlier with the Montpellier vitalists.

7. See Philippe Pinel's introductions to *Nosographie philosophique, ou La Méthode de l'analyse appliquée à la médecine* (1797), 5th ed. (Paris, 1813), i–cxx, and *Traité médico-philosophique sur l'aliénation mentale, ou La Manie* (Paris, 1800), v–lvi. See Cabanis's "Histoire physiologique des sensations," in *Rapports du physique et du moral de l'homme* (1802; reprint, Geneva: Slatkine Reprints, 1980), 102–80.

8. Useful historical accounts of the Montpellier physicians who dominated medicine at this time include Paul Delaunay, *Le Monde médical parisien au dix-huitième siècle* (Paris: Jules Rousset, 1905); Louis Dulieu, *La Médecine à Montpellier* (Avignon: Presses Universelles, 1975); Roger, *Les Sciences de la vie dans la pensée française au XVIIIe siècle*, 585–682; Haigh, *Xavier Bichat*, 15–65; and Elizabeth A. Williams's chapter "Montpellier Vitalism and The Science of Man" in *The Physical and the Moral*, 20–66.

9. It should be noted that the sensible organizing principle to which the Montpellier vitalists subscribed was not synonymous with the nervous system: their notion of sensibility was more diffuse than that of their British counterparts, whom Christopher Lawrence discusses in "The Nervous System and Society in the Scottish Enlightenment," in *Natural Order: Historical Studies of Scientific Culture*, ed. Barry Barnes and Steven Shapin (Beverly Hills, Calif.: Sage Publications, 1979), 19–40. Lawrence makes

a provocative analogy between the theory of sympathetic sensibility elaborated by such Scottish medical thinkers as Whytt, Cullen, and Brown and the hierarchical vision that the Edinburgh intellectual elite held of their community. In France, however, one can find no such neat homology between the model of the sensible body and images of the social body, primarily because, as Lawrence observes (34–35), the notion of sensibility that predominated there was not so neurally centralized.

10. Claude-Nicolas Le Cat, *Traité des sensations et des passions en général, et des sens en particulier* (Paris, 1767), 89–93, 206. See also the peculiar work attributed to Le Cat entitled *Mémoire posthume sur les incendies spontanés de l'économie animale* (Paris, 1813).

11. Théophile de Bordeu, *Recherches sur les maladies chroniques* (1775), in *Oeuvres complètes de Bordeu* (Paris, 1818), 2:806.

12. See Marin-Jacques-Clair Robert, *Traité des principaux objets de la médecine* (Paris, 1766), xxvii.

13. Ménuret de Chambaud, "Oeconomie animale," in *Encyclopédie, ou Dictionnaire raisonné des sciences, des arts et des métiers* (Paris, 1751–65; reprint, New York: Pergamon Press, 1969), vol. 2, tome 11, pp. 360–61. Hereafter cited as "OA." Ménuret includes a cross-reference to the *Encyclopédie*'s entry for "Sensibilité" at this point in his discussion, one of many instances of his use of such cross-references. The way in which the Montpellier medical Encyclopedists made use of such cross-indexing to highlight sensibility and philosophical medicine is discussed later in this chapter.

14. The full title of Lacaze's treatise is *Idée de l'homme physique et moral, pour servir d'introduction à un traité de médecine* (Paris, 1755). Hereafter cited as "Lacaze."

15. Claude-Nicolas Le Cat also equated the "ethereal" fluid in the nerves and semen with the substance in fire, light, and electricity; see his *Traité de l'existence, de la nature et des propriétés du fluide des nerfs, et principalement de son action dans le mouvement musculaire* (Berlin, 1753), 37–38. Many natural philosophers—especially those who favored the theory of epigenesis, like Buffon (who is quoted on this point by Lacaze, 74)—maintained that both sexes have semen. In *De la nature*, 3 vols. (Amsterdam, 1761–64), Jean-Baptiste-René Robinet went so far as to elaborate a whole cosmology of semen, which he believed could be detected throughout nature, in rocks and other inanimate bodies as well as in animals. On eighteenth-century epigenesis and seminalist theories, see Roger, *Les Sciences de la vie*, 457–528 and 642–51.

16. Several scholars have singled out Lacaze's work as central in some manner. Despite his well-founded reservations about Lacaze's originality, Jacques Roger observes that "Lacaze was apparently the first to have dared to shake off the yoke of medical mechanism, in a book published in Paris." *Les Sciences de la vie*, 639. François Azouvi describes Lacaze's treatise as a landmark in the growing identification between pathology and femininity; see "La Femme comme modèle de la pathologie au XVIIIème siècle," *Diogènes* 115 (1971), 25–40. See also Jean Starobinski, "La Vie et les aventures du mot 'réaction,'" *Modern Language Review* 70 (1975), xxi–xxxi; Marion Hobson, "Sensibilité et spectacle: Le contexte médical du *Paradoxe sur le comédien* de Diderot," *Revue de Métaphysique et de Morale* 82, no. 2 (1977), 145–64; and Williams, *The Physical and the Moral*, 41–45.

17. Henri Fouquet, "Sensibilité, Sentiment (Médecine)," in *Encyclopédie*, vol. 3, tome 15, p. 38.

18. Fouquet ends his article with a diatribe, inspired in part by Robert Whytt's critique of Haller's *Mémoires*, against the cruel vivisections that had been the basis of Haller's laboratory assays of sensibility (ibid., 52). See Haller's response in his entry on sensibility in the *Supplément* to the *Encyclopédie*, vol. 5, tome 4, pp. 776–79.

19. Bordeu describes this episode in a letter written in May 1754 to his mother: see letter 128 in Théophile de Bordeu, *Correspondance*, ed. Martha Fletcher (Montpellier: Presses de l'Université Paul Valéry, 1977), 2:114–19. See also the letters from Lacaze that immediately precede and follow this letter (ibid., pp. 114 and 120–21), and Martha Fletcher's biographical comments (pp. 69–71).

20. This article was a reprinted version of Bordeu's *Recherches sur les crises*, first written in 1743; see Bordeu, *Oeuvres complètes* (Paris, 1818), 1:237.

21. In his *Recherches sur les maladies chroniques* (1775), Bordeu developed the idea of therapeutic crisis expressed some twenty years earlier in his *Encyclopédie* article "Crise" and asserted that chronic diseases could be "simplified" by the physician into more treatable acute illnesses that would resolve themselves critically. The process Bordeu proposed for this conversion involved using specific mineral waters, whose sources were located in his native region of Béarn, where (not incidentally) his father practiced as both a physician and a spa director; see Bordeu, *Correspondance*, 1:205–10.

22. This is the position taken by William Coleman in "Health and Hygiene in the *Encyclopédie*." Coleman emphasizes the series of *Encyclopédie* articles devoted to hygiene, most of which were written by Arnulfe d'Aumont, another graduate of the Montpellier medical faculty.

23. Wilda Anderson, *Diderot's Dream* (Baltimore: Johns Hopkins University Press, 1990), 91–124, provides a perceptive analysis of the article "Encyclopédie," where Diderot explains the cross-referencing system that he built into the work.

24. Ménuret signed seventy of his articles by name or with an *m*. The rest of the articles that can be attributed to him are either referred to as his in other articles or are extremely similar in style and theme to those known to be his. My count of his contributions corresponds to that given in R. N. Schwab and W. E. Rex, eds., "Inventory of Diderot's *Encyclopédie*," *Studies on Voltaire and the Eighteenth Century* 93 (1972), 216–17. Jacques Roger was one of the first scholars to emphasize Ménuret's role in the *Encyclopédie*; see *Les Sciences de la vie*, 631–41. See also Maxime Laignel-Lavastine, "Les Médecins collaborateurs de *l'Encyclopédie*," *Revue d'histoire des sciences* 4 (1951), 353–58, and Pierre Astruc, "Les Sciences médicales et leurs représentants dans *l'Encyclopédie*," ibid., 359–68.

25. "Séméiotique," in *Encyclopédie*, vol. 2, tome 14, p. 937. Hereafter cited as "Sém."

26. Ménuret, "Prognostic," ibid., vol. 3, tome 13, p. 429.

27. "Observation," ibid., vol. 2, tome 11, pp. 313–23. The *m* signature that designates Ménuret as an author in the *Encyclopédie* appears only at the end of "Observations thérapeutiques"; that entry, however, is a continuation of the main article "Observation" in both style and format.

28. This part of Ménuret's discussion reflects the methodological debate that was then raging over the virtues of experimental investigative methods in natural philosophy. See, by contrast, d'Alembert's article "Expérimental," ibid. vol. 5, tome 6, pp. 298–301, which was written to praise the king's recent establishment of a university chair in experimental physics. See also Haller's *Supplément* article "Oeconomie animale," ibid., vol. 5, tome 4, pp. 104–5, in which he defends vivisectionist experimentation in physiology.

29. See aphorisms 15–27 of *De l'interprétation de la nature* (1753), in *Oeuvres philosophiques de Diderot* (Paris: Garnier, 1964), 189–95. Diderot, in fact, takes a much more qualified view of the philosophical potential of observation alone: he speaks sarcastically of the plodding, unimaginative observer who "will spend his whole life observing insects, without seeing anything new" (190), and praises instead the "spirit of divination by which one sniffs out [*subodore*], so to speak, unknown procedures, new experiments, unknown results" (197).

30. "Pouls," in *Encyclopédie*, vol. 3, tome 13, pp. 205–40.

31. Ménuret de Chambaud, *Nouveau traité du pouls* (Paris, 1768), ix.

32. *Recherches sur le pouls par rapport aux crises*, in *Oeuvres complètes de Bordeu*, 1:421. A very similar passage appears in "Pouls," 237–38. Bordeu's discovery of the natural principles of diagnostic pulse-taking was prompted, as he recounts, by stumbling upon a recently translated foreign treatise on pulses, M. Nihell's annotated version of the observations of Solano de Luques, an early-eighteenth-century Spanish physician. Bordeu, however, recasts the practice to fit the new Montpellier doctrine of the reactive animal economy and insists that the pulse is a phenomenon of sensibility, not motility. Interestingly, in his overview of existing work on pulses, Bordeu cites Glisson, Wepfer, Baglivi, and Hecquet but deliberately leaves out Haller, who had by then been widely heralded as the greatest living authority on the question.

33. Bordeu devotes the first five chapters of the *Recherches sur le pouls* to explaining how he devised a nomenclature of pulses that would take into account the anatomical architechtonics of the body—that is, the upper/lower axis at the diaphragm and the right/left axis—as well as the natural variations caused by age, sex, and temperament. He maintains that each body type and temperament has its own natural pulse which evolves with age; hence this assertion about the female pulse: "The natural pulse of women is, in general, more *lively* and closer to that of children and youth, than is the pulse of men; it has its particular degrees, *its youth, its middle age, its old age*." Ibid., 262.

34. Ibid., 263.

35. Bordeu, *Recherches sur l'histoire de la médecine*, in *Oeuvres complètes*, 2:663. Haller's disciple J. G. Zimmermann presented a similar portrait of the "enlightened" physician in his well-known treatise *On Experience in the Medical Art* [*Von der Ehfahrung in der Arzneykunst*], of 1763–64. Owsei Temkin analyzes this work in "Zimmermann's Philosophy of the Physician," in *The Double Face of Janus and Other Essays in the History of Medicine* (Baltimore: Johns Hopkins University Press, 1977), 239–45.

36. Bordeu, *Recherches sur l'histoire de la médecine*, 680–84. Although Bordeu praises Montesquieu as a great philosophical thinker, he undertakes in his *Recherches sur*

l'histoire de la médecine to correct the rigid physiological determination that informed Montesquieu's system. Paul Hoffmann emphasizes this aspect of Bordeu's thinking in "L'Idée de liberté dans la philosophie médicale de Théophile de Bordeu," *Studies on Voltaire and the Eighteenth Century* 88 (1972), 769–87.

37. An interesting example of the up-to-the-minute philosophical bent of the Montpellier physicians is found in the *Encyclopédie* article "Spasme," in which Ménuret de Chambaud discusses the epidemic of convulsions that overtook certain fervent members of the Jansenist sect after the closing of the Parisian cemetery of Saint-Médard in 1732; he refers his readers to Philippe Hecquet's medical treatise on the subject, *Le Naturalisme des convulsions* (1733). For more on this odd epidemic, see Georges Benrekessa, "Hystérie, 'crises' et convulsions au XVIIIe siècle: Age des Lumières, éclipses du sujet," *Revue des sciences humaines* 208, no. 4 (1987), 113–40, and Cathérine Laurence-Maire, *Les Convulsionnaires de Saint-Médard: Miracles, convulsions et prophètes à Paris au XVIIIe siècle* (Paris: Gallimard, 1985).

38. See, for example, François Dagognet, *La Maîtrise du vivant* (Paris: Hachette, 1988), especially the chapter "L'Obstacle naturaliste," 15–48. See also Clément Rosset, *L'Anti-nature* (Paris: Presses Universitaires de France, 1973), esp. 275–308.

39. Georges Canguilhem defends the historical role that vitalism has played in the ongoing evolution of biomedical theory; see his essay "Quelques aspects du vitalisme" in *La Connaissance de la vie*, 2d ed. (Paris: Vrin, 1985), 83–100. See also Judith Schlanger's *Les Métaphores de l'organisme* (Paris: Vrin, 1971).

40. Charles Daremberg, *Histoire des sciences médicales* (Paris: Ballière, 1870), 2:1015, 1157. Although Daremberg attacks a whole list of eighteenth- and nineteenth-century physician-philosophers, including Tissot, Pomme, Richerand (Bordeu's editor), and Cabanis, his prime target is Pierre Roussel, Bordeu's student and hand-picked intellectual successor.

41. Jean Senebier, *Essai sur l'art d'observer*, 2d ed. (Geneva, 1802), 187.

42. See, for example, Herbert Dieckmann's classic essay "Théophile Bordeu und Diderots *Rêve de d'Alembert*," *Romanische Forshungen* 52 (1938), 55–122. Dieckmann rightly concludes that Bordeu was an important source of Diderot's conviction that natural philosophers had to find ways of interrogating nature that were free of mechanistic thinking (66–67). However, Dieckmann discusses only one brief passage from the *Rêve* in any detail and does not address the issue of how Bordeu's specific ideas are creatively adapted by Diderot. See also Jean Varloot's introduction to the *Rêve de d'Alembert* in Denis Diderot, *Le Neveu de Rameau / Le Rêve de d'Alembert* (Paris: Editions Sociales, 1972), 186–227.

43. Yvon Belaval reads the *Rêve* as an audaciously ironic joke on the real-life d'Alembert and Mlle. de l'Espinasse; see "Les Protagonistes du *Rêve de d'Alembert*," *Diderot Studies* 3 (1961), 27–53.

44. *Recherches anatomiques sur la position des glandes et sur leur action*, in Bordeu, *Oeuvres complètes*, 1:36–208, hereafter cited as *Glandes*.

Martha Fletcher, the editor of Bordeu's *Correspondance*, describes the *Recherches sur les glandes* as "a 'bomb' of 520 pages launched against the mechanists who formed a compact majority at the Faculty of Paris." Bordeu, *Correspondance*, 2:69. Bordeu's letters are indeed full of references to the strategies he used to garner the most attention, even negative attention, for his publications.

45. Curiously, Bordeu ascribes the same sexualized capriciousness to cows as well as women: "Those who have often seen cows being milked, or who have been curious enough to undertake to do it themselves, must have noticed that, as shepherds put it, not everyone has the *knack for it*. One should not go and squeeze the teat harshly, but rather tickle it softly and stretch it; one then sees the cow settle into her position, spread her thighs a bit, and the milk flows marvelously" (*Glandes*, 128). He then recounts the old farmers' tale that some nasty cows have been known to refuse to nurse their calves after being "seduced" by snakes: "It is a received truth in the Pyrenees that snakes have the talent of tickling cows so well that, once cows have (as they say) sampled these animals, they cannot stand the presence either of their calf or of the farmer who comes to milk them; there may be some exaggeration in that story" (129).

46. François Duchesneau proposes the term "machina nervosa" to describe Bordeu's model of the organism and examines the objections that were made against this model by both Haller and Bordeu's primary successor at Montpellier, Paul Joseph Barthez; see *La Physiologie des Lumières*, 361–430.

47. The tendency to deemphasize this aspect of Bordeu's biomedical theory is evident in Haigh, "Vitalism, the Soul, and Sensibility"; Roselyne Rey, "La Théorie de la sécrétion chez Bordeu, modèle de la physiologie et de la pathologie vitalistes," *Dix-huitième siècle* 23 (1991), 45–58; and Duchesneau, *La Physiologie des Lumières*, 361–84.

48. An even more curious reformulation of this scenario appears in Bordeu's "Analyse médicinale du sang," this time in an interuterine setting:

One can also argue that the embryo rubs himself against the internal surface of the womb, and that he licks it, so to speak, or rather that he sucks it until the point that, being pressed up against it, he flatters and tickles the womb continuously. The orgasm of the womb and the *incubatory* effort increase in relation to this process. It is this effort that inspires Nature's decision to develop milk in the womb over the course of the pregnancy . . . Just as the embryo must solicit the womb during pregnancy, so too, the infant must keep the breasts spellbound as he nurses; without this regular source of irritation, the womb returns to the daily work of menstruation, and to the passion of the preparative measures related to procreation, of which the passion for forming milk is, so to speak, a part. All of these phenomena are directed by the sensible system and by the vital flame. It is up to anatomists to discover the paths and organs involved in these functions. (Bordeu, *Recherches sur les maladies chroniques*, 953–54)

49. Denis Diderot, *Le Rêve de d'Alembert*, in *Oeuvres complètes*, ed. Herbert Dieckmann et al. (Paris: Hermann, 1987), 17:154, hereafter cited as *RA*. Curiously, the editor of this edition, Jean Varloot, interprets this scene as proof that "it is the gentlemanly Bordeu, sparing of technical words, an obliging but rigorous interpreter, whom Diderot recalled when creating his character" (*RA*, 36).

50. At the end of *Recherches sur les glandes,* Bordeu mentions a third system of bodily coordination that resides in what he calls "the cellular tissue" (*Glandes,* 208). He would develop that idea fully in the *Recherches sur le tissu muqueux ou l'organe cellulaire, et sur quelques maladies de la poitrine* (1767), in Bordeu, *Oeuvres complètes,* 2:735–96.

51. Denis Diderot, *Rameau's Nephew and D'Alembert's Dream,* trans. Leonard Tancock (London: Penguin, 1966), 217; RA, 185. The English translation is hereafter cited as *Dream.*

52. Diderot repeats this point (and its illustration) in the chapter "Volonté," in *Eléments de physiologie,* ed. Jean Mayer (Paris: Librairie Marcel Didier, 1964), 263–65.

53. "They eat every day at the same hour; they get up and go to bed at designated hours; they get hungry at fixed times; they awake and go to sleep at precise hours; and what is most remarkable is that, if they happen to miss the moment that has been appointed for one of their functions, they find their systems upset until they have resumed their usual schedule" (*Glandes,* 185–86).

54. On Maupertuis's monadology, see Duchesneau, *La Physiologie des Lumières,* 243–58.

55. On Diderot's use of this conceptual metaphor, see Anderson, *Diderot's Dream,* 53–58; Aram Vartanian, "Diderot and the Phenomenology of the Dream," *Diderot Studies* 8 (1966), 245–46; and Jacques Chouillet, *Diderot, poète de l'énergie* (Paris: Presses Universitaires de France, 1984), 226–44.

56. Wilda Anderson, "Diderot's Laboratory of Sensibility," *Yale French Studies* 67 (1984), 72–91; Anderson, "Good, Solid Philosophy," in *Diderot's Dream,* 42–76. See also Rosalina de la Carrera's complementary reading of the *Rêve de d'Alembert* in *Success in Circuit Lies: Diderot's Communicational Practice* (Stanford: Stanford University Press, 1991), 127–66.

57. Aram Vartanian observes that "as occasion demands, d'Alembert becomes Diderot, Diderot becomes Bordeu, Bordeu becomes d'Alembert, and so on. One is tempted to say that each of them has surrendered a portion of his separate existence, and now functions 'organologically' in a sort of intellectual continuum." Vartanian, "Diderot and the Phenomenology of the Dream," 239. Although Vartanian is wrong to leave Mlle. de l'Espinasse out of the process of intellectual and physical convergence that occurs in the *Rêve de d'Alembert,* he offers a suggestive interpretation of how Diderot exploits the dream state to put forth a new vision of science and natural philosophy.

58. Anderson, *Diderot's Dream,* 39. Anderson's stauchly antivitalist reading of Diderot's materialism is compelling but not fully satisfying: she generates her basic model of Diderotian sensibility almost entirely out of the the the brute physical principle of elasticity that Diderot discusses in the early text *De l'interprétation de la nature.* Although she is correct to note that biological reflection is largely absent from *De l'interprétation de la nature,* that point is far more difficult to maintain about texts like the *Rêve de d'Alembert.* And while Diderot did, as Anderson emphasizes, insist that there is a natural continuum between the behavior of matter at the preorganic "molecular" stage and the phenomenon of sensibility at the organic and intellectual levels, his explo-

rations into physiology cannot be fully explained by a single physico-chemical theory. For a different view of Diderot's materialism, see M. Wartofsky, "Diderot and the Development of Material Monism," *Diderot Studies* 2 (1952), 279–329, especially his discussion of how Diderot diverges from both consistently mechanistic materialists like d'Holbach and vitalist materialists like Maupertuis.

59. "He was holding his right hand to make it look like the tube of a microscope, and his left, I think, represented the mouth of some receptacle. He looked down the tube into the receptacle and said: 'That Voltaire can joke as much as he likes, but the Eelmonger [Needham] is right; I believe my own eyes, and I can see them, and what a lot of them there are darting to and fro and wriggling about!' . . . He compared the receptacle, in which he could see so many instantaneous births, to the universe, and in a drop of water he could see the history of the world . . . Then he went on: 'In Needham's drop of water everything begins and ends in the twinkling of an eye'" (*Dream*, 173–74; *RA*, 127–28).

60. For another interpretation of how knowledge is quite literally embodied in the *Rêve de d'Alembert* and other texts by Diderot, see Daniel Brewer, *The Discourse of Enlightenment in Eighteenth-Century France: Diderot and the Art of Philosophizing* (Cambridge: Cambridge University Press, 1993), 168–203.

61. When Mlle. de l'Espinasse is told by Bordeu that "it would be useful to strip you of your present organization" in order to demonstrate his lesson on the inception of organic sensations, she enthusiastically replies: "If it became customary to go out into the street stark naked I should not be the first nor the last to conform. So treat me just as you like, so long as I can learn" (*Dream*, 189; *RA*, 148).

62. Dr. Bordeu will, however, later exclaim with evident irritation: "Aha! Having been a man for four minutes you take to your cap and petticoats and go all feminine again" (*Dream*, 230; *RA*, 202).

63. Wilda Anderson attributes Dr. Bordeu's unwitting sexual seduction to his mistaken belief that he is "'all mind'—only a diagnosing doctor who sees the phenomenon and analyzes it but is not affected by it . . . In the *Rêve*, Bordeu, in spite of his vision of himself, is at least as responsive to Mlle de l'Espinasse as she is to him. He simply does not realize it, because he knows to be aware of invasion [by sensibility] on the physical level, but he has been seduced by the growing acuity of her responses on the intellectual level. Ironically, it is on the intellectual level, where he diagnoses, that he has so superbly trained himself to be sensitive" (*Diderot's Dream*, 72). I will return to Diderot's two-level use of sensibility while discussing *La Religieuse* in Chapter 5.

64. This includes, of course, the various monstrous beings discussed by d'Alembert, Dr. Bordeu, and Mlle. de l'Espinasse (*RA*, 161–62, 167). On this subject see Emita Hill, "Materialism and Monsters in *Le Rêve de d'Alembert*," *Diderot Studies* 10 (1968), 67–93. See also Michel Baridon's analysis of how the interlocutors' very voices function as scientific instruments, in "L'Imaginaire scientifique et la voix humaine dans *Le Rêve de d'Alembert*," in *L'Encyclopédie, Diderot, l'esthétique: Mélanges en hommage à Jacques Chouillet*, ed. Sylvain Auroux, Dominique Bourel, and Charles Porset (Paris: Presses Universitaires de France, 1991), 113–21.

65. See, for example, Anderson, *Diderot's Dream*, 56–62.

66. Leo Spitzer, "The Style of Diderot," in *Linguistics and Literary History* (New York: Russell and Russell, 1962), 135–91.

67. Jean Starobinski, "Le Philosophe, le géomètre, l'hybride," *Poétique* 21 (1975), 8–23.

Chapter 3: The Medicalization of Enlightenment

1. Peter Gay, "The Enlightenment as Medicine and as Cure," in *The Age of Enlightenment: Studies Presented to Theodore Besterman*, ed. W. H. Barber (Edinburgh: St. Andrews University Publications, 1967), 375–86. Gay asserts that "medicine was philosophy at work; philosophy was medicine for the individual and for society" (380); he does not, however, delve into the way that eighteenth-century French medicine was shaped by its convergence with contemporary philosophy.

2. Enlightenment philosophes of the progressionist school generally spoke of perfectibility in terms of advancing the natural progress of reason in the human race. See for example the history of human progress that Turgot sketches in his "Second Discours, sur les progrès successifs de l'esprit humain" (1750), in *Oeuvres de Turgot* (Paris, 1844), 2:597–611. See also Michel Baridon, "Les Concepts de nature humaine et de perfectibilité dans l'historiographie des Lumières de Fontenelle à Condorcet," in *L'Histoire au dix-huitième siècle: Actes du Colloque d'Aix-en-Provence* (Aix-en-Provence: Edisud, 1980), 353–74.

3. Antoine Le Camus, *La Médecine de l'esprit* (Paris, 1769), 2d ed., 2 vols. Hereafter cited as *Méd.*

4. A translation of the two essays that comprise *De regimine mentis* appears in J. L. Rather's *Mind and Body in Eighteenth-Century Medicine: A Study Based on Jerome Gaub's "De regimine mentis"* (Berkeley and Los Angeles: University of California Press, 1965).

5. Gaub bitterly denounces La Mettrie at the outset of his 1763 essay as "a little Frenchman—a Mimus or Momus?—[who] brought forth a repulsive offspring, to wit, his mechanical man, not long after sitting before this chair and hearing me speak" (Gaub, 115).

6. Le Camus is less optimistic about the question of whether scholars can really achieve such a balance in their vital fluids in his "Mémoire sur le cerveau, où l'on développe le principe de la génération": he asserts here that, because lovemaking requires robust subjects who are not using their vital cerebro-seminal in higher activities, "men of letters are not very fertile and are ill-suited to sexual activity. They dissipate their spirits in study and use their brain for another purpose . . . The Philosophes who have sought to raise their souls to the most sublime contemplations have avoided all commerce with women." *Mémoire sur divers sujets de médecine* (Paris, 1760), 45.

7. All of society's institutions, asserts Le Camus, contribute to the "extinction of the beautiful species" of men. "Mémoire sur la conservation des hommes bien faits," in *Mémoire sur divers sujet de médecine*, 297.

8. Charles Augustin Vandermonde, *Essai sur la manière de perfectionner l'espèce humaine* (Paris, 1756), xvi, hereafter cited as *Essai*.

9. Another notable eighteenth-century treatise on procreative techniques was Michel Procope-Couteau's semifacetious *L'Art de faire des garçons par M. *** (Docteur en Médecine à l'Université de Montpellier)* (1748), 2d ed. (Montpellier, 1755). Procope-Couteau suggested that couples who wanted to produce a male child should lean toward the right testicle and ovary while making love; this would direct the vital spirits to the proper, "masculine" side, whereas leaning to the left would necessarily produce a girl. A later treatise written in this recipe-like vein was L. J. M. Robert's *Essai sur la mégalantrogénésie, ou L'Art de faire des enfants d'esprit qui deviennent de grands hommes* (Paris, 1801). For more on the eighteenth-century interest in producing superior offspring, see Jocelyne Livi, "La Cuisine de la procréation," in *Vapeurs de femmes: Essai historique sur quelques fantasmes médicaux et philosophiques* (Quentiny-Dijon: Navarin, 1984), 34–47, and Jean-Louis Fischer, "La Callipédie, ou L'Art de faire de beaux enfants," *Dix-huitième siècle*, no. 23 (1991), 141–58.

10. Vandermonde is uncommonly egalitarian in his views concerning enlightenment for the lower classes as well: he asserts that peasants are inferior to their more cultivated urban counterparts only in the breadth of their sensations—not, he emphasizes, in their basic constitution of mind (*Essai*, 287–88).

11. Pierre Roussel mentions both Vandermonde and Le Camus in his lengthy overview of the new philosophically minded generation of medical theorists; see the preface to his *Système physique et moral de la femme* (Paris, 1775), xxiii–xxvii.

12. Le Camus is included on the list of "authors I must read" that Diderot made in 1778 as he was assembling his personal compendium of physiological principles; see Jean Mayer's remarks on Le Camus in his introduction to the *Eléments de physiologie* (Paris: Librairie Marcel Didier, 1964), xlvii–xlviii, hereafter cited as *EP*. See also Roselyne Rey, "Diderot et la médecine de l'esprit," in *Colloque international Diderot (1713–1784)*, ed. Anne-Marie Chouillet (Paris: Aux amateurs des livres, 1985), 287–96.

13. Diderot espouses a theory of mind and body quite similar to that propounded by Gaub and Le Camus: "Is the soul happy, sad, angry, tender, secretive, or voluptuous? *it is nothing without the body; I defy anyone to explain anything without the body*" (*EP*, 58; my emphasis). However, he also observes at the end of the *Eléments de physiologie* that "all sensations, all affections being corporal, it follows that there is a physical medicine that is equally applicable to the body and to the soul; but I believe it to be almost impracticable, because the only way of preventing the dangers of such a practice would be to bring a fully perfected physiology to bear upon the relation between the whole and the organs, between the organs and their correspondence: in a word, one would almost have to apply physiology down to the elementary molecule" (*EP*, 301–2).

14. "Up to now there have only been a few general remedies that one can trust, like diet, exercises, distraction, and time, and nature; the rest could be more frequently harmful than helpful, with all due respect to M. Le Camus, his wisdom, and the intrepidity with which he prescribes bleedings, purgation, waters, baths, infusions, *décoctions*, and the entire battery of the healing art, which the great physicians use so spar-

ingly" (*EP*, 299–300). The remedies Diderot attacks here are cited in *La Médecine de l'esprit* as ways to fortify sensible fibers that have turned overly soft and limp, as in afflictions like cachexia and consumption (*Méd.*, 223).

15. Denis Diderot, *Réflexions sur le livre "De l'esprit" par M. Helvétius*, in Diderot, *Oeuvres complètes* (Paris: Hermann, 1981), 9:304. The objections Diderot makes here to Helvétius's philosophy of mind are developed in his *Réfutation suivie de l'ouvrage d'Helvétius intitulé "L'Homme"* (1773); see P. Vernière's excerpted version of this text in Diderot, *Oeuvres philosophiques* (Paris: Garnier, 1964), 563–620.

16. Claude Adrien Helvétius, *De l'esprit, or Essays on the Mind and Its Several Faculties* (London, 1807), xlii.

17. Diderot, *Réflexions sur le livre "De l'esprit,"* 308.

18. For a more modernist interpretation of the mind-body question as treated in eighteenth-century medicine, see Carmelina Imbroscio, "Recherches et réflexions de la médecine française du dix-huitième siècle sur des phénomènes psychosomatiques," *Studies on Voltaire and the Eighteenth Century* 190 (1980), 494–501.

19. As G. S. Rousseau and Roy Porter put it, "An ominous cloud hovered over the Enlightenment: the fear that, for all their faith in humanity, all their secular evangelizing, all their optimistic demythologizing crusades, the human animal himself might not prove fit for the programs of education, organization, and consciousness-raising that the *philosophes* were mobilizing." Rousseau and Porter, "Introduction: Toward a Natural History of Mind and Body," in *The Languages of Psyche: Mind and Body in Enlightenment Thought,* ed. G. S. Rousseau (Berkeley and Los Angeles: University of California Press, 1990), 39–40.

20. As Antoinette Emch-Dériaz notes in her useful biography, Tissot's treatise on the health of "literary persons" went through six reeditions (the last in 1859); was translated into English, German, and Italian; and belonged to a trilogy of works that Tissot wrote to address the health problems specific to particular groups. See Emch-Dériaz, *Tissot: Physician of the Enlightenment* (New York: Peter Lang, 1992), 55–94, 331–32.

21. Samuel-Auguste-André-David Tissot, *De la santé des gens de lettres* (Geneva: Slatkine, 1981), 16, hereafter cited as *SGL*.

22. For various perspectives on how the image of the writer as sickly and hypochondriacal has resounded through nineteenth- and twentieth-century literature and literary autobiography, see the essays included in the series "Médecins et Littérateurs," ed. Jean Decottignies, in the *Revue des sciences humaines*, nos. 198 (1985) and 208 (1987).

23. Interestingly, Tissot used the same technique of the graphic tableau in his treatise on masturbation, as a means of "terrifying by examples"; see S. A. Tissot, *Onanism, or A Treatise upon the Disorders Produced by Masturbation, or The Dangerous Effects of Secret and Excessive Venery,* trans. A. Hume, M.D. (1766; reprint, New York: Garland Publishing, 1985), xi. On this treatise, see Ludmilla Jordanova, "The Popularization of Medicine: Tissot on Onanism," *Textual Practice* 1, no. 1 (1987), 68–79; R. MacDonald, "The Frightful Consequences of Onanism: Notes on the History of a Delusion," *Journal of the History of Ideas,* no. 28 (1967), 423–31; and Théodore Tarc-

zylo, *Sexe et liberté au siècle des Lumières* (Paris: Presses de la Renaissance, 1983), 114–28 et passim.

24. Tissot proposes a curious comparison between the brain in the man of letters and the calloused hands that a manual laborer develops: "In workers the parts that work become callous; in men of letters it is the brain itself, and they often become incapable of tying together any ideas, and age well before their time" (*SGL*, 51–52).

25. Tissot, *Onanism*, 75.

26. Tissot concludes this part of his discussion by commenting, "While I reprimand those who engage passionately in scholarship, I have not had in mind those who cultivate the sciences wisely; and if one exposes oneself to the most unfortunate ailments when one sacrifices everything to the love of letters, one exposes oneself to shame by remaining in a state of ignorance" (*SGL*, 245).

27. In works like *The English Malady, or A Treatise of Nervous Diseases of All Kinds* (London, 1733), Cheyne did not so much reprimand scholars for being hypocondriacal as empathize with them very personally. On Cheyne and the other "hyp doctors" who were prominent in eighteenth-century England, see Roy Porter, "Barely Touching: A Social Perspective on Mind and Body," in Rousseau, *The Languages of Psyche*, esp. 54–74; G. J. Barker-Benfield, *The Culture of Sensibility: Sex and Society in Eighteenth-Century Britain* (Chicago: University of Chicago Press, 1992), ch. 1; and John Mullan, *Sentiment and Sociability: The Language of Feeling in the Eighteenth Century* (Oxford: Clarendon Press, 1988), ch. 5.

28. Speaking of women, Tissot maintains:

> Continuous reading produces all the nervous illnesses; perhaps, out of all the causes that have harmed the health of women, the main one has been the infinite increase in novels over the past hundred years. From the moment they are in diapers until the most advanced old age, women read novels with such ardor that they fear being distracted even for a minute, they do not budge from their places, and often stay up very late to satisfy this passion, which absolutely ruins their health. I won't even talk about those women who are themselves authors, and the number of them is rising every day. A girl who reads rather than running at the age of ten, will be when she is twenty a vaporous woman and not a good wet-nurse. (*SGL*, 183–84)

Aside from this diatribe, however, there are virtually no references in *De la santé des gens de lettres* to women scholars.

29. François Azouvi uses this phrase to describe Tissot's overall medical project, in his introduction to *De la santé des gens de lettres*, iii.

30. Tissot also wrote several treatises on diseases that afflicted the population at large, including *L'Inoculation justifiée* (1754), *Avis au peuple sur sa santé* (1761), *L'Histoire de la fièvre bileuse* (1755), *Lettre sur la maladie noire* addressed to the Swiss physician Zimmermann (1760), and *Lettre à Haller sur la petite vérole, l'apoplexie et l'hydropisie* (1761).

31. Théodore Tarczylo entitles the second part of his *Sexe et liberté au siècle des Lu-*

328 NOTES TO PAGES 107–113

mières, "L'Invention d'une maladie," to underscore the amount of fiction involved in the construction of the antimasturbatory movement that arose so forcefully in the eighteenth century, both in medical and in theological discourse (99–159).

32. See Tissot, *Essai sur les maladies des gens du monde* (1770) in *Oeuvres de M. Tissot: Nouvelle édition augmentée et imprimée sous ses yeux* (Lausanne, 1788), 4:24–25. I consider Tissot's health scale in greater detail in Chapter 6, while examining how Tissot and Rousseau deployed such dichotomies as "natural" versus "denaturing" to prescribe an ethical mode of life—one in which sensibility would be an instrument of true, morally sound edification rather than of excess and disorder.

33. The manner in which intellectual vigor affects physical vigor was still being debated well into the nineteenth century. For example, in *Les Avantages d'une constitution faible, aperçu médical* (Paris, an X [1802]), Fouquier de Maissemy argues that a frail physique is actually an advantage for both health and intellectual achievement; and in *Coup-d'oeil sur la dégénération qui s'est opérée dans le tempérament des hommes* (Paris, 1811), G. G. Lafont-Gouzi invokes both Tissot and Rousseau to support the idea that the current race of Western men are more feeble, decadent, and diseased than their predecessors because of the ongoing cult of knowledge.

Chapter 4: The Novel of Sensibility before 1750

1. Frank Baasner, "The Changing Meaning of 'Sensibilité,'" *Studies in Eighteenth-Century Culture* 15 (1986), 77–96.

2. On the moral vocabulary associated with sensibility, see John S. Spink, "'Sentiment,' 'sensible,' 'sensibilité': Les Mots, les idées, d'après les 'moralistes' français et britanniques du début du dix-huitième siècle," *Zadagnienia Rodzajów Literackich* 20 (1977), 33–47. See also Angelica Goodden's chapter "The Language of the Emotions," in *The Complete Lover: Eros, Nature, and Artifice in the Eighteenth-Century French Novel* (Oxford: Oxford University Press, 1989), 188–241. Thomas Di Piero argues that the French novel originally rose as a form of aristocratic fiction; see *Dangerous Truths and Criminal Passions: The Evolution of the French Novel, 1569–1791* (Stanford: Stanford University Press, 1992).

3. Philip Stewart uses the phrase "verbal chessboard" to describe the art of lovemaking in eighteenth-century worldly literature; see *Le Masque et la parole: Le langage de l'amour au XVIIIe siècle* (Paris: José Corti, 1973), esp. 100–116 and 148–84. See also Peter Brooks's reading of how the worldly moral and communication code operate in Crébillon, in *The Novel of Worldliness* (Princeton: Princeton University Press, 1969), 11–43, and see Angelica Goodden's remarks on Crébillon in *The Complete Lover*, 203–5, 212–16, and 231–37.

4. Claude Prosper Jolyot de Crébillon, *The Wayward Head and Heart*, trans. Barbara Bray (London: Oxford University Press, 1963), 8 (*Les Égarements du coeur et de l'esprit* [Paris: Garnier Flammarion, 1985], 74). Because Crébillon's vocabulary of sensibility is sometimes poorly rendered in the English translation of *Les Égarements*, I have provided those portions of the text in brackets where necessary. Unless otherwise

noted, references are to the English translation, cited as *Wayward*; the French edition is cited as *ECE*.

5. Brooks, *The Novel of Worldliness*, 28–29.

6. Thomas M. Kavanagh characterizes Meilcour at this point as "caught up in an immobilizing oscillation of antithetical feelings . . . Having lost faith in Versac, he has lost the ability to live a story whose assumed ending will provide the significance of each of its episodes." *Enlightenment and the Shadows of Chance: The Novel and the Culture of Gambling in Eighteenth-Century France* (Baltimore: Johns Hopkins University Press, 1993), 210.

7. In *The Unintended Reader: Feminism and Manon Lescaut* (Cambridge: Cambridge University Press, 1986), Naomi Segal constructs an elaborate feminist-psychoanalytic interpretation of the novel based on the distinct gender and class differences between its "intended" and "unintended" readers.

8. Antoine-François Prévost d'Exiles, *Manon Lescaut*, trans. Donald Frame (New York: New American Library, 1983), 19, hereafter cited as *ML*. I have occasionally modified Frame's translation.

9. There is clearly a parallel between the fear expressed here over becoming duped by a touching story and the episode surrounding Maria Rezati in Prévost's *Histoire d'une Grecque moderne* (1741; Paris: Garnier Flammarion, 1990), 192–97. In that episode, the French ambassador who serves as both protagonist and narrator refuses to be moved by Maria's tale of suffering because he questions whether she is truly worthy of sympathy, yet he responds with automatic sympathy to the story of her noble lover (another chevalier). See Elena Russo's incisive reading of this novel in *Skeptical Selves: Empiricism and Modernity in the French Novel* (Stanford: Stanford University Press, 1996), 22–66.

10. Renoncour establishes his fatherly credentials at the outset of his prefatory narrative: although of a solitary temperament, he was traveling at his daughter's behest when he first stumbled upon the spectacle that brought him into contact with des Grieux (*ML*, 33).

11. The brotherly character Tiberge is, of course, a special case: he is subject to the most frequent solicitations for help and sympathy from des Grieux. Although he is never convinced by des Grieux's rhetoric, Tiberge never fails to lend him money; he can therefore be seen both as des Grieux's mirror opposite (the good, morally upright son of the aristocracy) and as a surrogate father figure.

12. See on this point the chapter "The Code of Sensibility," in R. A. Francis, *Abbé Prévost's First-Person Narrators*, vol. 306 of *Studies on Voltaire and the Eighteenth Century* (1993), 151–68.

13. There is an interesting resonance between this passage and de Jaucourt's description in the *Encyclopédie* of the expanded moral existence that sensibility can produce: "Sensitive souls have more existence than others: joys and sorrows are multiplied for them." "Sensibilité (Morale)," in *Encyclopédie* (1751–65; reprint, New York: Pergamon Press, 1969), vol. 3, tome 15, p. 52.

14. The passage continues: "I did not dread it, I who expose myself to it so willingly

by giving up my fortune and the comforts of my father's house, I who have cut out even necessities of my own so as to satisfy her little whims and caprices" (*ML*, 72). Significantly, des Grieux's lofty rhetoric of sentiment is contaminated here by the rival language of economic exchange—a mode of exchange in which he is equally duplicitous, in that he uses his noble physiognomy, good manners, and seeming innocence to play on the sympathies of wealthy people.

15. Manon's death scene has attracted a wealth of semiotic and psychoanalytic readings, including Jacques Proust, "Le Corps de Manon," *Littérature*, no. 4 (1971), 5–21, and Sylvère Lotringer, "Manon l'écho," *Romanic Review*, no. 63 (1972), 92–110. See also Jean Rousset's comments about the inexpressibility of sentiment that burdens most of Prévost's characters, in *Narcisse romancier* (Paris: Corti, 1973), 136–37.

16. Kavanagh, "Chance, Reading, and the Tragedy of Experience: Prévost's *Manon Lescaut*," in *Enlightenment and the Shadows of Chance*, 158. Although Kavanagh recognizes the ruse involved in des Grieux's insistence that he is a helpless and hapless victim of fate, he suggests that des Grieux's ruse is a natural, universal response to the chaos of a chance-driven world.

17. Lionel Gossman, "Prévost's *Manon*: Love in the New World," *Yale French Studies* 40 (1969), 91–102.

18. Take, for example, the character M. de T., who emulates des Grieux's "bad boy" habits up to a point but refuses to take part in the mission of rescuing Manon along the route from Paris to Havre-de-Grace, for fear of ruining his reputation (*ML*, 161–62).

19. Moved by paternal sentiment, the father promptly sets about restoring order in his son's life: he joins forces with the other offended father, M. de G . . . M . . . senior, and goes with him to speak to the chief of police, of whom they make two requests—"one, to let [des Grieux] out of the Châtelet at once; the other, to lock up Manon for the rest of her days or send her to America" (*ML*, 159). Interestingly, when he is released from prison, des Grieux is too intimidated to inquire in the presence of these fathers about what has happened to Manon.

20. Kavanagh, *Enlightenment and the Shadows of Chance*, 157.

21. The novel opens with a transparently symbolic scene in which the two-year-old Marianne is pulled, crying and bloodied, from beneath the body of a young noblewoman who has just been assassinated, along with her husband and entire adult entourage, by highway robbers. Pierre Carlet de Chamblain de Marivaux, *La Vie de Marianne* (Paris: Garnier Flammarion, 1978), 52, hereafter cited as *VM*. Quotations are taken from the English translation, *The Virtuous Orphan*, trans. Mary Mitchell Collyer (Carbondale: Southern Illinois University Press, 1965). I have frequently modified the English translation and incorporated missing portions of the text in brackets.

22. Leo Spitzer, "A propos de *La Vie de Marianne* (Lettre à M. Georges Poulet)," *Romanic Review* 44 (1953), 102–26.

23. Brooks, *The Novel of Worldliness*, 132–33. What Brooks means by sentimentalist is a preromantic, effeminate, "vapid miniaturist" of the human heart—a false image of Marivaux that he finds in works like Ruth Kirby Jamieson, *Marivaux: A Study in Sensibility*, 2d ed. (New York: Octagon Books, 1969).

24. David Denby, *Sentimental Narrative and the Social Order in France, 1760–1820* (Cambridge: Cambridge University Press, 1994), 96.

25. John Heckman, "*Marianne*: The Making of an Author," *MLN* 86, no. 4 (1971), 509–22.

26. This is the type of passage that Georges Poulet singles out to support his argument that astonishment is the definitive state of existence for the Marivaudian being; see Poulet's study of Marivaux in *La Distance intérieure* (Paris: Plon, 1952), 1–34. Overlooking the constructive meaning that was ascribed to sensibility by the empiricist philosophers contemporary with Marivaux, Poulet anachronistically equates Marivaudian sensibility with an existential brand of sensationalism espoused by twentieth-century phenomenologists.

27. J. S. Spink does a useful analysis of the connections between Marivaux and eighteenth-century philosophy, in "Marivaux: The 'Mechanism of the Passions' and the 'Metaphysic of Sentiment,'" *Modern Language Review* 73 (1978), 278–90.

28. Poulet, *La Distance intérieure*, 21–22.

29. Marianne herself underscores the instrumental role played by her ability to inspire sympathy: she notes that, at this early stage of her life, "I had no other resource than arousing compassion" (*VM*, 235; my translation).

30. Those qualities are highlighted in the novel's portrait of Mme. de Miran (*VM*, 170–72). See Peter Brooks's perceptive analysis of portraiture and *marivaudage*, in *The Novel of Worldliness*, 103–10.

31. The sympathetic old abbess of part 6 gives Marianne this concise explanation of why interclass marriages are threatening to the aristocracy: "The difference of conditions is a necessary thing in life. And it could no longer subsist, all order would cease, if such unequal (and without exaggeration I may say, such monstrous) marriages as yours, child, were tolerated" (*Virtuous Orphan*, 223; *VM*, 273).

32. The minister's reaction is prefigured by a small but encouraging incident that takes place as Marianne waits to be summoned into the minister's chambers: a young officer who has "a presence extremely noble" is so struck when he sees her that he gazes at her ardently and murmurs, "Did you ever see anything so lovely?" (*Virtuous Orphan*, 235; *VM*, 286).

33. The hostile relative who appears in this episode is one of a mere handful of well-born characters in *La Vie de Marianne* who explicitly refuse to accord Marianne the standard title of respect for a noble girl: "'Mademoiselle!' cried the ill-natured relation with a mocking air, 'Mademoiselle! I think I have heard her called Marianne, or Miss What-do-you-call-her, for as nobody knows her origin, we cannot tell who she is'" (*Virtuous Orphan*, 242; VM, 296). To retaliate, Marianne the narrator refers to this woman in comically vindictive terms as "the long, meager relation" who speaks "with a tone even more sour and disagreeable than her looks" (*Virtuous Orphan*, 242; *VM*, 295).

34. Marianne describes Valville here as a "very honest man but born extremely susceptible to impressions. He meets with a dying beauty who touches him and snatches me from his heart" (*Virtuous Orphan*, 280; *VM*, 336). The beauty in question is Mlle. Varthon, whom Valville first lays eyes on as she is fainting; he rushes to her assistance,

just as he had with Marianne in part 2, and is immediately smitten (*VM*, 315–18). See Madeleine Therrien's structural comparison of these two episodes, in "La Problématique de la féminité dans *La Vie de Marianne*," *Stanford French Review* 11 (1987), 56–57.

35. Cf. Heckman, "*Marianne*: The Making of an Author," 520–21.

36. The final ingredient in that myth is inscribed on the novel's title page, where the author is identified as "Mme la Comtesse de ***"—an aristocratic designation that tempts us into believing that Marianne's qualities were at last officially recognized by polite society.

37. See, for example, Joan Hinde Stewart's introduction to *Gynographs: French Novels by Women of the Late Eighteenth Century* (Lincoln: University of Nebraska Press, 1993), 6–7.

38. Janet Gurkin Altman, for example, argues that the *Lettres d'une Péruvienne* should not be read according to the norms of romantic narrative nor according to the norms of typical eighteenth-century fictions of the cultural outsider. Rather, she asserts, it should be seen as a highly original "narrative of mental activity" that is not only comparable but superior to those written by philosophes like Condillac and Buffon. Altman, "Graffigny's Epistemology and the Emergence of Third-World Ideology," in *Writing the Female Voice: Essays on Epistolary Literature*, ed. Elizabeth C. Goldsmith (Boston: Northeastern University Press, 1989), 177. Using an overly polemical intellectual history to frame her analysis, Altman depicts Zilia as an intellectual heroine who embodies a female, "third-world" ideology that valorizes cultural difference and peaceful, nonhegemonic coexistence. See also Altman's "A Woman's Place in the Enlightenment Sun: The Case of F. de Graffigny," *Romance Quarterly* 38, no. 3 (1991), 261–72.

Thomas M. Kavanagh provides an insightful review of the history of how Graffigny's novel has been read, and of the renaissance it has recently enjoyed among literary critics, in chapter 4 of *Esthetics of the Moment: Literature and Art in the French Enlightenment* (Philadelphia: University of Pennsylvania Press, 1996), esp. 63–72.

39. According to John C. O'Neal, the philosophical dimension of the *Lettres d'une Péruvienne* resides in the way it both embraces and subverts a properly sensationalist aesthetics; see *The Authority of Experience: Sensationist Theory in the French Enlightenment* (University Park: Pennsylvania State University Press, 1996), 125–46.

40. Julia V. Douthwaite, *Exotic Women: Literary Heroines and Cultural Strategies in Ancien Régime France* (Philadelphia: University of Pennsylvania Press, 1992), 110–20.

41. Jack Undank, "Graffigny's Room of Her Own," *French Forum* 13, no. 3 (1988), 298–99.

42. Douthwaite, *Exotic Women*, 112, 119; Undank, "Graffigny's Room of Her Own," 304. Although he later takes issue with the "heterosexual antagonisms" that underlie most feminist approaches to Graffigny's novel, Undank practices a similar kind of sex-based oppositional criticism here by sexualizing the concepts of sensibility and reason in a way that is not entirely appropriate for the *Lettres d'une Péruvienne*.

43. Cf. Douthwaite, *Exotic Women*, and Altman, "Graffigny's Epistemology." Lahontan launched the vogue of primitivism with his highly successful philosophical di-

alogue *Dialogues curieux entre l'auteur et un sauvage de bon sens qui a voyagé* (1703). On the meanings that Enlightenment writers attached to the "savage" versus the "civilized," see Tzvetan Todorov, *Nous et les autres: La Réflexion française sur la diversité humaine* (Paris: Seuil, 1989), 297–314; Michèle Duchet, *Anthropologie et histoire au siècle des Lumières* (Paris: Maspero, 1971), 13–20; Jean Starobinski, "Le Mot 'civilisation,'" in *Le Remède dans le mal: Critique et légitimation de l'artifice à l'âge des Lumières* (Paris: Gallimard, 1989), 11–59; and Anthony Pagden, "The Savage Decomposed," in *European Encounters with the New World: From Renaissance to Romanticism* (New Haven: Yale University Press, 1993), 117–40.

44. Françoise de Graffigny, *Letters from a Peruvian Woman*, trans. David Kornacker (New York: Modern Language Association of America, 1993), 13, hereafter cited as *LP* followed by the letter number (when appropriate) and page number.

45. On the significance of the *quipus* and letter-writing in this novel, see Douthwaite, *Exotic Women*, 113–14; Altman, "Graffigny's Epistemology," 187–95; and Nancy K. Miller, *Subject to Change: Reading Feminist Writing* (New York: Columbia University Press, 1988), 137–57.

46. Zilia contends that the French "contribute to their girls' natural oversensitivity and weakness through childish compassion for the little accidents that befall them" (*LP*, letter 34, p. 143). As Bernard Bray and Isabelle Landy-Houillon point out in their "Notice" to the *Lettres d'une Péruvienne* (Paris: Garnier-Flammarion, 1983), 244, this sharply critical, feminist letter was added to the 1752 edition, after the novel's terrific success had been assured.

47. Many modern Graffigny critics have underscored the originality of the dénouement that she gives to this novel, according to which Zilia escapes all of the conventional plot endings for eighteenth-century literary heroines; see particularly Elizabeth MacArthur, "Devious Narratives: Refusal of Closure in Two Eighteenth-Century Epistolary Novels," *Eighteenth-Century Studies* 21, no. 1 (1987), 1–20. On the sequels that were written by other authors to "correct" Graffigny's ending, see English Showalter, "Les *Lettres d'une Péruvienne*: Composition, publication, suites," *Archives et Bibliothèques de Belgique* 54, nos. 1–4 (1983), 14–28; and Douthwaite, *Exotic Women*, 126–28.

48. Altman, "Graffigny's Epistemology," 194.

49. See Jean Ehrard's discussion of the false equation between "nature" and "virtue," in Marivaux, Prévost, Mme. de Lambert, and other writers of this period, in *L'Idée de nature en France à l'aube des Lumières* (Paris: Flammarion, 1970), 200–223.

50. See, for example, Spitzer, "A propos de *La Vie de Marianne*," 122.

Chapter 5: Organic Sensibility in Diderot's Theory and Practice of Fiction

1. Jacques Roger asserts that between 1754, when Diderot published *De l'interprétation de la nature*, and 1769, when he composed the *Rêve de d'Alembert*, Diderot's thinking on the origins and originality of living matter became less metaphysically ma-

terialist and more specifically biomedical. Roger, *Les Sciences de la vie dans la pensée française au XVIIIe siècle* (Paris: Albin Michel, 1963), 618. Jean Mayer observes that Diderot compiled and revised his notes from his copious readings in physiology, anatomy, and medicine during a period that stretched from 1765 until at least 1780; see the introduction to Diderot, *Eléments de physiologie*, ed. Jean Mayer (Paris: Librairie Marcel Didier, 1964), ix–lxxxi, hereafter cited as *EP.*

Among the many intriguing fragments included in the *Eléments de physiologie* is the 1778 list, "Authors I must read" (*EP*, 342–43), which features most of the theorists— including Haller, Bordeu, Bonnet, Roussel, and La Mettrie—who were involved in establishing the primacy of sensibility and/or irritability in all physiological and pathological functions. See also Jean Mayer, *Diderot homme de science* (Rennes: Imprimerie bretonne, 1959).

2. Jacques Chouillet emphasizes the numerous interconnections between the techniques and principles Diderot developed for the theater and those that he used in the novel *La Religieuse*; see *La Formation des idées esthétiques de Diderot* (Paris: Armand Colin, 1973), 418–552.

3. Georges May, *Diderot et "La Religieuse"* (New Haven: Yale University Press; Paris: Presses Universitaires de France, 1954), 111–12, 206–7.

4. The notion that Diderot was intent on pathologizing women and/or their sexuality has been advanced by Elisabeth de Fontenay in "Diderot gynéconome," *Digraphe* 7 (1976), 29–50; Marie-Hélène Huet, *Monstrous Imagination* (Cambridge: Harvard University Press, 1993), 82–95; and Anne Deneys-Tunney, *Écritures du corps: De Descartes à Laclos* (Paris: Presses Universitaires de France, 1992), 131–91.

5. The hoax that inspired *La Religieuse* is recounted in the novel's "Préface-Annexe," first written for the *Correspondance littéraire* of 1770 and then revised by Diderot sometime between 1780 and 1782; it appeared along with the novel in the original edition of *La Religieuse* in 1796. The classic study of this hoax is Herbert Dieckmann's "The 'Préface-Annexe' of *La Religieuse*," *Diderot Studies* 2 (1952), 21–147. See also Rosalina de la Carrera's more recent analysis in *Success in Circuit Lies: Diderot's Communicational Practice* (Stanford, Calif.: Stanford University Press, 1992), 11–38.

6. Diderot had serious reservations about the conventional novel; see Roger Kempf, *Diderot et le roman, ou Le Démon de la présence* (Paris: Seuil, 1964), esp. 15–39. The classic study of the novel's dubious reputation during the eighteenth century is Georges May, *Le Dilemme du roman au XVIIIe siècle* (New Haven: Yale University Press; Paris: Presses Universitaires de France, 1963).

7. "Until the present day," Diderot continues, "a novel was considered a frivolous tissue of fanciful events, the study of which was dangerous to our tastes and our morals." Denis Diderot, "An Eulogy of Richardson," in *Diderot's Thoughts on Art and Style*, trans. Beatrix L. Tollemache (London: J. Macqueen, 1896), 266. Hereafter cited as "ER." I have occasionally modified this translation.

8. On Diderot's use of the absorption conceit in his art criticism, see Michael Fried, *Absorption and Theatricality: Painting and Beholder in the Age of Diderot* (Chicago: University of Chicago Press, 1980), esp. 73–105 and 118–32. On absorption in

Diderot's dramatic theory, see David Marshall, *The Surprising Effects of Sympathy: Marivaux, Diderot, Rousseau, and Mary Shelley* (Chicago: University of Chicago Press, 1988), 105–34.

9. As Diderot puts it, "The charm and interest of the story make even the thoughtful reader less conscious (than he would otherwise be) of Richardson's delicate art" ("ER," 281).

10. Rosalina de la Carrera emphasizes the double-edged strategy underlying Diderot's unveiling of the mechanisms of fiction; see *Success in Circuit Lies*, 11–38.

11. On the dialogical in Diderot, see Carol Sherman, *Diderot and the Art of Dialogue* (Geneva: Droz, 1976); Jean Starobinki, "Diderot et la parole des autres," *Critique* 296 (1972), 3–22; Christie McDonald, *The Dialogue of Writing: Essays in Eighteenth-Century French Literature* (Waterloo, Ont.: Wilfred Laurier University Press, 1984), 63–73; and Jay Caplan, *Framed Narratives: Diderot's Genealogy of the Beholder* (Minneapolis: University of Minnesota Press, 1985).

12. Brooks points out that Diderot's emphasis on depicting everyday life "should not be read as a recommendation of naturalistic 'realism.' On the contrary, Diderot wants to exploit the dramatics and excitement discoverable within the real, to heighten in dramatic gesture the moral crises and peripeties of life." Peter Brooks, *The Melodramatic Imagination: Balzac, Henry James, Melodrama, and the Mode of Excess* (New Haven: Yale University Press, 1976), 13.

13. These are the qualities singled out for producing and judging art by Dorval of Diderot's *Entretiens sur "Le Fils naturel,"* in *Paradoxe sur le comédien, précédé des "Entretiens sur 'Le Fils naturel'"* (Paris: Garnier Flammarion, 1981), 60.

14. See in particular Rousseau's comments on the effects of theater, in Jean-Jacques Rousseau, *Lettre à d'Alembert sur les spectacles* (Paris: Gallimard-Folio, 1987), esp. 157–67.

15. Diderot also insists on the real value of moving aesthetic experiences in his *Discours sur la poésie dramatique*: "The poet, the novelist, the actor go to the heart in a roundabout way and strike the soul all the more surely and powerfully because it offers itself up to the blow. Yes, the pains they use to touch me are imaginary, but they touch me nonetheless. Every line of the *Homme de qualité retiré du monde*, of the *Doyen de Killerine*, and of *Cléveland* arouses my interest in the misfortunes of virtue, and costs me tears." Denis Diderot, *Oeuvres complètes*, ed. Herbert Dieckmann et al. (Paris: Hermann, 1975–), 10:338.

16. Although Diderot does not use the term here, he is referring implicitly to the notion of an artistic "modèle idéal" that he elaborates in the *Paradoxe sur le comédien*.

17. Diderot applies this aesthetic principle to the theater in the *Discours sur la poésie dramatique*: "It is not words that I want to take away from the theater, but impressions ... An excellent play is one whose effect lingers within me." *Oeuvres*, 10:339.

18. In his introduction to the Hermann edition of the *Éloge*, Jean Sgard suggests that this "friend" is a persona adapted from a self-portrait Diderot sketched in a letter to his mistress Sophie, where he told almost exactly the same anecdote regarding these two missing sections from *Clarissa* but cast himself as the reader. Diderot, *Éloge de*

336 NOTES TO PAGES 160-165

Richardson in *Oeuvres complètes*, ed. Herbert Dieckmann et al. (Paris: Hermann, 1975–), 13:182–83.

19. On the *scène muette*, see Diderot's *Entretiens sur "Le Fils naturel,"* 48–49, 61, 81–94. See also Peter Brooks's discussion of the "aesthetics of muteness" in *The Melodramatic Imagination*, 62–68.

20. On the moral ambiguity implicit in Diderot's aesthetics of intensity, see Jacques Chouillet, *Diderot, poète de l'énergie* (Paris: Presses Universitaires de France, 1984), 84–104, and Fried, *Absorption and Theatricality*, 80–81.

21. Théophile de Bordeu, "Crise," reprinted as *Recherches sur les crises* in Bordeu, *Oeuvres complètes* (Paris, 1818), 1:217.

22. Bordeu's remarks at the end of "Crise" (252) on ordinary practitioners and academic physicians are quite condescending. Predictably, many members of the eighteenth-century Parisian medical community were offended by these comments—most notably Michel-Philippe Bouvart, who openly detested Bordeu and was, perhaps not coincidentally, cast by Diderot in the unflattering role of the despotic doctor M. B . . . of *La Religieuse*. Bouvart's antipathy escalated into a professional quarrel that plagued Bordeu throughout his life. See Anthelme-Balthasar Richerand's account of this quarrel in his "Notice sur la vie et les ouvrages de Bordeu," in Bordeu, *Oeuvres complètes*, 1:xiii–xxi.

23. Ménuret de Chambaud, "Observation," in *Encyclopédie*, vol. 2, tome 11, p. 320.

24. Rita Goldberg has also explored the analogy Diderot makes between the artist and the scientist; see *Sex and Enlightenment: Women in Richardson and Diderot* (Cambridge: Cambridge University Press, 1984), 172–75. Although Goldberg notes that there is something distinctly medical about the narrative tone of *La Religieuse*, her reading of how this affects the novel's plot differs considerably from mine.

25. Denis Diderot, *The Paradox of Acting*, trans. William Archer (New York: Hill and Wang, 1957), 17, hereafter cited as *PC*. I have occasionally modified Archer's translation.

26. Diderot, *Le Paradoxe sur le comédien*, 131. This passage is omitted in Archer's translation. In the *Rêve de d'Alembert*, Dr. Bordeu observes: "Now, the superior man who has unfortunately been born with this kind of [sensitive] disposition will constantly strive to suppress it, dominate it, master its impulses and to maintain the hegemony of the center of the network. Then he will keep his self-possession amid the greatest dangers and judge cooly but sanely. He will omit nothing which might fit in with his aim or serve his ends. He will be difficult to take by surprise; by forty-five he will be a great king, statesman, politician, artist and especially a great actor, philosopher, poet, musician, or doctor; he will be master of himself and everything around him." Denis Diderot, *Rameau's Nephew and D'Alembert's Dream*, trans. Leonard Tancock (London: Penguin, 1966), 212–13.

27. On the function of alienation in Diderot's aesthetic theory, see Philippe Lacoue-Labarthe, "Diderot, le paradoxe et la mimésis," *Poétique* 43 (1980), 267–81; and Lionel Gossman and Elizabeth MacArthur, "Diderot's Displaced *Paradoxe*," in *Diderot: Di-*

gression and Dispersion, ed. Jack Undank and Herbert Josephs (Lexington, Ky.: French Forum, 1984), 106–29.

28. Grimm's comment, originally made in the *Correspondance littéraire* of 1770, is included in the "Préface-Annexe" to *La Religieuse*; see Denis Diderot, *La Religieuse,* in *Oeuvres complètes,* 11:31, hereafter cited as *Rel.*

29. Herbert Josephs, "Diderot's *La Religieuse:* Libertinism and the Dark Cave of the Soul," *MLN* 91 (1976), 734–55.

30. Leo Spitzer, "The Style of Diderot," in *Linguistics and Literary History* (New York: Russell and Russell, 1962), 166.

31. Diderot, *Memoirs of a Nun,* trans. Francis Birrell (London: Elek Books, 1959), 143, hereafter cited as *Nun.* I have occasionally modified Birrell's translation.

32. Flavio Luoni has attempted to rescue Spitzer from his very clear conflation of Diderot's stylistic representation of the physiological, and the putative psycho-physiology of Diderot the man; see "*La Religieuse:* Récit et écriture du corps," *Littérature,* no. 54 (1984), 79–99.

33. Sarah Kofman regards Suzanne's insistence on her own superior qualities in a Freudian manner, diagnosing Suzanne as a daughter figure who is obsessed with being singled out as favorite by a succession of mother figures; see *Séductions: De Sartre à Héraclite* (Paris: Editions Galilée, 1990), 40–41. Jay Caplan does a more persuasive interpretation of the psychodynamics involved in *La Religieuse* by focusing upon the way that Suzanne's "interesting" qualities—her innocence, her tears and suffering, and especially her "naturalness"—are designed to act upon the novel's designated narratee, who is not a maternal figure but the Marquis de Croismare, rhetorically constructed as a "Family Man"; see *Framed Narratives,* esp. 45–59. See also Roger Kempf's remarks on the role that this novel assigns to the Marquis de Croismare as privileged reader, in *Diderot et le roman,* 36–37.

34. See Fried, *Absorption and Theatricality,* 31, 96–97.

35. Caplan, *Framed Narratives,* 49.

36. Anne Deneys-Tunney rightly underscores the importance of pantomime in such passages of *La Religieuse*; see *Écritures du corps,* 149–55, 179–91. However, she reaches the debatable conclusion that what happens to Suzanne when her body becomes the object of an external gaze is that she is "dispossessed" of her own gaze and thus plunged into a psychological condition of hysteria. Although Suzanne observes several cases of psycho-physiological disorder that are comparable to hysteria as eighteenth-century thinkers understood it, she never becomes a patient in this novel but, rather, remains a semidetached observer.

37. Many critics have addressed the problem of Suzanne's often incongruous "innocence." Georges May, *Diderot et "La Religieuse,"* 204–11, tries to explain it as a careless lapse in literary verisimilitude on Diderot's part. Others have viewed it as a willful blindness on either Suzanne's or the author's part, or an unwillingless to speak the truth about lesbianism; see, for example, Vivienne Mylne, "What Suzanne Knew: Lesbianism and *La Religieuse,*" *Studies on Voltaire and the Eighteenth Century* 208 (1982),

167–73, and Walter E. Rex, "Secrets from Suzanne: The Tangled Motives of *La Religieuse*," in *The Attraction of the Contrary: Essays on the Literature of the French Enlightenment* (Cambridge: Cambridge University Press, 1987), 125–35.

38. See Georges May's analysis of this famous portrait in "Diderot, artiste et philosophe du décousu," in *Europäische Aufklärung Herbert Dieckmann zum 60. Geburtstag*, ed. Hugo Friedrich and Fritz Schalk (Munich: Fink Verlag, 1967), 165–88.

39. Some critics have attributed the contagious quality of such episodes to Suzanne herself, who (they argue) exerts an unwitting fatal effect upon those characters who come into physical contact with her. See, in this vein, Luoni, "*La Religieuse:* Récit et écriture du corps," 93–99; Josephs, "Diderot's *La Religieuse*," 748; and Marshall, *The Surprising Effects of Sympathy*, 89–92.

40. See Caplan, *Framed Narratives*, 45–59, and May, *Diderot et "La Religieuse,"* 98–114, 197–237.

41. Speaking of Mme. ***, Dom Morel observes: "She was not made for her state, and this is what happens sooner or later as a result. When one resists the general penchant of one's nature, that constraint diverts it into irregular passions, which are all the more violent for being ill-founded. It is a sort of madness" (*Nun*, 180).

42. See, for example, the celebrated passage from the "Préface-Annexe" that describes Diderot as having been moved to a state of tearful bereavement over Suzanne's tale as he was writing it (*Rel.*, 31).

43. Diderot, *De l'interprétation de la nature* (1753), in *Oeuvres philosophiques de Diderot*, ed. P. Vernière (Paris: Garnier, 1964), 197.

44. On the peculiar manner in which Diderot intertwines the philosophical and the licentious, see Aram Vartanian, "Erotisme et philosophie chez Diderot," *Cahiers de l'association internationale des études françaises* 13 (1960), 367–90.

45. Brooks, *The Novel of Worldliness*, 169–71.

46. See Pierre Trahard, "Dans l'ombre de Jean-Jacques," in *Maîtres de la sensibilité française au XVIIIe siècle* (Paris: Boivin, 1933), 4:7–45.

Chapter 6: The Moral Hygiene of Sensibility

1. Various scholars have ventured interpretations of how the *morale sensitive* project informs Rousseau's oeuvre; see, for example, Pierre Burgelin, *La Philosophie de l'existence chez Jean-Jacques Rousseau* (Paris: Presses Universitaires de France, 1952), 356–67, and Marcel Raymond, *Jean-Jacques Rousseau: La Quête de soi et la rêverie* (Paris: Corti, 1962), 35–49, where the *morale sensitive* is compared to both Condillacian sensationalism and Proustian involuntary memory.

2. Jean-Jacques Rousseau, *Discours sur les sciences et les arts* and *Discours sur l'origine et les fondements de l'inégalité parmi les hommes*, in *Oeuvres complètes*, ed. Bernard Gagnebin et al., vol. 3 (Paris: Pléiade, 1964), 1–237.

3. Jean-Jacques Rousseau, *The Confessions*, trans. Christopher Kelly, vol. 5 of *The Collected Writings of Rousseau*, ed. Christopher Kelly, Roger D. Masters, and Peter G.

Stillman (Hanover: University Press of New England, 1990–95). Hereafter cited as *Conf.* I have occasionally modified the English translation.

4. Jean-Jacques Rousseau, *Rousseau, Judge of Jean-Jacques: Dialogues*, trans. Judith R. Bush, Christopher Kelly and Roger D. Masters, vol. 1 of *The Collected Writings of Rousseau*. Hereafter cited as *Judge.* I have occasionally modified the English translation.

5. Jean-Jacques Rousseau, *Deuxième Dialogue*, in *Oeuvres complètes*, 1:804.

6. In his remarks on the vocabulary of *sensibilité* in Rousseau's writings, Jean Sgard notes the term's jointly biological and metaphysical connotations but reaches the debatable conclusion that Rousseau ultimately distanced himself from a sensualist or materialist definition of the property; see Michel Gilot and Jean Sgard, ed., *Le Vocabulaire du sentiment dans l'oeuvre de Jean-Jacques Rousseau* (Geneva: Slatkine, 1980), 3–5, 12–15.

7. Jean-Jacques has the same Pythagorean culinary tastes as Julie of *La Nouvelle Héloïse:* "Good food and good wine please him greatly, but his preference is for things that are simple, common, without special preparation, but well chosen from their species" (*Judge*, 114).

8. See, for example, R. Laforgue's "Etude sur Jean-Jacques Rousseau," *Revue française de psychanalyse* 1 (1927), 370–402, and more recently, the chapter *"Julie* and the Pathology of Conscience," in Asher Horowitz, *Rousseau, Nature, and History* (Toronto: University of Toronto Press, 1987), 135–65.

9. Ménuret de Chambaud, "Observateur," in *Encyclopédie* (New York: Pergamon Press, 1969), vol. 3, tome 11, p. 310; Jean Senebier, *Essai sur l'art d'observer* (1775), 2d ed. (Geneva, 1802).

10. Denis Diderot, *Eléments de physiologie*, ed. Jean Mayer (Paris: Librairie Marcel Didier, 1964), 302.

11. Samuel-Auguste-André-David Tissot, *De la santé des gens de lettres* (1768), introd. François Azouvi (Geneva: Slatkine, 1981), 7. The view of morality and medicine as intimately interconnected was popular throughout the French Enlightenment, from La Mettrie to Pierre Cabanis. See, on this subject, the chapter "Moral Theory in Medical Terms," in Kathleen Wellman, *La Mettrie: Medicine, Philosophy, and Enlightenment* (Durham, N.C.: Duke University Press, 1992), 213–45.

12. See, for example, the anonymous article "Hygiène," in *Encyclopédie*, vol. 2, tome 8, p. 385. William Coleman discusses this article in "Health and Hygiene in the *Encyclopédie:* A Medical Doctrine for the Bourgeoisie," *Journal of the History of Medicine* 29 (1974), 399–421. On Tissot's use of the doctrine of the non-naturals in his "occupation-specific" treatises, see Antoinette Emch-Dériaz, "The Non-Naturals Made Easy," in *The Popularization of Medicine, 1650–1850,* ed. Roy Porter (London: Routledge, 1992), 134–59.

13. See Jacques Domenech's chapter "La Morale du sentiment," in *L'Ethique des Lumières: Les fondements de la morale dans la philosophie française du XVIIIe siècle* (Paris: Vrin, 1989), 57–98.

14. Roy Porter describes that anxiety in these terms: "Might the progress of civilization be leading not to the promised land of salubrity but to the sickbed? . . . The so-

lution, theorized by philosophes and physicians alike, was that civilization might itself be the provocation of sickness." Roy Porter, *Doctor of Society: Thomas Beddoes and the Sick Trade in Late-Enlightenment England* (London: Routledge, 1992), 89.

15. Jean-Jacques Rousseau, *Dialogues, ou Rousseau Juge de Jean-Jacques*, in *Oeuvres complètes*, ed. Bernard Gagnebin et al., vol. 1 (Paris: Pléaide, 1959), 918–20. According to his *Confessions*, Rousseau's skepticism about medicine also took the form of intense dislike for certain physicians, most particularly Théodore Tronchin and Théophile de Bordeu; see *Les Confessions*, ibid., 472, 550.

16. See letter 3789 in *Correspondance générale de Jean-Jacques Rousseau*, ed. Théophile Dufour (Paris: Armand Colin, 1927), 8:75. Over the course of their correspondence, Rousseau and Tissot exchanged glowing praise for each other's works—most particularly Rousseau's *Emile* (1761) and Tissot's *Onanisme* (1758) and *Avis au peuple* (1767). See *La Correspondance complète de Jean-Jacques Rousseau* (Geneva: Institut Voltaire, 1971), vol. 11, entries 1908 (June 23, 1762), 1946 (July 3, 1762), 1966 (July 8, 1762), 1983 (July 11, 1762), 1994 (July 14, 1762), and 2022 (July 22, 1762); and vol. 37, entries 6520 (January 5, 1769) and 6536 (February 1, 1769).

17. Tissot's biographer Charles Eynard, *Essai sur la vie de Tissot* (Lausanne, 1839), 85, notes that, whereas Haller and Bonnet regarded Rousseau as a somewhat inconsistent and pompous philosopher, Tissot was unqualifiedly enthusiastic about him.

18. Serge A. Thériault, *Jean-Jacques Rousseau et la médecine naturelle* (Montreal: Les Editions Univers, 1979). Thériault approaches *La Nouvelle Héloïse* as a "novel constructed entirely according to the therapeutic principles of natural medicine" (53)—that is, as a barely fictional work that anticipates modern-day principles of naturism, like the avoidance of stress, agrobiology, emphasis on wholesome alimentation and exercise, and so on.

19. Anne-Charles Lorry, for example, declared that contemporary Europeans lived in a fallen, post-Adamic state of bodily frailty and exacerbated their delicateness by indulging their passions and eating "unreasonable" diets. Lorry, *Essai sur les alimens, pour servir de commentaire aux livres diétiques d'Hippocrates* (Paris, 1757), 2:18, 33. The most celebrated physician to the Parisian smart set was the Genevan doctor Théodore Tronchin, who popularized such healthful practices as daily constitutional walks (called *tronchiner*) and easy-moving skirts (*tronchines*) that worldly women could wear to take their exercise. For more on Tronchin, see Henri Tronchin, *Théodore Tronchin (1709–1781), un médecin du XVIIIe siècle* (Geneva: Kundig, 1906), esp. ch. 2.

20. The Encyclopedist Arnulfe d'Aumont exempted the robust from the highly regimented existence that all other modern people had to lead in order to stay healthy; see "Régime," in *Encyclopédie*, vol. 3, tome 14, p. 12.

21. Antoinette Emch-Dériaz points out this resemblance in her useful biographical study *Tissot, Physician of the Enlightenment* (New York: Peter Lang, 1992), 56–57. On the Physiocrats, see Elizabeth Fox-Genovese, *The Origins of Physiocracy: Economic Revolution and Social Order in Eighteenth-Century France* (Ithaca, N.Y.: Cornell University Press, 1976).

22. Tissot was deeply worried about the declining birth rate and vigor of the rural

population and believed that the cause of this decline was not so much disease as the se-ductions of city life. See his remarks in the *Avis au peuple sur sa santé*, 3d ed. (Paris, 1767), 6–9, and his condemnation of social trends like the increase in *luxe*, in *De la santé des gens de lettres*, 185–86.

23. Samuel-Auguste-André-David Tissot, *Essai sur les maladies des gens du monde* (1770), in *Oeuvres de M. Tissot: Nouvelle édition augmentée et imprimée sous ses yeux* (Lausanne, 1788), 4:ix, hereafter cited as *MGM*.

24. Ironically, the success of Tissot's *Essai sur les maladies des gens du monde* trans-formed his beloved home city of Lausanne into something of a worldly *tourbillon*; see Charles Eynard, *Essai sur la vie de Tissot*, 222.

25. Commenting on the *Essai sur les maladies des gens du monde*, Antoinette Emch-Dériaz notes: "Between the lines lurked a Tissot who was lashing out at the system of privileges. Openly he wrote of health, but behind his rhetoric about natural life and the effects that the Galenic non-naturals have on the health of the peasant and the aristocrat, Tissot was denouncing an unnatural state of affairs not only confined to the human body but also present in the body politic." *Tissot, Physician of the Enlightenment*, 72.

26. Tissot's disapproval of fancy food was shared by Anne-Charles Lorry, who rec-ommended that worldly people stick to "a light, moistening, and barely seasoned diet." *Essai sur les alimens*, 2:211. It also resembles the position taken in both the hygienic and culinary articles of the *Encyclopédie*; see Jean-Claude Bonnet, "Le Réseau culinaire dans l'*Encyclopédie*," *Annales E.S C.* 31, no. 5 (1976), 891–914.

27. Michel Delon has examined the legacy of this particular formula in "'Fatal présent du ciel qu'une âme sensible': Le Succès d'une formule de Rousseau," in *"La Nouvelle Héloïse" aujourd'hui* (Reims: A l'Écart, 1991), 53–64. For the passage itself, see Jean-Jacques Rousseau, *La Nouvelle Héloïse*, in *Oeuvres complètes*, vol. 2 (Paris: Pléiade, 1964), pt. 1, letter 26, p. 89 (hereafter cited as *NH*, followed by part, letter, and page number); translated by Judith H. McDowell as *Julie, or The New Eloise* (University Park, Pa.: Pennsylvania State University Press, 1968), 71. Because McDowell's English transla-tion is greatly abridged, I will also refer to the more quaint but comprehensive anony-mous translation *Eloisa: A Series of Original Letters* (London, 1810), 3 vols. I have occa-sionally modified both McDowell's translation and the 1810 version. References will be given in the text both to the appropriate English translation and to the French original.

28. See Anne Deneys-Tunney's chapter "Julie ou le corps abject" in *Écritures du corps* (Paris: Presses Universitaires de France, 1992), 193–282, and Peter Brooks, *Body Work: Objects of Desire in Modern Narrative* (Cambridge: Harvard University Press, 1993), esp. 38–49. Claude Labrosse offers yet another interpretation of the body in Rousseau's novel by approaching it as the locus of a process of acculturation; see "Jean-Jacques Rousseau et le corps dans *La Nouvelle Héloïse*," in *Corps création* (Lyon: Presses Universitaires de Lyon, 1980), 105–15.

29. Paul de Man, "Allegory (Julie)," in *Allegories of Reading: Figural Language in Rousseau, Nietzsche, Rilke, and Proust* (New Haven: Yale University Press, 1979), 188–220.

30. Marie-Hélène Huet, *Le Héros et son double* (Paris: Corti, 1975), 80–101.

31. Clearly, the notion of nature coexists paradoxically with Rousseau's near-obsession with control over the human being's senses and ambient milieu, as Jean Starobinski underscores: "It requires a masterpiece of artifice to arrange the world in such a way that virtue can be achieved naïvely and effortlessly, impelled solely by the senses." Starobinski, *Jean-Jacques Rousseau: Transparency and Obstruction*, trans. Arthur Goldhammer (Chicago: University of Chicago Press, 1988), 214 (translation slightly modified). On the highly artificial way in which Rousseau stages the natural in *Emile*, see Josué Harari, *Scenarios of the Imaginary: Theorizing the French Enlightenment* (Ithaca, N.Y.: Cornell University Press, 1987), 102–32.

32. In his tendency to swing from one emotional extreme to the other, Saint-Preux bears a striking constitutional resemblance to "Jean-Jacques" as described in the *Deux-ième Dialogue:* "The kind of sensibility I have found in him . . . creates inconsistent men who are often in contradiction with themselves" (*Judge*, 116).

33. Jean Starobinski sees the maternal, sympathetic nature of the Clarens society as an instance of the "transparency of consciences" that Rousseau held to be a moral ideal; see *La Transparence et l'obstacle* (Paris: Gallimard, 1971), 107–8.

34. Tissot put milk and other "simple" foods at the center of the diet he prescribed to restore the health of the recovering masturbator: "A healthy palate, which has all the sensibility it should have, can only enjoy simple dishes; complicated, fancy prepara-tions are unbearable for it, yet it finds in the least flavorful foods a savor which dulled organs cannot appreciate . . . Those who return to such simple foods for reasons of health consequently find in them unexpected delights." Tissot, *Onanism, or A Treatise upon the Disorders produced by Masturbation, or The Dangerous Effects of Secret and Ex-cessive Venery*, trans. A. Hume, M.D. (1766; New York: Garland Publishing, 1985), 135.

35. Saint-Preux applies the same "you are what you eat" logic to national distinc-tions, suggesting that Italians are effeminate because they eat so many greens, the En-glish are hard and inflexible because they are meat-lovers, the Swiss have mixed moral traits because they consume a lot of milk and beer, and the French are flexible because they eat everything (*NH*, 4.10.453). For an interesting analysis of Rousseau's culinary theories, see Jean-Claude Bonnet, "Le Système de la cuisine et du repas chez Rous-seau," *Poétique* 22 (1975), 244–67.

36. Interestingly, Tissot likewise condemns the extravagant lengths to which some people go to procure exotic wines: "The map of the places that have furnished the wines served on some splendid tables will soon cover the entire universe, and will be for the sensible man a very striking tableau of the extravagant and murderous customs of his century." *MGM*, 14.

37. The theological system Julie forges just before her fatal accident makes sensi-bility an earthly extension of spiritual communication: "Finding nothing in this globe capable of giving it satisfaction, my avid soul seeks an object in another world: in ele-vating itself to the source of sentiment and existence, its languour is vanishing; it is be-ing re-animated; it is acquiring new strength and new life" (*Eloisa*, 3:237; *NH*, 6.8.694).

Chapter 7: Moral Anthropology

1. The rediscovery of moral anthropology among modern historians is due largely to the work of Yvonne Kniebehler; see her study "Les Médecins et la 'nature féminine' au temps du Code civil," *Annales E.C.S.*, no. 4 (1976), 824–45. The 1857 *Catalogue des sciences médicales* lists some twenty-nine different treatises, most written between 1761 and 1850, on the distinctions between the "natural history" of man versus woman; see the *Catalogue des sciences médicales de la Bibliothèque Impériale* (Paris, 1857), 1:348–49.

2. Thomas Laqueur, *Making Sex: Body and Gender from the Greeks to Freud* (Cambridge: Harvard University Press, 1990), 5–6.

3. Londa Schiebinger, *The Mind Has No Sex? Women in the Origins of Modern Science* (Cambridge: Harvard University Press, 1989), 189–244.

4. Schiebinger discusses most of these subjects in *The Mind Has No Sex?* esp. chs. 6–8, and in *Nature's Body: Gender in the Making of Modern Science* (Boston: Beacon Press, 1993), ch. 5. See also Laqueur, *Making Sex*, esp. chs. 5 and 6; Maurice Bloch and Jean H. Bloch, "Women and the Dialectics of Nature in Eighteenth-Century Thought," in *Nature, Culture and Gender*, ed. Carol P. MacCormack and Marilyn Strathern (Cambridge: Cambridge University Press, 1980), 25–41; and Ludmilla Jordanova, "Sex and Gender," in *Inventing Human Science: Eighteenth-Century Domains*, ed. Christopher Fox, Roy Porter, and Robert Wokler (Berkeley and Los Angeles: University of California Press, 1995), 152–83.

5. Many nineteenth-century physicians of the moral anthropological school situated their work in the wake of the *Système physique et moral de la femme*. Roussel's hagiographer J. L. Alibert called him a true *médecin philosophe* largely because of his "sagagious" vision of sensibility's many repercussions; see Alibert's "Eloge de Pierre Roussel"—first written in 1803, shortly after Roussel's death—in *Système physique et moral de la femme, ou Tableau philosophique de la constitution, de l'état organique, du tempérament, des moeurs et des fonctions propres au sexe*, 7th ed. (Paris, 1820), x–xi.

6. Thomas Laqueur, for example, asserts that "Roussel and Moreau and Cabanis wrote as part of the Napoleonic retrenchment in matters of family and gender, arguing that corporeal differences demanded the social and legal differences of the new Code." Laqueur, *Making Sex*, 196. Laqueur seems to finesse the issue of chronology here: Roussel published his treatise fourteen years before the Revolution and was dead by the time Napoleon came to power. Dorinda Outram also emphasizes the primacy of politics in determining models of the body in *The Body and the French Revolution* (New Haven: Yale University Press, 1989).

7. See book 5 of Jean-Jacques Rousseau, *Émile*, in *Oeuvres complètes*, ed. Bernard Gagnebin et al., vol. 4 (Paris: Pléiade, 1969), pp. 692–868. Cabanis went to particular lengths to establish Rousseau, along with Roussel, as a precursor for all subsequent inquiries into women's nature; see Pierre-Jean-Georges Cabanis, *Rapports du physique et du moral de l'homme* (Geneva: Slatkine Reprints, 1980), 244.

8. Michel Foucault, *Madness and Civilization: A History of Insanity in the Age of Reason*, trans. Richard Howard (New York: Pantheon, 1965), 153–54.

9. Foucault's definition of the vapors exemplifies his problematic approach to early modern biomedical theory: it is supported with a citation taken not from a French medical treatise, but from *Observations on the Nature, Causes and Cure of the Disorders which have been commonly call'd Nervous, Hypochondriac, or Hysteric* (Edinburgh, 1765), by the British physician Robert Whytt, who placed far greater emphasis on sympathies than did most of his French counterparts.

10. Cf. François Azouvi,"La Femme comme modèle de la pathologie au XVIIIe siècle," *Diogènes,* no. 115 (1981), 25–40.

11. For a perceptive study of Cabanis's larger medical doctrine, see Martin Staum, *Cabanis: Enlightenment and Medical Philosophy in the French Revolution* (Princeton: Princeton University Press, 1980).

12. Included among the "female illnesses" that preoccupied eighteenth-century physicians were menstruation, conception, late births, childbirth, breast-feeding, and the phenomenon of the so-called "convulsionaries." See Lindsay Wilson, *Women and Medicine in the French Enlightenment: The Debate over "Maladies des Femmes"* (Baltimore: Johns Hopkins University Press, 1993), and Jocelyne Livi, *Vapeurs de femmes: Essai historique sur quelques fantasmes médicaux et philosophiques* (Quentiny-Dijon: Seuil/Navarin, 1984).

13. Joseph Raulin, *Traité des affections vaporeuses du sexe* (Paris, 1758), viii.

14. Pierre Hunauld was one of the few eighteenth-century theorists to explain the vapors in a way similar to that of the ancients: he maintained that they arose from an efflorescence of the "prolific spirits" which was then pathologically communicated throughout the body; see Hunauld, *Dissertation sur les vapeurs et les pertes de sang* (Paris, 1756), 56–60. Hunauld's efflorescence theory was harshly criticized by Raulin (Raulin, xiii).

15. Raulin, *Traité des affections vaporeuses du sexe,* 42: Pierre Pomme, *Traité des affections vaporeuses des deux sexes,* 4th ed. (Lyon, 1769).

16. See, for example, Paul Hoffmann, *La Femme dans la pensée des Lumières* (Paris: Ophrys, 1977), 176; G. S. Rousseau, "Nymphomania, Bienville, and the Rise of Erotic Sensibility," in *Sexuality in Eighteenth-Century Britain,* ed. Paul-Gabriel Boucé (Manchester: Manchester University Press, 1982), 95–119; and Wilson, *Women and Medicine in the French Enlightenment,* 125–59. Ilza Veith, by contrast, insists that eighteenth-century medical theorists "clung firmly to the somatic etiology" of hysteria. Veith, *Hysteria: The History of a Disease* (Chicago: University of Chicago Press, 1965), 170.

17. One might argue that the vapors were replaced by the assorted disorders that nineteenth-century physicians classified under the rubric of "mental alienation," a concept that entailed a distinctly different set of medical and cultural assumptions. See on this point Michel Foucault, *Histoire de la folie à l'âge classique* (Paris: Gallimard, 1972), 381–400. On psychiatry in nineteenth-century France, see Jan Goldstein, *Console and Classify: The French Psychiatric Profession in the Nineteenth Century* (Cambridge: Cambridge University Press, 1987).

18. The implied presence of popular readers is particularly evident in Hunauld's

Dissertation sur les vapeurs et les pertes de sang, which takes the form of a dialogue between a "very vaporous lady" and her physician.

19. Edme-Pierre Chauvot de Beauchêne, *De l'influence des affections de l'âme dans les maladies nerveuses des femmes, avec le traitement qui convient à ces maladies,* 2d ed. (Amsterdam and Paris, 1783).

20. M. Bressy, *Recherches sur les vapeurs* (London and Paris, 1789), ii.

21. According to Antoinette Emch-Dériaz, Tissot wrote an unfinished, unpublished treatise entitled *Des maladies des femmes.* He did not, however, include any specific chapter on the vapors in his plans for this work. See Tissot, *Physician of the Enlightenment,* 88–94.

22. Jean-Baptiste Pressavin, *Nouveau traité des vapeurs* (Lyon, 1770), 208.

23. See D. T. de Bienville, *La Nymphomanie, ou La Fureur utérine* (1771), 2d ed. (Amsterdam, 1780), 133–36, and Beauchêne, 213–14.

24. Pressavin expresses a related concern about the remedies that some physicians used to treat the vapors: "The abusive use of dampening medications [*humectants*] would make the two sexes almost as similar in physical constitution as in moral character." "Avant-Propos" to Pressavin, *Nouveau traité des vapeurs,* unpaginated. He also expresses concern that the vogue of overmedication might spread to the working classes and rob working-class men of the vigor necessary to perform their trades.

25. Jean-André Venel, *Essai sur la santé et sur l'éducation médicinale des filles destinées au mariage* (1776), cited in Hoffmann, *La Femme dans la pensée des Lumières,* 193.

26. On the rhetoric and symbolism surrounding breast-feeding in eighteenth-century France, see Ludmilla Jordanova, "Natural Facts: An Historical Perspective on Science and Sexuality," in *Sexual Visions: Images of Gender in Science and Medicine between the Eighteenth and Twentieth Centuries* (Madison: University of Wisconsin Press, 1989), 29–30.

27. On the prevalence of *ennui* in this period, see Robert Mauzi, "Les Maladies de l'âme au XVIIIe siècle," *Revue des sciences humaines,* no. 100 (1960), 459–93.

28. See Jean-Jacques Rousseau, *Lettre à d'Alembert sur les spectacles* (Paris: Gallimard-Folio, 1987), esp. 158–68, 197–212, and 297–312.

29. A trend closely related to the "back to the countryside" movement in mid-eighteenth-century medical discourse—particularly that devoted to the vapors and other chronic nervous ailments—was the rising popularity of trips to the seashore, cold and hot thermal baths, and other forms of hydrotherapy. Alain Corbin maintains that "even more than the countryside . . . the ocean represents irrefutable nature, which is beyond the realm of [civilized] ornamentation and over which dissimulation has no influence." *Le Territoire du vide: L'Occident et le désir du rivage, 1750–1840* (Paris: Aubier, 1988), 76.

30. Beauchêne injects yet another unmistakable echo of Rousseau into his conclusion: "How I would love for women to have spectacles suited to increasing their physical exercise . . . How I would love an outdoor spectacle, performed in groves, in the shade of their trees, where the illusions of perspective would extend the happy ideas with which women should be occupied!" (Beauchêne, 215).

31. Foucault, *Madness and Civilization*, 157.

32. Roussel praises both of these medical faculties for having liberated medicine from its conceptual enslavement to iatromechanism. Roussel, *Système physique et moral de la femme, ou Tableau philosophique de la constitution, de l'état organique, du tempérament, des moeurs et des fonctions propres au sexe*, 7th ed. (Paris, 1820), liv–lv; hereafter cited as *SF*. This edition also contains Roussel's *Fragment du "Système physique et moral de l'homme"* (hereafter cited as *FH*) and his *Essai sur la sensibilité*.

33. Paul-Victor de Sèze, *Recherches physiologiques et philosophiques sur la sensibilité ou la vie animale* (Paris, 1786).

34. Cabanis, *On the Relations between the Physical and Moral Aspects of Man*, ed. George Mora, trans. Margaret Duggan Mora (Baltimore: Johns Hopkins University Press, 1981), 1:33, hereafter cited as "Cabanis." I have occasionally modified this translation.

35. Sex comes second—after age but before temperament, illness, regimen and climates—in the series of six memoirs (memoirs 4–9) in which Cabanis examines the forces that affect the way that sensations and ideas are formed (Cabanis, 1:171–357, 2:363–519).

36. Schiebinger, *The Mind Has No Sex?* 206.

37. See Jordanova's discussion of the "assymetrical" teleology implicit to moral anthropology, in "Natural Facts," 28–29.

38. Le Doeuff's essay—subtitled "From Imaginary Knowledge to the Learned Imagination"—originally appeared in her book *L'Imaginaire philosophique* (Paris: Payot, 1980), 181–222. References are taken from Michèle Le Doeuff, "Pierre Roussel's Chiasmas: From Imaginary Knowledge to the Learned Imagination," in *The Philosophical Imagination*, trans. by Colin Gordon (Stanford: Stanford University Press, 1989), 138–70, hereafter cited as "LD."

39. Le Doeuff's presentation of Roussel's stance on female bone anatomy (LD, 145–46) is deceptive because she cites only part of the passage in which he discusses comparative pelvic bone structure (*SF*, 6). In fact, the difference that Roussel deemphasizes concerns not the structure of female versus male pelvic bones (as Le Doeuff claims), but their mobility. As Londa Schiebinger has demonstrated, the skeletal anatomists of this period tended, like Roussel, not to deny sexual differences in bone structure, but to exaggerate them—particularly in their depictions of the female pelvis, chest, and head; see Schiebinger, "More Than Skin Deep: The Scientific Search for Sexual Difference," in *The Mind Has No Sex?* 188–213.

40. After noting that Roussel views menstrual flow as a cultural phenomenon (*SF*, 118), Le Doeuff comments: "When Roussel treats menstruation as an acquired characteristic produced by dietary excess, his denial [*dénégation*] of the genital character of this phenomenon is something more than a simple denial" (LD, 140). However, the theory underlying Roussel's perspective on menstruation is not so much phallocentric as hydraulic: paraphrasing the theory of the early-eighteenth-century physician Georg-Ernst Stahl, Roussel asserts that menstruation is a feminine version of a nosebleed—a process that serves the function of regulating the vital fluids made plethoric

by civilization's overstimulating effects on the body (*SF,* 109, 119–22). Moreover, far from being wildly speculative about menstruation (as Le Doeuff suggests), Roussel simply repeats his century's admittedly curious ideas concerning woman's reproductive cycles. On this point see Laqueur, *Making Sex,* 207–27.

41. Rousseau, *Emile,* 697.

42. Théophile de Bordeu, *Recherches sur le tissu muqueux, ou l'organe cellulaire, et sur quelques maladies de poitrine* (1767), in *Oeuvres complètes* (Paris, 1818), 2:735–96.

43. Bordeu explains the theory of heavily dosed centers of sensibility in his *Recherches sur le tissu muqueux,* 752. For a broader view of the Enlightenment idea that vital energy is distributed in doses in the body and throughout the universe, see Michel Delon, *L'Idée d'énergie au tournant des Lumières (1770–1820)* (Paris: Presses Universitaires de France, 1988).

44. Jordanova, "Body Image and Sex Roles," in *Sexual Visions,* 58.

45. Jordanova, "Natural Facts," 28–29.

46. Cabanis sounds a similar theme in his explanation of women's weakness: "The weakness of the woman not only enters into the system of her existence as an essential element of her relations with the man, but is above all necesary, or at least very useful, for conception, for pregnancy, for delivery, for the lactation of the newborn child, and for the care necessary for raising him during the first years of his life" (Cabanis, 1:235).

47. See, for example, his analysis of how modesty and coquetry function as part of the "institution of nature" in women (*SF,* 101–6).

48. As time went on, moral anthropologists tended to underscore the sexes' mental differences in increasingly absolutist terms: "Man acts and thinks, and woman loves and tends to others. The former was endowed by nature with genius and strength; the latter received a more pleasant privilege, in the form of her bewitching graces and sweet attachment to those around her. Woman cannot compete with man in terms of bodily strength and intellectual elevation." Julien-Joseph Virey, *Histoire naturelle du genre humain* (Paris, an IX [1801]), quoted by Jocelyne Livi in *Vapeurs de femmes,* 175; my translation. See also the comparison Virey makes between men's and women's artistic capacities in his semi-medical, semi-aesthetic treatise *De l'influence des femmes sur le goût dans la littérature et les beaux-arts* (Paris, 1810).

49. De Sèze paints a similarly dramatic tableau of would-be women scholars: he warns women that, by undertaking serious mental labor, they expose themselve not only to vapors and melancholy, but also to apoplexy (de Sèze, 228).

50. As Roussel reminds women in the conclusion to his *Système physique et moral de la femme,* "A woman only has a right to all of the advantages that society gives its members, when she has fulfilled all of her social duties; and a woman has only done half of her task when she does not nourish the child she brings into the world. A woman is worthy of the rank she enjoys only when, after having beautified society through her charms, she has helped to increase society's strength by giving it strong and healthy citizens" (*SF,* 222).

51. Jean-Antoine-Nicolas de Caritat de Condorcet, *Esquisse d'un tableau des progrès de l'esprit humain,* trans. June Barraclough as *Sketch for a Historical Picture of the*

Progress of the Human Mind (London: Weidenfeld and Nicolson, 1955), 8. On the term *perfectibility* and the concepts to which it is linked, see Henry Vyverberg, *Historical Pessimism in the French Enlightenment* (Cambridge: Harvard University Press, 1958), esp. chs. 9–10; Robert Nisbet, *History of the Idea of Progress* (New York: Basic Books, 1980); and Michel Baridon, "Les Concepts de nature humaine et de perfectibilité dans l'historiographie des Lumières de Fontenelle à Condorcet," in *L'Histoire au dix-huitième siècle: Actes du Colloque d'Aix-en-Provence* (Aix-en-Provence: Edisud, 1980), 353–74.

52. Jean-Jacques Rousseau, *Discours sur l'origine et les fondements de l'inégalité parmi les hommes* (1754), trans. Judith R. Bush et al. as "Discourse on the Origins of Inequality (Second Discourse)," in *The Collected Writings of Rousseau*, ed. Roger D. Masters and Christopher Kelly (Hanover: University Press of New England, 1992), 26. In a useful editorial note to this passage, Jean Starobinski notes that Rousseau was among the first to use the neologism *perfectibilité* in writing; see Rousseau, *Discours sur l'origine de l'inégalité*, in *Oeuvres complètes* (Paris: Pléiade, 1964), 3:1317.

53. Rousseau, *Discours sur l'origine de l'inégalité*, 138–39. The threat of denaturation is, of course, even more dire for woman according to Rousseau's theoretical system, largely because, as in Roussel's medical doctrine, woman is more fully anchored in nature than is her male counterpart by virtue of her maternal duties. See in this regard book 5 of Rousseau's *Emile*, 692–703.

54. Roussel's medico-philosophical "solution" to the question of enlightenment seems to confirm the thesis advanced by Erica Harth that "with the erosion of dualism by the materialism and mechanism that were paradoxically initiated by Descartes, the slogan 'the mind has no sex' lost some of its vigor. Dualism unsexes the mind; materialistic monism reconnects it to the (sexed) body." Harth, *Cartesian Women: Versions and Subversions of Rational Discourse in the Old Regime* (Ithaca, N.Y.: Cornell University Press, 1992), 169. See also Christine Battersby, "Genius and the 'Female Sex' in the Eighteenth Century," *Studies on Voltaire and the Eighteenth Century* 264 (1989), 909–12, and Lieselotte Steinbrügge, *The Moral Sex: Woman's Nature in the French Enlightenment*, trans. Pamela E. Selwyn (New York: Oxford University Press, 1995). Genevieve Lloyd takes a longer perspective on this dichotomy in *The Man of Reason: "Male" versus "Female" in Western Philosophy* (Minneapolis: University of Minnesota Press, 1984).

55. Nineteenth-century physicians continued to use sensibility as a criterion for positing hierarchical differences between different types of beings: Jean-Baptiste Mège, for example, asserted that sensibility is "greater in the man of color than in the white man, greater in the city-dweller than in the peasant, greater in women than in men, and greater in children than in the elderly." Mège, *Alliance de l'hygie et de la beauté, ou L'Art d'embellir, d'après les principes de la physiologie* (Paris, 1818), 233. See Londa Schiebinger's analysis of how the notion of a "great chain of being" informed the way that the naturalists of this period approached both sex and race, in *Nature's Body*, esp. chs. 4–5.

Chapter 8: Sensibility, Anthropology, and *Libertinage* in Laclos and Sade

1. Ludmilla Jordanova, "Natural Facts: An Historical Perspective on Science and Sexuality," in *Sexual Visions* (Madison: University of Wisconsin Press, 1989), 27.

2. On the question of irony in Laclos's work, see Irving Wohlfarth's astute analysis "The Irony of Criticism and the Criticism of Irony," *Studies on Voltaire and the Eighteenth Century* 120 (1974), 269–317. On Laclos's complex relationship to Rousseau, see Laurent Versini, *Laclos et la tradition* (Paris: Klincksieck, 1968), 330–33, 534–37, 581–617 et passim; Peter Brooks, *The Novel of Worldliness* (Princeton: Princeton University Press, 1969), 172–218; and Joan DeJean, *Literary Fortifications: Rousseau, Laclos, Sade* (Princeton: Princeton University Press, 1984), 214–31.

3. Gilbert Lely proposes two hypotheses to explain this omission: first, Sade may have neglected to mention *Les Liaisons dangereuses* out of literary jealousy; and second, given that both Laclos and Sade spent seven months in 1794 at the Picpus sanatorium, they may have met and had a quarrel whose memory was still fresh in Sade's mind when he wrote his "Idée sur les romans." Lely, *La Vie du Marquis de Sade* (Paris: Pauvert, 1965), 659–61.

4. Jean Fabre examines the rhetorical strategies involved in Sade's essay, in *Idées sur le roman de Madame de Lafayette au Marquis de Sade* (Paris: Editions Klincksieck, 1979), 195–216. Madelyn Gutwirth does the same for Laclos's correspondence with Mme. Riccoboni in the first part of her essay "Laclos and 'Le sexe': The Rack of Ambivalence," *Studies on Voltaire and the Eighteenth Century* 189 (1980), 247–96.

5. "Correspondance entre Madame Riccoboni et M. de Laclos, avril 1782," in Laclos, *Oeuvres complètes*, ed. Laurent Versini (Paris: Pléiade, 1979), 757; hereafter cited as "R-L."

6. See Laurent Versini's hypotheses on the relation between Laclos's novel and those of Richardson and Crébillon, respectively, in *Laclos et la tradition*, 455–78, 481–519, et passim. Laclos professed to have a particular reverence for Richardson's novel *Clarissa:* in addition to having the libertine Valmont of *Les Liaisons dangereuses* make an explicit comparison between his seduction of Mme. de Tourvel and the fate of Richardson's heroine (see letters 107 and 110), Laclos referred to *Clarissa* as "the most profound of our novels"; see his essay "Sur le roman théâtral de M. Lacratelle aîné," in *Oeuvres complètes*, 508.

7. Some critics have drawn upon Laclos's personal writings to support the thesis that he was, in fact, a sincerely sensitive soul with "Rousseauistic" tendencies: see, for example, Versini, *Laclos et la tradition*, 613–15, and René Pomeau, "Le Mariage de Laclos," *Revue d'histoire littéraire de la France* 64, no. 1 (1964), 60–72.

8. In a note on this passage, Laurent Versini explains that *énergie* as used here was synonymous with *efficacité* in Laclos's day. Laclos, *Oeuvres complètes*, 1590 n. 2.

9. Riccoboni, clearly tired of the argument, does not write again, except to end the correspondence ("R-L," 768).

10. Denis Diderot, *Éloge de Richardson* in *Oeuvres complètes*, ed. Herbert Dieckmann et al. (Paris: Hermann, 1975–), 13:195.

11. Pierre Roussel, *Système physique et moral de la femme*, 7th ed. (Paris, 1820), 19.

12. Laclos, "Des femmes et de leur éducation," in *Oeuvres complètes*, 389–443. These essays, never published in Laclos's lifetime, are based on the copious notes he took while reading a variety of philosophical and anthropological works, most particularly Rousseau's *Discours sur l'origine de l'inégalité parmi les hommes* (1754) and Buffon's *Histoire naturelle* (1749–88).

13. For a more thorough interpretation of Laclos's essays on women, see Gutwirth, "Laclos et 'Le sexe,'" 281–96.

14. Sade uses Rousseau to illustrate the second of these principles: "Rousseau, to whom Nature had granted in refinement and sentiment what she had granted only in wit to Voltaire, treated the novel in another way altogether. What vigor, what energy in *La Nouvelle Héloïse*! . . . love was etching with its flaming torch every burning page of *Julie*." Donatien-Alphonse-François de Sade, "Reflections on the Novel," in *The 120 Days of Sodom and Other Writings*, trans. Austryn Wainhouse and Richard Seaver (New York: Grove Press, 1966), 105. For the corresponding French text, see "Idée sur les romans," in *Les Crimes de l'amour* (Paris: Gallimard, 1987), 37–38. References to the English translation, which I have occasionally modified, will be made using the abbreviation "Reflections." References to "Idée sur les romans" will be made using the abbreviation "Idée."

15. Sade's declaration that the novelist reveals truths deeper than those uncovered by history recalls the very similar argument made in Diderot's *Éloge de Richardson*, 201–2. Josué V. Harari examines the obsession with writing and truth-telling that informs both Sadian narrative and the libertine scenarios enacted by Sade's characters, in *Scenarios of the Imaginary: Theorizing the French Enlightenment* (Ithaca, N.Y.: Cornell University Press, 1987), 133–93. See also A. M. Laborde's chapter "La Triade nature, libertin, romancier," in *Sade romancier* (Neuchâtel: La Baconnière, 1974), 13–27.

16. Michel Delon uses the concept of energy to underscore the often overlooked connections that existed between eighteenth-century sentimentalism and libertinism: "The libertine and the *homme sensible*, such as they are presented in fiction, are on a quest for emotion—sensual and intellectual emotion for the first figure, sensitive and moral for the second; in both cases, what is unique about this emotion is its depth, its intensity. Both figures place great value on the energy that allows them to impose their will or increase their sensibility." *L'Idée d'énergie au tournant des Lumières* (Paris: Presses Universitaires de France, 1988), 441.

17. D. A. F. de Sade, "Justine, or Good Conduct Well Chastised," in *The Complete Justine, Philosophy in the Bedroom, and Other Writings*, trans. Richard Seaver and Austryn Wainhouse (New York: Grove Press, 1965), 455; hereafter cited as "Justine." I have occasionally modified the English translation.

18. I thank David Harrison of the University of Wisconsin for pointing out the progressive modifications in Sade's definition of nature in the "Idée sur les romans" and for noting how the novelist's role changes with each metaphoric transformation.

19. The trope of travel clearly informs the opening narrative structure of Sade's short story "Ernestine," whose narrator is a Frenchman traveling in Sweden. Upon descending into the mines of Tapberg, the narrator encounters the Count Oxtiern and insists on hearing his terrible story, saying, "Monsieur, the failings of man teach me to know him better; my sole purpose in traveling is to study. The further he has deviated from the barriers which Nature or man-made laws have imposed upon him, the more interesting is he as a subject of study, the more worthy to be examined and the more deserving of my compassion." "Ernestine, A Swedish Tale," in *The 120 Days of Sodom and Other Writings*, 729. On the somewhat dubious function of travel in Sadian narrative, see Philippe Roger, "La Trace de Fénelon," in *Sade: Écrire la crise*, ed. Michel Camus and Philippe Roger (Paris: Belfond, 1983), 149–73, and Roland Barthes, *Sade, Fourier, Loyola* (Paris: Seuil, 1971), 153–54.

20. Jean Deprun was one of the first modern critics to stress Sade's conceptual debt to the naturalists and biomedical theorists of the eighteenth century; see Deprun, "Sade et la philosophie biologique de son temps," in *Le Marquis de Sade* (Paris: Armand Colin, 1968), 189–203.

21. On the determining power of convention in *Les Liaisons dangereuses*, see Peter Brooks, *The Novel of Worldliness*, 172–218; Roy Roussel's chapter "*Les Liaisons dangereuses* and the Myth of the Understanding Man," in *The Conversation of the Sexes: Seduction and Equality in Selected Seventeenth- and Eighteenth-Century Texts* (New York: Oxford University Press, 1986), 94–123; and Susan Winnett, *Terrible Sociability: The Text of Manners in Laclos, Goethe, and James* (Stanford: Stanford University Press, 1993), ch. 2, 40–96. On psychological determinism in Laclos, see Georges Daniel, *Fatalité du secret et fatalité du bavardage: La Marquise de Merteuil, Jean-François Rameau* (Paris: Nizet, 1966), 7–99. On the militaristic structure of the libertines' seductions, see DeJean, *Literary Fortifications*, 191–201, 232–62. Finally, on the semiotic determinism of the novel's epistolary form, see Tzvetan Todorov, *Littérature et signification* (Paris: Larousse, 1967).

22. Joan DeJean, by contrast, describes resistance as part of "a complex, often multi-layered defensive apparatus" on which the novel's libertines base their conduct. *Literary Fortifications*, 235. On the manner in which the conventional meanings of femininity and masculinity are undermined in *Les Liaisons*, see Roussel, *The Conversation of the Sexes*.

23. Charles Baudelaire, "Notes analytiques et critiques sur *Les Liaisons dangereuses*," in *Oeuvres posthumes* (Paris: Louis Conard, 1939), 333–34.

24. Brooks, *The Novel of Worldliness*, 176.

25. Pierre Choderlos de Laclos, *Les Liaisons dangereuses*, trans. Douglas Parmée (Oxford: Oxford University Press, 1995), letter 9, pp. 23–24. All further references will be made to this translation, using the abbreviation *LLD*. I have occasionally modified the English translation.

26. "Yes, I love watching, contemplating that prudent woman launched unwittingly and inexorably on a steep and slippery slope which is carrying her down despite herself and forcing her to follow me . . . Oh, at least let me have time to contemplate this touching struggle between love and virtue" (*LLD*, letter 96, pp. 200–201).

27. Similarly, in the famous epistle Valmont writes on the back of the prostitute Émilie, he exploits the discursive style of the sentimentally tormented lover in a series of double entendres on expressions like "trouble," "delirium," transports," "intoxication," and so on (*LLD*, letter 48, pp. 93–94).

28. See DeJean's analysis of the "Rousseauian" school of Laclos critics in *Literary Fortifications*, 214–15, and Wolfarth's discussion of the *libertin* analogy in "The Irony of Criticism," esp. 270–86.

29. Wolfarth, "The Irony of Criticism," 282. Wolfarth finds the *libertin* analogy particularly pronounced in the interpretations of Jean Rousset and Georges Poulet. See Jean Rousset's reading of *Les Liaisons dangereuses* in *Forme et signification* (Paris: José Corti, 1962), 93–99, and Georges Poulet's in *La Distance intérieure* (Paris: Plon, 1952), 70–80.

30. See, for example, Merteuil's disdainful remarks in letters 81 and 85 about the excessively systematic methods of seduction used by Valmont and Prévan. See also Mme. de Volanges's efforts to rationalize why the roué Valmont is received in polite Parisian society: "Far from being ostracized by decent people, he's admitted and even warmly welcomed in what is known as 'good society' . . . Certainly Monsieur de Valmont comes to my house and he is accepted everywhere. This is one more absurdity to add to the thousand and one others condoned by society" (*LLD*, letter 32, pp. 61–62).

31. André Malraux emphasizes the mythological quality of Merteuil's and Valmont's shared ideology of superintelligence and absolute mastery; see Malraux, *Le Triangle noir* (Paris: Gallimard, 1970), 30–31. See also Jean-Luc Seylaz, *"Les Liaisons dangereuses" et la création romanesque chez Laclos* (Geneva: Droz, 1958), 76, 129, et passim.

32. Jean Giraudoux, "Choderlos de Laclos," in *Littérature* (Paris: Grasset, 1941), 73.

33. See Versini's comment on this passage in *Les Liaisons dangereuses* in Laclos, *Oeuvres complètes*, 1352 n. 2.

34. Roussel, *The Conversation of the Sexes*, 100, 108–113.

35. Aram Vartanian, "The Marquise de Merteuil: A Case of Mistaken Identity," *L'Esprit Créateur* 3, no. 4 (1963), 172–80.

36. See, for example, Anne Deneys-Tunney, *Ecritures du corps* (Paris: Presses Universitaires de France, 1992), 306–13.

37. In "The Sensationist Aesthetics of the French Enlightenment," *L'Esprit créateur* 28, no. 4 (1988), 95–105, John C. O'Neal ventures the dubious hypothesis that the statue of Condillac's *Traité des sensations* is itself feminized. O'Neal relies on a stereotypical supposition that in eighteenth-century French philosophy and literature alike, sensibility was understood as a primarily female trait. This is certainly not true of the sensationalist narratives of mental development that Merteuil is appropriating in letter 81 of *Les Liaisons dangereuses:* the Statue-Man fables to which this letter alludes were either strictly gender-neutral or masculinized. That is not to say that Merteuil's feminine twist on those fables is entirely original: Pierre Roussel does something quite similar in the *Système physique et moral de la femme.*

38. Georges Daniel astutely points out that (initially at least) "Mme. de Merteuil does not wear a mask because she has something to hide" but rather "cultivates the art

of dissimulation . . . as a vocation." Daniel, *Fatalité du secret et fatalité du bavardage au XVIIIe siècle*, 18.

39. See, for example, Baudelaire, "Notes analytiques," 336, and Roussel, *The Conversation of the Sexes*, 100.

40. Joan DeJean makes a suggestive link between Merteuil's intimate knowledge of the human heart and that which Sade requires of the novelist in his "Idée sur les romans"; see *Literary Fortifications*, 248, 326.

41. See, for example, letter 63, where Merteuil relates how she succeeded in simultaneously manipulating the sensibilities of Danceny, Cécile, and Mme. de Volanges, by arranging for the young lovers' illicit correspondence to be discovered by la Volanges senior.

42. Aram Vartanian, for one, contends that Merteuil is mythical because she personifies the fearful possibility that a gifted, willful woman might achieve full erotic emancipation and thus "breach the distinction between the masculine and the feminine." Vartanian, "The Marquise de Merteuil," 177. That interpretation is complicated, however, by the fact that the distinction between the masculine and the feminine is already blurred by the notion of sensibility that is at play in *Les Liaisons dangereuses*.

43. See, for example, Vartanian, "The Marquise de Merteuil," 178–79, and Roussel, *The Conversation of the Sexes*, 111–12.

44. See also the erotic tableau that Merteuil sketches in letter 63, where she describes the now-desolate Cécile crying in her nightclothes and seeking comfort in Merteuil's arms (119). This letter is central to establishing the sexual quadrille that eventually forms in the novel, involving Merteuil, Valmont, Cécile, and Danceny. Valmont jokingly suggests his erotic connection to Danceny in letter 115, where, after describing how he dictated a love letter that Cécile was struggling to write to Danceny, he exclaims: "The things I'm doing for Danceny! I'll have been his friend, his confidant, his rival . . . and his mistress!" (260).

45. The incredible degree of Cécile's "stupid ingenuousness" is confirmed when Valmont reports that Cécile has had a miscarriage, without ever knowing that she was pregnant: "Perhaps never before has any girl preserved such innocence while doing her damnedest to lose it. Ah me, that little girl doesn't waste much time using her head!" (letter 140, p. 312).

46. Hence the nasty witticism that the novel's conventional characters spread around about Merteuil: "The Marquis de ***, who never misses a chance to say something unkind, when talking of her yesterday said that her illness had turned her inside out and that now her soul was showing on her face. Unfortunately everyone thought that the remark was apt" (letter 175, p. 370).

47. David B. Morris rightly points out that libertine sensibility in Sade is paradoxical, inasmuch as it is "simultaneously hypersensitive and numb"; see "The Marquis de Sade and the Discourses of Pain: Literature and Medicine at the Revolution," in *The Languages of Psyche*, ed. G. S. Rousseau (Berkeley and Los Angeles: University of California Press, 1990), 323–24. See also Morris's chapter on Sade in his book *The Culture of Pain* (Berkeley and Los Angeles: University of California Press, 1991), 224–43.

48. Clairwil explains her temperament to Juliette in these terms: "'My soul is hard, and I am far from believing sensibility preferable to the apathy I luckily enjoy. Oh, Juliette,' she continued, donning her clothes, 'you perhaps entertain illusions regarding this dangerous softheartedness, this compassion, this sensibility, the having whereof is thought creditable by so many imbeciles." *Juliette*, trans. Austryn Wainhouse (New York: Grove Press, 1968), 277. I have occasionally modified the English translation.

49. In his analysis of Sadian apathy, Philippe Roger emphasizes that it is founded upon a materialist rejection of the cultural-moral values that were associated with sensibility in the eighteenth century: "Apathy is a mechanical procedure, whose mainspring is becoming accustomed to doing evil, to seeing pain, and so on; this procedure must facilitate the transition between the stereotypical moral person and the free being of libertinism . . . Being apprenticed in voluptuousness entails acquiring a counterculture that is composed of automatisms and pleasure-giving habits; this counterculture comes to take the place of the anterior 'conscience,' the one associated with 'sensibility.'" Roger, *Sade: La Philosophie dans le pressoir* (Paris: Grasset, 1976), 54–55. Roger explains that Sadian apathy revolves around a process of reconverting sensibility, by de-moralizing the so-called "sensible fiber" made popular by materialist writers like Diderot and d'Holbach, so that the notion of fiber can become purely physio-anatomical and erotic (Roger, 64).

50. See, for example, Marcel Hénaff, *Sade: L'Invention du corps libertin* (Paris: Presses Universitaires de France, 1978), 30. Sade was indeed an avid reader of eighteenth-century medical treatises, as is evident in the catalog that Alice M. Laborde has published of one of his earliest library collections: *La Bibliothèque du Marquis de Sade au château de La Coste (en 1776)* (Geneva: Editions Slatkine, 1991). In addition to La Mettrie's *Oeuvres philosophiques* (1751), indicated in entry 430 on p. 130, the collection includes two works written or inspired by Tissot: his *De la santé des gens de lettres*, and a work by Marc-Philippe Dutoit de Mambrini entitled *L'Onanisme, ou Discours philosophique et moral sur la luxure artificielle* (Lausanne, 1760), which Laborde describes as having been reprinted in the wake of the enormous popular response to Tissot's treatise on the same subject (cf. entries 289 and 290, p. 96). Sade also possessed *Mélanges de physique et de morale* (Paris, 1763) by the Montpellier physician Louis de Lacaze (see entry 271, p. 91).

51. Sade wrote two other versions of *Justine*: a *conte philosophique* entitled *Les Infortunes de la vertu*, written in 1787 but not published until 1930, and *La Nouvelle Justine, ou Les Malheurs de la vertu, suivie de L'Histoire de Juliette, sa soeur* (1797). Gilbert Lely notes the analogy between the systematically pessimistic conception of human nature that Sade put forth for the first time in the *Justine* of 1791 and the philosophy that imbues *Les Liaisons dangereuses*; see Lely, *La Vie du Marquis de Sade*, 578–610.

52. Justine (who hides her identity by calling herself Thérèse) is portrayed in platitudinously glowing terms at the outset of the narrative: "Hers was of a pensive and melancholy character . . . Full of tenderness, endowed with an astonishing sensibility instead of with the art and finesse of her sister [Juliette], she was ruled by an ingenu-

ousness, a candor that were to cause her to tumble into not a few pitfalls. To so many qualities this girl joined a sweet countenance . . . a virginal air, large blue eyes very soulful and appealing, a dazzling fair skin, a supple and resilient body, a touching voice, teeth of ivory and the loveliest blond hair" (*Justine*, 459).

53. Sade, *Aline et Valcour*, in *Oeuvres complètes du Marquis de Sade* (Paris: Au Cercle du Livre Précieux, 1966), 5:259.

54. See Josué V. Harari's analysis of the highly methodical procedures of writing and theorizing by which the Sadian libertine trains his or her imagination, in *Scenarios of the Imaginary*, 133–60.

55. See, for example, the description of Coeur-de-Fer and the portraits of the monks Dom Severino and Antonin in Sade, *Justine, ou Les malheurs de la vertu* (Paris: Librairie Générale Française, 1973), 46, 55, 163–65.

56. As J. Harari points out, "There is no corporeal eroticism for Sade . . . the libertine libido is always placed under the government of thought." *Scenarios of the Imaginary*, 145. Harari cites in this regard Roland Barthes, who says of Sade: "What makes the value of sex is intelligence. Intelligence is both an *effervescence of the head* . . . and a guarantee of capacity, for intelligence orders, invents, refines." *Sade, Fourier, Loyola*, trans. Richard Miller (Berkeley and Los Angeles: University of California Press, 1989), 170.

57. Morris, "The Marquis de Sade and the Discourses of Pain," 292.

58. *Justine, ou Les Malheurs de la vertu*, 143–44.

Conclusion

1. David Denby uses Baculard d'Arnaud as one of his case studies of eighteenth-century sentimentalism, in *Sentimental Narrative and the Social Order in France, 1760–1820* (Cambridge: Cambridge University Press, 1994), 8–25.

2. On those debates, see Claire Salomon-Bayet, *L'Institution de la science et l'expérience du vivant* (Paris: Flammarion, 1978).

3. Frank Baasner, *Der Bergriff 'sensibilité' im 18. Jahrhundert: Aufstieg und Niedergang eines Ideals* (Heidelberg: Carl Winter Universitätsverlag, 1988), 339–86. On the complicated question of how sensibility and sentimentalism operated in the rhetoric of the Revolution, see also Pierre Trahard, *La Sensibilité révolutionnaire (1789–1794)* (Paris: Boivin, 1936), and Denby, *Sentimental Narrative and the Social Order*, 139–65.

4. Cited in Baasner, *Der Begriff 'Sensibilité,'* 388.

5. Quoted from de Staël, *De l'Allemagne* (1815) in Denby, *Sentimental Narrative and the Social Order*, 208; my translation. Denby's chapter 6 (194–239) is a useful study both of Mme. de Staël's sociopolitical thought and of the selective use she made in her novels of certain eighteenth-century sentimentalist conventions. See also Simone Balayé, "A Propos du 'préromantisme': Continuité ou rupture chez Mme. de Staël," in *Le Préromantisme: Hypothèque ou hypothèse?* ed. Paul Viallaneix (Paris: Klincksieck, 1975), 153–68.

6. Pierre Simon Ballanche fils, *Du sentiment considéré dans ses rapports avec la littérature et les arts* (Lyon and Paris, 1801), 84.

7. See Roland Mortier, "Le Traité *Du Sentiment* de P. S. Ballanche: Un Programme littéraire antiphilosophique et post-Révolutionnaire," in *Approches des Lumières: Mélanges offerts à Jean Fabre* (Paris: Klincksieck, 1974), 319–31.

8. Étienne de Senancour, *Rêveries sur la nature primitive de l'homme* [1799–1800] (Paris: E. Cornély, 1910), 58–59. Senancour adds in a footnote: "This universal sensibility is unknown to the sentimental man, who, because of the weakness of his faculties and the narrow sphere of his conceptions, remains insensitive to almost all of the impressions of nature, which is almost inaccessible to him" (59). Senancour's Rousseauistic effort to give a primitivist, antisocial cast to "true" sensibility has obvious resonances with Bernardin de Saint-Pierre's *Paul et Virginie* (1788), a novel that was extremely popular throughout the next century, in which sentimentalism and exoticism combined with a highly teleological brand of naturalism.

9. Michel Delon notes that both François Marie Charles Fourier and Pierre Maine de Biran used the metaphor of Christopher Columbus's discovery of America to describe their own quests for a "new world"—a new social world in the case of Fourier and a new metaphysical world for Biran; see Delon, *L'Idée d'énergie au tournant des Lumières (1770–1820)* (Paris: Presses Universitaires de France, 1988), 456–57.

10. Mona Ozouf, "La Révolution française et la formation de l'homme nouveau," in *L'Homme régénéré: Essais sur la Révolution française* (Paris: Gallimard, 1989), 116–57.

11. On the organicist paradigm that marked thinking in nineteenth-century economic theory, biology, medicine, history, and sociology, see Georges Gusdorf's chapter "Organisme" in *Fondements du savoir romantique* (Paris: Payot, 1982), 427–46, and Judith Schlanger, *Les Métaphores de l'organisme* (Paris: Vrin, 1971).

12. See Roselyne Rey, "Le Vitalisme de Julien-Joseph Virey," in *Julien-Joseph Virey, naturaliste et anthropologue*, ed. Claude Bénichou and Claude Blanckaert (Paris: Vrin, 1988), 31–59. Rey bases her reading of Virey's "Romantic" brand of vitalism on texts like his article "Nature," included in the *Dictionnaire des sciences médicales par une société de médecins et de chirurgiens*, 60 vols. (Paris, 1812–22), 35:240–98.

13. The classic study of *Idéologie* as a philosophy is François Picavet's dated but still useful *Les Idéologues* (Paris, 1896). See also the discussion "Sentimentalism and 'Idéologie,'" in Denby, *Sentimentalism and the Social Order*, 166–93; and the various essays included in *L'Institution de la raison: La Révolution culturelle des Idéologues*, ed. François Azouvi (Paris: Vrin, 1992).

14. On the ambitious expansion of philosophical/anthropological medicine during this period, see Elizabeth A. Williams, *The Physical and the Moral* (Cambridge: Cambridge University Press, 1994), 67–114, and Sergio Moravia, "Philosophie et médecine à la fin du XVIIIe siècle," *Studies on Voltaire and the Eighteenth Century* 89 (1972), 1089–1151.

15. Roselyne Rey describes the disintegration of the close relationship that had existed among early-nineteenth-century physiology, philosophy, and medicine in these terms: "The juncture between these fields, which would henceforth be separated, was possible only because a certain philosophy of knowledge converged with the dissolution of the old [pedagogical] institutions and the subsequent establishment of new

structures. With the new distribution of chairs decreed by the law of 1811, and with the creation of the Academy of Medicine in December 1820, that unity would be lost in France, and remain so for a long time thereafter." "La Transmission du savoir médical," in *L'Institution de la raison,* 148–49.

16. See Jean-Jacques Süe, *Recherches physiologiques et expériences sur la vitalité* (Paris, an VI [1797]), 59–75. For a fuller account of the guillotine debate, see Dorinda Outram, "The Guillotine, the Soul, and the Audience for Death," in *The Body and the French Revolution: Sex, Class, and Political Culture* (New Haven: Yale University Press, 1989), 106–23.

17. On mesmerism as a theory and as a sociopolitical phenomenon, see particularly Robert Darnton, *Mesmerism and the End of the Enlightenment in France* (Cambridge: Harvard University Press, 1968), and François Azouvi, "Magnétisme animal: La Sensation infinie," *Dix-huitième siècle,* no. 23 (1991), 107–18. See also F. Azouvi, "Le Mesmérisme: Des Lumières à l'illuminisme," in *Lumières et illuminisme,* ed. Mario Matucci (Pisa: Pacini Editore, 1984), 133–40; Georges Benrekassa, "Hystérie, 'crises' et convulsions au XVIIIe siècle: Age des Lumières, éclipses du sujet," *Revue des Sciences humaines* 79, no. 208 (1987), 113–40; and Robert Amadou's remarks throughout his critical edition of Franz Anton Mesmer, *Le Magnétisme animal* (Paris: Payot, 1971).

18. Azouvi, "Magnétisme animal," 114–16.

19. I am paraphrasing the description of the magnetizer's "conductive" role provided by C. Deslon, one of Mesmer's French disciples, who is cited by Azouvi in "Magnétisme animal," 110. On the fluidist metaphor that was used in mesmerism and assorted biomedical doctrines from Descartes to Freud, see Jean Starobinski, "Note sur l'histoire des fluides imaginaires (des esprits animaux à la libido)," *Gesnerus* 23 (1966), 176–87. See also François Roustang's very insightful reflections on animal magnetism, somnabulism, and modern psychotherapy in *Influences* (Paris: Minuit, 1990), 57–79.

20. See Darnton, *Mesmerism and the End of the Enlightenment in France,* 83–125. The cultural and literary repercussions of mesmerism in the nineteenth century were enormous; Honoré de Balzac, for example, placed animal magnetism at the center of the plot of his novel *Ursule Mirouët* (1841). Maria A. Tatar discusses Balzac and other literary reflections of the nineteenth-century mesmerist movement in *Spellbound: Studies on Mesmerism and Literature* (Princeton: Princeton University Press, 1978); see esp. 152–88.

21. Maine de Biran's remarks on mesmerism are included in his "Discours à la Société médicale de Bergerac" (1807) in *Oeuvres* (Paris: Vrin, 1984), 5:82–123. See Roustang's discussion of this text in *Influences,* 71–76.

22. Biran set about redefining sensibility as early as 1801, when he wrote the first draft of *Influence de l'habitude sur la faculté de pensée.* For a thorough examination of the evolution of Biran's philosophy of the mind and soul, see Henri Gouhier's classic study, *Les Conversions de Maine de Biran* (Paris: Vrin, 1947).

23. On Bichat's work and its import for nineteenth-century physiology, anatomy, and medicine, see Elizabeth Haigh, *Xavier Bichat and the Medical Theory of the Eighteenth Century* (London: Wellcome Institute for the History of Medicine, 1984), and

François Duchesneau, *La Physiologie des Lumières* (The Hague: Martinus Nijhoff Publishers, 1982), 431–76.

24. Williams, *The Physical and the Moral*, 100. Williams provides a useful analysis of the implications of Bichat's principle of vital energy and theory of temperament for the medical science of man in nineteenth-century France. Roselyne Rey underscores the paradoxical nature of Bichat's insistence that the passions were situated in the organic, unconscious half of human life and could act upon the conscious half only through "sympathetic," pathological repercussion; see "La Transmission du savoir médical," 138–48.

25. See Bichat, *Recherches physiologiques sur la vie et la mort* (Paris: Gauthier-Villars, 1955), 85–90, 126–51, et passim. I have examined elsewhere the manner in which the terms of Bichat's binary physiological system are applied and inverted in Balzac's *Louis Lambert*; see my "Pathological Inversions: Balzac and Bichat," *Romantic Review* 79, no. 3 (1988), 422–42.

26. Virey delivered this discourse to the Academy of Medicine on February 18, 1840; it was reprinted in the *Gazette médicale* of March 7, 1840. See Rey, "Le Vitalisme de J-J. Virey," 50–53, and Geneviève Fraisse, "Le Genre humain et la femme chez J.-J. Virey, ou 'Une Certaine Harmonie d'inégalités correspondantes,'" in Bénichou and Blanckaert, *Julien-Joseph Virey, naturaliste et anthropologue*, 183–206.

27. See, for example, Pierre-Antoine Prost, *Essai physiologique sur la sensibilité* (Paris, 1805), and François-Joseph-Victor Broussais, *De l'irritation et de la folie, ouvrage dans lequel les rapports du physique et du moral sont établis sur les bases de la médecine physiologique* (Paris and Brussels, 1828).

28. I cite Elizabeth Williams's paraphrase of Alibert's "De l'influence des causes politiques sur les maladies et la constitution physique de l'homme" (1795), provided in *The Physical and the Moral*, 91–92.

29. Fréderic Bérard, *Doctrine des rapports du physique et du moral, pour servir de fondement à la physiologie dite intellectuelle et à la métaphysique* (Paris, 1823), cited in L. S. Jacyna, "Medical Science and Moral Science: The Cultural Relations of Physiology in Restoration France," *History of Science* 25 (1987), 123; Jacyna's translation.

30. See Daniel Pick, *Faces of Degeneration: A European Disorder, c.1848–c.1918* (Cambridge: Cambridge University Press, 1989).

31. In his "Introduction aux *Etudes philosophiques*" Felix Davin ("assisted," apparently, by the rather overbearing Balzac) compared Balzac's "physico-moral" mission as a novelist to the investigations of history's greatest scientists; see Balzac, *La Comédie humaine* (Paris: Pléaide, 1979), 10:1209.

32. Honoré de Balzac, *The Wild Ass's Skin*, trans. Herbert J. Hunt (London: Penguin Books, 1977), 245. I have slightly modified the English translation. L. S. Jacyna gives a short but interesting interpretation of this scene from the perspective of medical history in "Medical Science and Moral Science," 138–39.

33. See Roland Mortier's cogent remarks on the problems underlying the "Preromanticist" critical approach, in "Unité ou scission du siècle des Lumières?" in *Clartés et ombres du siècle des Lumières* (Geneva: Droz, 1969), 114–24.

ℬibliography

The listing that follows is divided into two parts: a list of primary sources and a list of secondary works. This is a complete listing of all works cited in the notes and of a few additional sources. In most cases, the English translations cited for French works are available translations, not translations of the specific French edition cited.

To avoid numerous instances of full citation of frequently cited sources— e.g., multivolume complete works or the *Encyclopédie,* from which many articles are cited—such sources are listed in full as separate entries, with only a brief citation followed by "q.v." used in the citation of sources derived from the larger work.

Primary Works

d'Alembert, Jean. "Expérimental." In *Encyclopédie* (q.v.). Vol. 1, tome 6.

——. *Preliminary Discourse to the Encyclopedia of Diderot.* Trans. Richard N. Schwab with the collaboration of Walter E. Rex. Indianapolis: Bobbs-Merrill, 1963.

Alibert, J. L. "Eloge de Pierre Roussel." In Pierre Roussel, *Système physique et moral de la femme* (q.v.).

d'Aumont, Arnulfe. "Régime." In *Encyclopédie* (q.v.). Vol. 3, tome 14.

Ballanche, Pierré Simon fils. *Du sentiment considéré dans ses rapports avec la littérature et les arts.* Lyon and Paris, 1801.

Balzac, Honoré de. *La Peau de chagrin* (1831). In *La Comédie humaine.* Vol. 10. Paris: Pléaide, 1979. (English translation: *The Wild Ass's Skin.* Trans. Herbert J. Hunt. London: Penguin Books, 1977.)

Beauchêne, Edme-Pierre Chauvot de. *De l'influence des affections de l'âme dans les maladies nerveuses des femmes, avec le traitement qui convient à ces maladies* (1781). 2d ed. Amsterdam and Paris: Mequignon, 1783.

Bichat, Xavier. *Recherches physiologiques sur la vie et la mort* (1800). Paris: Gauthier-Villars, 1955.

Bienville, D.T. de. *La Nymphomanie, ou La Fureur utérine* (1771). 2d ed. Amsterdam: M. M. Rey, 1780.

Boerhaave, Herman. *Institutions de médecine*. Trans. Julien Offray de La Mettrie. Paris: Huart, Briasson, et Durand, 1743–50.

Bonnet, Charles. *Essai analytique sur les facultés de l'âme* (1759). In *Oeuvres d'histoire naturelle et de philosophie*. Vol. 6. Neuchâtel: Samuel Fauche, 1779–83.

Bordeu, Théophile de. *Correspondance*. Ed. Martha Fletcher. Montpellier: Presses de l'Université Paul Valéry, 1977.

———. *Oeuvres complètes*. 2 vols. Paris: Caille et Ravier, 1818. Contains *Recherches anatomiques sur la position des glandes et sur leur action* (1752), *Recherches sur les crises* (1743), *Recherches sur l'histoire de la médecine* (1767), *Recherches sur les maladies chroniques* (1775), *Recherches sur le pouls par rapport aux crises* (1757), *Recherches sur le tissu muqueux, ou l'organe cellulaire*, ... (1767).

Bressy, M. *Recherches sur les vapeurs*. London and Paris: Planche, 1789.

Broussais, François-Joseph-Victor. *De l'irritation et de la folie, ouvrage dans lequel les rapports du physique et du moral sont établis sur les bases de la médecine physiologique*. Paris: Delaunay; Brussels: Librairie médicale française, 1828.

Buffon, George-Louis Leclerc de. *Oeuvres philosophiques de Buffon*. Paris: Presses Universitaires de France, 1954.

Cabanis, Pierre-Jean-Georges. *Rapports du physique et du moral de l'homme* (1802). Geneva: Slatkine Reprints, 1980. (English translation: *On the Relations between the Physical and Moral Aspects of Man*. Trans. Margaret Duggan Mora. Ed. George Mora. Baltimore: Johns Hopkins University Press, 1981.)

Catalogue des sciences médicales de la Bibliothèque Impériale. 2 vols. Paris, 1857.

Cheyne, George. *The English Malady, or A Treatise of Nervous Diseases of All Kinds*. London: Strahan and Leake, 1733.

Condillac, Abbé de. *Traité des sensations* (1754). Paris: Fayard, 1984. (English translation: *Condillac's Treatise on the Sensations*. Trans. Geraldine Carr. Los Angeles: School of Philosophy, University of Southern California, 1930.)

Condorcet, Jean-Antoine-Nicolas de Caritat de. *Sketch for a Historical Picture of the Progress of the Human Mind [Esquisse d'un tableau des progrès de l'esprit humain* (1795)]. Trans. June Barraclough, London: Weidenfeld and Nicolson, 1955.

Crébillon, Claude Prosper Jolyot de. *Les Egarements du coeur et de l'esprit* (1736). Paris: Garnier Flammarion, 1985. (English translation: *The Wayward Head and Heart*. Trans. Barbara Bray. London: Oxford University Press, 1963.)

Davin, Felix. "Introduction aux *Etudes philosophiques*." In *La Comédie humaine*, by Honoré de Balzac, 10:1199–1218. Paris: Pléiade, 1979.

Diderot, Denis. *Discours sur la poésie dramatique* (1758). In *Oeuvres complètes* (q.v.). Vol. 10.

———. *Eléments de physiologie* (1837). Ed. Jean Mayer. Paris: Librairie Marcel Didier, 1964.

———. *Éloge de Richardson* (1761). Introd. Jean Sgard. In *Oeuvres complètes* (q.v.). Vol. 13. (English translation: "An Eulogy of Richardson." In *Diderot's Thoughts on Art and Style*. Trans. Beatrix L. Tollemache. London: J. Macqueen, 1896.)

———. *De l'Interprétation de la nature* (1753). In *Oeuvres philosophiques*. Ed. Paul Vernière. Paris: Garnier, 1964.

———. *Lettre sur les sourds et muets* (1751). In *Oeuvres complètes* (q.v.). Vol. 4.

———. *Le Paradoxe sur le comédien, précédé des "Entretiens sur 'Le Fils naturel.'"* Paris: Garnier-Flammarion, 1981. (English translation: *The Paradox of Acting*. Trans. William Archer. New York: Hill and Wang, 1957.)

———. *Oeuvres complètes*. Ed. Herbert Dieckmann, Jacques Proust, Jean Varloot, et al. 33 vols. Paris: Hermann, 1975–.

———. *Réflexions sur le livre "De l'esprit" par M. Helvétius*. In *Oeuvres complètes* (q.v.). Vol. 9.

———. *Réfutation suivie de l'ouvrage d'Helvétius intitulé "L'Homme"* (1773). In *Oeuvres philosophiques*. Ed. Paul Vernière. Paris: Garnier, 1964.

———. *La Religieuse* (1760; 1780–82). In *Oeuvres complètes* (q.v.). Vol. 11. (English translation: *Memoirs of a Nun*. Trans. Francis Birrell. London: Elek Books, 1959.)

———. *Le Rêve de d'Alembert* (1769). In *Oeuvres complètes* (q.v.). Vol. 17. (English translation: *Rameau's Nephew and D'Alembert's Dream*. Trans. Leonard Tancock. London: Penguin, 1966.)

Encyclopédie, ou Dictionnaire raisonné des sciences, des arts et des métiers. Ed. Denis Diderot and Jean d'Alembert. 17 tomes. Paris: Briasson, David, Le Breton, and Durand, 1751–65. Reprint: New York: Pergamon Press, 1969.

Fabre, Pierre. *Essai sur les facultés de l'âme, considérées dans leur rapport avec la sensibilité et l'irritabilité de nos organes*. Paris: Vente, Mérigot, and Buisson, 1785.

Fouquet, Henri. "Sensibilité, Sentiment (Médecine)." In *Encyclopédie* (q.v.). Vol. 3, tome 15.

Fouquier de Maissemy. *Les Avantages d'une constitutions faible, apperçu* [sic] *médical*. Paris: Gilles, 1802.

Gaub, Jerome. *De regimine mentis* (1747 and 1763). Translated in J. L. Rather, *Mind and Body in Eighteenth-Century Medicine: A Study Based on Jerome Gaub's "De regimine mentis."* Berkeley and Los Angeles: University of California Press, 1965.

Graffigny, Françoise de. *Lettres d'une Péruvienne* (1747). Introd. Bernard Bray and Isabelle Landy-Houillon. Paris: Garnier-Flammarion, 1983. (English translation: *Letters from a Peruvian Woman*. Trans. David Kornacker. New York: Modern Language Association of America, 1993.)

Haller, Albrecht von. *A Dissertation on the Sensible and Irritable Parts of Animals* (1755). Introd. Owsei Temkin. Baltimore: Johns Hopkins Press, 1936.

———. *First Lines of Physiology* (1786). Introd. Lester King. New York: Johnson Reprint Corp., 1966.

———. *Mémoires sur la nature sensible et irritable des parties du corps animal*. 4 vols. Lausanne: Bousquet, 1756–60.

———. "Oeconomie animale." In *Supplément* (q.v.) to *Encyclopédie*. Vol. 5, tome 4.

———. "Physiologie." In *Supplément* (q.v.) to *Encyclopédie*. Vol. 5, tome 4.

———. *Réflexions sur le système de la génération de M. de Buffon*. Geneva: Barrillot, 1751.

————. "Sensibilité." In *Supplément* (q.v.) to *Encyclopédie*. Vol. 5, tome 4.

Hélvetius, Claude Adrien. *De l'esprit, or Essays on the Mind and Its Several Faculties.* Trans. unspecified. London: M. Jones, 1807.

Hunauld, Pierre. *Dissertation sur les vapeurs et les pertes de sang.* Paris: Leloup, 1756.

"Hygiène." In *Encyclopédie* (q.v.). Vol. 2, tome 8.

Jaucourt, Louis de. "Sensibilité." In *Encyclopédie* (q.v.). Vol. 3, tome 15.

Lacaze, Louis de. *Idée de l'homme physique et moral, pour servir d'introduction à un traité de médecine.* Paris: Guérin et Delatour, 1755.

Laclos, Pierre-Ambroise-François Choderlos de. "Correspondance entre Madame Riccoboni et M. de Laclos" (1782). In *Oeuvres complètes* (q.v.).

————. "Des femmes et de leur éducation." In *Oeuvres complètes* (q.v.).

————. *Les Liaisons dangereuses* (1782). In *Oeuvres complètes* (q.v.). (English translation: *Les Liaisons dangereuses.* Trans. Douglas Parmée. Oxford: Oxford University Press, 1995.)

————. *Oeuvres complètes.* Ed. Laurent Versini. Paris: Pléaide, 1979.

————. "Sur le roman théâtral de M. Lacratelle aîné" (1824). In *Oeuvres complètes* (q.v.).

Lafont-Gouzi, G. G. *Coup-d'oeil sur la dégénération qui s'est opérée dans le tempérament des hommes.* Paris: Gabon, 1811.

La Mettrie, Julien Offray de. *L'Homme machine* (1748). Paris: Editions Denoël/Gonthier, 1981. (English translation: *Man a Machine.* Trans. Gertrude Bussey and M. W. Calkins. La Salle, Ill.: Open Court Publishing Co., 1943.)

————. *Le Petit Homme à longue queue* (1751). Reprinted in *Corpus* 5/6 (1987), 181–93.

Le Camus, Antoine. *La Médecine de l'esprit* (1753). 2d ed. Paris: Ganeau, 1769.

————. "Mémoire sur la conservation des hommes biens faits." In *Mémoire sur divers sujets de médecine.* Paris: Ganeau, 1760.

————. "Mémoire sur le cerveau, où l'on développe le principe de la génération." In *Mémoire sur divers sujets de médecine.* Paris: Ganeau, 1760.

Le Cat, Claude-Nicolas. *Mémoire posthume sur les incendies spontanés de l'économie animale.* Paris: Migneret, 1813.

————. *Traité de l'existence, de la nature et des propriétés du fluide des nerfs, et principalement de son action dans le mouvement musculaire.* Berlin: Académie de Berlin, 1753.

————. *Traité des sensations et des passions en général, et des sens en particulier.* Paris: Vallert-La Chapelle, 1767.

Locke, John. *An Essay concerning Human Understanding* (1689). Ed. Peter H. Nidditch. Oxford: Clarendon Press, 1975.

Lorry, Anne-Charles. *Essai sur les aliments, pour servir de commentaire aux livres diétiques d'Hippocrates.* 2 vols. Paris: Vincent, 1757.

Maine de Biran, Pierre. "Discours à la société de Bergerac" (1807). In *Oeuvres.* Vol. 5. Paris: Vrin, 1984.

————. *Mémoire sur la décomposition de la pensée* (1805). In *Oeuvres.* Vol. 3. Paris: Vrin, 1984.

Marivaux, Pierre Carlet de Chamblain de. *La Vie de Marianne* (1731–41). Paris: Garnier Flammarion, 1978. (English translation: *The Virtuous Orphan*. Trans. Mary Mitchell Collyer. Carbondale: Southern Illinois University Press, 1965.)

Marquet, François Nicolas. *Nouvelle méthode facile et curieuse, pour apprendre par les notes de musique à connoître le pouls de l'homme et ses différens changemens* (1747). 2d ed. Paris: Didot, 1769.

Mège, Jean-Baptiste. *Alliance de l'hygie et de la beauté, ou L'Art d'embellir, d'après les principes de la physiologie*. Paris: Crochard, 1818.

Ménuret de Chambaud, Jean-Jacques. *Nouveau traité du pouls*. Paris: Vincent, 1768.

———. "Observateur." In *Encyclopédie* (q.v.). Vol. 2, tome 11.

———. "Observation." In *Encyclopédie* (q.v.). Vol. 2, tome 11.

———. "Oeconomie animale." In *Encyclopédie* (q.v.). Vol. 2, tome 11.

———. "Pouls." In *Encyclopédie* (q.v.). Vol. 3, tome 13.

———. "Prognostic." In *Encyclopédie* (q.v.). Vol. 3, tome 13.

[Ménuret de Chambaud, Jean-Jacques?]. "Séméiotique." In *Encyclopédie* (q.v.). Vol. 2, tome 14.

Mesmer, Franz Anton. *La Magnétisme animal*. Ed. Robert Amadou. Paris: Payot, 1971.

Pinel, Philippe. *Nosographie philosophique, ou La Méthode de l'analyse appliquée à la médecine* (1797). 5th ed. Paris: Brosson, 1813.

———. *Traité médico-philosophique sur l'aliénation mentale, ou La Manie*. Paris: Richard, Caille et Ravier, 1800.

Pomme, Pierre. *Traité des affections vaporeuses des deux sexes* (1760). 4th ed. Lyon: Benoît Duplain, 1769.

Pressavin, Jean-Baptiste. *Nouveau traité des vapeurs*. Lyon, 1770.

Prévost d'Exiles, Antoine-François, abbé de. *Histoire d'une Grecque moderne* (1741). Paris: Garnier Flammarion, 1990.

———. *Manon Lescaut* (1731). Trans. Donald Frame. New York: New American Library, 1983.

Procope-Couteau, Michel. *L'Art de faire des garçons par M. *** (Docteur en Médecine à l'Université de Montpellier)* (1748). 2d ed. Montpellier: Maugiron, 1755.

Prost, Pierre-Antoine. *Essai physiologique sur la sensibilité*. Paris: Demonville, 1805.

Raulin, Joseph. *Traité des affections vaporeuses du sexe*. Paris: Jean-Thomas Hérissart, 1758.

Richerand, Anthelme-Balthasar. "Notice sur la vie et les ouvrages de Bordeu." In Théophile de Bordeu, *Oeuvres complètes*. Vol. 1. Paris: Caille et Ravier, 1818.

Robert, L. J. M. *Essai sur la mégalantrogénésie, ou L'Art de faire des enfants d'esprit qui deviennent de grands hommes*. Paris: Debray, 1801.

Robert, Marin-Jacques-Clair. *Traité des principaux objets de la médecine*. Paris: Lacombe, 1766.

Roussel, Pierre. *Essai sur la sensibilité*. In *Système physique et moral de la femme* (q.v.).

———. *Fragment du "Système physique et moral de l'homme."* In *Système physique et moral de la femme* (q.v.).

———. *Système physique et moral de la femme, ou Tableau philosophique de la constitu-*

tion, de l'état organique, du tempérament, des moeurs et des fonctions propres au sexe (1775). 7th ed. Paris: Caille et Ravier, 1820.

Robinet, Jean-Baptiste-René. *De la nature.* 3 vols. Amsterdam: E. Van Harrelvelt, 1761–64.

Rousseau, Jean-Jacques. *The Collected Writings of Rousseau.* 5 vols. Ed. Christopher Kelly, Roger D. Masters, and Peter G. Stillman. Hanover, N.H.: University Press of New England, 1990–95.

———. *Les Confessions* (1782–88). In *Oeuvres complètes* (q.v.), vol. 1. (English translation: *The Confessions.* Trans. Christopher Kelly. In *The Collected Writings of Rousseau* [q.v.], vol. 5.)

———. *La Correspondance complète de Jean-Jacques Rousseau.* Geneva: Institut Voltaire, 1971.

———. *Correspondance générale de Jean-Jacques Rousseau.* Ed. Théophile Dufour. Paris: Armand Colin, 1927.

———. *Dialogues, ou Rousseau Juge de Jean-Jacques* (1772). In *Oeuvres complètes* (q.v.), vol. 1. (English translation: *Rousseau, Judge of Jean-Jacques: Dialogues.* Trans. Judith R. Bush, Christopher Kelly, and Roger D. Masters. In *The Collected Writings of Rousseau* [q.v.], vol. 1.)

———. *Discours sur les sciences et les arts* (1750). In *Oeuvres complètes* (q.v.), vol. 3.

———. *Discours sur l'origine et les fondements de l'inégalité parmi les hommes* (1754). In *Oeuvres complètes* (q.v.), vol. 3. (English translation: "Discourse on the Origins of Inequality [Second Discourse]." Trans. Judith R. Bush, Roger D. Masters, Christopher Kelly, and Terence Marshall. In *The Collected Writings of Rousseau* [q.v.], vol. 1.)

———. *Emile* (1762). In *Oeuvres complètes* (q.v.), vol. 4.

———. *Lettre à d'Alembert sur les spectacles* (1758). Paris: Gallimard-Folio, 1987.

———. *La Nouvelle Héloïse* (1758). In *Oeuvres complètes* (q.v.), vol. 2. (English translations: *Julie, or The New Eloise.* Trans. Judith H. McDowell. University Park: Pennsylvania State University Press, 1968. Also, *Eloisa: A Series of Original Letters.* Trans. unspecified. 3 vols. London: John Harding, 1810.)

———. *Oeuvres complètes.* Ed. Bernard Gagnebin, Marcel Raymond, et al. 5 vols. Paris: Pléaide, 1959–95.

Sade, Donatien-Alphonse-François de. *Aline et Valcour* (1795). In *Oeuvres complètes du Marquis de Sade,* vol. 5. Paris: Au Cercle du Livre Précieux, 1966.

———. "Ernestine." In *Les Crimes de l'amour* (1800). Introd. Michel Delon. Paris: Gallimard, 1987.

———. *Histoire de Juliette, ou Les Prospérités du vice* (1797). In *Oeuvres complètes du Marquis de Sade,* vol. 8. Paris: Au Cercle du Livre Précieux, 1966. (English translation: *Juliette.* Trans. Austryn Wainhouse. New York: Grove Press, 1968.)

———. "Idée sur les romans." In *Les Crimes de l'amour* (1800). Introd. Michel Delon. Paris: Gallimard, 1987. (English translation: "Reflections on the Novel." In *The 120 Days of Sodom and Other Writings.* Trans. Austryn Wainhouse and Richard Seaver. New York: Grove Press, 1966.)

———. *Justine, ou Les Malheurs de la vertu* (1791). Paris: Librairie Générale Française, 1973. (English translation: "Justine, or Good Conduct Well Chastised." In *The Complete Justine, Philosophy in the Bedroom, and Other Writings.* Trans. Richard Seaver and Austryn Wainhouse. New York: Grove Press, 1965.)

Senancour, Etienne de. *Rêveries sur la nature primitive de l'homme* (1799–1800). Paris: E. Cornély, 1910.

Senebier, Jean. *Essai sur l'art d'observer* (1775). 2d ed. Geneva: Paschoud, 1802.

Sèze, Paul-Victor de. *Recherches physiologiques et philosophiques sur la sensibilité ou la vie animale.* Paris: Prault, 1786.

Süe, Jean-Jacques. *Recherches physiologiques et expériences sur la vitalité.* Paris: Fuchs, an VI [1797].

Supplément to *Encyclopédie, ou Dictionnaire raisonné des sciences, des arts et des métiers.* 4 tomes. Amsterdam: M. M. Rey; Paris: Panckouche, 1776–77. Reprint: New York: Pergamon Press, 1969.

Tissot, Samuel-Auguste-André-David. *Avis au peuple sur sa santé.* Paris: Didot, 1767.

———. *De la santé des gens de lettres* (1768). Introd. François Azouvi. Geneva: Slatkine, 1981.

———. *Essai sur les maladies des gens du monde* (1770). In *Oeuvres de M. Tissot, Nouvelle édition augmentée et imprimée sous ses yeux,* vol. 4. Lausanne: Grasset, 1788.

———. *De l'onanisme* (in Latin, 1758; in French, 1760). Translated as *Onanism, or A Treatise upon the Disorders produced by Masturbation, or The Dangerous Effects of Secret and Excessive Venery.* Trans. A. Hume, M.D. 1766; reprint, New York and London: Garland Publishing, 1985.

Turgot, Anne Robert Jacques, Baron de. "Second Discours, sur les progrès successifs de l'esprit humain" (1750). In *Oeuvres de Turgot,* vol. 2. Paris: Guillaumin, 1844.

Vandermonde, Charles Augustin. *Essai sur la manière de perfectionner l'espèce humaine.* Paris: Vincent, 1756.

Virey, Julien-Joseph. "Du contraste entre le pôle génital et le pôle cérébral dans l'homme et dans la série des animaux." *Gazette médicale,* March 7, 1840.

———. *De l'influence des femmes sur le goût dans la littérature et les beaux-arts.* Paris: Deterville, 1810.

———. *Histoire naturelle du genre humain, ou Recherches sur ses principaux fondemens physiques et moraux.* 2 vols. Paris: F. Dufart, an IX [1801].

———. "Nature." In *Dictionnaire des sciences médicales par une société de médecins et de chirurgiens,* vol. 35. Paris: Pantoucke, 1812–22.

Whytt, Robert. *Observations on the nature, Causes and Cure of the Disorders which have been commonly call'd Nervous, Hypochondriac, or Hysteric.* Edinburgh, 1765.

Secondary Works

Altman, Janet Gurkin. "Graffigny's Epistemology and the Emergence of Third-World Ideology." In *Writing the Female Voice: Essays on Epistolary Literature.* Ed. Elizabeth C. Goldsmith. Boston: Northeastern University Press, 1989.

————. "A Woman's Place in the Enlightenment Sun: The Case of F. de Graffigny." *Romance Quarterly* 38, no. 3 (1991), 261–72.

Amrine, Frederick. "Introduction: The Evolution of Literature and Science as a Discipline." In *Literature and Science as Modes of Expression.* Dordrecht, Holland: Kluwer Academic Publishers, 1989.

Anderson, Lorin. *Charles Bonnet and the Order of the Known.* Dordrecht, Holland: D. Reidel Publishing Co., 1982.

Anderson, Wilda. *Diderot's Dream.* Baltimore: Johns Hopkins University Press, 1990.

————. "Diderot's Laboratory of Sensibility." *Yale French Studies* 67 (1984), 72–91.

Astruc, Pierre. "Les Sciences médicales et leurs représentants dans l'*Encyclopédie*." *Revue d'histoire des sciences* 4 (1951), 359–68.

Atkinson, Geoffrey. *The Sentimental Revolution: French Writers of 1690–1740.* Seattle: University of Washington Press, 1965.

Auroux, Sylvain. "Condillac, inventeur d'un nouveau matérialisme." *Dix-huitième siècle* 24 (1992), 153–63.

Azouvi, François. "La Femme comme modèle de la pathologie au XVIIIème siècle." *Diogènes* 115 (1971), 25–40.

————. "Magnétisme animal: La Sensation infinie." *Dix-huitième siècle* 23 (1991), 107–18.

————. "Le Mesmérisme: Des Lumières à l'illuminisme." In *Lumières et illuminisme.* Ed. Mario Matucci. Pisa: Pacini Editore, 1984.

Azouvi, François, ed. *L'Institution de la raison: La Révolution culturelle des Idéologues.* Paris: Vrin, 1992.

Baasner, Frank. *Der Bergriff 'Sensibilité' im 18. Jahrhundert: Aufstieg und Niedergang eines Ideals.* Heidelberg: Carl Winter Universitätsverlag, 1988.

————. "The Changing Meaning of 'Sensibilité': 1654 till 1704." *Studies in Eighteenth-Century Culture* 15 (1986), 77–96.

Balayé, Simone. "A Propos du 'préromantisme': Continuité ou rupture chez Mme de Staël." In *Le Préromantisme: Hypothèque ou hypothèse?* Ed. Paul Viallaneix. Paris: Klincksieck, 1975.

Baridon, Michel. "Les Concepts de nature humaine et de perfectibilité dans l'historiographie des Lumières de Fontenelle à Condorcet." In *L'Histoire au dix-huitième siècle: Actes du Colloque d'Aix-en-Provence.* Aix-en-Provence: Edisud, 1980.

————. "L'Imaginaire scientifique et la voix humaine dans *Le Rêve de d'Alembert*." In *L'Encyclopédie, Diderot, l'esthétique: Mélanges en hommage à Jacques Chouillet.* Ed. Sylvain Auroux, Dominique Bourel, and Charles Porset. Paris: Presses Universitaires de France, 1991.

Barker-Benfield, G. J. *The Culture of Sensibility: Sex and Society in Eighteenth-Century Britain.* Chicago: University of Chicago Press, 1992.

Barthes, Roland. *Sade, Fourier, Loyola.* Paris: Seuil, 1971. Trans. Richard Miller. Berkeley and Los Angeles: University of California Press, 1989.

Battersby, Christine. "Genius and the 'Female Sex' in the Eighteenth Century." *Studies on Voltaire and the Eighteenth Century* 264 (1989), 909–12.

Baudelaire, Charles. "Notes analytiques et critiques sur *Les Liaisons dangereuses*." In *Oeuvres posthumes*. Paris: Louis Conard, 1939.

Belaval, Yvon. "Les Protagonistes du *Rêve de d'Alembert*." *Diderot Studies* 3 (1961), 27–53.

Benrekessa, Georges. "Hystérie, 'crises' et convulsions au XVIIIe siècle: Age des Lumières, éclipses du sujet." *Revue des sciences humaines* 208, no. 4 (1987), 113–40.

Bloch, Maurice, and Jean H. Bloch. "Women and the Dialectics of Nature in Eighteenth-Century Thought." In *Nature, Culture, and Gender*. Ed. Carol P. MacCormack and Marilyn Strathern. Cambridge: Cambridge University Press, 1980.

Boas, Marie. "The Establishment of the Mechanical Philosophy." *Osiris* 10 (1952), 412–541.

Bonnet, Jean-Claude. "Le Réseau culinaire dans l'*Encyclopédie*." *Annales E.S.C.* 31, no. 5 (1976), 891–914.

———. "Le Système de la cuisine et du repas chez Rousseau." *Poétique* 22 (1975), 244–67.

Brewer, Daniel. *The Discourse of Enlightenment in Eighteenth-Century France: Diderot and the Art of Philosophizing*. Cambridge: Cambridge University Press, 1993.

Brissenden, R. F. *Virtue in Distress: Studies in the Novel of Sentiment from Richardson to Sade*. London: Macmillan Press, 1974.

Brooks, Peter. *Body Work: Objects of Desire in Modern Narrative*. Cambridge: Harvard University Press, 1993.

———. *The Melodramatic Imagination: Balzac, Henry James, Melodrama, and the Mode of Excess*. New Haven: Yale University Press, 1976.

———. *The Novel of Worldliness*. Princeton: Princeton University Press, 1969.

Brown, Theodore M. "From Mechanism to Vitalism in Eighteenth-Century English Physiology." *Journal of the History of Biology* 7, no. 2 (1974), 179–216.

Burgelin, Pierre. *La Philosophie de l'existence chez Jean-Jacques Rousseau*. Paris: Presses Universitaires de France, 1952.

Canguilhem, Georges. "La Constitution de la physiologie comme science." In *Etudes d'histoire et de philosophie des sciences*. 5th ed. Paris: Vrin, 1983.

———. *La Formation du concept de réflexe aux XVIIe et XVIIIe siècles*. 2d ed. Paris: Vrin, 1977.

———. "Qu'est-ce que la psychologie?" *Cahiers pour l'analyse*, nos. 1–2 (1966), 77–93.

———. "Quelques aspects du vitalisme." In *La Connaissance de la vie*. 2d ed. Paris: Vrin, 1985.

Caplan, Jay. *Framed Narratives: Diderot's Genealogy of the Beholder*. Minneapolis: University of Minnesota Press, 1985.

Carrera, Rosalina de la. *Success in Circuit Lies: Diderot's Communicational Practice*. Stanford: Stanford University Press, 1992.

Chouillet, Jacques. *Diderot, poète de l'énergie*. Paris: Presses Universitaires de France, 1984.

———. *La Formation des idées esthétiques de Diderot*. Paris: Armand Colin, 1973.

Christie, John. "The Human Sciences: Origins and Histories." *History of the Human Sciences* 6, no. 1 (1993), 1–12.

Cole, F. J. *Early Theories of Sexual Generation*. Oxford: Clarendon Press, 1930.

Coleman, William. "Health and Hygiene in the *Encyclopédie:* A Medical Doctrine for the Bourgeoisie." *Journal of the History of Medicine* 29 (1974), 399–421.

Conger, Syndy McMillen, ed. *Sensibility in Transformation: Creative Resistance to Sentiment from the Augustans to the Romantics*. Rutherford, N.J.: Fairleigh Dickinson University Press, 1990.

Cooter, Roger. "The Power of the Body: The Early Nineteenth Century." In *Natural Order: Historical Studies of Scientific Culture*. Ed. Barry Barnes and Steven Shapin. Beverly Hills, Calif.: Sage Publications, 1979.

Corbin, Alain. *Le Territoire du vide: L'Occident et le désir du rivage, 1750–1840*. Paris: Aubier, 1988.

Dagognet, François. *Le Catalogue de la vie*. Paris: Presses Universitaires de France, 1970.

———. *La Maîtrise du vivant*. Paris: Hachette, 1988.

Daniel, Georges. *Fatalité du secret et fatalité du bavardage: La Marquise de Merteuil, Jean-François Rameau*. Paris: Nizet, 1966.

Daniel, Stephen L. "Literature and Medicine: In Quest of Method." *Literature and Medicine* 6 (1987), 1–12.

Daremberg, Charles. *Histoire des sciences médicales*. 2 vols. Paris: Baillière, 1870.

Darnton, Robert. *Mesmerism and the End of the Enlightenment in France*. Cambridge: Harvard University Press, 1968.

Dawson, Virginia. *Nature's Enigma: The Problem of the Polyp in the Letters of Bonnet, Trembley, and Réamur*. Philadelphia: American Philosophical Society, 1987.

Decottignies, Jean, ed. "Médecins et Littérateurs." In *Revue des sciences humaines* 198 (1985) and 208 (1987).

DeJean, Joan. *Literary Fortifications: Rousseau, Laclos, Sade*. Princeton: Princeton University Press, 1984.

Delaunay, Paul. *Le Monde médical parisien au dix-huitième siècle*. Paris: Jules Rousset, 1905.

Delon, Michel. "'Fatal présent du ciel qu'une âme sensible': Le Succès d'une formule de Rousseau." In *La Nouvelle Héloïse aujourd'hui*. Reims: A l'Écart, 1991.

———. *L'Idée d'énergie au tournant des Lumières (1770–1820)*. Paris: Presses Universitaires de France, 1988.

De Man, Paul. *Allegories of Reading: Figural Language in Rousseau, Nietzsche, Rilke, and Proust*. New Haven: Yale University Press, 1979.

Denby, David. *Sentimental Narrative and the Social Order in France, 1760–1820*. Cambridge: Cambridge University Press, 1994.

Deneys-Tunney, Anne. *Écritures du corps: De Descartes à Laclos*. Paris: Presses Universitaires de France, 1992.

Deprun, Jean. "Sade et la philosophie biologique de son temps." In *Le Marquis de Sade*. Paris: Armand Colin, 1968.

Desaive, Jean-Paul, Jean-Pierre Goubert, Emmanuel Le Roy Ladurie, Jean Meyer, Otto Muller, and Jean-Pierre Peter. *Médecins, climat, et épidémies à la fin du XVIII-ème siècle*. Paris: Mouton et Ecole Pratique des Hautes Etudes, 1972.

Dieckmann, Herbert. "The *Préface-Annexe* of *La Religieuse*." *Diderot Studies* 2 (1952), 21–147.

———. "Théophile Bordeu und Diderots *Rêve de d'Alembert*." *Romanische Forshungen* 52 (1938), 55–122.

Di Piero, Thomas. *Dangerous Truths and Criminal Passions: The Evolution of the French Novel, 1569–1791*. Stanford: Stanford University Press, 1992.

Domenech, Jacques. *L'Ethique des Lumières: Les Fondements de la morale dans la philosophie française du XVIIIe siècle*. Paris: Vrin, 1989.

Douthwaite, Julia V. *Exotic Women: Literary Heroines and Cultural Strategies in Ancien Régime France*. Philadelphia: University of Pennsylvania Press, 1992.

Duchesneau, François. *La Physiologie des Lumières: Empirisme, modèles, et théories*. The Hague: Martinus Nijhoff Publishers, 1982.

Duchet, Michèle. *Anthropologie et histoire au siècle des Lumières*. Paris: Maspero, 1971.

Duden, Barbara. "A Repertory of Body History." In *Fragments for a History of the Human Body*, vol. 3. Ed. Michael Feher. New York: Zone, 1989.

Dulieu, Louis. *La Médecine à Montpellier*. Avignon: Presses Universelles, 1975.

Elias, Norbert. *The Civilizing Process*. Trans. Edmund Jephcott. New York: Urizen Books, 1978.

Emch-Dériaz, Antoinette. "The Non-Naturals Made Easy." In *The Popularization of Medicine, 1650–1850*. Ed. Roy Porter. London: Routledge, 1992.

———. *Tissot, Physician of the Enlightenment*. New York: Peter Lang, 1992.

Erämetsä, Erik. "A Study of the Word 'Sentimental' and of Other Linguistic Characteristics of Eighteenth-Century Sentimentalism in England." *Annales Academiae Scientiarum Fennicae*, ser. B, 74, no. 1 (1951).

Erhard, Jean. *L'Idée de nature en France à l'aube des Lumières*. Paris: Flammarion, 1970.

Eynard, Charles. *Essai sur la vie de Tissot*. Lausanne: Ducloux, 1839.

Fabre, Jean. *Idées sur le roman de Madame de Lafayette au Marquis de Sade*. Paris: Editions Klincksieck, 1979.

Figlio, Karl M. "The Historiography of Scientific Medicine." *Comparative Studies in Society and History* 19 (1977), 262–86.

———. "The Metaphor of Organization: An Historiographical Perspective on the Bio-Medical Sciences of the Early Eighteenth Century." *History of Science* 14 (1976), 17–53.

———. "Theories of Perception and the Physiology of Mind in the Late Eighteenth Century." *History of Science* 12 (1975), 177–212.

Fischer, Jean-Louis. "La Callipède, ou L'Art de faire de beaux enfants." *Dix-huitième siècle* 23 (1991), 141–58.

Fontenay, Elisabeth de. "Diderot gynéconome." *Digraphe* 7 (1976), 29–50.

Foucault, Michel. *L'Archéologie du savoir*. Paris: Gallimard, 1969.

———. *Histoire de la folie à l'âge classique* (1961). Paris: Gallimard, 1972. (English translation: *Madness and Civilization: A History of Insanity in the Age of Reason.* Trans. Richard Howard. New York: Pantheon, 1965.)

————. *Histoire de la sexualité.* 3 vols. Paris: Gallimard, 1976–84.

————. *Les Mots et les choses.* Paris: Gallimard, 1966.

————. *La Naissance de la clinique.* Paris: Presses Universitaires de France, 1963.

————. *L'Ordre du discours.* Paris: Gallimard, 1971.

————. *Surveiller et punir.* Paris: Gallimard, 1975.

Fox-Genovese, Elizabeth. *The Origins of Physiocracy: Economic Revolution and Social Order in Eighteenth-Century France.* Ithaca, N.Y.: Cornell University Press, 1976.

Fraisse, Geneviève. "Le Genre humain et la femme chez J.-J. Virey, ou 'Une certaine harmonie d'inégalités correspondantes.'" In *Julien-Joseph Virey, naturaliste et anthropologue.* Ed. Claude Bénichou and Claude Blanckaert. Paris: Vrin, 1988.

Francis, R. A. *Abbé Prévost's First-Person Narrators.* Vol. 306 of *Studies on Voltaire and the Eighteenth Century* (1993).

French, R. K. *Robert Whytt, the Soul, and Medicine.* London: Wellcome Institute for the History of Medicine, 1969.

Fried, Michael. *Absorption and Theatricality: Painting and Beholder in the Age of Diderot.* Chicago: University of Chicago Press, 1980.

Gay, Peter. "The Enlightenment as Medicine and as Cure." In *The Age of Enlightenment: Studies Presented to Theodore Besterman.* Ed. W. H. Barber. Edinburgh: St. Andrews University Publications, 1967.

Gelfand, Toby. "The Decline of the Ordinary Practitioner and the Rise of the Modern Medical Profession." In *Doctors, Patients, and Society: Power and Authority in Medical Care.* Ed. M. S. Staum and D. E. Larsen. Waterloo, Ont.: Historical Reflections Press, 1981.

Giraudoux, Jean. "Choderlos de Laclos." In *Littérature.* Paris: Grasset, 1941.

Goldberg, Rita. *Sex and Enlightenment: Women in Richardson and Diderot.* Cambridge: Cambridge University Press, 1984.

Goldstein, Jan. *Console and Classify: The French Psychiatric Profession in the Nineteenth Century.* Cambridge: Cambridge University Press, 1987.

Goodden, Angelica. *The Complete Lover: Eros, Nature, and Artifice in the Eighteenth-Century French Novel.* Oxford: Oxford University Press, 1989.

Gossman, Lionel. "Prévost's *Manon*: Love in the New World." *Yale French Studies* 40 (1969), 91–102.

Gossman, Lionel, and Elizabeth MacArthur. "Diderot's Displaced *Paradoxe.*" In *Diderot: Digression and Dispersion.* Ed. Jack Undank and Herbert Josephs. Lexington, Ky.: French Forum, 1984.

Goubert, J. P., ed. *La Médicalisation de la société française, 1770–1830.* Waterloo, Ont.: Historical Reflections Press, 1982.

Gouhier, Henri. *Les Conversions de Maine de Biran.* Paris: Vrin, 1947.

Grosrichard, Alain. "Une Expérience psychologique au dix-huitième siècle." *Cahiers pour l'analyse* 1–2 (1966), 101–24.

Gusdorf, Georges. "Organisme." In *Fondements du savoir romantique.* Paris: Payot, 1982.

————. "Le Progrès de la conscience médicale." In *Dieu, la nature, l'homme au siècle des Lumières*. Paris: Payot, 1972.

Gutwirth, Madelyn. "Laclos et 'Le sexe': The Rack of Ambivalence." *Studies on Voltaire and the Eighteenth Century* 189 (1980), 247–96.

Haigh, Elizabeth. "Vitalism, the Soul, and Sensibility: The Physiology of Théophile Bordeu." *Journal of the History of Medicine* 31 (January, 1976), 30–41.

————. *Xavier Bichat and the Medical Theory of the Eighteenth Century*. London: Wellcome Institute for the History of Medicine, 1984.

Hall, Thomas. *Ideas of Life and Matter: Studies in the History of General Physiology, 600 B.C.–1900 A.D.*. Chicago: University of Chicago Press, 1969.

————. "On Biological Analogs of Newtonian Paradigms." *Philosophy of Science* 35, no. 1 (1968), 6–27.

Hannaway, Caroline. "The Société Royale de Médecine and Epidemics in the Ancien Régime." *Bulletin of the History of Medicine* 46 (1972), 257–73.

Harari, Josué. *Scenarios of the Imaginary: Theorizing the French Enlightenment*. Ithaca, N.Y.: Cornell University Press, 1987.

Harth, Erica. *Cartesian Women: Versions and Subversions of Rational Discourse in the Old Regime*. Ithaca, N.Y.: Cornell University Press, 1992.

Hatfield, Gary. "Remaking the Science of Mind: Psychology as Natural Science." In *Inventing Human Science: Eighteenth-Century Domains*. Ed. Christopher Fox, Roy Porter, and Robert Wokler. Berkeley and Los Angeles: University of California Press, 1995.

Heckman, John. "*Marianne:* The Making of an Author." *MLN* 86, no. 4 (1971), 509–22.

Hénaff, Marcel. *Sade: L'Invention du corps libertin*. Paris: Presses Universitaires de France, 1978.

Hill, Emita. "Materialism and Monsters in *Le Rêve de d'Alembert*." *Diderot Studies* 10 (1968), 67–93.

Hobson, Marion. "Sensibilité et spectacle: Le Contexte médical du *Paradoxe sur le comédien* de Diderot." *Revue de métaphysique et de morale* 82 (1977), 145–64.

Hoffmann, Paul. *La Femme dans la pensée des Lumières*. Paris: Ophrys, 1977.

————. "L'Idée de la liberté dans la philosophie médicale de Théophile de Bordeu." *Studies on Voltaire and the Eighteenth Century* 88 (1972), 769–87.

Horowitz, Asher. "Julie and the Pathology of Conscience." In *Rousseau, Nature, and History*. Toronto: University of Toronto Press, 1987.

Huet, Marie-Hélène. *Le Héros et son double*. Paris: Corti, 1975.

————. *Monstrous Imagination*. Cambridge: Harvard University Press, 1993.

Imbroscio, Carmelina. "Recherches et réflexions de la médecine française du dix-huitième siècle sur des phénomènes psychosomatiques." *Studies on Voltaire and the Eighteenth Century* 190 (1980), 494–501.

Jacyna, L. S. "Medical Science and Moral Science: The Cultural Relations of Physiology in Restoration France." *History of Science* 25 (1987), 111–46.

Jamieson, Ruth Kirby. *Marivaux: A Study in Sensibility*. 2d ed. New York: Octagon Books, 1969.

Jones, Chris. *Radical Sensibility: Literature and Ideas in the 1790s.* London: Routledge, 1993.

Jones, Colin. "Montpellier Medical Students and the Medicalisation of Eighteenth-Century France." In *Problems and Methods in the History of Medicine.* Ed. Roy Porter and Andrew Wear. London: Croom Helm, 1987.

Jordanova, Ludmilla. "Body Images and Sex Roles." In *Sexual Visions: Images of Gender in Science and Medicine between the Eighteenth and Twentieth Centuries.* Madison: University of Wisconsin Press, 1989.

———. "Natural Facts: An Historical Perspective on Science and Sexuality." Ibid.

———. "The Popularization of Medicine: Tissot on Onanism." *Textual Practice* 1, no. 1 (1987), 68–79.

———. "Sex and Gender." In *Inventing Human Science: Eighteenth-Century Domains.* Ed. Christopher Fox, Roy Porter, and Robert Wokler. Berkeley and Los Angeles: University of California Press, 1995.

Josephs, Herbert. "Diderot's *La Religieuse*: Libertinism and the Dark Cave of the Soul." *MLN* 91 (1976), 734–55.

Kavanagh, Thomas M. *Enlightenment and the Shadows of Chance: The Novel and the Culture of Gambling in Eighteenth-Century France.* Baltimore: Johns Hopkins University Press, 1993.

———. *Esthetics of the Moment: Literature and Art in the French Enlightenment.* Philadelphia: University of Pennsylvania Press, 1996.

Keele, K. D. "The Search for the Sensorium Commune." In *Anatomies of Pain.* Springfield, Ill.: Charles C. Thomas, 1957.

Kempf, Roger. *Diderot et le roman, ou Le Démon de la présence.* Paris: Seuil, 1964.

King, Lester S. "Boissier de Sauvages and Eighteenth-Century Nosology." *Bulletin of the History of Medicine* 11 (1966), 43–51.

———. "Stahl and Hoffmann: A Study in Eighteenth-Century Animism." *Journal of the History of Medicine* 19 (1964), 118–30.

Kniebehler, Yvonne. "Les Médecins et la 'nature féminine' au temps du Code civil." *Annales E.C.S.* 4 (1976), 824–45.

Kofman, Sarah. *Séductions: De Sartre à Héraclite.* Paris: Editions Galilée, 1990.

Kuhn, Thomas. "Second Thoughts on Paradigms." In *The Essential Tension: Selected Studies in Scientific Tradition and Change.* Chicago: University of Chicago Press, 1977.

———. *The Structure of Scientific Revolutions* (1962). 2d ed. Chicago: University of Chicago Press, 1970.

Laborde, Alice M. *La Bibliothèque du Marquis de Sade au château de La Coste (en 1776).* Geneva: Editions Slatkine, 1991.

———. *Sade romancier.* Neuchâtel: La Baconnière, 1974.

Labrosse, Claude. "Jean-Jacques Rousseau et le corps dans *La Nouvelle Héloïse*." In *Corps création.* Lyon: Presses Universitaires de Lyon, 1980.

Lacoue-Labarthe, Philippe. "Diderot, le paradoxe et la mimésis." *Poétique* 43 (1980), 267–81.

Laforgue, R. "Etude sur Jean-Jacques Rousseau." *Revue française de psychanalyse* 1 (1927), 370–402.

Laignel-Lavastine, Maxime. "Les Médecins collaborateurs de l'*Encyclopédie*." *Revue d'histoire des sciences* 4 (1951), 353–58.

Lanson, Gustave. *Histoire de la littérature française*. Paris: Hachette, 1912.

———. *Nivelle de la Chaussée et la comédie larmoyante*. Paris: Hachette, 1887.

Laqueur, Thomas. *Making Sex: Body and Gender from the Greeks to Freud*. Cambridge: Harvard University Press, 1990.

Laurence-Maire, Cathérine. *Les convulsionnaires de Saint-Médard: Miracles, convulsions et prophètes à Paris au XVIIIe siècle*. Paris: Gallimard, 1985.

Lawrence, Christopher. "The Nervous System and Society in the Scottish Enlightenment." In *Natural Order: Historical Studies of Scientific Culture*. Ed. Barry Barnes and Steven Shapin. Beverly Hills, Calif.: Sage Publications, 1979.

Le Doeuff, Michèle. *L'Imaginaire philosophique*. Paris: Payot, 1980. (English translation: *The Philosophical Imagination*. Trans. Colin Gordon. Stanford: Stanford University Press, 1989.)

Lely, Gilbert. *La Vie du Marquis de Sade*. Paris: Pauvert, 1965.

Lesch, John. *Science and Medicine in France: The Emergence of Experimental Physiology, 1790–1855*. Cambridge: Harvard University Press, 1984.

Lindeboom, G. A. "Boerhaave's Concept of the Basic Structure of the Body." *Clio Medica* 5 (1970), 203–8.

———. *Hermann Boerhaave: The Man and His Work*. London: Methuen, 1968.

Livi, Jocelyne. *Vapeurs de femmes: Essai historique sur quelques fantasmes médicaux et philosophiques*. Quentiny-Dijon: Navarin, 1984.

Lloyd, Genevieve. *The Man of Reason: "Male" versus "Female" in Western Philosophy*. Minneapolis: University of Minnesota Press, 1984.

Lotringer, Sylvère. "Manon l'écho." *Romanic Review* 63 (1972), 92–110.

Luoni, Flavio. "*La Religieuse:* Récit et écriture du corps." *Littérature* 54 (1984), 79–99.

MacArthur, Elizabeth. "Devious Narratives: Refusal of Closure in Two Eighteenth-Century Epistolary Novels." *Eighteenth-Century Studies* 21, no. 1 (1987), 1–20.

MacDonald, R. "The Frightful Consequences of Onanism: Notes on the History of a Delusion." *Journal of the History of Ideas* 28 (1967), 423–31.

Malraux, André. *Le Triangle noir*. Paris: Gallimard, 1970.

Marshall, David. *The Surprising Effects of Sympathy: Marivaux, Diderot, Rousseau, and Mary Shelley*. Chicago: University of Chicago Press, 1988.

Marx, Jacques. *Charles Bonnet contre les Lumières, 1738–1850*. Vols. 156–57 of *Studies on Voltaire and the Eighteenth Century* (1976).

Mauzi, Robert. "Les Maladies de l'âme au XVIIIe siècle." *Revue des sciences humaines* 100 (1960), 459–93.

May, Georges. "Diderot, artiste et philosophe du décousu." In *Europäische Aufklärung Herbert Dieckmann zum 60. Geburtstag*. Ed. Hugo Friedrich and Fritz Schalk. Munich: Fink Verlag, 1967.

―――. *Diderot et "La Religieuse."* New Haven: Yale University Press; Paris: Presses Universitaires de France, 1954.

―――. *Le Dilemme du roman au XVIIIe siècle.* New Haven: Yale University Press; Paris: Presses Universitaires de France, 1963.

Mayer, Jean. *Diderot homme de science.* Rennes: Imprimerie bretonne, 1959.

McDonald, Christie. *The Dialogue of Writing: Essays in Eighteenth-Century French Literature.* Waterloo, Ont.: Wilfred Laurier University Press, 1984.

Miller, Nancy K. *Subject to Change: Reading Feminist Writing.* New York: Columbia University Press, 1988.

Moravia, Sergio. "From *Homme Machine* to *Homme Sensible*: Changing Eighteenth-Century Models of Man's Image." *Journal of the History of Ideas* 39, no. 1 (1978), 45–60.

―――. "Philosophie et médecine à la fin du XVIIIème siècle." *Studies on Voltaire and the Eighteenth Century* 89 (1972), 1089–1151.

Morris, David B. *The Culture of Pain.* Berkeley and Los Angeles: University of California Press, 1991.

―――. "The Marquis de Sade and the Discourses of Pain: Literature and Medicine at the Revolution." In *The Languages of Psyche: Mind and Body in Enlightenment Thought.* Ed. G. S. Rousseau. Berkeley and Los Angeles: University of California Press, 1990.

Mortier, Roland. "Le Traité *Du Sentiment* de P. S. Ballanche: Un Programme littéraire antiphilosophique et post-Révolutionnaire." In *Approches des Lumières: Mélanges offerts à Jean Fabre.* Paris: Klincksieck, 1974.

―――. "Unité ou scission du siècle des Lumières?" In *Clartés et ombres du siècle des Lumières.* Geneva: Droz, 1969.

Mullan, John. *Sentiment and Sociability: The Language of Feeling in the Eighteenth Century.* Oxford: Clarendon Press, 1988.

Mylne, Vivienne. "What Suzanne Knew: Lesbianism and *La Religieuse*." *Studies on Voltaire and the Eighteenth-Century* 208 (1982), 167–73.

Nisbet, Robert. *History of the Idea of Progress.* New York: Basic Books, 1980.

O'Neal, John C. *The Authority of Experience: Sensationist Theory in the French Enlightenment.* University Park, Pa.: Pennsylvania State University Press, 1996.

―――. "The Sensationist Aesthetics of the French Enlightenment." *L'Esprit créateur* 28, no. 4 (1988), 95–105.

Outram, Dorinda. *The Body and the French Revolution: Sex, Class, and Political Culture.* New Haven: Yale University Press, 1989.

Ozouf, Mona. *L'Homme régénéré: Essais sur la Révolution française.* Paris: Gallimard: 1989.

Paganini, Gianni. "Psychologie et physiologie de l'entendement chez Condillac." *Dix-huitième siècle* 24 (1992), 165–78.

Pagden, Anthony. "The Savage Decomposed." In *European Encounters with the New World: From Renaissance to Romanticism.* New Haven: Yale University Press, 1993.

Peter, Jean-Pierre. "Malade et maladies à la fin du XVIIIème siècle." *Annales E.S.C.* 22, no. 4 (1967), 711–51.

―――. "Les Mots et les objects de la maladie: Remarques sur les épidémies et la médecine dans la société française du XVIIIème siècle." *Revue historique* 246 (1971), 13–38.

Picavet, François. *Les Idéologues*. Paris: Alcan, 1896.

Pick, Daniel. *Faces of Degeneration: A European Disorder, c.1848–c.1918*. Cambridge: Cambridge University Press, 1989.

Pomeau, René. "Le Mariage de Laclos." *Revue d'histoire littéraire de la France* 64, no. 1 (1964), 60–72.

Porter, Roy. "Barely Touching: A Social Perspective on Mind and Body." In *The Languages of Psyche: Mind and Body in Enlightenment Thought*. Ed. G. S. Rousseau. Berkeley and Los Angeles: University of California Press, 1990.

———. *Doctor of Society: Thomas Beddoes and the Sick Trade in Late-Enlightenment England*. London: Routledge, 1992.

———, ed. *The Popularization of Medicine, 1650–1850*. London: Routledge, 1992.

Porter, Roy, and G. S. Rousseau. "Introduction: Toward a Natural History of Mind and Body." In *The Languages of Psyche: Mind and Body in Enlightenment Thought*. Ed. G. S. Rousseau. Berkeley and Los Angeles: University of California Press, 1990.

Poulet, Georges. *La Distance intérieure*. Paris: Plon, 1952.

Proust, Jacques. "Le Corps de Manon." *Littérature* 4 (1971), 5–21.

Ramsey, Matthew. "The Popularization of Medicine in France, 1650–1700." In *The Popularization of Medicine, 1650–1850*. Ed. Roy Porter. London: Routledge, 1992.

Raymond, Marcel. *Jean-Jacques Rousseau: La Quête de soi et la rêverie*. Paris: Corti, 1962.

Rex, Walter E. "Secrets from Suzanne: The Tangled Motives of *La Religieuse*." In *The Attraction of the Contrary: Essays on the Literature of the French Enlightenment*. Cambridge: Cambridge University Press, 1987.

Rey, Roselyne. "Diderot et la médecine de l'esprit." In *Colloque international Diderot (1713–1784)*. Ed. Anne-Marie Chouillet. Paris: Aux amateurs des livres, 1985.

———. "La Théorie de la sécrétion chez Bordeu, modèle de la physiologie et de la pathologie vitalistes." *Dix-huitième siècle* 23 (1991), 45–58.

———. "Le Vitalisme de Julien-Joseph Virey." In *Julien-Joseph Virey, naturaliste et anthropologue*. Ed. Claude Bénichou and Claude Blanckaert. Paris: Vrin, 1988.

Ridgeway, R. S. *Voltaire and Sensibility*. Montreal: McGill-Queen's University Press, 1973.

Riley, James C. *The Eighteenth-Century Campaign to Avoid Disease*. Basingstoke, Hampshire: Macmillan, 1987.

Roberts, Marie Mulvey, and Roy Porter, eds. *Literature and Medicine during the Eighteenth Century*. London: Routledge, 1993.

Roe, Shirley A., ed. *The Natural Philosophy of Albrecht von Haller*. New York: Arno Press, 1981.

Roger, Jacques. *Les Sciences de la vie dans la pensée française au XVIIIe siècle*. Paris: Albin Michel, 1963.

Roger, Philippe. *Sade: La Philosophie dans le pressoir*. Paris: Grasset, 1976.

———. "La Trace de Fénelon." In *Sade: Écrire la crise*. Ed. Michel Camus and Philippe Roger. Paris: Belfond, 1983.

Rosen, George. "The Philosophy of Ideology and the Emergence of Modern Medicine in France." *Bulletin of the History of Medicine* 20, no. 2 (1946), 328–39.

Rosset, Clément. *L'Anti-nature*. Paris: Presses Universitaires de France, 1973.

Rothfield, Lawrence. "Medicine and Mimesis." In *Vital Signs: Medical Realism in Nineteenth-Century Fiction*. Princeton: Princeton University Press, 1992.

Rousseau, G. S. "Discourses of the Nerve." In *Literature and Science as Modes of Expression*. Ed. Frederick Amrine. Dordrecht, Holland: Kluwer Academic Publishers, 1989.

———. "Literature and Medicine: Towards a Simultaneity of Theory and Practice." *Literature and Medicine* 5 (1986), 152–81.

———. "Medicine and Literature: Notes on Their Overlaps and Reciprocities." *Gesnerus* 43 (1986), 33–46.

———. "Medicine and Literature: The State of the Field." *Isis* 72 (1981), 406–24.

———. "Nerves, Spirits, and Fibres: Towards Defining the Origins of Sensibility." In *Studies in the Eighteenth Century, III: Papers Presented at the Third David Nichol Smith Memorial Seminar, Canberra 1973*. Ed. R. F. Brissenden and J. Eade. Canberra: Australian National University Press, 1976. Reprinted with a postscript in *The Blue Guitar* 2 (1976), 125–53.

———. "Nymphomania, Bienville, and the Rise of Erotic Sensibility." In *Sexuality in Eighteenth-Century Britain*. Ed. Paul-Gabriel Boucé. Manchester, England: Manchester University Press, 1982.

Roussel, Roy. "*Les Liaisons dangereuses* and the Myth of the Understanding Man." In *The Conversation of the Sexes: Seduction and Equality in Selected Seventeenth- and Eighteenth-Century Texts*. New York: Oxford University Press, 1986.

Rousset, Jean. *Forme et signification*. Paris: José Corti, 1962.

———. *Narcisse romancier*. Paris: Corti, 1973.

Roustang, François. *Influences*. Paris: Minuit, 1990.

Rudolph, Gerhard. "La Méthode hallérienne en physiologie." *Dix-huitième siècle* 23 (1991), 75–84.

Russo, Elena. *Skeptical Selves: Empiricism and Modernity in the French Novel*. Stanford: Stanford University Press, 1996.

Salomon-Bayet, Claire. *L'Institution de la science et l'expérience du vivant*. Paris: Flammarion, 1978.

Schiebinger, Londa. *The Mind Has No Sex? Women in the Origins of Modern Science*. Cambridge: Harvard University Press, 1989.

———. *Nature's Body: Gender in the Making of Modern Science*. Boston: Beacon Press, 1993.

Schlanger, Judith. *L'Invention intellectuelle*. Paris: Fayard, 1983.

———. *Les Métaphores de l'organisme*. Paris: Vrin, 1971.

Schwab, R. N. and W. E. Rex, eds. "Inventory of Diderot's *Encyclopédie*." *Studies on Voltaire and the Eighteenth Century* 93 (1972).

Seylaz, Jean-Luc. "*Les Liaisons dangereuses*" *et la création romanesque chez Laclos*. Geneva: Droz, 1958.

Sgard, Jean, and Michel Gilot, eds. *Le Vocabulaire du sentiment dans l'oeuvre de Jean-Jacques Rousseau*. Geneva: Slatkine, 1980.

Sherman, Carol. *Diderot and the Art of Dialogue*. Geneva: Droz, 1976.

Showalter, English. "*Les Lettres d'une Péruvienne*: Composition, publication, suites." *Archives et Bibliothèques de Belgique* 54, nos. 1–4 (1983), 14–28.

Smith, I. H. "The Concept 'Sensibilité' and the Enlightenment." *Journal of the Australasian Universities Language and Literature Association* 27 (1967), 5–17.

Sontag, Otto, ed. *The Correspondence between Albrecht von Haller and Charles Bonnet*. Vienna: Hans Huber Publishers, 1983.

Spink, John S. "Marivaux: The 'Mechanism of the Passions' and the 'Metaphysic of Sentiment'." *Modern Language Review* 73 (1978), 278–90.

———. "'Sentiment,' 'sensible,' 'sensibilité': Les Mots, les idées, d'après les 'moralistes' français et britanniques du début du dix-huitième siècle." *Zagadnienia Rodzajów Literackich* 20 (1977), 33–47.

Spitzer, Leo. "A propos de *La Vie de Marianne* (Lettre à M. Georges Poulet)." *Romanic Review* 44 (1953), 102–26.

———. "The Style of Diderot." In *Linguistics and Literary History*. New York: Russell and Russell, 1962.

Stafford, Barbara Marie. *Body Criticism: Imaging the Unseen in Enlightenment Art and Medicine*. Cambridge: MIT Press, 1991.

Starobinski, Jean. "Diderot et la parole des autres." *Critique* 296 (1972), 3–22.

———. "La littérature, le texte et l'interprète." In *Faire de l'histoire: Nouvelle approches*. Ed. Jacques Le Goff and Pierre Nora. Paris: Gallimard, 1974.

———. "Monsieur Teste Confronting Pain." In *Fragments for History of the Human Body*, vol. 3. Ed. Michael Feher. New York: Zone, 1989.

———. "Le Mot 'civilisation.'" In *Le Remède dans le mal: Critique et légitimation de l'artifice à l'âge des Lumières*. Paris: Gallimard, 1989.

———. "Note sur l'histoire des fluides imaginaires (des esprits animaux à la libido)." *Gesnerus* 23 (1966), 176–87.

———. "Le Philosophe, le géomètre, l'hybride." *Poétique* 21 (1975), 8–23.

———. "A Short History of Bodily Sensation." In *Fragments for a History of the Human Body*, vol. 3. Ed. Michael Feher. New York: Zone, 1989.

———. *La Transparence et l'obstacle*. Paris: Gallimard, 1971. (English translation: *Jean-Jacques Rousseau: Transparency and Obstruction*. Trans. Arthur Goldhammer. Chicago: University of Chicago Press, 1988.)

———. "La Vie et les aventures du mot 'réaction.'" *Modern Language Review* 70 (1975), xxi–xxxi.

Staum, Martin. *Cabanis: Enlightenment and Medical Philosophy in the French Revolution*. Princeton: Princeton University Press, 1980.

Steinbrügge, Lieselotte. *The Moral Sex: Woman's Nature in the French Enlightenment*. Trans. Pamela E. Selwyn. New York: Oxford University Press, 1995.

Stewart, Joan Hinde. *Gynographs: French Novels by Women of the Late Eighteenth Century*. Lincoln: University of Nebraska Press, 1993.

Stewart, Philip. *Le Masque et la parole: Le Langage de l'amour au XVIIIe siècle*. Paris: José Corti, 1973.

Tarczylo, Théodore. *Sexe et liberté au siècle des Lumières*. Paris: Presses de la Renaissance, 1983.

Tatar, Maria A. *Spellbound: Studies on Mesmerism and Literature*. Princeton: Princeton University Press, 1978.

Temkin, Owsei. "The Philosophical Background of Magendie's Physiology." *Bulletin of the History of Medicine* 20, no. 1 (1946), 10–35.

———. "Zimmermann's Philosophy of the Physician." In *The Double Face of Janus and Other Essays in the History of Medicine*. Baltimore: Johns Hopkins University Press, 1977.

Thériault, Serge A. *Jean-Jacques Rousseau et la médecine naturelle*. Montreal: Les Editions Univers, 1979.

Therrien, Madeleine. "La Problématique de la féminité dans *La Vie de Marianne*." *Stanford French Review* 11 (1987), 51–61.

Todd, Janet. "The Attack on Sensibility." In *Sensibility: An Introduction*. London: Methuen, 1986.

Todorov, Tzvetan. *Littérature et signification*. Paris: Larousse, 1967.

———. *Nous et les autres: La Réflexion française sur la diversité humaine*. Paris: Seuil, 1989.

Trahard, Pierre. *Les Maîtres de la sensibilité française au XVIIIe siècle (1715–1789)*. 4 vols. Paris: Boivin, 1931–33.

———. *La Sensibilité révolutionnaire (1789–1794)*. Paris: Boivin, 1936.

Tronchin, Henri. *Théodore Tronchin (1709–1781), un médecin du XVIIIe siècle*. Geneva: Kundig, 1906.

Undank, Jack. "Graffigny's Room of Her Own." *French Forum* 13, no. 3 (1988), 297–318.

Varloot, Jean. Introduction to *Le Neveu de Rameau / Le Rêve de d'Alembert*. By Denis Diderot. Paris: Editions Sociales, 1972.

Vartanian, Aram. "Diderot and the Phenomenology of the Dream." *Diderot Studies* 8 (1966), 217–53.

———. "Erotisme et philosophie chez Diderot." *Cahiers de l'association internationale des études françaises* 13 (1960), 367–90.

———. "The Marquise de Merteuil: A Case of Mistaken Identity." *L'Esprit créateur* 3, no. 4 (1963), 172–80.

———. *La Mettrie's "L'Homme Machine": A Study in the Origins of an Idea*. Princeton: Princeton University Press, 1960.

———. "Trembley's Polyp, La Mettrie, and Eighteenth-Century French Materialism." *Journal of the History of Ideas* 11, no. 3 (1950), 259–86.

Veith, Ilza. *Hysteria: The History of a Disease*. Chicago: University of Chicago Press, 1965.

Versini, Laurent. *Laclos et la tradition*. Paris: Klincksieck, 1968.

Vila, Anne C. "The *médecin philosophe* as Drama Critic: Pierre Fabre's Natural History of French Theatre." *Studies on Voltaire and the Eighteenth Century* 314 (1993), 231–48.

———. "Pathological Inversions: Balzac and Bichat." *Romanic Review* 79, no. 3 (1988), 422–42.

Vincent-Buffault, Anne. *Histoire des larmes, XVIIIe–XIXe siècles.* Paris: Editions Rivages, 1986.

Vyverberg, Henry. *Historical Pessimism in the French Enlightenment.* Cambridge: Harvard Univeristy Press, 1958.

Wartofsky, M. "Diderot and the Development of Material Monism." *Diderot Studies* 2 (1952), 279–329.

Wellman, Kathleen. *La Mettrie: Medicine, Philosophy, and Enlightenment.* Durham, N.C.: Duke University Press, 1992.

Williams, Elizabeth A. *The Physical and the Moral: Anthropology, Physiology, and Philosophical Medicine in France, 1750–1850.* Cambridge: Cambridge University Press, 1994.

Wilson, Arthur M., Jr. "Sensibility in France in the Eighteenth Century: A Study in Word History." *French Quarterly* 13 (1931), 35–46.

Wilson, Lindsay. *Women and Medicine in the French Enlightenment: The Debate over "Maladies des Femmes."* Baltimore: Johns Hopkins University Press, 1993.

Winnett, Susan. *Terrible Sociability: The Text of Manners in Laclos, Goethe, and James.* Stanford: Stanford University Press, 1993.

Wohlfarth, Irving. "The Irony of Criticism and the Criticism of Irony." *Studies on Voltaire and the Eighteenth Century* 120 (1974), 269–317.

 *Index*

Daremberg, Charles, 63
degeneration (denaturation): and contemporary society, 47, 87, 99–100, 104–7, 215, 233, 256, 328n. 33; counteracting, 87–89, 105, 253; and excessive sensibility, 96, 182, 191–92, 229, 243, 253, 257; in nineteenth century, 301
DeJean, Joan, 273
delicacy: moral, 86, 113, 124, 128, 132, 140, 147, 149, 150, 158, 162, 212, 292; physical, 97, 188, 190, 191, 192, 229, 232, 233, 237, 247, 287, 264, 290, 340n. 19
De Man, Paul, 198
Denby, David, 129
Deneys-Tunney, Anne, 197
depopulation, 106, 189, 340–41n. 22
Descartes, 14, 32, 279
determinism, 44, 77, 253, 257, 258, 259, 270, 285, 286, 351n. 21
diaphragm. *See* animal (body) economy
Diderot, Denis, 2, 4, 6, 8, 9, 31, 41, 42, 51, 58, 62, 64, 65–66, 68–79, 83, 91–94, 151, 152–62, 164–81, 200, 236, 263, 266, 313n. 40; aesthetics in, 146, 152–81 *passim*, 236, 335n. 16; and biomedical theory, 65, 91–92, 152–55, 325n. 13, 333–34n. 1; and Bordeu, 65–66, 69, 70, 71–73; clinical language in, 153, 166–80; and *Encyclopédie*, 51–52, 152, 318n. 23; on intelligence, 92–94; materialism in, 70, 73, 153, 322–23n. 58; pantomime in, 160, 169, 336n. 19, 337n. 36; on reading, 154–64; on theater, 151, 152–53, 181, 334n. 2; theory of fiction, 6, 41, 151, 152–53, 155–62, 160–81 *passim*, 200–201, 236, 263, 266, 334nn. 2, 4; theory of sensibility, 152–81 *passim*; typology of great observers, 165, 174, 179; on women, 153, 334n. 4, 337n. 36; writing style of, 77, 153, 166–68, 337n. 32. Works: *Discours sur la poésie dramatique*, 153; *Éléments de physiologie*, 65, 92, 152, 153, 187; *Éloge de Richardson*, 10, 153, 154, 155–62, 164, 179, 263; *Entretiens sur "Le Fils naturel"*, 153, 236; "Jouissance," 167; *Le Fils naturel*, 152; *De l'interprétation de la nature*, 56, 180; *Paradoxe sur le comédien*, 165,

179; *Le Père de famille*, 152; *Réflexions sur le livre "De l'esprit" par M Helvétius*, 92–94; *La Religieuse*, 6, 10, 67, 75, 112, 153–55, 161, 162, 164, 166–80, 225; *Le Rêve de d'Alembert*, 9, 45, 57, 65–66, 69–79, 92, 152, 154, 165–66, 181, 211; *Salons*, 156
dimorphism, 10, 226, 242, 243, 263, 264, 267, 291, 292, 293. *See also* libertinism
disease: classifying, 44, 294; theory of, 14, 49, 53–55, 71–77, 163, 229–34. *See also* animal (body) economy; hygiene; medicine; nerves, and nervous system; physiology
Douthwaite, Julia V., 140–41
drame bourgeois, 9, 153, 236. *See also* theater
dualism, 14, 28, 240, 299, 300, 301, 348n. 54
Dubos, Jean-Baptiste, 2
Duclos, Charles Pinot, 2, 275

economy, and economics: domestic, 106, 193, 201, 211, 213; in Tissot, 189, 192, 193
education: Graffigny on, 141, 142, 146, 147–48; influence on intelligence, 84–85, 88–89, 90–93, 254; medical, 39–40; sensationalist theory of, 35–36, 38, 313n. 40
effeminacy, 10, 228, 232, 233, 234, 238, 257
Encyclopédie, 1, 3, 9, 29, 45, 47–65, 71, 152, 154, 155, 162, 167, 211, 329n. 13, 340n. 20; cross-references in, 51–52, 58, 317n. 13; and popularization of medical theory, 9, 51, 52–64; *Supplément* to, 14, 29
enlightenment: and ethics, 94, 141, 142, 146, 147–49, 182–24 *passim*; and improvement of human race, 81–94; medicalization of, 9, 80–107, 290; and physical constitution, 229, 240–57 *passim*; and quest for mental-moral improvement, 7–9, 81–88, 91, 94–107, 147–49, 181, 243, 253, 256–57, 259, 268, 287, 292, 328n. 33; reaction against, 295, 302; and social reform, 80, 164–65, 166, 180; and unitary theory of man, 293, 297, 302; and vogue of arts and sciences, 95, 103, 104–5. *See also* meliorism; perfectibility
Euler, Leonhard, 31

Rousseau, 227, 246, 343n. 7; and sensibility, 226–28, 240–57; teleology in, 225, 242, 243, 244–46, 249. *See also* complementarity; dimorphism

morale sensitive, 10, 182–86, 188, 196, 338n. 1; in Rousseau, 183–84, 186, 192, 202, 205, 210, 215, 219, 224

Moreau de la Sarthe, Jacques-Louis, 226
Morris, David B., 3, 291
"mucus" tissue, 246, 247–48

naturalism, 43, 63. *See also* medicine: "philosophical"
nature, state of, 141, 183, 187, 192, 263. *See also* men; women
nerves, and nervous system: in animal economy, 24, 49, 83, 90; and common sensorium, 29, 33–35; disorders of, 40, 98, 100–101, 104–5, 194, 228–33, 236–37, 239, 254; and irritability, 21, 23–24, 26; in libertines, 289–90; as locus of sensibility, 13, 23–25, 29, 59, 66–69, 90, 190; and pulses, 68, 72; in reader-spectator, 105, 236–37; and sex, 246–47, 257
Newton, Isaac, 31, 77, 309–10n. 16
"non-naturals," 43, 80, 187, 192, 193, 253, 299. *See also* hygiene; passions
novel(s): conventions of, 6–7, 155, 168, 174; effects of reading, 105, 200, 233, 236, 238, 264; evolution of, 6, 9–10, 111, 150–51, 181, 328n. 2; figure of "good" reader, 158–62, 179, 200–201; libertine, 227, 257, 258–92 *passim*, 293, 296; mission of novelist, 6–8, 105, 156–57, 161–62, 261–63, 264–65, 267, 268–69; moral utility of, 119–20, 157–62, 181, 200–201, 260, 266; and natural philosophy, 155, 162, 176–79, 181, 227, 257, 258, 259, 266, 269; philosophical, 154, 174–81, 258, 260, 267, 268
nymphomania. *See* vapors

observation: in Diderot, 73, 74–77, 162, 164–65, 166, 169–80; in Laclos, 260, 263, 274–75, 276, 280, 281; medical, 40, 50–51, 53–58, 60–62, 64–65, 162–63, 165, 186–87, 240; and natural philosophy, 5,

7, 27, 30–31, 319n. 29; in Rousseau, 183, 210; and semiotics, 53–57
organicism, 88, 296–97, 300, 356n. 11; and *Naturphilosophie*, 296. *See also* monism; vitalism
Ozouf, Mona, 296

pain: as measure of sensibility, 25; in Sade, 266, 291
paradigm: of body as text, 5; of complementarity, 226, 242, 291; meanings of term, 2, 303–4n. 4; sensibility as, 2, 5, 10, 17, 37, 81–82, 111–12, 151, 241, 293, 303n. 4
Pascal, Blaise, 97
passions: in Bichat, 301; effects on mind, 87; energy of, 2, 158, 162, 266, 268, 288, 290, 350n. 16; and "non-naturals," 80, 192, 193; in Rousseau, 202, 205, 206, 218; in Sade, 262–68; and vapors, 232, 233, 234, 236–37
peasantry: diet of, 192–93; and health, 70, 106–7, 187, 191–96, 287; mental-moral capacities of, 193–94, 325n. 10; in *La Nouvelle Héloïse*, 214–15
perfectibility, 5, 40, 81, 91, 92, 94–95, 253, 256–57, 268, 287, 296, 301, 324n. 2, 348n. 52; and progress, 256, 268, 301; and regeneration, 296
philosophe(s). *See* enlightenment; physician-philosophers
physical-moral relation(s): and aesthetic experience, 156, 158–59, 161, 165, 236; and education, 85–91, 93, 301; in hygiene, 38, 40, 86, 97, 103, 186, 192, 211; and operations of mind/soul, 10, 80, 93, 182–86, 187; the phrase, 182, 225; reciprocities in, 4, 95–98, 100–104, 182–83, 203, 212, 241, 244, 246–47, 250–52, 258, 264, 294
physician-philosophers (*médecins philosophes*), 80, 81, 91, 93, 94, 154, 162–65, 170, 183, 187, 188, 209, 241, 269, 287, 291, 301, 319n. 35; hierarchy of, 62, 164, 174; as seen in nineteenth century, 39, 63, 314n. 49
Physiocracy, and Physiocrats, 189, 200, 189, 201

Roussel, Pierre, 10, 45, 226–29, 234–35, 238, 240–41, 243–57, 264, 269, 287, 293; *Essai sur la sensibilité*, 229, 241; *Fragment du "Système physique et moral de l'homme"*, 228, 250, 253, 257; *Système physique et moral de la femme*, 10, 226–27, 228, 234, 240–41, 243–48, 250–55, 259
Roussel, Roy, 276

Sade, Donatien-Alphonse-François de, 3, 4, 6, 10, 42, 64, 97, 155, 227, 257, 258–60, 264–69, 286–92, 295; anthropology in, 267, 268, 287, 288–89, 291–92; apathy in, 286, 354n. 49; exoticism in, 267, 351n. 19; on history, 265; interest in medical theory, 287, 289–91, 351n. 20, 354n. 50; and Laclos, 260, 349n. 3, 354n. 51; materialism in, 287, 354n. 49; on nature, 265, 266–67, 289; on novel-writing, 6–8, 264–65, 267, 268–69; sensibility in, 286–92, 353n. 47; and sentimentalism, 264–65, 266, 268, 292; theory of fiction, 260, 264–69; "truth" in, 265–69, 291, 350n. 15. Works: *Aline et Valcour*, 267, 289; *Les Cent vingt journées de Sodome*, 266; *Les Crimes de l'amour*, 260, 266, 267; "Ernestine," 267; *Histoire de Juliette, ou Les Prospérités du vice*, 266, 286, 289–90; "Idée sur les romans," 7–8, 260, 264–68; *Justine, ou les malheurs de la vertu*, 112, 266, 286, 288–89, 290, 291
Schelling, Friedrich Wilhelm Joseph von, 296
Schiebinger, Londa, 226, 242
scholar(s): diet of, 85, 86, 87, 98–99, 102; health problems of, 40, 97–105, 287; image of, 85–87, 95–97, 99, 102–3, 104, 107, 326n. 22; lifestyle of, 40, 94–107; and procreation, 99–100, 290, 324n. 6; women as, 254–55. *See also* studious life
"sciences of man" (human sciences), 1, 5, 56–57, 63, 150, 240, 256, 294, 297
semiotics (medical), 14, 39–40, 45, 51, 52–62, 72, 163, 186–87, 197; in diagnosis and prognosis, 40, 53–55, 62, 64, 162–64, 294; in Diderot, 154–55, 166–80;

and sense organs, 54, 61–62. *See also* pulse, and pulse-taking
Senancour, Étienne de, 296
Senebier, Jean, 64–65, 186
sensationalism (philosophy of mind, psychology), 2, 8, 13–14, 30–38, 40, 44, 45, 58, 64, 82–83, 91, 130, 240, 250, 280, 293, 297, 299, 331n. 26, 332n. 39, 338n. 1, 352n. 27; and "analysis," 30–31, 33–36, 45, 58, 64; and associationism, 312n. 37; and experiments on children, 313n. 40; and Statue-Man fable, 32–36, 280, 352n. 27
sensibility: absence of, 135–37, 144, 165, 166, 175, 194, 209–10, 271, 281, 286; ambiguities of, 1, 5, 6, 9–10, 112–28, 136–37, 154, 176–80, 225, 242–43, 256–57, 295, 296; in Britain, 3, 305n. 11, 316–17n. 9; in children, 247–48; and consciousness, 71, 130, 297, 299; and contagion, 171–80 *passim*, 199, 222, 274; cultivation of, 80, 86, 97, 98, 118, 147, 194, 195, 210, 287; dangers of, 1, 5, 10, 40–41, 46–47, 86, 97, 99, 104, 165–66, 171, 182, 193, 200, 208, 287; and disease, 50–51, 59, 71–72, 173–74, 176–77; and elitism, 112–13, 124, 127, 128, 150–51; eroticization of, 67–68, 75, 155, 205, 281, 289–92; fashionableness of, 2–3, 304n. 7; feminization of, 150; figure of *homme sensible*, 3, 125, 149, 183–86, 198–99, 203–204, 296; in formation of body, 48–50, 83–84, 246–48; in French Revolution, 295, 297, 355n. 3; hierarchy of sensible beings, 75–76, 162, 165, 170, 171, 199, 202–3, 205, 206, 210–11, 223–24, 241, 257, 348n. 55; and imagination, 218–19, 232, 235–37, 239, 302; and intensity of feeling, 123–25, 130, 142–43, 150, 203, 225, 233–35, 239, 249, 289, 292, 323n. 13; involuntary, 199, 205–6, 220, 224, 271, 272, 274, 275, 300; and irritability, 13–17, 21–28, 37–38, 106, 232, 300; libertine, 10, 269, 271, 274, 281–82, 285–92, 295, 353n. 47; local, 69–70, 71–72, 74, 76, 297 (*see also* vital centers); and love, 113, 118, 137, 145–48;

sensibility (*continued*)

and mental-moral edification, 95, 104–5,
182, 187, 207, 211, 221, 222, 295–96; and
"natural," 113, 132, 139, 140, 148–50,
185, 196, 199; nervous illness, 104–5,
194, 225, 228, 229–31, 232–33, 237, 239,
257 (*see also* vapors); in nineteenth century, 10, 294–302; physical variability
of, 3, 10, 42, 227, 241–42, 246–47,
255–57, 258, 287; in physician, 64,
162–64, 165; and race, 348n. 55; and
reason, 145, 295, 302; redefinition of,
226–27, 241, 249, 255–57, 282, 287, 288,
293–302; regulating, 87, 102, 145,
148–49, 182–83, 186, 195–96, 199, 200,
202, 204, 205, 210–17, 219, 271; and religion, 3, 295, 342n. 37; and the self, 128,
143, 271; and sociomoral virtues, 2, 9,
14, 44, 86–87, 111, 121, 182–83, 194, 209,
212, 218, 249–55, 290, 296; terms related
to, 2, 112

sentimentalism, 3, 6, 10, 128–40 *passim*,
154, 162, 179, 181, 264, 265, 292, 294,
295, 355nn. 3, 5; and exoticism, 356n. 8;
and libertinism, 10, 292; in Marivaux,
128–29, 133, 136, 139, 330n. 23; and
pathos, 127, 169, 177–78; in *La Religieuse*, 166, 168, 172, 177–78; and
tableau, 129, 133, 139, 160–61, 169, 172,
217, 221, 273

sex: and difference, 226–29, 233, 235, 238,
240–57, 258, 259, 261–64, 269, 274, 276,
279, 285, 286, 300, 346n. 39, 347n. 48;
influence on intelligence, 84, 90, 107,
250–57; and sensibility, 3, 10, 90, 225–57,
269, 287; separation of sexes, 215, 216.
See also complementarity; dimorphism

Sèze, Paul-Victor de, 10, 45, 226, 229, 240,
243, 246–52, 254, 287

sociability, 6, 99, 102–103, 112, 118, 159,
161, 296

society (civilization): debate on, 5, 40–41,
104–7, 182, 256, 264, 301; effects on
health, 40, 104–5, 182, 187, 188, 232,
233, 234–35, 236–38, 239; moral-
intellectual advantages of, 194, 195–96,
253, 256, 328n. 33; and state of nature,

183, 187, 192, 264, 289, 296, 356n. 8.
See also enlightenment; meliorism;
perfectibility

Spallanzani, Lazzaro, 64

spiritualism, 10, 25, 301. *See also* dualism;
Romanticism

Spitzer, Leo, 77, 128, 166–68

Staël, Germaine de, 295

Stahl, Georg-Ernst, 17, 43, 49, 315n. 3,
346–47n. 40

Starobinski, Jean, 4–5, 8, 77–78, 210

Steffens, Heinrich, 297

studious life: dangers of, 94, 95–107; effects
on women, 90, 254–55; and excess,
98–102; and hypochondria, 104, 327n.
27; and sociability, 99, 102–3

Süe, Jean-Jacques, 297

sympathy, 2, 46, 112, 113, 115–28, 129,
130–31, 133, 134, 136–40, 142, 144, 153,
159, 167, 168, 171, 172, 178, 179, 266,
272, 290, 297, 300; and deception,
119–20, 121, 125, 128, 130, 329n. 9,
323–30n. 14; organic, 68, 69, 83, 228,
297; and seduction, 167, 172, 178, 179;
and sensibility, 113, 119–27, 142, 153,
159, 172; and social class, 119–27; and
"tragedy" in Prévost, 122, 124, 125–27

taste: aesthetic, 157; and genius, 165; in
organs, 4, 68

temperament: influence on intelligence,
84–85, 93, 252–53; medical theory of, 41,
53, 186, 246, 247, 252–53, 269, 300

theater, 9, 41, 151, 152–53, 233, 236–37, 238,
294, 334n. 2

Tissot, Samuel-Auguste-André-David, 15,
42, 94–107, 187–96, 201, 211, 212, 215,
234, 246, 264, 290, 354n. 50; on diet,
192–93, 196, 212, 341n. 26, 342nn. 34,
36; discursive style of, 97, 99, 104–5; on
masturbation, 101–2, 106–7, 187, 212,
326–27n. 23, 342n. 34; patient types in,
97–107 *passim*, 187, 190–96 *passim*; on
peasantry, 106–7, 191–94; as physician-
philosopher, 187–89; physiological theory of, 94, 98, 100, 101–2, 188, 191;
remedies of, 102–3, 190–92, 195–96,

342n. 34; and Rousseau, 104–7, 187–88, 195–96, 201, 340n. 17, 342n. 34; social theory of, 189, 191; on worldliness, 188–96, 201, 232, 234. Works: *Avis au peuple sur sa santé*, 187; *De la santé des gens de lettres*, 9, 40, 95–107, 187, 290; "Discours préliminaire," 27–28; *Essai sur les maladies des gens du monde*, 10, 99, 106, 187–96, 211, 232; *De l'onanisme*, 101, 106

Trembley, Abraham, 310n. 22

Tronchin, Théodore, 264, 340nn. 15, 19

Turgot, Anne-Robert-Jacques, 81, 324n. 2

Undank, Jack, 140–41

Vandermonde, Charles Augustin, 9, 81, 88–94, 99, 102–3, 106

vapors, 10, 46, 76, 83, 86, 95, 228–40, 254, 257, 264; ancient notion of, 229, 344n. 14; and diet, 233, 236; and effeminacy, 228, 232, 233, 235; etiology of, 228, 229–31, 232, 233, 344n. 16; fashionableness of, 233; and gender, 229, 231, 233; history of, 231, 344n. 17; illnesses related to, 228, 231, 237; and nymphomania, 229, 257; remedies for, 234, 237–38, 345n. 24; role of imagination in, 232, 235–37, 239; role of passions in, 232, 233, 234, 235–37; and social reform, 232, 233, 234, 235–38; and theater-going, 233, 236–37; and urban life, 228, 229, 231–33, 234, 235–36

Vartanian, Aram, 26, 278

Venel, Gabriel, 50

Venel, Jean-André, 234

Versini, Laurent, 275

vie de relation, 10, 301

Virey, Julien-Joseph, 226, 300, 347n. 48

vital centers ("departments"), 50, 59, 69, 72, 246–47, 250

vital principle, 2, 16, 18, 27–28, 43, 46, 47, 240–41, 302, 315n. 3

vitalism, 2, 16, 37, 43, 51, 152, 227, 241, 247, 291, 293, 296–97, 299, 300–301, 302, 320n. 39; in nineteenth century, 296–97, 299, 300–301. *See also* Montpellier medical school; organicism; physiology

vivisection (animal experimentation), 24, 318n. 18

Voltaire, François-Marie Arouet, 64, 267

Whytt, Robert, 50, 308n. 6, 311n. 25, 318n. 18, 344n. 9

will (volition, *volonté*), 10, 25, 70, 76, 301

Williams, Elizabeth, 300

Wolfarth, Irving, 273–74

women: dietary preferences of, 212, 216; and education, 146, 263, 264, 284; health and illnesses of, 228, 229–40, 252, 254, 257, 317n. 16, 344n. 12; and high society, 234, 235–38; mental capacity of, 84, 90, 226, 250, 253–55, 256, 257, 259; "nature" of, 212, 225–26, 227, 234–57 *passim*, 264, 269, 347nn. 46, 47; as novelists, 105, 261, 262, 263, 265; and novel-reading, 105, 264; as scholars, 254–55; and sensibility, 92–94, 141, 145–47, 225, 228, 232–39, 246–57, 261–62, 264, 271, 274, 276, 279, 281, 284, 286; sexuality of, 153, 173; and sociability, 254–55; temperament of, 247, 252, 253; and theories of menstruation, 244, 246, 346–47n. 40; and vapors, 228, 229–40

worldliness, 102, 113–18, 185, 188–96, 201, 214–15, 264, 270, 282; and diet, 192–93, 194–96, 232–39; and gender, 232, 238–39; and health, 46, 189, 191–94, 232–40; and luxury, 231, 232; and mental-moral refinement, 194; *mondain* as medical type, 192–95, 232; and passions, 193–94; and seduction, 113–18; and sensibility, 192–96

Zimmermann, J. G., 64, 319n. 35

Library of Congress Cataloging-in-Publication Data

Vila, Anne C., 1961–
   Enlightenment and pathology : sensibility in the literature and medicine of
eighteenth-century France / Anne C. Vila.
     p.   cm.
   Includes bibliographical references and index.
   ISBN 0-8018-5677-9 (alk. paper). — ISBN 0-8018-5809-7 (pbk. : alk. paper)
    1. French literature—18th century—History and criticism.   2. Sentimentalism
in literature.   3. Senses and sensation in literature.   4. Medicine in literature.
   5. Enlightenment.   I. Title.
   PQ265.V48   1998
843'.509353—dc21   97-17346
                                                             CIP

Printed in the United States
88128LV00003B/64/A

9 780801 858093